Retirement Plans

**401(k)s, IRAs, and Other
Deferred Compensation Approaches**

The McGraw-Hill/Irwin Series in Finance, Insurance and Real Estate

Stephen A. Ross
Franco Modigliani Professor of Finance and Economics Sloan School of Management Massachusetts Institute of Technology Consulting Editor

FINANCIAL MANAGEMENT

Adair
Excel Applications for Corporate Finance
First Edition

Benninga and Sarig
Corporate Finance: A Valuation Approach

Block and Hirt
Foundations of Financial Management
Twelfth Edition

Brealey, Myers, and Allen
Principles of Corporate Finance
Eighth Edition

Brealey, Myers, and Marcus
Fundamentals of Corporate Finance
Fifth Edition

Brooks
FinGame Online 5.0

Bruner
Case Studies in Finance: Managing for Corporate Value Creation
Fifth Edition

Chew
The New Corporate Finance: Where Theory Meets Practice
Third Edition

Chew and Gillan
Corporate Governance at the Crossroads: A Book of Readings
First Edition

DeMello
Cases in Finance
Second Edition

Grinblatt (editor)
Stephen A. Ross, Mentor: Influence Through Generations

Grinblatt and Titman
Financial Markets and Corporate Strategy
Second Edition

Helfert
Techniques of Financial Analysis: A Guide to Value Creation
Eleventh Edition

Higgins
Analysis for Financial Management
Eighth Edition

Kester, Ruback, and Tufano
Case Problems in Finance
Twelfth Edition

Ross, Westerfield, and Jaffe
Corporate Finance
Eighth Edition

Ross, Westerfield, Jaffe, and Jordan
Corporate Finance: Core Principles and Applications
First Edition

Ross, Westerfield, and Jordan
Essentials of Corporate Finance
Fifth Edition

Ross, Westerfield, and Jordan
Fundamentals of Corporate Finance
Eighth Edition

Shefrin
Behavioral Corporate Finance: Decisions That Create Value
First Edition

White
Financial Analysis with an Electronic Calculator
Sixth Edition

INVESTMENTS

Adair
Excel Applications for Investments
First Edition

Bodie, Kane, and Marcus
Essentials of Investments
Sixth Edition

Bodie, Kane, and Marcus
Investments
Seventh Edition

Hirt and Block
Fundamentals of Investment Management
Eighth Edition

Hirschey and Nofsinger
Investments: Analysis and Behavior
First Edition

Jordan and Miller
Fundamentals of Investments: Valuation and Management
Fourth Edition

FINANCIAL INSTITUTIONS AND MARKETS

Rose and Hudgins
Bank Management and Financial Services
Seventh Edition

Rose and Marquis
Money and Capital Markets: Financial Institutions and Instruments in a Global Marketplace
Ninth Edition

Saunders and Cornett
Financial Institutions Management: A Risk Management Approach
Fifth Edition

Saunders and Cornett
Financial Markets and Institutions: An Introduction to the Risk Management Approach
Third Edition

INTERNATIONAL FINANCE

Eun and Resnick
International Financial Management
Fourth Edition

Kuemmerle
Case Studies in International Entrepreneurship: Managing and Financing Ventures in the Global Economy
First Edition

REAL ESTATE

Brueggeman and Fisher
Real Estate Finance and Investments
Thirteenth Edition

Corgel, Ling, and Smith
Real Estate Perspectives: An Introduction to Real Estate
Fourth Edition

Ling and Archer
Real Estate Principles: A Value Approach
Second Edition

FINANCIAL PLANNING AND INSURANCE

Allen, Melone, Rosenbloom, and Mahoney
Retirement Plans: 401(k)s, IRAs, and Other Deferred Compensation Approaches
Tenth Edition

Altfest
Personal Financial Planning
First Edition

Harrington and Niehaus
Risk Management and Insurance
Second Edition

Kapoor, Dlabay, and Hughes
Focus on Personal Finance: An Active Approach to Help You Develop Successful Financial Skills
First Edition

Kapoor, Dlabay, and Hughes
Personal Finance
Eighth Edition

Retirement Plans

401(k)s, IRAs, and Other Deferred Compensation Approaches Tenth Edition

Everett T. Allen, Jr., LLB
Retired Vice President and Principal Towers Perrin

Joseph J. Melone, Ph.D., CLU, CHFC, CPCU
President and Chief Executive Officer (RET.) AXA Financial

Jerry S. Rosenbloom, Ph.D., CLU, CPCU
Frederick H. Ecker Emeritus Professor of Insurance and Risk Management Academic Director, Certified Employee Benefit Specialist Program Wharton School University of Pennsylvania

Dennis F. Mahoney, CEBS, CFP®
Associate Academic Director, Certified Employee Benefit Specialist Program Wharton School University of Pennsylvania TIAA-CREF Institute Fellow

McGraw-Hill Irwin

Boston   Burr Ridge, IL   Dubuque, IA   New York   San Francisco   St. Louis
Bangkok   Bogotá   Caracas   Kuala Lumpur   Lisbon   London   Madrid   Mexico City
Milan   Montreal   New Delhi   Santiago   Seoul   Singapore   Sydney   Taipei   Toronto

McGraw-Hill
Irwin

RETIREMENT PLANS: 401(k)s, IRAs, AND OTHER DEFERRED COMPENSATION APPROACHES

Published by McGraw-Hill/Irwin, a business unit of The McGraw-Hill Companies, Inc., 1221 Avenue of the Americas, New York, NY, 10020. Copyright © 2008 by The McGraw-Hill Companies, Inc. All rights reserved. No part of this publication may be reproduced or distributed in any form or by any means, or stored in a database or retrieval system, without the prior written consent of The McGraw-Hill Companies, Inc., including, but not limited to, in any network or other electronic storage or transmission, or broadcast for distance learning.

Some ancillaries, including electronic and print components, may not be available to customers outside the United States.

This book is printed on acid-free paper.

1 2 3 4 5 6 7 8 9 0 DOC/DOC 0 9 8 7

ISBN 978-0-07-337742-1
MHID 0-07-337742-2

Editorial director: *Brent Gordon*
Executive editor: *Michele Janicek*
Editorial coordinator: *Katherine Mau*
Marketing manager: *Dean Karampelas*
Senior project manager: *Susanne Riedell*
Senior production supervisor: *Carol A. Bielski*
Lead designer: *Matthew Baldwin*
Lead media project manager: *Brian Nacik*
Cover design: *Matthew Baldwin*
Cover image: © *Digital Vision*
Typeface: *10/12 Times New Roman*
Compositor: *Laserwords Private Limited*
Printer: *R. R. Donnelley*

Library of Congress Cataloging-in-Publication Data

Retirement plans : 401(k)s, IRAs, and other deferred compensation approaches / Everett
    T. Allen, Jr. ... [et al.]. — 10th ed.
      p. cm. — (The McGraw-Hill/Irwin series in finance, insurance and real estate)
    Rev. ed. of: Pension planning. 9th ed. 2003.
    Includes index.
    ISBN-13: 978-0-07-337742-1 (alk. paper)
    ISBN-10: 0-07-337742-2 (alk. paper)
    1. Old age pensions—United States. 2. Pension trusts—United States. 3. Deferred compensation—United States. I. Allen, Everett T.
    HD7105.35.U6A44 2008
    332.024'0145—dc22

                                        2007014253

For Marie, Chris, Sam, Carlyn, Bob, and Lauren.
    Joseph J. Melone, Ph.D., CLU, ChFC, CPCU

For Lynn, Debra, Heather, and Amy.
    Jerry S. Rosenbloom, Ph.D., CLU, CPCU

For Josephine, the love of my life, and for our loving
children: Diana, Dennis, Matthew, Timothy, Judith Ann,
and Gabrielle. I also wish to express gratitude to my
mother and father, Joseph and Edna, for a lifetime of
love and support, and to Joe and Shaun for their many
positive influences on my life.
    Dennis F. Mahoney, CEBS, CFP®

Preface to *Retirement Plans,* Tenth Edition

Retirement planning has dramatically changed. This change will touch the lives of almost every individual in our society. These statements are not meant to dramatize the subject matter, to spark controversy or alarm, or even to spawn more sales of *Retirement Plans.* These are simple facts because human beings need resources to sustain our lives. A major income source in our later years flows from our retirement plans, because we see increased longevity in our society, and because our private retirement system affects the design of our complementary social insurance programs. With the movement away from traditional defined benefit plans to defined contribution plans, today's workers now bear the investment risk associated with their retirement income. This represents a major and dramatic transformation of our retirement system.

With the movement away from defined benefit plans and the predominant reliance on defined contribution plans, our society has embarked on a new era in capitalism and a not inconsequential social experiment. Although the U.S. private pension system did not require employers to sponsor a private plan, an employer's willingness to do so came with a number of prescribed responsibilities following the enactment of the Employee Retirement Income Security Act (ERISA) in 1974. While defined benefit structures dominated, the individual employee was shielded from many of the cares of retirement wealth management and even could rely on the federal government through the Pension Benefit Guaranty Corporation to provide an insurance program for her or his retirement income stream should the employer fail at managing the assets providing the funding within the pension plan.

Fast forward from the prior era to today's realities, where the once-supplemental 401(k) savings plan has become the primary foundational private retirement plan for many people. Here, employees are responsible for managing their retirement wealth and seeking means to ensure that their retirement income will last a lifetime. This challenge is exacerbated by increased longevity; skyrocketing medical costs; employers backing away from providing retiree medical programs; and social insurance programs, such as Social Security and Medicare, that face uncertainty and challenge. Add to this the potential necessity for expensive long-term custodial care at advanced ages, and today's generation of workers planning for retirement possesses unparalleled financial planning challenges.

How did this new retirement paradigm come about? The avalanche of defined benefit curtailments occurred during a time of unparalleled capital market optimism, when many investments in these programs were seeing dizzying ascendancy. Now that plan participants have seen a reversal of their fortunes and a return to more modest accumulations in their accounts, the reality of retirement planning is upon us. The questions that are being asked are many. Will defined contribution plans be able to adequately underwrite the retirement income streams needed for the Baby Boom generation? Will employees adequately diversify and proficiently manage their plan assets? Will employees save enough and avoid tempting opportunities to deplete their accounts prematurely? What will become of those individuals who plan poorly, make suboptimal choices, or neglect to accept the responsibility to plan for retirement?

Although the challenges are many, the opportunities also abound. Today's generation of workers possesses unprecedented access to information, far-reaching control over the management of their retirement resources, and empowerment to shape and safeguard their financial destinies. For those prepared for these challenges and willing to plan, retirement security can be a pleasant and prosperous reality.

The tenth edition of this text has been completely revised to align with this rapidly evolving and exciting new reality. The text moves away from its prior emphasis on retirement plan administrative functions to the shared responsibilities between plan sponsors and plan participants in creating and managing retirement wealth. Recognizing this dramatic change with primary reliance on defined contribution retirement savings plans, the text has been retitled as *Retirement Plans.* To some, the previous nine editions' title of *Pension Planning* connoted an emphasis on defined benefit plans. The change in title is intended to properly capture the broad spectrum of retirement savings plan structures that characterize the retirement planning landscape. These include 401(k) plans, 403(b) plans, 457 plans, Keogh plans, individual retirement accounts, profit sharing plans, and various other types of plans.

Retirement Plans includes updated information to portray the pervasive legislative change and governmental policy initiatives that have occurred. Most prominent is the Pension Protection Act (PPA) of 2006, whose comprehensive alteration of existing law restructures the foundational elements on which the private retirement system is anchored. Other legislation from recent years also is detailed because certain legislative themes emerge and often are carried forward with future passage of succeeding legislation. Providing an understanding of these themes from inception provides context for better understanding retirement and tax policy. Accordingly, the text describes the legal precepts of the Employee Retirement Income Security Act of 1974 (ERISA) and the policy directives instituted by the Economic Growth and Tax Relief Reconciliation Act of 2001 (EGTRRA). Also, certain elements of the Tax Increase Prevention and Reconciliation Act of 2006 (TIPRA) are referenced.

A number of new chapters have been added to this edition. Chapter 4, "Risk Management Through Retirement Planning," specifically examines the risks that individuals face in planning for retirement. This chapter also chronicles the breakthrough research that is being done by various individuals and organizations to better understand the nature of retirement risk.

In Part II, Chapter 5, "Overview of Defined Contribution Plan Types," provides a roadmap so that users of the text can gain a macro-picture of retirement plan savings structures and their use by different constituencies of retirement savers before embarking on a detailed discovery of the structures' intricacies. The actual study of plan structures now precedes detailed study of general plan qualification requirements. With this new presentation approach, the most prominent types of retirement savings plans, such as 401(k) plans, are brought forward in the book. Early on in Chapter 11, "Behavioral

Finance and Defined Contribution Plan Design," the exciting breakthroughs occurring in this new field of study are presented so practitioners and government policymakers can transform research findings into plan features and governmental regulations that enhance participant financial security. The Solo (k) plan is now covered in Chapter 13, having become a viable plan choice under the right circumstances.

Part III, "Special Purpose Retirement Planning Structures," takes a broad look at retirement savings vehicles outside of the qualified plan arena. Not only are IRAs and small-employer plans covered, but such programs as executive retirement arrangements and employee stock compensation plans are covered as well. Chapter 16, "Managing Retirement Assets in Multiple Plan Structures," looks at the planning involved as individuals move between employers throughout their careers and look at the merits of consolidating plan assets or rolling over assets into IRAs.

Part IV, "Defined Benefit Plans and Hybrid Retirement Plans," primarily dealing with administration of defined benefit plans, has been completely revised reflecting the expansive consequences of the Pension Protection Act of 2006 on defined benefit plan funding and other aspects of pension oversight.

Part V presents tax and legal requirements. Not only are the technical plan qualification requirements presented here, but a new Chapter 28, "Fiduciary Oversight and Plan Governance," authored by a noted retirement expert, explains translating these technical requirements into management practices that uphold the highest fiduciary standards and hallmarks of good stewardship.

Finally, Part VI, "Wealth Management and Distribution Planning," presents the new paradigm of retirement planning in a wealth management context. This section presents the emerging insights associated with integrating retirement planning as one manages total individual wealth from a comprehensive and holistic perspective.

The intent of this book, as was true in prior editions, is to advance the knowledge and best practices of retirement planning. This objective takes on a broader audience in our new world of shared responsibility involving not only plan sponsors, consultants, and retirement plan specialists, but also the individual plan participants empowered to manage their individual retirement wealth. Therefore, it also is hoped that the book— ultimately through education—will serve to enhance retirement security for all those using or participating in any type of retirement savings plan.

Acknowledgments

We want to express our appreciation once again to the many individuals who assisted us in the preparation of *Retirement Plans* and in prior editions of the related text, *Pension Planning*. Many of their contributions have survived in this tenth edition. We are also very much indebted to the individuals in the insurance, financial, and consulting professions who have reviewed portions of this text and made many valuable suggestions, and to the many teachers and students who over the years have given us extremely constructive comments and enabled us to improve the readability and quality of the text. Special thanks also are due representatives of The American College, the College for Financial Planning, the International Foundation of Employee Benefit Plans, the Society of Actuaries, the Employee Benefit Research Institute (EBRI), the Life Office Management Association, and the National Institute of Pension Administrators (NIPA) for their comments and review over the years. Also, the authors express their appreciation for the opportunity to participate with esteemed colleagues in a variety of meetings, symposia, and colloquia that shape our thinking and understanding of retirement planning. A special debt of gratitude in this regard is owed to Madeleine d'Ambrosio, CEBS; Anne Ollen, CEBS, Paul Yakoboski, Ph.D., at the TIAACREF Institute, and Theresa Bartlett, Certified Financial Planner Board of Standards. Also, two colleagues who were instrumental in initiating involvement at these organizations, Michele F. Davis and David Livran, CFP®, are to be thanked. Likewise, gratitude is expressed to our many colleagues at the American Institute for Chartered Property and Casualty Underwriters, with whom we have continuing professional experiences.

A special debt of gratitude is owed to Robert J. Myers, one of the world's leading authorities on Social Security for writing the appendix on Social Security and Medicare. Similarly, a special debt of gratitude is owed to Daniel J. Ryterband, CEBS, and Richard L. Alpern, both from Frederic W. Cook & Co. Inc., for the chapter on Section 457 plans. Thanks are also due to David Cole, consultant, with Frederic W. Cook & Co., for his work on a previous edition of the chapter. We would also like to thank Mary Komornicka, CEBS, ChFC, PMP, of WNK Consulting Ltd., who authored the chapter on fiduciary oversight and plan governance. Thanks also are due to Kristina Kananen, QPA, QKA, APA of Datair Employee Benefit Systems, Inc., for her helpful suggestions on nondiscrimination testing issues covered in Chapter 25.

In addition we would like to thank the many organizations and publishers that granted permission to use material provided in "Insights" throughout the book.

Also, the authors express their appreciation to G. Victor Hallman, a lecturer in financial and estate planning at the Wharton School of the University of Pennsylvania for his contribution to the chapter on employee stock compensation plans. This chapter is adapted from the seventh edition of *Personal Financial Planning,* which he co-authored. Thanks also are due to Dawn Bizzell, CEBS, an economist with the Pension Benefit Guaranty Corporation for her help in reviewing Chapter 22, "Plan Termination Insurance for Single-Employer Pension Plans." The authors greatly appreciate the cooperation of Towers Perrin in providing material from their books, *The Handbook of 401(k) Plan Management* and *The Handbook of Executive Benefits.*

The authors also would like to express their deep appreciation to Dr. Jack L. Van Derhei, Professor of Risk Management and Insurance, Temple University, for his excellent contributions as a co-author on editions six through eight. Not only are his direct contributions to prior editions of the book appreciated, but his widely reported research findings that continue to affect the field of retirement planning and continue to emerge in the subject matter of this book.

The authors also appreciate the many contributions made by Fina Maniaci, CEBS, manager of the CEBS Program, both directly and indirectly in bringing this project to fruition and for her review of material on Social Security. Appreciation is also due to Diana Krigelman for review of the manuscript.

The authors are extremely indebted to the able team at McGraw-Hill for their assistance in completing this book. Special thanks are owed to Michele Janicek, Editor. Michele's assistance and insights were invaluable. Also, gratitude is owed to Susanne Riedell, Senior Project Manager, Barbara Hari, and Katherine Mau.

Finally, we would be remiss if we were not to mention the tremendous void felt in writing the tenth edition of this book without our colleague, Everett T. Allen, Jr. Ev was an original author of *Pension Planning* and contributed significantly to its many editions throughout the years. We dedicated the ninth edition to Ev's memory. His writing was always clear, and his insightful commentary was always thoughtful and well reasoned. As we talk to colleagues in industry, we constantly meet individuals who were Ev's friends and clients. We enjoy hearing their memories of Ev, and we hope we live up to Ev's high standards of scholarship, professionalism, and integrity.

Joseph J. Melone

Jerry S. Rosenbloom

Dennis F. Mahoney

Contents

Retirement Plans

401(k)s, IRAs, and Other
Deferred Compensation Approaches

Chapter 1

The Dynamic, Ongoing Evolution of Private Pension Plans

After studying this chapter you should be able to:

- Describe the components of the tripod of economic security.
- Explain the economic problems encountered with old age.
- Discuss the factors that have contributed to the historical growth of the private pension system.
- Discuss the changing perceptions that unions have had of pension plans.
- Describe the economic rationales for private pensions.
- Cite the major acts of legislation and their impact in shaping the private pension system.

Individuals generally seek means to enhance their economic security. One cause of economic insecurity is the probable reduction of an individual's earning power at an advanced age. In the United States, this risk is met through one or more of the following means: personal savings (including individual insurance and **annuities**[1]), employer-sponsored pension plans (private plans), and social insurance programs. When combined, these three elements produce a multifaceted approach to economic security sometimes referred to as the **"tripod of economic security,"** the "three-legged stool of economic security," or the "pillars of economic security." The dramatic growth of private plans since the 1940s has focused considerable interest on this form of income maintenance.[2]

[1] An annuity is a contract with an insurance company whereby the insurance company pays an income for a specific time period, such as a number of years or for life, in exchange for an initial cash payment.

[2] *Private plans,* as used in this text, refer to plans established by private agencies, including commercial, industrial, labor, and service organizations, and nonprofit religious, educational, and charitable institutions. Social Security is covered in Appendix 1 at the end of the book.

Growth of Private Plans

The beginnings of industrial pension plans in the United States date back to the establishment of the American Express Company plan in 1875.[3] Benefits under this first private pension plan were equal to 50 percent of average pay earned in the final 10 years of employment, but could not exceed $500 annually.[4] The second formal plan was established in 1880 by the Baltimore and Ohio Railroad Company. During the next half century, approximately 400 plans were established. These early pension plans were generally found in the railroad, banking, and public utility fields. The development of pensions in manufacturing companies was somewhat slower, largely because most manufacturing companies were still relatively young and therefore not confronted with the superannuation problems of the railroads and public utilities.

Insurance companies entered the pension business with the issuance of the first group annuity contract by the Metropolitan Life Insurance Company in 1921.[5] The second contract was issued by the Metropolitan in 1924 to an employer who already had a retirement plan on a "pay-as-you-go" basis.[6] In 1924, The Equitable Life Assurance Society of the United States announced its intention of offering a group pension service, thus becoming the second company to enter the field.[7]

Although the beginnings of private pensions date back to the 1800s, the significant growth in these programs has come since the 1940s. In a recent year, the percentage of wage and salary workers ages 21–64 who participated in a pension plan reached 56.6 percent.[8] At year-end 2005, total U.S. retirement assets stood at $14.5 trillion. Of this $14.5 trillion, $3.7 trillion were held in defined contribution plans, $1.9 trillion were held in private defined benefit plans, $3.8 trillion were held in government retirement funds, $3.7 trillion were held in individual retirement accounts, and $1.4 trillion were held in fixed and variable annuities. It is worth noting there has been a significant increase in the relative growth of defined contribution plan assets. Defined contribution plans and individual retirement accounts made up 51 percent of all retirement assets in 2005, up from 39 percent in 1990.[9]

---

[3] Murray Webb Latimer, *Industrial Pension Systems* (New York: Industrial Relations Counselors Inc., 1932), p. 21.

[4] Hewitt Associates LLC, *Microhistory of Employee Benefits and Compensation 1794–2005* (Lincolnshire, IL, August 2005), p. 3.

[5] Kenneth Black, Jr., *Group Annuities* (Philadelphia: University of Pennsylvania Press, 1955), p. 9.

[6] Ibid., p. 11.

[7] Ibid.

[8] *EBRI Issue Brief No. 286* (Washington, DC: Employee Benefit Research Institute, October 2005), p. 1.

[9] Investment Company Institute, *Research Fundamentals, The U.S. Retirement Market, 2005*, vol. 15, no. 5 (Washington, DC: Investment Company Institute, July 2006), p. 2.

Retirement income in the United States is structured on the often-referenced "three-legged" stool of Social Security, employer-sponsored pension plans and personal savings. In addition to the fact that one or two of these "legs" is often missing or woefully inadequate, the matter has been exacerbated by a restructuring of employer-provided retirement income programs. There has been a massive shift from defined benefit (DB) pension plans to defined contribution (DC) plans. The result has been a transfer of much of the cost and risk of longevity and the attending decision-making requirements from employers to the often-unprepared employee. . . .

No group (human resources and employee-benefits professionals) is in a better position to help educate employees on the importance of retirement savings and to counsel employers on the importance and feasibility of sponsoring retirement income programs. . . .

The bottom line is that some progress has been made in encouraging small employers to sponsor pension plans and more is possible, and when employees have access to a plan, they participate to a high degree. However, under a system based on voluntary pension plan sponsorship by employers and voluntary participation by employees, a significant number of employees will always lack access or elect not to participate.

Source: John G. Kilgour, "Responding to Changing Retirement Savings Programs," *Compensation & Benefits Review,* 33, no. 5, September–October 2001, pp. 25–35. Copyright © 2001 by Sage Publications, Inc. Reprinted by permission of Sage Publications, Inc.

Economic Problems of Old Age

Longevity is a source of economic insecurity in that individuals may outlive their financial capacities to maintain themselves and their dependents. The extent to which an aged person will have the financial capacity to meet self-maintenance costs and those of dependents relies upon the standard of living desired during retirement years, employment opportunities, and other resources (e.g., personal savings, social insurance, and inherited assets) available to meet this contingency.

Standard of Living after Retirement

The assumption usually is made that the financial needs of an individual decrease after retirement. To some extent, this assumption is valid. The retired individual may have no dependent children, and a home and its furnishings generally have been acquired by retirement age. However, the actual aggregate reduction in the financial needs of a person upon retirement has probably been overstated. Personal expectations and preferences discourage any drastic change in one's standard of living upon retirement, and an increasing tendency exists for retired persons to remain fairly active, particularly in terms of civic, social, travel, and other recreational activities. Furthermore, urbanization, geographic mobility, demographics, and changing culture minimize the prospect of retired parents moving in with their children.

Another major factor preventing a decrease in the financial needs of retirees is the likely cost of long-term care. It is estimated that a person reaching age 65 will have a 40 percent probability of being in a nursing home before death.[10] Although the federal government briefly experimented with the possibility of assuming a greater portion of this burden through the Medicare Catastrophic Coverage Act of 1988, the manner in which this additional coverage was financed proved to be politically unpalatable and it was repealed the following year. The Health Insurance Portability and Accountability Act (HIPAA) of 1996 made employer-paid long-term care tax-excludable beginning in 1997. Also, employer premiums became tax deductible to employers and tax-free to employees, although employee premiums cannot be paid from a flexible spending account or by elective pretax contributions under a cafeteria plan. Although this favorable tax treatment is an incentive for some employers to provide long-term care coverage to employees, the expense of this benefit limits its use for many employers. Even if retirees are fortunate enough to have comprehensive health insurance coverage continued by their employers after retirement, changes in the accounting standards applied to these plans have caused modifications in the type of coverage, cost sharing, or financing of this benefit.

The authors are not suggesting that retired workers require income benefits equal to their earnings levels immediately preceding retirement, nor even the level of preretirement take-home pay. Presumably, at least at the higher income levels, these individuals have been allocating a portion of their take-home pay to individual savings. However, it is suggested that the reduction in standard of living after retirement is not very great; and, more important, the trend in social thinking seems to be in the direction of not expecting retired workers to have to take much of a reduction in standard of living after retirement. The effect of inflation also has militated against a lower standard of living. Therefore, it is questionable whether one should assume any significant decrease in basic financial needs upon retirement, at least for individuals in the low- and middle-income categories.

Employment Opportunities

In recent years the percentage of men participating in the labor force was 30.3 percent for ages 65–69 and 12.2 percent for those 70 or over. In this same time period the percentage of women participating in the labor force was 20 percent for ages 65–69 and 5.9 percent for those 70 and over.[11] Obviously, many reasons account for the withdrawal of the aged from the labor force. A large number of older workers voluntarily retire. If workers have the necessary financial resources, they may wish to withdraw from active employment and live out their remaining years of life at a more leisurely pace. Others find it necessary for reasons of health to withdraw from the labor force. The aging process takes its toll, and many individuals are physically unable to operate at the level of efficiency attainable at a younger age. Disabilities at the older ages tend to be more frequent and of longer duration.

[10] Anthony J. Gajda and Morris Snow, "Long-Term Care," *The Handbook of Employee Benefits,* ed. Jerry S. Rosenbloom, 5th ed. (New York: McGraw-Hill, 2001), p. 310.
[11] Metropolitan Life Insurance Company, *Mature Market Institute Demographic Profile: The 65+ Population* (Westport, CT, 2004), p. 3.

Voluntary retirement and the physical inability to continue employment are undoubtedly important reasons for the decrease in the percentage of older persons participating in the labor force. However, these are probably not the most important factors affecting employment opportunities for the aged. The effects of industrialization, expansive technological advances, and the development of the federal Old Age, Survivors, Disability, and Health Insurance (OASDHI) program, private pensions, and other employee benefit programs probably have had a more significant impact on this problem.

The rapid pace and dynamic evolution of industrial employment operated to the disadvantage of older persons. Automation and mass-production assembly lines put a premium on physical dexterity and mental alertness. Employers generally were of the opinion, justifiable or not, that younger workers were better suited to the demands of industrial employment. In an agricultural economy, on the other hand, the able-bodied older person could continue to work, at least on a part-time basis.

Similarly, as organizations adapt to the information systems age and increasingly look to enhance productivity through the use of computers, the Internet, and other technology applications, it appears that older workers will continue to be at risk. Some social philosophers expect that greater labor market dislocations will occur and postulate that the systems age could mean a decreasing need for mass labor.[12]

The OASDHI program and private pension plans, although created to alleviate the financial risk associated with excessive longevity, have actually aggravated the problem. These programs have tended to institutionalize age 65 as the normal retirement age, although the 1986 amendments to the Age Discrimination in Employment Act (ADEA) banned mandatory retirement (at any age) for most employees. The 1983 amendments to The Social Security Act are gradually raising the normal retirement age for Social Security benefits to age 67 by the year 2027.[13] At the time of publication, some Social Security reform proposals suggested that normal retirement age for Social Security benefits be linked to life expectancy and automatically increase as life expectancies rise. Also, some employers may hesitate to hire older workers on the assumption that these employees will increase pension and other employee benefit plan costs. It is difficult to generalize the impact of the older worker on employee benefit plan costs. Nevertheless, it must be recognized that an employer's attitude toward hiring older workers may be influenced by the assumption, justified or not, that employee benefit costs will be adversely affected.

Self-employed members of the labor force have greater control as to the timing of their retirement from active employment. For example, physicians and lawyers frequently continue in practice, at least on a part-time basis, until advanced ages. Owners of businesses also continue to be active in their firms until relatively old ages. The fact remains, however, that employment opportunities for the majority of older workers have

---

[12] Jeremy Rifkin, *The End of Work* (New York: Penguin Group, 2004), p. 5.

[13] The retirement benefits provided under The Social Security Act are discussed in detail in Appendix 1 at the end of this book.

become more limited. It is quite likely that this will be a temporary phenomenon for many employees given the expected impact of changing demographics and the potential shortage of certain segments of the workforce projected for the future.

Individual Savings of the Aged

If employment opportunities for the aged are decreasing and financial needs are still substantial at advanced ages, the need for savings becomes quite apparent. However, studies indicate that a substantial proportion of the homes owned by the aged are clear of any mortgage. Home ownership reduces the income needs of the aged insofar as normal maintenance costs and taxes are less than the amount of rent required for comparable housing accommodations. It has been estimated that the maintenance costs for an unencumbered home are about one-third to 40 percent less than the costs of renting comparable facilities. Furthermore, there is the possibility that the home can be used in part as an income-producing asset or that a home equity loan can be used to provide additional cash.

There is growing interest in the concept of a so-called **reverse annuity.** Under this approach, the home owner receives a lifetime monthly income in exchange for the title to the home at the home owner's death. The amount of the monthly annuity payment depends on the equity in the home and the life expectancy of the home owner.

Jacobs and Weissert were early researchers who analyzed the potential for using home equity to finance long-term care. Their results strongly suggested that a significant number of elderly Americans could use their homes' equity to meet their health care expenses. They also concluded that those in the highest risk group and those with the lowest incomes, who are often the same individuals, also could be significantly helped by the use of reverse annuity mortgages.[14]

As a result of the Housing and Community Development Act of 1987, the federal government began an experimental program in which the Department of Housing and Urban Development (HUD) insured a maximum of 2,500 reverse annuity mortgages. The experimental program was further extended. In 1993, the National Housing Act was amended and the mortgage insurance authority of the Federal Housing Authority (FHA) Reverse Mortgage program was made permanent. Throughout the 1990s, reverse mortgages insured by the HUD program grew dramatically. According to HUD Secretary Andrew Cuomo, the number of new reverse mortgages has quadrupled in the past decade.[15] Although the complexity of the HUD program, the inherent risks, and the small profit potential have reduced the number of original lenders, it is anticipated that the reverse annuity concept will become even more important in the future.[16]

---

[14] Bruce Jacobs and William Weissert, "Using Home Equity to Finance Long-Term Care," *Journal of Health Politics, Policy & Law* 12, no. 1 (Spring 1987), pp. 77–95. However, other researchers analyzed the potential of reverse annuity mortgages to increase the current income of the elderly and concluded that most low-income elderly also had little housing equity. See Steven F. Venti and David A. Wise, "Aging and the Income Value of Housing Wealth," *Journal of Public Economics* 44, no. 3 (April 1991), pp. 371–97.

[15] Ilyce R. Glink, "*The Latest on Reverse Mortgages.*" (ThinkGlink.com, January 31, 2002), p. 1.

[16] Robert J. Pratte, "A Mortgage for the 21st Century," *Mortgage Banking* 50, no. 8 (May 1990), pp. 45–52.

Personal savings rates have been running at historically low levels in recent years. The distribution of savings by savings media has changed considerably over the years. The change that is most pertinent to this discussion is the relative increase in private pension reserves in relation to purely individual forms of saving. Annual employer contributions to private pension funds now amount to a sizable amount.[17] It should be noted that many pieces of legislation in the late 80s and early 90s impacted overall pension contributions by changing the limits on allowable pension contributions for plan sponsors.[18] However, a major shift in tax policy resulted with the passage of the **Economic Growth and Tax Relief Reconciliation Act of 2001 (EGTRRA).** For the first time in several years, limits on allowable pension contributions were actually increased. The tremendous increases in disposable income over the last 50 years previously had not resulted in any increase in the proportion of personal savings. Although many questioned whether the expanded contribution limits of EGTRRA would be sustained following the tragedy of September 11th in 2001 and the subsequent economic costs related to the Iraq War, passage of the **Pension Protection Act (PPA) of 2006** made these expanded contribution limits permanent. Without inclusion of the PPA provision making the EGTRRA contribution limits permanent, these limits would have been rescinded after 2010 when the sunset provision of the EGTRRA legislation would have occurred. It will be interesting to see whether these expanded pension contribution limits, now made permanent by the PPA, have a sustained impact on personal savings.

There have been many forces at work that have restricted the growth of savings. Advertising, installment credit, and the media of mass communications encourage individuals to set their sights on a constantly increasing standard of living. This competition from consumption goods for current income dollars results in a lower priority being placed on the need for accumulating savings for old age. Also, the high levels of federal income tax rates reduce an income earner's capacity to save. Although tax rates were reduced by the Tax Reform Act of 1986 (TRA '86), they subsequently increased. EGTRRA reduced income tax rates again, although not as dramatically as TRA '86 did. Inflation was an additional deterrent to increased levels of saving. Inflation is a particularly serious threat to the adequacy of savings programs of persons who already are retired. For employed persons, increases in the cost of living may be offset, in part or in whole, by increases in current earnings; however, inflation protection is likely to be less comprehensive for most aged persons.[19] Therefore, the aged are faced with the alternatives of accepting a lower standard of living or more rapidly liquidating their accumulated savings. Although the initial years of the new millennium experienced low levels of inflation, it is important to realize the threat to purchasing power that an increased rate of inflation can mean.

---

[17] As the private retirement system has changed, many of these retirement assets are now in individual account types of plans.

[18] This reduction in allowable pension contributions results from the conflict between the social policy objectives of encouraging employers to provide pensions and the federal revenue loss occurring since pensions are afforded preferential tax treatment. At the end of this chapter is a more detailed discussion of legislation affecting pension contribution limits.

[19] Appendix 1 at the end of this book describes the inflation protection inherent in Social Security payments; Chapter 17 analyzes the techniques used by many private plan sponsors to provide partial ad hoc relief.

The proportion of individual (as opposed to group) savings, then, is decreasing at a time when the pattern of living for the aged is becoming increasingly more costly. Under such circumstances, the tremendous importance of pension programs in meeting the economic risk of old age is obvious.

Increasing Longevity

Still another dimension to the overall economic problem of old age is the number of aged in the population. The fact that life expectancy has been increasing is well recognized. However, that this increase in **longevity** is a recent and quite dramatic development often is not appreciated. Since 1900, life expectancy at birth has increased from 47 years to approximately 77.5 years. The rates of mortality at the earlier ages are now so low that further improvements in mortality at these ages would have little impact on further extensions of the average length of life. If additional improvements in longevity are to be realized, reductions in mortality at the older ages are required. This impediment to further extensions in life expectancy may be overcome if medical advances result from the current concentration of research in the areas of the chronic and degenerative diseases. Medical research in fields such as biotechnology and gene therapy may result in such advances.

One effect of the improvements in longevity in the twentieth century has been an absolute and relative increase in the population of persons age 65 and over. In 1900, there were approximately 3 million persons age 65 and over, whereas there were about 36 million such persons in 2005. The proportion of the U.S. population age 65 and over in 2005 was about 12.6 percent, whereas the proportion of the population in this age bracket in 1900 was about 4 percent.

Another important dimension in the analysis of the changing **demography** of the elderly—those age 65 and over—is their age distribution. A generation ago, 68 percent of the elderly were 65 to 74 years old, 27 percent were 75 to 84 years old, and only 5 percent were 85 or older. However, today's (2010) elderly population reflects a shift toward the upper end of the age scale: Approximately 19.1 percent are 85 or over; 38.6 percent are 75 to 84; and 42.3 percent are 65 to 74.[20]

The problem of old-age economic security, therefore, is of concern to an increasing number and percentage of the U.S. population.

Reasons for Growth of Private Pensions

From the preceding discussion it can be seen that the problem of economic security for the aged is a serious and increasingly important one. However, the mere existence of the problem does not explain the sustained growth of private pensions. In other words, given the existence of the old-age economic problem, why did employers and employees choose to meet the need, at least in part, through the vehicle of private pension programs? In a broad sense, the major reason is the fact that private pensions offer substantial

---

[20] *Statistical Abstract of the United States, 2007* (Washington, DC: U.S. Government Printing Office, December, 2006), p. 18. Note: 2010 data utilizes projections based on the 2000 census.

advantages to both employers and employees. Without this foundation of mutual benefit, the private pension movement could not have achieved the substantial and sustained growth it has enjoyed. In addition, for several decades, government officials have recognized the social desirability of pension programs and have acted to encourage the growth of these plans through favorable treatment under the tax system and by other means. As indicated in Chapter 3, some observers have noted that many legislative initiatives have tended to favor defined contribution over defined benefit approaches. The growth of these different types of plans and the historical impact of favorable legislation are chronicled in that chapter. However, it appears that this attitude of encouraging private pension growth through preferential tax treatment stalled when large federal budget deficits occurred in the 80s and 90s.

The specific factors generally considered as having influenced the growth of private pensions are discussed below. It must be recognized that the reasons giving rise to the establishment of one plan are sometimes quite different from those in the case of another plan. As noted above, a policy shift appeared to occur with the passage of EGTRRA. This policy of foregoing tax revenues with expanded contribution limits to retirement plans was bolstered with enactment of the PPA.

Increased Productivity

A systematic method of meeting the problem of **superannuated** employees can be easily justified on sound management grounds. Due to advanced age, an employee may reach a point where he or she experiences a diminishment in productivity. That is, at some advanced age, an employee's contribution to the productivity of the firm may be worth less than the compensation he or she is receiving.

The employer has several courses of action if an employee reaches this point. One, the employee can be terminated without any further compensation or any retirement benefits as soon as the value of the employee's services is less than the salary being paid. For obvious reasons, this course of action is seldom followed by employers. Two, the employer can retain the less-productive, superannuated employee in the employee's current position at the current level of compensation, the difference between the employee's productivity and salary being absorbed by the employer as a cost of doing business. This alternative is also undesirable and would undoubtedly be the most costly method of meeting the problem of less-productive, superannuated employees. Furthermore, the longer range indirect costs that would be incurred from the resultant inefficiencies and poor employee morale among the productive, active workers would be significant. Three, the employer could retain the less-productive, superannuated worker but transfer the employee to a less-demanding job at the same or a reduced level of compensation. In the former case, the direct costs would be similar to alternative two, but the indirect costs would be reduced in that a more capable person would now be staffing the more demanding position. If the employee's salary is reduced, the direct costs of superannuation also would be reduced.

Most employers who do not have a pension plan generally handle the problem of the less-productive, superannuated worker in the latter manner. The effectiveness of this approach to the problem has certain important limitations. First, a firm usually has only a limited number of positions to which such workers can be transferred. For a medium- or even large-sized firm, only a fraction of such employees can be efficiently employed. With the onset of the Systems Age and the increasingly higher levels of skill required in most jobs, the limitations of this solution are apparent. Furthermore, the less-productive, superannuated employee is generally still overpaid in the less-demanding jobs since, for practical purposes, salary reductions commensurate with the decrease in employee productivity are seldom made. Lastly, this approach does not solve the problem of productivity; it merely defers it, since a point will be reached where the employee's productivity is considerably below even a minimum level of wage.

The fourth alternative available to the employer in meeting the problem of productivity loss with superannuation is to establish a formal pension plan. A pension plan permits employers to provide less-productive, superannuated employees with an acceptable alternative to continued employment in a humanitarian and nondiscriminatory manner, and the inefficiencies associated with retaining employees beyond their productive years are reduced. Furthermore, the sense of security derived from the knowledge that some provision will be made, at least in part, for their retirement income needs should increase the morale and productivity of employees. Also, the systematic retirement of older workers will keep the channels of promotion open, thereby offering opportunity and incentive to the younger employees—particularly those aspiring to executive positions. Therefore, a pension plan should permit an employer to replenish the workforce.

The problem of productivity loss with superannuation, then, exists for most business firms. Any solution, except the unlikely alternative of arbitrary termination of older workers without any retirement benefit, results in some cost, direct or indirect, to the employer. Unfortunately, some employers assume that the retirement plan solution is the only approach that carries a price tag, but the hidden costs of the other alternatives must be recognized as well. The decision, therefore, is which solution is best suited to the needs and financial position of the employer. For a large number of employers, the formal retirement plan approach has proven to be the superior solution.

Tax Considerations

The bulk of the growth in private pension plans has occurred since 1940. One reason for the growth of these plans during the World War II and Korean War periods was that normal and excess-profit tax rates imposed on corporations during these years were extremely high. Since the employer's contributions to a qualified pension plan are deductible (within limits) for federal income tax purposes, a portion of the plan's liabilities could be funded with very little effective cost to the firm. Furthermore, the investment income earned on pension trust assets is exempt from federal income taxation until distributed.[21]

The tax advantages of qualified pension plans are attractive from the standpoint of employees covered under the plan; for example, the employer's contributions to a pension fund do not constitute taxable income to the employee in the year in which contributions are made. The pension benefits derived from employer contributions are taxed when distributed to the employee. In addition, under limited circumstances, distributions from a pension plan may be taxed on a favorable basis.

---

[21] For a complete discussion of the tax aspects of qualified pension plans, see Chapters 25 and 26.

Therefore, qualified pension plans generally offer significant tax advantages to participants; prior to 1988, employees in high income tax brackets received the greatest advantages.[22] Since the high-salaried senior officers of corporations often make the decision regarding the establishment and design of employee benefit plans, their role as participants under the plans may have influenced their decisions on these matters. However, in the case of large corporations, costs and other considerations minimized or eliminated the personal tax situations of key employees as factors influencing the establishment or design of a pension plan. In the case of a small, closely-held corporation, on the other hand, one can readily see how the tax implications for stockholder-employees might have been a decisive factor in the establishment and design of a pension plan. Lastly, tax considerations are certainly one reason, although not the most important, why some labor leaders negotiate for the establishment and liberalization of employee benefit programs in lieu of further wage increases.

The Tax Reform Act of 1986 and subsequent legislative initiatives have diminished the benefits available to highly compensated employees. As a result, there is a much greater interest in nonqualified plans for the highly compensated, and the number of employees covered by such arrangements has increased.[23]

Wage Stabilization

The second wartime development that helped to stimulate the growth of pensions was the creation of a **wage stabilization program** as part of a general price control effort. Employers competing for labor could not offer the inducement of higher wages. Under these conditions, union leaders found it difficult to prove to their memberships the merits of unionism.

Therefore, the War Labor Board attempted to relieve the pressure on management and labor for higher wage rates by permitting the establishment of fringe benefit programs, including pensions. This policy further stimulated the growth of pension plans during the period.

Union Demands

Labor leaders have had differing views over the years regarding the desirability of employer-financed pension plans. In the 1920s, labor generally did not favor such plans for its membership. It held the view that pensions represented an additional form of employer paternalism and were instituted to encourage loyalty to the firm.

---

[22] Up until 1986, the federal income tax law had 14 progressive tax brackets and a maximum rate of 50 percent. The Tax Reform Act of 1986 reduced the number of tax brackets to two (15 percent and 28 percent), effective in 1988. The maximum tax bracket was subsequently increased to 31 percent. The Omnibus Budget Reconciliation Act of 1993 created a further marginal income tax rate of 36 percent and imposed an additional 10 percent surtax on taxable income over $250,000, while increasing the alternative minimum tax rate. The combination of these changes has resulted in some individuals' experiencing marginal federal tax rates at, or exceeding in some cases, 42 percent. The Economic Growth and Tax Relief Reconciliation Act of 2001 (EGTRRA) reduced tax rates so that when fully phased in for year 2006 and later years, base rates would be 10 percent, 15 percent, 25 percent, 28 percent, 33 percent, and 35 percent.

[23] For a detailed discussion of nonqualified plans, see Chapter 14.

Labor leaders felt that the need would be best met through the establishment of a government-sponsored universal social security system; in the absence of that solution, unions should establish their own pension plans for their members. The former objective was achieved with the passage of The Social Security Act of 1935. By the 1930s, several unions had established their own plans. However, many of these plans were financed inadequately, a condition that became apparent during the depression years. Recognition of the financial burden of a pension program and enactment of wage controls led some labor leaders, in the early 1940s, to favor the establishment of employer-supported pension plans.

From 1945 to 1949, the rate of growth of new plans fell off markedly. During this postwar period, employee interest centered upon cash wage increases in an attempt to recover the ground lost during the period of wage stabilization. In the latter part of the 1940s, union leaders once again began expressing an interest in the negotiation of pension programs. The renewal of interest in pensions probably came about because of two factors. First, there was increasing antagonism on the part of the public toward what were viewed by many persons as excessive union demands for cash wage increases. The negotiation of fringe benefits was one way of possibly reducing pressures from this quarter. Second, some union leaders argued that Social Security benefits were inadequate, and a supplement in the form of private pension benefits was considered to be necessary. Also, certain labor officials believed the negotiation of employer-supported pensions would weaken the resistance of the latter toward liberalizations of Social Security benefit levels. Thus, pension demands became a central issue in the labor negotiations in the coal, automobile, and steel industries in the late 40s. Although unions had negotiated pension benefits prior to this period, it was not until the late 40s that a major segment of labor made a concerted effort to bargain for private pensions.

Labor's drive for pension benefits was facilitated by a National Labor Relations Board (NLRB) ruling in 1948 that employers had a legal obligation to bargain over the terms of pension plans. Until that time, there was some question as to whether employee benefit programs fell within the traditional subject areas for collective bargaining—that is, wages, hours, and other conditions of employment. The issue was resolved when the NLRB held that pension benefits constitute wages and the provisions of these plans affect conditions of employment.[24] Upon appeal, the court upheld the NLRB decision, although it questioned the assumption that such benefits are wages.[25] These decisions determined that an employer cannot install, terminate, or alter the terms of a pension plan covering organized workers without the approval of the authorized bargaining agent for those employees. Furthermore, management has this obligation regardless of whether the plan is contributory or non-contributory, voluntary or compulsory, and regardless of whether the plan was established before or after the certification of the bargaining unit.

Labor was quick to respond to these decisions, and the 1950s were marked by union demands for the establishment of new pension plans, the liberalization of existing

[24] *Inland Steel Company* v. *United Steelworkers of America,* 77 NLRB 4 (1948).
[25] *Inland Steel Company* v. *National Labor Relations Board,* 170 F (2d) 247, 251 (1949).

plans, and the supplanting of employer-sponsored programs with negotiated plans. Undoubtedly, labor's interest in private pensions has been an important factor in the tremendous growth in plans since 1949.

Business Necessity

Employers hire employees in a free, competitive labor market. Therefore, as the number of plans increases, employees come to expect a pension benefit as part of the employment relationship. Employers who do not have such a plan are at a competitive disadvantage in attracting and retaining human resources. Therefore, some employers feel they must install a plan even if they are not convinced that the advantages generally associated with a pension plan outweigh the cost of the benefit. Admittedly, this is a negative reason for instituting a plan. In other words, while these employers believe little evidence exists that pension plans truly result in improved morale and efficiency among their workforce, they feel there would clearly be an adverse employee reaction if they did not offer a pension. Also, in contrast to situations where a plan is established in response to labor demands, an employer may offer a pension plan as part of an employee relations objective aimed at keeping a union out of the firm.

Reward for Service

There is a tendency to argue that employers never provide any increase in employee benefits unless they can expect an economic return in some form. Although this philosophy may generally prevail in a capitalistic system, the fact remains that many employers have established plans out of a sincere desire to reward employees who have served the firm well over a long period of service. Also, some employers may feel a moral responsibility to make some provision for the economic welfare of retired employees.

Efficiency of Approach

Part of the growth of private pensions must be attributed to the belief that a formal group savings approach has certain inherent advantages. The advantages are not such that they eliminate the need for individual savings, but the merits of private pensions as a supplement to Social Security benefits and individual savings programs are indeed significant. First, the economic risk of old age derives from the fact that a point is reached when an employee is unable or unwilling to continue in active employment. A formal plan as an integral part of compensation arrangements and employment relationships, therefore, is quite logical. There is no additional wage cost to the employer to the extent that pension benefits are provided in lieu of other forms of compensation. If pension benefits are provided in addition to prevailing wage rates, the employer's extra wage costs resulting from the pension plan may be able to be passed on to the consuming public in the form of higher prices.

It has been argued that from a broad social point of view, the private pension system is the lowest cost method of providing economic security for the aged. In addition to the administrative efficiency of group savings arrangements, it is argued that the small increase in consumer prices that might be required to provide pension benefits is a relatively painless method of meeting the risk. In other words, the burden of retirement security is spread over a large number of people and over a long period of time. Still another aspect to the argument is the assumption that private pensions increase consumption levels among the aged, which in turn helps to maintain a high level of economic activity.

Last, private pensions constitute a form of forced savings. This advantage is extremely important in view of the apparent desire of many people to maintain a relatively high standard of living during their active employment years. Thus, it may be argued that it is economically more efficient if at least part of the risk is met through a forced savings private pension scheme.

Sales Efforts of Funding Agencies

For all these reasons, there has been a considerable demand over the years for private pensions. However, in many instances, the advantages of these programs have had to be called to the attention of specific employers. This function of creating effective demand for the pension product has been aggressively performed by those parties interested in providing services in this area. Insurance companies, through agents, brokers, and salaried representatives, were undoubtedly instrumental in the growth of pensions, particularly in the decades of the 20s and 30s. The trust departments of banks also are equipped to handle pension funds, and many corporate trustees and asset managers have been actively soliciting pension business, particularly since the early 1950s. Similarly, the sales efforts of mutual fund representatives in recent years, particularly with 401(k) plans, have contributed to the growth of private pension and savings plans.

Rationale of Private Pensions

The growth of private pensions is attributable, as seen above, to a variety of reasons. It is difficult to determine the extent of the growth contributed by each factor, but it seems reasonable to conclude that the dominant reasons leading to the establishment of specific plans have varied depending on the circumstances surrounding each case. In other words, productivity considerations have been dominant forces leading to the creation of some plans, while labor pressures, tax considerations, or other factors have encouraged the establishment of others. With such variety of motivation, it is difficult to characterize private pensions in terms of a single philosophy or rationale. Nevertheless, attempts have been made over the years to explain private pensions in terms of an underlying concept or philosophy.[26]

Early industrial pension plans were viewed as gratuities or rewards to employees for long and loyal service to the employer. Closely related to this view is the concept that private pensions constitute a systematic and socially desirable method of releasing employees who are no longer productive members of the employer's labor force. Regardless of the view taken, it is clear that these early plans were largely discretionary, and

---

[26] For an excellent discussion of pension philosophies, see Jonas E. Mittelman, "The Vesting of Private Pensions" (Ph.D. dissertation, University of Pennsylvania, 1959), ch. 2.

management made it quite evident that employees had no contractual rights to benefits under the plans. Continuation of the pension plan was dependent upon competitive conditions and management policy. Furthermore, management reserved the right to terminate benefit payments to pensioners for misconduct on the part of the beneficiary or for any other reasons justifying such action in the opinion of the employer.

Thus, the growth of early pensions might be best categorized by a single concept: business expediency. Business expediency, by the very nature of the concept, implies that the establishment of a plan is a management prerogative and that the primary motivation for the creation of such plans is the economic benefit, direct or indirect, that is accrued to the employer. But as the economy became more and more industrialized and pension plans became more prevalent, there was increasing expression of the view that employers had a moral obligation to provide for the economic security of retired workers. This point of view was expressed as early as 1912 by Lee Welling Squier, as follows: "From the standpoint of the whole system of social economy, no employer has a right to engage men in any occupation that exhausts the individual's industrial life in 10, 20, or 40 years; and then leave the remnant floating on society at large as a derelict at sea."[27]

This rationale of private pensions has come to be known as the **human deprecia-tion concept.** It was the point of view taken by the United Mine Workers of America in their 1946 drive to establish a welfare fund:

> The United Mine Workers of America has assumed the position over the years that the cost of caring for the human equity in the coal industry is inherently as valid as the cost of the replacement of mining machinery, or the cost of paying taxes, or the cost of paying interest indebtedness, or any other factor incident to the production of a ton of coal for consumers' bins . . . [The agreement establishing the Welfare Fund] recognized in prin-ciple the fact that the industry owed an obligation to those employees, and the coal miners could no longer be used up, crippled beyond repair, and turned out to live or die subject to the charity of the community or the minimum contributions of the state.[28]

This analogy between human labor and industrial machines also was made in the report of the president's fact-finding board in the 1949 steelworkers' labor dispute in support of its conclusion that management had a responsibility to provide for the secu-rity of its workers: "We think that all industry, in the absence of adequate government programs, owes an obligation to workers to provide for maintenance of the human body in the form of medical and similar benefits and full depreciation in the form of old-age retirement—in the same way as it does now for plant and machinery."[29] The report con-tinues as follows: "What does that mean in terms of steelworkers? It should mean the use of earnings to insure against the full depreciation of the human body—say at age 65—in the form of a pension or retirement allowance."[30]

---

[27] Lee Welling Squier, *Old Age Dependency in the United States* (New York: Macmillan, 1912), p. 272.

[28] United Mine Workers of America Welfare and Retirement Fund, *Pensions for Coal Miners* (Washington, DC, n.d.), p. 4.

[29] Steel Industry Board, *Report to the President of the United States on the Labor Dispute in the Basic Steel Industry* (Washington, DC: U.S. Government Printing Office, September 10, 1949), p. 55.

[30] Ibid., p. 65.

The validity of the human depreciation concept of private pensions has been challenged by many pension experts.[31] The process of aging is physiological and is not attributable to the employment relationship. Admittedly, the hazards of certain occupations undoubtedly shorten the life span of the employees involved. In those instances, the employer can logically be held responsible only for the increase in the rate of aging due to the hazards of the occupation. More important, the analogy between humans and machines is inherently unsound. A machine is an asset owned by the employer, and depreciation is merely an accounting technique for allocating the costs of equipment to various accounting periods. Employees, on the other hand, are free agents and sell their services to employers for a specified wage rate. An employee, unlike a machine, is free to move from one employer to another. The differences between humans and machines are so great that one must question the value of the analogy as a basis for a rationale of private pensions. As Dearing notes, "Any economic or moral responsibility that is imposed on the employer for the welfare of workers after termination of the labor contract should be grounded on firmer reasoning than is supplied by the machine-worker analogy."[32]

A more recent view of private pensions that has achieved broader acceptance is the **deferred wage concept.** This concept views a pension benefit as part of a wage package that is composed of cash wages and other employee fringe benefits. The deferred wage concept has particular appeal with reference to negotiated pension plans. The assumption is made that labor and management negotiators think in terms of total labor costs. Therefore, if labor negotiates a pension benefit, the funds available for increases in cash wages are reduced accordingly. This theory of private pensions was expressed as early as 1913:

> In order to get a full understanding of old-age and service pensions, they should be considered as a part of the real wages of a workman. There is a tendency to speak of these pensions as being paid by the company, or, in cases where the employee contributes a portion, as being paid partly by the employer and partly by the employee. In a certain sense, of course, this may be correct, but it leads to confusion. A pension system considered as part of the real wages of an employee is really paid by the employee, not perhaps in money, but in the forgoing of an increase in wages which he might obtain except for the establishment of a pension system.[33]

The deferred wage concept also has been challenged on several grounds. First, it is noted that some employers who pay the prevailing cash wage rate for the particular industry also provide a pension benefit. Thus, it can be argued that in these cases the pension benefit is offered in addition to, rather than in lieu of, a cash wage increase. Second, the deferred wage concept ignores the possible argument that the employer is willing to accept a lower profit margin to provide a pension plan for employees. Third, it is sometimes argued that if pension benefits are a form of wage, then terminated employees should be entitled to the part of the retirement benefit that has been earned to

---

[31] For example, see Dan M. McGill and Donald S. Grubbs, Jr., *Fundamentals of Private Pensions*, 6th ed. (Burr Ridge, IL: Richard D. Irwin, 1989), pp. 18–19. See also Charles L. Dearing, *Industrial Pensions* (Washington, DC: Brookings Institution, 1954), pp. 62–63 and 241–43; and Mittelman, "Vesting of Private Pensions," pp. 28–34.

[32] Dearing, *Industrial Pensions*, p. 243.

[33] Albert de Roode, "Pensions as Wages," *American Economic Review* III, no. 2 (June 1913), p. 287.

the date of termination. In practice, one finds that not all plans provide for the full and immediate vesting of all benefits. However, it can be argued that the deferred wage concept does not necessarily require the full and immediate vesting of benefits. Proponents of this concept view pension benefits as a wage, the receipt of which is conditioned upon the employee's remaining in the service of the employer for a specified number of years. This view of the pension benefit is similar, conceptually, to a pure endowment in which the policyholder receives the full face benefit of the policy if he or she lives to the maturity of the policy; however, the beneficiaries receive nothing if the policyholder dies prior to this time period. The consideration of the employee in this case is the reduction in cash wages accepted in lieu of the pension benefit.

In spite of the appeal of the deferred wage theory, it is questionable whether the private pension movement can be explained solely in terms of this concept. Indeed, there is probably no one rationale or theory that fully explains the reason for being of private pensions. This conclusion is not surprising since these plans are private, and the demands or reasons that give rise to one plan may be quite different from those leading to the introduction of another plan.

Legislative History and Recent Legal Changes

Employee benefits in general and pension plans in particular have been the subject of substantial legislative activity in recent years.

After many years of discussion and debate concerning reform of the private pension system, the **Employee Retirement Income Security Act of 1974 (ERISA)** became law on September 2, 1974. ERISA effected some of the most significant changes ever enacted in the private pension movement. These changes affected virtually all aspects of corporate and self-employed pension plans from a legal, tax, investment, and actuarial viewpoint. In addition, ERISA established new reporting, disclosure, and fiduciary requirements as well as a program of plan termination insurance. Another major feature of ERISA was the establishment of the individual retirement account (IRA) concept, which was initially designed for individuals not covered under a qualified retirement plan.

The Economic Recovery Tax Act of 1981 (ERTA) was one of the biggest tax reduction acts in history. It also included several provisions that affected retirement plans. Most notable were the provisions that greatly expanded IRA opportunities to anyone with personal service income, allowed for voluntary contributions to qualified plans, and increased contribution and deduction limits for both simplified employee pension (SEP) programs and Keogh (HR-10) plans. ERTA also made changes that affected stock ownership plans and executive compensation arrangements.

Following on the heels of ERTA came another massive act, the **Tax Equity and Fiscal Responsibility Act of 1982 (TEFRA)**, considered by some to be the biggest revenue-raising bill in history. TEFRA probably touched everyone in the United States in some manner and affected retirement plans in many ways. It reduced the maximum limits of pension plan benefits and contributions; brought about parity between corporate plans and plans for self-employed persons; introduced special restrictions on plans that are considered "top heavy," that is, plans that appear to be heavily weighted toward key employees; and provided for federal income tax withholding on pension and annuity payments.

After a one-year hiatus, in 1984 Congress passed two acts with significant implications for qualified retirement plans. The Deficit Reduction Act of 1984 (DEFRA) contained several provisions that substantially modified savings incentives. Cost-of-living adjustments for contribution and benefit limits were frozen for a second time. Estate tax exclusions for distributions from qualified plans and IRAs were repealed. Rules for cash-or-deferred plans, also known as 401(k) plans, were tightened. The Retirement Equity Act of 1984 (REACT) represented an attempt on the part of Congress to provide what was perceived by some as a more equitable distribution of retirement benefits from qualified plans. Young employees and females were the chief benefactors, as REACT required a reduction in the minimum age for mandatory participation, modified rules relating to breaks in service, changed the survivor benefit requirements, and allowed for the assignment of qualified plan benefits in divorce proceedings.

In the most pervasive changes since ERISA, the **Tax Reform Act of 1986** imposed new coverage tests and accelerated vesting requirements for qualified plans, changed the rules under which qualified plans can be integrated with Social Security, lowered limits for retirement benefits that begin before age 65, changed the timing and taxation of plan distributions, and terminated IRA deductions for many qualified plan participants. Substantial changes also were made with respect to employee stock ownership plans and executive compensation. Following the Tax Reform Act of 1986, Congress passed the Omnibus Budget Reconciliation Act of 1987 (OBRA '87), which made significant changes with respect to (1) minimum funding and maximum tax deductions for qualified plans and (2) plan termination obligations for defined benefit plans.

Under the Technical and Miscellaneous Revenue Act of 1988 (TAMRA), Congress provided the possibility that certain minimum participation requirements enacted in the Tax Reform Act of 1986 may be applied separately with respect to each separate line of business of an employer.[34] TAMRA also added an additional sanction for highly compensated employees, requiring them to include in their gross income for the year in which the minimum participation standard is not met an amount equal to their vested accrued benefit as of the close of that year.

The Omnibus Budget Reconciliation Act of 1989 (OBRA '89) made numerous changes in the statutory provisions that permitted a lender to an employee stock ownership plan (ESOP), or ESOP plan sponsor, to exclude 50 percent of the interest from its income for federal tax purposes.[35] OBRA also amended, among other things, provisions

---

[34] The Small Business Job Protection Act of 1996 modified minimum participation rules as they apply to separate lines of business. The act allowed that fewer than 50 employees could be participants in a defined benefit plan for a separate line of business if it otherwise would meet the requirements to qualify as a separate line of business.

[35] The Small Business Job Protection Act of 1996 repealed the interest income exclusion for ESOP loans that allowed banks, insurance companies, regulated investment companies, and certain corporations to exclude 50 percent of the interest received on ESOP loans. Repeal of the interest income exclusion became effective with loans where a contract for the loan agreement occurred on or after June 10, 1996.

pertaining to the Section 404(k) dividend deduction, the ESOP tax-free rollover, and the ESOP estate tax exclusion.

The Omnibus Budget Reconciliation Act of 1990 (OBRA '90) increased Pension Benefit Guaranty Corporation (PBGC) premiums as well as the excise tax on reversions of excess pension plan assets to the employer on termination of a pension plan. However, OBRA '90 presented an opportunity to increase corporate cash flow and possibly decrease near-term expenses through the use of excess pension assets to pay retiree health benefits. The existence of this opportunity depends on the funded status of a pension plan.

The Older Workers Benefit Protection Act of 1990 amended the Age Discrimination in Employment Act (ADEA) to apply to employee benefits but singled out early retirement incentive plans as allowable if they were voluntary, conformed with the purposes of the ADEA, and met certain minimum standards.

The Unemployment Compensation Amendments of 1992 (UCCA) instituted a 20 percent mandatory withholding tax on lump-sum distributions that are not directly transferred to a qualified type of retirement account and provided notification requirements that plan sponsors must distribute to participants requesting lump-sum distributions. Furthermore, these amendments liberalized the rollover rules, affording most taxable distributions eligibility for rollover treatment, and required plan sponsors to provide a direct rollover option by the end of the 1994 plan year.

The Omnibus Budget Reconciliation Act of 1993 (OBRA '93) lowered the allowable compensation limit for computation of qualified plan contributions to $150,000 from the $235,840 it had risen to through indexing. The law also limited the indexing of the $150,000 compensation cap to $10,000 increments, thus slowing its rise. This sharp reduction in the allowable compensation base that could be used in determining contributions to qualified pension, 401(k), and other retirement plans of highly compensated employees, caused increased interest in nonqualified plans for replacing lost benefits. The law uncapped the wage base on which employers would pay the 1.45 percent Medicare portion of the Federal Insurance Contributions Act (FICA) tax. Additionally, OBRA '93 increased the amount of Social Security benefits subject to taxation from 50 percent to 85 percent for middle- and higher-income individuals beginning in 1994.

The Uniformed Services Employment and Reemployment Rights Act of 1993 guaranteed a veteran's right to pension benefits that would have accrued during military service and clarified various pension issues that arise with a military leave.

The Retirement Protection Act of 1994 that was part of the General Agreement on Tariffs and Trade (GATT) had a number of provisions directly impacting retirement plans. A number of provisions were instituted to strengthen minimum funding for certain underfunded plans. Premiums to the Pension Benefit Guaranty Corporation (PBGC) were increased. Large underfunded plans were required to engage in additional disclosure to the PBGC and plan participants. Certain limitations were instituted on the use of actuarial assumptions for lump-sum distributions, and rounding rules were instituted for the upward indexing of inflation-indexed pension limits. Essentially, these limits were rounded down until inflation adjustments move them up to the next even multiple of $5,000 ($500 or $50, in some cases). These indexing features affected the cap on included compensation for pension contributions, dollar amounts for determining highly compensated employees in nondiscrimination testing, elective deferral, and Section 415 limits. Section 415 of the Internal Revenue Code (IRC) impacts allowable limits on contributions and benefits through retirement plans. The rounding rules slow the rate of escalation in cost-of-living increases.

Immediately before the 1996 congressional summer recess and the fall 1996 presidential election, several pieces of legislation were passed into law. This legislation included the Small Business Job Protection Act of 1996 and the Health Insurance Portability and Accountability Act of 1996. Within these pieces of legislation and some other enacted laws were considerable tax-related provisions that in combination represented the most sweeping alterations to the tax code since the Tax Reform Act of 1986. Most of the pension-related provisions were included in the **Small Business Job Protection Act (of 1996),** where these provisions were assembled thematically as pension simplification provisions. Many of these provisions were advanced as a necessary compromise to gain the support of the small business community for an increase in the minimum wage, although, because of bipartisan support for the pension simplification issue, many technical corrections to earlier legislation were included.

Among the major provisions in the Small Business Job Protection Act of 1996 were the following: the creation of the savings incentive match plans for employees (SIMPLE plans); a simplified definition of highly compensated employees (HCEs) for nondiscrimination testing purposes; simplified nondiscrimination testing procedures; the establishment of testing safe harbors for 401(k) plans; the repeal of family aggregation rules; a change in the definition of compensation used for computing the limitations of IRC Section 415; modification of plan distribution rules; an increase in the maximum tax deductible contribution for spousal IRAs, and several provisions of significance to plans for tax-exempt entities (403(b) plans) and state and local governments (457 plans).

The Health Insurance Portability and Accountability Act of 1996, although not primarily dealing with pensions, included some provisions that related to retirement security. For example, this act permitted penalty-free early distributions from an IRA for payment of certain medical expenses and health insurance premiums. The act also provided favorable tax treatment for qualified long-term care (LTC) insurance and non-insured LTC expenses, although long-term care employee premiums were prohibited from being sheltered under cafeteria plans.

In 1997 two major pieces of legislation were passed impacting employee benefits and pension plans. Most of the provisions affecting pensions and employee benefit plans were included in the **Taxpayer Relief Act of 1997,** the tax portion of the budget legislation. The spending portion of the legislation known as the Balanced Budget Act of 1997 included many changes related to the Medicare program.

The Economic Growth and Tax Relief Reconciliation Act of 2001 made extensive and far-reaching changes to retirement plans. Among the many changes to be phased in over several years were increased contribution, benefit, and deduction limits for all types of retirement savings vehicles; business credits for the startup of retirement plans;

tax credits to lower- and middle-income employees making contributions to retirement plans; greater parity between plans with elimination of the 403(b) exclusion allowance and various changes to eligible 457 (b) plans; greater contribution limits permitted for retirement plan participants who were age 50 and over; plan loans permitted for sole proprietors; S corporation shareholders and partners; a new provision allowing 401(k) and 403(b) plans to incorporate a feature called a "qualified Roth contribution program"; and greater portability for all types of retirement programs by providing for easier rollover of distributions between various types of plans. However, EGTRRA also introduced an element of uncertainty for these extensive retirement plan changes since the act contained a sunset provision stating that all the rule changes would not apply to taxable, plan, or limitation years after December 31, 2010. Effectively all these retirement plan rule changes that were phased in over the next several years would automatically be eliminated in 2011 unless further legislation was passed to extend or retain these changes. Therefore, EGTRRA created both great promise and great uncertainty concerning the expansion of tax incentives for retirement plans.

The **Job Creation and Worker Assistance Act of 2002** increased the interest rate range for computing a defined benefit plan's current liability; specified that contribution deduction limits applicable to employers that maintain a combination of plans do not apply when only elective contributions are contributed to an employer's defined benefit plan; clarified certain issues for rollovers of after-tax contributions; and conformed the percentage of compensation for allowable contributions to simplified employee pensions (SEPs) to the permissible deduction limit.

On August 17, 2006, President George W. Bush signed the Pension Protection Act of 2006 into law. The PPA was the most comprehensive pension legislation in decades. Some observers viewed the PPA as the most substantial pension legislation enacted since the passage of ERISA in 1974. The PPA made the retirement-related provisions of EGTRRA permanent, thus avoiding their sunset on the last day of December 2010. The PPA included new funding rules for defined benefit plans, rules applicable to cash balance plans and other "hybrid type" plans, and rules designed to increase participation in employer-sponsored defined contribution plans. Some of the PPA provisions were effective for plan years beginning in 2008, while others were effective immediately upon enactment or for plan years beginning in 2007.

Among the provisions related to DC plans were those that increased employee participation in these plans by providing employers with incentives to automatically enroll employees into defined contribution plans and to default automatic enrollees into certain balanced long-term investment vehicles or managed accounts. The PPA also affected DC plans by making all contributions subject to faster vesting schedules; allowing financial service providers to give personal investment advice to participants in 401(k) plans and individual retirement accounts; and requiring that DC plans provide participants with quarterly benefit statements if participants direct investments or annual statements if participants do not direct investments. Furthermore, additional diversification requirements were instituted for certain DC plans holding publicly traded employer stock if the plan was not a stand-alone employee stock ownership plan (ESOP). The PPA made permanent Roth 401(k) and Roth 403(b) contributions and allowed an exception to the 10-percent early withdrawal tax for distributions from an IRA, 401(k) plan, or other similar retirement arrangements to certain reservists who were called to active duty military service. To qualify for this exemption, a reservist had to be called up to active duty between September 11, 2001, and December 31, 2007, for a period longer than 179 days.

With regard to defined benefit plans, the PPA completely overhauled the funding rules for DB plans in an attempt to make these retirement plans more secure. These updated funding rules generally applied to plan years beginning in 2008, although transition rules applied to the 2006 and 2007 plan years. The PPA encouraged DB plans to create a funding cushion by increasing the limits on deductible contributions. The PPA also attempted to facilitate phased retirement arrangements by allowing plans to distribute retirement benefits to active employees before the plan's normal retirement age. The PPA permits the distribution of retirement benefits to active employees age 62 or older, even if the plan's normal retirement age is later than age 62. The PPA modified the ability to transfer excess assets from defined benefit plans to a separate account to fund retiree health benefits. Although such transfers could occur in the past to fund current year benefits, the PPA permitted such transfers after August 17, 2006 to fund future retiree health benefits as well.

Many changes, rulings, and regulations relating to these various pieces of legislation have occurred since their enactment. The legislation and the changes, as well as their impact on retirement plans, are discussed throughout this book.

Chapter Summary

- One cause of economic insecurity is the probable reduction of an individual's earning power at an advanced age. Most often, the problem of economic insecurity is remedied by the "tripod of economic security"—personal savings, employer-sponsored pensions, and social insurance programs.
- Although the assumption usually is made that financial needs decrease after retirement, the actual aggregate reduction in financial needs upon retirement is probably overstated.
- Private pensions have experienced dramatic growth since the 1940s for a number of reasons. Among the economic, sociological, and historical reasons for this growth are the following:
  - A systematic method of meeting the problem of superannuated employees can be justified on sound management grounds. Economists have theorized on the economic rationale of private pensions using the human depreciation concept and the deferred wage concept.
  - Tax considerations provide financial incentives for the provision of qualified pension plans.
  - Union demands and the actions of the War Labor Board when increases in wages were prohibited have contributed to pension growth.

- Employers may be motivated to provide pensions to compete in recruiting and retaining workers, or they may provide pensions to reward service or forestall unionization. At times employers have been encouraged to implement pensions by the sales efforts of funding agencies.

- Pension plans have been the subject of substantial legislative activity and the development of these plans is better understood when the provisions of these legislative acts are known. One of the most notable pieces of legislation is the Employee Retirement Income Security Act of 1974 (ERISA), which established a major foundation from a legal, tax, investment, and actuarial viewpoint. The Tax Reform Act of 1986 probably provided the most pervasive changes in pension regulation since the passage of ERISA. The Small Business Job Protection Act of 1996 contained many pension-related provisions that were linked as pension simplification initiatives. Within the Small Business Job Protection Act of 1996 were many technical corrections relating to earlier pension legislation. In 1997 the Taxpayer Relief Act and Balanced Budget Act were passed.

- The Economic Growth and Tax Relief Reconciliation Act of 2001 (EGTRRA) made extensive and far-reaching changes to retirement plans. Among the many changes to be phased in over several years were increased contribution, benefit and deduction limits for all types of retirement savings vehicles; business credits for the start-up of retirement plans; tax credits to lower- and middle-income employees making contributions to retirement plans; greater parity between plans with elimination of the 403(b) maximum exclusion allowance and various changes to eligible 457(b) plans; greater contribution limits permitted for retirement plan participants who were age 50 and over; plan loans permitted for sole proprietors; S corporation shareholders, and partners; a new provision allowing 401(k) and 403(b) plans to incorporate a feature called a "qualified Roth contribution program"; and greater portability for all types of retirement programs by providing for easier rollover of distributions between various types of plans. However, EGTRRA also introduced an element of uncertainty for these extensive retirement plan changes since the act contained a sunset provision stating that all the rule changes would not apply to taxable, plan, or limitation years after December 31, 2010.

- On August 17, 2006, President George W. Bush signed the Pension Protection Act (PPA) of 2006 into law. The PPA was the most comprehensive pension legislation in decades. Some observers viewed the PPA as the most substantial pension legislation enacted since the very passage of ERISA in 1974. The PPA made the retirement-related provisions of EGTRRA permanent, thus avoiding their sunset on the last day of December 2010. The PPA included new funding rules for defined benefit plans, rules applicable to cash balance plans and other "hybrid type" plans, and rules designed to increase participation in employer-sponsored defined contribution plans. Some of the PPA provisions were effective for plan years beginning in 2008, while others were effective immediately upon enactment or for plan years beginning in 2007.

• Among the provisions of the PPA related to defined contribution plans were those that increased employee participation in these plans by providing employers with incentives to automatically enroll employees into DC plans and to default automatic enrollees into certain balanced long-term investment vehicles or managed accounts. The PPA also affected DC plans by making all contributions subject to faster vesting schedules; allowing financial service providers to give personal investment advice to participants in 401(k) plans and individual retirement accounts; and requiring that DC plans provide participants with quarterly benefit statements if participants direct investments or annual statements if participants do not direct investments. Furthermore, additional diversification requirements were instituted for certain defined contribution plans holding publicly traded employer stock if the plan was not a stand-alone employee stock ownership plan (ESOP). With regard to defined benefit plans, the PPA completely overhauled the funding rules for DBPs in an attempt to make these retirement plans more secure.

Key Terms

annuities, p. *1*
deferred wage concept, p. *16*
demography, p. *8*
Economic Growth and Tax Relief Reconciliation Act of 2001 (EGTRRA), p. *7*
Employee Retirement Income Security Act of 1974 (ERISA), p. *17*
human depreciation concept, p. *15*

Job Creation and Worker Assistance Act of 2002, p. *21*
longevity, p. *8*
Pension Protection Act (PPA) of 2006, p. *7*
reverse annuity, p. *6*
Small Business Job Protection Act (of 1996), p. *20*
superannuated, p. *9*

Tax Equity and Fiscal Responsibility Act of 1982 (TEFRA), p. *17*
Taxpayer Relief Act of 1997, p. *20*
Tax Reform Act of 1986, p. *18*
tripod of economic security, p. *1*
wage stabilization program, p. *11*

Questions for Review

1. Describe the basic economic problems facing the aged.
2. Why have private pension plans grown so rapidly since the 1940s?
3. Explain the alternatives that exist for an employer dealing with less-productive super-annuated employees. What are the limitations of these alternatives?
4. Briefly describe the principal tax advantages of qualified pension plans.
5. Describe how wage stabilization during World War II affected private pension plans.
6. Explain the role played by the National Labor Relations Board (NLRB) in the development of pension plans.
7. Describe the merits of private pensions as a supplement to Social Security benefits and individual savings programs.

8. Briefly describe the impact of recent legislation on the design process for private pension plans.

Questions for Discussion

1. Economists have often argued that pension benefits are a form of deferred compensation accepted by employees in lieu of higher present wages. Assume that the employees of a firm ask you how much the pension benefit they earned this year is actually worth in current dollars. In general terms, how would you perform this valuation? What types of assumptions would you need to make? If the employees told you that they would forfeit the entire pension attributable to employer contributions if they were terminated within five years of the time they were originally hired, how would you factor this information into your analysis?

2. For several years it has been argued that one of the primary advantages of a pension plan for employees is that it allows them to avoid taxation on a portion of their total compensation during the time they are in a high tax bracket and to postpone the receipt—and consequently the taxation—of this money until after they retire. If, as was usually the case prior to the Tax Reform Act of 1986, the employee expected to be in a lower tax bracket after retirement, the tax savings inherent in this deferral could be substantial. However, if the federal income tax system evolved into a modified form of a flat tax system in which many taxpayers expected to be taxed at the same rate, regardless of when their money was received, does this necessarily imply that the tax advantages of private pension plans have ceased to be an important advantage for employees? (Hint: Even if all money received from a pension plan is taxed at the same rate, does the fact that money can accumulate at a before-tax rate of return, instead of an after-tax rate of return, affect the eventual amount of money received by the employee?)

3. The text suggests that a private pension plan allows the burden of retirement security to be spread out over a long period of time. Discuss how this specifically applies in the case of investment risk. Assume that there are only two forms of investments for retirement: a risk-free asset with a known rate of return, and a risky asset with a higher expected rate of return. Unfortunately, the risky asset may experience large decreases as well as increases in any particular year. If employees were to invest for their retirement on an individual basis, why might they be willing to choose the risk-free asset, knowing their expected accumulation at retirement will be smaller? In contrast, if employees allowed the employer to invest for their retirement through a defined benefit pension plan (in which the employee's retirement benefit is guaranteed regardless of the level of the pension assets), would the employer be as likely to choose the lower yielding, risk-free asset for the pension plan? (Hint: What is the relevant investment horizon for a pension plan if it is assumed to be an ongoing operation?)

Resources for Further Study

CCH Editorial Staff. "Legislation 2006: Pension Protection Act of 2006: Law, Explanation and Analysis." *Commerce Clearing House* (2006).

CCH Editorial Staff. "Pension Protection Act of 2006." *Commerce Clearing House* (2006).

Kilgour, John G. "Responding to Changing Retirement Savings Programs." *Compensation & Benefits Review,* September/October 2001.

Rosenbloom, Jerry S. "The Environment of Employee Benefit Plans." *The Handbook of Employee Benefits.* 6th ed. Jerry S. Rosenbloom, ed. New York: McGraw-Hill, 2005.

Salisbury, Dallas L. "Regulatory Environment of Employee Benefit Plans." *The Handbook of Employee Benefits.* 6th ed. Jerry S. Rosenbloom, ed. New York: McGraw-Hill, 2005.

www.ebri.org—website of the Employee Benefit Research Institute.

www.ifebp.org—website of the International Foundation of Employee Benefit Plans.

www.ici.org—website of the Investment Company Institute.

www.pensionresearchcouncil.org—website of the Pension Research Council at the Wharton School of the University of Pennsylvania.

Chapter 2

Strategic Plan Design

After studying this chapter you should be able to:

- Identify important environmental factors an employer should consider when designing a pension plan.
- Describe alternative plan design approaches to achieve employer goals and objectives.
- Explain techniques that may be used to make comparisons between the retirement plans of various employers.
- Identify opportunities to comply with legal requirements by modifying elements of plan design.
- Describe how the entire portfolio of benefits for a retiree may affect the goals and objectives set for the retirement plan.
- Explain the purpose of income-replacement objectives, why they are less than 100 percent of preretirement gross income, and why they may vary depending upon salary level.

It is reasonable to speculate that the first employee benefit plans were established to serve specific purposes—for example, to avoid "passing the hat" among employees when someone died. For many years, the design of these plans was influenced largely by the insurance industry's attitude toward underwriting, funding, and administration, since the plans were made available by insurers under the terms and conditions they chose to offer.

Over the years, many factors have influenced the design of employee benefit plans, and a body of law has emerged that affects these plans in terms of minimum requirements and permissible provisions. The taxation of contributions and benefits also has influenced plan design, and the process of collective bargaining and the interests of organized labor have been a major influence, as has the availability of alternate funding mechanisms. These, and other factors, including a growing degree of sophistication and knowledge of the field, have created an environment in which an employer has a wide degree of choice and flexibility in benefit plan design. In recent years, however, the increasing level of federal regulation has caused retirement plans to gravitate toward common plan provisions. For example, plans that have eligibility requirements almost always settle on the use of one year of service and a minimum age of 21.[1]

The cost of employee benefits is significant. A well-rounded program (including paid time off) can easily generate a total cost in the vicinity of 30 percent or more of an employer's base payroll. If the cost of statutory benefits also is included, total cost can easily reach 40 percent of payroll or more. Indeed, some companies have total benefit costs that approach 50 percent of payroll. The amounts accumulated under these plans also are of major importance. For example, the assets accumulated by some companies in their pension plans alone exceed their net worth.

Given the substantial costs involved in employee benefits plans, the importance they have to millions of workers, and the complex legal, tax, and funding environments that exist, it is most important that such plans be designed with particular care, that they be fully supportive of the employer's philosophy, goals, and objectives, and that they at least partially satisfy the perceived needs of the employees. This concept is of equal importance to small employers and to larger organizations.

The major focus of this text is on the various mechanisms that exist for the delivery of retirement benefits and the ways in which a specific retirement plan might be designed. However, matters that influence the design of a retirement plan also influence the design of other employee benefit plans. Thus, while the primary emphasis of this chapter is on retirement plans, the subject matter is broad enough to apply to all employee benefits.

In this chapter, some of the environmental considerations that can influence plan design are described first. Then employer philosophy and attitudes are discussed. The final portion of the chapter deals with specific employee benefit plan objectives.

Environmental Considerations

Before passage of the Tax Equity and Fiscal Responsibility Act of 1982 (TEFRA), the employer's legal status often influenced plan design. Federal tax law dealt differently with sole proprietorships, partnerships, Subchapter S corporations, nonprofit organizations, and regular corporations. For example, defined contribution pension or profit sharing plans generally were adopted by unincorporated organizations and by Subchapter S corporations because of the deduction limits previously imposed on these organizations. Often, these deduction limits and the potential benefits of a defined benefit pension plan caused such organizations to incorporate either on a regular basis or as a professional corporation or association. While the parity provisions of TEFRA eliminated most of the distinctions in tax law that formerly applied to partnerships and sole proprietorships, precedents established by prior practice and prior law still may continue to influence plan design for some organizations.

Section 501(c)(3) organizations need to take special matters into account when considering employee benefits. One such matter is that contributions are not deductible and will not operate to reduce plan costs. Thus, the "out-of-pocket" costs for a given level of employee benefits will be higher for a tax-exempt organization than they would be for

[1] See Chapter 26 for a discussion on the determination of service.

a profit-making corporation under like circumstances. Also, these organizations have frequently used defined contribution concepts because of the availability of tax-deferred annuities under Section 403(b) of the Internal Revenue Code.

The basic characteristics of the employer and its industry are part of the background for designing an employee benefit program. Is the firm a young, growing organization, or is it relatively mature? Is its history of profits stable and predictable, or have profits been, or are they likely to be, volatile? Does the firm anticipate moderate or significant growth, and what will its need for employees be in the foreseeable future? Is the industry highly competitive? Are profit margins narrow? Is the business cyclical? What are the firm's short- and long-term capital needs? The answers to these questions and others like them can be of great importance in structuring benefit plans that will both meet employee needs and offer funding patterns compatible with the employer's objectives and capabilities.

The characteristics of the individuals employed by the employer also play an important role in plan design. The distribution of employees by age, service, sex, and pay can have significant implications in terms of the type of benefit provided, cost levels generated, and similar matters.

An employer with diversified operations has special considerations when it comes to employee benefit plan design. For example, such an employer needs to consider whether the same benefit program is appropriate for all facets of the business. Factors such as cost, profit margins, competitive need, and geographic differences should be taken into account. Another factor related to this issue is the employer's attitude regarding the transfer of employees. A uniform program facilitates such transfers, while different plans at different locations may create impediments. Obviously, the employer's basic policy concerning employee transfers, whether encouraged or discouraged, bears on the matter. One approach used by some employers is to combine a basic or "core" program that applies in all areas of the business with a flexible or varying program of supplemental benefits to accommodate different industry needs.

The communities in which the employer does business also can be an environmental factor in plan design. This is less the case in large, urban areas, but it can become quite meaningful when the company is the dominant or a major employer in a discrete geographical area. In this case, the design and structure of an employee benefit plan could reflect the employer's degree of concern over the image it wishes to create in the communities in which it does business. If such a concern exists, it often indicates the need for liberal benefit provisions—not only by the employer's own industry standards, but by the standards established by different employers involved in the same communities.

The presence or absence of collective bargaining units also can be a significant consideration. The demands of labor, both on a local and a national or "pattern" basis, can influence plan design, even for nonbargaining employees. Many employers follow the practice of extending bargained-for benefits to nonbargaining unit employees, or they make the plans of the nonbargaining unit employees slightly better than those of the bargaining unit employees, to the extent that this does not violate labor laws. Others, however, treat the programs as totally separate, particularly in the context that benefit plans are part of total compensation and that basic salary and wage structures also are quite different between the two groups.

The foregoing is not intended to be an exhaustive discussion of environmental factors that influence plan design. Rather, it is intended to give some indication of the various items that should be considered. With these in mind, it is appropriate to turn to a discussion of employer philosophy and attitudes.

Employer Philosophy and Attitudes

Specific objectives for employee benefit plans should be considered in the context of the employer's philosophy and attitudes for the management of human resources. The following list of questions and observations, again not all-inclusive, is designed to suggest the nature of some of the items that need to be considered.

1. What is the employer's basic compensation philosophy? Many employers believe benefit plans are part of total compensation and that the cost and benefit structure of these plans should reflect the employer's basic attitude toward other compensation elements. Thus, the employer who has adopted a policy of paying high wages and salaries may very well adopt a liberal benefit program. On the other hand, an employer may choose to establish a benefit program that keeps total compensation costs at an acceptable level while presenting one element of compensation on a more favorable basis. For example, an employer may wish to establish highly competitive wages and salaries but, to keep total compensation costs in line, may provide only modest benefits. Such a compensation strategy, of course, can affect the type of employee attracted and also can influence matters such as turnover rates. It also is possible for an employer to adopt a reverse compensation strategy mix and have a liberal benefit program to go along with a cash compensation program that is not fully competitive. This type of compensation mix often is found in governmental units, where cash compensation is fixed by law and where incentive compensation may not be payable. Here, it is common to find liberal benefit programs.

2. Is the employer's basic attitude toward providing employee benefits one that emphasizes the protection and maintenance of income in the event of economic insecurity? Or is its attitude oriented more toward providing additional current, although tax-deferred, compensation? Most employers do not have a clear-cut and total preference for one or the other of these positions; however, one position might be of greater significance than the other. The employer's leaning toward one or the other of these two concepts can find expression in a number of plan decisions. For example, a preference for the **income-maintenance approach** could suggest the choice of a defined benefit pension plan integrated to the maximum extent with Social Security benefits[2] or the choice of a death benefit that provides an income

---

[2] The basic concept of integration is that the benefits of the employer's plan are dovetailed with Social Security benefits in such a manner that employees earning over the Social Security taxable wage base will not receive combined benefits under the two programs proportionately greater than the benefits for employees earning less than this amount. Although the benefit formula under the private plan may favor the higher paid employees, the additional amounts provided for them cannot exceed levels allowed under the Internal Revenue Code and supporting regulations. This concept is presented in more detail in Chapter 25.

benefit only to survivors of the employee's immediate family. A **compensation-oriented approach,** though, might suggest the use of a defined contribution plan as the basic program for providing retirement benefits. In recent years, as employers have shifted from "paternalistic" attitudes to ones that emphasize individual responsibility, there has been growing interest in the compensation-oriented approach.

3. Does the employer believe employees should share in the cost of meeting their own economic security needs? Many employers take the position that employees do have such a responsibility; they believe that benefits in the event of medical expense needs, death, disability, and retirement should come from three sources—the government, the employer, and the employee's own savings. Where desired, employee involvement can be in the form of direct employee contributions, or it can be recognized in indirect ways as, for example, when income-replacement objectives in a noncontributory pension plan are consciously set below what might otherwise be desired levels, or through the use of deductibles, coinsurance, or inside plan limitations in a medical expense plan. Also, an employer can view this issue from the perspective of the total employee benefit program, making some specific plans **contributory** and some **noncontributory,** with the overall employee contributions achieving a total level the employer feels is satisfactory.

4. A long-term, advance-funded retirement program involves certain risks. Two of the most important risks relate to the impact of inflation and investment results. The employer's attitude on who should bear these risks—the employer or the employees—can play a significant role in the choice between a defined benefit and a defined contribution pension plan.[3] Under the former, these risks are assumed by the employer, although the risk of inflation can be tempered by the choice of a formula that is not pay-related, or by the choice of a career-pay formula; under a defined contribution plan, the employee in effect assumes both of these risks. The growing use of defined contribution plans, along with the transfer of these risks to employees, has caused many employers to take steps to provide investment education for their employees.

5. The selection of specific retirement plan provisions (normal retirement age, early retirement age and subsidies, the treatment of **deferred retirement,** and the benefit levels provided in all these events) and the amount of postretirement life and medical expense insurance provided can influence the pattern of retirements in any organization. Many employers prefer to encourage employees to retire at or before normal retirement age for a variety of reasons, such as keeping promotional channels open. Others prefer to encourage deferred retirements and are reluctant

---

[3] A defined benefit plan is a pension plan under which the employer provides a determinable benefit, usually related to an employee's service and/or pay. Under this approach, the employer's cost is whatever is necessary to provide the benefit specified. A defined contribution plan is a pension plan under which the employer's contribution is fixed and this contribution is accumulated to provide whatever amount of benefit it can purchase. Thus, an employee's benefit becomes the variable, depending on factors such as age at entry, retirement age, and investment earnings (or losses). A defined contribution plan can involve a specific contribution or it can take the form of a profit sharing plan.

to see skilled workers leave while still capable of making important contributions to the firm's profitability. Still other employers take a neutral position and do not seek to exert any influence on the pattern of retirements in their organizations. In any event, this issue took on added significance after the 1986 amendments to the Age Discrimination in Employment Act (ADEA), which protect employment rights of all employees age 40 and over. This issue was further influenced by the 1983 Social Security amendments, which gradually extend the "normal" retirement age for Social Security benefits to age 67, at the same time reducing the level of benefits available from ages 62 through 66. This issue continues to be influenced by demographic considerations and a general recognition of the fact that the relative size of the workforce—over and under age 65—is changing. With these demographic shifts in mind, many employers might choose to encourage employees to remain in the workforce beyond age 65. This could be accomplished in many ways, including phased retirements, reduced-hour work schedules, part-time employment, and consulting arrangements.

6. A number of employers prefer to structure an employee benefit program on a basis that gives employees a wide choice of plans in which to participate and some control over the extent to which they participate in these plans. This can be accomplished on the basis of before-tax credits in the form of **flexible** or **"cafeteria" benefits,** or it can be accomplished by developing various layers of after-tax contributory coverage. Such employers believe this type of flexibility makes the program more meaningful to employees and more efficient, since benefits are delivered only when needed or desired. Other employers prefer not to become involved in the administrative complexities and costs associated with such flexibility, nor do they wish to absorb any additional costs associated with the adverse selection made possible by such choices. Also, those employers who have a paternalistic attitude might feel many employees would not want to make those choices or would not be able to make the right choices. However, the apparent trend in recent years has been toward the creation of individual responsibility and choice and away from paternalism.

7. An employer's position concerning the cost levels it can assume can be a major determinant for a plan's benefit levels and the various ancillary benefits that might be included. The assumption of any given level of cost commitment also involves a balancing of employee interests with those of the organization's owners or shareholders. Another aspect relates to the employer's attitude about the need for maintaining controls over future cost levels. A high degree of concern in this area, for example, might lead to the selection of alternatives such as a career-pay or a defined contribution pension plan, the use of pay-related deductibles in a medical plan, nonpay-related death benefits, or a medical plan structured using defined contribution concepts.

8. Whether the plan's benefits should be coordinated with Social Security benefits is a most important question. The employer's basic philosophy concerning this issue plays an important role in plan design. A great many employers believe that because of the very nature of Social Security benefits and their relatively larger value for

lower-paid employees, it would be impossible to achieve an equitable balancing of benefits and costs for employees at all pay levels without integrating pension and disability income plans in some fashion with the benefits provided by Social Security. Others believe the communication and administrative difficulties associated with integrated plans are such that integration is not desirable.

9. Should an employer provide a benefit program for executives that differs from that provided for its employees in general? Over the years, the majority of benefit programs have been applied across-the-board to all employees, and many employers still believe executives or highly paid employees should be treated the same as all employees. An increasing number of organizations, however, believe the unique needs of executives cannot be met by plans that must meet the nondiscrimination requirements of federal tax law. For example, it may be difficult for a firm to recruit a needed executive in midcareer because of the loss of pension benefits he or she would experience, since a large part of the executive's benefits would be frozen at the pay levels achieved with the prior employer. In such a case, a need may exist for the employer to have a retirement arrangement that restores the benefits that such an executive might potentially lose. Similarly, an employer might find it desirable to provide executives with a supplemental pension that applies the basic pension plan formula to the executive's incentive pay, if the basic pension relates to base compensation only. Due to the **nondiscrimination requirements** described in Chapter 25, special benefits for executives such as those described cannot be provided through a qualified, nondiscriminatory pension or profit sharing plan. Instead, these benefits must be provided through some form of **nonqualified supplemental pension arrangement** (these nonqualified arrangements are described in Chapter 14). Many employers also provide executives with additional death benefits, both before and after retirement, as well as with additional disability income protection.

10. An important question since the passage of the Employee Retirement Income Security Act of 1974 (ERISA) is whether the employer is willing to assume the **plan termination obligations** imposed upon the employer in the event of the termination of a defined benefit plan before all accrued and vested benefits have been funded. The impact this might have on net worth, credit ratings, and the ability to raise capital has caused a good deal of concern—particularly among small employers.[4] This potential liability can be avoided if a defined contribution pension plan is adopted and, indeed, the great majority of new tax-qualified plans adopted since the passage of ERISA have been of the defined contribution variety. In addition, the annual premium payable for plan termination insurance has become quite substantial—a minimum of $31 (in 2007) for single-employer plans and $8 for multiemployer plans per year per covered participant (including retired and terminated vested participants)—and the rate is considerably higher for plans with unfunded liabilities.

---

[4] The employer's liability on termination of a single-employer plan is quite complex and a detailed discussion of this topic is deferred until Chapter 22. It should be noted that an employer also can be exposed to a liability in the case of a negotiated multiemployer plan.

Employer Objectives

With the preceding in mind, it is appropriate to consider specific employer objectives. The following discusses major employer objectives, as well as some of the factors relating to such objectives. Obviously, not all of these objectives apply to each employer and, if they do have application, it is likely their relative importance may not be the same for each employer.

Attraction and Retention of Employees

Most employers recognize they must maintain some form of employee benefit program to attract and retain desirable employees. This is particularly so when the employer must compete with other employers for personnel.

Even so, many employers believe the presence of an adequate benefit program is not a positive influence in their efforts to attract and retain employees—at least to any significant extent. Rather, these employers reason the absence of such a program could have a negative effect on their recruiting and retention efforts. Put another way, these employers are of the opinion that an inadequate program can hinder their efforts to recruit and retain employees, while an overly generous program will not produce a corresponding increase in their ability to attract and hold desirable workers.

While this might be true as a general concept, it is worth noting that some benefit plans might have greater impact than others as far as employees are concerned. Thus, for example, the presence of a generous profit sharing plan might make employment with one employer more attractive than employment with another employer who offers a more conventional pension. In the same vein, employees might find the choice and value of a flexible (or cafeteria) benefit plan of more interest than a plan that offers a standard fare of benefits.

Meeting Competitive Standards

While the objective of having competitive employee benefit plans is closely related to the objective of being able to attract and retain good employees, it is somewhat broader in scope and can reflect employers' attitudes about their standing in their own industry and in the communities in which they operate. This objective also recognizes that, unlike other forms of compensation, employee benefit plans are highly visible and readily subject to external comparison.

An employer who wishes to have competitive employee benefit plans must establish standards for measuring these plans. Will competitiveness be measured against industry standards, geographic standards, or both? Many employers have a preference for measuring their plans against industry standards. However, it should be recognized that such standards are most appropriate for skilled or professional workers and for management personnel—those whose capabilities are more specific to the employer's own industry. For workers whose capabilities are more readily transferred from one industry to another, a more realistic standard would be those plans maintained by the local companies with which the employer competes for human resources. Thus, as a practical matter, most employers seek to compare their plans both on an industrywide and a geographic basis.

Having identified the standard against which the plans are to be measured, the employer also must decide upon the relative level of competitiveness to achieve. For example, the employer might decide the objective is to have an employee benefit program that meets the average of the companies that form its comparison base (or it can establish different positions for different plans). Conversely, the employer might decide it wishes to be a leader and have a program that is consistently among the best, or it might wish to rank somewhere between the 50th and 75th percentiles. And, of course, the employer might elect to lag somewhat behind other companies because of cost or other considerations.

Even though the comparison base has been identified and the relative ranking within this base established, there remains the important matter of determining the technique to be used to establish the relative standing of the different plans. One method used quite frequently is to make comparisons of the benefits actually payable to representative employees under different circumstances. For example, the benefits payable under a retirement plan at normal retirement age might be projected for several employees with differing pay, service, and age characteristics. This method is relatively simple in concept but should be used with caution. First, it shows benefits only and does not necessarily give any true indication of the relative cost of the plans involved. Also, by isolating a specific benefit, the importance and value of other benefits included in the same plan are not taken into account. For example, a company might be ranked as the highest in terms of benefits payable at normal retirement, but the other companies in the comparison may have much more valuable early retirement or survivor income benefits. Even if other benefits are illustrated and compared in the same way, the aggregate value of all benefits within the same plan may not be readily ascertainable. This method is also sensitive to the assumptions used in making the illustrations. If retirement benefits are being illustrated, for example, and if future pay increases are not taken into account, the benefit differences attributable to **final-pay** and **career-pay**[5] formulas will not be apparent (nor will there be any apparent difference between a final three-year average plan and a final five-year average plan).

Another method used is to compare actual costs to the employer for different benefit plans. The material used for this purpose usually is information acquired from both published and private surveys about actual employer cost patterns. A major difficulty with this approach is that there is often inconsistent reporting among different employers of the information requested. Also, actual contribution patterns do not necessarily reflect

---

[5] A final-pay provision bases benefits on the employee's earnings averaged, for example, over the last three or five years of employment, or over the three or five consecutive years in the 10-year period immediately prior to retirement during which the employee's earnings are the highest. By contrast, a career-pay provision bases benefits on the employee's earnings averaged over the entire career of employment. This concept is presented in detail in Chapter 17.

the real cost or value of the benefit involved. The cost reported, for example, might be the total annual cost of the plan, including employee contributions, and might reflect the specific characteristics of the employee group involved. In the case of retirement plans, significant differences may exist in annual contributions because of the choice of a prior actuarial method and a plan's "at risk" status. For example, two employers with identical plans might report significantly different annual costs because of these differences in funding.

A third method used for measuring plans uses uniform actuarial methods and assumptions and focuses on the relative value of the different benefits provided. This technique establishes the value of specific plans, specific benefits within a plan, and the aggregate value of all plans. The method also can establish these relative values on the basis of employer cost only or on the basis of combined employer and employee cost. By using uniform actuarial methods and assumptions, and by applying these to a database of employees held the same for all employer plans in the study, the actual differences in the value of different benefits are isolated and their relative values established. It should be noted that this technique does not establish actual costs or cost patterns; it simply establishes whether one particular benefit or plan is more valuable than another and the extent to which this is so.

Cost Considerations

Earlier in this chapter, reference was made to an employer's attitude on costs and how this can play a major role in plan design. Because a retirement plan often represents a major part of an employer's total benefit program cost, it is particularly important that the employer have specific objectives in this area.

It is important to distinguish between ultimate real cost and estimated annual accruals to meet funding requirements. With this distinction in mind, an employer may need to contribute more to meet actual liabilities under a plan that was not properly funded in the past.

The employer's objectives for these cost levels influence the choice of retirement plan formula as well as the inclusion and level of ancillary benefits. These objectives also may influence the decision as to whether the plan should be contributory and, if so, the level of employee contributions required.

There are other objectives an employer could have for matters concerning cost. The need for contribution flexibility might be one such objective and, if desired, could lead the employer to adopt a profit sharing plan. Another objective could relate to the employer's willingness to assume the costs associated with future inflation. The extent to which the employer wishes to limit its commitment might dictate the choice of a career-pay formula for a defined benefit plan or even the choice of a defined contribution plan of some type.

The need for a cost-efficient retirement program is an obvious objective. Thus, employers wish to avoid excessive or redundant benefits and to fund the plan in the most efficient manner possible. For this reason, many employers choose to coordinate benefits from all sources; for example, they may integrate their retirement plan benefits with those provided by Social Security.

More aware today than ever before of the total monies they have earmarked for employee compensation and benefits, more and more companies are analyzing the competitiveness of their total compensation programs. They are launching communication efforts to educate employees on the total value of their compensation and benefits packages. And some also are going to great lengths to educate their managers on the "Total Portfolio Approach," which views compensation as everything of value the company provides, including salary, short-term incentives, long-term incentives, benefits, and perquisites. They also are grouping all types of rewards and recognition systems under the total compensation "umbrella."

As costs and competitive pressures mount, organizations will need to examine the total cost impact of their compensation and benefits programs more strategically. As a result, the traditional development process for these programs will change: Companies will increasingly require new analyses and new measures of program competitiveness, and the corporate finance department will play a greater role in compensation decision making. . . .

For compensation and benefits managers specifically, four conditions are driving the need to change their focus:

- Compensation and benefit costs are a significant company expense.
- Companies desperately need to control fixed costs.
- Companies need to break the "entitlement mentality" among employees.
- Incremental increases to base salaries over time can be devastating to an organization's cost structure.

Source: Jack Dolmat-Connell, "A New Paradigm for Compensation and Benefits Competitiveness," pp. 52–53. Reprinted by permission of Sage Publications, Inc., from *Compensation & Benefits Review,* Sept./Oct. 1994. Copyright © 1994. Sage Publications, Inc., Thousand Oaks, CA. All rights reserved.

It also is possible that an employer may view a retirement plan as a tax shelter for the benefit of key employees. When this is the case, the employer's objective might be to maximize benefits and contributions within the limits permitted by federal tax law.

Other employee benefit plans also involve cost considerations. If postretirement death and medical expense benefits are to be provided, should these liabilities be prefunded, and, if so, how? Should inflation-sensitive benefits—medical expenses and pay-related death benefits—be subjected to some degree of control through plan design? What type of funding mechanism should be used to gain greater control over cash flow? Clearly, cost considerations are becoming an increasingly important factor in plan design and plan funding.

Compliance with Legal Requirements

Employee benefit plans have almost always been subject to some degree of regulation and other legal requirements. This has become much more the case since the advent of

ERISA, nondiscrimination laws, and the like. The enactment of the Tax Reform Act of 1986 also has had a major impact on the design of plans. More recently, the provisions of the Economic Growth and Tax Relief Reconciliation Act of 2001 and the Pension Protection Act of 2006 now have an effect on the design and administration of plans, as well. Thus, the design and maintenance of employee benefit plans must meet the requirements of federal tax law, nondiscrimination laws, securities laws, labor laws, and state insurance laws. In several areas, state as well as federal laws must be taken into account. Thus, an implicit, if not explicit, objective of any employee benefit plan is that it must comply with these legal requirements.

However, an employer often has a choice regarding the manner in which compliance is achieved. For this reason, it is desirable that the employer formulate specific objectives in this regard. The following examples should give at least some indication of areas where compliance choices are available.

1. The Age Discrimination in Employment Act (ADEA) prevents discrimination in employment for employees age 40 and over. However, this does not require all benefit plans to treat all employees alike regardless of age. It is possible, for example, to reduce life insurance coverage for active employees by reason of age (but only within cost-justified limits). Although it is no longer possible to terminate pension accruals in a defined benefit plan or to discontinue allocations in a defined contribution plan after an active employee has attained age 65, a plan may limit the amount of benefit provided under the plan or the number of years of service or plan participation taken into account. An employer should establish basic objectives regarding how its over-65, active employees will be treated and whether compliance with this law should be at or above the minimum level. The employer's decision is, of course, influenced by other objectives and attitudes, such as whether it is desirable to encourage earlier or deferred retirements, the firm's public relations posture, and the like.

2. Federal tax law permits the exclusion from a defined benefit pension plan of those employees who have less than one year of service or who are under age 21. Employers may include all employees in their plans or may seek to exclude the maximum number possible, depending upon their attitude regarding minimum compliance and other objectives.

3. An employer may wish to establish a defined benefit pension plan that includes incentive compensation for executives as part of the compensation base used to determine plan benefits, but it may not want to include overtime pay and shift differentials paid to other employees. It is unlikely the Internal Revenue Service would approve such a pay definition in a qualified pension plan. Compliance with the nondiscrimination requirements of federal tax law could be satisfied by designing the qualified plan with a nondiscriminatory definition of compensation that relates to base pay only and then instituting a nonqualified, supplemental executive retirement plan (SERP) that applies the base plan formula to incentive pay.

4. A savings plan can be designed so that some part of both employer and employee contributions can be invested in employer securities. Securities and Exchange

Commission (SEC) requirements are such that the plan will have to be registered before employee contributions may be invested in this manner. These requirements can be avoided if employer securities are purchased using only employer contributions.

Achieving Optimum Tax Benefits

Federal tax law is such that some advantages exist for distributions from employee benefit plans. This is particularly so in the case of tax-qualified retirement and profit sharing plans. Indeed, on the one hand, these tax advantages very often are the motivating force behind the adoption of a plan.

If an employer wishes to achieve the maximum tax advantages for a retirement program, this can find expression in many areas; for example, potential tax advantages exist depending upon the choice of benefit formula, the degree to which the plan is integrated with Social Security benefits, the level of funding needed, the funding instrument chosen, the adoption of both a defined benefit and a defined contribution plan, the use of a **target benefit plan,** and so on.[6]

The desire to maximize tax advantages also may affect other benefits and how they are funded. For example, a preretirement spousal benefit may be included as part of a retirement plan, or it may be funded by a separate group term life insurance program. If funded by life insurance, most of the benefit payments will escape income tax; however, the annual cost of insurance can represent taxable income to the employees under Section 79 of the Internal Revenue Code.[7] If the benefit is provided from retirement plan assets, the payments represent taxable income (except to the extent provided by employee contributions), but there will be no annual cost of insurance to be reported by the employee. The emphasis to be placed on these various tax considerations and the characteristics of the employee group involved influence the choice of how the benefit will be funded.

Efficiency of Design

The overall cost of employee benefits is quite substantial and, as noted earlier, can amount to one-third or more of an employer's payroll costs. For this reason, it is important for an employer to structure its employee benefit program so benefits are provided in

---

[6] A target benefit plan is one that combines the concepts of both defined contribution and defined benefit plans. The target benefit plan uses a defined benefit formula to determine an employee's projected pension at normal retirement date. A contribution to provide this benefit is then determined. This contribution is not adjusted for future experience. Instead, contributions are accumulated for each employee in an individual account and, depending upon actual investment results, can accumulate to provide a greater or smaller benefit than that originally projected. This approach has the advantage of determining the initial amount to be allocated to each employee on a basis that reflects the employee's age as well as compensation, while at the same time preserving the accumulation aspects of a defined contribution plan. This concept is presented in more detail in Chapter 21.

[7] Life insurance death benefits generally are income tax free. However, if paid in installments, the portion representing interest payments will be taxable.

The advent of FAS 106 caused employers to reexamine the design of their postretirement health care plans, with a view toward reducing and controlling their liabilities for these benefits. This type of analysis recognized that postretirement health care benefits are, in fact, a major form of retirement benefit—with costs, in many cases, being equal to or greater than the cost of conventional retirement income benefits. While in the process of considering design alternatives and cost control mechanisms, many employers recognized that their postretirement health care benefits were, in several key ways, inconsistent with the income benefits being provided by their retirement plans. For example,

- Most retirement plans do not provide for automatic benefit increases to respond to postretirement inflation adjustments. These increases, if any, are made on an "ad hoc" basis. By contrast, postretirement health care benefits usually were "defined benefit" in nature and were provided even though their cost was rising due to inflation. This had the effect of making postretirement health care benefits automatically indexed not only to inflation in general, but to the higher rates of inflation associated with health care.

- While some retirement plans do provide for spousal death benefits at employer cost, most do not, with such protection being provided only on a basis where the employee pays for its full cost. By contrast, a great many health care plans provided that if an employee died after retirement (or after early retirement eligibility), spousal protection was provided for life.

- The typical retirement plan requires that an employee complete a career of service—usually 25 to 30 years—in order to receive an optimal level of retirement benefits; the typical health care plan required only 5 to 10 years.

- The earlier an employee retires under a retirement plan, the greater will be the *reduction* in the employee's income benefits; the earlier an employee retired under a health care plan, the greater was the *value* of the employee's health care benefits.

These differences in plan provisions and benefits caused employers to reconsider their attitudes and objectives concerning their overall "retirement" programs, and they have caused many to revise or eliminate retiree health care benefits.

the most efficient manner possible and overlapping or redundant benefits are eliminated or, at least, minimized.

One of the most effective ways of doing this is to recognize that while any particular benefit plan has a primary focus (e.g., retirement, death, or disability), all benefit plans and some statutory plans must function in some fashion in the case of an event covered primarily by another plan. For example, the primary plan dealing with retirement is, of course, the employer's retirement plan. However, Social Security can be a major source of additional retirement income. Supplemental retirement income also can be provided by the employer's 401(k) or profit sharing plan if such a plan is in existence. The employer's group life insurance and medical expense plans may be the source of additional benefits for a retired employee. Viewing all these plans as a total retirement program can influence the choice of specific benefits and benefit levels. Thus, the existence of significant amounts of postretirement life insurance might suggest that, except for legally required joint and survivor protection, the normal payment of retirement benefits exclude any form of death benefit, such as a guarantee that benefits will be paid for a minimum period of time; otherwise, excessive or redundant postretirement death benefits might be provided.

The same approach can be applied to the events of preretirement death and disability. In the event of preretirement death, the primary plan is the employer's group life insurance plan. However, additional death benefits may be provided by way of continuation of medical expense coverage for the employee's dependents and, in certain cases, the retirement plan may be required to provide **preretirement survivor benefits.**[8] Social Security also can be a substantial source of survivor benefits, as can a profit sharing or 401(k) plan. In the case of disability, a need exists to coordinate the benefits available from the employer's plan (life insurance, short- and long-term disability income plans, 401(k) and profit sharing plans, and medical expense plans) with those available from Social Security and other statutory plans. Again, efficient plan design suggests the benefits from all these sources be coordinated to ensure overall benefits are in line with employer objectives.

Income-Replacement Ratios

Employer objectives as to **income-replacement ratios** are critical in the design of disability income and retirement plans.

In the case of disability income plans, the issues are not as complex. The benefit usually is not service related (although some plans are), and it is generally designed to replace a percentage of current pay. There are no restrictions on the ability of a plan to integrate with Social Security benefits, and it is customary to offset 100 percent of the employee's primary Social Security disability benefit. In fact, most plans offset 100 percent of the total Social Security benefit payable, including family benefits. In general, the plan formula recognizes that some part or all of the Social Security and plan benefits may be income tax free and that total after-tax income should provide adequate maintenance while at the same time creating an economic incentive for the employee to rehabilitate and return to active work. A typical formula might provide for a total, gross before-tax benefit (including Social Security) of 60 percent of current pay.

Establishing income-replacement objectives for a retirement plan is more complex. Before selecting a specific benefit formula, it is important for an employer to identify the amount of an employee's gross income to be replaced by the retirement plan and under what circumstances.

From the employee's viewpoint, it would be desirable to have a situation where total retirement income permits the full maintenance of the standard of living the employee enjoyed just prior to retirement. For most employees, some part of this income consists of Social Security benefits. Indeed, for employees at lower income levels, a substantial portion of preretirement gross income will be replaced by Social Security benefits. For

---

[8] The preretirement survivor benefit requirements for a qualified plan are described in Chapter 26.

example, the replacement ratios, defined as Social Security benefits relative to gross pay, exceed 70 percent for an individual whose final pay is $10,000. At a final pay level of $30,000, Social Security can replace over 30 percent. Even at $50,000, the replacement ratio is over 25 percent. As discussed later, the after-tax replacement ratios are even more significant.

An employee's personal savings, including equity in a home, also can be a source of retirement income. Also, many employers maintain supplemental profit sharing and 401(k) plans that can be a source of additional income. In the absence of any such plan, however, it must be recognized that many individuals will not be able to save meaningful amounts of money to assist in meeting their retirement needs.

Another factor that should be considered in setting income-replacement ratios is that some reduction in gross income can take place without causing a significant reduction in a retiree's standard of living. Tax considerations are one reason this is so. First, a retired employee is no longer paying a Social Security tax (unless he or she is in receipt of earned income). Moreover, Social Security benefits are income tax free for many individuals.[9] In addition, the standard deduction for federal taxes is increased for individuals age 65 or over. For example, the standard deduction for an unmarried taxpayer who is not a surviving spouse and is age 65 or over is increased by an additional standard deduction of $1,300 (in 2007). For a married taxpayer who is age 65 or over, the additional standard deduction is $1,050 (in 2007). Finally, retirement income is not subject to state or local taxes in many jurisdictions.

Another reason why some reduction in gross income can be tolerated is the removal of work-related expenses, such as commuting costs, the expense of maintaining a second car, lunch and clothing costs, and so on.[10] Also, many retired individuals no longer face the costs associated with child rearing (food, clothing, education, and the like), and many will have reduced housing costs because of the completion of mortgage payments and, in some localities, reduced real estate taxes.

With factors such as these in mind, most employers establish income-replacement objectives that generate something less than a 100 percent replacement of full preretirement gross income. Typically, these income-replacement objectives are set with several factors in mind:

1. They usually take the employee's (but not the spouse's) Social Security benefits into account.[11]

---

[9] Under the Social Security amendments of 1983 and the Omnibus Budget Reconciliation Act of 1993, between 50 and 85 percent of Social Security benefits can become taxable for individuals whose income exceeds threshold amounts. For a detailed discussion of the taxation of Social Security benefits, see Appendix 1.

[10] Projections as to the reduction in these expenses vary.

[11] It is not customary to take the spouse's Social Security benefit into account in setting objectives. To do so would be difficult since a direct recognition of this benefit would not be permitted by the Internal Revenue Service; to approximate its value on an across-the-board basis would result in inequity between employees who have a spouse and those who do not.

2. The objectives usually are higher for lower-paid employees than for higher-paid employees.
3. The objectives usually are set for the employee's pay level during the final year of employment or over a three- or five-year average just prior to retirement, when the employee's earnings are highest.
4. Full income-replacement objectives are set only for individuals who have completed what the employer considers to be a "career" of employment; individuals who have less than this amount of service with the employer have objectives proportionately reduced.

A few comments are appropriate for each of these points. As indicated earlier, Social Security benefits can be of great importance to individuals at lower income levels, and they take on added significance since all or a portion of the benefits may be income tax free. Further, the employer has shared in the cost of providing these Social Security benefits. Thus, even though the particular pension formula for the employer's plan may not directly reflect Social Security benefits, the accrual rates chosen can be designed to produce a net plan benefit that, when added to the employee's primary Social Security benefit, produces the desired result.

At one time, it was not uncommon for an employer to have a single income-replacement objective for employees at all pay levels. However, it was soon recognized that lower-income employees need a higher level of income replacement simply because of minimum income needs. Moreover, it was reasoned that higher-paid employees could accept lower income amounts without incurring a major reduction in living standards.

Most defined benefit plans use an employee's final average pay to determine benefit amounts. Typically, this is a five-year average, although some plans use a three-year average. It is common for employers who have such a plan to state their income-replacement objectives in terms of the pay base used in the plan. Some employers, however, actually set objectives in terms of the employee's pay in the final year of employment, with the result that the plan benefit, when expressed as a percentage of the final average pay used in the plan, is somewhat higher than the employer's actual objective. It also should be noted that employers who adopt career-pay plans or who adopt defined contribution plans often do so with final-pay income-replacement objectives in mind. Those who use career-pay plans frequently "update" accrued career-pay benefits to reflect current pay levels and to move benefits closer to objectives. Those with defined contribution plans find it more difficult to make such adjustments but often set contribution levels so that, under reasonable expectations for salary growth and investment return, final-pay objectives might be achieved. Unfortunately, the inherent nature of defined contribution plans is such that, in most situations, these objectives will either be exceeded or not met at all.

Understandably, most employers do not feel an obligation to provide a full level of benefits to short-service employees. Thus, it is common practice to set objectives and design benefit formulas so that proportionately smaller benefits are provided for those individuals who work for an employer for less than what the employer considers to be

TABLE 2.1
Illustrative Income-Replacement Objectives (Employee with 30 Years of Service)

Final Pay	Retirement Income as a Percentage of Final Pay*
Under $20,000	80–70%
$20,000 to $50,000	75–65
$50,000 to $75,000	70–60
$75,000 to $100,000	65–55
Over $100,000	60–50

* Including primary Social Security benefits.

a reasonable career. The number of years involved, of course, varies from employer to employer and reflects the nature of the employer's business and the degree of maturity it has achieved. However, career periods of from 25 to 35 years are common.

With these factors in mind, Table 2.1 sets forth a typical set of income-replacement objectives. These objectives are merely examples. What is appropriate for one employer may be inappropriate for another and, in any event, what one employer adopts as objectives necessarily reflects that employer's own philosophy and environment.

Other Objectives

The foregoing has discussed some of the major employer objectives associated with employee benefit plans. Other employer objectives also play an important role in plan design. Some of these additional objectives are discussed below.

Social Obligations

Many employers feel a strong sense of social responsibility to their employees and to society in general. The adoption of adequate and meaningful employee benefit plans is a form of meeting this responsibility.

Employee Incentives

It would be a rare employer who is not interested in improving employee productivity. Profit sharing plans and plans that involve ownership of employer securities are plans that can create employee incentives and, as a result, improve productivity. Beyond this, employee morale is an important factor that can influence productivity. As noted earlier, the presence of employee benefit plans may not be a positive force in recruiting and retaining employees, and they may not be a positive factor in creating improved morale. However, their absence could be a negative influence and, for this reason, most employers believe a benefit program, along with other positive compensation and human resource practices, is an important factor in maintaining employee morale at a proper level.

Corporate Identification

It may be desirable to have employees identify with overall employer business objectives. This might be accomplished by having employees acquire an ownership interest in the firm. Profit sharing plans, 401(k) plans with some employer stock, and employee stock ownership plans (ESOPs) can achieve this objective. By having all or part of an employee's account invested in employer securities, the employee is made aware of the company's progress and the importance of achieving satisfactory profit results. The employee also can have the opportunity to vote the shares credited to his or her account, and the employer has the additional opportunity of being able to communicate with the employee as a shareholder by sending annual reports, proxy statements, and the like.

Administrative Convenience

Generally, it is desirable that employee benefit plans be designed so that administrative involvement and cost are kept to a reasonable minimum. This objective has become especially important with increasing government regulations and requirements and as design and funding choices become greater and more complex. In this regard, employers should be aware of their own administrative capabilities, as well as those available from external sources.

Chapter Summary

- The design of original pension plans was largely influenced by the insurance industry's attitude toward underwriting, funding, and administration.
- More factors have come to influence the design of pension plans as the field has developed. Primary factors include:
  - A body of law affecting minimum requirements and permissible plan provisions.
  - Issues regarding the taxation of contributions and benefits.
  - Collective bargaining and the interests of organized labor.
  - Availability of alternate funding mechanisms.
  - Growing degree of sophistication and knowledge of the pension field.
  - Plan cost considerations.

- Given their substantial costs, their importance to millions of workers, and the complex legal, tax, and funding environment, pension plans should be designed and operated to be fully supportive of an employer's philosophy, goals, and objectives and the perceived needs of employees.
- An employer's philosophy and goals can be shaped by the environment in which it operates.
- Special objectives are established in the context of employer attitudes on matters such as:
  - Basic compensation philosophy.
  - The desired emphasis on the protection and maintenance of income.
  - Employee cost sharing.
  - Whether the employees or employer should bear the risks of inflation and investing.
  - Influencing retirement patterns.

- Flexibility of choice.
- Cost and funding controls.
- Coordination of plan and statutory benefits.
- The treatment of executives.
- The assumption of plan termination obligations.

- Employer objectives may include:
  - Attraction and retention of employees.
  - Meeting competitive standards.
  - Cost and funding controls.
  - Legal compliance.
  - Optimizing tax benefits.
  - Efficiency of design.
  - Income-replacement ratios.
  - Social obligations.
  - Employee incentives.
  - Corporate identification.
  - Administrative convenience.

- Employers can use income-replacement ratios, particularly with defined benefit plans, to establish quantifiable objectives that can be monitored to assess plan effectiveness.

Key Terms

career-pay/final-pay (benefit formulas), p. *35*
compensation-oriented approach, p. *31*
contributory/ noncontributory (benefit plans), p. *31*
deferred retirement, p. *31*

flexible or "cafeteria" benefits, p. *32*
income-maintenance approach, p. *30*
income-replacement ratios, p. *41*
nondiscrimination requirements, p. *33*

nonqualified supplemental pension arrangement, p. *33*
plan termination obligations, p. *33*
preretirement survivor benefits, p. *41*
target benefit plan, p. *39*

Questions for Review

1. Describe some of the environmental factors that should be considered in the pension plan design process.
2. Many employers believe employees should share in the cost of meeting their own economic security needs. This type of employee involvement in a private pension plan may take two alternative forms. Explain.

3. Describe the three techniques that may be used to establish the relative standing of various retirement plans.

4. What are some of the objectives an employer could have for matters concerning the cost of its pension plan?

5. An employer often has a choice in the manner in which compliance with legal requirements for pension plans is achieved. Give four examples of areas where compliance choices are available.

6. What are some of the plan design alternatives available to an employer who wishes to achieve maximum tax advantages for a retirement program?

7. An efficient pension plan design requires the identification of all sources of benefits for a retired employee. What plans should be considered as potential sources of benefits?

8. Why do some employers establish income-replacement objectives that generate something less than 100 percent of full preretirement gross income?

9. Identify the factors that are often considered by employers in setting income-replacement objectives.

10. Describe how retirement plans may be used to provide: *(a)* employee incentives, and *(b)* corporate identification.

Questions for Discussion

1. Assume that an employer wants to provide a reasonable combined replacement ratio (a ratio that combines both Social Security and private pension benefits in the numerator) for high-paid employees without providing an excessive replacement ratio for employees at lower income levels. Illustrate why it may be necessary for the employer to integrate the pension plan. (The mechanics of the integration procedure will be treated in Chapter 25.)

2. Provide a numerical example to explain why an executive might experience a loss of pension benefits under a final average defined benefit plan if he or she were to change jobs in midcareer.

3. The age at which unreduced Social Security retirement benefits may commence is scheduled to gradually increase from age 65 to a maximum of age 67. Assume that you are asked to give advice on how a firm's retirement benefits should be restructured as a result of this change. Discuss how your response will vary depending on the employer's objectives.

Resources for Further Study

CCH Editorial Staff. "Legislation: 2006: Pension Protection Act of 2006; Law, Explanation and Analysis." *Commerce Clearing House* (2006).

Hallman, G. Victor III. "Functional Approach to Designing and Evaluating Employee Benefits." In *The Handbook of Employee Benefits*. 6th ed. Jerry S. Rosenbloom, ed. New York: McGraw-Hill, 2005.

Stone, Gary K. "Risk Concepts and Employee Benefit Planning." *The Handbook of Employee Benefits*. 6th ed. Jerry S. Rosenbloom, ed. New York: McGraw-Hill, 2005.

Chapter 3

Defined Contribution versus Defined Benefit Plans

After studying this chapter you should be able to:

- Distinguish the fundamental differences between defined contribution and defined benefit plans.
- Explain the primary advantages of both defined contribution and defined benefit plans.
- Describe when employer objectives would be best served by a defined contribution or defined benefit approach.
- Discuss why certain employers have favored the defined contribution approach.
- Explain how specific federal legislation has tended to encourage the use of defined contribution plans.

Before discussing specific aspects of retirement plan design, it is important to recognize that an employer has two broad choices in selecting a plan to provide these benefits. One of these is the **defined benefit plan,** under which the employer provides a determinable benefit, usually related to an employee's service and/or pay. Under this approach, the employer's cost is whatever is necessary to provide the benefit specified. The second approach is the **defined contribution plan.** Here, the employer's contribution is fixed and accumulates to provide whatever amount of benefit it can purchase. Thus, an employee's benefit becomes the variable, depending upon factors such as level of contributions, age at entry, retirement age, and investment earnings (or losses). A defined contribution plan can involve a specific contribution (as in a money purchase pension plan), or it can take the form of a profit sharing, 401(k), or employee stock ownership plan (discussed in subsequent chapters of this text).

Although only the two polar types of pension plans are discussed in this chapter, it is important to note that in recent years some employers have adopted plans that combine features of both approaches. These plans, such as target benefit, cash balance, and other hybrid plans, will be best understood after the reader fully understands each of the specific features of a pension plan. Therefore, the discussion of these plans is deferred until Chapter 21.

The choice between a defined benefit and a defined contribution plan to provide or supplement retirement benefits is of great importance to employers and employees. Legislative developments in recent years have been a major factor influencing this decision. While a detailed discussion of various plan types is found in subsequent chapters of this text, it is important, at this stage, to provide an overview of the factors involved in making a choice between these two different approaches to providing retirement benefits. This chapter reviews the background and broad considerations involved, as well as the legislative activity that bears on this choice.

Background

The majority of employees covered by the private retirement system in the United States traditionally participated in defined benefit plans. There were some notable exceptions. Educational and other nonprofit institutions, for example, have historically favored defined contribution pension arrangements because of the unique tax benefits granted them under Section 403(b) of the Internal Revenue Code. Also, a number of profit-making organizations have opted for deferred profit sharing arrangements to serve as retirement plans. Nevertheless, the defined benefit approach was favored by most employers, both small and large, at least until the passage of the Employee Retirement Income Security Act of 1974 (ERISA). Since that time, however, the majority of all new plans established have been defined contribution in nature. Further, there has been a decline, in recent years, in the total number of defined benefit plans in effect. That is, the number of defined benefit plans terminated in each of these years exceeded the number of new defined benefit plans established during the same period.

The historical preference for defined benefit plans over defined contribution plans was based on many factors:

1. If an employer has specific **income-replacement objectives** in mind, these can be accommodated with a defined benefit plan. The defined contribution approach, on the other hand, may produce plan benefits that fail to meet or that exceed such objectives as they affect individual employees. This depends on a number of factors, such as length of participation, age at retirement, inflation, investment results, and the like.

2. By the same token, many employers wish to take Social Security benefits into account so that the combined level of benefits from both sources will produce desired results. Although defined contribution plans can be integrated with Social Security benefits by adjusting contribution levels, integration of benefits cannot be accomplished as efficiently as under defined benefit plans.

One method of weighing the value, efficiency, and sufficiency of retirement benefits is to examine the ratio of the income from retirement benefits available to a career employee at retirement to that employee's final preretirement wages. This wage replacement ratio should guide employers in determining both the level of benefits and basic plan design features.

Having a plan without a goal means that employers can never really evaluate the effectiveness of their retirement benefits once those benefits are delivered. Wage replacement goals can provide an important beginning step for the entire retirement plan design process. By choosing a wage replacement goal first, the employer can then examine a number of different plan designs to find the retirement plan that meets that goal at the lowest cost to the employer.

Source: Martha Priddy Patterson, "Retirement Benefits in 1995: KPMG's Third Annual Survey Findings," *Journal of Compensation and Benefits,* November–December 1995, pp. 19–20. Reprinted with permission from *Journal of Compensation and Benefits,* Copyright © 1995 by Warren, Gorham & Lamont, Park Square Building, 31 St. James Avenue, Boston, MA 02116-4112. 1-800-950-1211. All rights reserved.

3. The typical defined contribution plan provides that the employee's account balance is payable in the event of death and, frequently, in case of disability. This, of course, produces additional plan costs or, alternatively, lower retirement benefits if overall costs are held constant. An employer who is interested primarily in providing retirement benefits can use available funds more efficiently for this purpose under a defined benefit plan.

4. Some think a more equitable allocation of employer contributions occurs under a defined benefit plan, since the employee's age, past service, and pay all may be taken into account. Others think just the opposite, that allocations on the basis of pay only produce fairer results. This characteristic of defined contribution plans is one of the reasons they do not lend themselves to achieving consistent income-replacement objectives. It should be noted, however, that defined contribution plans can be structured with allocations weighted by age and service, thus achieving allocation patterns more consistent with those of defined benefit plans.

5. A defined benefit plan can be (and often is) structured to provide a benefit that is related to an employee's final pay, thus protecting the employee against the effects of preretirement inflation. Equivalent protection cannot be provided under a defined contribution plan. Thus, in a defined contribution plan, the risk of inflation is assumed by employees, who must rely primarily on investment results to increase the value of their benefits during inflationary periods.

6. This last comment raises another issue in the comparison of defined benefit plans and defined contribution plans. Investment risk and reward are assumed by the employer under the former, by employees under the latter. Risk can be minimized by use of selected investment media. Absent such protection, however, many people feel that it is inappropriate for the average employee to assume such risk for a major

component of his or her retirement security. Since employees often make investment choices that are quite conservative, their investment returns do not provide them with adequate inflation protection. In recent years, many employers have initiated educational programs to inform their employees about basic investment principles, with the hope and expectation that this will make their employees better investors. The Pension Protection Act also allows investment advice through fiduciary advisers.

7. The incremental value from year to year of a younger employee's **accrued benefit** under a defined benefit plan is relatively small; in the typical final-pay plan, the value of accrued benefits for older employees increases each year at a relatively substantial rate. By contrast, the increase in the amount of an employee's accrued benefit (his or her account balance) attributable to employer contributions under a typical defined contribution plan stays relatively constant from year to year as a percentage of pay. One effect of this is that employees who terminate employment at younger ages will receive greater benefits under a typical defined contribution plan than under a defined benefit plan. As a result, termination benefits can be more costly under the defined contribution approach. As noted earlier, however, it is possible to design defined contribution plans with allocation patterns that are weighted for age and service. If this is done, termination benefits will more closely resemble those of a defined benefit plan.

The defined contribution approach is, of course, not without its advantages. Deferred profit sharing plans, for example, offer employers maximum flexibility in cost commitment as well as opportunities to increase employee productivity. Through the use of employer securities as a plan investment, greater employee identification with the company and its goals also can be achieved. Additionally, if the employee group covered is relatively young, the defined contribution plan is apt to have greater employee relations value than a defined benefit plan. Another possible advantage of the defined contribution plan (unless it is a money purchase plan) is that employee contributions can be made on a **before-tax basis** under Section 401(k); defined benefit plans in the private sector permit employee contributions only on an **after-tax basis.**

Another factor to consider concerns the cost of plan administration. At one time, it was thought that defined contribution plans produced higher administrative costs because of the individual account record keeping required and because of the many transactions (e.g., loans, withdrawals, investment changes) that could take place. However, legislative activity, particularly the plan termination insurance provisions of the law, have caused the administrative cost of defined benefit plans to increase to the point where they may, indeed, be more expensive to administer than typical defined contribution plans. **Plan termination insurance premiums,** for example, are currently at a minimum of $31 (in 2007) for single-employer plans and $8 for multiemployer plans per year per participant (including retirees and vested terminated participants) and could be much higher depending on the plan's unfunded liabilities. In addition, the defined benefit plan has annual actuarial fees along with expenses associated with maintaining employee records, processing benefit payments, and so forth.

A rapidly growing public policy concern facing the United States is whether future generations of retired Americans, particularly those in the "baby boom" generation, will have adequate retirement income. One reason is that Social Security's projected long-term financial shortfall could result in a reduction in the current-law benefit promises made to future generations of retirees. Another reason is that many baby boomers will be retiring with employment-based defined contribution (DC) plans, as opposed to the "traditional" defined benefit (DB) plans that historically have been the predominant source of employer-provided retirement income.

These factors are likely to reduce the amount of life annuity benefits that future retirees will receive relative to current retirees, raising questions as to whether other sources of retirement income—such as individual account plans (DC plans and individual retirement accounts, or IRAs)—will make up the difference.

The Employee Benefit Research Institute developed a model to project retirement income. Under the model's baseline assumptions, both males and females are found to have an appreciable drop in the percentage of private retirement income that is attributable to defined benefit plans (other than cash balance plans). In addition, results show a clear increase in the income retirees will receive that will have to be managed by the retiree. This makes the risk of longevity more central to retirees' expenditure decisions.

The implications of these model results for retirees are significant. First, individuals—rather than the pension plan sponsor—increasingly will have to manage their retirement assets and bear the risk of investment losses. Second, since most retirees' non–Social Security retirement income will be distributed as a lump sum or in periodic payments (from a defined contribution plan or IRA) rather than as a regular paycheck for life (from a defined benefit plan), retirees will need either to purchase an annuity from an insurance company or carefully manage their individual rate of spending in order to avoid outliving their assets.

Source: "The Changing Face of Private Retirement Plans," Employee Benefit Research Institute Issue Brief no. 232, April 2001, Executive Summary. Reprinted with permission of the Employee Benefit Research Institute, © 2001 Employee Benefit Research Institute. All rights reserved.

Legislative Factors

Despite the advantages noted, since the passage of ERISA, a defined benefit plan now exposes an employer to significant financial liability if the plan is terminated when there are unfunded liabilities for vested benefits. An employer's net worth is subject to a lien in favor of the **Pension Benefit Guaranty Corporation (PBGC)** if necessary to meet any liabilities assumed by the PBGC in this event (the specifics of the employer's liability are discussed in Chapter 22). The problems of potential employer liabilities were exacerbated by the Multiemployer Pension Plan Amendments Act of 1980, which created substantial liabilities for an employer who wishes to or who must withdraw from a multiemployer plan that has **unfunded vested liabilities.** Here, the employer is liable for its share of unfunded vested liabilities (generally on the basis of the ratio of the employer's contributions to total contributions).

The vast majority of employees who are not covered by a private retirement program work for smaller companies. Clearly, these small employers, as well as newly formed companies, are apt to be reluctant to adopt a defined benefit plan and take on the potential liabilities that are imposed by ERISA. Many such employers will find the defined contribution alternative, which has no such liabilities, to be a more palatable approach—despite the possible advantages offered by a defined benefit arrangement.

In addition to the plan termination provisions of ERISA, which implicitly but significantly encourage the use of defined contribution plans, it is important to note that the federal government—knowingly or unknowingly—has emphasized the defined contribution approach in many other ways. For example:

1. Long-standing provisions of the Internal Revenue Code (IRC) permit and encourage the use of **tax-deferred annuities** (discussed in Chapter 9) for employees of educational and other nonprofit organizations.

2. The basic structure of the IRC, as it is applied to HR-10 or Keogh plans for the self-employed, is strongly oriented toward defined contribution plans. Even though amended to specifically sanction defined benefit plans, the defined contribution approach has proven to be the simplest and easiest way to take advantage of this law. Indeed, almost all such plans have used the defined contribution approach. The parity provisions of the Tax Equity and Fiscal Responsibility Act of 1982 (TEFRA) eliminated most of the distinctions in tax law that formerly applied to different organizations. However, precedents established by prior practice and prior law may still continue to influence plan design for unincorporated organizations.

3. The individual retirement arrangement (IRA) concept (described in Chapter 12) is totally a defined contribution approach.

4. Beginning in 1979, employers were permitted to adopt a **simplified employee pension (SEP).** A SEP uses the IRA concept but has higher contribution limits than an IRA and considerably less paperwork than a conventional retirement plan. Again, the defined contribution approach is mandatory. Similarly, the Small Business Job Protection Act of 1996 instituted savings incentive match plans for employees (SIMPLE plans) for small employers with 100 or fewer employees. SIMPLE plans can be structured either as IRAs or 401(k) plans—again, the defined contribution approach is mandatory. Enhancements made by the Economic Growth and Tax Relief Reconciliation Act of 2001 (EGTRRA) such as a new provision allowing 401(k) and 403(b) plans to incorporate a feature called a "qualified Roth contribution program" to these types of plans increase the appeal of these types of defined contribution plans.

5. **Employee stock ownership plans (ESOPs),** also defined contribution plans, have been the subject of special legislation. As described in Chapter 7, such plans, unlike defined benefit plans, can be instrumental in corporate debt financing. In addition, ESOPs have been the subject of special interest legislation—witness, for

example, the Regional Rail Reorganization Act of 1973, the Foreign Trade Act of 1974, the Chrysler Corporation Loan Guarantee Act of 1979, the Small Business Employee Ownership Act of 1980, and the Tax Reform Act of 1986.

6. The Revenue Act of 1978 added **Section 125** to the **IRC.** This Section permits the adoption of cafeteria or flexible benefit plans and provides that an employee can choose between taxable and nontaxable compensation elements without problems of constructive receipt if certain conditions are met. One of these conditions is that deferred compensation plans cannot be one of the choices. However, this Section has since been amended to allow the inclusion of profit sharing and stock bonus plans that meet the requirements of Section 401(k) of the IRC (described in Chapter 8). Thus, a flexible compensation plan can permit an employee to choose among welfare benefits (e.g., life insurance, disability income, medical expense), cash, deferred profit sharing, or savings plan benefits. This legislation further encourages the defined contribution approach. This area is particularly significant since flexible compensation plans have become a major factor in the employee benefit planning process.

7. Closely related to flexible compensation plans are the Section 401(k) cash/deferred profit sharing or savings plans. A key feature of these plans is that they permit the use of salary reduction arrangements—an approach that can be highly tax effective and that has captured the interest of many employers. Consequently, the growth of 401(k) plans has been dramatic. Employers who do not have pension plans may find the combination of tax savings for employees and the possible lesser financial obligations of the defined contribution approach to be an attractive way of establishing a retirement program. This could be particularly true when integrated with an overall flexible compensation program.

8. Defined benefit and money purchase pension plans must include both **pre- and postretirement joint and survivor benefits** for the benefit of the employee's spouse. These provisions are complex, and their administration can be cumbersome. By contrast, other defined contribution plans need not include these joint and survivor provisions if the plan provides that the employee's spouse is the beneficiary for 100 percent of the employee's account balance if the employee does not elect an annuity distribution from the plan, and all or any portion of the participant's account balance has not been transferred from a plan subject to the joint and survivor rules. These, and other requirements applicable to defined benefit plans (e.g., the anticutback rules), have made the design and administration of defined benefit plans much more complex than is the case for defined contribution plans.

Other Factors

Other legislation also may have an indirect effect that will encourage the growth of defined contribution plans. Some of the changes made by the 1983 Social Security amendments are a good example of how indirect legislation can affect the design of private retirement plans.

These amendments gradually change the normal retirement age for Social Security benefits from 65 to 67. While the earliest age for claiming Social Security retirement benefits has not increased beyond age 62, the reduction for early benefit commencement will be gradually increased as the normal retirement age increases. Moreover, workers will have an additional incentive to remain in the workforce beyond age 65, since delayed retirement credits have been increased and the earnings test has been liberalized (see Appendix 1: "Social Security and Medicare" for details).

These changes could affect the planning process associated with defined benefit plans. Most of these plans are designed to produce a specific amount of replacement income, together with primary Social Security benefits, when an employee reaches age 65. The actual income-replacement objectives may vary, but they usually reflect the employee's pay level and length of service. While replacement ratios generally are expressed in terms of before-tax income, they are often consciously set with reference to their after-tax value.

The fundamental concept of this planning process revolves around the coordination of two income sources—the private plan and Social Security—usually occurring around the time of the employee's 65th birthday. However, the idea that 65 is the typical retirement age has already begun to diffuse with trends toward early retirement. This diffusion will become even greater as the Social Security normal retirement age is changed, especially since mandatory retirement is no longer legal. What may emerge is a concept that retirement age will become highly subjective for each employee. Actual retirement age may range over a span that begins when employees are in their late 50s and extends until employees reach their early 70s. If retirement becomes spread over such a wide range, it will become increasingly difficult to maintain a plan design structure that is predicated on the majority of employees retiring at age 65 and the coordination of two income sources at this point. Thus, one of the broad but important implications facing employers is the potential need to rethink their approach to plan design and the basic delivery of retirement benefits. Nonintegrated plans and a greater use of defined contribution plans are examples of approaches that might be considered. These approaches allow an employer to opt for cost control in lieu of finely tuned benefit levels.

A mandatory private retirement system in the United States is still a long way off—if, indeed, it ever becomes a reality. Yet the possibility exists that such a system will become law. The last time this issue was studied was in 1981. At that time, a Presidential Commission on Pension Policy recommended that a mandatory minimum pension system be established. More specifically, the commission recommended that this program be in the form of a defined contribution plan. While the commission did not divulge all of its reasoning in support of this defined contribution recommendation, it is likely that it was perceived as the simplest and most acceptable way of moving into a mandatory system. A mandatory defined benefit program would present a host of issues concerning pay-related benefits, the recognition of prior service, and the imposition of related liabilities.

Many of the provisions of the Pension Protection Act of 2006 will serve to bolster the prominence of defined contribution plans as the bulwark of the private pension system. As the new millennium began, many adverse circumstances in the general economy resulted in harmful effects for private pension plans. Some funding issues directly related to pension plans were also problematic. The horrific events of September 11, 2001, the downturn in the economy, retreating equity prices, airlines seeking bankruptcy protection, corporate reporting and accounting scandals, abuses in executive compensation, widespread efforts to freeze or terminate traditional defined benefit pension plans, and increasing pension liabilities for the Pension Benefit Guaranty Corporation (PBGC) all meant difficulties for the U.S. private pension system. In the wake of these difficulties, calls for legislative reforms were heard. The Pension Protection Act (PPA) of 2006 was heralded as a necessary reform to safeguard pension benefits for American workers. Its overhaul of funding rules for defined benefit plans and its tougher requirements on underfunded plans, although well-intentioned, were unlikely to stem the exodus of employer sponsors from supporting the traditional defined benefit plans. In fact, some practitioners believe that these measures might serve to exacerbate flight from the traditional defined benefit plan. With the defined benefit plan in decline, several measures within the PPA show recognition that the defined contribution plan, which in the past, may have supplemented defined benefit plans, will need to provide more support for American workers in the future. Among the measures that will allow these plans to fulfill their destiny as primary retirement income sources are provisions providing for participant diversification rights, stipulations broadening access to investment advice, new rules for automatic participant enrollment, allowances for faster vesting, greater ease in moving plan balances through expanded plan portability, and the making permanent of many EGTRRA-enacted favorable retirement provisions.

The Future

Despite all the foregoing, defined benefit plans are still a significant part of the private and public pension systems. They are firmly entrenched in certain sectors such as the governmental sector. It is unlikely that many of these plans will be shifted—at least completely—to defined contribution plans. Some employers, for example, might opt to use a hybrid plan, such as a target benefit plan, that attempts to achieve a mix of the perceived advantages of both the defined benefit and defined contribution approaches. What also has happened is that employers with defined benefit plans have held them at current levels or "frozen" them, opting either to replace future earned pension benefits or to make benefit improvements via some kind of supplemental defined contribution arrangement (e.g., a salary reduction, Section 401(k) savings plan). For employers who do not yet have a pension plan, there has already been and is likely to be greater use of one form or another of the defined contribution approaches referred to in this chapter.

IRAs, ESOPs, SEPs, SIMPLE plans, flexible compensation plans, and Section 401(k) plans are all attractive and viable programs to consider. While defined benefit plans will remain a component in the United States private pension system, the defined contribution plan has taken on the more prominent role and is likely to continue as the predominant form of plan for most private employers.

Chapter Summary

- An employer has two broad choices in selecting a plan to provide pension benefits:
  - A *defined benefit plan,* under which the employer provides a determinable benefit, usually related to an employee's service and/or pay.
  - A *defined contribution plan,* where the employer's contribution is fixed and this contribution is accumulated to provide whatever amount of benefit it can purchase upon the employee's retirement.
- In recent years, some employers have adopted pension plans that combine the best features of both defined benefit and defined contribution approaches. These hybrid plans include cash balance and target benefit plans.
- Traditionally, defined benefit plans have covered the vast majority of employees. Employers creating new plans today tend to prefer defined contribution approaches. Defined benefit and defined contribution plan designs each involve distinct advantages.
- Investment risk and reward are assumed by the employer under a defined benefit plan and by employees under a defined contribution plan.
- Legislative factors have been important determinants impacting the growth of defined benefit and defined contribution plan designs. Since the passage of ERISA, extensive pension legislation has shaped employer preferences for distinct plan designs in many direct and indirect ways.
- Other factors, such as modification of the Social Security system (another component of the "tripod of economic security"), have affected and will continue to affect the design of private pension plans.

Key Terms

accrued benefit, p. *52*
after-tax basis, p. *52*
before-tax basis, p. *52*
defined benefit plan, p. *49*
defined contribution plan, p. *49*
employee stock ownership plans (ESOPs), p. *54*
income-replacement objectives, p. *50*

Pension Benefit Guaranty Corporation (PBGC), p. *53*
plan termination insurance premiums, p. *52*
pre- and postretirement joint and survivor benefits, p. *55*
Section 125 of the Internal Revenue Code (IRC), p. *55*

simplified employee pension (SEP), p. *54*
tax-deferred annuities, p. *54*
unfunded vested liabilities, p. *54*

Questions for Review

1. Describe the factors that will determine an employee's retirement benefit under the defined contribution approach.
2. Explain the primary advantages of a defined benefit plan.
3. Explain the primary advantages of a defined contribution plan.
4. Explain the ways in which the federal government has encouraged the defined contribution approach.
5. Explain how the 1983 Social Security amendments might affect use of the defined benefit approach.

Questions for Discussion

1. The text states that in the view of some, a more equitable allocation of employer contributions occurs under a defined benefit plan than under a defined contribution plan. Assume that a participant in a defined benefit pension plan, age 25, is currently paid $15,000 per year and he or she will retire at age 65. At that time, he or she will receive a pension benefit equal to 1 percent of his or her average salary in the last five years, times years of service. Compute the present value of the pension benefit accrued from working an additional year, as a percentage of the participant's compensation, at ages 30, 35, 40, 45, 50, 55, 60, and 64. Perform the calculations under two sets of assumptions: (*a*) the participant has no wage growth and the discount rate is 3 percent, and (*b*) the participant's wage growth is 7 percent and the discount rate is 10 percent. Graph the change in the present value of accrued benefits from an additional year's work (expressed as a percentage of compensation) against the participant's age under both scenarios. What conclusions can you draw about the allocation of employer contributions under defined benefit plans? (Notice that the discount rate exceeds the wage growth by 3 percent under both scenarios.)
2. Prepare a graph similar to the ones created in the preceding question for an employee participating in a defined contribution plan providing a contribution of 6 percent of compensation, and compare your results with the previous graphs. What conclusions can you draw about the allocation of employer contributions under a defined contribution plan vis-à-vis those of a defined benefit plan? What implications do these conclusions present for the retention of older employees?
3. Assume that you are an employee, age 25, and you are given your choice of participating either in the defined benefit plan described in Question 1 or the defined contribution plan described in Question 2. Which one would you prefer? Describe how you made the evaluation and any assumptions required.

Resources for Further Study

Allen, Everett T., Jr. and Dennis F. Mahoney. "Retirement Plan Design." *The Handbook of Employee Benefits.* 6th ed. Jerry S. Rosenbloom, ed. New York: McGraw-Hill, 2005.

CCH Editorial Staff. "Legislation 2006: Pension Protection Act of 2006: Law, Explanation, and Analysis." *Commerce Clearing House* (2006).

Perdue, Pamela D. "Going, Going, Gone: The Continuing Decline of the Traditional Defined Benefit Plan." *Journal of Pension Planning & Compliance* 26, no. 4 (Winter 2001).

Salisbury, Dallas L. "The Future of Employee Benefit Plans." *The Handbook of Employee Benefits.* 6th ed. Jerry S. Rosenbloom, ed. New York: McGraw-Hill, 2005.

Stevens, Paul Schott. "ICI President's Remarks Before the Economic Club of Chicago." www.ici.org/issues/ret/06_econ_stevens_spch.html. November 10, 2006.

Chapter 4

Risk Management through Retirement Planning

After studying this chapter you should be able to:

- Describe the various risks that individuals face during the later stages of life.
- Discuss how some of these risks can be viewed in isolation or related to other identifiable risks.
- Explain how the risks individuals face affect their employers and society at large.
- Discuss how the approach to managing these risks has changed over time.
- Contrast differences in the management of retirement investment risks depending on whether they are managed using defined benefit plans or defined contribution plans.

Introduction

As indicated in Chapter 1, certain economic problems accompany advanced age. As was stated, "longevity is a source of economic insecurity in that individuals may outlive their financial capacities to maintain themselves and their dependents."[1] Although there is recognition that there are increased risks with longevity, there is a need for greater precision in describing the nature of these risks if one is to adequately plan to manage them. This chapter describes several of these risks, details how these elements of risk are related to each other, and discusses the implications of risk management when handled by the individual planning for her or his retirement.

---

[1] See the discussion on increasing longevity in Chapter 1.

The Concept of Retirement Risk

What Is Retirement Risk?

Often when the idea of retirement or the phase of life commonly referred to as the "retirement years" is discussed, the idea of risk enters the discussion. But what is meant by *retirement risk*? When we talk about "retirement risk" are we simply describing a form of financial risk or investment risk? Or could "retirement risk" be something much larger and more complicated than simply a form of investment risk? Before trying to gain a more precise understanding of retirement risk, let us explore the basic premise concerning the notion of *retirement* generally.

The concept of **retirement** describes the phase of life following an extended period where we engage in some form of work activity attributable to labor. Although there are work activities that are charitable in nature, most forms of work result in income generation, providing resources to sustain the necessities and amenities of life. This income-generating activity can either be as an employee of some other person or organizational entity or working for oneself. The notion of retirement involves the basic concept that individuals will work for a period of time during which they will set aside assets or become entitled to benefits. Following this period of asset accumulation or period of earning benefits eligibility, these individuals will then cease working and use the assets or earned benefits to sustain their material resource needs.

The way in which the assets and/or benefits are accumulated and disbursed can vary. Sometimes the accumulation of resources or earning of benefits occurs through a governmental or social insurance program. Alternatively, the system can be operated and funded through a private employer. Even self-employed individuals can accumulate assets for their own retirement through such savings vehicles as individual retirement accounts (IRAs). "**Retirement security** is based on the fundamental idea that individuals will work for a number of years, build retirement assets and/or entitlement to benefits, and then retire and use the assets (and/or benefits) in their retirement years."[2] Although many individuals traditionally have retired at a specific age (namely, age 65), many people today will transition into retirement over an extended number of years, either through **phased-retirement** programs through their employer, or else by seeking and engaging in some form of part-time employment or alternative income-generating work arrangement following departure from their primary, previously held work arrangement.

Oftentimes when people discuss retirement risk they are describing the situation where retirees find themselves possessing inadequate resources to provide for their living needs. Of primary concern to many retirees is the possibility that they may deplete the resources set aside for retirement needs or find that the needs of retirement exceed either accumulated assets or benefits coverage. This is especially true when we look at the potentially financially disastrous consequences if we need to access long-term care services for an extended period of time or incur extensive medical care costs attributable to a major illness. So, is retirement risk properly described as a resource shortfall?

---

[2] Anna M. Rappaport and Monica Dragut, "High-Age Implications of Postretirement Risks, *Benefits Quarterly* (Fourth Quarter 2005), p. 13.

Retirement risk can certainly be attributable to a resource shortfall. It can also involve *longevity risk*. **Longevity risk** can be described as the situation where a person's extended life span exceeds expectations and results in the depletion of resources expected to be sufficient to meet the material needs of retirement. However, longevity risk is not the only source of resource shortfalls. Individuals can fail to adequately plan for retirement. Individuals may also lack sufficient resources during their working years to adequately make provision for their future retirement. Even individuals who believe they have adequately planned for retirement can see erosion or elimination of retirement resources occur because of such unanticipated financial conditions as rampant inflation or adverse investment results. So when we consider **retirement risk**, there are many interrelated attributes that either contribute to insecurity or serve as direct perils to the person whose life has entered the retirement phase. Figure 4.1 shows a listing of contributors to retirement insecurity that may collectively be considered as retirement risk. These elements comprise many of the more commonly identified contributors to retirement insecurity.

Contributors to Retirement Insecurity

As might be expected, there can be considerable overlap among the contributors to retirement insecurity. Many of the elements identified in Figure 4.1 are not independent of each other, and one element of risk may trigger other risks. Understanding these contributors to risks, their variability, and the extent to which the risks themselves can be transferred or diminished is key to creating or enhancing retirement security.

FIGURE 4.1   **Contributors to Retirement Insecurity**

Resource shortfalls resulting from:
- Inadequate planning and provision for resource needs
- Resource erosion or elimination
- Need expansion or enhancement
- Longevity risk

Cataclysmic events causing:
- Changes to the existing family unit or system (such as loss of a spouse)
- Adverse health consequences
- Need for long-term care services
- Interruption of ability to live independently
- Major shocks to retirement resource systems

Environmental changes such as:
- Changes in tax structure
- Alterations in social insurance systems
- Modifications of employer or self-maintained benefit programs
- Adaptations in the economy or investment risk

Loss of ability to independently manage risks and living needs brought about by:
- Ongoing difficulties or lack of adequate skill sets
- Deterioration of abilities (either rapidly occurring or progressive in nature)
- Cataclysmic events affecting ability to function independently

Sources of retirement risk have received increasing attention. There are rational explanations for the increased concern and study of retirement risks. First, increased longevity is making retirement risk an issue since longer life expectancies increase the possibility of outliving designated retirement resources. Life expectancy at high ages (i.e., those ages above age 85) increased more than 50 percent during the twentieth century.[3] This is not only an individual issue, but a societal issue as well, since increased longevity and the aging of populations puts increased strains on the social insurance systems of nations that are allocating resources to these social issues. As people age, health care costs increase.[4] So increased longevity poses not only a lengthening of the need for resources, but actually means increasing the magnitude of some needs such as the demand for health care services.

Second, the sheer number of people entering the retirement years is demanding a realignment of societal resources. The **baby boom** generation represents a substantial demographic cohort born between 1945 and 1963. By its large size relative to other age cohorts, it has major implications for the allocation of societal resources as a segment of its members enters the retirement phase of life.

Third, as noted in Chapter 3, there has been a dramatic shift from defined benefit plans to defined contribution plans in the private retirement system. This shift places more responsibility for risk management with the individual plan participant. Because a specific regular and recurring pension payment is not guaranteed when a defined contribution plan is used, this risk, broadly defined as *investment risk*, is borne by the individual participant. It has yet to be seen whether reliance on defined contribution plans will adequately provide for the retirement needs of this large demographic cohort of baby boomers. While there is an increasing number of people entering retirement with increased longevity and more costly health care needs, the structural design of the private pension system in the United States and other countries is changing. The trend in retirement plan change involves a migration to types of plans where the individual participant is responsible for investment risk.

Greater Concern about Retirement Risk

The Society of Actuaries (SOA) has noted that the concept of retirement risk is of greater importance where longevity has increased and where the retirement system has undergone a structural shift from a defined benefit approach to a defined contribution model.

> This transformation means an increasing number of Americans are more responsible for their own increasingly expensive security in retirement. Issues of personal responsibility are particularly hard-hitting as retirees reach advanced ages. Those over age 80 are more likely than younger retirees to have used up all assets other than Social Security and require long-term care or become dependent on others."[5]

[3] Ibid., p. 17.

[4] Uwe Reinhardt, "Does the Aging of the Population Drive the Demand for Health Care?," *Health Affairs* 22, no. 8 (November/December 2003), p. 28.

[5] Rappaport and Dragut, "High-Age Implications of Postretirement Risks, p. 12.

The SOA Committee on Postretirement Needs and Risks has undertaken to categorize postretirement risks and analyze the variability of these risks. In examining these risks, it was noted that some risks may be transferred by using insurance and existing financial products offered in the marketplace, while other risks cannot easily be alleviated with presently available insurance or financial products. In addition to the difficulties of managing some risks, the SOA Committee also noted the risk of inadequate information for decision making can sometimes thwart or impede successful risk management. According to the SOA Committee's categorization of postretirement risks, the components of retirement risks may be grouped into:

1. Financial and economic risks;
2. Business and employment risks;
3. Public policy risks; and
4. Risks related to longevity, outliving assets, and changes in family structure.[6]

Importance of Information Concerning Retirement Risk

The observation by the SOA Committee that an absence of information to facilitate decision making on managing retirement risk is important. When the information to make effective decisions is absent, this condition adds an additional risk component or potentially intensifies the severity of the other risks being managed. Both the adequacy of information and the competency of the person managing the risk are important. Even if individuals are of sound mind and possess the required skill-set to rationally attempt to manage these risks effectively, their well-intended efforts can be thwarted by the absence of adequate information. Second, the aging process itself can at some point diminish the individual retiree's ability to effectively manage these risks self-sufficiently even if the individual was originally capable of managing these risks. Any attempt to manage retirement risks must be conducted knowing the possible threat of insufficient information and should attempt to establish a means to manage risks that recognizes that at some point the individual retiree may be less-equipped to continue managing these risks. Therefore, risk management of retirement risks often involves establishing a decision system, such as using trustees or establishing a process to delegate decision making should the need arise in the future.

Although the particular approach to categorizing postretirement risks may vary, it is important to note that current thinking on retirement risk is that it does not merely involve the investment risk commonly associated with defined contribution plans, but also refers to a series of interrelated and overlapping contingencies that can threaten the retirement security of the individual and his or her family. Retirement risk can manifest itself as resource shortfalls limiting access to necessities of life or health care, but can also occur as a loss to independent living and the inability to manage life's resources effectively and in a self-sufficient manner. To adequately safeguard against these risks, a fuller discussion of the contributors to risk is provided in the next section.

---

[6] Society of Actuaries' 2001 Retirement Risk Study.

A Closer Look at Retirement Risk

Resource Shortfalls

Resource shortfalls can occur in retirement for a variety of reasons. One source of inadequate resources in retirement can occur from inadequate planning and provision made during the income earning years that precede the retirement years. Inadequate planning and provision may occur by necessity if the individual has inadequate or insufficient income during the income earning years and must devote all of his or her earned income resources to basic living requirements. Many individuals find themselves in this situation. Certain populations living at or below the poverty line are subject to this contributing risk factor. Certain constituency groups are especially prone to this condition.

For instance, it has been noted that in the 1990s and early beginnings of the new millennium when financial planners counseled women on retirement planning, oftentimes the resources available to women varied markedly depending on the women's particular age cohort. The women in the eldest age cohort may have served primarily or entirely as homemakers, with little direct compensation for work outside the home. Accordingly, apart from the resources acquired by a spouse, there were very limited resources that had been set aside for retirement. The next eldest demographic cohort likely possessed greater retirement resources, since this group may have participated in the workforce to a greater extent and had access to defined contribution plans or defined benefit plans subject to less lengthy vesting requirements at least during a portion of their work lives. Finally, the younger demographic age cohort had access to portable and less lengthy vesting requirements associated with retirement plans and had participated in these saving vehicles since their participation in the workforce. Also, their period of participation in the labor market had been continuous since entering the workforce and was likely to be less sporadic than the women who entered the workforce before them.[7]

Although some resource shortfalls occur because individuals do not have the means to save for retirement, there are many other situations in which resource shortfalls are the result of individuals simply failing to plan adequately even though they possess the necessary resources. Delaying current consumption and saving for retirement is never easy. It is always easier to currently consume rather than to save resources for future needs. Several studies suggest that U.S. savings rates could be higher.

Even if an individual has planned in advance and saved for retirement, asset erosion or elimination (or the reduced purchasing power of those assets) can occur, resulting in retirement resources shortfalls. This can occur because of many unexpected occurrences. Investment risk has become more of an issue because of the participant self-directed nature of many defined contribution retirement savings vehicles. This becomes more of a threat in the face of increased longevity. A stark reality of a defined contribution system is that investment risk is borne by the plan participants. As the retirement system has made a massive shift in moving from a system primarily anchored on defined benefit plans to one where a defined contribution approach has become the foundational element of most people's retirement security, there has been a major shift

---

[7] Martha Priddy Patterson, "Pension Envy: Why Retirement Planning for Women Is More Challenging, *The Journal of Retirement Planning* 3, no. 4 (July–August 2000), pp. 16–29.

in risk assumption to the individual employee. While this element is apparent because of the very nature of these types of plans, it is not clear whether the risk transferred can be managed as effectively by individuals, and whether defined contribution plans, as presently regulated by law, facilitate individuals properly managing the risks they have assumed.

The changing nature of private pensions has occurred over a series of years. If we look at the advent of this transformation, we see an initial movement away from defined benefit plans, followed by a continuous trend and potentially a precipitous drop in the provision of these pensions. This change has taken place as a number of other occurrences have taken place in the workplace. Although the movement away from this type of pension plan could be attributed to various causes, it has occurred as the whole notion of the employer–employee employment contract has changed. In some ways the idea of a portable defined contribution account that an employee transports with him or her from job to job seems compatible with the less stable and less enduring career patterns of today. Nevertheless, this new arrangement is a rather new development and will be tested as the large age cohort of baby boomers moves into retirement. Although some market watchers expect a cataclysmic consequence of this new model, other observers are far less suggestive of a "doomsday" scenario, although there are definitely potential problems with this type of retirement planning model.

Some accounts question how unprepared Americans are for the retirement years. Some studies point to a more optimistic outcome than is sometimes projected:

> So is the future of retirement in America a disaster in the making? The simple answer is no. Most forecasts suggest that the glass is at least half full. For example, the Center for Retirement Research at Boston College ... reported that six out of 10 working Americans are on track for retirement, while four out of 10 are at risk of not having enough on which to live comfortably. Another well-known study showed that half of workers surveyed were ready for retirement, while one-fourth needed to do more to prepare. Other research has settled somewhere in between. So depending on the survey, the glass is anywhere from 60% to 75% full.
>
> That isn't all that different from what we see when we look at today's retirees. About three in 10 rely on Social Security for more than 90% of their income—basically all they have. It can be a difficult life if you live on your own and can't rely on family for support. Another three in 10 receive anywhere from 50% to 90% of their income from Social Security. These individuals may have some supplemental pension or savings benefits, and their homes are their largest assets. In short, some will do fine, while others will struggle.
>
> Finally, there are the remaining four in 10 retirees, for whom Social Security plays a much smaller role. People in this group have meaningful savings, either from the workplace or personally. Many have pensions. Some also have significant earnings from work, despite being retired. As a group, this population is probably just fine.[8]

The author of this account goes on to summarize the situation of the baby boomer age cohort as being one where resources are unlikely to match expectations. He notes that the real crisis will be one of unfulfilled expectations:

[8] Stephen P. Utkus, "Brewing a Tempest in a Teapot," *On Wall Street* (August 1, 2006), pp. 1–2.

The bigger problem, it turns out, is the boomers' relative standard of living. They've grown accustomed to seeing their incomes climb much faster than those of their parents'. They expect a terrific retirement. But because they have saved less in percentage terms, they are going to discover that their retirement incomes won't go as far as they expected. Compared with earlier retirees, the boomers will have a higher level of retirement income, but it'll represent a smaller percentage of the amount they earned while working.

So boomers will be objectively better off but will feel relatively worse off. To put it bluntly, this isn't a crisis in the numbers; it's a crisis of expectations. It's not disaster that looms—just disappointment. And to deal with that disappointment, boomers will have two options: Be satisfied with a lower standard of living or work longer and continue to add to savings.[9]

Marketplace conditions can have major impact on the income streams that a defined contribution plan is able to produce. A study attempted to ascertain the merits of including international assets in defined contribution portfolios. Among the study's findings was that depending on prevailing market conditions, there could be very **disparate outcomes in income replacement ratios** relative to final salary. According to the study, a full-career employee investing identically 7 percent of salary throughout his or her career could see income replacement ratios at age 62 ranging from 51 percent to 115 percent of peak earnings. Interestingly, these two extremes were the actual replacement ratios that 62-year-old workers would have experienced if their terminal years of employment had been a mere three years apart (the actual years where this major variation occurred were 2000 and 2003). This variation demonstrates the possible effects of a major capital market correction relative to the commencement of retirement income disbursements.[10]

Although defined contribution holdings invested in a particular asset class may exhibit a long-term rate of return that approaches historical means, there can be substantial variation and **diversion from historical means** over shorter time periods. Accordingly, if an individual sees a major reversal and loss in a retirement account at the onset of retirement, the income needs in the immediately following years may serve to deplete resources before the asset class rebounds. Although an institutional investor or sponsor of a corporate defined benefit plan may withstand such a reversal by holding investments until the particular distressed segment of the market recovers; an individual needing immediate income may not have the luxury to await the rebound in asset values. Accordingly, the individual self-managing his or her account is often more at risk in such a situation and has fewer options to remedy the adverse conditions. Such adverse capital market conditions can result in significant asset reduction or elimination for the individual's self-managed account.

At the same time that retirement resources can be subject to immediate and severe elimination or reduction, various forms of investment risk may erode the value of

[9] Ibid., p. 2.

[10] Gary Burtless, "Risk and Reward of International Investing for Retirement Savers: Historical Evidence," prepared for the 8th Annual Joint Conference of the Retirement Research Consortium, *Pathways to a Secure Retirement*, Brookings Institution (August 7, 2006), p. 17.

TABLE 4.1
Effects of Inflation on Purchasing Power of $1,000

When inflation is (percent)	After 10 Years	After 20 Years	After 30 Years
3	$744	$554	$412
5	614	377	231
10	386	149	57

Source: Numbers appeared in Table I from "High-Age Implications of Postretirement Risks," by Anna M. Rappaport and Monica Dragut from *Benefits Quarterly*, Fourth Quarter 2005. Copyright 2005 International Society of Certified Employee Benefit Specialists. All rights reserved.

retirement assets over time. This is particularly true regarding the threat of inflation and its resultant **erosion in purchasing power.** The continuous erosive power of inflation can be particularly problematic for those individuals living on a fixed income whose purchasing power does not keep pace with inflation. Table 4.1 illustrates the eroding power of inflation that significantly reduces the effective purchasing power of $1,000 over varying time horizons with variations in the overall rate of inflation.

As can be seen from Table 4.1, over an extended period of time, even modest amounts of 3 to 5 percents of inflation can have a major detrimental adverse impact on investments. Portfolios of assets that fail to outpace inflation can be significantly reduced in terms of their ability to provide adequate purchasing power to retirees. Retirees who are self-managing their retirement accounts must target to outpace inflation.

Although the movement of private corporations away from a defined benefit to a defined contribution model is a new development in corporate America, the idea of a private pension system anchored on a defined contribution approach is not entirely an untried concept. Many tax-exempt organizations have utilized this approach—and with considerable success. In fact, the success of the 403(b) approach may hold considerable lessons for corporate entities. However, success depends on a number of factors: adequacy of contributions, the right array of investment options, financial education for plan participants and plan features that assist in protecting against poor decision making by participants, and important policies and practices related to eventual distribution of plan assets, among others.

It should be noted that governmental public policy is attempting in some degree to strengthen some safeguards for individual plan participants within this emerging private pension system where an increased reliance exists on participant-directed defined contribution accounts. Specifically, some of the provisions of the Pension Protection Act (PPA) of 2006 make tangible efforts to better serve the interests of defined contribution plan participants. The PPA expands the opportunities for plan sponsors to allow investment companies to provide financial advice to participants. The PPA also clarifies that defined contribution plan sponsors may automatically enroll participants in their plans and use default elections into more balanced investment portfolios. This clarification allows default investment elections so that long-term investment results will be superior to those that would generally be expected to be attained by defaulting participants into less-volatile money market accounts. In the past, plan sponsors were reluctant to default plan participants into more risky investments fearing liability for a fiduciary breach if participants incurred investment losses.

In addition to the resource elimination or erosion that can occur with retirement assets, retirees can undergo changes in their life situations that actually result in an **expansion of their needs for resources** during the retirement years. The idea of some cataclysmic health event (described in the next section) readily comes to mind. Such an event not only can result in large costs associated with health services, but can also necessitate the expense of continuing custodial care services as well. Apart from a catastrophic health event, merely affording health insurance to protect against these risks can strain the resources of retirees.

> Some studies have provided estimates of a lifetime of coverage valued at about $175,000 for an age-65 couple,[11] divided into costs for prescription drugs (42%), Medicare premiums (23%), and the remainder attributed to copays and deductibles. Though these estimates are highly uncertain, it is evident that retirees lacking employer-provided retiree health benefits will pay more—one study indicated that an average 20% of monthly incomes could be devoted to medical expenses. Access to a group retiree medical plan therefore helps cushion many retirees against a portion of these costs.[12]

Other events can also result in the need for greater resources throughout retirement. It has not been uncommon for families to see grown children undergo some transforming life event such as a divorce or job loss and need the assistance of retired parents. These events can result in unexpected need expansion that a retiree did not plan for during the working years. Major repairs to a home or the necessity to replace a vehicle can also place significant burdens on retiree resources.

Among all of the previously mentioned risks placing strains on retirement resources is the traditional threat from longevity risk. Simply stated, it is never known just how long an individual will live. Although individuals may know their life expectancy according to actuarial tables when commencing retirement, it is important to realize that such projections involve averages with significant members of the age cohort living beyond the stated life expectancy. To arrive at an average life expectancy, which is usually an approximation of median age at death, half the population under consideration will outlive the median age at death. Thus when planning for retirement, projected life span for an individual should always anticipate a lifetime that will proceed beyond that projected as the life expectancy.

Some basic observations can be made about the emerging factors concerning retirement realities:

[11] Paul Fronstin, and Dallas Salisbury, "Retiree Health Benefits: Savings Needed to Fund Health Care in Retirement." *Issue Brief, EBRI,* February 2003. (As reported in TIAA-CREF Institute Policy Brief: Reforming Retiree Benefits.)

[12] Patricia Neumann, "The State of Retiree Health Benefits: Historical Trends and Future Uncertainties." *The Henry J. Kaiser Family Foundation.* Testimony before the Special Committee on Aging, United States Senate, May 17, 2004. (As reported in TIAA-CREF Institute Policy Brief: Reforming Retiree Benefits.)

- Increasingly larger numbers of workforce participants are covered by defined contribution rather than defined benefit plans.
- People have been living longer and retiring earlier, although some reversal may be occurring in the trend toward earlier retirements.
- Health care costs, particularly for the aged who have higher utilization rates, have increased substantially.
- Employers, once willing to provide sizable support for retiree health care programs, have backed away from providing support in this area.
- Changes to family structures and longer life expectancies have resulted in more Americans needing access and support for long-term care services.

Cataclysmic Events

Although some of the cataclysmic events that could lead to retirement insecurity were mentioned in the previous section, we provide a fuller discussion of these elements in this section. Cataclysmic events that change the family structure often represent major risk for retirees. Death of a spouse is among the most common shocks to the retiree's family structure. Divorce of a spouse in retirement can also occur. Both of these events can create major challenges for retiree resources. When death or divorce occur, there can be a loss of benefits eligibility provided through the spouse or a reduction in resources. Some forms of annuities result in an income reduction upon the death of a co-annuitant.

As intimated earlier, a common threat for all aging retirees are the catastrophic health events that can incapacitate and/or require major care from health care providers. Also, the necessity for increased use of health services is correlated with age. As individuals age, generally there is some deterioration in health and a necessity for the utilization of more extensive and more expensive health care. Beyond the need for health care services, loss of function and ability to independently care for oneself can necessitate the use of custodial care.

Although the necessity to access custodial or long-term care would often result in the inability to live independently, the loss of the capability to live independently can occur separately from the need to access custodial care. An individual can lack the basic ability to live independently. Individuals can experience difficulties due to a decline in physical well-being, loss of mental acuity, or inability to cope with the demands of everyday living. A change in an individual's circumstances—whether it be caused by the loss of a spouse, the advent of health issues, or the need to make a major adjustment in daily living routines—can necessitate some form of assistance.

Catastrophic shocks can occur that not only affect the health and well-being of the retiree personally, but major and unexpected shocks can also affect the resource systems of retirees. Dramatic investment losses or the bankruptcy of a former employer that ends benefits coverage are threats that can dramatically alter the life situations of retirees. Economic cycles can result in periods of time where a number of businesses will experience bankruptcy. Changes in global competition can render whole industries unprofitable. These occurrences in the macro-economy can have direct consequences for individual retirees whose pensions or benefit coverage may be reduced or eliminated. In the beginning of the millennium, the airline industry was plagued by adverse business conditions, and a number of large carriers sought bankruptcy protection. Many airline pilots were affected by these bankruptcies. Although the pilots' defined benefit pensions were protected by plan termination insurance through the Pension Benefit Guaranty Corporation as described in Chapter 22, the actual pensions received by pilots were the guaranteed amounts that were significantly below their expectations. Many retiring airline pilots were forced to adjust their standard of living to accommodate this adverse shock to their retirement resources. The next section looks at how a variety of environmental changes in the macro-economy can result in risk and adverse living conditions for the individual retiree.

Environmental Change

Retirees are not insulated from environmental change. Several areas in the environment where change occurs can have important repercussions for the living circumstances of retirees. One area of tremendous importance to retirees involves tax law. Defined contribution plans afford retirees preferential tax treatment while assets compound tax deferred; Social Security benefits are free of income taxation if the retiree's income is below a certain level; and certain retirement savings vehicles such as Roth IRAs, Roth 401(k)s, and Roth 403(b)s make distributions that are entirely free of taxes if certain conditions have been met. Any alteration of the Tax Code at the federal, state, or local level that affects private retirement system benefits or the tax treatment of payments from social insurance programs can have a significant effect in altering the financial well-being of retirees.

Apart from modification of the tax treatment of social programs, more substantive alteration of these programs in terms of eligibility requirements or actual benefits paid can have major implications for retirees and their dependents.

Adjustments may also be made to the benefit programs provided by private or public sector employers. Like governmental social insurance programs, these private or publicly sponsored benefit programs play an important role in providing overall financial security to retirees. Any change in private sector or public employer benefit programs can have a major impact on the living conditions of retirees. In recent times major changes have occurred in the realm of retiree health care. Formerly, many more private sector employers provided health care to their retirees. However, as the costs of these programs have greatly expanded and as employers have become more cognizant of their escalating costs, many employers have ceased to provide these benefits. Medicare and Medicaid provide a substantial portion of health coverage to retirees.

> After retirement, many retirees age 65 and older receive Medicare benefits, a government program that pays about 60% of health care costs, and 13% receive Medicaid (a government program targeted mainly at the indigent). Since the government programs leave gaps, it is not unusual for the elderly to obtain additional coverage. For instance, 22% of the elderly in 2004 had individually purchased health "Medigap" insurance, and about 29% had employer-sponsored retiree health insurance. Traditionally, larger employers offered retiree medical plans along the lines of a "defined benefit" or indemnity model,

where reimbursement for hospital and major medical treatment was provided if Medicare did not pick up the costs.[13]

Many employers, particularly in the private sector are no longer providing retiree health care benefits.

Environmental change can also occur in financial markets causing increased investment risk for retirees. A major market decline or a prolonged period of under valuation of certain asset classes can be especially problematic for retirees.

Ability to Independently Manage Risks and Living Needs

Apart from actual risks that directly affect the health, well-being, or financial resources of retirees, retirees can eventually find it difficult to independently manage these risks on their own or need assistance to manage their own living needs. Managing one's life involves a fair amount of complexity. As people age, many times they reach a point where it becomes more challenging simply to manage their own affairs. The idea of managing the aforementioned risks involves certain organizational and cognitive aptitudes that may become more challenging for superannuated individuals. Inability to procure basic life necessities, including health care, or to navigate the systems that provide these benefits can result in a decreased quality of life. Accordingly, a retiree can at some point realize that additional services are necessary to allow him or her to cope with the activities of life. Such a realization can come progressively as he or she undergoes a gradual deterioration in abilities, or this can occur abruptly as a result of some major cataclysmic event. This might occur with the death of a spouse. This is especially the case when one spouse may have solely taken responsibility for certain family activities like family finances or the cooking of meals or home care. One person, without the presence of his or her spouse, may lack the requisite skill set that the deceased spouse possessed.

Alternatively, the realization that a person can no longer live independently may occur when he or she transitions into a new stage of life. For instance, an individual whose health care needs progress to a point where more frequent trips to the doctor are required on an ongoing basis, may find the logistics of scheduling and traveling to doctors' offices to be beyond his or her capabilities. At times such recognition may necessitate a major alteration in living conditions. Some retirees may find that relocation into some form of alternate living arrangement such as a life care community may be beneficial to alleviate the stress and rigors of daily living. A **life care community** generally is a living arrangement that encompasses housing and meal arrangements and offers contracts that cover all health care services from assisted living to hospital care and physician's visits, which are usually already covered by a resident's private health insurance and/or Medicare.

The ongoing difficulty of managing living needs may require a major transition to a new way of living. Depending on the availability of alternative living arrangements and

[13] Sylvester Schieber, "The Future of Retiree Health Benefits in Higher Education in the US." Presented at the April 2004 TIAA-CREF Institute Conference on Recruitment, Retention and Retirement, New York, April 1–2, 2004.

their affordability, retirees may have limited options when they experience an inability to manage the risks of retirement and/or the routine rigors of daily living.

Managing Retirement Risks

Once retirement risks are identified, efforts can be made to manage these risks. As we indicated earlier, most of these retirement risks are better managed if planned for in advance. Some of these risks can be managed using insurance or other financial products currently available in the marketplace. Selection of a strategy for managing these risks involves accessing adequate information and selecting the most appropriate alternative. Knowing that resources are necessary to live in retirement, assets can be accumulated over a person's working career.

Pension plans and other types of tax-advantaged savings vehicles generally provide the most efficient way to accumulate savings for retirement. Although all of the risks identified previously are not totally remedied by an accumulation of pension or retirement plan assets, the build-up of sufficient retirement savings will be an essential element of the risk management strategy for most individuals entering retirement. This book is primarily concerned with the alternative choices related to retirement savings vehicles and pension plans. The remainder of this book examines the distinguishing characteristics of various types of savings vehicles that allow individuals to accumulate resources for retirement. As there are a number of different types of plan structures, particularly for defined contribution savings, a knowledgeable professional can assist an individual in understanding the types of plans most appropriate for his or her given situation.

Sometimes the type of plan made available by a given employer is dictated by the legal structure of the organization. For instance, some organizations are restricted from offering a 401(k) plan. This would be the case with a governmental employer that may offer a 457(b) plan, allowing its employees to save for retirement by tax deferring part of their incomes. Even when an individual is limited by the type of plan offered by an employer, an employee may have various choices whether to tax-defer contributions into a plan or to make those contributions on an after-tax basis. Most employers also allow employees to supplement savings through the employer above and beyond their basic retirement plans. Employees wishing to save additional amounts must decide whether to save these additional amounts through the employer or to opt for a savings vehicle independent of the employer. Today some employers offer 401(k) plans that would take employee salary deferrals on a pre-tax basis and separate Roth 401(k) plans that would involve after-tax contributions and subsequent withdrawals on a tax-free basis.

Once a decision is made regarding the tax treatment of the monies saved, employees must decide how those monies will be invested within the employer's plan. Many employer plans allow employees to actually designate how monies will be invested from a menu of investment choices within the plan. Sometimes these choices involve different investment company choices and further choices of portfolios of investments once the particular fund family is selected. All involve different types of investments, different investment objectives, and different expenses for investment management.

Additionally if individuals decide to supplement their employer-sponsored retirement savings programs by saving outside the employer plan on their own, a whole series of decisions need to be made in terms of the appropriate retirement savings vehicle to use as a supplement. Individuals may qualify for an individual retirement account where they can make contributions on a tax-deductible basis. Alternatively, individuals may qualify to contribute to a Roth IRA, where the contributions are made on an after-tax basis but the ultimate future distributions are disbursed on a totally tax-free basis.

In essence, there is substantial choice and flexibility when it comes to saving for retirement. Substantial choice and flexibility means both responsibility and challenge for the individual planning for her or his retirement. As has been noted throughout this chapter, the current trend in public policy and marketplace conditions places more responsibility on the individual to manage his or her retirement risks.

Chapter Summary

- The concept of *retirement* describes the phase of life following an extended period where a person engages in some form of work activity attributable to labor. Although there are work activities that are charitable in nature, most forms of work result in income generation, providing resources to sustain the necessities and amenities of life. This income-generating activity can either be as an employee of some other person or organizational entity or working for oneself.

- The notion of retirement involves the basic concept that individuals will work for a period of time during which they will set aside assets or become entitled to benefits. Following this period of asset accumulation or period of earning benefits eligibility, these individuals will then cease working and use the assets or earned benefits to sustain their material resource needs.

- Oftentimes when people discuss *retirement risk*, they are describing the situation in which retirees find themselves possessing inadequate resources to provide for their living needs. Of primary concern to many retirees is the possibility that they may deplete the resources set aside for retirement needs or find that the needs of retirement exceed either accumulated assets or benefits coverage.

- Longevity risk can be described as the situation where a person's extended life span exceeds expectations and results in the depletion of resources expected to be sufficient to meet the material needs of retirement.

- While there is an increasing number of people entering retirement with increased longevity and more costly health care needs, the structural design of the private pension system in the United States and other countries is changing. The trend in retirement plan change involves a migration to types of plans where the individual participant is responsible for investment risk.

- Any attempt to manage retirement risks must be conducted knowing the possible threat of insufficient information and should attempt to establish a means to manage risks that recognizes that at some point the individual retiree may be less-equipped to continue managing these risks. Therefore, risk management of retirement risks often involves establishing a decision system, such as using trustees or establishing a process to delegate decision making should the need arise in the future.

- Retirement risk can manifest itself as resource shortfalls limiting access to necessities of life or health care, but it can also occur as a loss of independent living and the inability to manage life's resources effectively and in a self-sufficient manner.

- Although defined contribution holdings invested in a particular asset class may exhibit a long-term rate of return that approaches historical means, there can be substantial variation and diversion from historical means over shorter time periods. Accordingly, if an individual sees a major reversal and loss in a retirement account at the onset of retirement, the income needs in the immediately following years may serve to deplete resources before the asset class rebounds.

- A successful defined contribution type of retirement system depends on a number of critical factors. Among these factors are adequacy of contributions, the right array of investment options, financial education for plan participants and plan features that assist in protecting against poor decision making by participants, and important policies and practices related to eventual distribution of plan assets.

- There is substantial choice and flexibility when it comes to saving for retirement. Substantial choice and flexibility means both responsibility and challenge for the individual planning for her or his retirement.

- The current trend in public policy and marketplace conditions places more responsibility on the individual to manage his or her retirement risks.

Key Terms

asset erosion or elimination, p. *66*
baby boom, p. *64*
disparate outcomes in income replacement ratios, p. *68*
diversion from historical means in asset returns, p. *68*

erosion in purchasing power due to inflation, p. *69*
expansion of retiree resource needs, p. *70*
life care community, p. *73*
longevity risk, p. *63*
phased-retirement, p. *62*

resource shortfalls, p. *66*
retirement, p. *62*
retirement risk, p. *63*
retirement security, p. *62*

Questions for Review

1. Describe what is meant by the notion of retirement.
2. Describe the idea of retirement security.

3. How do individuals transition into retirement over an extended number of years?
4. What is longevity risk?
5. What is retirement risk?
6. What are the categories the Society of Actuaries has used to describe retirement risks?
7. What are the reasons for resource shortfalls in retirement?
8. Discuss events that can result in asset erosion or elimination in retirement.
9. Describe the view that holds the future of retirement in America is not a disaster in the making.
10. Using Table 4.1, show the effects of inflation on purchasing power over different time periods with different rates of inflation.
11. What factors allow for successful use of defined contribution plans by employers as primary retirement savings vehicles for their employees?
12. How costly is retiree health care?
13. List some basic observations about the emerging factors concerning retirement realities.
14. What factors can affect a retiree's ability to independently manage risks and living needs?
15. How do retirement plan selection and the choice of savings vehicles serve to assist in managing retirement risks?

Questions for Discussion

1. How may a plan participant protect retirement assets against the erosive effect on purchasing power due to inflation?
2. Discuss how retirement plan selection and the choice of savings vehicles may assist in managing retirement risk beyond basic income needs.

Resources for Further Study

Burtless, Gary. "Risk and Reward of International Investing for Retirement Savers: Historical Evidence." Prepared for the 8th Annual Joint Conference of the Retirement Research Consortium: *Pathways to a Secure Retirement*, held in Washington, DC, *The Brookings Institution,* August 10–11, 2006.

Davis, Debra A. "Do-It-Yourself Retirement: Allowing Employees to Direct the Investment of Their Retirement Savings." *University of Pennsylvania Journal of Labor and Employment*, Winter 2006.

Rappaport, Anna M., and Monica Dragut. "High-Age Implications of Postretirement Risks." *Benefits Quarterly,* Fourth Quarter 2005.

Rappaport, Anna M., "Society of Actuaries Research Provides Insight for Navigating a Treacherous Pension Environment." SOA website, http://www.soa.org, accessed June 9, 2006.

Rudolph, Max J., "Allow Investors to Own Their Retirement." SOA website, http://www.soa.org, accessed October 12, 2006.

Utkus, Stephen P., "Brewing a Tempest in a Teapot." *On Wall Street*, August 1, 2006.

Reinhardt, Uwe, "Does the Aging of the Population Drive the Demand for Health Care?" *Health Affairs*, November/December 2003.

Chapter 5

Overview of Defined Contribution Plan Types and Their Use in Retirement Plan Design

After studying this chapter you should be able to:

- Describe the general characteristics of defined contribution plans.
- Identify some basic differences among various types of defined contribution plans.
- Explain the factors that influence the amount of retirement benefit under a defined contribution plan.
- Explain the limitations on employers in terms of contribution levels and deductibility of contributions to defined contribution plans.
- Distinguish among various types of defined contribution plans.

To briefly review the discussion in Chapter 3, pension plans are either *defined benefit* or *defined contribution* in nature. Traditionally the majority of employees in the United States were covered by defined benefit plans, reflecting the fact that most large employers and almost all union-negotiated plans had used this approach. A defined benefit plan provided a fixed amount of pension benefit. The amount of each employee's benefit usually depended on length of service and pay level—for example, a pension of 1 percent of pay for each year of service. In collectively bargained plans, however, pay often was not taken into account; the monthly pension was typically a fixed dollar amount (such as $30) for each year of service. In any event, a defined benefit plan promised a fixed level of benefit and the employer contributed whatever was necessary to provide this amount.

By contrast, the defined contribution approach focused on contribution levels. The employer's contribution was fixed as a percentage of pay or as a flat dollar amount.[1] This contribution, along with any amounts contributed by the employee, was accumulated and invested on the employee's behalf. The amount of pension an employee received would thus vary depending on such factors as length of plan participation, the level of contributions, and investment gains and losses.

Since the passage of the Employee Retirement Income security Act (ERISA), there has been a growing interest in the defined contribution concept. In fact, the majority of all new plans established since the mid-1970s used the defined contribution approach. Even though many of these defined contribution plans had been supplemental in nature—and most had been profit sharing or stock bonus programs, including so-called savings plans and cash or deferred arrangements (CODAs)[2]—some of these plans had been true pension arrangements that used defined contribution concepts. These latter plans were called *money purchase* pension plans.

This chapter begins with a review of the general characteristics of defined contribution plans. It then considers the contribution structure of these plans. The chapter concludes with a discussion of the distinguishing characteristics of various types of defined contribution plans.

General Characteristics of the Defined Contribution Approach

Defined contribution plans differ from defined benefit arrangements. One example of this difference concerns the allocation of employer contributions. The amount an employer contributes for each employee under a defined contribution plan is usually expressed as a percentage of the employee's current pay (for the year involved), with the result that each employee, regardless of age, receives the same percentage-of-pay contribution. By contrast, the allocation of employer contributions under a final-pay defined benefit plan is such that age and prior service also are taken into account. Thus, the amount of aggregate employer contributions allocated to younger employees usually is much higher under a defined contribution plan than it is under a defined benefit plan. Some employers believe that this is an equitable allocation of their contributions. Others, however, feel that it is fairer to allocate contributions in such a way that older (and usually longer service) employees receive proportionately greater amounts. Regardless of how an employer views this issue, the fact remains that this type of allocation pattern can produce higher levels of severance benefits for employees who terminate at younger ages with a vested interest and, to this extent, higher plan costs. It should be noted, however, that it is possible to design a defined contribution plan so that contributions increase with

[1] This fixed contribution requirement is a characteristic of money purchase plans that distinguishes them from other defined contribution arrangements in which the employer's contribution is a variable that is related to profits or is made on a discretionary basis.

[2] Technically, the tax law only provides for pension, profit sharing, and stock bonus plans. Savings plans are *generally* not a recognized form of plan, as such, and are usually qualified as profit sharing plans. CODAs are not plans but rather are arrangements that are attached to an underlying profit sharing or stock bonus plan. Nevertheless, common usage refers to both savings plans and CODAs as though they were separate types of plans.

age and service, provided this does not produce discriminatory results. In such a plan, the pattern of allocations will more closely resemble that of a defined benefit plan.

Another example concerns the way in which defined contribution plans respond to inflation. In essence, the retirement benefits that might be provided to an employee are the result of contributions that are based on the employee's career average compensation. There will be some reflection of inflation that takes place during the employee's preretirement years, in that current and future contributions will take the accumulated effects of inflation into account. And, if the employee's account balance is invested in equity-type investments, some inflation protection may be provided by investment results.[3] Also, because of the very nature of the employer's commitment, no postretirement inflation protection is provided under a defined contribution plan. By contrast, the typical final-pay defined benefit plan provides for an initial level of income that reflects inflation up to the time of retirement. Further, some employers provide for "ad hoc" increases for their retirees, from time to time, under defined benefit arrangements.

A related comparison concerns investment risk. Under defined contribution plans, the employee both receives the benefit of all positive investment returns and bears the risk of all unfavorable results. Under a defined benefit plan, investment risk and reward is borne by the employer.

Contribution Structure

As previously noted, defined contribution plans do not provide a fixed benefit for employees. Instead, the employer (and any employee) contributions, together with investment income, are applied to provide as much in the way of pension benefits as possible. Since the cost of a given amount of benefit varies by entry age and retirement age, the benefits of any employee will depend on these factors as well as on contribution levels and investment results.

Defined contribution plans are often contributory. In this case, the employer's contribution is usually a match or multiple of the employee's contribution. For example, the plan could call for the employer and employee each to contribute 5 percent of the employee's compensation; or the employee's contribution could be set at 3 percent of compensation with the employer contributing 6 percent.

It should be noted that defined contribution plans have several inherent limitations when viewed from the perspective of providing retirement income. First, an employee who joins the plan at an older age will have only a short period of time to accumulate funds, with the result that the employee's benefit often will be inadequate. Table 5.1 indicates the results that could flow under a defined contribution plan and the disparity in benefits that could be produced. This table assumes that the compensation shown for each employee will continue until normal retirement; that the contribution made by the employer each year is 10 percent of the employee's pay; that this contribution will accumulate at 6 percent compound interest until retirement; and that the fund accumulated

---

[3] Many employees, however, tend to select relatively conservative investments (fixed income or guaranteed interest funds) when choices are made available to them, with the result that significant inflation protection may not be provided from this source—at least in many situations.

TABLE 5.1   Illustration of Defined Contribution Formula without Earnings Projection

Age at Entry	Normal Retirement Age	Pay	Contribution	Fund at Retirement	Monthly Benefit	Benefit as a Percentage of Pay
30	65	$12,000	$1,200	$141,745	$1,274	127%
40	65	14,000	1,400	81,419	732	63
45	65	9,500	950	37,043	333	42
53	65	30,000	3,000	53,646	482	19
55	65	12,000	1,200	16,766	151	15

at retirement will be applied under representative annuity purchase rates to provide a monthly pension benefit.

Table 5.1 also shows that younger employees have a much longer time to accumulate funds and thus receive a proportionately larger benefit. Moreover, the defined contribution plan has an additional weakness since, because of the effect of compound interest, greater weight is given to the employee's lower compensation at the younger ages than will be given to the higher compensation the employee receives when he or she is older.

An additional comment about the potential disadvantages of defined contribution plans has to do with their ability to respond to growth in an employee's earnings—particularly during periods of inflation. Table 5.1 projects benefits for employees on the assumption that earnings will remain constant. This is not a realistic assumption since, in all probability, most employees will receive a number of pay increases over their working careers. Thus, it is important to illustrate and compare the results depicted in Table 5.1 with what would be the case if all assumptions remained the same except for future pay growth. This comparison for the same group of employees is set forth in Table 5.2, which assumes that earnings will grow at the rate of 4 percent a year. As can

TABLE 5.2   Illustration of Defined Contribution Formula with and without Projection of Pay

Age at Entry	Pay		Fund at Retirement		Monthly Benefit		Benefit as Percentage of	
	Pay at Entry	Final Pay	With Flat Pay	With Projected Pay	With Flat Pay	With Projected Pay	Entry Pay	Final Pay
30	$12,000	$45,532	$141,745	$237,864	$1,274	$2,139	127.4%	56.4%
40	14,000	35,886	81,419	120,652	732	1,085	62.7	36.3
45	9,500	20,015	37,043	51,156	333	460	42.1	27.6
53	30,000	46,184	53,646	65,375	482	588	19.3	15.3
55	12,000	17,080	16,766	19,754	151	178	15.1	12.5

be seen, the potential benefit, as a percentage of final pay, is considerably lower when future earnings growth is taken into account.

Another observation about the deficiencies of a defined contribution plan is that the employee's benefit under this approach can only be estimated. This lack of certainty as to benefits could prove to be an unsatisfactory employee relations feature of such a plan. Also, the variation in benefit levels for different employees makes it difficult, if not impossible, to design a contribution formula that produces benefit levels uniformly responsive to employer objectives. As a final observation, a defined contribution plan is a career-pay plan; however, unlike the practice for career-pay defined benefit plans, it is relatively uncommon for an employer to update accrued benefits to take inflation into account.

Integration with Social Security

Section 401(l) of the Internal Revenue Code (IRC) permits most qualified plans to "integrate" or coordinate contributions and/or benefits with the benefits provided by Social Security. In essence, this provision of the law provides for a limited form of discrimination in that it permits plans to provide higher contributions or benefits for higher-paid employees so as to compensate for the fact that the relative value of Social Security decreases as pay goes up.

Thus, a defined contribution plan can have two employer contribution levels—one level for pay up to a specified amount and another higher contribution level for pay in excess of that amount. Section 401(l) requires that the difference between these two employer contribution levels cannot exceed a certain amount—called the **permitted disparity.**

The point at which the contribution percentage changes is called the plan's **integration level.** The law permits the use of an integration level in any plan year of any amount up to the Social Security taxable wage base at the beginning of that year.

When a plan's integration level equals the Social Security taxable wage base or is set at a level at or below 20 percent of this taxable wage base, the contribution percentage for pay above this amount may exceed the contribution percentage for pay below this amount by the lesser of (1) 5.7 percent and (2) the percentage applicable to pay below the wage base. In other words, when the contribution percentage applicable to pay below the integration level is equal to or less than 5.7 percent, the contribution percentage for pay above the integration level cannot be more than twice the lower contribution percentage; if the lower percentage is greater than 5.7 percent, the higher percentage cannot be more than the lower percentage plus 5.7 percent.

Thus, for example, if the lower contribution percentage is 4 percent, the higher percentage cannot exceed 8 percent; if the lower percentage is 6 percent, the higher percentage cannot exceed 11.7 percent. Table 5.3 shows illustrative maximums for plans that are integrated at the Social Security wage base or at or below 20 percent of this amount.

If a plan's integration level is between 20 and 100 percent of the Social Security taxable wage base, the 5.7 percent standard in these rules is reduced. If the plan's integration level is more than 80 percent of the Social Security taxable wage base, it is reduced to 5.4 percent; if the integration level is between 20 and 80 percent of the wage base, it is reduced to 4.3 percent.

It should be noted that if a money purchase plan is part of an arrangement that involves an ESOP, this portion of the program may be integrated. Also, if a plan fails to meet the specific requirements of Section 401(l), it may still be able to qualify if it can pass the nondiscrimination tests of Section 401(a)(4) of the IRC.

TABLE 5.3
Defined Contribution Plan Integration Limits (If Integration Level Is at Social Security Taxable Wage Base or at or below 20 Percent of This Amount)

If Lower Contribution Percentage Is:	Upper Contribution Percentage Cannot Exceed:
1.0%	2.0%
2.0	4.0
3.0	6.0
4.0	8.0
5.0	10.0
5.7	11.4
6.0	11.7
7.0	12.7
8.0	13.7

Section 415 Limitations

The annual additions to an employee's account (employer and employee contributions plus any reallocated forfeitures) cannot exceed the lesser of (1) $45,000 (in 2007) indexed to increase with changes in the consumer price index (CPI) or (2) 100 percent of compensation.

Deduction Limits

Under the Economic Growth and Tax Relief Reconciliation Act (EGTRRA), there is a uniform limit of 25 percent of compensation for all defined contribution plans.

Overview of Retirement Plan Structures

Plan Variety in the Private Pension System

Throughout the remainder of this text, various types of pension plans and retirement savings vehicles are explained. At this point, it is hoped that readers will obtain an overview that will serve as a reference point or type of "road map" in understanding the diversity of forms that are presently permissible when designing a retirement plan. Throughout the text, an attempt is made to present some history as to how these various retirement forms evolved over time. This evolutionary history is often helpful in recognizing certain inconsistencies and variations between various retirement savings vehicles.

Attempts to Build a More Consistent and Less Complicated System

At some point, this complicated road map may be rendered obsolete and may be viewed only as providing historical perspective on retirement planning structures if legislative initiatives to simplify the retirement planning landscape are successful. Many legislators and observers agree that the system has become unwieldy. Such complication makes it difficult for employers and participants alike to use these structures to the fullest extent and to ensure that they are keeping their plans up to date and complying with all legal requirements. This complicated system also makes it difficult at times for federal regulators to enforce public policy as intended. Complexity also is inefficient and costly.

Defined Benefit versus Defined Contribution Structure

Defined Benefit Payout Formula Variation

At the most elementary level, retirement plans can be segmented into defined benefit and defined contribution structures as described in Chapter 3. Whereas defined benefit plans may be described in terms of a variety of forms that the benefit formula will take, there are not a variety of different legal forms that apply to defined benefit plans. In terms of defined benefit formulas, they typically are based either on a final-pay or career-pay basis. As noted in Chapter 17, defined benefit formulas can be further segmented in terms of types of formulas: flat amount formulas, flat percentage of earnings formulas, flat amount per year of service formulas, and percentage of earnings per year of service formulas.

Defined Contribution Legal Structure Variation

With defined contribution plans, there is a considerable amount of variety in legal structures. The Internal Revenue Code primarily segments qualified plans into three major types of plans: money purchase pension plans, profit sharing plans and stock ownership plans. Although these three major categories are used throughout the IRC in explaining distinguishing characteristics in plan types and the necessity for compliance with plan qualification requirements (as described in Chapters 25, 26, and 27), other variations are possible. First let us distinguish some essential characteristics of these major types of plans and then discuss variations that are possible in utilizing these basic plan types.

Money Purchase Pension Plans (MPPs)

Money purchase plans are defined contribution plans that traditionally have served as pension plans. These types of plans are required to maintain individual accounts for employees. The plans are subject to the defined contribution annual addition limits of Section 415 of the IRC. MPPs are not subject to the plan termination provisions of Title IV of the Employee Retirement Income Security Act (ERISA) that apply to defined benefit plans. Employer contributions to MPPs generally must be made on an after-tax basis, although pre-ERISA money purchase pension plans could allow contributions on a pre-tax basis. Prior to passage of the Economic Growth and Tax Relief Reconciliation Act of 2001, these types of plans were used quite frequently. These plans involved a fixed contribution from the employer either on a percentage-of-pay basis or as a fixed-dollar amount. Once the fixed contribution was established, an employer was required to make this contribution annually unless the plan was amended. These plans were often coupled with profit sharing plans (described next). The reason for the pairing of these two types of plans was to achieve the maximum deductible contribution allowable under the law. Prior to the passage of EGTRRA, profit sharing plans were only permitted to receive contributions of 15 percent of compensation. Profit sharing plans are able to determine their annual contribution on an annual basis. Accordingly, employers could have discretion each year on whether they would make their contributions into the profit sharing plan. Often an employer sponsored both a profit sharing plan, where a 15 percent contribution was made (on a discretionary basis) and an additional 10 percent contribution was made into the MPP to achieve the maximum allowable deduction under the law. EGTRRA changed the law permitting a full 25 percent contribution into profit sharing plans. Henceforth, an employer could obtain the maximum allowable deduction under the law and still have the flexibility whether to make any plan contribution in a given year. As described in the box, "Possible Obsolescence of Money Purchase Pension Plans," in Chapter 6, there are still possible uses for MPPs, but the frequency of this use has declined considerably since the passage of EGTRRA.

Profit Sharing Plans (PSPs)

Profit sharing plans are defined contribution type plans that can be structured with either a discretionary formula or a predetermined formula for employer contributions into the plan. These plans also often allow employee contributions as well. Sometimes they are structured with an employer "matching" formula, where the employee must contribute in order to receive the employer match. As stated earlier, employer contributions could range up to a full 25 percent of compensation, but may also be set lower. There is considerable variation in the design of profit sharing plans. These plans can entail employer contributions only, used by employers to reward employees for achieving certain performance targets. These plans can also be structured and used as the employer's primary retirement plan. Many of these plans may require employee contributions to receive an employer match. Section 401(k) of the IRC allows employees to make plan contributions on a pre-tax basis. 401(k)s are not really a type of plan, but must be coupled with an underlying type of plan. Most often 401(k) provisions are coupled with profit sharing plans. An employer also may choose not to make any type of employer contribution and may offer a 401(k) provision attached to a profit sharing plan, affording its employees the opportunity to save their own funds for retirement on a pre-tax basis.

Stock Ownership Plans (SOPs)

In many ways, **stock ownership plans** may be compared to the aforementioned profit sharing plans. However, the main distinguishing characteristic of this type of plan is that it is created to invest primarily in employer securities. Whereas most qualified plans must prudently diversify plan assets to comply with the fiduciary standards of ERISA, a stock ownership plan is free of this requirement and can invest up to 100 percent of plan assets in qualifying employer securities. Although there are variations on possible SOP plan designs, special requirements as well as special favorable characteristics are permitted under the law for so-called **leveraged employee stock ownership plans (ESOPs).** A primary favorable benefit is that a leveraged ESOP is used in conjunction with debt financing.

401(k) Plans

As indicated in the section on PSPs, although **401(k) plans** are typically referred to in common usage as a type of retirement plan, in actuality Section 401(k) is a provision of the IRC that is coupled with an underlying plan structure to permit employees to contribute a portion of their salary into the plan on a tax-deferred basis. Since first being permitted under the law in the mid- to late 1970s, 401(k) type plans have grown among private employers to become the preeminent and most widely utilized retirement savings vehicle. Since 401(k) plans can be configured with employee contributions only, or with a variety of employee and employer contribution formulas, these plans offer employers considerable flexibility in terms of plan designs. These plans afford employees attractive tax-deferral opportunities but also place stipulations on employee opportunities to access plan funds once contributed to the plan. However, loan features are available that allow employees to access plan funds without having to face the severe tax consequences of early withdrawals under certain hardship conditions.

403(b) Plans

Whereas 401(k) plans are widely used among for-profit employers, certain not-for-profit employers at times during the past could not offer 401(k) tax deferral opportunities to their employees. However, Section 403(b) of the IRC, affords these types of employers the opportunity to offer their employees similar tax deferral opportunities. Though 403(b) type plans were first formalized in the 1950s and have a much longer history than 401(k) plans, they are often compared with 401(k) plans. Allowable employers under section 403(b) include nonprofit organizations qualified under Section 501(c)(3) of the IRC, public school systems, public colleges, and public universities. Originally Section **403(b) plans** restricted underlying plan investments to insurance contracts and annuities. The ability to offer mutual fund products under 403(b) plans was made allowable following ERISA's passage in 1974. Increasingly, the trend toward uniformity in plan requirements has made 403(b) plans subject to many of the same requirements that apply to 401(k)s.

457 Plans

In the same way that not-for-profit employers were precluded from offering their employees 401(k) tax deferral opportunities, state and municipal governmental employees are similarly prohibited from participating in 401(k) plans. The Revenue Act of 1978 made provision for similar tax deferral opportunities for these workers through the use of nonqualified deferred compensation plans by creating IRC Section 457. It is important to note that nonqualified deferred compensation **457 plans** exhibit considerable differences from the ERISA-mandated requirements of the law that apply to tax-qualified plans. Later, the requirements of Section 457 were also applied to nonqualified deferred compensation plans offered by tax-exempt employers. Although the requirements of Section 457 as applied to both governmental and tax-exempt employers were uniform originally, changes in the plan objectives associated with these different types of employers have resulted in the divergence of plan rules depending on whether the employer is a governmental or tax-exempt entity.

Small Employer Plans

Whereas the foregoing plans apply to several different types of employers, federal legislators have been repeatedly frustrated since many smaller private sector employers fail to offer retirement plans to their employees. It has been thought that many small employers have refrained from sponsoring qualified plans and offering them to their employees because of the complexity associated with complying with plan qualification requirements. Accordingly, legislative attempts have been made to offer retirement savings vehicles to smaller employers that offer similar tax favored benefits but without all of the complicated requirements associated with qualified plans. A variety of **small employer plans** would fall within the category of plan types with more simplified compliance requirements. These include **simplified employee pensions (SEPs)** and **savings incentive match plans for employees (SIMPLEs). Keogh plans** allow unincorporated employers to receive the same benefits as incorporated employers offering qualified plans. (Keoghs can be offered as either defined benefit or defined contribution type plans, although the majority of Keogh plans are defined contribution type plans.) The variety of these small employer plan offerings are indicative of legislators' continuing attempts to encourage small employer participation in the private retirement plan system and the number of small employers willing to sponsor a plan falling short of public policy objectives.

Individual Retirement Accounts (IRAs)

For those saving for their own retirement needs outside of their employer, **individual retirement accounts (IRAs)** are used. These accounts were originally made available at the time that ERISA was enacted into law in 1974. Subsequently, Congress has made considerable changes in the law regarding IRAs, and these changes have resulted in the offering of different types of IRAs. The original traditional type of IRA allowed taxpayers to reduce their taxable income and receive a tax deduction by the amount of their contribution into the IRA. Later Congress only permitted tax-deductible IRAs if the taxpayer's income fell below certain thresholds depending on tax filing status. The result of this requirement was that IRAs could be either deductible or nondeductible in nature. Then, as a result of the Taxpayer Relief Act of 1997, another type of nondeductible IRA, the **Roth IRA,** became available in 1998. Contributions to Roth IRAs are not tax deductible when made, but earnings accumulate tax deferred initially and subsequently are distributable tax-free if certain conditions are met. Like deductible and nondeductible traditional IRAs, a Roth IRA contribution must be made by the due date for the filing of the taxpayer's income tax return, not including extensions. Withdrawals of regular annual Roth contributions are tax free at any time since taxes have already been paid on these amounts. Withdrawals of earnings from Roth IRAs are tax free (rather than tax deferred) if the distribution is considered to be a qualified distribution. A qualified distribution is a distribution that is made at least five years from the first of the year in which the Roth account was established and meets at least one of the triggering conditions for distribution under the law.

Chapter Summary

- The amount an employer contributes for each employee under a defined contribution plan is usually expressed as a percentage of the employee's current pay (for the year involved), with the result that each employee, regardless of age, receives the same percentage-of-pay contribution. By contrast, the allocation of employer contributions under a final-pay defined benefit plan is such that age and prior service also are taken into account.

- Under defined contribution plans, the employee both receives the benefit of all posi- tive investment returns and bears the risk of all unfavorable results. Under a defined benefit plan, investment risk and reward is borne by the employer.
- Defined contribution plans have several inherent limitations when viewed from the perspective of providing retirement income. First, an employee who joins the plan at an older age will have only a short period of time to accumulate funds, with the result that the employee's benefit often will be inadequate. The defined contribution plan has an additional weakness since, because of the effect of compound interest, greater weight is given to the employee's lower compensation at the younger ages than will be given to the higher compensation the employee receives when he or she is older. An additional potential disadvantage of defined contribution plans has to do with their ability to respond to growth in an employee's earnings—particularly during periods of inflation. Another observation about the deficiencies of a defined contribution plan is that the employee's benefit under this approach can only be estimated. This lack of certainty as to benefits could prove to be an unsatisfactory employee relations feature of such a plan.
- Section 401(l) of the IRC permits most qualified plans to "integrate" or coordinate con- tributions and/or benefits with the benefits provided by Social Security. In essence, this provision of the law provides for a limited form of discrimination in that it permits plans to provide higher contributions or benefits for higher-paid employees so as to compen- sate for the fact that the relative value of Social Security decreases as pay goes up.
- With defined contribution plans, there is a considerable amount of variety in legal structures. There are money purchase pension plans, profit sharing plans, stock own- ership plans, leveraged employee stock ownership plans (ESOPs), 401(k)s, 403(b)s, 457 plans, small employer plans [comprised of simplified employee pensions (SEPs), savings incentive match plans for employees (SIMPLE plans), and defined contribu- tion Keoghs], and various types of individual retirement accounts (IRAs) including Roth IRAs.

Key Terms

401(k) plans, p. *86*
403(b) plans, p. *87*
457 plans, p. *87*
individual retirement
   accounts (IRAs), p. *88*
integration level, p. *83*
Keogh plans, p. *88*
leveraged employee
   stock ownership plans
   (ESOPs), p. *86*

money purchase plans
   (MPPs), p. *85*
permitted disparity, p. *83*
profit sharing plans
   (PSPs), p. *86*
Roth IRAs, p. *88*
savings incentive match
   plans for employees
   (SIMPLEs), p. *88*

Section 401(l) of the IRC,
   p. *83*
simplified employee
   pensions (SEPs), p. *88*
small employer plans,
   p. *88*
stock ownership plans
   (SOPs), p. *86*

Questions for Review

1. What characteristics of a defined contribution plan distinguish it from defined benefit plans?

2. What are the factors that ultimately influence the amount of retirement benefit an employee might receive under a defined contribution plan?
3. Describe the Section 415 limitations that apply to defined contribution plans.
4. What deduction limits apply to a defined contribution plan?
5. Describe the variety of legal forms available under defined contribution plans.

Questions for Discussion

1. Describe the permitted disparity limitations that apply to a defined contribution plan that is integrated with Social Security benefits.
2. Evaluate the efficiency of a defined contribution plan as an employer's primary vehicle for providing retirement benefits.

Resources for Further Study

Donovan, Kevin J.; and Gucciardi, Joan. "Designing Plans after EGTRRA." *Journal of Pension Benefits* 9, no. 1 (Autumn 2001).

Employee Benefit Research Institute. "History of 401(k) Plans: An update," www.ebri. org/pdf/publications/facts/0205fact.a.pdf. Washington DC: EBRI (February 2005).

Knowledge@Wharton. "Hands-off: Holders of 401(k) Retirement Accounts Are Not Your Typical Investors." http:knowledge.wharton.upenn.edu/article. cfm?articleid=1405#. Philadelphia: The Wharton School (March 8, 2006).

Knowledge@Wharton. "How Can Employers Improve Defined Contribution Plans?" http:knowledge.wharton.upenn.edu/article.cfm?articleid=1578#. Philadelphia: The Wharton School (October 18, 2006).

Towers Perrin. "From Responsibility to Action–Making Benefit Change Work." Towers Perrin HR Services (2007).

www.psca.org—website of the Profit Sharing/401(k) Council of America.

www.403bwise.com—website of information on 403(b) plans.

www.457bwise.com—website of information on 457(b) plans.

Chapter 6

Profit Sharing Plans and Money Purchase Pension Plans

After studying this chapter you should be able to:

- Describe the characteristics of profit sharing plans and money purchase pension plans.
- Explain the purposes of these plans and how their purposes influence elements of plan design.
- Discuss contribution requirements imposed on profit sharing and money purchase pension plans by the Internal Revenue Code.
- Explain allowable and customary approaches to allocating employer contributions in profit sharing and money purchase pension plans.
- Describe what happens to forfeited nonvested contributions in profit sharing and money purchase pension plans.
- Discuss allowable and customary approaches regarding withdrawals from profit sharing plans.

Profit sharing plans constitute an important component in the overall structure of employee benefit programs in the United States. The requirements imposed by the Employee Retirement Income Security Act (ERISA) as to minimum funding and employer liabilities for plan terminations resulted in a growing interest in **individual-account retirement programs.** Profit sharing and savings plans have considerable appeal since they embody the individual account concept without imposing any fixed commitment on employers to provide any specific level of benefits. Thus, one has seen greater use of profit sharing plans in lieu of pension plans or a greater use of basic pension plans plus a supplemental savings or profit sharing program. Particularly in today's competitive business climate, with its primary emphasis on pay-for-performance, profit sharing plans are well-suited to supply this component of total compensation on a tax-deferred basis.

Definition of Profit Sharing

Many definitions of profit sharing have been suggested. One broad concept is that a profit sharing plan is one in which the company's contributions are based upon business profits, regardless of whether the benefit payments are made in cash, are deferred, or are a combination of the two. This definition suggests three basic profit sharing plan approaches, which may be defined as follows: (1) **current** (cash)—profits are paid directly to employees in cash, check, or stock as soon as profits are determined (e.g., monthly, quarterly, semiannually, or annually); (2) **deferred**—profits are credited to employee accounts to be paid at retirement or upon other stated dates or circumstances (e.g., disability, death, severance, or under withdrawal provisions); and (3) **combined**— part of the profit is paid out currently in cash and part is deferred. This can take place under one plan with both current and deferred features or under two separate plans—one cash and the other deferred—covering, by and large, the same employee groups.

The definition of a profit sharing plan as set forth in federal income tax regulations is as follows:

> A profit sharing plan is a plan established and maintained by an employer to provide for the participation in his profits by his employees or their beneficiaries. The plan must provide a definite predetermined formula for allocating the contributions made to the plan among the participants and for distributing the funds accumulated under the plan after a fixed number of years, the attainment of a stated age, or upon the prior occurrence of some event such as layoff, illness, disability, retirement, death, or severance of employment.[1]

The qualification of profit sharing plans for tax exemption under Section 401 of the Internal Revenue Code (IRC), then, is restricted to deferred or combination-type plans. Current or cash profit sharing plans (approach [1] above), therefore, are not treated in this chapter. Also, combination cash or deferred plans (approach [3] above), because of the unique requirements of federal tax law that apply to such plans, are treated separately in Chapter 8. Thus, this chapter relates only to tax-qualified deferred profit sharing plans (approach [2] above).

Qualification Requirements

The qualification requirements for profit sharing plans are, for the most part, identical to those for pension plans, which are described in Chapters 25 and 26. However, this chapter discusses these requirements in terms of their application to profit sharing plans. This discussion relates only to plans that are not top heavy. The special requirements applicable to top-heavy plans, that is, plans in which the sum of account balances of key employees exceed 60 percent of the sum of account balances for all covered employees or plans that are part of a top-heavy group, are covered in Chapter 26.

---

[1] Reg. 1.401(b)(1)(ii).

Coverage Requirements

In order to qualify and thus receive favorable tax treatment under the IRC, a profit sharing plan must be for the **exclusive benefit** of employees or their beneficiaries. Therefore, a plan will not qualify if the coverage requirements result in discrimination in favor of the highly compensated employees—that is, the plan must meet the coverage requirements of Section 410(b) of the IRC. Restriction of coverage by type of employment (e.g., salaried employees, hourly employees, sales representatives) is permitted, provided that such coverage requirements do not result in prohibited discrimination.

Relatively few profit sharing plans impose a minimum age requirement, but practically all profit sharing plans specify a service requirement as a condition for participation in the plan. The IRC permits the use of a minimum age of up to 21 and a service requirement of up to one year (two years if the plan provides for full and immediate vesting and is not a cash or deferred arrangement).

Contribution Requirements

The Internal Revenue Code does not require as a condition for qualification that a profit sharing plan include a **definite predetermined contribution formula.** And, for plan years beginning after December 31, 1985, it is no longer necessary that contributions be based on profits. In the absence of such a formula, however, the regulations require that **substantial and recurring contributions** be made if the requirement of plan permanency is to be met.

Contributions under a profit sharing plan may be made on a discretionary basis (e.g., as determined annually by the board of directors of the company) or in accordance with a definite predetermined formula. The **discretionary contribution approach** offers the advantage of contribution flexibility. The board of directors can adjust contributions in view of the firm's current financial position and capital needs. Also, the discretionary approach precludes the possibility that contribution payments will exceed the maximum amount currently deductible for federal income tax purposes (to be discussed later in this chapter). If the amount of contribution is discretionary, the plan often imposes certain minimums and maximums. For example, the plan may provide that contributions cannot exceed 15 percent of profits but can be discretionary up to that limit; or it may stipulate that contributions cannot exceed 10 to 30 percent of profits, with the percentage to be determined by a board of directors.

There are advantages in using a definite predetermined formula. A definite formula promotes increased employee morale and feelings of security. Without a definite formula, employees may feel unsure of receiving a share of what they have helped to produce.

Whether the definite formula or discretionary contribution approach is used, management still must determine the extent to which employees are to directly or indirectly share in the firm's profits. In arriving at this decision, management must take into account factors such as the objectives of the plan, the nature of the firm's business, the pattern of profits, and the age and service composition of the employee group. Obviously, a good deal more thought must be given to this matter if a definite contribution formula is used.

The contribution commitment under definite-formula plans generally is expressed as a fixed percentage or a sliding scale of percentages of profits. The specified percentages usually are applied to profits before taxes, although a base of after-tax profits can be used. The sliding scale formula provides for higher percentage contributions for higher levels of profits. A percentage-of-compensation formula also can be used.

Whether the definite formula or discretionary contribution approach is used, the plan usually specifies some limitation on the amount of annual contribution. One reason is to give priority to a minimum rate of return on capital for stockholders. Limitations on contributions can be expressed in several different ways. For example, the plan may provide that no contribution will be made in years in which dividend payments are less than a specified amount, or unless aggregate profits exceed a stated amount, or when profits are less than a given percentage of the firm's capital funds. Many plans also impose the limitation that contributions in any one year cannot exceed the maximum amount deductible for federal income tax purposes by the employer.

Employee Contributions

It is conceptually illogical to *require* employee contributions under profit sharing plans. Furthermore, in those plans that require employee contributions, the employer's contribution usually is based on the amount of the employee's contribution. For these reasons, contributory plans generally are referred to as thrift or savings plans to distinguish them from traditional profit sharing plans. For a more complete discussion of these plans, see Chapter 8.

Even though employee contributions usually are not required under profit sharing plans, it is quite common to permit them on a "voluntary" basis, with employees being given this option regardless of the level of employer contributions involved. When allowed, these voluntary contributions may be made as **elective deferrals** under Section 401(k) of the IRC or as contributions from after-tax income. If made as elective deferrals, the plan must meet the actual deferral percentage (ADP) test requirements of Section 401(k) unless the plan is designed to meet safe harbor requirements; if made as after-tax contributions, the plan must meet the actual contribution percentage (ACP) test requirements of Section 401(m).

Allocations to Employee Accounts

It was noted above that the Internal Revenue Service (IRS) does not require a plan to include a definite contribution formula as a condition for qualification. However, it is necessary that the plan include a definite **allocation formula** to become qualified. Since contributions to the plan generally are based on profits, a method or formula is needed to determine the amount to be credited to each participant's account.

The employer must decide the basis upon which the contributions to the plan are to be divided among the various participants. The allocation of contributions to the account of each participant usually is made on the basis of compensation or a combination of compensation and service. If compensation is used, then allocations are made on the basis of the proportion of each participant's compensation to the total compensation of all participants. For example, if employee A earns $10,000 a year and the total annual compensation for all participants is $200,000, employee A will be credited with 5 percent of the employer's total annual contributions because $10,000 is 5 percent of $200,000. Under a formula that reflects both compensation and service, a unit of credit might, for example, be given for each year of service and an additional unit given for each $100 of compensation. With 20 years of service, employee A would have 20 units of service and 100 units of compensation. Therefore, employee A's share of contributions is determined by the fraction of 120 over the total number of units similarly calculated for all participants. The most popular allocation formulas are those based on compensation, although many plans use a combination of compensation and years of service.

The IRS requires a definite allocation formula in qualified plans so that it may determine whether contributions are shared in a nondiscriminatory manner. The plan also must meet the nondiscrimination requirements of Section 401(a)(4) of the IRC. The typical profit sharing plan, however, generally will have no trouble in meeting these requirements since such a plan usually allocates contributions on the basis of a uniform percentage of pay. Where this is the case, and if the same vesting schedule and years of service definition apply to all participants, the plan will be considered to meet the nondiscrimination requirements. (For purposes of these requirements, a plan having an integrated allocation formula that meets the permitted disparity requirements of Section 401(l) will be considered to have a uniform percentage allocation formula.) If the allocation formula is weighted for age and/or service and for units of pay that do not exceed $200, the plan will meet the nondiscrimination requirements if the average of the allocation rates for highly compensated employees (HCEs) does not exceed the average of the allocation rates for the nonhighly compensated employees (NHCEs). Otherwise, the plan will have to meet the testing requirements of Section 401(a)(4).

The allocation formula is used to determine the employee's share of contributions for accounting or record-keeping purposes. The contribution dollars are not segregated on behalf of each participant. Contributions are received, administered, and invested by the trustee as unallocated assets. The balance in each participant's account represents the participant's share of the assets of the fund at that moment. An exception is the case where the trust permits each participant's account to be invested in "earmarked" investments. Whether the participant is currently entitled to all or a part of the money credited to his or her account depends upon the provisions of the plan.

Finally, the allocation of employer contributions is subject to the contribution and benefit limitations of the IRC. These limits are described in Chapter 26.

Under many profit sharing plans, there may be some forfeited amounts when employees terminate with less than full vesting. These forfeitures may be used to reduce employer contributions. More typically, in profit sharing plans, they are re-allocated among remaining participants. These reallocations generally are based on the pay of each remaining participant in relation to the total pay of all remaining participants. The IRS will not permit reallocations on the basis of the account balances of the remaining participants if such a procedure would produce discrimination in favor of HCEs. However, the investment income of a profit sharing plan may be allocated on the basis of account balances. Thus, it is possible to have different allocation formulas for contributions, forfeitures, and investment income.

Integration with Social Security

As mentioned earlier, profit sharing plans seldom are integrated with Social Security benefits. While these plans *can* be integrated with Social Security benefits subject to the

IRC requirements for defined contribution plans,[2] no portion of a plan that consists of a cash or deferred arrangement (CODA) may be integrated. It should be noted that the maximum deductible amount that can be allocated to each participant's account in any one year pertains to the aggregate of employer contributions and forfeitures of nonvested accumulations during the year. In nonintegrated profit sharing plans, the maximum deductible annual contribution is 25 percent of compensation. Furthermore, if the plan is not integrated, forfeitures may be reallocated among remaining participants without reducing the 25 percent maximum. Last, if an employer has integrated both its pension and profit sharing plans covering any of the same employees, the integration under both plans cannot exceed 100 percent of the integration capability of a single plan. The objective of this requirement is to avoid the discrimination in favor of HCEs that would otherwise result.

Provision for Distributions

As indicated earlier, the definition of profit sharing in the federal income tax regulations permits distributions "after a fixed number of years, the attainment of a stated age, or upon the prior occurrence of some event such as layoff, illness, disability, retirement, death, or severance of employment."

The primary objective of many deferred profit sharing plans is to permit the employee to build up an equity in the fund to enhance his or her economic security after retirement. The law requires that the accumulations credited to the employee's account vest in full at normal retirement age, regardless of the employee's length of service. Most plans also fully vest the amounts credited to the employee upon death, while a lesser but still significant number of plans provide full and immediate vesting upon the occurrence of total and permanent disability.

Whether an employee is entitled to a distribution from the fund upon voluntary termination of employment or upon being laid off depends upon the vesting provisions of the plan. Of course, if the plan is contributory, the employee is always entitled, at a minimum, to a return of the benefit attributable to his or her contributions upon death, total and permanent disability, or severance of employment.

The value of employer-provided contributions under a deferred profit sharing plan also must vest upon severance of employment in accordance with the requirements of the IRC. Thus, the plan must satisfy one of the alternative minimum vesting schedules.[3]

Withdrawals during Active Employment

Some plans also permit participants to withdraw a portion of their vested benefits in the plan prior to separation of employment.[4] The regulations permit distributions from a qualified profit sharing plan "after a fixed number of years." The IRS has interpreted this to mean that accumulations cannot be distributed in less than two years. In other words, if contributions have been credited to an employee's account for three years, he

---

[2] The IRC requirements for integrated defined contribution plans are described in Chapter 25.

[3] See Chapter 26 for a full discussion of these minimum vesting requirements.

[4] Contributions made on an elective deferral basis are subject to the withdrawal restrictions described in Chapter 8.

or she can withdraw an amount equal to the first year's contribution and the investment income credited in that year (assuming that the plan permits such withdrawals). Tax law also permits the withdrawal of funds upon the happening of an event such as hardship or, as interpreted by the IRS, upon the completion of five years of plan participation. The right to withdraw may be restricted to employee contributions, or it may apply to the vested portion of accumulations attributable to employer contributions. Of course, the participant must report the withdrawn amount as taxable income in the year in which it is received (except to the extent it is considered to be a return of the employee's own contributions), and such amount will be taxable as ordinary income. Moreover, an additional tax of 10 percent of the taxable portion of the distribution could be assessed on distributions before the participant reaches age 59½ unless certain conditions are met. Although a withdrawal provision may be desirable in a plan, care should be exercised, since a provision that is too liberal could result in defeating the long-term savings objective of the plan.

Loans

Loan provisions also are found in some deferred profit sharing plans. Under a loan provision, a participant generally is entitled to borrow up to a specified percentage (50 percent, for example) of the vested portion of his or her account (including any employee contributions). The loan provision has an advantage over a withdrawal provision in that repayment of the loan will permit achievement of the objective of a long-term program geared toward retirement. However, some employers may prefer the withdrawal provision, since such a provision might help in avoiding possible employee dissatisfaction that could result from the feeling that they must pay interest on the use of "their own money." The loan provision is also advantageous in that, if IRS requirements are met, the sums borrowed are not subject to federal income tax. However, the interest payments are not deductible for federal income tax purposes. The law requires that loans be available to all participants on a reasonably equivalent basis and that a loan not be made available to HCEs in a percentage greater than that made available to other employees. The law also requires that the loan bear a reasonable rate of interest, be adequately secured, and be made only by the plan (and not by a third party, such as a bank, with the employee's account balance as security). If the loan provision meets the requirements of the Department of Labor (DOL) and the IRS, the loan will be exempted from the prohibited transactions provisions of ERISA and the IRC. If a loan is made and is not exempted, this could constitute a prohibited transaction and could be in violation of the legal requirement that a plan prohibit assignments and alienations; this could result in a plan disqualification.

A loan to an employee will be treated as a taxable distribution unless certain requirements are met. These requirements involve the amount of the loan (or accumulated loans), the agreement concerning loan terms, and the time period for repayment. The maximum amounts that can be borrowed without being considered a distribution depend upon the amount of the employee's vested interest in his or her account balance. If it is (1) $10,000 or less, the entire vested interest is available; (2) between $10,000 and $20,000, $10,000 is available; (3) between $20,000 and $100,000, 50 percent of the vested interest is available; or (4) $100,000 or more, $50,000 is available. The $50,000 limitation on loans from qualified plans is reduced by the excess of the highest outstanding loan balance during the preceding one-year period over the outstanding balance on the date a new loan is made.[5]

The loan must be evidenced by a legally enforceable agreement setting forth the amount, term, and repayment schedule of the loan.

As to the time period for repayment, the loan, by its terms, must be repaid within five years; substantially level amortization of the loan is required, with payments made at least quarterly. If the loan is used to acquire a dwelling unit (which is to be used as a principal residence of the participant) and meets the amount limitation, the five-year time limit does not apply.

Investment Options

It is possible for the assets of a profit sharing plan to be invested in a single fund, with all employees sharing proportionately in the investment gains and losses of that fund. But, in fact, few plans are designed and operated in this fashion. Most plans allow employees to direct the investment of their accounts and to choose from among several different investment options. These options typically include two or more of the following: a guaranteed interest contract or arrangement, a corporate bond or fixed income fund, a government bond fund; one or more equity funds (with varying degrees of risk), and an employer stock fund. Larger employers might have even more funds to choose from and might include, for example, a real estate fund. Some employers make these choices available by arranging for a choice among several of the funds offered by an investment company.

A major reason for permitting these choices is to limit the employer's fiduciary responsibility. Some statutory relief from this liability can be obtained by complying with regulations issued by the DOL. In general, these regulations require that a plan offer at least three diversified categories of investment with materially different risk and return characteristics and that participants have the right to change investments at least quarterly—more often if needed because of the volatility of a particular fund. Regulatory liability protection can be afforded to employer stock if the shares are publicly traded in a recognized market and if the plan also offers the three required options; however, all purchases, sales, voting, and related share activities must be implemented confidentially through a fiduciary. It should be noted that failure to comply with the DOL regulations does not mean that fiduciaries are automatically liable—it simply means that the regulatory safe harbor for liability attributable to participants' investment choices will not be available. Also, compliance does not relieve the employer from responsibility for ensuring that the investments are prudent and properly diversified.

If employer stock is an investment choice and can be purchased with employee contributions, the requirements of the Securities and Exchange Commission (SEC) will have to be met. These requirements are discussed in Chapter 27.

A plan also can be written to permit employees to invest part of their account balances in life and health insurance. When this is done, and when a participant is investing

---

[5] The Department of Labor has taken the position that a loan cannot exceed 50 percent of the employee's vested account balance. Because of this conflict between the DOL and the IRS, most plans limit the loan to 50 percent of the vested account balance and ignore the $10,000 minimum.

Evaluating the Costs of Plan Loans to Employees

Loan provisions have proven attractive to many employees who feel they are getting a "break" in the form of a no-cost loan since they are paying interest to themselves—as the loan is repaid, both principal and interest are credited to their accounts. This, of course, is not the case. Assuming that the rate of interest charged by the plan is the same as the rate the employee would pay to a commercial lender, there is no difference in the cost of the loan. In fact, making the loan from the plan could be more costly. When a loan is made from the plan, the employee's account balance, to the extent of the loan, is credited only with the interest charged by the plan. If the account would have been credited with a higher rate of return during the loan period had a loan not been made, the employee will have lost this additional investment income. This amount, compounded over the years remaining until a distribution is made, could add significantly to the real cost of the loan—over and above the interest rate charged.

This result can be avoided (or at least minimized) if the employee adjusts the investment mix of his or her account balance to treat the loan amount as part of the fixed income portion of the total account. For example, an employee with an account balance of $50,000 might be invested 80 percent in common stock ($40,000) and 20 percent in fixed income investments ($10,000). If the employee takes a loan of $10,000 and does not adjust the portfolio, the typical plan would reduce her mix so that $32,000 would be invested in stock and $8,000 would be invested in fixed income investments. The loan, however, is a fixed income investment, making a total of $18,000 in this category. She could counter this effect by directing that all of the remaining account balance ($40,000) be invested in stock, thus restoring the original mix with the expectation of not reducing overall returns.

funds that have accumulated for less than two years, additional IRS requirements must be met. These requirements are that such amounts, when used to purchase life or health insurance, must be incidental. The IRS has defined **incidental insurance benefits** as follows:

1. If only ordinary life insurance contracts are purchased, the aggregate premiums in the case of each participant must be less than one-half the total contributions and forfeitures allocated to his or her account.
2. If only accident and health insurance contracts are purchased, the payments for premiums may not exceed 25 percent of the funds allocated to the employee's account.
3. If both ordinary life and accident and health insurance contracts are purchased, the amount spent for the accident and health premiums plus one-half of the amount spent for the ordinary life insurance premiums may not, together, exceed 25 percent of the funds allocated to the employee's account.

In addition, the purchase of an ordinary life insurance contract will be incidental only if the plan requires the trustee to convert the entire value of the life insurance contract at or before retirement into cash; provides periodic income so that no portion of such value may be used to continue life insurance protection beyond retirement; or distributes the contract to the participant.

Other Requirements

Qualified profit sharing plans, like qualified pension plans, must meet the requirements of the IRC. Thus, they must be in writing, be permanent, be communicated to employees, and preclude diversion or recapture by the employer of contributions to the plan. A qualified profit sharing plan must treat service as required by ERISA and permit employees to buy back their benefits under stated conditions. It also must include a number of other features, such as a prohibition against assignments (with the exception of certain specified events), the protection of an employee's benefits in the event of plan merger or consolidation, and the payment of benefits by prescribed times. The plan also must comply with the top-heavy provisions of the law.

The requirement that a qualified pension plan provide definitely determinable benefits obviously does not apply in the case of qualified profit sharing plans. Also, certain other provisions of ERISA are not applicable to qualified profit sharing plans—for example, the minimum funding standards and the plan termination insurance requirements.

Limits on Deductibility of Employer Contributions

The limits on the deductibility of employer contributions to a profit sharing plan are set forth in **Section 404 of the IRC.**

For profit sharing plans, the **maximum deductible contribution** is equal to 25 percent of the compensation paid or otherwise accrued during the employer's taxable year to all covered employees for years beginning after 2001 as a result of Economic Growth and Tax Relief Reconciliation Act (EGTRRA). The maximum deductible contribution for profit sharing plans had previously been 15 percent of the compensation paid or otherwise accrued during the employer's taxable year to all covered employees for years prior to 2002.[6] Carryover provisions apply in profit sharing plans when the contribution in one taxable year is greater than the deductible limit for that taxable year. This type of carryover is called a **contribution carryover.** Thus, if a contribution is made in a given year in excess of the allowable deduction for that year, the employer will be allowed to take a deduction for such excess payment in a succeeding taxable year if it does not bring the deduction for the succeeding year to over 25 percent of the participating payroll for that succeeding year. However, any excess contribution is subject to a 10 percent penalty tax.

If both a pension plan (defined benefit or money purchase) and a profit sharing plan exist, with overlapping payrolls, the total amount deductible in any taxable year under

---

[6] If the contribution to the profit sharing plan was less than the allowable 15 percent, the difference between the amount actually paid in and the 15 percent limit (called a "credit carryover") could be contributed and deducted in succeeding years, but only if the carryover was accumulated before 1987. The credit carryover contribution in any later year could not exceed the allowable percent of the compensation paid or otherwise accrued during such later year. Also, there was an overall annual limitation when a credit carryover was involved. This overall limit was and is 25 percent of current covered payroll.

both plans cannot exceed 25 percent of the compensation paid or accrued to covered employees for that year.[7] When excess payments are made in any taxable year, the excess may be carried forward to the succeeding taxable year, subject to the limitation that the total amount deducted for that succeeding taxable year (including the deduction for the current contribution) cannot exceed 25 percent of the compensation paid or accrued for that subsequent year.

The 25 percent overall limitation can be achieved by a profit sharing plan alone since a currently deductible profit sharing contribution must not exceed 25 percent of the payroll of the participating employees for years beginning after 2001.[8] The 25 percent overall limitation does not eliminate the requirement that a currently deductible pension contribution must not exceed the amount that would have been the limit had only a pension plan been in effect.

Taxation of Distributions

The taxation of distributions from a qualified profit sharing plan is identical to the tax treatment of distributions from a qualified pension plan, discussed in detail in Chapter 31. However, the tax treatment of distributions of securities of the employer should be mentioned here because investing a portion of trust assets in the securities of the employer is a common practice under profit sharing plans. Securities of the employer include stocks, bonds, and debentures issued by the employer's parent or subsidiary corporations. If a total distribution (defined in Chapter 31) of the employee's account is made under qualifying conditions, the employee can elect to include either the market value of the employer securities or their cost basis to the trust as taxable income at the time of distribution. In other words, the employee need not be taxed on the unrealized appreciation at the time of distribution unless he or she so elects. If the employee elects to defer taxation, the unrealized appreciation, along with any subsequent increase in the value of the securities, is taxed as a capital gain when the securities are sold. If the securities are held until the employee's death prior to EGTRRA's elimination of the estate tax in 2010 (remember, as of this writing the estate tax would re-emerge in 2011), the employee's heirs will have a cost basis in the securities equal to their market value at the time of death (i.e., the appreciation in value unrealized at the time of death will not be taxed as income). If the securities of the employer are included in a distribution that does not meet qualifying conditions, only the portion of the securities attributable to employee contributions can be valued on the basis of cost to the trust.

---

[7] This 25 percent limit will be increased to the extent larger contributions are required by the IRC's minimum funding standards, as described in Chapter 19.

[8] See the insight box on page 103 describing the popularity in years before 2002 of combination plans involving money purchase pension plans and profit sharing plans. The insight box explains how increasing the maximum deductible contribution from 15 percent to 25 percent for years beginning after 2001 favors profit sharing plans alone in many situations.

Termination of a Plan

Although a qualified profit sharing plan must be permanent, the IRS does permit inclusion of a provision giving the employer the right to amend or terminate the plan. However, if the vesting schedule is changed, any participant with at least three years of service must be given the election to remain under the preamendment vesting schedule. If the plan is terminated for reasons other than "business necessity" within a few years after its inception, this action will be considered by the IRS as evidence that the plan, from its inception, was not a bona fide program for the exclusive benefit of employees in general. If business necessity exists, the employer may terminate the plan without adverse tax consequences.

If a plan is terminated, all assets in the fund are vested immediately in plan participants. Since all plan assets are allocated to specific participants, no problem exists regarding any order of priorities in the distribution of the fund. Each participant is entitled to the balance in his or her account.

Upon termination of the plan, the trustees will determine, in accordance with plan provisions, a method of distributing the plan assets. The participants' shares may either be distributed in a lump sum; distributed in installments over a period of years; used to purchase immediate or deferred annuities (either fixed or variable); or distributed in kind.

Money Purchase Pension Plans

Decreased Utilization of Money Purchase Pension Plans

As explained more fully in the box entitled "Possible Obsolescence of Money Purchase Pension Plans" on the following page, there has been decreased utilization of these plan structures. Although these types of plans are less likely to be utilized today, their prior prevalence and distinguishing characteristics merit the following overview.

General Characteristics

In a sense, **money purchase pension plans** are hybrids. Because they technically are pension plans, they are treated for many purposes in much the same fashion as defined benefit plans. They are, for example, subject to the minimum funding and joint and survivor requirements of the tax law that apply to defined benefit arrangements. In other areas, however, the tax law treats money purchase plans as defined contribution arrangements. Thus, individual accounts must be maintained for employees, the plans are subject to the annual addition limits of Section 415 of the Internal Revenue Code (IRC), and they are not subject to the plan termination provisions of Title IV of ERISA.

Although they are treated differently for different tax law purposes, money purchase plans are fundamentally defined contribution plans. For this reason, they have many of the same basic characteristics that are found in all defined contribution plans— particularly when contrasted with defined benefit arrangements.

Prior to the passage of the Economic Growth and Tax Relief Reconciliation Act of 2001 (EGTRRA), it was common for many self-employed individuals to sponsor money purchase pension plans paired with profit sharing plans. The reason these types of plans were common in Keoghs or HR-10 plans was that the combination provided the maximum deductible contribution with the most flexibility. A profit sharing plan in the past only allowed a 15 percent of pay contribution and deduction. The advantage of the profit sharing plan was, and still is, that the annual contribution can be discretionary, and the individual need not make a contribution if cash is scarce. The money purchase pension plan, however, requires a fixed annual contribution. The combination money purchase pension plan paired with a profit sharing plan allowed a self-employed person to reach the maximum deduction of 25 percent of pay with a fixed annual contribution of 10 percent to the money purchase plan and a discretionary contribution of 15 percent of pay to the profit sharing plan. EGTRRA increased the allowable deductible contribution to a profit sharing plan from 15 percent of pay to 25 percent of pay. Therefore, it appears that a profit sharing plan alone allows both the maximum deductible contribution and the most flexibility with a discretionary contribution.

Some practitioners believe the money purchase pension plan will become obsolete. However, there are still some applications for money purchase pension plans. Because money purchase pension plans are subject to minimum funding standards, they provide plan participants with added security regarding plan contributions. This may be important in certain situations such as with collectively bargained plans or if employers are concerned with the perception that future plan contributions will not occur. Some participants will obviously prefer the money purchase pension plan over the profit sharing plan with the assurance of annual contributions. Also, target benefit plans that comply with safe harbor requirements, must be money purchase plans.*

* These examples of situations where use of a money purchase pension plan is appropriate were referenced in Amy L. Cavanaugh, "The Money Purchase Plan: R.I.P.," *Journal of Pension Benefits* 9, no. 1 (Autumn 2001), p. 48.

Some of the more specific or typical characteristics of money purchase plans are as follows:

- In establishing the plan, the employer agrees to make a fixed contribution each year for each eligible employee. This contribution is usually expressed as a percentage of pay, although it may be a flat dollar amount. This constitutes a definite commitment on the part of the employer and the contribution must be made each year, regardless of profits, and cannot be varied except by plan amendment.
- The plan may require employees to make contributions to participate. If so, these contributions can be made only from after-tax income—that is, salary reductions or elective deferral contributions cannot be made under a money purchase plan. When employees do contribute:
  - The contribution rate is fixed (unlike the typical savings plan, where the employee can choose from among different levels of participation).

- The employer's contribution rate is often set with reference to what employees are contributing—for example, at two times the employee contribution rate.
- Regardless of whether employees are required to make mandatory contributions in order to participate, they may be permitted to make **voluntary contributions,** that is, contributions that do not generate any type of employer contribution.
- **Forfeitures** that arise when partially vested or nonvested employees terminate employment may be used to reduce employer contributions or may be reallocated among the remaining plan participants; the customary practice in money purchase plans is to use these contributions to reduce the employer contributions due next.[9]
- Both employer and employee contributions are transferred to a trustee (or an insurance company under a group annuity type of contract), where they are invested on behalf of the employees.
- Individual accounts are established for participating employees. Each account is credited with employer and employee contributions, reallocated forfeitures (if applicable), and its proportionate share of investment gains and losses.
- As with other types of defined contribution plans, employees frequently are given a choice of several investment funds in which to invest their account balances.
- An employee's benefit, at any given time, is whatever can be provided by his or her vested account balance at that time. If the employee retires, the employee will usually have the option of receiving this account balance in a lump sum or in the form of monthly installments—over a period equal to the employee's life expectancy or the joint life expectancy of the employee and his or her spouse, if married.
- The employee's account balance (even if not otherwise vested) usually is payable in full in the event of the employee's death.
- Unlike conventional profit sharing and savings plans, a money purchase plan generally cannot make distributions until the employee has severed employment. Thus, **in-service withdrawals** are not permitted.
- While it is possible for a money purchase plan to provide for loans to employees, this practice is unusual. In general, money purchase plans focus on their role as retirement vehicles; permitting loans could be viewed as being inconsistent with this fundamental purpose.

Contribution Structure

Money purchase plans do not provide a fixed benefit for employees. Instead, the employer (and any employee) contributions, together with investment income, are applied to provide as much in the way of pension benefits as possible. Since the cost of a given amount of benefit varies by entry age and retirement age, the benefits of any employee will depend on these factors as well as on contribution levels and investment results.

In the past, the employee's gender also was a factor in determining the amount of retirement benefit that could be provided under a money purchase plan. If a male and

[9] Prior to the Tax Reform Act of 1986, forfeitures under money purchase plans could be used only to reduce employer contributions.

female employee were the same age and had exactly the same amount accumulated under such a plan, the male employee would receive a higher lifetime pension than the female employee. This was because the female employee was expected to live longer and, in anticipation of this, the same initial amount was expected to be paid over a longer period of time. Because of this difference in life expectancies, the actuarial value of the pension, in both cases, was considered to be the same. In 1983, however, the Supreme Court ruled (in *Arizona Governing Committee* v. *Norris*) that life annuities under an employer-sponsored defined contribution plan must be provided on a uniform basis.[10]

Tax Law Provisions

Money purchase plans are subject to almost all of the tax law provisions applicable to qualified plans. The following is a brief discussion of the major tax law provisions that are different as they apply to money purchase plans. In some instances, the discussion is in terms of how money purchase plans are treated differently from other types of defined contribution plans.

Nondiscrimination in Contributions and Benefits

When a money purchase plan involves after-tax employee and matching employer contributions, an actual contribution percentage (ACP) test must be satisfied each year in accordance with the terms of Section 401(m) of the IRC.[11] The ACP test also applies to voluntary after-tax employee contributions even when there is no employer match. This test limits the participation of highly compensated employees (HCEs) so that their average contribution percentages cannot exceed the average contribution percentages of the nonhighly compensated employees (NHCEs) by more than a stipulated amount. In general, the ACP for HCEs cannot be more than 125 percent of the ACP for NHCEs. An alternative limitation permits the ACP for HCEs to be as much as two times the ACP for NHCEs, but not more than two percentage points higher. If the portion of the plan that is subject to this test meets its requirements each year, this portion will satisfy the nondiscrimination in contributions and benefits requirements of Section 401(a)(4) of the IRC.

If the ACP test is not applicable to employer contributions because there are no mandatory employee contributions, this portion of the plan must satisfy the nondiscrimination requirements of Section 401(a)(4) of the IRC.[12] However, the regulations prescribe two safe harbors that can be met in order to satisfy these requirements. The first safe harbor is for plans with a uniform contribution formula—where contributions equal the same percentage of pay or the same dollar amount for every covered employee—and will apply

---

[10] It should be noted that employees can buy annuities from insurance companies on the open market (i.e., apart from the qualified plan). At this time, insurers are not required to offer such annuities on a unisex basis, although legislation that would require this has been proposed. Even though not required to do so, however, many insurers provide for unisex premiums.

[11] The complete details of this test are discussed in Chapter 8, since the ACP test is similar to the actual deferral percentage (ADP) test applicable to elective deferrals under cash or deferred arrangements (CODAs) and, quite often, the two tests must both be made for the same plan. Also, if this plan meets certain safe harbor requirements, ACP testing will not be required for the matching employer contributions.

[12] These requirements are discussed in Chapter 25.

to most money purchase plans. To use this safe harbor, the same vesting schedule and definition of years of service must apply to all participants. Also, if the plan integrates with Social Security benefits by providing a higher contribution percentage for pay above a specified level than for pay below that level, the plan will be deemed to satisfy this safe harbor if the plan meets the permitted disparity requirements of Section 401(l).

The second safe harbor applies to nonintegrated "uniform points plans" (other than employee stock ownership plans [ESOPs]) that allocate contributions based on a formula weighted for age and/or service and units of pay that do not exceed $200. This safe harbor is available to such plans if the average of the allocation rates for HCEs does not exceed the average of the allocation rates for the NHCEs.

Section 415 Limitations

The annual additions to an employee's account (employer and employee contributions plus any reallocated forfeitures) cannot exceed the lesser of (1) $45,000 indexed to increase with changes in the consumer price index (CPI) or (2) 100 percent of compensation. Further, a combined Section 415 limitation was applicable for years prior to 2000 if the employer also maintained a defined benefit plan.[13]

Joint and Survivor Requirements

The joint and survivor requirements (both pre- and postretirement) that apply to defined benefit plans apply as well to money purchase plans. It should be noted that other forms of defined contribution plans are exempted from these requirements (1) if the employee's spouse is the beneficiary for 100 percent of the employee's account balance unless the spouse consents in writing to the designation of another beneficiary; (2) if the employee does not elect an annuity distribution and (3) the plan cannot have received a transfer from a pension plan. This exemption is also available to money purchase plans that are part of an employee stock ownership plan (ESOP).

Before-Tax Contributions

The CODA feature of Section 401(k) of the IRC, which permits employees to make elective deferrals and thus make before-tax contributions, is not available to money purchase plans. These elective deferral contributions can be made only in conjunction with profit sharing and stock bonus and savings plans that are qualified as profit sharing plans. If a savings plan is qualified as a money purchase pension plan, as was occasionally the case (although extremely rare today), the elective deferral option would not be available (nor would the plan be able to permit in-service withdrawals).

Forfeitures

The amounts forfeited when an employee terminates employment with less than full vesting can be applied in two ways under a money purchase plan. These amounts can be used to reduce employer contributions or they can be reallocated among the remaining employees. As was indicated earlier, the customary practice with money purchase pension plans was to reduce employer contributions. This was due to a prohibition on reallocating contributions to other employees before 1987.

[13] The Section 415 limitations are discussed in Chapter 26.

Employer Securities

Generally, defined benefit plans are prohibited from having more than 10 percent of their assets invested in qualifying employer securities. Profit sharing and stock bonus plans, on the other hand, are permitted to invest up to 100 percent of their assets in qualifying employer securities if the plans so provide. Money purchase plans, even though they are defined contribution plans, are subject to the same 10 percent limitation that applies to defined benefit plans.[14]

In-Service Distributions

As noted in an earlier discussion, since it is a pension plan, a money purchase plan is not permitted to make distributions to employees on an in-service basis. In general, these plans can make distributions only in the event of termination of employment (including retirement, death, and disability). They also may make distributions upon termination of the plan. In this regard, they differ significantly from other types of defined contribution arrangements that are qualified as profit sharing or stock bonus plans.

Minimum Funding Standards

Again, because a money purchase plan is a pension plan, it is subject to the minimum funding requirements of the IRC. While an actuarial valuation is not required, the plan is still subject to funding requirements. In normal circumstances (absent a funding waiver), the required contribution must be made in full each year. As a result, the money purchase plan can be viewed as being the most rigid of all plans in terms of funding flexibility.

Deduction Limits

Prior to EGTRRA there were no specific deduction limits, as such, for money purchase plans. The general concept that the amount contributed must represent reasonable compensation applied, of course, and there was a practical limit in that Section 415 stipulated that the maximum annual addition to an employee's account could not exceed a certain amount. Also, if another plan(s) existed, there would be a maximum combined deductible limit for all plans of 25 percent of covered payroll. Under EGTRRA, there is a uniform limit of 25 percent of compensation for all defined contribution plans.

Chapter Summary

- Profit sharing plans have considerable appeal since they embody the individual account concept without imposing any fixed commitment on employers to provide

---

[14] A limited grandfathering provision is provided for money purchase plans in existence on September 2, 1974, and provides for investing more than 10 percent of their assets in employer securities.

any specific level of benefits. The IRC does not require that a qualified profit sharing plan include a definite predetermined contribution formula. In the absence of such a formula, the regulations require that contributions be made on a substantial and recurring basis in order for plan permanency to be established. Though plans are not required to provide a definite contribution formula, it is necessary that such plans include a definite allocation formula to become qualified.

- A profit sharing plan must be for the exclusive benefit of employees or their beneficiaries and is generally subject to the same coverage and qualification requirements attributable to pension plans.

- Contributions under a profit sharing plan may be made on a discretionary basis or in accordance with a definite predetermined formula. Both of these approaches have relative advantages and disadvantages from both an employee and employer perspective. It is conceptually illogical to require employee contributions under profit sharing plans, although some plans provide for voluntary employee contributions. Such voluntary contributions may be made as elective deferrals on a pretax basis under Section 401(k) of the IRC or as after-tax contributions.

- Some profit sharing plans permit distributions after a fixed number of years while employees are still actively employed. The IRS has interpreted this requirement to mean that accumulations cannot be distributed in less than two years. Distributions also can be made upon the occurrence of an event such as hardship or the completion of five years of participation. Loan provisions also are allowable in qualified profit sharing plans as long as plans meet certain requirements prescribed by the IRS and DOL.

- For profit sharing plans, the maximum deductible contribution is equal to 25 percent of the compensation paid or otherwise accrued to all covered employees during the employer's taxable year, for years beginning after 2001 as a result of EGTRRA.

- Money purchase pension plans involve characteristics of defined benefit pension plans and defined contribution arrangements. On the defined benefit side, minimum funding and joint and survivor requirements of the tax law apply. On the defined contribution side, individual accounts must be maintained, plans are subject to the annual addition limits of IRC Section 415, and plans are exempt from the plan termination provisions of Title IV of ERISA.

- The employer contribution to a money purchase pension plan constitutes a definite commitment on the part of the employer, and the contribution must be made each year—regardless of profits—and cannot be varied except by plan amendment. These employer contributions may be a fixed dollar amount but are more commonly expressed as a percentage of pay.

- Since the passage of ERISA, money purchase plans requiring employee contributions can make these contributions only on an after-tax basis. A plan involving after-tax employee and matching employer contributions is subject to the actual contribution percentage (ACP) test each year.

Key Terms

allocation formula, p. *94*

combined (approach), p. *92*

contribution carryover, p. *100*

current (approach), p. *92*

deferred (approach), p. *92*

definite predetermined contribution formula, p. *93*

discretionary contribution approach, p. *93*

elective deferrals, p. *94*

exclusive benefit, p. *93*

forfeitures, p. *104*

in-service withdrawals, p. *104*

incidental insurance benefits, p. *99*

individual-account retirement programs, p. *91*

maximum deductible contribution, p. *100*

money purchase pension plans, p. *102*

profit sharing plans, p. *91*

Section 404 of the IRC, p. *100*

substantial and recurring contributions, p. *93*

voluntary contributions, p. *104*

Questions for Review

1. What are the typical participation requirements found in a profit sharing plan? Explain.

2. What contribution requirements are imposed by the IRC on profit sharing plans?

3. What advantages can be ascribed to a definite predetermined contribution formula for a profit sharing plan?

4. Describe a common approach for allocating employer contributions that recognizes both compensation and length of service.

5. What usually happens to forfeited amounts of nonvested contributions in a profit sharing plan? Explain.

6. Is a profit sharing plan obligated to permit participants to withdraw a portion of their vested benefits prior to separation from employment? Explain.

7. Explain a typical loan provision that may be included in a profit sharing plan.

8. Can a qualified profit sharing plan be terminated? Explain.

9. What is meant by an incidental insurance benefit under a profit sharing plan?

10. What characteristic of a money purchase plan distinguishes it from other defined contribution plans?

11. Why are money purchase plans utilized less frequently than in the past?

Questions for Discussion

1. Discuss the conditions under which an employer may desire to establish a profit sharing plan.

2. Assume that an employer has had a profit sharing plan for several years and that the reaction of the employees toward the plan has been unsatisfactory. Discuss the plan

design flexibility available for a profit sharing plan that may be used by the employer to improve the employees' reaction without increasing the employer's annual cost.

3. Assume that a publicly held firm decides to sponsor a profit sharing plan that will incorporate a definite predetermined contribution formula. Discuss how you would establish such a formula, keeping in mind the need to be equitable to stockholders, bondholders, and employees.

Resources for Further Study

Cavanaugh, Amy L. "The Money Purchase Plan: R.I.P." *Journal of Pension Benefits* 9, no. 1 (Autumn 2001).

Donovan, Kevin J., and Gucciardi, Joan. "Designing Plans after EGTRRA." *Journal of Pension Benefits* 9, no. 1 (Autumn 2001).

Kline, Alissa. "Pooling the Profit." Business First of Buffalo (February 23, 2007).

Kozol, George B. "Advantages of 401(k)—Profit Sharing Plans." *The CPA Journal* (March 2005).

Krass, Stephen J. *The Pension Answer Book: 2006 Edition.* New York: Panel Publishers, 2006.

Palmer, Bruce A. "Profit Sharing Plans." *The Handbook of Employee Benefits.* 6th ed. Jerry S. Rosenbloom, ed. New York: McGraw-Hill, 2005.

Profit Sharing/401(k) Council of America. *50th Annual Survey of Profit Sharing and 401(k) Plans.* Chicago: PSCA, 2007.

www.psca.org—website of the Profit Sharing/401(k) Council of America.

Chapter 7

Employee Stock Ownership Plans (ESOPs)

After studying this chapter you should be able to:

- Describe the characteristics of employee stock ownership plans (ESOPs).
- Explain the potential advantages an employer might realize in adopting a leveraged ESOP.
- Describe the special requirements that are imposed on an ESOP that are not imposed on other types of qualified plans.
- Explain the rationale for the special requirements that are imposed on ESOPs.
- Discuss how fiduciary requirements such as the diversification requirement apply to an ESOP.
- Distinguish how an ESOP might be used differently by a large, publicly held company and a small, privately held business.

Overview

ESOP Defined

In a broad sense, an employee stock ownership plan (ESOP) could be defined as any type of qualified employee benefit plan (including profit sharing and savings) that invests some or all of its assets in employer securities. The definition of ESOP contained in the law, however, is much narrower in scope. Specifically, the Internal Revenue Code (IRC) defines an ESOP as a qualified stock bonus plan or a combination qualified stock bonus plan and defined contribution (money purchase) plan designed to invest primarily in employer securities.[1] Internal Revenue Service (IRS) regulations, in turn, define a **stock bonus plan** as a plan established and maintained by an employer to provide benefits similar to those of a profit sharing plan except that the contributions by the employer are not necessarily dependent upon profits and the benefits are distributable in the stock of the employer company. (Cash distributions are permitted; however, the employee must have the right to demand a distribution in the form of employer securities.) The plan must formally state that it is an ESOP and that assets are to be invested primarily in employer securities.

Simple or Nonleveraged ESOP

ESOPs have existed for many years, but it was not until the 1970s that these plans began to grow in popularity. Much of the early interest in the plans was attributable to the "tax credit" ESOP where the plan was financed with an employer tax credit and, typically, where there was no additional employer contribution. The tax credit for these plans expired on January 1, 1987, however, so that no additional funding of these plans is now taking place. Nevertheless, some of these plans continue to exist in terms of their accrued benefits and many have been modified or incorporated into other qualified plan arrangements such as savings plans or cash or deferred arrangements (CODAs).

---

[1] The phrase "designed to invest primarily in employer securities" has never been defined by the government, but most practitioners believe that this requirement will be met if more than 50 percent of the plan's assets are so invested when viewed over the life of the plan.

NONLEVERAGED ESOP

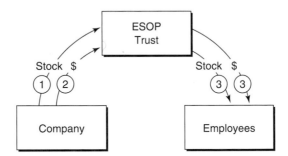

1. Each year, company gives stock to ESOP.
2. Or, each year, company gives cash to ESOP to buy stock. Employees pay nothing. ESOP holds stock for employees and periodically notifies them of how much they own and how much it is worth.
3. Employees collect stock or cash according to a vesting schedule when they retire or otherwise leave the company.

Source: Robert W. Smiley, Jr., and Ronald J. Gilbert, *Employee Stock Ownership Plans,* © 1989, pp. 1–3. Reprinted with permission from Warren, Gorham & Lamont, Park Square Building, 31 St. James Avenue, Boston, MA 02116-4112. 1-800-950-1211. All rights reserved.

Leveraged ESOP

The ongoing interest in ESOPs is largely attributable to the so-called **leveraged ESOP,** where the plan is used in conjunction with debt financing. As a result of the Tax Reform Acts of 1984 and 1986, leveraged ESOPs offer several significant tax advantages not available to other types of qualified retirement plans. In exchange for these privileges, however, they must meet a unique set of qualification rules.

LEVERAGED ESOP

1. Bank lends money to ESOP with company guarantee.
2. ESOP buys stock from company.
2A. Or, ESOP buys stock from existing shareholders.
3. Company makes annual tax deductible contributions to ESOP, which in turn repays bank.
4. Employees collect stock or cash when they retire or leave company.

Source: Robert W. Smiley, Jr., and Ronald J. Gilbert, *Employee Stock Ownership Plans,* © 1989, pp. 1–5. Reprinted with permission from Warren, Gorham & Lamont, Park Square Building, 31 St. James Avenue, Boston, MA 02116-4112. 1-800-950-1211. All rights reserved.

To set up a leveraged employee stock ownership plan, a trust is created by the employer and the trustee acquires funds through a loan. The loan may be made directly to the trustee by the lending institution, in which case the loan is usually guaranteed by the employer because the trust cannot generate income (other than investment income) on its own. Alternatively, the employer can borrow the funds directly from the lending institution and immediately lend the same amount to the trustee in what is termed a **back-to-back arrangement.** In either case, the trustee uses the borrowed funds to purchase employer stock, usually directly from the employer.

The stock purchased by the trustee is held in an **unallocated suspense account** and is pledged as collateral for the loan. The employer then makes contributions to the plan for the benefit of employees. The plan uses these contributions to repay the loan, including interest. As the loan is repaid, shares of stock are released from the suspense account and allocated to the individual accounts of eligible employees. In most situations, the number of shares released is determined under what is termed the **fractional method.** This method reflects the ratio of the amount of the current principal and interest payment to the total current and future principal and interest payments. A second method relates only to current and future principal payments and may be used if the loan duration is less than 10 years.

This type of loan under an ESOP is exempt from the prohibited transaction provisions of the Employee Retirement Income Security Act (ERISA), provided the loan is made primarily for the benefit of participants in the plan and the interest is not in excess of a reasonable rate. In this regard, the regulations note that these loans "will be subject to special scrutiny by the Department of Labor (DOL) and the Internal Revenue Service to ensure that they are primarily for the benefit of plan participants and beneficiaries."[2] Also, ESOPs are exempt from the diversity requirements of the fiduciary provisions of ERISA; they are not, however, exempt from the prudency requirements, nor are they exempt from the requirement that fiduciaries must act solely for the exclusive benefit of employees and their beneficiaries.

Advantages and Disadvantages of a Leveraged ESOP   Significant advantages (including tax advantages) exist for ESOPs, and they can serve many useful purposes. An ESOP can be an effective employee benefit plan capable of satisfying important employer objectives. It also can be an effective device for converting a public company to a private organization, for disposing of a corporate division (the selling corporation would establish a new corporation that, in turn, would establish an ESOP for the purpose of raising capital and purchasing the division), and for providing **estate liquidity** to a major shareholder.

Many employers will find leveraged ESOPs attractive because they can put relatively large blocks of stock into presumably friendly hands. While this could be an advantage in case of a takeover attempt, a leveraged ESOP must still exist primarily for employee benefit purposes and takeover protection can only be incidental.

Using a leveraged ESOP gives the employer the advantage of avoiding some of the expenses and complexities of selling stock to the public and/or existing shareholders. Also, the plan may create a proprietary interest on the part of employees and can supplement existing compensation and benefit plans.

Advocates of the leveraged ESOP often claim that since employer contributions are tax deductible, the debt created in conjunction with the ESOP is retired with pretax dollars and, as a result, the ESOP is a tax-efficient way to raise capital (as contrasted with conventional debt and equity financing). This claim is, at best, an over-simplification. Technically, the *trust* and not the employer has incurred the debt, with the employer having contingent liability as the guarantor of the loan. The debt is retired by the trust using contributions made by the employer. The employer is entitled to a deduction only because its contributions are being made to a qualified plan for the benefit of employees. Thus, while the debt is being retired indirectly with pre-tax dollars, it must be clearly understood that the way it is being done is by a charge to earnings. This could result in

[2] DOL Reg. 54.49975–7(b)(2).

lower net income and lower earnings per share for the firm. There also could be a dilution in share value as well as cash flow implications. Also, it must be remembered that employer contributions (and resulting expenses) often will continue under the ESOP long after the debt has been retired. In short, careful analysis is necessary to fully evaluate the financial implications of a leveraged ESOP.

From an employer's viewpoint, there is the potential disadvantage that no portion of the stock held in the unallocated suspense account can revert to the employer if the trust is terminated prematurely. Also, there may be some risk of disqualification because of failure to meet the "exclusive benefit" requirements of the law. Another potential drawback to the employer is that an ESOP could be an inefficient compensation tool if the stock appreciates in value because the company foregoes a tax deduction for capital appreciation on shares that under a typical nonleveraged plan would have been made in future years. This same aspect, however, can produce an advantage to employees, particularly to highly compensated employees (HCEs), since this appreciation in the value of stock will not be a part of the employee's annual addition under Section 415.

An additional advantage to employees is that with an ESOP there is a greater assurance of employer contributions than with a profit sharing plan. There is a potential disadvantage to employees, however, in that their financial security may be too closely tied to the fortunes of the employer.

As will be seen in the next portion of this chapter, there are several tax advantages for both employers and employees associated with ESOPs. These advantages can be quite valuable and place ESOPs in a unique category in terms of qualified plan benefits.

Like any other employee benefit plan, careful consideration should be given to the employer's objectives and the plan's relative advantages and disadvantages before it is adopted. Even though financial aspects may be the driving force behind a plan's adoption, it must always be remembered that an ESOP is still an employee benefit plan and should thus accommodate the employer's overall human resource philosophy and objectives.

ESOP Qualification Requirements

At the outset, it should be recognized that an ESOP is a qualified plan, and as such it must meet the general requirements applicable to all qualified plans. These requirements are described in Chapters 25 and 26. In addition, ESOPs must meet a number of special requirements, and there are unique provisions of the tax law that apply only to ESOPs. The major ESOP requirements and tax law provisions are described in the following section.

Employer Securities Requirements

ESOP assets may be invested only in **qualifying employer securities.** In general, this includes both common and convertible preferred stock that are publicly tradable. In the case of stock that is not readily tradable on an established securities market, the term means common stock having a combination of voting power and dividend rights equal to or greater than (1) that class of the employer's common stock having the greatest voting power and (2) that class of the employer's stock having the greatest dividend rights.

Voting Rights

Participants must be given the right to vote shares that have been allocated to their accounts. In the case of a closely held company, **voting rights** generally have to be given only for major issues: mergers, consolidations, recapitalization, reclassification, liquidation, and the dissolution or sale of substantially all of the firm's assets. However, if the shares of the closely held company were acquired with the proceeds of a loan where the lender was able to exclude 50 percent of interest from income, all voting rights on allocated shares must be given to participants.[3] The voting requirements for closely held companies can be satisfied by providing each participant with one vote, regardless of the number of shares actually allocated, and voting all shares held by the plan (whether or not allocated) in proportion to the vote.

Rights of First Refusal

Stock may be made subject to a **right of first refusal** in favor of the employer, the ESOP, or both. However, the stock must not be publicly traded at the time the right may be exercised. Also, the selling price and other terms under the right must not be less favorable to the seller than the greater of the value of the stock or the purchase price and other terms offered by a buyer, other than the employer or ESOP, making a good faith offer to purchase the security. The right of first refusal must lapse no later than 14 days after the stockholder gives written notice that an offer by a third party to purchase the stock has been received.

Put Options

A **put option** is not required for publicly traded stock. Otherwise, such an option is required and, under this option, the employee will have the right to require the employer to repurchase the stock. This put option must be exercisable only by the employee (or his or her donee, the employee's estate, or a distributee from the employee's estate).

The put option may not bind the plan, but it may grant the plan the option to assume the rights and obligations of the employer at the time it is exercised. The put must be exercisable for at least 60 days following the distribution of the stock and, if not exercised, for a second period of at least 60 days in the plan year following the distribution. The price must be determined under a fair valuation formula.

If an employer is required to repurchase employer stock that is distributed to the employee as part of a total distribution of the entire amount of the employee's account within one taxable year, the payment may be made in substantially equal periodic payments over a period not exceeding five years. The payments may not be made less frequently than annually and must begin no later than 30 days after the option is exercised. In addition, the employer must provide adequate security and pay reasonable interest on the unpaid amount. If the employer is required to repurchase the stock as part of an

---

[3] The Small Business Job Protection Act of 1996 repealed the interest income exclusion for ESOP loans that allowed banks, insurance companies, regulated investment companies, and certain corporations to exclude 50 percent of the interest received on ESOP loans. Repeal of the interest income exclusion became effective with loans where a contract for the loan agreement occurred on or after June 10, 1996.

installment distribution, it must pay for the stock in full within 30 days after the option is exercised. A separate put option exists for each installment.

Valuation of Securities

Stocks must be valued at fair market value, which presents no difficulty if stock is regularly traded in a recognized market. If the stock is closely held or not publicly traded, an acceptable procedure must be developed for appraising and determining the fair market value of the stock. Generally, determination of fair market value must be on at least an annual basis and independently arrived at by a person who customarily makes such appraisals and who is independent of any party to a transaction involving a right of first refusal or a put option.

Nondiscrimination Testing/Integration with Social Security

An ESOP cannot be combined with other plans to satisfy the coverage and non discrimination requirements of the IRC, except for the purposes of the average benefits test.[4] Similarly, the portion of a plan that is an ESOP and the portion that is not must be treated as separate plans.

The contributions (and allocations) made for employees under an ESOP may *not* be integrated with Social Security benefits.

Diversification Requirement

Employees who are at least age 55 and who have completed at least 10 years of participation must be given the opportunity to diversify their investments by transferring from the employer stock fund to one or more of three other investment funds.[5] The right to diversify need be granted only for a 90-day window period following the close of the plan year in which the employee first becomes eligible to diversify and following the close of each of the next five plan years. This right is limited to shares acquired after 1986 and is further limited to 25 percent of such shares until the last window period, when up to 50 percent of such shares may be eligible for **diversification.**

The Pension Protection Act of 2006 (PPA) changed the **diversification requirements** for many plans holding employer stock. Stand-alone ESOPs in public companies and all closely held company ESOPs were exempted from these requirements. However, if a public company holds employer stock in its 401(k) plan or has a KSOP type of plan, which is a plan that combines an ESOP and a 401(k) plan, the diversification requirements enacted as part of the PPA would be applicable. In a KSOP, a company will match employee contributions with stock rather than cash. Essentially to qualify for the exemption, the plan would need to be qualified as an ESOP that does not permit either employee pre-tax deferrals under Internal Revenue Code (IRC) Section 401(k), or employee after-tax or employer matching contributions under IRC Section 401(m). The exception regarding closely held company ESOPs would only apply if the plan sponsor or any parent corporation of the plan sponsor has not issued any publicly traded security. These diversification requirements, when applicable, allow employees to diversify out of employer stock at any time if the employer stock was purchased through employee deferrals, or after three years of service if the employer stock was purchased with employer

---

[4] See the discussion of these requirements in Chapter 25.

[5] Alternatively, amounts subject to the right of diversification may be distributed from the plan.

contributions. The diversification requirements generally are phased in over a three-year period for company stock acquired with employer contributions prior to January 1, 2007. However, pretax employee elective deferrals, employee after-tax contributions invested in company stock, and employer contributions on behalf of participants who had three years of service and had attained age 55 before the first plan year beginning after December 31, 2005, would have an immediate right to diversify these pre–January 1, 2007, holdings.

The diversification requirements, if applicable, require plan sponsors to provide each participant and beneficiary with a notice not later than 30 days prior to the first date that the participant is permitted to diversify his or her holdings of company stock.

Section 415

An employee's annual addition limit under Section 415 is determined on the basis of the employer's contributions to the plan and not on the value of the stock at the time it is allocated to the employee's account. Also, stock dividends, since they are considered to be investment income, are not counted toward the annual addition limit when they are added to the employee's account.

In the case of a leveraged ESOP, if no more than one-third of the deductible employer contribution for the year is allocated to HCEs, repayments of interest on the loans and reallocated forfeitures derived from leveraged shares will not be considered part of the annual addition either.

Accelerated Vesting

As a result of the PPA, all defined contribution plans are required to vest nonmatching employer contributions on at least a three-year cliff or on a six-year graded vesting schedule (20 percent after each of years 2 through 6) effective in 2007. Prior to the enactment of the PPA, the minimum permitted vesting schedules involved either a five-year cliff approach or a seven-year graded vesting basis (20 percent after each of years 3 through 7) for nonmatching employer contributions. The Economic Growth and Tax Relief Reconciliation Act of 2001 (EGTRRA) already had made the three-year cliff and six-year graded vesting schedules the applicable standard for matching employer contributions. Although the three-year cliff and six-year graded vesting schedules generally would apply to ESOPs, the PPA exempted certain ESOPs from this requirement. If an ESOP had an outstanding loan on September 26, 2005, which was incurred for the purpose of acquiring qualified employer securities, the faster vesting schedules are not applicable to any plan year beginning before the earlier of (1) the date the loan is fully repaid or (2) the date on which the loan was, as of September 26, 2005, scheduled to be fully repaid.

Distribution Requirements

As noted earlier, an ESOP generally is required to make distributions to employees in the form of employer securities. Cash payments may be established in a plan as the normal form of distribution, but the participant must have the right to elect to receive stock. (This requirement does not apply to other investments into which the participant has elected to diversify his or her account balance.)

Employers must consider a number of issues in administering a dividend pass-through feature. Will minimums be imposed on the pass-through? Are the appropriate plan accounts clearly designated as ESOP accounts and eligible for the dividend pass-through? Will it be necessary to coordinate the pass-through with concurrent in-service withdrawals? Are dividends to be passed through for terminated participants? These questions illustrate the administrative considerations involved when including a pass-through provision in an ESOP.

Like all qualified plans, an ESOP cannot force distribution of a participant's account (if more than $5,000) until the later of age 62 or the plan's normal retirement age, and it must observe the minimum distribution rule requirements. Unlike other qualified plans, ESOPs are required to permit accelerated distributions for stock acquired after 1986 when participants terminate employment. Unless otherwise requested by the participant, ESOPs must distribute such stock by the end of the year following the later of (1) the year in which the participant dies, retires, or becomes disabled; or (2) the fifth plan year following the year of termination for any other reason. (Longer periods are allowed if the participant's account balance exceeds $500,000 [indexed]. In 2007, the indexed amount was $915,000, and an ESOP sponsor could extend the payout period by one additional year [not to exceed five additional years] for each $180,000 [in 2007, as indexed] or a fraction thereof, by which the employee's account balance exceeded $915,000.) The employer may delay distribution of stock acquired under a loan until the plan year following the plan year in which the loan has been repaid in full.

Joint and Survivor Requirements

Money purchase pension plans generally are subject to the qualified joint and survivor rules. A money purchase plan that is part of an ESOP, however, will be exempt from these rules to the same extent as other defined contribution plans if (1) the participant's account balance is payable in full to his or her spouse unless the spouse consents in writing to the designation of another beneficiary, (2) the participant does not elect benefits in the form of a life annuity, and (3) all or any portion of the participant's account balance has not been transferred from a plan subject to the joint and survivor rules.

Dividends

As a general rule, a corporation will not be allowed a tax deduction for dividends paid to shareholders. These dividends normally are paid out of after-tax income. If dividends are passed through or paid in cash to employees on a current basis under an ESOP, however, the employer will be able to claim a tax deduction for the dividends so paid.[6] This particular feature has attracted the attention of many employers who are considering establishing an ESOP for a conventional employer stock fund under a CODA.

Cash dividends also are deductible if they are used to repay an ESOP loan where the shares on which the dividends are paid have been acquired with the proceeds of such a

---

[6] Dividends so paid to employees will be taxable; however, they will not be subject to the 10 percent early distribution tax.

loan. If the dividends are for allocated shares, participants must receive an allocation of employer securities with a fair market value equal to or greater than the amount of such dividends.

As a result of the Economic Growth and Tax Relief Reconciliation Act of 2001, cash dividends may also be deducted by a C corporation when they are reinvested in qualified employer securities at the election of plan participants and their beneficiaries.

EGTRRA expanded the situations whereby a plan could deduct the payment of dividends. Prior to the passage of EGTRRA, dividends were only deductible (1) if paid in cash directly to plan participants or their beneficiaries, (2) if paid to the plan and subsequently disbursed in cash to plan participants and beneficiaries no later than 90 days following the close of the plan year in which the dividends were paid to the plan, or (3) when the dividends were used to make a leveraged ESOP's loan payment. This provision was added to the law as a savings incentive to encourage ESOPs to allow plan participants and beneficiaries to retain and reinvest the dividend proceeds in the plan without the firm loosing a tax deduction.

At the same time that EGTRRA expanded the deductibility of dividends, the law provided the Internal Revenue Service with greater authority to disallow deductions for dividends determined to be unreasonable. In the case of a dividend paid on common stock that is primarily and regularly traded on an established securities market, the dividend will generally be considered reasonable. For common stock not traded on an established securities market, the reasonableness of a dividend involves comparing the dividend rate on ESOP-held stock with the dividend rate for comparable corporations whose stock trades on an established market. Such characteristics as type of industry, size of corporation, earnings level, capital structure, and dividend history would be relevant.

The IRS released final regulations that disallow employer deductions of dividends used to pay for the redemption of employer securities held by an ESOP or related person. These regulations deal with the application of stock reacquisition expenses and deductions for dividends paid on employer securities. These regulations effectively prohibit a double deduction for the same dividend and apply to amounts paid or incurred on or after August 30, 2006. These regulations clarified issues that arose following a court decision in the *Boise Cascade Corporation* v. *United States* case, where the court effectively permitted payments made by a corporation to redeem stock held by its ESOP that were subsequently distributed to plan participants to be treated as deductible as dividends.

Deductibility of Employer Contributions

In the case of a nonleveraged ESOP, the normal deduction limits apply to employer contributions. Prior to the passage of EGTRRA, 15 percent of covered compensation could be deducted in the case of a conventional stock bonus plan. Under a leveraged ESOP, in this prior era, the employer was able to contribute and deduct up to 25 percent of covered payroll on an annual basis for principal repayments on the loan. In addition, contributions made for the entire amount of loan interest also were deductible. For plan years following December 31, 2001, with the passage of EGTRRA, the amount deductible for stock bonus plans has risen from 15 percent to 25 percent of covered compensation giving it parity with the leveraged ESOP. The leveraged ESOP still holds an advantage in that the entire amount of the loan interest is still deductible.

Deferral of Gain on Stock Sales to ESOPs

A shareholder of a closely held company may be able to sell stock to the ESOP and to defer recognition of the gain on such sale if certain conditions are met. One such condition is that immediately after the sale, the ESOP must own at least 30 percent of the total value of outstanding employer securities or 30 percent of each class of outstanding stock. Also, the employer stock must have been held by the selling shareholder for more than one year and must not have been received as a distribution from a qualified plan or pursuant to stock options.

To qualify for the deferral, the selling shareholder must reinvest the entire proceeds in either debt securities or stock of another domestic corporation that does not have passive investment income in excess of 25 percent of its gross receipts for the preceding taxable year. Also, 50 percent of the new corporation's assets must be used in the active conduct of a trade or business. This reinvestment must occur within a period beginning 3 months before and ending 12 months after the sale to the ESOP.

The selling shareholder (and family members) and any other person owning more than 25 percent of any class of the employer securities will not be able to participate in the ESOP if this option is exercised.

Chapter Summary

- The Internal Revenue Code defines an ESOP as a qualified stock bonus plan or a combination qualified stock bonus plan and defined contribution (money purchase) plan designed to invest primarily in employer securities.
- IRS regulations define a stock bonus plan as a plan established and maintained by an employer to provide benefits similar to those of a profit sharing plan except that contributions by the employer are not necessarily dependent on profits and the benefits are distributable in the stock of the employer. (Cash distributions are permitted; however, the employee must have the right to demand a distribution in the form of employer securities.)
- The phrase in the IRC definition of an ESOP, "designed to invest primarily in employer securities," has never been precisely defined by the government. Most practitioners believe that this requirement will be met if more than 50 percent of the plan's assets are so invested when viewed over the life of the plan.
- An ESOP may use debt financing, thus creating the so-called leveraged ESOP. A leveraged ESOP offers special exemptions from certain prohibitions that apply to other qualified plans. For example, ESOPs are exempt from the diversity requirements of the fiduciary provisions of ERISA. However, ESOPs are *not* exempt from the prudency requirements, nor are they exempt from the requirement that fiduciaries act solely for the exclusive benefit of employees and their beneficiaries.
- There are many good reasons for the creation of an ESOP. An ESOP can be an effective employee benefit plan. An ESOP can be an effective device for converting a

public company to a private organization. Similarly, an ESOP can be used to dispose of a corporate division. An ESOP also may be useful for providing estate liquidity to a major shareholder. A leveraged ESOP can put relatively large blocks of stock into presumably friendly hands, an advantage in the case of a takeover attempt.

- While enjoying special advantages, an ESOP also is subject to a number of important requirements. In addition to the general requirements applicable to qualified plans, other unique provisions apply. An ESOP cannot be combined with other plans in applying the coverage and nondiscrimination requirements of the IRC, except for the purposes of the average benefit test. Similarly, the portion of a plan that is an ESOP and the portion that is not must be treated as separate plans. Contributions made for employees under an ESOP may *not* be integrated with Social Security benefits.

- Other unique requirements attributable to ESOPs involve the stipulation that participants be given the right to vote shares that have been allocated to their accounts; the ability of a sponsoring employer to make stock subject to a right of first refusal by the employer, the ESOP, or both when the participant seeks to sell the stock; and the necessity to provide a put option to have the employer repurchase the stock if the ESOP stock is not publicly traded.

Key Terms

back-to-back arrangement, p. *113*
diversification, p. *117*
estate liquidity, p. *114*
fractional method, p. *114*
leveraged ESOP, p. *113*

PPA diversification requirements, p.*117*
put option, p. *116*
qualifying employer securities, p. *115*
right of first refusal, p. *116*

stock bonus plan, p. *112*
unallocated suspense account, p. *113*
voting rights, p. *116*

Questions for Review

1. Describe a back-to-back loan that is sometimes entered into under a leveraged ESOP.
2. Identify the potential advantages that might accrue to an employer who adopts a leveraged ESOP.
3. Describe the potential advantages and disadvantages that might accrue to employees under a leveraged ESOP.
4. What types of securities meet the definition of qualifying employer securities in the case of a company whose stock is not readily tradeable on an established securities market?
5. What voting rights must be given to employees when the stock of an ESOP is the stock of a closely held company?
6. Under what circumstances may stock held under an ESOP be made subject to a right of first refusal?

7. Under what circumstances must stock held under an ESOP be subject to a put option?

8. Describe the diversification requirement that must be included in an ESOP.

9. Under what circumstances may an employer be allowed a tax deduction for dividends paid for stock held under an ESOP?

Questions for Discussion

1. ESOP loans are exempted from some of the fiduciary requirements of ERISA. Which fiduciary requirements continue to apply to these loans and from which requirements are they exempted? What rationale exists for granting these exemptions?

2. ESOP advocates often claim that a leveraged loan allows the employer to retire debt with pretax dollars. Explain why this is an oversimplification of the financial aspects of a leveraged ESOP.

3. Describe the special tax advantages that have been granted to leveraged ESOPs and why these plans have received more favorable tax treatment than other qualified plans.

Resources for Further Study

CCH Editorial Staff. "Legislation 2006: Pension Protection Act of 2006: Law, Explanation and Analysis." *Commerce Clearing House* (2006).

CCH Editorial Staff. "Pension and Benefits—9/15/06—News and Information." *Commerce Clearing House* (September 15, 2006).

CCH Editorial Staff. "Pension Protection Act of 2006." *Commerce Clearing House* (2006).

Katten, Muchin, Rosenman, LLP, Client Advisory. "Pension Protection Act of 2006 Impacts ESOPs." (August 22, 2006).

Hart, Michael A. "ESOPs in Corporate Acquisitions: What Every Buyer Should Know about the Target Company's ESOP." *Benefits Law Journal* 14, no. 1 (Spring 2001).

Kornfeld, Judith. "ESOP Repurchase Obligation Issues in S Corporations." *Journal of Pension Benefits* 8, no. 3 (Spring 2001).

Rodrick, Scott S. *ESOP Valuation.* 3rd ed. Oakland, CA: The National Center for Employee Ownership, October 2005.

Rodrick, Scott S. *Leveraged ESOPs and Employee Buyouts.* 5th ed. Oakland, CA: The National Center for Employee Ownership, February 2005.

Rodrick, Scott S. *Selling to an ESOP.* 8th ed. Oakland, CA: The National Center for Employee Ownership, 2005.

Rodrick, Scott; and Corey Rosen. *The ESOP Reader*. 4th ed. Orlando, FL: Harcourt, 2005.

Smiley, Robert W., Jr.; and Gregory K. Brown. "Employee Stock Ownership Plans (ESOPs)." *The Handbook of Employee Benefits*. 6th ed. Jerry S. Rosenbloom, ed. New York: McGraw-Hill, 2005.

www.nceo.org—website of the National Center for Employee Ownership.

Chapter 8

Cash or Deferred Arrangements (CODAs) under Section 401(k)

After studying this chapter you should be able to:

- Describe the advantages of CODAs from both employer and employee perspectives.
- Describe the characteristics of cash or deferred arrangements.
- Explain the applicability of the ADP and ACP tests to CODAs.
- Describe the safe harbor and simplified testing options available for CODAs.
- Describe the special nonforfeitability requirements that apply to CODAs.
- Explain the limitations on withdrawals that apply to CODAs.
- Discuss how CODA deferrals impact Social Security taxes and benefits.

Although once viewed primarily as supplemental savings vehicles, cash or deferred arrangements under Section 401(k) of the Internal Revenue Code (IRC) have grown in prominence to take the premier position as the centerpiece in many a workers' approach to retirement planning. No longer are 401(k) plans perceived only as supplemental savings programs that might complement another retirement plan such as a defined benefit pension plan. For many employees, the 401(k) plan serves as the foundation for retirement. Many of these 401(k) plans serving as primary retirement plans involve employer matching contributions that are contingent on the employee making her or his own contribution toward retirement savings. In this way, both employer and employee assume a role in providing the necessary resources for retirement income. Although 401(k) plans may still be designed and offered as a supplemental savings vehicle, the widespread elimination of defined benefit plans and the migration by employers to defined contribution structures coupled with 401(k) provisions has made these "plans" the predominant employer-sponsored retirement plan. Although the term *401(k) plan* is commonly used to describe these types of arrangements, a 401(k) plan in reality is not a distinct type of retirement plan. A 401(k) provision allows a participant to elect whether to receive direct taxable compensation from an employer or to defer receipt of this compensation and have it contributed into a trust or fund where it will be deposited and invested on behalf of the participant. Most often 401(k) provisions are attached to profit sharing plans. Profit sharing plans were described in Chapter 6.

Because of the overwhelming popularity and widespread utilization of 401(k) plans as primary employer-sponsored retirement plans, their critical importance to the retirement security of millions of workers in the private pension system is well understood and appreciated by workers, employers, and government policymakers. Increasingly, federal legislation has been designed to safeguard 401(k) plans and ensure that they are administered in a fashion that will result in long-term financial security for the participants who depend on them. Many provisions enacted into law as part of the Pension Protection Act of 2006 (PPA) can be seen as furthering this policy objective. Although several provisions of the PPA relate to funding protections for traditional defined benefit plans, other provisions applicable to defined contribution plans will have very significant and enduring effects on future retirement security. Some observers noted the provisions related to defined contribution plans as signaling a recognition by governmental policymakers that defined contribution structures, primarily 401(k) plans, represent the future underpinnings of financial security for today's generation of workers.

There are many significant defined contribution provisions within the legislation. For instance, there are guidelines allowing plan sponsors to permit the investment companies administering their plans to provide more comprehensive investment advice to participants. There also are stipulations allowing workers to diversify out of employer stock. The law provides clarifications on automatic enrollment for plan participants who fail to enroll in their employer's plan upon hire and guidance on default investments that are more conducive to long-term capital appreciation for enrollees who have failed to make investment selections. The law also requires more accelerated vesting schedules for all defined contribution plans. Throughout this chapter, a comprehensive treatment of 401(k) plans discusses the origins of these plans, their evolution to date, issues in administering CODAs, governmental policy regarding these plans, and future directions for these pivotally important retirement savings programs.

Advantages and Disadvantages of CODAs

The advantages of CODAs are significant. From an employer's viewpoint, CODAs have all the advantages normally associated with any employee benefit plan. Thus, they should be of material value in attracting and retaining employees, improving employee morale, achieving a better sense of corporate identification (when employer securities are involved), and so forth. In addition, they can serve specific corporate objectives. Some employers have increased 401(k) contributions rather than direct compensation as part of their overall compensation strategy. Other employers have instituted or enhanced 401(k) plans when modifying or discontinuing other employee benefit plans, such as retiree health care.

Enron Corporation Bankruptcy and the Reform of 401(k) Plans   1

In reaction to the bankruptcy of Enron Corporation, there was widespread clamor for reform of regulations governing 401(k) plans. The reason for this call to reform involved the fact that many Enron employees nearly lost their entire retirement savings when the company collapsed. Under the Enron plan, employees received company stock as a match to their employee contributions. Most employees were unable to diversify the company stock they received as a plan match. Although employees could diversify their own contributions on which they received the company match, many employees chose not to do so since Enron stock had performed so well in prior years. Another complicating factor was that Enron Corporation was in the process of switching 401(k) plan administrators and was in the midst of a "blackout period" when the company stock began to plummet downward. Under the rules applicable at the time of the Enron collapse, employees were unable to switch out of company stock during the "blackout period" while a new vendor was taking on its role as the 401(k) administrator. Employees could only watch in horror as they saw the value of their retirement savings dramatically disappear.

President Bush weighed in on this issue by creating a Task Force on Retirement Security. The task force was charged with developing new safeguards to protect the pensions of American workers. Many issues that were identified by the Task Force on Retirement and subsequently recommended by the President were enacted into law as part of the Pension Protection Act of 2006 (PPA). Because of the more prominent role of 401(k) plans, if the PPA were to be effective, it had to safeguard the resources being accumulated and managed within 401(k) and other defined contribution plans. Hence the legislation addressed such issues as:

- Participant rights to diversify out of employer stock.
- More frequent and timely information reporting on assets held in these accounts.
- Reducing vesting requirements for all types of defined contribution plans.
- Facilitating investment advice for plan participants.
- Allowing automatic enrollment and more balanced default investments.

From the viewpoint of employees, the first and foremost advantage of a CODA involves taxes. If a conventional savings plan is converted to a CODA, the participating employees can realize an immediate increase in take-home pay. But of more importance is the fact that contributions are accumulating under a tax shelter. This means that an employee can receive investment income on amounts that otherwise would have been paid in taxes. Over a period of years, the cumulative effect of this can be quite substantial. Finally, when amounts are distributed and subject to tax, the actual amount of tax paid might be considerably less than would otherwise have been the case. Installment distributions could be taxed at a lower effective tax rate (due to lower levels of taxable income and indexed tax brackets).

Employees also have the flexibility of determining, on a year-to-year basis, whether to take amounts in cash or defer these amounts under the plan. Since employee needs and goals change from time to time, this element of flexibility can be quite important.

The disadvantages of CODAs also should be recognized. From the employer's viewpoint, these plans involve complex and costly administration. Also, the employer must be prepared to deal with employee relations and other problems that can occur in any year that the plan fails to satisfy the ADP and ACP tests. These plans also will involve a greater communications effort than is associated with conventional employee benefit plans.

From the viewpoint of employees, the disadvantages of CODAs are not as great. In fact, the only significant disadvantage is that elective contributions are subject to withdrawal limitations and the possible application of the early distribution tax (described in Chapter 31). This could be of major importance to some employees, particularly those at lower pay levels, and could be a barrier to their participation in the plan.

The Future

CODAs have already become an important part of the employee benefit planning process. A majority of organizations already have established CODAs or converted existing plans to CODAs in the past. Many others are actively moving in this same direction. There is every reason to believe that the growth of these plans will continue in the foreseeable future. Although it appears that there will be certain legislative changes and governmental regulations affecting the operation of CODAs both in the near term and in the more distant future, the essential characteristics of 401(k) plans likely will remain intact.

CODAs are an interesting and tax-efficient way of providing employee benefits. They are consistent with the growing concept that employee benefit plans need to be flexible and need to address the varying needs of employees at different times during their careers. There seems little doubt that they will continue to be a major factor in the employee benefit planning process of the future.

Cash or deferred arrangements (CODAs) are not an entirely new concept. They have existed since the 1950s. However, they were originally beset with legislative and regulatory doubt during the mid-1970s. The Revenue Act of 1978, along with proposed regulations issued by the IRS in 1981, opened the way for these plans, and their growth since 1981 has been significant.

The following sections review the legislative history of these plans, the technical requirements they must meet, and some special considerations that must be taken into account. General matters of plan design and tax qualification that apply equally to CODAs as well as to other tax-qualified plans are not discussed in the remainder of this chapter since they are covered elsewhere in the book. As previously noted, it should be remembered that a 401(k), although often referred to as a type of retirement plan, is not in actuality a specific type of plan. Rather a 401(k) provision is attached to another type of plan allowing an employee a choice of receiving an employer contribution in cash or having it deferred under the plan and/or the choice of making his or her own contribution to a plan from before-tax income. This allows the employee to avoid any federal tax on these amounts until they are received in the form of a plan distribution. A 401(k) provision can be added to a conventional deferred profit sharing plan, a savings plan, a stock bonus plan, an employee stock ownership plan, a pre-ERISA money purchase plan, or a rural electric cooperative plan.

Legislative History of CODAs

Before 1972, the IRS provided guidelines for qualifying cash option CODAs in a series of revenue rulings. In essence, more than half of the total participation in the plan had to be from the lowest paid two-thirds of all eligible employees. If this requirement was met, employees who elected to defer were not considered to be in constructive receipt of the amounts involved, even though they had the option to take cash. Salary reduction plans satisfying these requirements also were eligible for the same favorable tax treatment.

In December 1972, the IRS issued proposed regulations stating that any compensation that an employee could receive as cash would be subject to current taxation even if deferred as a contribution to the employer's qualified plan. Although primarily directed at salary reduction plans, the proposed regulations also applied to cash option profit sharing plans.

As the gestation period for ERISA was coming to an end, Congress became increasingly aware of the need to devote additional time to the study of the CODA concept. As a result, ERISA included a section providing that the existing tax status for CODAs was to be frozen until the end of 1976. Plans in existence on June 27, 1974, were permitted to retain their tax-favored status; however, contributions to CODAs established after that date were to be treated as employee contributions and, as a result, were currently taxable.

Unable to meet its self-imposed deadline, Congress extended the moratorium on CODAs twice; the second time, the deadline was extended until the end of 1979.

The Revenue Act of 1978 enacted permanent provisions governing CODAs by adding Section 401(k) to the IRC, effective for plan years beginning after December 31, 1979. In essence, CODAs are now permitted, as long as certain requirements are met.

This legislation, in itself, did not result in any significant activity in the adoption of new CODAs. It was not until 1982, after the Internal Revenue Service issued proposed regulations in late 1981, that employers began to respond to the benefit-planning opportunities created by this new legislation. By providing some interpretive guidelines for Section 401(k), and by specifically sanctioning **salary reduction plans,** the IRS opened the way for the adoption of new plans and for the conversion of existing, conventional plans. For example, many employers converted existing after-tax savings plans to CODAs to take advantage of the Section 401(k) tax shelter on employee contributions.

The Tax Reform Act of 1984 provided some subtle modifications to Section 401(k). Among other things, it made it clear that CODAs could not be integrated with Social Security. The 1984 legislation also extended cash or deferred treatment to pre-ERISA money purchase plans, although contributions were limited to the levels existing on June 27, 1974.

The changes imposed by the Tax Reform Act of 1986 were much more substantive. In addition to reducing the limit on elective deferrals, this legislation provided a new definition of highly compensated employees; restricted the actual deferral percentage (ADP) test; established a new test for after-tax and matching employer contributions; imposed an additional tax on early distributions; and reduced the employer's flexibility in designing eligibility requirements for these arrangements.

Another law affecting CODAs was the Small Business Job Protection Act of 1996. Among other things, this legislation simplified the ADP test and created safe harbor arrangements that can eliminate the need for ADP testing.

The Economic Growth and Tax Relief Reconciliation Act of 2001 (EGTRRA) had far-reaching impact on CODAs. A number of favorable provisions applicable to CODAs were included as part of the Act. Among the most notable provisions, EGTRRA increased the elective deferral limit in 2002 and scheduled further escalation through 2006 at which time its increases would be indexed in $500 increments; catch-up contributions were permitted, allowing employees age 50 and older at the end of a tax year to electively defer even greater amounts; the multiple-use test applying to plans needing to conduct both the ADP and ACP tests was repealed for years beginning after 2001; the 401(k) ADP nondiscrimination safe harbor was broadened making it a top-heavy safe harbor; a "qualified Roth contribution program" could be added to 401(k) plans beginning after 2005 whereby participants electing to have all or a portion of their elective deferrals designated as after-tax "Roth contributions" would not be taxed on qualified distributions when they occur in the future; and the "same desk rule" was eliminated, allowing employees continuing in the same job for a different employer following liquidation, merger, consolidation, or other corporate transaction to receive a distribution on the basis of having separated from "employment" rather than "service." Generally the changes affecting 401(k) plans enacted into law with EGTRRA were intended to allow individuals to save more for retirement, make plan administration less complex allowing the offering of such plans to be broadened, enhance the portability of retirement benefits in such plans, reduce administrative burdens for employers sponsoring 401(k)s, and bring greater parity among all types of retirement savings vehicles.

As indicated at the beginning of this chapter, the PPA of 2006 made many significant changes in the law related to defined contribution plans generally, with many of these changes having important implications for 401(k) plans.

1. Employer contributions to defined contribution plans for years beginning after 2006 must vest at least as rapidly as either a three-year cliff or a six-year graded vesting schedule. For 401(k) plans providing employer-matching contributions, this provision was irrelevant because these more compressed vesting schedules already were required for employer-matching contributions. However, if a 401(k) plan provided employer contributions where an employee contribution was not required to receive the employer match, this provision would have an impact.

2. The PPA also required that, beginning after 2006, defined contribution plans of publicly traded companies that hold publicly traded employer securities allow participants to diversify account balances that are invested in employer securities. Generally, the diversification requirements allow participants to immediately diversify investments resulting from elective deferrals and after-tax contributions. Participants who have completed three years of service must be permitted to diversify the investment of any employer contributions. To comply with these requirements, plans must offer at least three diversified investment options other than employer securities, and plans must permit diversification elections to be made at least quarterly. Plans already providing more liberal diversification provisions

related to employer securities are not exempt from these rules and must comply with the diversification notice requirements instituted under the PPA. Generally, plans must provide a notice to participants of their right to diversify at least 30 days prior to the date that participants become eligible to diversify.

3. The PPA amended ERISA to explicitly provide that ERISA preempts any state wage and hour law that directly or indirectly prohibits or restricts automatic enrollment features in defined contribution plans. However, to qualify for this preemption, the plan sponsor must notify employees of their rights and obligations under the automatic enrollment arrangement, including their right to opt out of the arrangement or to elect to have contributions made at a different percentage. In administering the automatic enrollment feature, employers must give employees a reasonable amount of time, after receipt of the notice and before the first elective contribution is made, to make such an election. The notice must also describe default investment options for the automatic contributions. The Department of Labor has issued proposed regulations providing default investment guidelines.

4. The PPA also added a new optional nondiscrimination safe harbor plan design for plans using an automatic enrollment feature effective for plan years beginning after 2007.

5. The PPA made a change in the notice and consent rules applicable when a plan distribution occurs. Previously, the distribution notice was required to be given to a participant no less than 30 days and no more than 90 days before a distribution occurred. The PPA extended the 90-day period to 180 days and also mandated that the notice describe the consequences of a failure to defer receipt of the distribution.

6. The PPA also expanded conditions that would allow hardship distributions. The PPA directed the IRS to modify hardship rules to provide that events constituting hardships for a plan participant's spouse or dependent would also constitute hardship when occurring to the participant's beneficiary under the plan.

7. Finally, the PPA made the provisions of EGTRRA affecting retirement plans that were scheduled to expire after 2010 permanent.

Technical Requirements

IRC **Section 401(k)** states that a qualified CODA is any arrangement that:

1. Is part of a profit sharing or stock bonus plan, a pre-ERISA money purchase plan, or a rural electric cooperative plan[1] that meets the requirements of Section 401(a) of the IRC.

---

[1] For purposes of IRC Section 401(k), the term *rural electric cooperative plan* means any pension plan that is a defined contribution plan and that is established and maintained by a rural electric cooperative or a national association of such cooperatives. For further details, see IRC Section 457(d)(9)(B).

2. Allows covered employees to elect to have the employer make contributions either to a trust under the plan on behalf of the employees or directly to the employees in cash.
3. Subjects amounts held by the trust to certain specified **withdrawal limitations,** when those amounts are attributable to employer contributions made pursuant to an employee's election.
4. Provides that accrued benefits derived from such contributions are **nonforfeitable.**
5. Does not require, as a condition of participation in the arrangement, that an employee complete a period of service with the employer maintaining the plan in excess of one year.

As a tax-qualified plan, a CODA must meet all of the nondiscriminatory requirements generally applicable to such plans. The special requirements for CODAs are covered in the following discussion. Before discussing these requirements, however, it is important to understand the difference between the different types of employee and employer contributions that can be made under a CODA:

- **Elective contributions** are amounts an employee authorizes the employer to contribute to a CODA on a pretax basis—either by way of salary reduction, in the case of a typical savings plan, or through an election to defer, in the case of a cash option profit sharing plan. Elective contributions are sometimes called pretax contributions or elective deferrals.
- **After-tax employee contributions** consist of money an employee is deemed to have received and taken as income.
- **Matching contributions** are employer contributions made when an employee authorizes an elective deferral or makes an after-tax employee contribution.
- **Nonelective contributions** are employer contributions made on behalf of eligible employees regardless of whether they have made elective deferrals.
- **Qualified nonelective contributions (QNECs)** are nonelective contributions to which two special rules apply: (1) the contribution must be fully vested at all times, and (2) it generally may not be distributed to the employee on an in-service basis for any reason before the employee reaches age 59½.
- **Qualified matching contributions (QMACs)** are matching contributions that meet the same rules a nonelective contribution must meet to become a QNEC.
- **Safe harbor contributions** are employer contributions made to allow a plan to meet safe harbor requirements and avoid the need for ADP testing. Like QNECs, they must be fully vested and are subject to distribution restrictions.

The passage of EGTRRA in 2001 created new types of contributions that could be made to CODAs. Passage of the PPA of 2006 made these types of contributions permanent. The following types of contributions are now specifically permitted and made permanent:

- **Employee catch-up contributions** are increased elective deferrals permissible for employees who are at least age 50 before the end of the tax year. At the time

EGTRRA was enacted, employee catch-up contributions were scheduled to increase as follows:

Year	Allowable Catch-up
2002	$1,000 additional
2003	$2,000 additional
2004	$3,000 additional
2005	$4,000 additional
2006	$5,000 additional
Years following 2006	Additional amounts are indexed in $500 increments

In 2007 employee catch-up contributions were $5,000. Employee catch-up contributions are not subject to any other contribution limits and are not taken into account in applying other contribution limits to other contributions or benefits under a plan. An employer will not fail the IRC Section 401(a)(4) nondiscrimination rules if the plan allows all eligible plan participants to make the same election regarding catch-up contributions. However, all plans maintained by related employers are treated as one plan if the employers are treated as a single employer. According to the Conference Committee report, an employer can make matching contributions with respect to catch-up contributions, although these matches would be subject to all the rules typically applicable to matching contributions. It should be noted that one of the major motivations for allowing catch-up contributions was to aid women approaching retirement whose savings may have been insufficient because of career interruptions and absences from the workforce.

- **Designated Roth contributions** are employee contributions effective for tax years beginning after 2005 whereby an employee elects to have all or a portion of his or her annual elective deferral treated as an after-tax "Roth contribution." To allow for such an election, an employer must incorporate a "qualified Roth contribution program" as part of the 401(k) plan. A 403(b) plan (see Chapter 9) may also offer such a program. The advantage to employees in electing to have all or a portion of their elective deferrals treated as designated Roth contributions is that, although these monies will be taxed currently when contributed into the plan, qualified distributions from a designated Roth account (both contributions and subsequent investment earnings) are not subject to taxation when disbursed.

Because these Roth contributions are treated as elective deferrals, they fully and immediately vest. Roth contributions are subject to the withdrawal restrictions that generally prohibit payment from the account prior to the participant's retirement, separation from service, death, disability, or the occurrence of another distributable event authorized by the Internal Revenue Service. The Conference Committee report indicates Congressional intent that designated Roth contributions may only be made prospectively and that employees may not make retroactive designations of prior year elective deferrals into Roth contributions. Designated Roth contributions are treated as elective deferrals for purposes of the ADP test. A 401(k) or 403(b) plan offering the option of a qualified Roth contribution program must establish, for each participating employee, a separate "designated Roth account" that will hold designated Roth contributions and earnings allocable to those contributions.

Type of Plan

As already mentioned, a CODA may be part of a profit sharing or stock bonus plan. This, of course, includes savings plans. The only qualified, defined contribution plan that cannot be established as a CODA is a post-ERISA money purchase or defined contribution pension plan.[2]

As a practical matter, most CODAs fall into one of two categories—either cash or deferred profit sharing plans or savings plans. CODAs also can be subdivided into plans that involve employer contributions only, both employer and employee contributions, and employee contributions only. Plans involving only employee contributions are not used to a great extent, largely because of the difficulty these plans experience in satisfying the special nondiscrimination tests described later in this chapter.

Individual Limitations

There is a limitation on exclusion for elective deferrals for any taxable year. This limit was initially set at a fixed dollar amount and was indexed to changes in the consumer price index. At the time of EGTRRA's passage in 2001, the limit on elective deferrals was set at $10,500. EGTRRA increased the elective deferral limit for 2002 and scheduled it to increase in subsequent years according to the following schedule:

Year	Elective Deferral Limit
2002	$11,000
2003	$12,000
2004	$13,000
2005	$14,000
2006	$15,000
Years following 2006	Additional amounts are indexed in $500 increments

The elective deferral limit for CODAs was $15,500 in 2007.

It should be noted that any excess amounts are included in the employee's gross income. This limitation applies to the aggregate elective deferral made in a taxable year to all CODAs.

[2] CODAs are not available as state or local government plans unless they were adopted before May 6, 1986. Tax-exempt organizations were previously subject to similar limitations; however, the Small Business Job Protection Act of 1996 repealed these limitations, and tax-exempt organizations were able to adopt CODAs beginning in 1997.

A second limit caps the amount of pay that can be taken into account for most qualified plan purposes, including the determination of contributions and benefits. Initially, this limit was set at $200,000 and was indexed to increase with changes in the CPI. By 1993, the limit had reached $235,840. The Omnibus Budget Reconciliation Act of 1993 (OBRA '93) reduced the limit to $150,000, effective in 1994. The limit was still indexed to changes in the CPI; however, changes took place only when accumulated changes due to movement in the CPI amounted to at least $10,000. For 2001, this limit had reached $170,000. EGTRRA increased this limit on includible compensation from $170,000 in 2001 to $200,000 in 2002 and revised the indexing so that it would increase in $5,000 increments in years after 2002. In 2007 the limit on includable compensation was $225,000.

Nondiscrimination in Coverage and Contributions

A CODA will not have a tax-qualified status unless the employees eligible to benefit under the arrangement satisfy the coverage provisions described in Chapter 25 and the contributions under the plan are deemed to be nondiscriminatory. To satisfy the non-discrimination-in-contributions requirement, an **actual deferral percentage (ADP) test** must be met; if after-tax employee contributions and/or employer matching contributions are involved, an **actual contribution percentage (ACP) test** also must be met. These tests (except for the ACP test for after-tax employee contributions) will not have to be performed, however, if safe harbor contributions are made, as described later in the chapter.

The ADP test is a mathematical test that must be satisfied by the close of each plan year. The first step in applying this test is to determine the **actual deferral percentage** for each eligible employee. This is done by dividing the amount of contribution deferred at the employee's election (plus, at the election of the employer, any QNECs or QMACs) by the amount of the employee's compensation. This percentage is determined for all eligible employees, whether or not they are actually participating. Thus, the ADP for a nonparticipating but eligible employee is zero. For purposes of this test, the compensation used must meet one of the four acceptable definitions of compensation found in the regulations.[3]

The next step is to divide the eligible employees into two groups—the highly compensated employees (HCEs) and all other eligible nonhighly compensated employees (NHCEs). For each of these groups, the actual deferral percentages are mathematically averaged. If the average ADP for the HCEs does not exceed the average ADP for the NHCEs by more than the allowable percentage, the test is satisfied for the year. The basic test is that the ADP for HCEs cannot be more than 125 percent of the ADP for NHCEs. An *alternative* limitation can produce a higher ADP for the HCEs in many situations. This **alternative limitation** permits the ADP for HCEs to be as much as two times the ADP for the NHCEs, but not more than two percentage points higher. The allowable percentages are set forth in Table 8.1. Table 8.2 shows the permissible ADPs for HCEs at various levels, assuming whichever of the above tests permits the highest result.

---

[3] These definitions are described in Chapter 25. It should be noted, however, that even though one of these definitions must be used for testing, the plan may use another nondiscriminatory definition of compensation for purposes of determining plan contributions.

TABLE 8.1
Allowable ADP
Percentages for HCEs

If the ADP for NHCEs Is	Then the ADP for HCEs May Not Exceed	
	Basic Test	Alternative Limit
1%	1.25%	2.0%
2	2.50	4.0
3	3.75	5.0
4	5.00	6.0
5	6.25	7.0
6	7.50	8.0
7	8.75	9.0
8	10.00	10.0
9	11.25	11.0
10	12.50	12.0
11	13.75	13.0
12	15.00	14.0

For years prior to 1997, these steps had to be followed using compensation and deferrals for the current year—both for NHCEs and HCEs. Beginning with the 1997 plan year, employers were allowed to conduct the ADP test using actual deferral percentages of NHCEs for the prior year. Employers are not required to use prior-year percentages; however, if an employer elects to use current-year percentages, this election can be changed only in accordance with IRS regulations.

Beginning with the 1999 plan year, the ADP test could be performed excluding any NHCEs who participate before attaining age 21 and completing one year of service (the

TABLE 8.2
Permissible ADPs for
HCEs

If the ADP for NHCEs Is	Then the ADP for HCEs May Not Exceed
1%	2%
2	4
3	5
4	6
5	7
6	8
7	9
8	10
9	11¼
10	12½

maximum statutory eligibility requirements permitted), as long as the plan separately passes the 410(b) coverage tests for all participants in that age/service group.

It should be noted that the ADP test determines a maximum average deferral percentage for the HCEs. It does not necessarily indicate the maximum deferral percentage for an *individual* in this group. As long as the average deferral percentage for the highly compensated employees is less than or equal to the maximum allowed, it will be permissible for an individual in this group to defer an amount in excess of that limitation.

If any highly compensated employee is a participant under two or more CODAs of the employer, all such CODAs will be treated as one CODA for purposes of determining the employee's actual deferral percentage.

A similar test, known as the actual contribution percentage (ACP) test, applies to any after-tax employee contributions and any employer matching contributions.

In addition to making safe harbor contributions and/or using prior year actual deferral percentages of NHCEs, there are several ways in which an employer can minimize or eliminate the possibility that a plan will not meet the ADP and ACP tests. The following lists some of the techniques that might be used for this purpose.

1. The plan can be designed so that it is in automatic compliance. For example, the employer might make an automatic 5 percent QNEC contribution for all employees. Employees may then be given the option of contributing up to 1.0 percent of pay by way of salary reduction. The plan will always satisfy the ADP test since the ADP for the HCEs will never exceed the 125 percent basic test.

2. The plan also could be designed to encourage maximum participation from the NHCEs. This could be done under a savings plan, for example, by providing for higher levels of employer contributions with respect to lower pay levels or with reference to lower rates of contribution.

3. Limits may be placed on the maximum amounts that might be deferred or contributed.

4. A mandatory minimum deferral or contribution may be required from all participating employees.

5. The plan could include a provision allowing the employer to adjust prospective deferrals or after-tax contributions (either upward or downward) if the plan is in danger of failing to meet the tests.

6. The employer may make additional QNEC or QMAC contributions at the end of the plan year to the extent necessary to satisfy the applicable test.

7. Contributions for a plan year could be determined in advance of the plan year and, once established on a basis that satisfies the test, requirements could be fixed on an irrevocable basis (except, possibly, that NHCEs could be given the option of increasing their contributions).

Safe Harbors—ADP/ACP Testing

A CODA plan sponsor no longer had to worry about nondiscrimination tests for elective contributions starting in 1999 if the employer satisfied one of two safe harbors by either (1) providing certain matching contributions to NHCEs or (2) making a contribution of 3 percent of compensation for all NHCEs, regardless of whether these employees contributed to the plan. Also, ACP testing was not required for matching contributions starting in 1999 if (1) the plan provided for a safe harbor matching contribution and (2) no match was provided on contributions in excess of 6 percent of compensation. (The ACP test still is required, however, for after-tax employee contributions.)

The safe harbor matching contribution must be at least 100 percent of the first 3 percent of pay contributed and 50 percent of the next 2 percent of pay contributed. Other formulas for matching contributions will qualify for this safe harbor treatment if the formula provides an amount of matching contribution at least as large as the safe harbor formula and the percent matched does not increase as the employee's contribution increases. In addition, the rate of match for HCEs cannot be greater than the rate of match for NHCEs.

To meet the safe harbor requirements, eligible employees must be informed of their opportunity to participate in the CODA prior to the beginning of the year and the matching contributions used to satisfy the safe harbor must be fully vested and subject to the same restrictions on distributions as QNECs or QMACs—that is, they can be distributed only on account of separation from service, death, disability, or attainment of age 59½.[4]

While these safe harbors eliminate the need and expense of annual testing, as well as the necessity of recharacterizing (described later) or refunding excess contributions, they can result in additional plan costs caused by the full-vesting and annual-notice requirements. As noted in footnote 4, according to IRS notice 2000-3 a plan sponsor now has the option to make a decision as late as 30 days before the end of the plan year whether to treat a 401(k) as a safe harbor plan. Essentially this allows the plan sponsor until 30 days before the end of the plan year to decide whether to subject the 401(k) to ADP testing and possible remedial actions, or instead, make the 3 percent nonelective contribution and avoid testing altogether.

The PPA added another safe harbor option for 401(k) plans that contain an automatic enrollment feature. Accordingly, 401(k) plans with an automatic enrollment feature can avoid nondiscrimination testing for both elective deferrals and matching contributions. To qualify for this safe harbor, deferrals must be at least 3 percent of compensation in the participant's first year of participation, and subsequently increase by 1 percentage point each year until the deferrals reach 6 percent in the fourth year and remain at least at 6 percent thereafter. The automatic deduction cannot exceed 10 percent, and the percentages must be applied uniformly to all automatically enrolled employees. For NHCEs, the employer also must provide either (1) a nonelective contribution equal to at least 3 percent of the employee's compensation or (2) a matching contribution of 100 percent of at least 1 percent of the participant's compensation and 50 percent of the employee's deferrals between 2 and 6 percent of compensation. The

---

[4] Initially when the concept of safe harbor plans was introduced, an employer needed to have safe harbor language in the plan before the beginning of the plan year. IRS notice 2000-3 changed this rule allowing a nonsafe harbor 401(k) plan that uses the current-year testing method to be amended into a safe harbor plan as late as 30 days before the end of the plan year. To take advantage of this option, the safe harbor contribution must be in the form of a 3 percent of pay nonelective contribution. Notice to eligible employees before the beginning of the year must advise them that the plan sponsor might choose to amend the plan into a safe harbor plan.

matching rate for HCEs cannot exceed the matching rate for NHCEs. When a plan utilizes this safe harbor, employer contributions must be 100 percent vested within two years. It should be noted that this safe harbor option grants the employer more time to vest such contributions than does the previously described safe harbor that was made available in 1999. An employer could opt to add automatic enrollment to an existing safe harbor plan following the provisions made available in 1999. If this were done, the employer's contributions under the existing safe harbor would become vested immediately.

Since passage of the PPA, 401(k) plans with automatic enrollment features complying with the Act could comply with nondiscrimination testing in one of three ways:

1. The more complicated and more extensive testing which examines each eligible participant's deferrals.
2. The previously available safe harbor permitted beginning in 1999.
3. The "automatic enrollment" safe harbor where employer contributions could range from 3 to 10 percent of the participant's compensation.

Treatment of Excess Deferrals and Contributions

Excess deferrals may arise if the amount deferred by an employee exceeds the allowable elective deferral limit for the year in question. Excess contributions may arise as a result of a plan's failure to meet the ADP or ACP test.

Excess deferrals due to the elective deferral limit may be allocated among the plans under which the deferrals have been made by March 1 following the close of the taxable year, and the plan may distribute the allocated amount back to the employee by April 15. Although such a distribution will be included in the employee's taxable income for the year to which the excess deferral relates, it will not be subject to the 10 percent excise tax that might otherwise apply to distributions prior to age 59½; however, even though distributed, this amount will generally have to be taken into account by the employer when applying the ADP test for the year. Any income on the excess deferral will be treated as earned and received in the taxable year in which the excess deferral was made. Any excess deferral not distributed by this date (April 15 of the following year) will remain in the plan, subject to all regular withdrawal restrictions. Moreover, the amount will again be treated as taxable income when it is later distributed.

If excess contributions arise because of the ADP or ACP tests, there are several ways in which the problem can be addressed. The first, of course, is for the employer to make additional contributions to the extent necessary to satisfy the test requirements. Alternatively, if it is the ADP test that has been failed, the employer can **recharacterize the excess deferrals** as after-tax employee contributions; in this event, however, they will then be subject to the ACP test requirements. A third method is to refund the excess contributions using the method prescribed in the regulations.[5] For plan years beginning after December 31, 2007, corrective distributions for failure to satisfy the ADP or ACP tests are taxable in the year of distribution and need not include the differential period income if

[5] Prior to 1997, this method required the HCE or HCEs with the highest rate of deferral to be reduced first and to the extent necessary to satisfy the test. Beginning in 1997, refunds must be made starting with those HCEs who have made the highest dollar amount of contribution.

distributed within the period prescribed to avoid the 10 percent excise tax. For purposes of the law, an excess attributable to a failure of the ADP test is called an **excess contribution.** An excess attributable to failure of the ACP test is called an **excess aggregate contribution.**

If contributions are to be returned, there are two critical dates to keep in mind. The first such date is 2½ months after the end of the plan year in which the excess has occurred. If excess contributions or excess aggregate contributions are returned by that time, the amount generally will be considered as income on the earliest date that amounts deferred for the plan year being tested would otherwise have been received in cash. A return of after-tax contributions, of course, will not be taxable; however, other returned amounts, including investment income on both after-tax and elective deferrals, will be taxable. The amounts distributed will not attract the 10 percent excise tax that might otherwise apply to early distributions.

The second critical date that relates to the return of excess contributions is the last day of the plan year following the plan year in which the excess has occurred. If the required amounts are distributed after the first critical date and before the second critical date, the amount returned is taken into income in the year of distribution. In addition, the employer is subject to a 10 percent penalty tax on the amount of principal involved (but not on investment earnings).

If excess contributions are not returned by the second critical date, the consequences could be serious. If the excess is an excess contribution, the CODA portion of the plan could lose its qualified status for the years in question, with the result that *all* employees could be taxed on amounts they could have received in cash. If the excess is an excess aggregate contribution, the entire plan could lose its qualified status for the years in question; this could entail a loss of deductions, the taxation of plan investment income, and the taxation of all employees to the extent of their vested account balances.

Nonforfeitability Requirements

The value of all elective and any after-tax employee contributions to a CODA must be fully vested at all times. QNECs, QMACs, and safe harbor contributions allowed in 1999 also must be fully vested at all times. (Note the safe harbor contributions under the automatic enrollment safe harbor need not vest for two years.) The value of other employer contributions must vest in accordance with one of ERISA's prescribed vesting standards. It should be noted, however, that the vested amount of elective contributions cannot be considered for this purpose. Thus, the vesting of employer contributions must be accomplished independently.

As mentioned previously, if employer contributions are fully vested from the outset (and if they are subject to withdrawal restrictions), they may be taken into account when applying the ADP test.

Limitations on Withdrawals

A common provision in many profit sharing and savings plans is one that permits an employee to make a withdrawal of some part of the vested account balance while still actively employed. Sometimes, this withdrawal right is limited to hardship situations;

more often than not, however, a withdrawal can be made for any reason and is typically subject to some period of suspension from plan participation.

In the case of a CODA, the ability to make in-service withdrawals is severely limited. The value of elective contributions may be distributable only upon death, disability, separation from service, the termination of the plan (provided no successor plan other than an employee stock ownership plan [ESOP] or a simplified employee pension [SEP] plan has been established), or certain sales of businesses by the employer. Distributions of elective contributions will be permitted after the employee has attained age 59½ or before this age in the case of a hardship. For hardship withdrawals, however, the amount available is limited to the elective contributions themselves; investment income on such contributions can be included only to the extent that it was earned prior to December 31, 1988 (for calendar year plans). Safe harbor contributions are subject to similar withdrawal restrictions. Also, it should be noted that if employer contributions (QNECs and QMACs) have been included in the ADP test, the withdrawal restrictions on these amounts are even greater; any such contributions and any investment income earned on such contributions are withdrawable for hardship only to the extent that they were made or earned before the end of the last plan year ending before July 1, 1989.

Limiting the withdrawal of elective contributions to hardship cases only can be of significance to many employers, since it could have a negative effect on the participation of lower-paid employees, thus creating problems in meeting the ADP and ACP tests. The regulations define hardship in a very narrow way. Specifically, these regulations require that the hardship be caused by "immediate and heavy financial needs" of the employee. Further, they require that the withdrawal must be necessary to satisfy the financial need.

As indicated earlier, the PPA expanded conditions that would allow hardship distributions. The PPA directed the IRS to modify hardship rules to provide that events constituting hardships for a plan participant's spouse or dependent would also constitute hardship when occurring to the participant's beneficiary under the plan.

The regulations permit each of these conditions to be met on a "facts and circumstances" basis, but they also provide for the use of safe harbors. For determining immediate and heavy financial need, the following events are acceptable:

- The incurring of certain medical expenses by the employee, the employee's spouse, certain dependents of the employee, as defined in Section 152 of the IRC, or the participant's beneficiary; or the need for "upfront" funds to obtain certain medical services for these individuals.
- The purchase (excluding mortgage payments) of a principal residence for the employee.
- Payment of room and board, tuition, and related educational fees for the next 12 months of postsecondary education for the employee or the employee's spouse or dependents.
- The need to prevent either the eviction of the employee from his or her principal residence or foreclosure on the mortgage of the employee's principal residence.

The PPA allowed penalty-free withdrawals from retirement plans to individuals called to active military duty for a period in excess of 179 days beginning after September 11, 2001, and before December 31, 2007.

The regulatory safe harbor for the second requirement, that the withdrawal be necessary to satisfy the financial need, includes four conditions:

1. The distribution must not exceed the amount of the need.
2. The employee must have obtained all distributions (other than hardship distributions) and all nontaxable loans currently available under all plans maintained by the employer.
3. The plan (and other plans maintained by the employer) must provide that the employee's elective and after-tax contributions will be suspended for at least 6 months after receipt of the distribution.[6]
4. The plan and all other employer plans must limit the employee's elective contributions for the calendar year immediately following to no more than the excess, if any, of that year's elective contribution limit over the amount electively contributed in the year of the distribution.

A plan may use a facts and circumstances approach, rely on the safe harbors, or use a combination of both in designing and administering a hardship withdrawal provision.

It should be noted that some amounts might still be available for nonhardship, in-service withdrawals. As already noted, employer contributions may be withdrawn (unless they are designated to be part of the ADP test). Also, the value of any after-tax employee contributions may be withdrawn, as may the value of any contributions (employer and employee) made to a plan before it became a CODA. Finally, even elective contributions may be withdrawn on a nonhardship basis after the employee attains age 59½.

Separate Accounting

The regulations state that all amounts held by a plan that has a CODA will be subject to the CODA nonforfeitability and withdrawal requirements unless a separate account is maintained for benefits specifically subject to these requirements. Included are amounts contributed for plan years before 1980, contributions not subject to a deferral election, and contributions made for years when the CODA is not qualified.

The passage of EGTRRA provided for another separate accounting requirement for plan years beginning after 2005 if employers choose to offer a "qualified Roth contribution program" in connection with a 401(k) plan. A 401(k) or 403(b) plan offering the option of a qualified Roth contribution program must establish, for each participating employee, a separate "designated Roth account" that will hold designated Roth contributions and earnings allocable to those contributions.

---

[6] The safe harbor suspension of elective deferrals and after-tax contributions following hardship distributions was originally set at 12 months. EGTRRA reduced this period of time to 6 months for years beginning after December 31, 2001.

Loans

Because of the restrictions on the in-service withdrawal of elective contributions, many employers have included loan provisions in their CODA programs. The legal requirements for loans are the same for CODAs as they are for profit sharing plans. These requirements were discussed at length in Chapter 6, so they are not repeated here.

Other Considerations

The preceding discussion dealt with the requirements of federal tax law for the qualification of CODAs and the income tax treatment of elective contributions. There are, however, other issues that must be addressed. The following section discusses the status of elective contributions for purposes of Social Security, other employer-sponsored plans, and state and local taxes. It also discusses the deduction limits for 401(k) contributions, the treatment of excess deferrals, and the effect of such contributions on deduction limits.

Social Security

Originally, elective contributions to a CODA were not considered to be wages for purposes of Social Security. Thus, they were not subject to Social Security (Federal Insurance Contributions Act [FICA]) tax, nor were they taken into account when calculating Social Security benefits.

This was changed by the 1983 Social Security amendments. Elective contributions are now considered as wages for Social Security (and federal unemployment insurance) purposes. Thus, FICA taxes are paid on such amounts under the taxable wage base, and they are taken into account when calculating an employee's Social Security benefits.

Other Employer-Sponsored Plans

A matter of some concern to employers in the past was the question of whether an employee's elective contributions should be considered as part of the compensation base for purposes of other tax-qualified plans. This uncertainty was resolved in 1983 when the Internal Revenue Service ruled that the inclusion (or exclusion) of elective contributions under a CODA as compensation in a defined benefit pension plan does not cause the pension plan to be discriminatory.

Employers also maintain other pay-related employee benefit plans. These include short- and long-term disability income plans, group term life insurance, survivor income benefits, and, in some cases, health care plans. There appear to be no legal reasons that pay, for the purpose of determining benefits under these plans, cannot be defined to include elective contributions made under a CODA. If such contributions are to be included, care should be taken to ensure that necessary plan and/or insurance contract amendments are made so that compensation is properly defined.

A CODA will not be qualified if any other benefit provided by the employer (other than the employer's matching contribution) is conditioned, either directly or indirectly, on the employee's electing to have the employer make or not make contributions under the arrangement in lieu of receiving cash.

State and Local Taxes

The treatment of elective contributions under state and local tax laws is not completely uniform. For years, many states followed principles of federal tax law in the treatment of employee benefits. This practice also was followed by many local governments that impose some form of income tax.

With the increased use of individual retirement accounts (IRAs) in recent years, and with the publicity that CODAs have received, there has been growing concern among state and local tax authorities over the potential loss of tax revenue. As a result, the question of state and local taxation of elective contributions has become an important issue.

At this time, most state and local authorities have indicated that they will follow federal tax law. However, a few have announced that elective contributions will be taxable and subject to employer withholding. It seems reasonable to expect that other state and local authorities might adopt this latter position.

Deduction Limits

Section 404 of the IRC imposes limits on the amount an employer can deduct for contributions made to qualified plans. For profit sharing plans prior to 2002, this limit was 15 percent of covered payroll. However, EGTRRA increased the allowable limit to 25 percent of covered payroll beginning in 2002. If the employer has both a defined benefit plan and a defined contribution plan, the combined limit is 25 percent of the covered payroll.

Elective contributions previously affected the maximum deduction in two ways. First, they reduced the amount of the covered payroll to which the percentage limitations applied, thus reducing the dollar amount available as a maximum deduction. Second, they were considered to be employer contributions, and thus they reduced the amount otherwise available for the employer to contribute and deduct.

EGTRRA modified the definition of compensation beginning in 2002 to allow greater employer deductible contributions. Elective deferrals to qualified cash or deferred arrangements, which were previously excluded from the definition of compensation, are now included. Also, elective deferrals to cash or deferred arrangements are no longer deemed employer contributions and they are, therefore, not subject to the employer deduction limitations.

It should be noted that the changes enacted into law as part of EGTRRA not only affected 401(k) plans for larger employers, but also had a profound effect on the smallest of employers—a one-person firm. Because of the EGTRRA changes, the so-called, Solo(k) plan became viable. This use of a 401(k) for the one-person firm is described in Chapter 13.

Effect of Elective Deferrals on Deductible Employer Contributions: Pre- and Post-EGTRRA

For most employers, the effect of elective deferrals on deductible employer contributions in the past did not create problems. Employers who maintained liberal plans, however, may have found that the level of elective contributions permitted might have to be limited in order to preserve the ability to make regular, deductible employer contributions.

The problem was exacerbated by similar elective contributions made by employees for health care benefits and qualified transportation fringe benefits, and to flexible spending accounts (FSAs) for health and dependent care. These contributions also reduced covered payroll for purposes of determining deductible limits and contributions to the CODA. The following example illustrates the impact of these factors both pre- and post-EGTRRA:

Payroll before Elective Contributions			$1,000,000
Elective Contributions for			
CODA	$ 80,000		
Health care	55,000		
FSA health care	25,000		
FSA dependent care	25,000		
Qualified transportation fringe benefits	5,000		
Total	$190,000		
		Pre-EGTRRA	**Post-EGTRRA**
Payroll base for computing employer deductible contribution		$810,000	$890,000
Deductible employer contribution:			
Pre-EGTRRA: 15% of payroll base		$121,500	
Post-EGTRRA: 25% of payroll base			$222,500
Pre-EGTRRA reduction of employer contribution for employee elective deferrals		(80,000)	0
Allowable employer contribution		$ 41,500	$222,500

In this example, if the employer matched elective contributions on a dollar-for-dollar basis, pre-EGTRRA the employer would not be able to contribute the full $80,000 necessary to accomplish this result. In fact, it would barely be able to make a 50 percent match.

Post-EGTRRA, however, the employer's ability to match or to provide nonelective contributions is dramatically increased. The ability to provide this much higher level of deductible contributions results from (1) the increased contribution limit available to profit sharing plans from 15 percent of pay to 25 percent of pay, (2) the exclusion of elective deferrals from the payroll base for computing employer deductible contributions, and (3) the fact that employee elective deferrals no longer are counted as employer contributions.

Chapter Summary

- Although cash or deferred arrangements have existed since the 1950s, their most significant growth has occurred since 1981, after the Revenue Act of 1978 amended the Internal Revenue Code by adding Section 401(k). In late 1981, proposed regulations were issued clarifying uncertainties regarding these arrangements.

- Distinctions between different types of employer and employee contributions to CODAs are important because the nature of these contributions determines the applicability of either the actual deferral percentage test or the actual contribution percentage test for nondiscrimination testing purposes.

- Excess contributions arising from a plan's failure to meet the ADP or ACP test can have important implications. Although certain remedial actions are permitted within specified time frames, certain defects, if not remedied, can result in plan disqualification.

- The value of all elective and any after-tax employee contributions, QNECs, QMACs, and safe harbor contributions allowed in 1999 to a CODA must be fully vested at all times. The value of other employer contributions must vest in accordance with ERISA's prescribed vesting standards. The PPA of 2006 allows for safe harbor contributions in connection with automatic enrollment that must vest in two years.

- The ability to make in-service withdrawals is severely limited in the case of a CODA. The value of elective contributions is distributable only upon death, disability, separation from service, the termination of the plan (provided no successor plan other than an ESOP or a SEP has been established), or certain sales of businesses by the employer. Distributions of elective contributions will be permitted after the employee has attained age 59½ or before this age in the case of hardship. Similar withdrawal restrictions apply to QNECs, QMACs, and safe harbor contributions.

- Internal Revenue Service regulations define hardship in a narrow way and require that the hardship be caused by the immediate and heavy financial needs of the employee. Further, they require that the withdrawal be necessary to satisfy the financial need. Although the regulations permit each of these conditions to be met on a "facts and circumstances" basis, the regulations provide for the use of safe harbors for determining both "immediate and heavy financial need" and the means "necessary to satisfy the financial need."

Key Terms

excess aggregate
   contribution, p. *140*
excess contribution, p. *140*
matching contributions,
   p. *132*
nonelective contributions,
   p. *132*
nonforfeitable, p. *132*

qualified matching
   contributions
   (QMACs), p. *132*
qualified nonelective
   contributions (QNECs),
   p. *132*
recharacterization of
   excess deferrals, p. *139*

safe harbor contributions,
   p. *132*
salary reduction plans,
   p. *129*
Section 401(k), p. *131*
withdrawal limitations,
   p. *132*

Questions for Review

1. Explain the advantages and limitations of a CODA from the viewpoint of employees.
2. Explain the disadvantages of a CODA from the viewpoint of the employer.
3. What requirements must be satisfied by a CODA for it to be qualified under the IRC?
4. Explain the steps involved in the ADP test.
5. May contributions (expressed as a percentage of compensation) for the higher-paid employees under a qualified CODA be larger than contributions for their lower-paid colleagues? Explain.
6. Describe the safe harbor contribution requirements for CODAs.
7. Explain the vesting requirements for contributions to a qualified CODA.
8. Describe the impact of CODA deferrals on Social Security taxes and benefits.
9. May elective contributions to a CODA be considered as part of the compensation base for purposes of other tax-qualified plans? Explain.
10. Describe how elective contributions to a CODA will affect the employer's deduction limits.

Questions for Discussion

1. Discuss the conditions under which an employer may wish to establish a CODA.
2. Assume that an employer has had a CODA for several years and that the reaction of the employees toward the plan has been unsatisfactory. Discuss the plan design flexibility available for a CODA that may be used by the employer to improve the employees' reaction without increasing the employer's annual cost.
3. Discuss how the dollar limit on elective contributions is likely to affect plan design for CODAs.

Resources for Further Study

Benna, Ted. "401(k) Plans: From Inception to the Present Day." *The Handbook of Employee Benefits.* 6th ed. Jerry S. Rosenbloom, ed. New York: McGraw-Hill, 2005.

Buckley, Allen. "401(k) Plan Loans and Participant Bankruptcy." *Journal of Pension Benefits* 8, no. 4 (Summer 2001).

CCH Editorial Staff. "2001 Tax Legislation: Law, Explanation, and Analysis." *Commerce Clearing House Pension Plan Guide* (2001).

CCH Editorial Staff. "Legislation 2006: Pension Protection Act of 2006: Law Explanation and Analysis." *Commerce Clearing House* (2006).

Hoffman, Craig. "IRS Notice 2000-2—the New and Improved 401(k) Safe Harbor Plan." *Journal of Pension Benefits* 7, no. 3 (Spring 2000).

Holden, Sarah, and Jack L. Van Derhei. "Investment of Defined Contribution Plan Assets." *The Handbook of Employee Benefits.* 6th ed. Jerry S. Rosenbloom, ed. New York: McGraw-Hill, 2005.

Palmer, Bruce A. "Profit Sharing Plans." *The Handbook of Employee Benefits.* 6th ed. Jerry S. Rosenbloom, ed. New York: McGraw-Hill 2005.

Pianko, Howard. "The 401(k) Plan Sponsor/Fiduciary: Understanding Aggregate Fees Received by Service Providers." *Journal of Pension Planning & Compliance* 27, no. 3 (Fall 2001).

Thompson Publishing Editorial Staff. "The Pension Protection Act of 2006: Essential Insights." Thompson Publishing Group (2006).

Chapter 9

Section 403(b) Plans

After studying this chapter you should be able to:

- Identify the required statutory features of a Section 403(b) plan.
- Detail the eligibility requirements that qualify an organization to establish a 403(b) plan.
- Specify the funding instruments permitted by IRC Sections 403(b) and 403(b)(7).
- Explain the IRC rules and tax aspects for distributions from 403(b) plans.

Introduction

A 403(b) plan is a retirement mechanism for employees of public educational institutions and certain nonprofit tax-exempt organizations that permits thousands of eligible organizations to provide their employees an opportunity to save for retirement on a tax-deferred basis.

A 403(b) plan can be structured in different ways. First, a 403(b) plan can be structured on a fully contributory and elective basis without employer contributions. Second, a plan can be structured involving employer contributions with or without employee contributions. Employer contributions come in three varieties: (1) fixed contributions without mandatory employee contributions; (2) fixed contributions on a matching basis requiring employee contributions (meaning that an employee will not receive an employer match unless the employee makes a contribution); and (3) variable contributions where an employer contributes to the 403(b) and may use it, in a sense, as a means of rewarding employees for achieving performance targets, much like a profit sharing plan is used. All three variations of employer contributions can permit voluntary, unmatched employee contributions.

Under most 403(b) plans, participating employees can elect to have their salaries reduced, pursuant to a **salary reduction agreement** with the employer, and have the amount of the reduction applied to purchase **403(b) annuities** (or mutual funds) within the limits established by law. Often referred to as a **tax-deferred**

annuity (TDA) plan or supplemental retirement annuity (SRA) plan, this type of 403(b) arrangement is intended as a voluntary tax-deferred savings plan using salary reduction, and it generally does not involve employer contributions. Under this arrangement, once the employee decides how much to contribute (within permitted limits), a salary reduction agreement for that amount is entered into with the employer. The amount by which the employee's salary is reduced is then contributed by the employer to the TDA on behalf of the employee. Although the savings under a TDA are intended for retirement purposes, some or all of the accumulated funds in these programs can be made available to employees prior to retirement in the event of financial hardship, as defined by Internal Revenue Service (IRS) regulations and under other specified circumstances.

If an employer contributes to a 403(b) plan in the form of matching contributions and/ or discretionary contributions (similar to profit sharing plans) in addition to employees' tax-deferred salary reduction contributions, the arrangement sometimes makes up the **employer's basic retirement plan.**

The remainder of this chapter reviews the key features and legal requirements of Section 403(b) plans.

Requirements of a 403(b) Plan under the Internal Revenue Code (IRC)

The Present Statute

To qualify for the favorable tax treatment provided in the law, plans must comply with the statutory requirements of Section 403(b) of the IRC as amended, which provides, in relevant part, that:

> If an annuity contract is purchased for an employee by an employer described in Section 501(c)(3)... or for an employee... who performs services for an educational organization described in Section 170(b)(1)(A)(ii), by an employer which is a State, a political subdivision of a State, or an agency or instrumentality of any one or more of the foregoing..., the employee's rights under the contract are nonforfeitable, except for failure to pay future premiums (and) except in the case of a contract purchased by a church, such contract is purchased under a plan which meets the nondiscrimination requirements... then amounts contributed by such employer for such annuity contract... shall be excluded from the gross income of the employee for the taxable year.

ERISA amended Section 403(b) of the IRC to add Section 403(b)(7), which further provides in relevant part:

> For purposes of this title, amounts paid by an employer... to a custodial account... shall be treated as amounts contributed for an annuity contract for (the) employee if the amounts are to be invested in **regulated investment company stock** (mutual fund shares) to be held in that custodial account.

The essential requirements to achieve the desired tax advantages similar to qualified retirement plans are as follows:

1. The employer must be a qualified educational or nonprofit organization or a public school system (or public college or university).
2. The participant must be a bona fide employee.
3. The participant's rights under the contract must be nonforfeitable.
4. The contributions paid in any year must not exceed the exclusion allowance for the years prior to 2002, the limits under IRC Section 415, the annual limit on salary reduction contributions, or the maximum amount permitted under the nondiscrimination requirements.
5. The plan must meet the nondiscrimination requirements applicable to plans involving employer contributions. For plans that include only voluntary employee salary reductions, IRS regulations simply require that the opportunity to make salary reduction contributions be effectively available to essentially all employees.
6. The annuity contract must be purchased by the employer, or the employer must make a deposit to a custodial account that will purchase mutual fund shares.

The next section analyzes these essential requirements of a 403(b) plan in greater detail.

Qualified Employers

If the employee is to qualify for tax-deferred treatment, his or her employer must be one of the following:

1. A nonprofit organization qualified under Section 501(c)(3) of the Internal Revenue Code (e.g., a tax-exempt hospital, church, school, charitable organization, or other such organization or foundation).
2. A public school system or public college or university (e.g., one operated by a state, or by a county, city, town, school district, or other political subdivision or agency of a state). As used in this chapter, the term *public school system* includes such public colleges and universities.

Only those tax-exempt organizations that meet the requirements of Section 501(c)(3) are qualified employers for purposes of a 403(b) plan. In the case of questions concerning the qualification of an organization, a ruling should be sought from the IRS.[1]

Eligible Employees

To be eligible for participation in a 403(b) plan, an individual must be a **bona fide employee** of a qualified nonprofit organization or a public school system. The individual may be the top-paid or the lowest-paid employee. He or she may be a seasonal,

[1] If the activity of an organization is such that if it were not publicly operated, it could qualify under Section 501(c)(3), and if it has sufficient independence from the state, and so on, it may be able to obtain a ruling that it is a counterpart of a Section 501(c)(3) organization.

part-time, or full-time employee, but must be an *employee*—not an independent contractor. This point requires particular attention in connection with certain professional people (such as radiologists, pathologists, and anesthesiologists) who may or may not, in certain circumstances, be employees.[2] Clerical, administrative, supervisory, and custodial employees of public school systems as well as teachers qualify.[3]

Nonforfeitable Employee Rights

Nonforfeitability under a 403(b) plan essentially requires that the benefits under the plan belong to and be payable to the employee. Without a trust, the employee's rights under an annuity contract, whether under the employer's basic retirement plan or a supplemental tax-deferred retirement annuity plan, would appear to be nonforfeitable if ownership of the contract is vested solely in the employee. The same would appear to be true if there is some form of joint ownership of the contract, together with an agreement between the employer and the employee whereby the employee cannot be deprived of benefits provided by annuity premiums previously paid, even though the employer may exercise control over the time of receipt of those benefits.

As a practical matter, it would appear that nonforfeitability would require that ownership ordinarily be vested solely in the employee, thus leaving him or her free of any restrictions or problems that might arise as a result of insolvency or change of management of the employer. As sole owner of the contract, the employee is free to exercise any of his or her contractual rights, subject, of course, to restrictions on **transferability.** Thus, when an insurance company product is involved, the employee may be free, within the limitations of the contract, to elect a reduced paid-up annuity, to exchange the contract for a reduced annuity with an earlier maturity date, to surrender the contract in order to transfer the proceeds to another issuer, or to borrow from the insurer against its cash value.

However, group annuity contracts are also sometimes used to fund 403(b) plans. In that case, generally, the employer is the contract holder. Nevertheless, in such a contract there are provisions that specify that the rights of participating employees are nonforfeitable.

Contributions

Two types of contributions can be made under 403(b) arrangements. These often are referred to as nonelective and elective contributions.

Nonelective contributions are those that the employer makes on behalf of the participant to the employer's basic retirement plan. **Elective contributions** to 403(b)

---

[2] Some professionals in the service of tax-exempt organizations may be barred by ethical or legal considerations from meeting the tests for the required employer–employee relationship. See Revenue Ruling 66–274, 1966–2 CB 446 for an outline of criteria used in determining the relationship between a physician and a hospital. Also, see *Ravel* v. *Comm'r.*, 26 TCM 885 (1967) and *Azad* v. *U.S.*, 388 F 2d 74 (1968).

[3] In addition, the regulations provide that one who is elected or appointed to certain public offices may qualify if there is a requirement that to hold the office such person must be trained or experienced in the field of education. For example, a commissioner or superintendent of education generally will be eligible, but a regent or trustee of a state university or a member of a board of education is not eligible. Reg. 1.403(b)-1(b)(5).

plans are those voluntary contributions made by an eligible employee to a tax-deferred annuity under a salary reduction agreement made with his or her employer. Elective contributions also include those contributions an employee must make to receive employer matching contributions under the employer's basic retirement plan. Previously only one such salary reduction agreement per year was permitted by Internal Revenue Code (IRC) regulations. Once the employee elected the amount to be contributed for the year, he or she generally could not change the amount until the next taxable year. The Small Business Job Protection Act of 1996 repealed this prior prohibition on multiple salary reduction agreements for plan years beginning after December 31, 1995. Participants in 403(b) plans now may enter into salary reduction agreements more frequently than once per year. Effectively participants may enter into salary reduction agreements as frequently as the plan permits, provided the amounts are not currently available, meaning the compensation has not been paid to the employee or the compensation is not able to be received at the employee's discretion.

Both nonelective and elective contributions must be made by the employer and are excluded from the employee's gross income for the current year as long as such contributions do not exceed the limitations outlined below and discussed further in the next several sections of this chapter.[4]

Four possible limitations on the amount that can be contributed to a 403(b) arrangement are:

- An elective deferral limit on contributions made pursuant to salary reduction arrangements.
- An annual exclusion allowance limitation for years prior to 2002.
- An annual limit on total contributions (Section 415 annual limit).
- An annual limit on includible compensation (Section 401(a)(17)).

Limitation on Salary Reduction Contributions

The maximum amount an individual may contribute on an annual basis to all 403(b) plans in which he or she participates (pursuant to a salary reduction agreement) is determined by Internal Revenue Code Section 402(g). At the time of Economic Growth and Tax Relief Reconciliation Act's (EGTRRA) passage in 2001, the limit on elective deferrals was set at $10,500. EGTRRA increased the elective deferral limit for 2002 and scheduled it to increase in subsequent years according to the following schedule:

Year	Elective Deferral Limit
2002	$11,000
2003	$12,000
2004	$13,000
2005	$14,000
2006	$15,000
Years following 2006	Additional amounts are indexed in $500 increments

[4] In addition to certain other tax penalties that may apply, contributions to a custodial account (but not to an annuity contract) in excess of these limits generally are subject to a 6 percent excise tax under IRC Section 4973.

In 2007, the 402(g) limit had reached $15,500.

It should be noted that the 402(g) limit moves in tandem with the limit for 401(k) cash or deferred arrangement (CODA) elective deferrals (see Chapter 8). The 401(k) elective deferral limit reached the 403(b) level in 1996. Since that time the 403(b) and 401(k) elective deferral limits are now at the same level and are indexed to increase together. The elective deferral limit does not apply to contributions made by an employer to a 403(b) plan. The employee's 402(g) limit, however, would be reduced by any additional elective deferrals the employee may have made as a participant in a 401(k) plan, a SIMPLE plan, or a simplified employee pension (SEP) plan. Formerly if an individual also contributed to a deferred compensation (IRC Section 457[b]) plan sponsored by the employer, the 402(g) limit was reduced to the lower 457(b) limit for the total salary deferral amounts contributed to both the TDA and the Section 457 plans.

With the passage of EGTRRA, the amount that could be contributed to a 457(b) plan was decoupled from the 402(g) elective deferral limit for 403(b) plans for years beginning after 2001. The net result of this change in the law was to permit employees eligible for both types of plans to be able to contribute twice as much money on a pretax basis using both a 403(b) and a 457(b) deferred compensation plan.

In special cases, an annual amount above the 402(g) limit may be contributed by an employee to a 403(b) plan under a salary reduction agreement. Under this **special "catch-up" election,** an employee of a qualifying organization[5] who has entered into a salary reduction agreement with the employer and has at least 15 years of service with the organization may make additional contributions above the 402(g) limit in an amount not to exceed the smallest of the following:

- $3,000.
- $15,000 decreased by the amount of additional salary reduction contributions made previously by the employee under these special rules.
- The excess of $5,000 times years of service minus prior tax-deferred employee contributions.

Under this special catch-up election, an eligible employee can contribute a maximum of $15,000 of additional contributions through the employer after fulfilling the 15-year service requirement, but cannot, in any event, contribute more than an additional $3,000 in any single year.

EGTRRA also provided a type of employee catch-up contribution in years after 2001 for employees who were at least age 50 before the end of the tax year. These employee catch-up contributions allow for increased elective deferrals. At the time EGTRRA was enacted, employee catch-up contributions were scheduled to increase as follows:

---

[5] A qualifying organization allowing for catch-up elections is more limited than the universe of employers that are permitted to offer 403(b) plans. Generally an employee must work for an educational organization, a hospital, a home health service agency, a health and welfare service agency, or a church or related organization to be eligible for catch-up elections.

Year	Allowable Catch-up
2002	$1,000 additional
2003	$2,000 additional
2004	$3,000 additional
2005	$4,000 additional
2006	$5,000 additional
Years following 2006	Additional amounts are indexed in $500 increments

In 2007, the allowable catch-up contribution remained at $5,000.

Employee catch-up contributions are not subject to any other contribution limits and are not taken into account in applying other contribution limits to other contributions or benefits under a plan. An employer will not fail the Code IRC Section 401(a)(4) nondiscrimination rules if the plan allows all eligible plan participants to make the same election regarding catch-up contributions. However, all plans maintained by related employers are treated as one plan if the employers are treated as a single employer. According to the Conference Committee report, an employer can make matching contributions with respect to catch-up contributions, although these matches would be subject to all the rules typically applicable to matching contributions. It should be noted that one of the major motivations for allowing catch-up contributions was to aid women approaching retirement whose savings may have been insufficient because of career interruptions and absences from the workforce.

Exclusion Allowance

Historically in years prior to 2002, 403(b) plan sponsors needed to be concerned with the calculation of the maximum **exclusion allowance** in order to determine the amount that could be contributed by an employee on a tax deferred basis to a 403(b) plan. This was a particularly cumbersome calculation because the plan sponsor was required to keep detailed records of prior plan contributions for each employee over the employee's entire career history with the employer. The methodology for calculation of the maximum exclusion allowance was contained in the Internal Revenue Code and even predated the passage of the Employee Retirement Income Security Act (ERISA) in 1974. When other limits subsequently were passed into law and made applicable to 403(b) plans, such as the Section 415 limits and the 402(g) limit on elective deferrals, the calculation became even more cumbersome. This resulted in complexity for 403(b) plan administrators since the calculation involved computation of all these multiple limits and a determination of which limit was the controlling limit on employee elective deferrals. The calculation was further complicated by the creation of alternative limits (alternative limits A, B, and C and other special catch-ups) when new limits came into being. The passage of the Economic Growth and Tax Relief Reconciliation Act of 2001 considerably simplified administration of 403(b) plans since it eliminated the exclusion allowance for years beginning after 2001. The alternative limits A, B, and C, which allowed some employees to make additional contributions, also were repealed.

Since the calculation of the maximum exclusion allowance was of such importance historically in administering 403(b) plans, a chapter appendix was included in the ninth edition of this text illustrating the steps of the calculation. Since elimination of this calculation was part of EGTRRA and the law contained a sunset provision automatically repealing all tax law modifications after 2010, it was within the realm of remote possibility that the maximum exclusion allowance, without further tax law change, would reemerge in 2011. This possibility was removed with the passage of the Pension Protection Act (PPA) of 2006, which made the retirement planning provisions of EGTRRA permanent.

IRC Section 415 Limit

EGTRRA increased the **IRC Section 415 limit** for defined contribution plans to the lesser of $40,000 or 100 percent of compensation in 2002. After that, the Section 415 limit was indexed in $1,000 increments. The Section 415 limit includes both employer and employee contributions as well as any forfeitures that result from nonvested terminations and the allocation of these forfeited amounts to the accounts of remaining participants. In 2007, this indexed limit was the lesser of $45,000 or 100 percent of compensation.

IRC Section 401(a)(17) Limit on Includible Compensation

The limit on the maximum amount that can be taken into account when calculating retirement plan contributions or benefits, or when conducting nondiscrimination testing (see nondiscrimination testing discussion in Chapter 25), is determined by the IRC Section 401(a)(17) limit. EGTRRA increased this compensation limit to $200,000 in 2002 and indexed its escalation in future years in $5,000 increments instead of the $10,000 increments that existed pre-EGTRRA. In 2007, this indexed limit was $225,000.

Limits on Elective Deferrals under Section 402(g)

As noted earlier in the chapter, EGTRRA changed the limit on elective deferrals for 2002 and scheduled its rise over the next several years.

EGTRRA also made provision for employees who attained age 50 by the end of the tax year to contribute additional elective deferral amounts for years beginning after 2001. Also of significance was EGTRRA's provision decoupling the limit for 403(b) and 457(b) plans for years after 2001, allowing employees eligible for both plans to effectively double their elective deferral limit. The elective deferral limit, however, generally does apply to the sum of the employee's other elective deferrals for the taxable year, including CODAs, SIMPLE plans, and salary reduction simplified employee pensions (SARSEPs). EGTRRA also allowed employee contributions effective for tax years beginning after 2005 whereby an employee can elect to have all or a portion of his or her annual elective deferral treated as an after-tax "Roth contribution." In order to allow for such an election, an employer must incorporate a "qualified Roth contribution program" as part of the 403(b) plan. A 401(k) plan (see Chapter 8) may also offer such a program. The advantage to employees in electing to have all or a portion of their elective deferrals treated as designated Roth contributions is that, although these monies will be taxed currently when contributed into the plan, qualified distributions from a designated Roth account (both contributions and subsequent investment earnings) are not subject to taxation when disbursed. Since these Roth contributions are treated as elective deferrals, they are fully and immediately vested. Roth contributions are subject to the withdrawal restrictions that generally prohibit payment from the account prior to the participant's retirement, separation from service, death, disability, or the occurrence of another distributable event authorized by the Internal Revenue Service. The Conference Committee report indicated congressional intent that designated Roth contributions may only be made prospectively and that employees may not make retroactive designations of prior-year elective deferrals into Roth contributions. Designated Roth contributions are treated as elective deferrals for purposes of the nondiscrimination testing, described in Chapter 25. A 403(b) or 401(k) plan offering the option of a qualified Roth contribution program must establish, for each participating employee, a separate "designated Roth account" that will hold designated Roth contributions and earnings allocable to those contributions.

If the employee makes an elective deferral in excess of the dollar limit for a taxable year, the excess must be allocated by the employer among the plans under which the deferrals were made by March 1 of the following year. The excess contributed, including any investment income thereon, must then be distributed by the plans to the employee by April 15. Such distributions (and investment income) will be included in the employee's taxable income for the year in which the excess deferral was made, but it will not be subject to the 10 percent penalty tax for premature distributions.

If the distribution is *not* made by the April 15 deadline, however, the excess deferral will be included in the employee's taxable income for the year in which the excess deferral was made and will be taxed *again* in the year it is actually distributed to the employee.

Plans that failed to apply the elective deferral limit previously risked plan disqualification and loss of their tax-favored status. The Small Business Job Protection Act of 1996 clarified that the limits on elective deferrals apply to each individual 403(b) *contract* rather than the 403(b) *plan* as a whole. This distinction is important since it clarifies that excess deferrals could subject individual contracts to loss of tax-favored treatment, but that contracts where deferrals are not excessive will not be negatively affected. This clarification was applicable for plan years beginning after December 31, 1995.

Nondiscrimination Requirements

For plan years after 1988, 403(b) annuity arrangements, except for church plans, are generally subject to extensive IRC nondiscrimination rules as outlined by the Tax Reform Act of 1986 (TRA '86). TRA '86 basically enacted three nondiscrimination rules that have an impact on 403(b) annuity plans. Two of the nondiscrimination rules generally incorporate the rules designed to prevent discrimination in favor of highly compensated employees (HCEs) under qualified retirement plans. These rules apply only to contributions to 403(b) annuities made *other than* pursuant to a salary reduction agreement entered into by the employee (i.e., under the employer's basic retirement plan). The third rule applies only to salary reduction contributions.

The first nondiscrimination rule effective for plan years after 1988 generally applies the same rules and regulations governing coverage that apply to qualified retirement plans to nonsalary reduction contributions made to 403(b) plans. In addition, such contributions are subject to the IRC Section 401(a)(17) limit on compensation that can be taken into account. These rules are discussed in detail in Chapters 25 and 26.

The second nondiscrimination rule requires that employer and nonsalary reduction employee contributions meet the actual contribution percentage (ACP) test that compares contributions for highly compensated employees and nonhighly compensated employees. This test is basically the same as applied to 401(k) plans and is discussed in detail in Chapter 8.

The final nondiscrimination rule, which applies only to salary reduction contributions, as discussed above, requires that if the employer permits employees to make such contributions, this opportunity must generally be made available to all employees except for certain nonresident aliens; employees covered by a Section 457 plan, a 401(k) plan, or another 403(b) plan sponsored by the same employer; employees who normally work fewer than 20 hours per week; collectively bargained employees; students performing certain services; and employees whose maximum salary reduction contributions under the plan would not exceed $200. Unlike qualified retirement plans, 403(b) plans are not permitted to impose minimum age and service requirements before employees can make salary reduction requirements.

Annuity Contract Purchased by an Employer

In speaking of "an annuity . . . purchased . . . by an employer," the law gives no indication of what constitutes an annuity contract or a purchase by an employer. However, the IRS has stated that insurance companies or mutual funds must be used.[6] From the insurance company standpoint, it would appear to make no difference whether such a contract used for a 403(b) plan is a single-premium or annual-premium contract or whether it provides for fixed or variable annuity payments, provides for immediate or deferred payments, or includes a refund provision.

The regulations under IRC Section 403(b) provide, however, that "an individual contract issued after December 31, 1962, or a group contract which provides incidental life insurance protection may be purchased as an annuity contract." The expression *incidental life insurance protection* presumably has the same meaning as it has with respect to insurance purchased under qualified plans.[7] The IRS also has ruled that a modified endowment policy with an annuity rider providing a preretirement death benefit with an actuarial value of less than that of a typical retirement income policy meets the incidental death benefit test.[8]

Also, since December 31, 1962, the term *annuity* includes a so-called *face-amount certificate* but does not include a contract or certificate issued after that date that is transferable.[9] The regulations spell out in some detail what is meant by the term

[6] Revenue Ruling 82–102.
[7] For a discussion of the meaning of incidental life insurance under qualified plans, see Chapter 6.
[8] Rev. Rul. 74–115, IRB 1974-11, 9.
[9] IRC 401(g), which reads in its entirety as follows: For purposes of this section and Sections 402, 403, and 404, the term *annuity* includes a face-amount certificate, as defined in Section 2(a)(15) of the Investment Company Act of 1940 (15 USC Sec. 80a-2); but it does not include any contract or certificate issued after December 31, 1962, which is transferable, if any person other than the trustee of a trust described in Section 401(a) which is exempt from tax under Section 501(a) is the owner of such contract or certificate.

nontransferable, and the language of the regulations has been used as a guide by insurers in appropriately wording their contracts.

Thus, any annuity contract, individual or group, ordinarily issued by an insurance company may be used to provide a tax-deferred annuity, provided it contains an appropriate restriction respecting transferability.

Contracts that require periodic level premium payments have been developed to accommodate the needs of the market. One can now find contracts with premiums payable for only 9 or 10 consecutive months of a year, which have been designed to coincide with the payroll schedules of educational institutions. However, most annuity contracts issued today allow flexible premium payments. Therefore, they are readily adaptable to varying incomes (hence, varying elective deferrals) and variable frequency of payment.

It would appear that the payment of premiums satisfies the **purchase requirement** of the statute. Thus, a qualified employer may assume the payment of premiums on an individual annuity contract already owned by one of its employees and will be considered as having purchased a tax-deferred annuity for the employee in each year that premiums are so paid, provided that the contract contains the requisite restriction on transferability.

ERISA, as mentioned previously, by adding Section 403(b)(7), substantially expanded the range of permissible investments to include custodial accounts of regulated investment companies (mutual funds) as well as insurance company annuities or separate accounts.

Distributions and Taxation

Regular and Premature Distributions

For plan years after 1988, distributions from 403(b) arrangements of contributions made pursuant to an employee's salary reduction agreement and any investment income on such contributions are subject to basically the same restrictions as elective deferral contributions made to qualified 401(k) plans (see Chapter 8).[10] Hence, distributions of salary reduction contributions on behalf of an employee and investment earnings on such contributions credited to a TSA after 1988 generally may be made from a 403(b) plan under the following circumstances:[11]

- Attainment of age 59½.
- Death or disability.
- Separation from service.
- Financial hardship.

[10] See John J. McFadden, *Retirement Plans for Employees* (Burr Ridge, IL: Richard D. Irwin), pp. 269–70.

[11] If the account is *invested* in a custodial account (mutual fund), the withdrawal limitations apply to all 403(b) contributions, and only salary reduction contributions may be distributed in the event of hardship. If the account is invested in an annuity contract, the withdrawal limitations apply only to salary reduction contributions and investment earnings thereon credited after 1988.

Note, however, that in the case of a distribution on account of financial hardship, *only* salary reduction contributions made by an employee, and not any investment earnings thereon, may be distributed. The PPA requires that new rules be issued to modify whether a participant has suffered a hardship if certain medical events occur involving the participant's beneficiary under the plan.

Distributions from a 403(b) plan, unless rolled over (discussed later in this chapter) to an individual retirement account (IRA) or another 403(b) plan, are taxed for federal income tax purposes as ordinary income in the year received.

In addition to the ordinary income tax due in the year a distribution is received, a premature distribution penalty tax of 10 percent of the taxable amount distributed generally applies to any distribution from a 403(b) plan before age 59½. The penalty tax would not apply, however, to premature (pre-age 59½) distributions made under the following conditions:

- To an employee who separates from service at or after age 55 and who receives the distribution upon separation from service to the employer.
- Upon the employee's death or disability.
- Upon the employee's separation from service to his or her employer, if the employee receives a distribution in substantially equal periodic payments over his or her life expectancy or over the joint life expectancies of the individual and his or her beneficiary.
- If the employee rolls the distribution over to an IRA or another tax-favored retirement plan.
- To pay medical expenses that are deductible for federal income tax purposes (currently those over 7.5 percent of the employee's adjusted gross income) under IRC Section 213.
- To someone other than the employee under a qualified domestic relations order (QDRO) (see Chapter 26).
- To an individual who is a reservist or national guardsman and who was ordered or called to active duty for a period in excess of 179 days or for an indefinite period and that is made during the period beginning on the date of the order or call to duty and ending at the close of the active duty period. (This provision is applicable to individuals ordered or called to duty after September 11, 2001, and before December 31, 2007.)

Hence, the 10 percent penalty tax applies to nonmedical financial hardship distributions if made prior to age 59½.

Time When Distributions Must Commence

An employee generally must begin receiving distributions from a 403(b) annuity plan by the later of (1) the April 1 following the year in which the individual attains age 70½ or (2) the calendar year following the year in which the employee retires.[12] If sufficient records are maintained to segregate an employee's pre-1987 account balance, however, and if the 403(b) plan so provides, any amounts credited prior to January 1, 1987, need not be distributed until age 75. If a distribution is taken in periodic payments, a minimum distribution must be made based on the individual's life expectancy or the joint life expectancies of the individual and his or her beneficiary. A penalty tax of 50 percent of the difference between the minimum required distribution and the actual distribution received is imposed on the employee if the distribution is less than that required by law.

EGTRRA did not modify the minimum distribution rules, but instructed the Treasury Department to modify the life expectancy tables to more accurately reflect actual current life expectancies. On April 17, 2002, the Treasury Department issued updated regulations regarding minimum distributions. The updated life expectancy tables were included in these regulations.

Taxation of Distributions

Any lump sum distribution from a 403(b) plan is taxable to the participant at ordinary income tax rates. Neither capital gains income tax rates nor income averaging opportunities, available to qualified plan lump-sum distributions before the year 2000, are available for a 403(b) plan distribution. The only part of the distribution that may not be subject to taxation would be any cost basis the employee may have in the distribution because of taxes previously paid by the employee on his or her plan contributions or for any incidental life insurance costs (PS 58 costs) on life insurance included and already subjected to taxation.

Installment payments under a 403(b) plan are taxed in accordance with the annuity rules applicable for qualified plans. See Chapter 31 for a complete discussion of the annuity rules.

---

[12] Previously, employees who continued to work past age 70½ were not required to receive distributions from their accounts while continuing in active employment. This was changed with the Tax Reform Act of 1986 (TRA '86). Though certain employees were excluded from having to take distributions if continuing to work, TRA '86 generally required distributions to commence by April 1 of the year following the year in which an employee attained age 70½ regardless of whether the individual continued in active employment. Employees participating in church or governmental plans remaining in active service and employees who reached age 70½ prior to 1988 were excluded from these distribution requirements. Effectively, the Small Business Job Protection Act of 1996 replaced the minimum distribution rules mandated by TRA '86 with the rules in effect prior to TRA '86. Therefore those still working are no longer required to commence distributions at age 70½ unless the individual is a 5 percent owner or the retirement plan in question is an individual retirement account. These new distribution rules became effective for years beginning after December 31, 1996. It should be noted that a participant receiving distributions under the TRA '86 rules who was continuing to work could be permitted to stop receiving minimum distributions, although the new law did not mandate that this option be offered by plan sponsors.

Loans

Because of the restrictions and limitations on distributions from 403(b) plans previously described, loan provisions are very popular under such plans. Loans under 403(b) plans generally are permitted on the same basis and with the same limits as under qualified retirement plans (see Chapter 6). Basically, such loans must meet the following IRC requirements:

- Loans generally may not exceed the lesser of 50 percent of the participant's account balance or $50,000 (reduced by the amount of any principal repayments on any other loans outstanding during the prior year).
- Loans must bear a reasonable rate of interest.
- Loans must be repaid within five years except for a loan used in the purchase of the employee's principal residence.
- Loan repayments must be made at least quarterly.
- Loans must be on a level amortization basis.

Transfers, Rollovers, and Increased Portability

Transfers

Transferability generally refers to the ability to move some or all of the participant's 403(b) accumulated plan assets among different funds or providers sponsored by the employer—subject, of course, to the plan provisions. In addition, a participant may be allowed to transfer his or her 403(b) plan assets to another 403(b) plan without federal income tax consequences, again subject to possible restrictions imposed by the existing plan and the new plan.

Rollovers

Under IRC Section 403(b)(8), distributions from a 403(b) plan are not includable in an employee's gross income if they are properly rolled over. The basic requirements applicable to a valid rollover are that the employee, pursuant to the plan's usual distribution rules, receives all or a portion of his or her interest in the plan in an eligible rollover distribution; the employee rolls any portion of the distribution into another eligible plan or to an individual retirement account; and if property other than money is distributed, the employee transfers the same property he or she received. In addition, the employee must complete the rollover within 60 days of his or her receipt of the eligible rollover distribution.

For purposes of this discussion, an **eligible rollover distribution** is any distribution of all or a portion of an employee's interest in a 403(b) plan, but it does *not* include (1) any distribution required to be made under the required minimum distribution rules; (2) certain periodic distributions;[13] or (3) any distribution made on account of hardship. Unless made in the form of a direct rollover (i.e., where, pursuant to the employee's instructions, the distribution is paid by the payor plan directly to another plan or IRA and not to the employee), an eligible rollover distribution is subject to mandatory 20 percent federal income tax withholding. The payor (i.e., the insurer or custodian) must withhold the tax even if the employee intends to, and actually does, roll the distribution over upon receiving it. In that case, the employee will be taxed on the amount withheld unless he or she includes other funds equal to the withholding amount in the amount ultimately rolled over.

Increased Portability

Prior to 2002, 403(b) plan assets could only be rolled over to another 403(b) plan or to an IRA. Beginning in 2002 as a result of changes made by EGTRRA, rollover distributions could occur between qualified plans, 403(b), and eligible governmental 457(b) plans. Also, as was permitted previously for qualified and 403(b) plans, eligible distributions

---

[13] Any distribution that is part of a series of substantially equal periodic payments made at least annually over the life or life expectancy of the employee (or the joint lives or life expectancies of the employee and his or her beneficiary), or for a period of at least 10 years, is not an eligible rollover distribution.

from governmental 457(b) plans could also be rolled over to IRAs. The mandatory 20 percent withholding rule is applicable to distributions from rollover-eligible governmental 457(b) plans if distributions fail to be directly rolled over. Rollovers from contributory IRAs (see Chapter 12) may also be made into 403(b) plans, qualified plans, or eligible governmental 457(b) plans. Previously if an individual wanted to roll over 403(b) balances to a Roth IRA, the individual had to first transfer the assets to a traditional IRA and subsequently re-transfer the funds to the Roth IRA. Following passage of the PPA, direct rollovers from 403(b) plans to Roth IRAs are permissible after December 31, 2007. For tax years prior to 2010, such rollovers are subject to a limitation of $100,000 in adjusted gross income of the taxpayer. In 2010 and later years, this adjusted gross income limitation will no longer apply. After-tax contributions from a qualified defined contribution plan (401[a], 403[a] or 401[k] plan) can be directly rolled over (but not indirectly rolled over, that is, in a rollover made within the 60-day period following a distribution) to another qualified defined contribution plan. Such after-tax amounts may be rolled over directly or indirectly to an IRA. The receiving qualified defined contribution plan must account for such after-tax amounts separately, but a receiving IRA does not. However, when EGTRRA was passed, it did not appear that distributions of after-tax amounts could be rolled over to 403(b) or governmental 457(b) plans. The Pension Protection Act of 2006 specifically clarifies that, effective for tax years after 2006, after-tax amounts may be rolled over tax-free from a qualified retirement plan to a tax-sheltered annuity.

The law permits the Treasury Department to extend the 60-day rollover period where the failure to make a rollover within 60 days is attributable to casualty, disaster, or events beyond the reasonable control of the participant.

Beginning in 2007, a nonspouse beneficiary was able to roll over a 403(b) account balance to an "inherited" IRA. Previously, only surviving spouses had this option. However, a nonspouse beneficiary of an "inherited" IRA must begin distributions according to the minimum distribution rules described in Internal Revenue Code Section 401(a)(9) rather than according to the special rules applicable to spouses allowing a deferral of distributions until he or she attains age 70½.

Regulations Providing 403(b) Guidance

In 2004, the Internal Revenue Service issued proposed regulations for 403(b) plans. These regulations were extensive, and they were important because they represented the first comprehensive 403(b) plan guidance in more than 40 years. The main provisions within the proposed regulations related to written documentation requirements, return of excess employee deferrals, new required employer communication and transfer rules, time limits on when funds needed to be deposited into 403(b) accounts, allowance for employer contributions to former employees following severance of employment, coordination of catch-up limits, Roth contributions, restrictions on life insurance as part of the plan, and clarifications on 403(b) plan terminations. As can be seen from this list, these proposed regulations were extremely substantive in scope. However, studies conducted indicated that many plan sponsors had serious misconceptions resulting from these comprehensive proposed regulations. Therefore, on August 29, 2006, the IRS announced that the general effective date for the regulations would be extended. They would not become effective before January 1, 2008, and actually could take effect later than this date. Importantly, the IRS indicated that the proposed regulations could not be relied upon as guidance in administering 403(b) plans prior to their effective date as set forth in the final regulations. Accordingly, the proposed regulations currently have no legal authority and cannot be used to guide plan sponsors in administering the plans they oversee. Plan sponsors of 403(b) plans should be vigilant when further guidance is forthcoming from the IRS as of January 1, 2008, or later.

Chapter Summary

- A tax-favored retirement mechanism exists for employees of public educational institutions and certain nonprofit tax-exempt organizations. To avail themselves of the favorable tax treatment, plans must comply with the statutory requirements of Section 403(b) of the IRC. ERISA amended Section 403(b) of the IRC adding Section 403(b)(7) to allow investments in regulated investment company stock (mutual funds) as well as annuity contracts.
- In order to offer 403(b) arrangements to its employees, an employer must be either a nonprofit organization qualified under Section 501(c)(3) of the IRC or a public school system or public college or university.
- Limitations apply to the amount that can be contributed to a 403(b) arrangement. These limitations are:
  - A limit on elective deferrals for contributions made pursuant to salary reduction agreements.
  - An annual exclusion allowance limitation (prior to 2002).
  - An annual limit on total contributions (Section 415 annual limit).
- Additionally, employer contributions to a 403(b) plan cannot be calculated using compensation that exceeds the allowable limit prescribed by Section 401(a)(17).
- For plan years after 1988, Section 403(b) plans, other than church plans, generally became subject to the extensive IRC nondiscrimination rules mandated by the Tax Reform Act of 1986.
- Distributions from 403(b) arrangements of contributions made pursuant to an employee's salary reduction agreement and any investment income on such contributions are subject to basically the same restrictions as elective deferral contributions made to qualified 401(k) plans.
- Any lump-sum distribution from a 403(b) plan is taxable to the participant at ordinary income tax rates.
- Rollover distributions may occur between qualified plans, 403(b) plans, eligible governmental 457(b) plans, and IRAs.

Key Terms

403(b) annuities, p. *149*
bona fide employee,
   p. *151*
elective contributions,
   p. *152*
eligible rollover
   distribution, p. *163*
employer's basic
   retirement plan, p. *150*
exclusion allowance, p. *155*

IRC Section 415 limits,
   p. *156*
nonelective contributions,
   p. *152*
nonforfeitability, p. *152*
nontransferable, p. *159*
purchase requirement,
   p. *159*
regulated investment
   company stock, p. *150*

salary reduction
   agreement, p. *149*
special "catch-up"
   election, p. *154*
tax-deferred annuity
   (TDA), pp. *149–150*
transferability, p. *152*

Questions for Review

1. Briefly summarize the provisions of the tax code that permit one to set up a tax-deferred annuity.
2. What are the essential requirements to achieve the desired tax shelter for a 403(b) plan? Explain.
3. What does it mean when the IRC requires that the employee's rights be nonforfeitable? Explain.
4. Explain how the elimination of the maximum exclusion allowance in 2002 affected the administration of 403(b) plans.
5. What nondiscrimination tests apply to 403(b) plans?
6. When must distributions commence from a 403(b) plan?

Questions for Discussion

1. Discuss the conditions under which an employer may desire to establish a 403(b) plan.
2. Discuss how the elective deferral limitation has affected plan design for 403(b) annuities.
3. Discuss how the nondiscrimination requirements have affected plan design for 403(b) annuities.
4. Discuss the effects of EGTRRA and the PPA on 403(b) plans.

Resources for Further Study

CCH Editorial Staff. "Legislation 2006: Pension Protection Act of 2006: Law, Explanation, and Analysis." *Commerce Clearing House* (2006).

Cumming, Chris. "Tax-Exempt Entities: When Two Retirement Plans Are Better than One: Making the Most of Paired 401(k)–403(b) Plans." *Journal of Pension Benefits* 8, no. 4 (Summer 2001).

Davis, Michele F. "Section 403(b) Plans for Nonprofit Organizations." *The Handbook of Employee Benefits*. 6th ed. Jerry S. Rosenbloom, ed. New York: McGraw-Hill, 2005.

www.tiaa-cref.org—website of Teachers Insurance and Annuity Association.

www.tiaa-crefinstitute.org—website of the TIAA-CREF Institute.

10

Section 457 Deferred Compensation Plans[1]

Daniel J. Ryterband[2]

Richard L. Alpern

After studying this chapter you should be able to:

- Describe which employers and employee groups utilize Section 457 plans.
- Distinguish between eligible Section 457(b) plans and ineligible Section 457(f) plans.
- Explain the reasons why Section 457 plans are not subject to the same Internal Revenue Service (IRS) requirements that normally apply to qualified retirement plans.
- Discuss how state and local governments use Section 457 plans differently than tax-exempt employers.
- Identify various plan sponsor administrative requirements when offering Section 457 plans.

Background

Deferred compensation plans allow employees to postpone receiving income for future service until some later date—most commonly at retirement. Deferred amounts and income earned generally are not taxed until either paid or **made available** to plan participants. Deferred amounts generally are considered made available when participants acquire an immediate, nonforfeitable right to them.

[1] Minor modifications have been made to update the chapter for applicable provisions of the Pension Protection Act (PPA) of 2006.

[2] This chapter originally appeared as Chapter 34 in *The Handbook of Employee Benefits,* 6th ed., Jerry S. Rosenbloom, ed. (New York: McGraw-Hill Companies, Inc, 2005).

Deferred compensation plans can be structured as pure deferred compensation plans, supplemental benefit arrangements, or a combination of both. In **pure deferred compensation plans,** employees enter into an agreement with their employer to reduce present compensation or to forego a raise or bonus in return for the employer's promise to pay benefits at a future date. In **supplemental benefit plans,** the employer pays an additional, supplemental benefit (sometimes based on a qualified retirement plan benefit formula), without reducing the employee's present compensation, raise, or bonus.

When properly structured, deferred compensation plans shield participants' deferred income from what are termed the tax "doctrines" of economic benefit and constructive receipt. The doctrine of **economic benefit** generally states that an economic benefit results when an economic or financial benefit, even though not in cash form, is provided to an employee as compensation, such as when an employee receives beneficial ownership of amounts placed with a third party, or when assets are unconditionally and irrevocably paid into a fund to be used for the employee's sole benefit. The doctrine of **constructive receipt** generally states that income, although not necessarily received in hand by an individual, is considered received and, therefore, currently taxable when it is credited to an account or set aside so it may be drawn upon at any time and amounts receivable are not subject to substantial limitations or restrictions.[3] Generally, events triggering economic benefit or constructive receipt result in deferred amounts becoming available to plan participants, and thus, subject to current taxation. A mere **unsecured promise to pay,** however, does not constitute receipt of income.[4]

Introduction to Section 457 Plans

Section 457 plans are nonqualified deferred compensation plans available only to state and local **government employers** (including rural electrical cooperatives) and nongovernment organizations exempt from tax under Internal Revenue Code (IRC) Section 501. Examples of **tax-exempt organizations** under Section 501 include nongovernmental schools, private hospitals, labor unions, farmers' cooperatives, and certain trade associations, business leagues, private clubs, and fraternal orders. For the most part, they are nonprofit organizations serving their members or a public or charitable cause.

The Revenue Act of 1978 created IRC Section 457, allowing employees of state and local governments to defer a portion of compensation annually in plans meeting specified requirements. The Tax Reform Act of 1986 (TRA '86) extended Section 457's provisions to nonqualified deferred compensation plans of nongovernment tax-exempt employers. Section 457 limits deferral opportunities for employees of eligible employers.

Eligible employers generally use Section 457 plans in two ways:

1. As pure deferred compensation plans that allow participants to reduce their taxable salary in a manner similar to that of private-sector 401(k) plans. (401[k] plans generally are not available to state and local government organizations.)
2. As supplemental benefit plans that provide executives with supplemental retirement income.

[3] Reg. Sec. 1.451-2(a).
[4] Rev. Rul. 60-31, 1960-1 CB 174; Rev. Rul. 69-650, 1969-2 CB 106.

Plans meeting the complex requirements of Section 457 as well as related laws and regulations receive favorable federal and state tax treatment (deferral of tax, including deferral of income, Social Security, Medicare, and unemployment taxes for plans of governmental employers).[5] Section 457 classifies plans as either "eligible" or "ineligible," each subject to the following specific requirements. **"Eligible"** plans are known as **Section 457(b) plans,** whereas **"ineligible"** plans are known as **Section 457(f) plans.**

Eligible Plan Requirements

In eligible plans of government employers, deferred income and its earnings are tax free until paid to participants or beneficiaries.[6] In eligible plans of nongovernment tax-exempt employers, deferred income and its earnings are tax free until paid *or made available* to participants or beneficiaries.[7]

Eligibility for Plan Participation

Plan participation must be limited to employees and independent contractors performing service for the employer.[8] Before deferring compensation that is paid or made available in any given month, participants must have previously entered into an agreement authorizing the deferrals.[9] Therefore, an active worker must wait until the beginning of the month after entering into an agreement before deferring any income paid or made available in that month. New employees can make deferrals in their first month of employment if they enter into an agreement on or before their first day of employment.[10] It is not necessary to execute a new agreement for each month. Under a special rule, accumulated sick pay, vacation pay, and back pay that is payable before severance from employment can be deferred as long as the deferral agreement is entered into before the date on which the pay is currently available (as described in the Section 401[a] regulations).[11]

Maximum Annual Deferral

The Economic Growth and Tax Relief Reconciliation Act of 2001 (EGTRRA) increased the plan ceiling, or maximum annual deferral to $11,000 for 2002 or 100 percent of includable compensation,[12] whichever is less.[13] The $11,000 limit increases each year by $1,000 to $15,000 in 2006, and is subsequently adjusted annually in amounts rounded down to the nearest $500 (based on general cost of living increases).[14] Includable

---

[5] IRC Sec. 3121(a)(5)(E), 3121(v)(3), 3306(b)(5)(E).

[6] IRC Sec. 457(a)(1)(A).

[7] IRC Sec. 457(a)(1)(A), 457(a)(1)(B).

[8] IRC Sec. 457(b)(1), Reg. Sec. 1.457-2(d).

[9] IRC Sec. 457(b)(4).

[10] Reg. Sec. 1.457-2(g).

[11] Reg. Sec. 1.457-1(d)(1).

[12] IRC Sec. 457(b)(2).

[13] All provisions of EGTRRA of 2001 will expire on 12/31/2010 unless extended by a future act of Congress.

[14] IRC Sec. 457(e)(15)(A), 457(e)(15)(B).

compensation is payment for service performed for the employer which is currently includable in gross income.[15] In general, participants with total compensation in excess of the dollar maximum ($15,500 for 2007; increased as described earlier) can defer a maximum of $15,500 in 2007, and participants with total compensation less than $15,500 in 2007 can defer up to 100 percent of compensation. Deferred amounts exceeding this limit generally are treated as made available and subject to normal taxation in the taxable year deferred.

For purposes of the plan ceiling, deferred income must be taken into account at its current value in the plan year deferred, unless the deferred income is subject to a substantial risk of forfeiture. In that event, the deferred income would be taken into account in the plan year in which the risk of forfeiture lapses.[16]

Catch-Up Provision

Since 2002, participants age 50 and older at the end of the plan year have been allowed to make an additional $1,000 contribution above the dollar limits described earlier (not to exceed 100 percent of includable compensation). The $1,000 catch-up amount increased each year by $1,000 until it reached $5,000 in 2006, and subsequently will be adjusted annually in amounts rounded down to the nearest $500 (based on general cost of living increases).[17] In 2007, the catch-up amount remained at $5,000.

During any or all of the three taxable years ending before the year the participant reaches normal retirement age, the **"catch-up" provision** described is superseded by an amount equal to twice the otherwise applicable limit or, if less, the participant's normal ceiling plus aggregate unused annual ceiling amounts for deferrals in prior years.[18] For example, a 62-year-old participant, with gross compensation of $30,000 in an eligible plan with a normal retirement age of 65, who has underutilized deferrals in prior years by $10,000 could elect to defer a maximum of $25,500 for 2007. This amount is computed by adding the underutilized prior year deferrals of $10,000 to the normal limit of $15,500 (which is less than twice the normal limit).

Normal retirement age must be specified in the plan in order to use the increased catch-up provision. It may be defined as any age on or after the earlier of age 65 and the age at which the participant has the right under the employer's pension plan to immediate, unreduced retirement benefits. As an alternative, the plan is permitted to provide that a participant may designate a normal retirement age within the range described in the prior sentence. However, normal retirement age may not be defined as an age later than 70½.[19]

Coordination with Other Plans

Prior to EGTRRA, maximum deferrals in eligible 457(b) plans were required to be coordinated with amounts excluded from income under other types of deferral arrangements, such as 401(k) plans, 403(b) plans, savings incentive match plans for employees

---

[15] IRC Sec. 457(e)(5).
[16] IRC Sec. 457(e)(6), Reg. Sec. 1.457-2(b).
[17] IRC Sec. 414(v)(B), Sec. 414(v)(C).
[18] IRC Sec. 457(b)(3).
[19] Reg. Sec. 1.457-2(f)(4).

(SIMPLE plans), and simplified employee pensions (SEPs). Effective in 2002, the requirement to coordinate deferrals no longer applies.[20] Therefore, participants could defer the Section 457(b) plan ceiling irrespective of contributions to other plans. The Pension Protection Act (PPA) of 2006 made this provision of EGTRRA, which no longer required coordinating maximum annual deferrals with other plans, permanent rather than "sunsetting" after 2010.

Funding Requirements

In plans maintained by tax-exempt organizations, deferred amounts and earnings must remain the sole property of the employer until made available to participants, subject only to the claims of the employer's general creditors.[21] However, plans maintained by government organizations are required to hold all plan assets in a trust, custodial account, or annuity contract for the exclusive benefit of participants and their beneficiaries.[22] The terms of the trust must make it impossible for plan assets or income to be diverted to any purpose other than participant benefits until all liabilities of the plan have been satisfied. The trust requirement is designed to prevent loss of participant retirement benefits to the claims of the government's general creditors. Before the trust requirement was instituted as part of the Small Business Job Protection Act of 1996, participant benefits were held as employer assets and subject to the general claims of the plan sponsor's creditors.

Investment Options Available to Participants

In government plans, which are required to irrevocably set aside assets to pay participant benefits through a formal trust, custodial account, or annuity contract, participants are generally permitted to choose among various investment alternatives offered under the plan. In plans maintained by tax-exempt organizations, in which deferred amounts and earnings must remain the property of the employer until distributed to the participant, only "informal" funding is permitted. In these plans, employers can earmark assets and allow the participants to direct investment, but they cannot be given a secured interest in the purchased assets. As a result, participants in plans sponsored by tax-exempt organizations can exercise some ownership rights, but remain at risk that the employer may be unable to pay promised benefits.

Most employers that offer eligible 457(b) plans offer participants a variety of investment choices, including equity, bond, and money market funds; guaranteed interest contracts; bank deposit accounts; and fixed- and variable-annuity contracts.

Insurance companies are the predominant investment manager. Other managers include mutual funds, brokerage firms, banks, and investment advisers. In-house investment management is uncommon. Investment managers frequently are responsible for plan implementation, administration and record keeping, and participant enrollment as well, but these functions can be contracted to service providers or performed in-house.

[20] EGTRRA Sec. 615(a).
[21] IRC Sec. 457(b)(6).
[22] IRC Sec. 457(g).

Availability of Loan Provisions

Participant loans are not permitted in eligible 457(b) plans maintained by tax-exempt employers because participants have no secured, nonforfeitable benefit from which to secure the loan and assets must remain subject to the employer's general creditors until made available. However, in plans maintained by government employers, participant loans may be permitted under the general terms that apply to qualified retirement plans (e.g., 401[k] plans). Whether the availability or making of a loan or the failure to repay a loan from a government employer is treated as a distribution depends on the facts and circumstances, including whether the loan has a fixed repayment schedule, whether the loan bears interest, and whether there are payment safeguards that would be followed by a prudent lender.[23]

Availability of Benefits

Plan benefits generally cannot be made available (other than through a loan feature in a plan maintained by a government employer or a qualified domestic relations order (QDRO)[24]) until the participant has a severance from employment or is faced with an "unforeseeable emergency," or until the calendar year when the participant attains age 70½, if later.[25] Severance from employment generally occurs at the employee's termination, disability, death, or retirement. Independent contractors are considered separated from service when their contracts expire, assuming the expiration constitutes a good-faith and complete termination of the contractual relationship. If the employer expects to renew the contract or hire the independent contractor as an employee, separation from service generally has not occurred.[26]

An unforeseeable emergency is a severe financial hardship of the participant, the participant's spouse, participant's beneficiary, or the participant's dependent resulting from a sudden and unexpected illness, loss of property because of casualty, or other similar extraordinary and unforeseeable circumstance outside participant control. Sending a child to college or purchasing a new home are not considered unforeseeable emergencies.[27] In addition, participants may not withdraw money if insurance, liquidation of the participant's assets, or discontinuing plan deferrals will relieve the hardship. Emergency withdrawals are permitted only in amounts necessary to satisfy the emergency need, including the amount of any taxes or penalties reasonably anticipated to result from the distribution.[28] The PPA of 2006 mandated that new rules regarding hardship distributions be issued permitting distributions for certain medical events involving a participant's beneficiary. The PPA also made permanent the EGTRRA provisions scheduled to sunset after 2010 that allow early distribution from a Section 457 plan pursuant to a qualified domestic relations order.

[23] Reg. Sec. 1.457-6(f)(2).
[24] IRC Sec. 414(p)(11).
[25] IRC Sec.457(d)(1).
[26] Reg. Sec. 1.457-6(b)(2).
[27] Reg. Sec. 1.457-6(c)(2)(i).
[28] Reg. Sec. 1.457-6(c)(2)(iii).

An exception to these rules is available for participants of tax-exempt employers with account balances up to $5,000, excluding the portion of such account balance attributible to rollover contributions (and the earnings allocable thereto), if no amount has been distributed to the participant during the two-year period that precedes the distribution and there has been no prior plan distribution to the participant.[29] Although this provision formerly applied to both governmental and tax-exempt employers, Section 457(e)(9) was amended by EGTRRA so that it now applies only to tax-exempt employers.

Plan Distributions

In general, distributions from eligible plans must begin within 60 days after the later of the close of the plan year in which a participant attains or would have attained the plan's normal retirement age or the day the participant separates from service.[30] Eligible 457(b) plans are subject to the same distribution beginning-date requirements as qualified plans. As such, plan distributions must begin no later than April 1 of the calendar year following the calendar year in which the employee either retires or attains age 70½, whichever is later.[31]

Eligible 457(b) plan distributions (and amounts considered made available in plans maintained by tax-exempt organizations) are subject to regular income tax withholding as wages, and payments are reported on Form W-2.[32] However, amounts made available are not taxed if the participant or beneficiary irrevocably elects before the amounts would be considered made available to defer payment until a later date.[33] For example, if a plan provides that distributions will be paid in a lump sum 60 days after severance of employment unless, within 30 days after severance, the participant elects to defer payment; if a participant elects during the 30-day period to defer payment until age 65, the amount is not treated as made available (even though the person had the right to receive it) and remains tax deferred until received. A participant or beneficiary who has made such an election may make one additional election to defer payment before it would have commenced under the initial deferral election; an election to accelerate payment is not permissible.[34] An election of a method of payment may be made at any time before amounts are distributed.[35]

Former participants may have any amount made payable to them transferred to another eligible 457(b) plan without having amounts includible in gross income.[36] Additionally, former government plan participants may roll over plan distributions to an individual retirement plan, a qualified plan, or an annuity plan without having amounts includible in gross income.[37] Conversely, distributions from an individual retirement

---

[29] IRC Sec. 457(a)(2), Sec. 457(e)(9), Sec. 72(t)(9).

[30] IRC Sec. 402(c)(Reg. Sec. 1.457-2(i)(1).

[31] IRC Sec. 457(d)(2) and 401(a)(9).

[32] Notice 2003-20, IRB 2009-19; Rev. Rul. 82-46, 1982-1 CB 158.

[33] Reg. Sec. 1.457-7(c)(2)(i) and (ii).

[34] Reg. Sec. 1.457-7(c)(2)(iii).

[35] Reg. Sec. 1.457-7(c)(2)(iv).

[36] IRC Sec. 457(e)(10).

[37] IRC Sec. 457(e)(16).

plan, a qualified plan, or an annuity plan may be rolled over into government 457(b) plans.[38] The rollovers from and into another type of plan must be made within 60 days of distribution.[39] However, the 60-day rollover period is extended where failure to comply is due to casualty, disaster, or other events beyond the reasonable control of the participant.[40] Former participants may elect a trustee-to-trustee transfer of eligible 457(b) plan distributions to a defined benefit governmental plan if such transfer is for the purchase of permissive service credit or a repayment to which Section 415 does not apply without having amounts includible in gross income.[41] The PPA of 2006 clarified that the term "permissive service credit" allows participants to purchase credit for periods of time even if no service is performed, subject to limits on nonqualified service. Essentially this allows participants to purchase permissive service credit that relates to benefits to which they would not otherwise be entitled to receive under the plan made after 1997. This provision is effective for transfers occurring after 2001.

Distributions from 457 plans are exempt from the 10 percent penalty tax on withdrawals made before age 59½ except for portions attributable to rollovers from another type of plan.[42] The PPA of 2006 directed the IRS to issue regulations on how a governmental 457 plan can meet the requirements of the minimum required distribution rules.

IRS Approval

Unlike qualified plans, eligible 457(b) plans need not apply to the Internal Revenue Service (IRS) for approval but can and often apply for private letter rulings indicating the plan meets the requirements of Section 457. Plans not administered according to the law can lose the tax benefit of deferral. State and local government plans that do not comply with the statutory requirements of eligible 457 plans must be amended as of the first plan year beginning more than 180 days after IRS notification of any inconsistencies. A plan not amended within this grace period will be treated as an ineligible plan and becomes subject to the rules of Section 457(f). There is no grace period for plans of nongovernmental tax-exempt employers that must maintain compliance at all times to maintain favorable tax treatment.[43]

Ineligible Plan Requirements

Ineligible 457 plans are governed by separate rules under Section 457(f). To receive tax-preferred treatment in an ineligible plan, amounts deferred must be subject to a **"substantial risk of forfeiture."** Unlike eligible plans, ineligible plans place no limits on the amount of deferrals made. Employers, therefore, can use ineligible plans to allow employees a contribution level above the eligible plan limit or to provide supplemental

---

[38] IRC Sec. 402(c)(8)(B).

[39] IRC Sec. 402(c)(3)(A).

[40] IRC Sec. 402(c)(3)(B).

[41] IRC Sec. 402(e)(17)(A), 402(e)(17)(B).

[42] IRC Sec. 72(t).

[43] IRC Sec. 457(b) last paragraph, Reg. Sec. 1.457-2(1).

retirement benefits to selected executives. However, ineligible plans are better suited for employer contributions than for salary reduction because of the "substantial risk of forfeiture" provision. If an employer maintains both an eligible and an ineligible plan, it is preferable that they be maintained and administered separately for cost and compliance reasons.

Ineligible 457(f) plan deferred amounts are included in participant or beneficiary gross income in the first taxable year where there is no substantial risk of forfeiture, even if amounts are not received.[44] For a substantial risk of forfeiture to exist, a person's right to receive deferred amounts must be conditioned on future performance of substantial services.[45] Whether the risk of forfeiture is substantial depends on the facts and circumstances of each situation. For example, a substantial risk of forfeiture likely exists when rights to deferred payment are lost at termination of employment for any reason, but a requirement that rights are lost only at termination for cause or committing a crime generally would not create a substantial risk. If any portion of the plan consists of a transfer of property described in Internal Revenue Code Section 83, including stock options, the rules of Section 83 apply instead of the rules under Section 457.[46]

Beginning in 2005, amounts deferred under ineligible 457(f) plans must also satisfy the requirements of IRC 409A, which was added by the American Jobs Creation Act of 2004, with respect to deferral elections and distributions. If the requirements are not met, deferred amounts will also be subject to an additional tax in the first taxable year in which there is no substantial risk of forfeiture equal to 20 percent of the deferred amounts and any earnings credited to the amounts (and may also be subject to additional tax equal to interest at the underpayment rate on the deferred amounts and earnings).[47] The Act's requirements are applicable to amounts deferred after 2004, as well as previously deferred amounts that are not vested as of December 31, 2004, subject to certain transition rules.[48]

Taxation of distributions or amounts made available in ineligible plans is determined under IRC Section 72 annuity rules.[49]

Nondiscrimination Issues

Unlike qualified retirement plans (e.g., 401[k] plans), Section 457 plans are not subject to complex IRS rules that require benefits to be nondiscriminatory. As a result, 457 plans can be offered on a discriminatory basis with participation limited to only a few employees or even to a single employee.

The requirement that 457 plans maintained by tax-exempt employers be unfunded, however, limits availability to certain employee groups in such plans. This is because Title

---

[44] IRC Sec. 457(f)(1)(A).

[45] IRC Sec. 457(f)(3)(B).

[46] Reg. Sec. 1.457-11(d).

[47] IRC Sec. 409A(1).

[48] Sec. 855(d) of P.L. 108-357.

[49] IRC Sec. 72 and 457(f)(1)(B), Reg. Sec. 1.457-11(a)(4).

I of the Employee Retirement Income Security Act (ERISA) requires that plans be funded, which conflicts with the Section 457 requirement that plans be unfunded. Tax-exempt employers' plans generally are subject to Title I requirements and, therefore, must fall within one of the special Title I exceptions to meet both ERISA and Internal Revenue Code (IRC) requirements. This conflict generally requires nongovernment tax-exempt employer 457 plans to restrict participation to a select group of management or highly compensated employees ("top hat" plans) to avoid ERISA's funding requirements.[50] Nongovernment tax exempt employers have used ineligible 457(f) plans to provide "restoration" plan benefits (i.e., contributions above IRS limits in qualified 401[k] plans or 403[b] plans) for their highly paid employees. Beginning in 2002, nongovernment tax-exempt employers could also use eligible 457(b) plans as an additional executive compensation benefit since eligible 457(b) plans no longer needed to coordinate their elective deferral limits with the elective deferrals under other types of plans.

457 Plan Reporting and Disclosure

State and local government employer 457 plans are exempt from ERISA's reporting and disclosure requirements.[51] These employers do not have to comply with requirements for summary plan descriptions, summary annual reports and summary descriptions of material plan modifications, annual registration statements, and annual reports, and other materials frequently requested by participants. Certain returns and reports (such as Form W-2 and 1099-MISC), however, must be filed with the IRS, and participants and beneficiaries must receive information about their benefits when they terminate employment or receive benefit distributions.

Nongovernmental tax-exempt employer plans must meet ERISA's requirements for reporting and disclosure.[52] However, tax-exempt employer plans maintained for a select group of management or highly compensated employees can satisfy ERISA's reporting and disclosure requirements through an alternative compliance method under Department of Labor regulations. Under this method, a statement must be filed with the Secretary of Labor declaring the plan is maintained primarily to provide deferred compensation for a select group of management or highly compensated employees. Plan documents must be provided upon request to the Department of Labor.[53]

Deferred Arrangements Not Considered Deferred Compensation Plans

A 1987 IRS notice interpreted Section 457 requirements as applying to all deferred arrangements. This was interpreted as meaning benefits such as accrued sick time and vacation not used in the present year (as well as elective deferrals of compensation)

---

[50] IRS Notice 87-13, 1987-1 CB 432.

[51] ERISA Sec. 4(b)(1).

[52] ERISA Sec. 4(a), 201, 301, and 401.

[53] Labor Reg. Sec. 2520.104-23.

would be subject to Section 457 restrictions.[54] The dollar value of these benefits that employees received then would directly reduce their allowable compensation deferral amount in eligible plans. Under this interpretation, state and local government and tax-exempt employers were severely restricted in providing deferred compensation and supplemental retirement benefits. Section 457 was later amended so that the following plans generally are excluded from Section 457 restrictions and are not considered as providing compensation deferral:[55]

1. Vacation and sick leave.
2. Compensatory time.
3. Severance pay.
4. Disability pay and death benefits.

To be exempt from Section 457, an arrangement must be legitimate and not an indirect method of deferring cash amounts.

Deferred Compensation Plans Not Subject to Section 457

Certain deferred compensation plans of state and local government and tax-exempt employers generally are not subject to Section 457 restrictions if certain conditions are met. In general such amounts would be subject to the requirements of IRC Section 409A, except to the extent vested as of December 31, 2004, or as otherwise provided in IRS guidance.

Nonelective Deferred Compensation of Nonemployees

Plans providing nonelective deferred compensation for services not performed as an employee (e.g., independent contractors) are exempt from Section 457 restrictions for tax years beginning after December 31, 1987. To be considered nonelective, a plan must be uniform for all participants, offer no variations or options, and cover all persons with the same relationship to the employer.[56] For example, if a hospital gives a nonemployee doctor deferred compensation, the deferred compensation is considered nonelective only if all other nonemployee doctors are offered coverage by the same plan.

Church and Judicial Deferred Compensation Plans

Deferred compensation plans of churches and church-controlled organizations for their employees generally are exempt from Section 457 requirements for tax years beginning after December 31, 1987.[57]

State judges' government deferred compensation plans use the tax rules for funded and unfunded nonqualified deferred compensation plans, rather than Section 457 rules, if certain requirements are met. In addition, participants are not subject to the substantial

---

[54] IRS Notice 87-13, 1987-1 CB 432.
[55] IRC Sec. 457(e)(11).
[56] IRC Sec. 457(e)(12).
[57] IRC Sec. 457(e)(13), 3121(w)(3)(A), 3121(w)(3)(B).

risk of forfeiture rule for ineligible plans.[58] Qualified state judicial plans must have existed continuously since December 31, 1978, and must require:

1. All eligible judges to participate and contribute the same fixed percentage of compensation.
2. The plan to provide no judge with an option that would affect the amount of includible compensation.
3. Retirement benefits to be a percentage of the compensation of judges holding similar positions in the state.
4. Benefits paid in any year not to exceed either 100 percent of a participant's average compensation for the highest three years, or if less, $180,000 adjusted for inflation ($180,000 in 2007).[59]

Nonqualified state judicial plans that do not meet these requirements are taxed as ordinary Section 457 deferred compensation plans.

Nongovernment Tax-Exempt Employer Deferred Compensation Plans

Grandfather provisions may apply to nongovernment tax-exempt employer plans in certain cases. Amounts deferred in tax-exempt employers' plans in taxable years beginning before January 1, 1987, generally are exempt from Section 457 restrictions. Amounts deferred after December 31, 1986, are exempt from Section 457 restrictions if deferrals are based on an agreement that on August 16, 1986, was in writing and stipulated deferrals of a fixed amount (or a fixed percentage of a fixed base amount) or an amount determined by a fixed formula. For example, participants who were deferring 5 percent of compensation according to a written plan on August 16, 1986, must make all subsequent deferrals at 5 percent for the amount to be considered fixed. An example of a fixed formula is a deferred compensation plan designed as a defined benefit plan in which deferrals to be paid in the future are in the form of an annual benefit equal to 1 percent per year of service times final average salary. Changes in the fixed amount or fixed formula result in loss of grandfathered status.[60]

Nonelective Government Employer Deferred Compensation Plans

A grandfather provision also is available to amounts deferred before July 14, 1988, in nonelective government plans by participants covered by a written agreement. To avoid Section 457 restrictions, the agreement must stipulate determination of annual deferrals as a fixed amount or by a fixed formula. Amounts deferred on or after July 14, 1988, are exempt from Section 457 restrictions until the tax year ending after the effective date of an agreement modifying the fixed amount or fixed formula.[61]

---

[58] Sec. 1107(c)(4) of P.L. 99-514 (TRA '86).
[59] Sec. 252 of P.L. 97-248 (TEFRA).
[60] IRS Notice 87-13, 1987-1 CB 432.
[61] Sec. 6064(d)(3) of P.L. 100-647 (TAMRA).

Collectively Bargained Deferred Compensation Plans

Collectively bargained plans of both state and local government and nongovernment tax-exempt employers allowing nonelective income deferral may be excluded from Section 457 restrictions if certain conditions are met. To be grandfathered, a plan must cover a broad group of employees; have a definite, fixed, and uniform benefit structure; and have been in existence on December 31, 1987. A plan loses grandfathered status upon the first material plan modification only if the sponsor changes the benefit formula or expands the class of participants. This grandfather rule generally applies only to union employees participating in a nonqualified, nonelective plan under a collective bargaining agreement. The rule also is available to nonunion employees if, as of December 31, 1987, participation was extended to a broad group of nonunion employees on the same terms as the union employees and union employees account for at least 25 percent of total compensation.[62]

Taxation of Nonelective Deferred Compensation Subject to Section 457

The preceding discussion on deferred compensation plans not subject to Section 457 indicates that, under certain circumstances, nonelective deferred compensation is exempt from Section 457 rules and current taxation. However, many employees of state and local governments and nongovernment tax-exempt employers are taxed on nonelective deferred compensation before they are entitled to receive it. For example:

> A nonprofit organization hires an employee under a five-year employment agreement to pay $50,000 annually. Assuming the employee works the entire five-year period, an additional $10,000 will be paid annually in years six through 10. Under Section 457 rules, the employee would be taxed in year six on the entire present value of all five $10,000 payments. If we assume the discounted present value of the $10,000 payments equals approximately $41,000[63] and the entire amount is subject to 28 percent tax, $11,480 would be paid in tax in Year 6 even though only $10,000 is actually received.

This results in current taxation on amounts the taxpayer:

1. Has not yet received.
2. Has no current right to receive.
3. May not actually ever receive.

Because similar rules do not apply to private-sector employers, this practice places state and local government and nongovernment tax-exempt employers at a disadvantage in recruiting employees.

---

[62] IRS Notice 88-98, 1988-2 CB 421.

[63] Calculated using a 7 percent discount rate, the present value of $10,000 received annually over five years equals $41,001.97.

Conclusion

Most 457 plans are maintained by state and local government employers for the purpose of salary reduction. Without these plans, governmental employers would be precluded from offering salary deferral opportunities that are common among for-profit employers.

Section 457 plans used for purposes other than salary reduction are less common but are rapidly gaining in importance. Nongovernment tax-exempt employers can use eligible 457(b) plans to provide supplemental retirement benefits and salary continuation to certain high-paid executives. Amounts deferred under eligible 457(b) plans are no longer coordinated with amounts deferred under other deferral arrangements since the passage of EGTRRA. Nongovernment tax-exempt employers can also use ineligible 457(f) plans to provide supplemental retirement benefits and salary continuation to certain high-paid executives. These plans function to:

1. Provide benefits over IRC Section 415 limits on contributions to, or benefits from, qualified plans.
2. Offset the effect of the $225,000 maximum compensation cap (as of 2007) of IRC Section 401(a)(17) when determining benefits or contributions to qualified plans.
3. Give valued employees additional death and disability benefits.
4. Impose "golden handcuffs" on valued employees or enhance early retirement benefits.
5. Increase benefits for executives recruited in midcareer who are unable to accrue maximum pension benefits in a qualified plan by normal retirement age.
6. Reward key employees for their contributions to the organization.

Keen competition for talented employees forces employers to design plans attractive to an increasingly mobile workforce. For state and local government and nongovernment tax-exempt employers, 457 plans play an important part in meeting overall employee benefit plan objectives. A successful program, however, requires compliance with the complex requirements governing design, operation, and administration of Section 457 plans.

Chapter Summary

- Deferred compensation plans allow employees to postpone receiving income for future service until some later date—most commonly at retirement. Deferred compensation plans can be structured as pure deferred compensation plans, supplemental benefit arrangements, or a combination of both.
- Deferred compensation plans shield participants' deferred income from what are termed the tax "doctrines" of economic benefit and constructive receipt.
- Section 457 plans are nonqualified deferred compensation plans available only to state and local governmental employers (including rural electrical cooperatives) and nongovernment organizations exempt from tax under Internal Revenue Code Section 501.

- Eligible employers generally use Section 457 plans in two ways:
    a. As pure deferred compensation plans that allow participants to reduce their taxable salary in a manner similar to that of private-sector 401(k) plans, since 401(k) plans generally are not available to state and local government organizations.
    b. As supplemental benefit plans that provide executives with supplemental retirement income.

- Section 457 classifies plans as either "eligible" or "ineligible." "Eligible" plans are known as Section 457(b) plans, whereas "ineligible" plans are known as Section 457(f) plans. In eligible plans of government employers, deferred income and its earnings are tax free until paid to participants or beneficiaries. In eligible plans of nongovernment tax-exempt employers, deferred income and its earnings are tax free until paid or made available to participants or beneficiaries. In an ineligible plan, amounts deferred must be subject to a "substantial risk of forfeiture." Unlike eligible plans, ineligible plans place no limit on the amount of deferrals made. Employers, therefore, can use ineligible plans to allow employees a contribution level above the eligible plan limit or to provide supplemental retirement benefits to selected executives. However, ineligible plans are better suited for employer contributions than for salary reduction because of the "substantial risk of forfeiture" provision.

- For eligible Section 457(b) plans maintained by tax-exempt organizations, deferred amounts and earnings must remain the sole property of the employer until made available to participants, subject only to the claims of the employer's general creditors. However, eligible Section 457(b) plans maintained by government organizations are required to hold all plan assets in a trust, custodial account, or annuity contract for the exclusive benefit of participants and their beneficiaries.

- Most Section 457 plans are maintained by state and local government employers for the purpose of salary reduction. Without these plans, governmental employers would be precluded from offering salary deferral opportunities that are common among for-profit employers. Section 457 plans used for purposes other than salary reduction are less common but are rapidly gaining in importance. Nongovernment tax-exempt employers can use eligible 457(b) plans to provide supplemental retirement benefits and salary continuation to certain high-paid executives. Nongovernment tax-exempt employers can also use ineligible Section 457(f) plans to provide supplemental retirement benefits and salary continuation to certain high-paid executives.

Key Terms

catch-up provision, p. *171*

constructive receipt, p. *169*

economic benefit, p. *169*

eligible Section 457(b) plans, p. *170*

government employers, p. *169*

ineligible Section 457(f) plans, p. *170*

made available, p. *168*

pure deferred compensation plans, p. *169*

"substantial risk of forfeiture," p. *175*

supplemental benefit plans, p. *169*

tax-exempt organizations, p. *169*

unsecured promise to pay, p. *169*

Questions for Review

1. What is the purpose of a deferred compensation plan?
2. Distinguish between deferred compensation plans structured as pure deferred compensation plans and those structured as supplemental benefit arrangements.
3. Explain the tax "doctrines" of economic benefit and constructive receipt.
4. Which types of organizations may utilize Section 457 plans?
5. How do eligible employers generally use Section 457 plans?
6. Can independent contractors participate in eligible Section 457 plans?
7. Explain how coordination between maximum deferrals in eligible 457(b) plans and amounts excluded from income under other types of deferral arrangements has changed over time.
8. Describe the different funding requirements of eligible 457(b) plans depending on whether the sponsor is a tax-exempt organization or a governmental organization.
9. Can all eligible 457(b) plans offer loans to their participants?
10. Describe the characteristics of ineligible 457(f) plans.
11. What types of benefits generally are excluded from Section 457 restrictions and are not viewed as providing compensation deferral?

Questions for Discussion

1. Compare and contrast governmental Section 457 plans to similar types of plans utilized by for-profit corporate employers in the private sector.
2. How might tax-exempt employers utilize Section 457 plans as part of their executive compensation total rewards to compete for executive talent in the private sector?

Resources for Further Study

CCH Editorial Staff. "Legislation 2006: Pension Protection Act of 2006: Law, Explanation and Analysis." *Commerce Clearing House* (2006).

Deloitte Editorial Staff. "Overview of Final Section 457 Regulations." *Deloitte's Washington Bulletin*, (July 23, 2003).

Kline, S. Howard. "'Rolling Vesting' May Remain Viable for Ineligible Section 457 Plans Notwithstanding Section 409A," *Tax Advisory*: Buchanan, Ingersoll & Rooney, PC, (August, 2006).

Ryterband, Daniel J. and Richard L. Alpern. "Section 457 Deferred Compensation Plans." *The Handbook of Employee Benefits*. 6th ed. Jerry S. Rosenbloom, ed. New York: McGraw-Hill, 2005.

11

Behavioral Finance Impacts on Defined Contribution Plan Designs

After studying this chapter you should be able to:

- Summarize some of the inroads that behavioral finance has made in explaining the actions and decisions of individual investors as they save and invest for retirement.
- Describe some of the unique challenges that a defined contribution retirement system faces related to individual responsibility and behavioral choice by plan participants.
- Explain how plan sponsor thought is evolving in reaction to behavioral finance findings and their implications for plan design of defined contribution retirement plans.
- Discuss legislative and regulatory initiatives advanced by governmental policymakers that allow plan sponsors to use behavioral finance findings to increase retirement security for plan participants.
- Explain specific features being used by retirement plan designers to capitalize on behavioral finance findings and the specific outcomes these specific features seek to achieve when implemented in a retirement plan.
- Describe the receptivity of retirement plan stakeholders to these new behavioral finance features and the marketplace evolution in accepting these features.

This chapter introduces the field of study known as **behavioral finance** or behavioral economics. This field of study is relatively new and is concerned with economic decision making by individuals and groups of individuals. Behavioral finance is highly relevant to retirement plan design, particularly because the private pension system has shifted from a defined benefit basis to a system where defined contribution structures are in the majority. The defined contribution plan designs that have evolved in the market, have to a large extent, depended on the individual plan participant to make a series of complex decisions that determine his or her long-term retirement security. In the past, many economic models assumed that individuals were rational decision makers who could be expected to pursue their own self-interest. Accordingly, there was the underlying assumption that individuals would adequately provide for their own retirement security if given the option to participate and manage assets through a well-designed, defined contribution retirement plan.

Unfortunately, reality does not align with this assumption. Many workers who are eligible to participate in a well-designed retirement plan fail to enroll. Many individuals even forego generous employer-matching contributions by not participating in the plans offered by their employers. Even those workers who do enroll and participate in the plan often contribute at a level that will not provide an income stream in retirement that is commensurate with their preretirement earnings history. Many of the investment choices made in self-directing the underlying assets within defined contribution plans also appear to be less than optimal. Investors do not adequately diversify, they have shown a propensity to concentrate too much of their portfolios in employer stock, they do not adjust asset allocations over time, and they will not rebalance portfolios on a regular basis to limit risk. Asset allocations may be too conservative or are concentrated in market sectors whose volatility will be highly damaging over a market cycle. Some employees trade too often in their accounts and seem to be insensitive to exorbitant fund expense ratios. The same irrational behavior that seems to pervade employees' careers when they should be accumulating sufficient retirement resources to sustain them during the retirement years appears to pervade their choices when it comes to disbursing assets during the retirement years. As was noted in Chapter 4 when retirement risks were chronicled, employees will withdraw lump sums, underestimate life expectancies, make distribution decisions inconsistent with life circumstances, and generally run the risk of exhausting the resources they have stockpiled for retirement. In short, both during the accumulation period and during the distribution period, those individuals directing their retirement accounts using defined contribution plans appear to make poor decisions.

Behavioral finance seeks to explain the behavior and decisions of individuals. To the extent that behavioral finance can explain individual decision making and investor choices, those designing retirement plans for employers may incorporate these behavioral finance findings as they draft plan provisions. In fact, the whole realm of retirement planning seems like a highly practical area in which to apply the research findings of behavioral finance. Employers engaging in retirement plan design and attempting to promote the long-term financial security of their workers appear to be capable of extracting immense benefit from the research findings of behavioral finance. Not only have employers seen value in behavioral finance, but also legislators and government regulators have referenced behavioral finance findings when enacting legislation and issuing regulatory guidance. Governmental policymakers have seen the value in behavioral finance research in assisting them to establish requirements for retirement plans that will create the proper incentives to guide the decisions of individual plan participants. This was evidenced by references to behavioral finance research in the proposed rules on default investment alternatives described later in the chapter.

What Is Behavioral Finance?

Behavioral finance and behavioral economics are fields of study that apply the use of scientific research techniques to understand social, cognitive, and emotional biases that affect and influence economic decision making. These fields of study concentrate on the decisions of individual and collective economic agents and study whether the decisions they make are entirely rational or seem to lack rationality. The economic models developed by behavioral theorists combine the study of psychology with neoclassical economic theory. Although classical economics recognized that psychological elements have influenced how economic agents perceive "utility," or the derived sense of benefit from their decisions, neoclassical economists moved away from placing prominence on these psychological factors. Neoclassical economists sought to position economics as a more rigorous discipline, much like a physical science. Their models tended to assume rational economic agents who sought to maximize their profit or utility. Still, many prominent economic thinkers during the neoclassical period included psychological factors as influencing certain economic decisions. However, certain economic thinkers started in-depth research on decision-making using findings from psychology. A seminal academic research paper was written by Amos Tversky and Daniel Kahneman in 1979.[1] It used cognitive psychological techniques to explain a number of documented anomalies in rational economic decision making. In 2002, Daniel Kahneman was awarded the Nobel Prize in Economics "for having integrated insights from psychological research into economic science, especially concerning human judgment and decision-making under uncertainty."[2]

There are certain key themes that have emerged in the study of behavioral economics although the field is still in its infancy. Among these key themes are the following:

- **Heuristics:** People often make decisions based on approximate, so-called rules of thumb that are not entirely grounded in strictly rational analyses. These shortcuts to decision making can result from difficulty in assembling all of the relevant information to make the decision or from limitations on the decision maker's capabilities or competencies. This theme indicates that decision outcomes often fall short of the optimal positive determinations suggested by neoclassical economists. In an attempt to develop scientifically rigorous economic models during the neoclassical period, the realities and limitations posed by information gaps and agent abilities were avoided and ignored.

- **Framing:** The way a problem or decision is presented to the decision maker will affect his or her action. Similar to the first theme, the outcome that results is less than optimal. Importantly, decision makers seem to be influenced by the depiction of the choice, and their decisions appear to be susceptible to manipulation. This theme has both negative and positive implications. On the negative side, it suggests that economic agents' decisions can be flawed and are far less reliable and

---

[1] Amos Tversky and Daniel Kahneman, "Prospect Theory: Decision Makeup Under Risk," *Journal of Risk and Uncertainty* 5, no. 4 (1992), pp. 297–323.

[2] *Behavioral Finance,* Wikipedia (February 3, 2007), p. 2.

logical than previously envisioned by neoclassical economists. On the positive side, however, is the potential promise that decisions framed differently can guide decision makers to make more optimal choices.

- **Market inefficiencies:** There are explanations for observed market outcomes that diverge from what would be expected if market efficiency were present.[3] The real-life outcomes that previously appeared as aberrations that were unexplainable by well-conceived economic modeling are now seen as explainable once social, cognitive, and emotional biases are recognized. No longer must observable conditions in the real world be deemed unexplainable or mysteriously incongruent with logical economic modeling. The introduction of a more accurate portrayal of human economic agents explains market conditions.

Essentially these themes depict a world in which individuals make decisions that result in outcomes that are far different from the rational expectations portrayed by neoclassical economists. These themes depict a world in which individuals make decisions with incomplete information, are likely to be influenced by the way the decision is presented, and make suboptimal choices as a result. Although this model is one of suboptimal choice and inefficiency, it allows for the facilitation of better decision making by framing the decisions differently. The application of behavioral finance is very appropriate in the context of self-directed, defined contribution plan management. With these types of plans, individual participants are faced with the opportunity to make decisions that will enhance their long-term financial security.

Behavioral Finance and Retirement Planning

As noted in previous chapters, the United States and some other countries have retirement systems that primarily involve voluntary private pensions and retirement savings vehicles sponsored by employers. Although certain hybrid plans combining elements of defined benefit and defined contribution plans exist, most retirement plans are either defined benefit or defined contribution in structure. Defined benefit plans entail a set formula that dictates a participant's benefit at retirement. The vast majority of these employer-sponsored defined benefit pension plans have historically been entirely financed through employer contributions and did not require employees to contribute their personal savings into these plans. In contrast, defined contribution plans have no established formula to determine a benefit but rely on the accumulation of assets over time to provide an account whose distributions will fund retirement. Contributions into the account as well as investment results over time will determine the adequacy of the resource base that will fund retirement distributions.

When employers are using a defined contribution type of plan as the primary retirement plan, they will frequently make employer contributions into these plans but often also will require employees to contribute in order to receive an employer match. The fact that employees can save on a tax-deferred basis using a 401(k) provision, as explained in Chapter 8, makes saving through 401(k) plans a highly efficient way to accumulate

---

[3] Ibid., pp. 2–3.

resources for retirement needs. The 401(k) plan has become the most common type of defined contribution plan. The majority of 401(k) plans allow their participants to direct the selection of investments among various choices.

The relative importance of defined contribution retirement plan structures has surpassed use of the defined benefit model. According to a Department of Labor Study published in 2005, considerably more than twice as many workers are active participants in defined contribution plans than are participants in defined benefit plans.[4] If the defined contribution structures in use are examined, one can see that a considerable amount of responsibility rests with the individual participant. Essentially the worker must choose to participate, to set a contribution rate, to select various investments, and ultimately to decide how funds are withdrawn from the account. All of these decisions are complex determinations. With the shift in emphasis from defined benefit plans to defined contribution approaches and with the elements of defined contribution plan design that place many responsibilities for decision making on the individual participant, the study of behavioral finance and behavioral economics is very relevant to the study and design of retirement plans.

Behaviorists and Investment Decision Making[5]

Through research, behaviorists have uncovered several insights regarding individual investor patterns of decision making. Some of these insights show a passive avoidance of decision making by individuals, while others show anomalies when individuals make active choices regarding investments. Behaviorists have determined that individuals have certain proclivities and tendencies that forestall them from even approaching the subject and initiating action that is in their long-term interest. But even if individuals surpass the passive factors resulting in inactivity, their active choices are less than optimal. This section lists both factors resulting in inactivity as well as factors resulting in suboptimal active choices:

Factors Resulting in Inactivity

Individual Investors Are Loss-Averse

Prospect theory as developed by Kahneman and Tversky found that individuals suffer more remorse as a result of losses than they experience satisfaction or pleasure for their gains.[6] Essentially individuals do not rate gains and losses of equal magnitude equally. Tversky and Kahneman tried to measure the disparity in **loss aversion** versus gain satisfaction. They found that on average, if a loss and gain were of the same magnitude, individuals felt more remorse for losses by a factor of 2 or 2.5 times the satisfaction felt

[4] John Turner, "Lessons from Behavioral Finance," *Benefits Quarterly* (Fourth Quarter 2006), p. 24.

[5] Jodi DiCenzo, "Behavioral Finance and Retirement Plan Contributions: How Participants Behave, and Prescriptive Solutions," Employee Benefit Research Institute Issue Brief No. 301 (January 2007). This issue brief provides considerable detail on the specific behavioral biases affecting decisions by retirement plan participants.

[6] Tversky and Kahneman, "Advances in Prospect Theory: Cumulative Representation of Uncertainty." Journal of Risk and Uncertainty. No. 5, (1992), pp. 297–323.

for a gain. The implication of this finding is that convincing individuals to forego present consumption for a future payment at a later date may be difficult. In short, it is a challenge from the outset to convince many individuals to save for retirement.

Hyperbolic Discounting

Apart from sheer loss aversion that results from foregoing current consumption, individuals tend to overemphasize immediate desires and rewards at the expense of their longer-term needs. Not surprisingly, the present needs consistently present themselves as more pressing. **Hyperbolic discounting** is the human tendency, when faced with uncertainty, to sharply reduce the importance of the future in the decision-making process. Consequences that occur at a later time, good or bad, tend to have a lot less bearing on choices when they occur in the future. Survey results have shown that 25 percent of workers who have access to a defined contribution plan fail to contribute at all, while fewer than 10 percent will contribute at the maximum level allowed under the law.[7] Furthermore, consumption levels tend to progress upward as income levels increase. Individuals have a proclivity to spend more as they earn more.

Procrastination and Inertia

Individuals have a tendency to delay making decisions and have difficulty once they delay a decision to take action to change their course or direction. Inactivity in decision making tends to have a "stickiness" that demands more effort to overcome once a decision is delayed, deferred, or avoided. **Procrastination** may result from a bias toward the status quo that is described next. At times, a decision to maintain the status quo may make rational sense, but at other times, particularly when the cost of a delayed decision is high, the preferential bias toward the status quo is clearly irrational. For instance, when an employee is willing to forego an employer match in a 401(k) plan, procrastination and **inertia** are clearly irrational.

Status Quo Bias

Closely related to procrastination and perhaps overlapping with procrastination and inertia is **status quo bias.** When comparing actively making decisions or taking a positive step or decisive move, individuals have a proclivity to prefer the status quo, or the prevailing condition. As cited in the previous example, status quo bias is not irrational when the decision is cost-neutral or when uncertainty is so pronounced that the likelihood of a gainful outcome is highly suspect or unsure. However, an assured receipt of an employer matching contribution within a 401(k) plan is neither a cost-neutral situation nor an uncertain outcome. Quite the contrary: it is a delayed decision carrying a very high cost, especially when the effects of compounding are considered. However, the compounding effect is probably masked due to hyperbolic discounting.

Complexity

The decisions regarding selecting of investments and planning for retirement tend to involve a high level of **complexity** and are not easy for individuals to solve. When individuals attempt to save, invest, and plan for retirement, they need to make decisions

[7] John Turner, "Lessons from Behavioral Finance," *Benefits Quarterly* (Fourth Quarter 2006), p. 25.

under uncertainty. These decisions involve weighing a number of competing factors, assigning priorities to these factors, projecting certain trends and expectations into the future, and performing complicated computations that individuals cannot easily intuitively assign values. In short, even if one desires to plan for retirement, reducing the problem to a manageable basis is not an easy exercise. In fact, many individuals find the nature of the decision to entail such complication, that they need significant professional assistance to design their personal plan if they are to plan effectively.

Choice Overload

Many times when individuals approach this complicated decision they are faced with a large and perplexing set of alternative choices. The decision is complicated enough, but the innumerable different possible scenarios and the proliferation of options within retirement planning structures expand the possible choices that individuals may select. The sheer volume of choices, or **choice overload,** often serves to result in a "paralysis of analysis" and an inability to settle on a decisive course of action.[8]

Factors Resulting in Suboptimal Active Choices

Bounded Rationality

Even if individuals do not succumb to choice overload and look to make concrete decisions, the odds against making optimal choices are formidable, a condition known as **bounded rationality.** Individuals have limitations regarding their mental capabilities to deal with problems involving the high degree of complexity that appears to be inherent in retirement planning. Neoclassical economists minimized the existence of constraints on human intelligence and problem-solving ability. Their insistence on human rationality and logic ignored the difficulties presented by complex problems and uncertain outcomes. Hence, their portrayal of economic agents assumed capabilities exceeding the skill-set of many individuals.

Overweighting of Past Performance

Investors seem to **overweight past performance** as an indicator of future performance, particularly when reviewing the performance of mutual funds. Funds routinely caution prospective investors that past performance is not a guarantee of future performance. Nevertheless, investors tend to disregard this caution. In a sense, investors may be relying on the only information, or what they consider the best information, they possess regarding a gauge of the fund's performance. However, all too often the investor is more likely to experience reversion to the mean in future years, rather than continued above-average performance by a given fund manager. It also should be noted that fund families often heavily advertise those funds within their family of funds that have turned in a stellar performance. Many investors may be reacting to the advertising stimuli they are receiving to a greater extent, rather than making a reasoned determination as to where to best direct their investable funds.

---

[8] Jodi DiCenzo, "Behavioral Finance and Retirement Plan Contributions: How Participants Behave, and Prescriptive Solutions," Employee Benefit Research Institute Issue Brief No. 301 (January 2007), pp. 7–10.

Effects of Savings Anchors

Not only are workers making decisions about how to invest their retirement assets, but workers also are making determinations regarding the appropriate level at which to save for retirement. This decision has enormous implications as to whether there will be sufficient resources to fund a comfortable retirement. Similar to investing decisions, savings decisions seem to be subject to certain biases, and anchors involve an initial starting point or level from which the decision maker adjusts. When one examines the level at which individuals save for retirement, one can identify the starting points from which individuals begin their decision process. Researchers have noted that so-called **savings anchors** vary with age and income. Those who are closer to retirement and possess higher incomes appear to anchor their savings to the maximum allowed under the law. Conversely, workers who are further from retirement and possess lower incomes tend to anchor their savings to the minimum level of contribution necessary to receive the full employer match. In both of these situations, it appears that the level of saving is affected more by the anchor and perhaps by affordability than by a computation of the necessary funds to sustain a certain income level during the retirement years.[9]

Investor Overconfidence

Many investors demonstrate an undue level of confidence that markedly contrasts with reality. In other words, those investors whose investing records appear to be abysmal seem to indicate in surveys that they are the most confident about their investing abilities. Researchers have found an inverse correlation between **investor overconfidence** and knowledge. Seemingly in agreement with this finding is the observation that in a retirement confidence survey, a significant percentage of those who were confident about their retirement were, in fact, not saving anything toward their retirement!

Peer Influence

Peers seem to have an effect on whether individuals choose to participate in retirement plan offerings. A study suggested the potency of **peer influences** by noting the high rates of participation within certain work groups at an employer. Peer effects would seem at odds with the view that saving and investing decisions are made by economic agents using a rational process.

Inappropriate Risk Discounting

Investors underestimate the risk of certain investments. Such **inappropriate risk discounting** seems to manifest itself when investors have a keen sense of familiarity with an investment. This is particularly true when one observes the risk that investors attach to company stock held within their retirement plans. Although a concentration of one's retirement investments in company stock fails to be a diversified investment and is even more risky since it is correlated with one's source of income, individuals have repeatedly shown a preference to concentrate their 401(k) holdings in company stock. This is risky

---

[9] Paul Yakoboski and Jack VanDerhei, "Contribution Rates and Plan Features: An Analysis of Large 401(k) Plan Data," EBRI Issue Brief Number 174 Employee Benefit Research Institute (June 1996), pp. 1–16.

since the individual may lose his or her job if the company experiences financial difficulties and simultaneously may see the value of his or her retirement plan plummet.[10]

Disposition Effect

When it comes to selling or disposing of assets, individuals appear to have biases against selling assets at a loss. Therefore, they will often liquidate assets that have appreciated and retain those investments where the market price has declined. This **disposition effect** does not mean that investors are rationally evaluating assets in terms of their long-term intrinsic value. Rather, many investors appear to be avoiding the regret they would experience in recognizing a loss. These investors show a propensity to hold onto some marginal or inferior investments while disposing of the more superior investments.[11]

Behavioral Finance: Research Findings to Actual Plan Designs

Once the elements of behavioral finance are recognized and the effects of social, cognitive, and emotional biases are explained, attempts can be made to mitigate the problematic aspects that accompany behavioral biases. In other words, prescriptive constructs can be implemented that will lessen the effects of human bias. This is particularly true in an area like retirement planning, where employer plan sponsors have wide latitude in designing their plan offerings. Employers have a vested interest in the success of their employees' retirement planning decisions, particularly for larger employers that perceive well-operating retirement plans as facilitating the ongoing replenishment of their workforce. The well-executed retirement decisions of employees will result in beneficial outcomes for employee and employer alike. Increased retirement plan wealth will allow for successful exodus from the active workforce and migration into retirement status by employees. This movement into retiree status on a systematic basis is a desirable outcome for the ongoing productive economic enterprise in need of rejuvenating its workforce. Since the United States and some other industrial societies are rooted in a reliance on private retirement systems, governmental policymakers will also see enhanced decision making by empowered plan participants as a worthy social objective. It should not be surprising that government policymakers are willingly embracing the findings of behavioral finance and enacting legislation that capitalizes on its findings.

   As previously noted, behavioral finance is a relatively young and recently developing field of study. Nevertheless, even at this recent juncture in its development, its findings have already been translated into social policy. The most comprehensive and far-reaching overhaul in pension policy over the last 30 years occurred with passage of the Pension Protection Act of 2006 (PPA), which was permeated with numerous provisions whose basis for enactment can be rationalized and justified using the precepts and findings of behavioral finance research. Not only can a supposition be made that these

[10] DiCenzo, "Behavioral Finance and Retirement Plan Contributions: How Participants Behave, and Prescriptive Solutions," pp. 7–13.

[11] Rhonda Evans, "Understanding Behavioral Finance," *The Inside Edition* (April 26, 2005), pp. 2–3.

policy determinations were made with a consideration of findings in behavioral finance research, but direct reference to behavioral finance research is included in some of the governmental regulations that have been issued to date interpreting the PPA. Specifically, the regulations explaining default investment alternatives under participant-directed individual account plans that were issued on September 27, 2006, made reference to several behavioral finance research studies. Before providing detailed explanations of these regulations, certain plan design approaches that have evolved in the marketplace as well as PPA provisions rooted in behavioral finance are presented.

Remedial Benefit Design Using Behavioral Finance Findings

Individual economic agents are not quite as logical as postulated by neoclassical economists. When making saving and investment decisions, individuals are prone to make less than optimal choices because of social, cognitive, and emotional biases. Therefore, plan sponsors, insurance companies, investment companies, and consultants who assist in designing retirement plans are now attempting to design the plans so as to mitigate the detrimental effects these biases can cause. Some of the more popular approaches introduced into the marketplace and clarified through governmental legislation and regulation are explained in this section.

Life Cycle Funds

Life cycle funds typically are mutual funds that are designed to facilitate asset allocation decisions based on the age of the plan participant. There are two basic types of lifestyle funds: **static allocation funds** and **targeted-maturity funds**.[12] When the static allocation approach is utilized, these funds maintain a fixed-asset allocation. A series of funds are typically offered to plan participants, with some funds being aggressive in terms of their risk level and other fund offerings exhibiting progressively less risk, until a decidedly minimal risk and more conservative fund is the final offering within the array of funds. Investors would determine which fund is appropriate for them given their individual risk tolerance. Often it would be suggested that individuals would be capable of using the more aggressive funds at younger ages, and it would generally be appropriate for individuals to transition into the less aggressive funds as they age and approach retirement. The second approach offers a series of funds with target retirement dates designated. An individual would select a fund with the approximate or exact year in which they are expecting to retire. Unlike the static allocation funds where an individual must take action to move from the more aggressive fund to less aggressive funds as he or she approaches retirement, the targeted-maturity funds automatically rebalance and shift investments from aggressive to more conservative asset allocations as the target date approaches. The final allocation as of the targeted date is often intended to remain intact throughout the retirement years.

---

[12] Catherine D. Gordon and Kimberly A. Stockton, "Funds for Retirement: The 'Life-Cycle' Approach," Vanguard Investment Counseling & Research, The Vanguard Group (2006), p. 2.

Progressive Increases in Savings Rates

Under the **progressive increases in savings rates** approach (suggested by Thaler and Benartzi), decisions are made considerably in advance of pay raises to commit to increased retirement savings at those future times when pay is raised. The proposed Save More Tomorrow (SMT) Program involves the following actions:

> First, employees are approached about increasing their retirement plan contribution rates a considerable time before their scheduled pay increase. Second, if employees join, their contribution to the plan is increased beginning with the first paycheck after a raise. This feature mitigates the perceived loss aversion of a cut in take-home pay. Third, the contribution rate continues to increase on each scheduled raise award date until the contribution rate reaches a preset maximum. Fourth, the employee is able to opt out of the plan at any time. This possibility to exit the plan is seen as necessary to make employees comfortable with joining the plan.[13]

Automatic Enrollment

Many employees who are eligible for participation in an employer-sponsored retirement plan fail to enroll. Some of these employees may let a considerable period of time elapse between their initial time of allowed eligibility and the date when they actually sign up for the plan. Many employees will even forego employer-matching contributions that they could have received if they had enrolled when they first became eligible to enroll. The practice of **automatic enrollment** involves a requirement that an individual become a plan member when initially eligible unless the individual makes a negative election to the contrary to decline plan participation. This approach requires action by the individual to decline participation rather than the traditional approach that required action to become a plan member.

Default Investments

The issue of deciding on **default investments** is closely related to the practice of automatic enrollment. For a plan sponsor who has adopted the practice of automatically enrolling employees who become eligible for plan participation and fail to enroll, a contribution into a defined contribution plan that is self-directed by the employee presents a problem. Once a contribution is placed into the plan, a decision must be made concerning how the contribution is invested. In the past there was considerable concern as to how the plan sponsor should direct the investment of these funds. In the absence of instructions from the employee, should the employer make investments that were unlikely to sustain any losses as would be the case with a money market investment? Or, alternatively, should an employer invest using asset classes whose historical rate of return would provide a superior long-term outcome over an extended time horizon? As described later, the passage of the PPA brought greater clarity to this issue through its provisions on default investments and its mandate for the subsequently issued regulations.

It should be noted that many of the approaches suggested in this section assist the individual by calling for fewer active decisions on her or his part. Rather, the plan takes

---

[13] Richard H. Thaler and Shlomo Benartzi, "Save More Tomorrow: Using Behavioral Economics to Increase Employee Saving," *Journal of Political Economy* 112, no. 1 (2004), pp. 164–187.

action unless otherwise instructed by the participant and attempts to implement these steps systematically to serve the best long-term interest of the plan participants. For instance, a targeted-maturity life cycle fund avoids choice overload and investment decision biases by having the participant make a single election related to anticipated retirement date. Once this decision is made, appropriate initial asset allocations are made given the time horizon until retirement. Subsequently, these asset allocations are rebalanced on a systematic basis over the employee's career until a more conservative asset allocation is achieved at the point of retirement. In the same way that employees are freed from making a series of decisions regarding investments, the necessary decisions on increasing savings could be implemented using Thaler's and Benartzi's SMT program. With this program an employee would be assured that savings levels would continuously increase until the desired savings target was achieved. The sense of loss aversion would be avoided because the incremental adjustments to savings would be predetermined yet would not occur until an individual was receiving a pay raise. The SMT uses several biases to work toward the employee's long-term best interests. Hyperbolic discounting serves a favorable end when the lag between signup and startup of plan participation is lengthened. Loss aversion is avoided because there is no cut in take-home pay. Escalating contribution rates use inertia and status quo bias to assist in keeping people in the plan.[14] For those employees who have failed to initiate action to join the plan, the use of automatic enrollment and default investments builds to favorable long-term retirement resources without the individual having taken any action. As can be seen from this discussion, behavioral finance uses the social, cognitive, and emotional biases that have traditionally hampered employee welfare and redirects these biases in such a way as to promote outcomes that enhance employee retirement security.

Legislation and Regulation Encouraging Behavioral Finance Plan Designs[15]

The PPA of 2006 provided relief from liability to fiduciaries who invest participant assets in certain types of default investment alternatives in the absence of participant investment direction. The PPA directed that such regulations provide guidance on the appropriateness of designating default investments that include a mix of asset classes consistent with capital preservation or long-term capital appreciation, or a blend of both. Under the law, a participant in an individual account plan is treated as exercising control over the assets in the account if the sponsor invests in default investments and conforms to the requirements of the regulations. This exercise of control applies to the amount of contributions and earnings on the contributions when, in the absence of an election by the participant, the plan sponsor invests the assets in accordance with the regulations prescribed by the U.S. Secretary of Labor. These regulations were issued on September 27,

[14] Ibid., pp. 164–187.

[15] Department of Labor Employee Benefits Security Administration, "Default Investment Alternatives Under Participant Directed Individual Account Plans; Proposed Rule," 29 CFR Part 2550 (September 27, 2006), pp. 56806–56824.

2006, and were entitled, "Default Investment Alternatives Under Participant Directed Individual Account Plans."

If the plan sponsor is to receive relief from liability, each participant must receive, within a reasonable period of time before each plan year, a notice explaining the employee's right under the plan to designate how contributions and earnings will be invested and explaining how, in the absence of any investment election by the participant, such contributions and earnings will be invested. Additionally, participants must have a reasonable period of time after receipt of such notice and before the beginning of the plan year to make such a designation. Such a notice must be sufficiently accurate and comprehensive to apprise the employee of such rights and obligations, and be written in a manner calculated to be understood by the average employee eligible to participate.

The relief provided by the proposed regulation is conditioned on the use of certain investment alternatives, but the limitations of the proposed regulation are not to be construed to indicate that the use of investment alternatives not identified in the regulation as qualified default investment alternatives are imprudent. The regulation specifically indicated that investments in money market funds, stable value products and similarly performing investment vehicles may be prudent for some participants or beneficiaries. There are six conditions to qualify for this fiduciary relief. The six conditions are as follows:

Condition 1

Assets must be invested in a **qualified default investment alternative.** There are five requirements for a qualified default investment alternative:

1. A qualified default investment alternative shall not hold or permit the acquisition of employer securities. There are two exceptions to this prohibition, however. First, it does not apply to employer securities held or acquired by an investment company registered under the Investment Company Act of 1940 or a similar pooled investment vehicle subject to regulation. Essentially, this exception allows for holdings in mutual funds and other pooled funds. Without this exception, it would become onerously complex to make sure that no diversified mutual fund held any stock of the employer in question. Second, there is an exception for employer securities acquired as a matching contribution from the employer or plan sponsor or at the direction of the participant or beneficiary. This exception ensures that an investment management service will not be precluded from serving as a qualified default investment alternative merely because the account of a participant or beneficiary holds employer securities acquired as matching contributions from the employer or plan sponsor, or acquired as a result of prior direction by the participant or beneficiary, provided that the investment management service has the authority to dispose of such securities.
2. A qualified default investment alternative may not impose financial penalties or otherwise restrict the ability of a participant or beneficiary to transfer, in whole or in part, his or her investment from the qualified default investment alternative to any other investment alternative available under the plan.
3. A qualified default investment alternative must either be managed by an investment manager as specified under ERISA, or by an investment company registered under

the Investment Company Act of 1940. The Labor Department believes that when plan fiduciaries are relieved of liability for underlying investment management or asset allocation decisions, those responsible for the investment management or asset allocation decisions must be investment professionals who acknowledge their fiduciary responsibilities and liability under ERISA. For this reason, the regulation requires that, except in the case of registered investment companies, those responsible for the management of a qualified default investment alternative be "investment managers" as defined by ERISA.

4. A qualified default investment alternative must be diversified so as to minimize the risk of large losses.

5. A qualified default investment alternative conditions relief on the use of one of three types of investment products, portfolios, or services. In defining qualified default investment alternatives, the U.S. Department of Labor presumes that the only objective and readily available information available to the plan sponsor that is relevant to making an investment decision on behalf of the participant is age. For this reason, the investment objectives of the qualified default investment alternatives are not required to consider other factors, such as risk tolerances, other investment assets, etc. The three types of investment products, portfolios or services include:

   a. An investment fund product or model portfolio that is designed to provide varying degrees of long-term appreciation and capital preservation through a mix of equity and fixed-income exposures based on the participant's age, target retirement date (such as normal retirement age under the plan), or life expectancy. Such products and portfolios change their asset allocation and associated risk levels over time with the objective of becoming more conservative (i.e., decreasing risk of losses) with increasing age. An example of such a fund or portfolio may be a life cycle or targeted-retirement-date fund or account. It should be noted that the reference to an investment fund product or model portfolio was used to allow for a stand-alone product, or a fund of funds offering, comprised of various investment options otherwise available under the plan for participant investments. When a fund of funds portfolio is used, it is likely that money market, stable value, and similarly performing capital preservation vehicles play a role in comprising the mix of equity and fixed-income exposures.

   b. An investment fund product or model portfolio that is designed to provide long-term appreciation and capital preservation through a mix of equity and fixed-income exposures consistent with a target level of risk appropriate for participants of the plan as a whole. For purposes of this alternative, asset allocation decisions for such products and portfolios are not required to take into account the age of an individual participant, but rather focus on the demographics of the participant population as a whole. An example of such a fund or portfolio may be a **balanced fund.** As noted in item 5a, a stand-alone or fund-of-funds approach are both acceptable under this alternative.

   c. An investment management service where an investment manager allocates the assets of a participant's individual account to achieve varying degrees of long-term appreciation and capital preservation through a mix of equity and fixed-income exposures, offered through investment alternatives available under the plan, based on the participant's age, target retirement date (such as normal retirement date under the plan), or life expectancy. Such portfolios change their asset allocation and associated risk levels over time with the objective of becoming more conservative (i.e., decreasing risk of losses) with increasing age. An example of such a service may be a **managed account.**

Condition 2

The participant or beneficiary on whose behalf assets are being invested in a qualified default investment alternative had the opportunity to direct the investment of assets in his or her account but did not direct the assets.

Condition 3

The participant or beneficiary on whose behalf an investment in a qualified default investment alternative may be made is furnished a notice within a reasonable period of time (at least 30 days), in advance of each subsequent plan year. The required notice can be furnished in the plan's summary plan description, summary of material modifications, or as a separate notification.

Condition 4

The terms of the plan must require that any material provided to the plan relating to a participant's or beneficiary's investment in a qualified default investment alternative (e.g., account statements, prospectuses, proxy voting material) be provided to the participant or beneficiary.

Condition 5

Any participant or beneficiary on whose behalf assets are invested in a qualified default investment alternative must be afforded the opportunity, consistent with the terms of the plan (but in no event less frequently than once within any three-month period), to transfer, in whole or in part, such assets to any other investment alternative available under the plan without financial penalty. This provision ensures that participants and beneficiaries on whose behalf assets are invested in a qualified default investment alternative have the same opportunities as other plan participants and beneficiaries to direct the investment of their assets. This provision does not confer greater rights on participants or beneficiaries' whose accounts are invested in qualified default investment alternatives by the plan than are otherwise available under the plan with respect to the timing of investment decisions.

Condition 6

The plan must offer participants and beneficiaries the opportunity to invest in a broad range of investment alternatives as specified in the Section 404(c) regulation. The Department of Labor (DOL) believes that participants and beneficiaries should have access to a sufficient range of investment alternatives to achieve a diversified portfolio with aggregate risk and return characteristics at any point within the range normally appropriate for the pension plan participant or beneficiary. The DOL believes that the application of the broad range of investment alternatives standard of the Section 404(c) regulation accomplishes this.

It is expected that more retirement plan sponsors will adopt automatic enrollment or change their current practices regarding automatic enrollment. Plan sponsors will introduce or conform their existing default investment policies to align with the qualified default investment alternatives identified in the regulations. To date, many plan sponsors have already made some of these types of investment alternatives available to plan participants as either default investments or as choices they can actively select. Increased use of these investment choices indicates that plan participants are receptive to these types of investment choices.

Chapter Summary

- Behavioral finance and behavioral economics are fields of study that apply the use of scientific research techniques to understand social, cognitive, and emotional biases that affect and influence economic decision making. These fields of study concentrate on the decisions of individual and collective economic agents and study whether the decisions they make are entirely rational or seem to lack rationality. The economic models developed by behavioral theorists combine the study of psychology with neoclassical economic theory.

- There are certain key themes that have emerged in the study of behavioral economics although the field is still in its infancy. Among these key themes are the following:

  - *The theme of heuristics:* People often make decisions based on approximate, so-called rules of thumb that are not entirely grounded in strictly rational analyses. These shortcuts to decision making can result from difficulty in assembling all of the relevant information to make the decision or from limitations on the decision maker's capabilities or competencies.

  - *The theme of framing:* The way a problem or decision is presented to the decision maker will affect his or her action. Importantly, decision makers seem to be influenced by the depiction of the choice, and their decisions appear to be susceptible to manipulation.

  - *The theme of market inefficiencies:* There are explanations for observed market outcomes that diverge from what would be expected if market efficiency were present.

- With the shift in emphasis from defined benefit plans to defined contribution approaches and with the elements of defined contribution plan design that place many responsibilities for decision making on the individual participant, the study of behavioral finance and behavioral economics is very relevant to the study and design of retirement plans.

- Through research, behaviorists have uncovered several insights into individual investor patterns of decision making. Some of these insights show a passive avoidance of decision making by individuals, while others show anomalies when individuals make active choices regarding investments.

- Once the elements of behavioral finance are recognized and the effects of social, cognitive, and emotional biases are explained, attempts can be made to mitigate the problematic aspects that accompany behavioral biases. In other words, prescriptive constructs can be implemented that will lessen the effects of human bias. This is particularly true in an area like retirement planning, where employer plan sponsors have wide latitude in designing their plan offerings.

- The Pension Protection Act of 2006 (PPA) was permeated with numerous provisions whose basis for enactment can be rationalized and justified using the precepts and findings of behavioral finance research. Not only can a supposition be made that these policy determinations were made with a consideration of findings in behavioral finance research, but direct reference to behavioral finance research is included in some of the governmental regulations that have been issued to date interpreting the PPA.

- Life cycle funds are mutual funds that are designed to facilitate asset allocation decisions based on the age of the plan participant. There are two basic types of lifestyle funds: static allocation funds and targeted-maturity funds. When the static allocation approach is utilized, these funds maintain a fixed-asset allocation. A series of funds are typically offered to plan participants, with some funds being aggressive in terms of their risk level and other fund offerings exhibiting progressively less risk, until a decidedly minimal risk and more conservative fund is the final offering within the array of funds. The second approach offers a series of funds with target retirement dates designated. An individual would select a fund with the approximate or exact year in which they are expecting to retire. Unlike the static allocation funds, where an individual must take action to move from the more aggressive fund to less aggressive funds as one approaches retirement, the targeted-maturity funds automatically rebalances and switches investments from aggressive to more conservative asset allocations as the target date approaches. The final allocation as of the targeted date is often intended to remain intact throughout the retirement years.

- The practice of automatic enrollment involves a requirement that an individual become a plan member when initially eligible unless the individual makes a negative election to the contrary to decline plan participation. This approach requires action by the individual to decline participation rather than the traditional approach that required action to become a plan member.

- The issue of deciding on default investments is closely related to the practice of automatic enrollment. For a plan sponsor who has adopted the practice of automatically enrolling employees who become eligible for plan participation and fail to enroll, a contribution into a defined contribution plan that is self-directed by the employee presents a problem. Once a contribution is placed into the plan, a decision must be made concerning how the contribution is invested.

- The PPA of 2006 provided relief from liability to fiduciaries who invest participant assets in certain types of default investment alternatives in the absence of participant investment direction. The PPA directed that such regulations provide guidance on the appropriateness of designating default investments that include a mix of asset classes consistent with capital preservation or long-term capital appreciation, or a blend of both. Under the law, a participant in an individual account plan is treated as exercising control over the assets in the account if the sponsor invests in default investments and conforms to the requirements of the regulations.

- The relief provided by the proposed regulation is conditioned on the use of certain investment alternatives, but the limitations of the proposed regulation should not be construed to indicate that the use of investment alternatives not identified in the regulation as qualified default investment alternatives would be imprudent. A qualified default investment alternative conditions relief on the use of one of three types of investment products, portfolios, or services. Examples of investment alternatives meeting these conditions are (1) a life cycle or targeted-retirement-date fund or account, (2) a balanced fund, and (3) a managed account.

Key Terms

automatic enrollment, p. *194*

balanced fund, p. *197*

behavioral finance, p. *184*

bounded rationality, p. *190*

choice overload, p. *190*

complexity, p. *189*

default investments, p. *194*

disposition effect, p. *192*

framing, p. *186*

heuristics, p. *186*

hyperbolic discounting, p. *189*

inappropriate risk discounting, p. *191*

inertia, p. *189*

investor overconfidence, p. *191*

life cycle funds, p. *193*

loss aversion, p. *188*

managed account, p. *198*

market inefficiencies, p. *187*

overweighting past performance, p. *190*

peer influence, p. *191*

procrastination, p. *189*

progressive increases in savings rates, p. *194*

qualified default investment alternative, p. *196*

savings anchors, p. *191*

static allocation life cycle funds, p. *193*

status quo bias, p. *189*

targeted-maturity life cycle funds, p. *193*

Questions for Review

1. What is behavioral finance?
2. What are some of the key themes that have emerged in the study of behavioral economics?
3. In the context of making investment decisions, distinguish between passive factors resulting in inactivity and active choices that are less than optimal.
4. Discuss types of biases that result in investors being passive or inactive about investing.
5. Discuss types of biases that result in investors making active choices that are less than optimal.

6. How can the identification of investor biases be helpful in improving individual investor decision making?

7. Has behavioral finance had an impact on employers offering defined contribution retirement plans?

8. Have behavioral finance research findings had an impact on governmental policy relative to defined contribution retirement plans? Explain.

9. List and explain some remedial benefit design features using behavioral finance research findings.

10. How does the Pension Protection Act of 2006 (PPA) encourage plan sponsors to invest assets in a way consistent with capital preservation and/or long-term capital appreciation in the absence of participant investment direction?

11. What six conditions are used to qualify a fiduciary for relief from fiduciary liability when investing participant assets in default investment alternatives?

12. What are the five requirements for a default investment to be deemed a qualified default investment alternative?

Questions for Discussion

1. Discuss what behavioral biases seem to affect an employee population participating in a defined contribution retirement plan you are familiar with, and describe prescriptive enhancements that could be made to the plan to lessen the effects of these behavioral biases.

2. Discuss the merits of the alternative choices a plan sponsor has regarding a qualified default investment alternative and what factors should determine which one of these choices is selected.

Resources for Further Study

Department of Labor Employee Benefits Security Administration, "Default Investment Alternatives Under Participant Directed Individual Account Plans; Proposed Rule," 29 CFR Part 2550 (September 27, 2006).

DiCenzo, Jodi. "Behavioral Finance and Retirement Plan Contributions: How Participants Behave, and Prescriptive Solutions," EBRI Issue Brief No. 301 (January 2007).

Evans, Rhonda. "Understanding Behavioral Finance: How to Minimize Plan Participant Investing Errors," *The Inside Edition* (April 26, 2005).

Greer, Boyce. "The Case for Age-Based Lifecycle Investing." Fidelity Investments Viewpoint Investment Concepts White Paper (2006).

Gordon, Catherine D.; and Kimberly A. Stockton. "Funds for Retirement: The 'Life-Cycle' Approach." Vanguard Investment Counseling & Research (2006).

Powell Goldstein LLP. "Pension Protection Act of 2006: Changes for Defined Contribution Plans." Client Alert: Employee Benefits & Executive Compensation (December 15, 2006).

Thaler, Richard H.; and Shlomo Benartzi. "Save More Tomorrow: Using Behavioral Economics to Increase Employee Saving." The Anderson School at UCLA (August 2001).

Turner, John. "Lessons from Behavioral Finance: Designing 401(k) Plans That Encourage Retirement Savings." *Benefits Quarterly* (Fourth Quarter 2006).

Wikipedia, *Behavioral Finance* (February 2007).

Chapter 12

Individual Retirement Arrangements

After studying this chapter you should be able to:

- Explain the characteristics and features of individual retirement accounts (IRAs).
- Distinguish between the various types of IRAs.
- Describe the eligibility requirements for the various types of IRAs.
- Discuss the contribution limits applicable to various types of IRAs.
- Explain the tax issues related to IRA distributions.
- Discuss prohibited transactions and other prohibitions related to IRAs.

Despite the rapid growth of the private pension system, more than 40 million American workers were not covered by qualified pension or profit sharing plans at the beginning of 1974. Congress, in recognition of this fact, included provisions in the Employee Retirement Income Security Act (ERISA) that would enable such individuals to establish their own retirement plans on a tax-deferred basis beginning in 1975. **Individual retirement arrangements (IRAs)** are defined contribution-type plans. An eligible individual could make tax-deductible contributions (up to prescribed limits) under such a plan, and the investment income earned on the contributions generally would be currently sheltered from income tax. Such contributions and investment income would be taxed as ordinary income as they were received or made available.

Over the years, Congress has made numerous changes regarding the workings of IRAs. As a result of these changes, there now are different types of IRAs with varying characteristics, various features, and differing tax treatments. This chapter describes the various types of IRAs available under current tax law and explains the distinct attributes of each type. IRAs remain a popular way for individuals to manage their own retirement assets. Often using IRAs to receive rollovers from other retirement planning vehicles, individuals bridge the gap between a qualified plan distribution on separation from service and drawing down retirement income. Funds transferred into an IRA in such a transaction continue to compound on a tax-deferred basis without being subject to current taxation.

IRAs also are used as funding vehicles by some employers (both incorporated and unincorporated) that sponsor simplified employee pension (SEP) plans and savings incentive match plans for employees (SIMPLE plans), discussed in Chapter 13. In lieu of using the more traditional qualified plans, employers use these more simplified retirement planning vehicles because, under present law, the requirements that must be met by a qualified pension plan are considerably more complex than the requirements applicable to SEPs and SIMPLE plans.

The Small Business Job Protection Act of 1996 eliminated the creation of salary reduction simplified employee pension (SARSEP) plans after December 31, 1996. Employers who created SARSEPs before January 1, 1997, can continue their use, including offering these arrangements to employees hired after January 1, 1997. The curtailment of SARSEPs resulted from the creation of SIMPLE plans, discussed in the next chapter. SIMPLE plans can be configured using either IRAs or 401(k) plans. A thorough understanding of IRAs is necessary to fully understand these simpler retirement structures that use IRAs as a basis on which the employer plan is built.

The Taxpayer Relief Act of 1997 created Roth IRAs, named after Senator William V. Roth, Jr., a sponsor of the 1997 act. Roth IRAs have unique tax advantages distinguishing them from the classic, or traditional IRAs. These unique tax advantages and differing requirements necessitate that Roth IRAs be separately presented.

In this chapter we look at traditional deductible IRAs, nondeductible IRAs, employer-sponsored IRAs, deemed IRAs[1] under employer plans, and Roth IRAs. As stated previously, IRAs can serve as the underlying plan structure for other plans such as SEPs, SARSEPs, and SIMPLEs. A detailed discussion of these IRA uses within the context of plans for the self-employed is reserved until these plans are discussed in Chapter 13.

General Eligibility and Contribution Limits

This section of the chapter discusses eligibility to establish an individual retirement arrangement and the various contribution limits. Also discussed are requirements relative to distributions and rollover provisions.

Eligibility to Establish IRAs

To be eligible to establish an individual retirement arrangement (IRA), an individual must have **earned income** from personal services—investment income does not qualify for such a plan.[2] If both an individual and spouse have compensation or self-employment income during a taxable year, each spouse may establish his or her own IRA. Community property laws do not apply to IRAs. If an individual is married and otherwise eligible to make IRA contributions and has a nonworking spouse, an IRA

---

[1] These are traditional or Roth IRAs allowed by EGTRRA starting in plan years beginning after 2002 to be implemented by employers without affecting the employer's other retirement plan offerings. Essentially these deemed IRAs permit employees to save for retirement conveniently through payroll withholdings.

[2] All alimony and separate maintenance paid under a divorce or separation instrument and includable in gross income is a compensation substitute for IRA purposes.

for the nonworking spouse also may be established, subject to certain limitations discussed later. IRAs also may be established by rollover contributions. For example, individuals who receive distributions from qualified plans, governmental 457(b) plans, or 403(b) arrangements[3] may roll over the funds received into an IRA. Also, funds invested in an IRA may be rolled over to another IRA. A death beneficiary of a qualified plan participant, a governmental 457(b) plan participant, a 403(b) arrangement owner, or an IRA owner also can establish an IRA by rolling over the death benefit.[4] A spouse receiving amounts from a qualified plan, governmental 457(b) plan, 403(b) arrangement, or an IRA in certain divorce-related circumstances also may roll over such amounts received into IRAs. Both the Economic Growth and Tax Relief Reconciliation Act of 2001 (EGTRRA) and the Pension Protection Act (PPA) of 2006 expanded the situations under which a plan distribution could be rolled over into an IRA. An expanded discussion of situations allowing for eligible rollovers is contained later in the chapter.

No restrictions exist on the number of individual retirement arrangements an individual may establish; however, the aggregate contributions made to all plans in a given year must not exceed the allowable contribution limits. As a practical matter, the combination of the maximum permissible contribution under law and the minimum contribution requirements of the financial institutions offering such plans effectively limits the number of plans that can be operated at the same time. (See the section, Selection of Funding Arrangement, p. 213.)

Contribution Limits

There is no dollar limit applied to **rollover contributions to IRAs.** Accordingly, the material in this portion of the chapter applies only to nonrollover contributions (referred to as "regular annual" IRA contributions).

Regular annual IRA contributions were limited to $2,000 or 100 percent of earned income for the taxable year, whichever was less prior to 2002. With the passage of EGTRRA in 2001, the annual contribution limit for IRAs was increased to $3,000 beginning in 2002. Additionally, beginning in 2002 EGTRRA allowed for IRA catch-up contributions for any taxpayers who were age 50 or older. When EGTRRA was passed, regular annual IRA contributions and IRA catch-up contributions were scheduled to increase in future years as noted in Table 12.1.

In any event, an individual ceases to be eligible to make regular annual contributions to either a traditional deductible or nondeductible IRA beginning with the taxable year in which the individual attains age 70½. Roth IRAs (discussed later in the chapter) permit regular annual contributions beyond age 70½ provided the individual has income from personal services as mentioned previously.

---

[3] See Chapter 9 for a discussion of 403(b) plans and Chapter 10 for a discussion of 457(b) plans.

[4] Prior to the passage of the Pension Protection Act of 2006, only spousal beneficiaries could roll over death benefits from various other retirement plans into IRAs. The PPA allows distributions from these retirement arrangements to an individual retirement account or individual retirement annuity for a nonspouse beneficiary for distributions occurring after December 31, 2006.

TABLE 12.1   Regular Annual and Catch-up Contributions for Traditional and Roth IRAs as Enacted by EGTRRA

Year	Regular Contribution Limit	Annual Contribution Limit for Individuals 50 and Over
2001	$2,000	$2,000 (No catch-up permitted by law)
2002–2004	$3,000	$3,500 (Including a $500 catch-up)
2005	$4,000	$4,500 (Including a $500 catch-up)
2006–2007	$4,000	$5,000 (Including a $1,000 catch-up)
2008 and later	$5,000 (Indexed in future years in $500 increments.)	$6,000 (Including a $1,000 catch-up) (Indexed in future years in $500 increments.)

If both an individual and spouse have compensation, then each spouse is eligible to contribute to his or her separate IRA up to the lesser of 100 percent of earned income or the allowable annual dollar limit, whichever is less, as shown in Table 12.1.

An otherwise eligible individual also may set up and contribute to one or more IRAs for a nonworking spouse or a spouse who elects to be treated as having no compensation for the year. Under a spousal IRA plan of this type, the spouses must file a joint income tax return. Originally, if one spouse had no compensation, a married couple was restricted to a combined maximum annual IRA contribution of $2,250 when IRAs were limited to a $2,000 annual contribution. The Small Business Job Protection Act of 1996 (SBJPA) created new spousal IRA rules effective for tax years beginning after December 31, 1996. Under the new rules, nonworking spouses were able to contribute up to the full $2,000 limit existing at the time of the SBJPA's enactment. A combined maximum contribution of $4,000 was allowable—$2,000 for each spouse. Deductibility of this $4,000 was limited if the working spouse earned more than $40,000 and participated in an employer-sponsored retirement program as discussed in the next section. With the passage of EGTRRA, each spouse could contribute up to the applicable annual limit for any given year as shown in Table 12.1. There was also the additional benefit that each spouse could make a catch-up contribution if the spouses individually met the age 50 threshold by the end of the tax year.

The PPA allowed for the normal catch up amount to be tripled for tax years beginning in 2007 through 2009 (i.e., $3,000 rather than $1,000 in 2007) in situations where the employer filed for bankruptcy protection and the employer (or another person) was subject to indictment or conviction from related business transactions. An eligible individual must have been a participant in the employer's 401(k) plan for at least six months prior to the filing of the bankruptcy case, and the employer must have made matching contributions of at least 50 percent of the employee's contributions with the employer's stock. Taxpayers using this provision are not allowed to also benefit from the otherwise available catch-up rules for persons who are age 50 or older.

Regular IRA contributions to the IRA of the nonworking spouse can no longer be made beginning within the calendar year the nonworking spouse reaches age 70½. If the employee-spouse is younger, he or she can continue to make annual IRA contributions to his or her own IRA until the year he or she reaches age 70½.

Distinguishing IRAs: Contribution Deductibility and Taxation of Distributions

Deductibility of IRA Contributions

Individuals may deduct the full amount of their regular annual contributions to IRAs if they do not actively participate in a qualified plan.

If either the taxpayer or his or her spouse is an active participant[5] in an employer-maintained plan for any part of a plan year ending with or within the taxable year, the maximum[6] IRA contribution deduction is reduced (but not below zero) based on adjusted gross income (AGI), calculated without regard to any IRA contributions.[7] The phase-out thresholds that apply to the deduction on contributions to a traditional IRA by individuals who are active participants in an employer-sponsored retirement plan were unchanged by EGTRRA, but the thresholds continued to increase as a result of the previously enacted provisions of the Taxpayer Relief Act of 1997. Table 12.2 illustrates the income ranges subject to phase out of deductible contributions in a traditional IRA.

To compute the amount of the deductible contribution to a single or married taxpayer filing a joint return, the following calculation is made:

$$\text{Applicable annual contribution limit from Table 12.1} \quad \times \quad \frac{\text{Modified AGI} - \text{Lower limit of phase out from Table 12.2}}{\$10{,}000 \text{ or (Other difference in the phase out range from Table 12.2 if not equal to } \$10{,}000)}$$

In the case of contributions to an employed individual's IRA and a nonworking spousal IRA, the maximum tax deduction for the married couple (after application of the AGI test, as noted in Table 12.2) is limited to the lesser of 100 percent of earned income or twice the allowable annual dollar limit shown in Table 12.1.

---

[5] The determination of whether an individual is an active participant is made without regard to whether the individual's rights under the plan are nonforfeitable.

[6] This figure could be doubled if a nonworking spouse contributed the full amount to an individual retirement account as allowed for tax years following December 31, 1996, by the Small Business Job Protection Act of 1996. Beginning in 1998 a taxpayer was not precluded from making a contribution to a deductible IRA solely because the spouse was a participant in a qualified employer-sponsored retirement plan, but the maximum contribution was phased out for incomes above a certain level. (See Table 12.2 for a detailed description of the phase-out limits in various years.)

[7] No dollar limitation will be reduced below $200 until the limitation is completely phased out.

TABLE 12.2   **Annual Phase-out Limits on Taxpayer Deductions of Regular Annual Contributions to Traditional IRAs**

Year	Single Taxpayers		Married Taxpayers Filing Jointly	
	Where Phase out Starts	Where Deduction Is Completely Eliminated	Where Phase out Starts	Where Deduction Is Completely Eliminated
2001	$33,000	$43,000	$53,000	$ 63,000
2002	$34,000	$44,000	$54,000	$ 64,000
2003	$40,000	$50,000	$60,000	$ 70,000
2004	$45,000	$55,000	$65,000	$ 75,000
2005	$50,000	$60,000	$70,000	$ 80,000
2006	$50,000	$60,000	$75,000	$ 85,000
2007	$52,000	$62,000	$83,000	$103,000
2008 and later	Amounts indexed.		Amounts indexed.	

Nondeductible IRA contributions also may be made if they are designated as such on the taxpayer's return. Although these contributions will be made from after-tax income, they will benefit from the compounding of tax-sheltered investment income during the time they remain in the IRA. Because the annual limit on regular contributions to any working individual's IRA is limited to the applicable dollar amount shown in Table 12.1 (or the earned income for the year, if under the allowable dollar amount), nondeductible contributions cannot exceed the same allowable dollar amount or earned income limit. Taxpayers may elect to treat contributions as nondeductible even though they are eligible to make deductible contributions. If taxpayers make any deductible contributions, nondeductible contributions may be made against the remaining limit.

Because the IRA contribution deduction is against gross income, it may be taken even though the individual does not itemize deductions. If the individual's employer makes the contribution other than as a SEP or SIMPLE employer plan contribution directly to the IRA on behalf of the individual,[8] the amount still must be reported as earnings and then taken as a deduction against gross income. This contribution will be subject to Federal Insurance Contributions Act (FICA) or Social Security tax and Federal Unemployment Tax Act (FUTA) tax but not to withholding taxes.

Individual IRA contributions must be made before the due date for the individual's filing of the federal income tax return for the taxable year for which the deduction is claimed (disregarding any filing extensions).

Any **excess contribution** is subject to a nondeductible 6 percent excise tax in addition to current income taxation. The excise tax continues to be applied each year until the

---

[8] See a discussion of SEPs and SIMPLE plans in Chapter 13.

excess contribution is withdrawn from the IRA. For example, if an individual makes an excess contribution of $100 to an IRA in 20X1, an excise tax of $6 is imposed for 20X1 and for each year thereafter until the excess contribution is withdrawn.

Because of the restrictions on distributions from an IRA (discussed in a later section of this chapter), the question arises whether the withdrawal of an excess contribution is itself a taxable event. If the excess contribution is withdrawn before the tax return filing date for the year for which the contribution was made, the withdrawn excess amount is not included in taxable income, and the 10 percent premature distribution tax is not applied. However, earnings must be withdrawn and are taxable and potentially subject to penalty.

Any excess contributions not taken as a distribution may be eliminated in later years by contributing less than the maximum allowable deduction in such years. For example, if an individual contributed an excess of $100 over the allowable limit in one year (as depicted in Table 12.1), the situation can be remedied by contributing $100 less than the allowable limit in the following year. If excess contributions are not eliminated through these steps, the excess amounts will be subject to a cumulative 6 percent excise tax each year until they are eliminated.

Roth IRAs

History and Distinguishing Characteristics from Traditional IRAs

As previously mentioned, the Taxpayer Relief Act of 1997 introduced another type of nondeductible IRA, the **Roth IRA,** that could be used beginning in 1998. Like traditional IRAs, Roth IRAs permit the same regular annual contribution limit as does a traditional IRA. (The annual contribution limits are noted in Table 12.1.) If a taxpayer makes regular annual contributions to any other IRAs, for instance, to either a traditional deductible or nondeductible IRA, the maximum annual contribution limit to the Roth IRA is reduced by those contributions. The rules permitting a regular annual contribution to a Roth IRA are unique to this particular retirement savings vehicle. Unlike a traditional IRA, regular annual contributions can be made to a Roth IRA at any age (even beyond age 70½), provided the contributions do not exceed earned income for that particular year. The income phase out on the ability to make regular annual contributions to a Roth IRA applies even if an individual is not an active participant in an employer-sponsored retirement plan. A single taxpayer must have adjusted gross income (AGI) of less than $99,000 in 2007 in order to make a full annual contribution to a Roth IRA (a partial contribution can be made if AGI is between $99,000 and $114,000 in 2007). A married taxpayer must have adjusted gross income (AGI) of less than $156,000 in 2007 in order to make a full annual contribution to a Roth IRA (a partial contribution can be made if AGI is between $156,000 and $166,000 in 2007). If a married taxpayer files his or her income tax return as married filing separately, he or she is ineligible to make a regular annual Roth contribution once AGI exceeds $10,000; a phased contribution is permissible if income is $10,000 or lower.

Contributions to Roth IRAs are not tax deductible when made, but earnings accumulate tax deferred. Like deductible and nondeductible traditional IRAs, a Roth IRA contribution must be made by the due date for the filing of the taxpayer's income tax return, not including extensions. Withdrawals of regular annual Roth contributions are tax free at any time since taxes have already been paid on these amounts. Withdrawals of earnings from Roth IRAs are tax free (rather than tax deferred) if the distribution is considered to be a qualified distribution. A qualified distribution is a distribution that is made at least five years from the first of the year in which the Roth account was established and meets at least one of the following other requirements:

1. The taxpayer has attained age 59½.
2. The taxpayer is disabled.
3. The taxpayer has died and payment is made to a beneficiary or to the individual's estate.
4. The distribution is made to pay first-time home buyer expenses and does not exceed $10,000.

Generally under other circumstances, withdrawals of earnings are taxable and would be subject to the additional early distribution federal tax of 10 percent. However, if a withdrawal of earnings meets one of the conditions to be excepted from the early withdrawal penalty tax, this 10 percent additional federal tax would not apply. Later in the chapter, the exceptions to the 10 percent early withdrawal tax are explained.

Conversion of a Traditional IRA into a Roth IRA

The owner of a traditional IRA may convert it into a Roth IRA if his or her modified adjusted gross income (AGI) does not exceed $100,000 prior to 2010 as either a single person or as a married person filing a joint return in the year that the **conversion** occurs. Modified AGI excludes income attributable to the conversion itself and also excludes any minimum required distributions from traditional IRAs in the year of conversion.[9] The full amount of a traditional IRA or a partial lesser amount can be converted. A taxpayer making such a conversion will be subject to taxation in the year of conversion for any proceeds of the account which have been converted that would be subject to taxation upon distribution. A conversion that is subject to taxation is also subject to income tax withholding unless the account owner makes an election in writing not to have withholding occur. Though a traditional IRA that is converted into a Roth IRA is subject to regular federal income taxation, it is not subject to the 10 percent penalty tax on premature distributions.

The Tax Increase Prevention and Reconciliation Act of 2006 removed the $100,000 modified adjusted gross income limitation to be eligible to convert a traditional IRA to a Roth IRA effective for tax years beginning after December 31, 2009. This provision was applicable to both individual filers and married couples filing jointly. For conversions occurring in 2010, unless the taxpayer elects otherwise, the amount included in gross income as a result of the conversion would be included ratably in 2011 and 2012. However, if the converted amounts then were distributed from the Roth account before 2012, the amount deferred ratably until 2012 would be accelerated and shown in gross income earlier. Following

---

[9] This can be an important exclusion in computing modified AGI, especially for an older person attempting to make a conversion.

2010, conversions from a traditional IRA to a Roth IRA would be included in gross income in the year of conversion.

IRA Administrative Issues

Funding

An individual may establish an individual retirement savings plan (either traditional or Roth) by making contributions to one or more of the following:

1. An individual retirement account.
2. An individual retirement annuity.
3. A U.S. retirement bond (permitted prior to May 1, 1982, and therefore not applicable to Roth IRAs because these funding mechanisms predated the introduction of Roth IRAs).

IRA contributions must be made in cash. Thus, the contribution of existing property (e.g., existing mutual fund shares) is not permitted.

The following material discusses each of these approaches in greater detail, as well as the restrictions of the Internal Revenue Code for prohibited transactions and unrelated business income.

Individual Retirement Account (IRA)

This type of plan entails the establishment of a trust or a custodial account. The trustee or custodian may be a bank or another person or organization that demonstrates to the satisfaction of the Internal Revenue Service that the IRA account will be administered in accordance with the law.

There are some restrictions on investments in such an IRA. The assets cannot be invested in life insurance contracts. (There is a limited exception for endowment contracts with incidental life insurance features that were issued before 1979.) Also, IRA investments in collectibles, such as antiques, works of art, stamps, coins, and the like, are not permitted. Most IRA accounts are invested in assets such as bankpooled funds, savings accounts, certificates of deposit, savings and loan association accounts, mutual fund shares, exchange traded funds (ETFs), face-amount certificates, and insured credit union accounts. A **self-directed IRA** arrangement also can be established. Under this approach a corporate trustee is selected (which generally charges fees for the services provided). The individual is free to make the investment decisions, within the constraints outlined here, for his or her IRA.

The key requirements of an individual retirement account are as follows:

1. The regular annual contribution must be made in cash and must not exceed the allowable amount permitted by law in a given year as previously shown in Table 12.1.
2. The entire value of the account must be nonforfeitable.
3. No part of the funds may be invested in life insurance contracts or collectibles, other than legal tender gold and silver coins minted by the United States.

4. The assets in the account must not be commingled with any other property (except the assets of other qualified trusts).
5. Distributions must be made in accordance with the restrictions imposed by the law.

IRAs may be set up by adopting either IRS Form 5305 for Individual Retirement Trust Accounts or IRS Form 5305A for Individual Retirement Custodial Accounts. Alternatively, if the trustee or custodian wishes to use its own agreement, it may do this and submit the agreement to the IRS for approval on Form 5306. An individual who uses such approved plans does not need to submit his or her individual plan for IRS approval.

Individual Retirement Annuity

Under this type of plan, the individual's contribution is invested through the purchase of a **flexible premium annuity IRA** from a legally licensed life insurance company.

The annuity contract must involve flexible premiums and may be participating or nonparticipating. Also, the annuity may be fixed or variable. The key requirements of a flexible premium annuity IRA are as follows:

1. The annual premium must not be fixed and must not exceed the allowable amount permitted by law in a given year as previously shown in Table 12.1.
2. The contract must be nontransferable.
3. The individual's interest in the contract must be nonforfeitable.
4. Dividends must be used before the end of the next year to purchase additional benefits or to reduce future premiums.
5. Distributions must be made in accordance with the restrictions imposed by law.

Selection of Funding Arrangement

Selection of the appropriate funding arrangement involves many of the same considerations taken into account in the selection of a funding instrument for a qualified pension plan. Thus, the individual must give consideration to potential investment return as well as investment risk. The expenses associated with the particular funding arrangement also must be taken into account as must benefit security and services provided.

Investment Advice to IRA Owners

Since the Pension Protection Act of 2006 (PPA) instituted an exemption from the prohibited transaction rules, IRA account owners will have greater access to receive investment advice after 2006. Under the exemption, a qualified "fiduciary adviser" may provide personally tailored investment advice to IRA account owners if certain conditions are met. The exemption provision stipulates that the advice be provided by an adviser whose compensation does not vary with the investment option chosen or through a computer model that is certified by an independent third party. In the case of an IRA (as opposed to an employer-sponsored plan), the computer model exception will only be available if and when the Labor Department concludes that a viable model for this purpose exists. For purposes of this provision, references to IRAs are expansive including health savings accounts (HSAs), Archer medical savings accounts (MSAs), and Coverdell education savings accounts (ESAs).

Prohibited Transactions

Individual retirement savings plans are subject to the prohibited transactions provisions of ERISA. If the individual engages in a prohibited transaction, the plan will be disqualified as of the first day of the taxable year in which the transaction occurred. The individual must then include the fair market value of the assets of the plan (determined as of the first day of such year) in ordinary income where applicable. In addition, if the individual has not attained age 59½ (or is not disabled), an additional 10 percent tax will be levied where applicable since this is treated as a premature distribution. Generally speaking, fiduciaries and parties in interest are prohibited from engaging in the following:

1. Selling, exchanging, or leasing property.
2. Lending money or extending credit.
3. Furnishing goods, services, or facilities.
4. Transferring to or using plan assets.

There are, of course, exceptions to the prohibited transaction rules. One of the more significant exceptions permits a financial institution to provide ancillary services where this is done without interference with the interests of the participants and beneficiaries, where not more than reasonable compensation is charged, and where adequate internal safeguards exist to prevent provision of services in an excessive or unreasonable manner.

Except for the individual (and his or her beneficiary), a party in interest who engages in a prohibited transaction will be subject to an excise tax of 10 percent of the amount involved. If the situation is not corrected within the time allowed (90 days unless extended by the IRS), a further excise tax of 100 percent of the amount involved will be levied.

If an individual has an individual retirement annuity and borrows any money under or by use of that annuity contract, the annuity will lose its tax-exempt status as of the first day of the taxable year in which the transaction occurred. The fair market value of such annuity when applicable (as of the first day of such taxable year) will have to be included in the individual's gross income for such year. If the individual has not attained age 59½ or is not disabled at such time, this also will be considered to be a premature distribution, and the additional tax of 10 percent of the amount involved where applicable will be levied.

If an individual has an individual retirement account and uses all or any portion of the account as security for a loan, the portion so used will be treated and taxed as a distribution. Again, if the individual has not attained age 59½ or is not disabled, the 10 percent additional tax also will be levied where applicable.

Unrelated Business Income

An individual retirement arrangement is subject to federal income tax on any **unrelated business income** that arises from the conduct of any trade or business that is not substantially related to the exempt purpose of the plan. If a plan develops such unrelated business income, the plan will not be disqualified; however, such income will be subject to tax.

Distributions

The law contains very specific provisions that relate to distributions from traditional IRAs. In general, these provisions are designed to support the basic purpose of such plans—that they should provide retirement income. Thus, premature distributions are discouraged. On the other hand, the individual is expected to begin receiving payments by age 70½ and is encouraged to draw down benefits over his or her remaining lifetime (or the joint lifetimes of the individual and his or her beneficiary). As indicated previously, Roth IRAs are exempt from the minimum distribution rules. Therefore, the owner of a Roth IRA can hold assets in the account until death without being subject to any penalty taxes. Upon the death of the Roth IRA owner, a designated beneficiary of the account would be required to commence distributions.

The following material discusses payment requirements, the taxation of distributions, and the treatment of premature distributions and rollovers.

Required Distributions

Distribution from a traditional IRA must commence no later than April 1 of the calendar year after the calendar year in which the individual attains age 70½. Although the Small Business Job Protection Act of 1996 no longer requires participants in qualified plans to begin receiving distributions after attaining age 70½ if they are still employed, 5 percent owners and traditional IRA holders are exempted from these modified distribution rules. Accordingly, the holder of a traditional IRA must still commence distributions following attainment of age 70½. Distribution may be in the form of a lump sum, a life annuity or joint life annuity, or in periodic payments not to exceed the life expectancy of the individual or the joint life expectancy of the individual and a designated beneficiary. If the owner of the traditional IRA dies before the entire interest is distributed, the required distribution to the beneficiary depends on whether distributions to the traditional IRA owner had already been required to start by the date he or she died. If they have, the remaining portion of the interest is distributed at least as rapidly as under the method of distribution being used at the date of death. If they have not, the entire interest of the traditional IRA owner must be distributed to a designated beneficiary commencing in the year following the year in which the employee's death occurred and the distribution must occur over the life of such beneficiary, or over a period not extending beyond the life expectancy of such beneficiary. If a designated beneficiary is not named, the entire interest of the account must be distributed within five years of the account owner's death regardless of who or what entity receives the distribution.[10] Also, under the minimum distribution rules that were amended in 2001 and further revised in 2002 by the Internal Revenue Service, the determination of a designated beneficiary is not made until September 30 of the year following the IRA owner's death, allowing for postmortem estate planning.[11] If the designated beneficiary is the surviving spouse of the traditional IRA owner, additional flexibility exists. In this case, distributions do not have to begin

---

[10] It should be noted that although this particular discussion began by detailing distribution requirements for a traditional IRA, once the IRA owner is deceased the rules related to minimum distributions for a beneficiary would also be applicable for beneficiaries of Roth IRAs.

[11] A detailed discussion of tax issues and distribution planning is contained in Chapter 31.

prior to the time the traditional IRA owner would have attained age 70½. The spouse also may be able to roll over the death benefit to his or her IRA or treat the deceased owner's IRA as his or her own. Additionally, the spouse may then consider conversion to a Roth IRA. The PPA allows rollover by nonspouse beneficiaries to an IRA. However, the PPA does not afford the nonspouse beneficiary the same distribution flexibilities applicable to a spouse.

If traditional IRA assets are not distributed at least as rapidly as described above, an excise tax will be levied. This excise tax will be 50 percent of the **excess accumulation.** The excess accumulation is the difference between the amount that was distributed during the year and the amount that should have been distributed under the rules described earlier.[12]

Taxation of Distributions

Traditional IRA distributions (to an individual or his or her beneficiary) are taxable under IRC Section 72. Generally, traditional IRA distributions are fully includable as ordinary income if they have been made on a deductible basis, but if nondeductible contributions have been made, a portion of each distribution is treated on a tax-free basis. Individuals making nondeductible contributions must keep records that will enable them to establish the amount excludable from income. Lump-sum distributions do not qualify for long-term capital gains treatment, nor did they qualify for the special five-year averaging treatment made available to qualified plans before the year 2000. Federal and some state income tax withholding may be required from any traditional IRA distributions.

Premature Distributions

If a traditional IRA owner takes a distribution from a traditional IRA before attaining age 59½, it is considered to be a **premature distribution.** The taxable amount of the premature distribution is included in the individual's gross income in the year of receipt, and an additional nondeductible tax penalty of 10 percent of the taxable amount of the premature distribution also applies.

As described previously, this would not be an issue for a Roth IRA if it involved contributions to the plan, because tax would have already been paid on the contributions and contributions may be withdrawn at any time. However, the 10 percent penalty tax is applicable to earnings withdrawn from a Roth account prematurely that are not considered qualified distributions. If the withdrawal of Roth IRA earnings occurs either within the five-year period commencing from the first of the year in which the Roth account was established, or if the withdrawal occurs after this five-year period, but does not involve at least one of the relevant conditions permitting for a distribution, the distribution would not be considered a qualified distribution. The relevant conditions permitting a qualified distribution include:

1. The taxpayer has attained age 59½.
2. The taxpayer is disabled.
3. The taxpayer has died and payment is made to a beneficiary or to the individual's estate.

---

[12] An excess accumulation tax can apply to withdrawals that are not taken from a Roth IRA when the IRA owner has died and a designated beneficiary needs to receive distributions.

4. The distribution is made to pay first-time home buyer expenses and does not exceed $10,000.

However, certain conditions allow premature distributions from traditional IRAs and nonqualified distributions from Roth IRAs to be exempted from the 10 percent early distribution tax.

Conditions Exempting IRA Distributions from Penalty Taxes

The 10 percent penalty does not apply to distributions made on account of the IRA owner's death or disability. For purposes of the law, an individual is considered to be disabled "if he or she is unable to engage in any substantial gainful activity by reason of any medically determinable physical or mental impairment which can be expected to result in death or to be of long-continued and indefinite character."

There is also an exception for **substantially equal periodic payments** made at least annually over the life or life expectancy period of the individual or joint lives or life expectancies of the individual and a beneficiary. This payment pattern cannot be stopped or changed before the later of the IRA owner's reaching age 59½ or five years from the date of the first payment, or the penalty may be retroactively applied.

The 10 percent penalty tax does not apply if a withdrawal is made on account of an Internal Revenue Service levy on the account to collect taxes. Likewise, a payment made as a timely corrective distribution from an IRA would be exempted from penalty tax. In the case of a payment made to an alternate payee pursuant to a qualified domestic relations order (QDRO), a penalty tax is waived. Although the QDRO rules apply to retirement plans and do not apply to IRAs, the transfer of an individual's interest in an IRA to the individual's spouse or former spouse under a divorce or separation agreement is not considered to be a taxable transfer. As such, this distribution would be similarly exempted because the penalty tax applies only to amounts includible in income.

The Health Insurance Portability and Accountability Act of 1996 (HIPAA) instituted certain exceptions that would allow early distribution from an IRA free of the 10 percent penalty tax. For distributions occurring after December 31, 1996, the penalty tax does not apply to distributions from an IRA that are used to pay medical expenses in excess of 7.5 percent of adjusted gross income. Similarly, the penalty tax does not apply to distributions from an IRA used to pay health insurance premiums after separation from employment. In order to be excused from the 10 percent penalty tax, the individual must have received unemployment compensation for at least 12 consecutive weeks under a federal or state program and the IRA withdrawal must occur during any tax year in which the unemployment compensation is received or in the following tax year. Self-employed individuals are treated as qualifying for this exception if they meet all the requirements for receiving unemployment compensation except for the fact that they are self-employed.[13]

The Taxpayer Relief Act of 1997 exempted a withdrawal from the 10 percent penalty tax in 1998 and later years if the withdrawal was for qualified education expenses of the taxpayer, spouse, child, or grandchild; or if the withdrawal is for the purchase of a first home (limited to $10,000).

[13] CCH Editorial Staff, "1996 Tax Legislation: Law and Explanation," *Commerce Clearing House Pension Plan Guide,* no. 1123, August 1996, p. 107.

Rollovers

Under certain conditions, the law permitted amounts to be rolled over on a tax-deferred basis from one plan to another. Such rollovers could be made to an IRA from a qualified plan, a 403(b) arrangement, or another IRA. Rollovers could be made from one IRA to another IRA and, in some circumstances, from an IRA to a qualified plan or 403(b) arrangement.

EGTRRA further expanded the portability of retirement plans beginning in 2002. Beginning at this time, the rollover of distributions was allowed between qualified plans, 403(b) arrangements, and eligible governmental 457(b) plans. The law also allowed eligible rollover distributions from eligible governmental 457(b) plans to be rolled over into IRAs. Rollovers of contributory or conduit IRAs (those IRAs having received rollover contributions from other plans) into qualified plans, 403(b) plans, or eligible governmental 457(b) plans also was allowed. The law also made provision so that after-tax contributions from a qualified defined contribution plan could be directly rolled over (but not indirectly rolled over within a 60-day period following distribution by way of a regular rollover which is defined below) to another qualified plan. These after-tax contributions from a qualified defined contribution plan could be either rolled over directly or indirectly via a regular rollover into an IRA. For a qualified defined contribution plan to receive after-tax amounts, it was required to separately account for such amounts in its record keeping. An IRA receiving rolled-over after-tax contributions was not required to separately account for these amounts.

Even with these expanded opportunities to roll over after-tax balances among various types of retirement plans, it was still prohibited to move after-tax balances from qualified retirement plans into either defined benefit plans or 403(b) plans. However, the PPA relaxed these prohibitions for tax years beginning after December 31, 2006. After-tax contributions from qualified retirement plans can be rolled over to defined benefit plans or 403(b) plans as long as such a transaction occurs through a direct trustee-to-trustee rollover and if the transferee plan separately accounts for the after-tax contributions and earnings thereon.

Rollover contributions to an IRA must be **eligible rollover distributions.** That is, rollover contributions may include any distribution except a required minimum distribution (see Chapters 31 and 9 for discussion of minimum distributions from a qualified plan or 403(b) arrangement, respectively), or any distribution that is part of a series of substantially equal periodic payments over the IRA owner's life, life expectancy, or a period of at least 10 years. If an individual rolls over to an IRA a distribution that is not eligible to be rolled over, a 6 percent excise tax may be imposed on the amount rolled over until it is removed.

There are two methods of making rollover contributions to an IRA—a direct rollover and a regular or indirect rollover. In a **direct rollover,** the individual instructs the plan trustee or contract issuer to transfer funds directly to the IRA. In a **regular rollover,** the individual receives a check for the eligible rollover distribution from the plan trustee or the contract issuer (net of the required 20 percent federal income tax withholding) and within 60 days of receipt contributes up to the amount of the eligible rollover distribution as a rollover contribution to an IRA. The benefit of using the direct IRA rollover method is that there is no 20 percent federal income tax withholding. An individual using the regular rollover method can contribute the 20 percent withholding amount to the IRA from his or her own funds to retain the tax-deferred rollover of the entire amount of the eligible rollover distribution.

A distribution from an IRA that is reinvested in another IRA within 60 days of receipt also is not taxable to the individual. Rollover contributions are not eligible for the regular IRA contribution deduction. Also, IRA distributions that are required to be distributed at or after age 70½ may not be rolled over. It does not matter whether all or only a portion of the transferor IRA is rolled over into one or more recipient IRAs.

IRA-to-IRA rollovers are limited to one in any 12-month period beginning on the date amounts are received. This limit is applied by tracing the funds rolled over, as illustrated in the following example.

If an IRA owner has two IRAs, IRA-1 and IRA-2, and he or she rolls over the assets of IRA-1 into a new IRA-3, the owner also may make a rollover from IRA-2 into IRA-3 or into any other IRA within one year after the rollover distribution from IRA-1. These are both rollovers because the IRA owner did not receive more than one distribution from either IRA within one year. However, the IRA owner cannot, within the one-year period, again roll over the assets he or she rolled over into IRA-3 into any other IRA. Any distributions from IRA-3 made within the particular one-year period will not qualify as rollovers. They are taxable distributions and may be subject to the 10 percent tax on premature distributions.

Because of the peculiar limits on IRA-to-IRA rollovers, a number of IRA owners prefer to conduct direct transfers from one IRA to another directly.

Special Tax-Free Distributions from IRAs

The Pension Protection Act of 2006 permits IRA owners who are at least age 70½ to make tax-free distributions of up to $100,000 per year from their IRAs to public charities for tax years 2006 and 2007. Such amounts are treated as qualified charitable distributions only if a distribution under Internal Revenue Code (IRC) Section 170 would otherwise be allowable.

Estate Tax

For federal estate tax purposes, the entire value of an IRA is included in the decedent's gross estate, though the decedent's estate can avail itself of the marital deduction. EGTRRA repealed the federal estate tax for years beginning after 2009. However, since EGTRRA's estate tax provisions "sunset" in years after 2010 unless further legislation is passed, the federal estate tax is presently scheduled to reemerge in 2011.

Employer-Sponsored IRAs

Although the IRA is viewed primarily as a device for facilitating individual retirement savings, an employer—including a self-employed person—may sponsor an IRA for some or all employees. Sponsoring an IRA or facilitating IRA contributions through payroll deductions is not the same as establishing a SEP plan. A labor union also may sponsor an IRA plan for its members. No requirement exists that an **employer-sponsored IRA** be available to all employees or be nondiscriminatory in benefits. The contributions to the IRA may be made as additional compensation or by payroll deduction. Any amount contributed by an employer to an IRA is taxable to the employee as additional compensation income. The employee is then eligible for the IRA tax deduction up to the allowable annual dollar limitation for a given year, unless the "active participation in a qualified plan" rules apply,[14] in which case the contributions may be nondeductible in whole or in part. The amounts contributed are additional compensation and subject to FICA (Social Security) and FUTA taxes. No federal income tax withholding is required if the employer believes the employee will be entitled to the offsetting IRA tax deduction.

An employer-sponsored IRA may use separate IRA trusts or annuity plans for each employee, or a single account may be used. However, the single account must provide a separate accounting for each participant's interest. Either a commingled trust fund or a nontrusteed group annuity contract with individual certificates may be used. In an employer-sponsored IRA, the prohibited transaction rules apply to transactions between the employer or other disqualified person and the IRA itself. Such prohibited transactions are subject to the ERISA penalties. The entire IRA plan or trust will not be disqualified as a result of a prohibited transaction involving an individual participant. If the individual participant engages in a prohibited transaction with the employer-sponsored IRA, only his or her individual portion of the IRA becomes disqualified, much as if he or she maintained the IRA separately.

An employer sponsoring an IRA may request a determination letter from the IRS. Furthermore, the same reporting, disclosure, and fiduciary requirements applicable to qualified plans under ERISA may apply to an employer sponsoring an IRA plan if the employer endorses the IRA.[15] However, the participation, funding, and vesting rules of ERISA do not apply. Each participant always is 100 percent vested in his or her IRA. If an employer makes no actual contribution to employee IRAs, but merely provides certain facilities, such as payroll deductions or checkoffs, or allows the actual sponsor (e.g., an insurer or labor union) to publicize the program among employees, the reporting and disclosure requirements will not apply to the employer.

Deemed IRAs

EGTRRA created a new form of IRA beginning in 2003. Under this arrangement an employer sponsoring a qualified plan, 403(b) arrangement, or governmental 457(b) plan could add an IRA feature to its plan. Such a feature would allow employees to make voluntary employee contributions to either traditional or Roth IRAs established as separate "add-on" accounts. These add-on accounts or annuities are deemed to be either a traditional or Roth IRA, and are not subject to the normal rules applicable to the particular retirement plan to which they are attached. The **deemed IRAs** are subject to the reporting and other requirements generally applicable to IRAs under the Internal Revenue Code.

Reporting and Disclosure

An individual having an IRA is not subject to any reporting and disclosure requirements except in years in which a rollover has occurred, nondeductible contributions have been

[14] For a Roth IRA, the active participation rules do not apply. Only income limitations govern ability to contribute to a Roth IRA.

[15] The criteria for an employer endorsement are found in Department of Labor Regulation Section 2510.3-2.

made, or one of the penalty taxes is payable. The issuer, trustee, or custodian of an IRA must provide annual reports of the value of the IRA as of the close of the calendar year, as well as reporting any distributions from the IRA. Distributions may be reported as fully taxable even though they are not because nondeductible contributions have been made. In such a case, the individual must provide documentation of the amount included.

Nonrefundable Tax Credits for Certain Retirement Savers

In an effort to encourage lower- and middle-income workers to save for their retirement, EGTRRA provided nonrefundable tax credits to individuals who are 18 years of age or over, unless they are full-time students or claimed as dependents on another taxpayer's tax return beginning in 2002. The credit may be claimed for tax years beginning in 2002 and was scheduled to expire after 2006. These credits were made permanent by the Pension Protection Act of 2006. The credit is claimed on the taxpayer's tax return and applies to the first $2,000 in retirement plan contributions. Those retirement plan contributions eligible for the credit would include contributions to traditional and Roth IRAs as well as elective contributions made to SEPs, SIMPLEs, 401(k)s, 403(b)s, and eligible governmental 457(b) plans.

The PPA indexed the adjusted gross income limits needed to qualify for these non-refundable tax credits beginning in 2007 and allowed taxpayers to direct the Internal Revenue Service after 2006 to deposit any tax refund attributable to the saver's credit into a retirement plan or individual retirement account.

Chapter Summary

- In recognition of the fact that a significant number of American workers were not covered by the private pension system, Congress enabled individuals to establish their own retirement plans on a tax-deferred basis using individual retirement arrangements beginning in 1975. Provisions allowing for individual retirement arrangements were enacted into law as part of the Employee Retirement Income Security Act (ERISA), which was passed into law in 1974.

- Over time, there have been many modifications to the original enabling legislation that created individual retirement arrangements. As a result, there are various types of individual retirement arrangements with their own distinct features and tax implications. These various IRAs include traditional deductible IRAs, traditional nondeductible IRAs, employer-sponsored IRAs, deemed IRAs "added on" to employer plans, and Roth IRAs.

- To be eligible to establish an individual retirement arrangement (IRA), an individual must have earned income from personal services—investment income does not qualify for such a plan. However, alimony and separate maintenance paid under a divorce or separation instrument is treated as a compensation substitute and can serve as the basis for an IRA contribution.

- Individual retirement arrangements must be defined contribution-type plans. Regular annual contributions are limited to a fixed dollar amount set for any given year by law or 100 percent of earned income for the taxable year, whichever is less. An individual with a nonworking spouse can contribute a combined amount which is double what a single taxpayer could contribute with a spousal IRA, although no more than the applicable dollar amount for a single individual can be contributed to the IRA of either spouse. The deductibility of IRA contributions depends upon participation in a qualified plan and family income level.

- The Taxpayer Relief Act of 1997 introduced another type of nondeductible IRA—the Roth IRA—that could be used beginning in 1998. Roth IRAs are subject to the same regular annual contribution limits as traditional IRAs. Eligibility to make a Roth IRA regular annual contribution is related to income limits and does not depend on participation in an employer-sponsored retirement plan. Roth IRAs make available the possibility that "qualified distributions," including earnings which have accumulated tax deferred while in the account, will be distributed tax free if certain conditions are met.

- Distributions must commence from a traditional IRA no later than April 1 of the calendar year after the calendar year in which the account owner attains age 70½. However, a Roth IRA does not require minimum distributions on the part of the original account owner while living, though a designated beneficiary receiving the proceeds of a Roth account is subject to taking minimum distributions. If assets are not distributed from IRAs as needed to meet the required minimum distribution requirements, they are subject to an excise tax of 50 percent on any excess accumulation that should have been distributed from the account. Some distributions from individual retirement accounts also can be subjected to a 10 percent early distribution tax if taken before the account owner attains age 59½ unless he or she qualifies for exemption from this penalty tax.

- An individual having an IRA is not subject to any reporting and disclosure requirements except in years in which a rollover has occurred, nondeductible contributions have been made, or one of the penalty taxes is payable. The issuer, trustee, or custodian of an IRA must provide annual reports of the value of the IRA as of the close of the calendar year, as well as reporting any distributions from the IRA. Distributions may be reported as fully taxable even though they are not because nondeductible contributions have been made. In such a case, the individual must provide documentation of the amount included.

- The PPA allowed taxpayers to direct the Internal Revenue Service after 2006 to deposit any tax refund attributable to the saver's credit into a retirement plan or individual retirement account.

Key Terms

conversion, p. *211*	employer-sponsored IRA, p. *219*	individual retirement arrangements (IRAs), p. *204*
deemed IRAs, p. *220*		
direct rollover, p. *218*	excess accumulation, p. *216*	nondeductible IRA contributions, p. *209*
earned income, p. *205*	excess contribution, p. *209*	
eligible rollover distributions, p. *218*	flexible premium annuity IRA, p. *213*	premature distribution, p. *216*

regular annual IRA
   contributions, p. *206*
regular rollover, p. *218*
rollover contributions to
   IRAs, p. *206*

Roth IRAs, p. *210*
self-directed IRA, p. *212*
substantially equal
   periodic payments,
   p. *217*

unrelated business income,
   p. *214*

Questions for Review

1. Describe the reason Congress first made individual retirement arrangements available.
2. Summarize the various types of IRAs that have developed over time.
3. What conditions must be met for an individual to be eligible to establish an IRA?
4. Can an individual be covered by a corporate qualified pension plan and also by an IRA? Explain the consequences with respect to the deductibility of the IRA contribution.
5. What is a prohibited transaction under ERISA? Explain when this concept can be relevant for IRAs.
6. Are there any restrictions on the period of time over which distributions from a traditional IRA can be made? How would your answer differ for a Roth IRA? Explain.
7. Describe a premature distribution from an IRA and explain the tax penalties that could result from a premature distribution. Explain how the tax implications are different for traditional IRAs and Roth IRAs.
8. What conditions must be met for distributions from a Roth IRA to be considered "qualified distributions" that can be received tax free?
9. Is it possible for a person to receive a lump-sum distribution from a qualified pension or profit sharing plan and transfer the funds tax free to an individual retirement savings plan? If so, what are the federal income tax results?
10. How have EGTRRA and the PPA resulted in increased portability of retirement plans, and what role do IRAs play in pension portability? Explain.

Questions for Discussion

1. Discuss the evolution of IRAs over time and the possible governmental policy concerns that have resulted in this evolution.
2. The IRA deduction limitation will undoubtedly decrease the participation of employees in this arrangement. Discuss how this is likely to affect plan design for qualified plans.
3. Discuss the various approaches to funding IRA plans.
4. Evaluate the relative advantages and disadvantages of traditional IRAs and Roth IRAs. If you were serving as a financial adviser, when would you recommend the use of each?

Resources for Further Study

Altieri, Mark P.; and Richard A. Naegele. "Creditors' Rights, Tax-Qualified Plans, and IRAs." *Journal of Pension Planning & Compliance* 26, no. 4 (Winter 2001).

Bickley, Mary C.; and William H. Rabel. "Individual Retirement Arrangements (IRAs), Simplified Employee Pensions (SEPs), SIMPLE Plans, and HR-10 (Keogh) Plans." *The Handbook of Employee Benefits.* 6th ed. Jerry S. Rosenbloom, ed. New York: McGraw-Hill, 2005.

CCH Editorial Staff. "1996 Tax Legislation: Law and Explanation." *Commerce Clearing House Pension Plan Guide* 1188, no. 1123 (August 1996).

CCH Editorial Staff. "2001 Tax Legislation: Law, Explanation, and Analysis." *Commerce Clearing House Pension Plan Guide* (2001).

CCH Editorial Staff. "Legislation 2006: Pension Protection Act of 2006: Law, Explanation and Analysis." *Commerce Clearing House* (2006).

Department of the Treasury, Internal Revenue Service, 26 CFR Parts 1, 54, and 602, "Required Distributions from Retirement Plans; Final Rule." (April 17, 2002).

Hansen, Kenneth A. "IRS Makes Qualified Plan and IRA Required Minimum Distributions Smaller and More Uniform." *Journal of Retirement Planning* 4, no. 3 (May/June 2001).

Chapter 13

Keogh Plans, SEPs, SIMPLE Plans, and Solo 401(k) Plans

After studying this chapter you should be able to:

- Describe various types of tax-favored retirement plans for self-employed individuals and other simplified retirement savings vehicles.
- Note distinctions between self-employed individuals and owner-employees.
- Detail the distinct plan features applicable to Keoghs, simplified employee pension (SEP) plans, savings incentive match plans for employees (SIMPLE plans), and solo 401(K) plans.
- Understand the tax effects of transferring assets between various types of plans.

Other chapters in this book cover retirement plans for employees of incorporated businesses, and Chapter 12 describes individual retirement arrangements (IRAs). The focus in this chapter is on plans for two additional groups of workers: (1) self-employed individuals and (2) the employees of self-employed individuals. Tax-favored retirement plans have been provided in the law for these groups in the form of Keogh (HR-10) plans for the self-employed and their employees. As noted in Chapter 12, individual retirement arrangements are available for other individuals planning for their own retirement. In addition, simplified employee pension (SEP) plans may be used by all employers to provide retirement plans for their employees using IRAs as funding vehicles.

Retirement planning for the self-employed and other individuals planning for their own retirement was affected by the pension simplification provisions of the Small Business Job Protection Act of 1996, a predominant theme of which was to make retirement savings vehicles less complex administratively and more accessible to small businesses. In recognition of the fact that pension plan coverage is far less prevalent among small employers than among medium- and larger-sized firms, Congress was interested in permitting a retirement plan that would not be subject to the same rigors as tax-qualified plans. Although this is true of the aforementioned SEPs, overall participation rates in these arrangements have been somewhat disappointing and have not resulted in a broader level of pension coverage among small employers. Accordingly, the savings incentive match plans for employees (SIMPLE plans) were introduced. SIMPLE plans were first made available in 1997. SIMPLE plans can be designed as either individual retirement accounts or 401(k)-type plans. This chapter describes the historical evolution of these various retirement plan structures, their tax requirements, and their usefulness and appropriateness for accumulating retirement resources.

Finally, a unique plan called the solo 401(k) plan is explained. This plan has limited applicability and is generally only appropriate for one-person or two-person firms. The solo 401(k) is not so much a distinct type of plan but involves using a 401(k) plan for the one-person or two-person firm. Prior to 2002, combinations of other tax-qualified plans—specifically use of both a money purchase pension plan and a profit sharing plan together without a 401(k) provision—permitted greater tax sheltering possibilities. However, changes in the law that occurred with the passage of the Economic Growth and Tax Relief Reconciliation Act of 2001 (EGTRRA) resulted in the use of a profit sharing plan with a 401(k) provision as a viable option in these situations resulting in higher tax-sheltering possibilities.

The PPA allows small employers to offer a combined defined benefit and defined contribution plan utilizing a 401(k) plan effective January 1, 2010. This new plan is called a "DB/K plan".

Plans for the Self-Employed

For many years, corporate employees enjoyed the tax benefits of qualified pension and profit sharing plans, while self-employed individuals (such as partners and sole proprietors) were denied these tax benefits even though they were permitted to establish tax-favored plans for their employees. For approximately 11 years, Congress considered a number of different bills in an effort to remove this tax inequity; the culmination of these efforts occurred in 1962 with the passage of the Self-Employed Individuals Tax Retirement Act, more popularly known as Keogh or HR-10.

This law permitted a self-employed individual to establish a qualified pension or profit sharing plan in which self-employed individuals may participate, but it entailed many restrictions and limitations when compared with the choices available to corporate employees. Because of the restrictions and limitations in **Keogh (HR-10) plans,** many unincorporated businesses incorporated primarily for the tax savings possible under corporate retirement plans. Over the years since 1962, several pieces of legislation liberalized some of the limitations of Keogh plans, and in 1982, the Tax Equity and Fiscal Responsibility Act of 1982 (TEFRA) essentially allowed retirement plans for the self-employed to include many provisions that parallel those of corporate plans. The provisions that applied only to Keogh plans following the passage of TEFRA in 1982 were:

- Employer contributions allocable to the purchase of life, accident, health, or other insurance protection on behalf of a self-employed person were not deductible.
- Loans to owner-employees were prohibited.

A few other special provisions discussed in the remainder of this chapter also applied to Keoghs. However, the passage of the Economic Growth and Tax Relief Reconciliation

Act of 2001 brought further parity by removing the prohibition on loans for owner-employees. Effective for plan years beginning after December 31, 2001, the prohibited transaction exemption that applies to participant loans under qualified plans was expanded to cover owner-employees.

Plan Provisions

Eligibility

Only a sole proprietor or a partnership may establish a Keogh plan; a common-law employee or an individual partner cannot. This does not preclude, however, a proprietor or partnership from setting up a retirement plan with only the common-law employees participating.

If an owner-employee wishes to establish and participate in a Keogh plan, he or she must cover all employees who are at least 21 years of age and have one year of service with the employer. A two-year waiting period can be used if the plan provides 100 percent vesting after the two-year period. Keogh plans must meet the same nondiscrimination coverage and participation requirements as other qualified plans. These rules (discussed in detail in Chapters 25 and 26) can be especially important for owner-employees under Keogh plans.

Contribution and Benefit

Keogh plans can be established either on a defined benefit or a defined contribution basis. If a defined benefit Keogh plan is used, the same limit applies as for a defined benefit corporate pension plan; that is, the limit is the lesser of 100 percent of the average of the participant's highest three consecutive calendar years of earnings or $180,000 in 2007 (as indexed for inflation in $5,000 increments under Internal Revenue Code (IRC) formulas).

For defined contribution Keogh plans, the maximum annual contribution is the lesser of 100 percent of the participant's compensation or $45,000 in 2007 (as indexed for inflation in $1,000 increments under Internal Revenue Code formulas). For the self-employed person, defined contribution plan "compensation" is the self-employed person's "earned income from self-employment" less one-half the self-employment tax (not to exceed $225,000 in 2007).

For example, assume in 2007 George Jones was a sole proprietor with two employees each earning $20,000 per year. Mr. Jones's gross revenue for the year was $230,000, and all business expenses before Keogh contributions were $50,000. The Keogh contribution rate is 10 percent. Therefore, the Keogh contribution for each employee was $2,000. George Jones's Keogh contribution would be determined as follows:

Gross revenue	$230,000
Minus business expenses	−50,000
Net income	$180,000
Minus contributions for two employees	−4,000
Net profit	$176,000

George Jones had no other income. Based on his earned income, his total self-employment tax was $12,228. George Jones's contribution would be determined as follows:

$$\text{Contribution for George Jones} = \text{Keogh contribution rate} \times \frac{(\text{Earned income} - \tfrac{1}{2} \text{ Self-employment taxes})}{1 + \text{Keogh contribution rate}}$$

Therefore,

$$\text{Total contribution for George Jones} = 0.10(\$176{,}000 - \$6{,}114) \div 1.10$$

$$= \$16{,}988.60 \div 1.10$$

$$= \$15{,}444.18$$

However, the $15,444.18 contribution may not exceed the lesser of 100 percent of earned income less one-half the self-employment tax (which in this example is $176,000 − $6,114 − $15,444.18) up to $225,000 (in 2007), or $45,000 (in 2007). Because ($176,000 − $6,114 − $15,444.18) was less than $200,000 and is also less than 100 percent of earned income from self-employment and $45,000, the contribution of $15,444.18 is appropriate.

Deductions for Contributions

Contributions made before the due date of the self-employed individual's tax return for the prior year (including extensions) are treated as made for the prior year as long as the plan was established by the end of the prior year, the contributions are designated as applying to the prior year, and the contributions are deducted on the prior year's tax return. The owner's deductions for contributions made on behalf of nonowner employees to a Keogh plan are calculated no differently from those of a corporate employer for its employees under a qualified plan. The owner's deduction for contributions for himself or herself is based on the owner's earned income from self-employment, which takes into account the deduction for one-half the self-employment tax and the deduction for contributions to the plan on the owner's own behalf. In a profit sharing plan, for example, the maximum deductible contribution for the self-employed individual is 20.0000 percent of earned income, less one-half the self-employment tax, before subtracting the amount of the contribution.[1]

Taxation of Distributions

Distributions are taxable in exactly the same fashion as distributions made from a qualified plan established by a corporate employer. Distributions in the form of periodic payments generally had been taxable as ordinary income in accordance with the annuity rules of Section 72 of the Internal Revenue Code. However, the Small Business Job

---

[1] Section 401(c)(2) defines compensation for defined contribution plans as net earnings subject to self-employment tax less one-half the self-employment tax less the pension deduction under Section 404. If this is calculated algebraically disregarding the self-employment tax, 25 percent becomes 0.25/1.25 or 20.0000 percent.

Protection Act of 1996 introduced a simplified method for determining the investment in contract when a distribution occurs from a qualified retirement plan, qualified annuity, or tax-sheltered annuity. Under the simplified method, the employee's nontaxable component of each year's distribution generally equals the nontaxable investment in contract as of the annuity start date, divided by the number of anticipated payments to be received as indicated in the following table:

Primary Annuitant's Age When Annuity Commences	Number of Anticipated Annuity Payments*
55 or younger	360
56 to 60	310
61 to 65	260
66 to 70	210
71 or older	160

* If the annuity contract itself specifies the number of payments to be received, the contractual number of payments would be divided into the investment in contract. This simplified method for determining the nontaxable portion of each annuity distribution took effect 90 days after the signing of the Small Business Job Protection Act, which occurred in August 1996.

The self-employed individual's cost basis for this purpose generally will be the sum of contributions that he or she was not able to deduct.

For years where income averaging was still available, lump sum distributions to or on behalf of self-employed individuals on account of death, disability, or after attainment of age 59½ were the same for regular or common-law employees; this was not applicable to other separations. The Small Business Job Protection Act of 1996 abolished five-year income averaging for lump sum distributions occurring in tax years after December 31, 1999. It should be noted that individuals who became age 50 before January 1, 1986, still may avail themselves of 10-year averaging and capital gains provisions under prior law.

Death Benefits

If a life insurance benefit is provided by the plan, the beneficiary of a plan participant may consider the pure insurance portion of the benefit (i.e., the excess of the face amount over the cash value of the contract) as income tax–free life insurance proceeds. The cash value of the contract, however, as well as any other form of cash distribution under the plan, is considered taxable income to the beneficiary. The beneficiary's cost basis is the same as the plan participant's cost basis at the time of his or her death. However, the term costs of insurance protection that were not deducted by the proprietorship would not be a cost basis to the beneficiary. The tax treatment of the distribution is the same as that described for distributions to the plan participant.

Loans

Loans from Keogh plans generally are permitted on the same basis as for qualified retirement plans. As indicated in the beginning of the chapter, plan loans were not permitted to self-employed individuals who were owner-employees prior to 2002. Owner-employees are sole proprietors and partners owning more than 10 percent of either the capital or profit interest in a partnership. This prohibition on loans to owner-employees was changed by EGTRRA. Effective for plan years beginning after December 31, 2001, the prohibited transaction exemption that applies to participant loans under qualified plans was expanded to cover owner-employees. This change in the law now allows owner-employees to take loans. Owner-employees include owners of sole proprietorships, partnerships, or S corporations. Some tax practitioners have indicated that the ability to access plan loans may provide an incentive for some owner-employees to form Keoghs rather than to use a SEP or a SIMPLE IRA as a retirement plan. Both the SEP and the SIMPLE IRA which use IRAs as funding sources for participant accounts are prohibited from making loans, as is the case with all IRAs.

Whereas all owner-employees are self-employed individuals, not all self-employed individuals are owner-employees. The distinction is in the amount of proprietary interest held by the individual. An **owner-employee** is a self-employed individual who owns the entire interest in an unincorporated business (a sole proprietor) or a partner who owns more than 10 percent of the capital or profit interest of the partnership. Thus, a partner owning 10 percent or less of the capital or profit interest of a partnership is not an owner-employee, even though he or she is a self-employed individual. This distinction was very important regarding plan loans prior to 2002 because the provisions of the law were more restrictive for self-employed individuals who also were owner-employees.

Within the definition of owner-employee is any stockholder employee in a Subchapter S corporation.

Rollovers

Tax-free rollovers from a Keogh plan to another Keogh plan, to an employer-sponsored retirement plan, a 403(b) plan, a governmental 457(b) plan, or to an individual retirement account are permitted.

Simplified Employee Pension Plans

Congress, in an attempt to encourage the adoption of private pension plans, created the concept of **simplified employee pension (SEP) plans.** In effect, SEPs are individual retirement accounts with higher contribution limits than those normally applicable to these arrangements. Further, they allow an employer to adopt a retirement program with a minimum of paperwork and regulatory compliance. Over the years, Congress has made changes in contribution limits and plan requirements.

This part of the chapter provides a brief overview of the tax law provisions applicable to SEPs. It also includes a discussion of the eligibility requirements applicable to these plans, the deductibility of contributions, and the use of salary reduction arrangements. Because SEPs are IRAs, unless otherwise noted the IRA rules discussed in Chapter 12 generally apply.

General Tax Law Requirements

The general authority for SEPs is found in Sections 408(j) and (k) of the IRC, which provide for an increase in the normal IRA limit if certain requirements are met. Thus, a SEP is treated, under the law, as an IRA with higher limits.

The employer establishing a SEP can be an incorporated entity or a self-employed individual. For the employer, a SEP is a plan that uses individual retirement accounts or annuities to provide retirement benefits for employees. The employer must notify the employees of the plan. A SEP program is a defined contribution plan; the defined benefit approach is not permitted for these plans. The SEP must be a formally adopted program having the following characteristics:

- It must be in writing and must specify the requirements for employee participation. Further, it must specify when the employee makes contributions and how each eligible employee's contribution will be computed.

- The employer must make contributions to the SEP for any employee who is at least 21 years of age, has worked for the employer during at least three of the last five years, and has received at least $500 in 2007, indexed for cost-of-living increases, in compensation from the employer for the year.

- Employer contributions may not discriminate in favor of any highly compensated employee (see Chapter 25).

- Employer contributions may be discretionary from year to year. However, the plan document must specify a definite allocation formula.

- Each employee must be fully vested in his or her account balance at all times.

- The program may not restrict the employee's rights to withdraw funds contributed to his or her SEP at any time (i.e., the program must give unrestricted withdrawal rights to the employees).

- The employer may not require that an employee leave some or all of the contributions in the SEP as a condition for receiving future employer contributions.

- In 2001, contributions for an individual in a SEP were limited to the lesser of 15 percent of compensation or $35,000. The amount of includible compensation on which SEP contributions could be based was $170,000 in 2001. EGTRRA increased the percentage of compensation allowance for SEPs from 15 percent of compensation to 25 percent of compensation beginning in 2002. The Section 415 limit was changed by EGTRRA to the lesser of 100 percent of compensation or $40,000 for 2002. The limit on includible compensation was increased to $200,000 in 2002. In 2007 the Section 415 limit had increased to $45,000 and the limit on includible compensation to $225,000. Also, the amount allocated or contributed in total by the employer for the employee under a SEP and other qualified pension or profit sharing plans may not exceed the Section 415 limits. In addition, an employee may make a regular contribution to an IRA, and this is not aggregated with the SEP contributions for purposes of the 25 percent or Section 415 limits.[2]

- The top-heavy provisions of the law apply to SEP programs; however, a special provision allows employers to elect to measure aggregate employer contributions,

[2] Although the allowable contribution limit for SEPs was raised from 15 percent of compensation to 25 percent of compensation at the time of EGTRRA's passage, another section of the Internal Revenue Code dealing with the maximum amount an employer could deduct for a SEP was not changed from 15 percent by EGTRRA. However, the Job Creation and Worker Assistance Act of 2002 increased the percentage for computing the deduction limit from 15 percent to 25 percent. Now the deduction limit and contribution limit are the same.

instead of aggregate account balances, to test if the SEP has exceeded the 60 percent limit discussed in Chapter 26.

• Because they are IRAs, SEPs cannot permit employees to make loans.

Eligibility

For an IRA funded by employer contributions to be treated as a SEP, the employer must contribute to the SEP of each eligible employee. As long as the employee satisfies the eligibility criteria mentioned earlier, the employer must make contributions on the employee's behalf. The employer does not have to make a contribution, however, for (1) members of a collective bargaining unit if retirement benefits were the subject of good-faith bargaining and (2) certain nonresident aliens with no United States income source.

Controlled group rules apply to SEPs, and if the employer is a member of a controlled group, SEP contributions must be made for all eligible employees of each one of the businesses that make up the group.

Contributions

Employer contributions to a SEP must bear a uniform relationship to total compensation not in excess of $225,000 in 2007, indexed to the consumer price index. However, employer contributions under a SEP may be integrated with Social Security benefits under the same "permitted disparity" rules that apply to defined contribution plans (described in Chapter 25).

The maximum contribution limit to a SEP is 25 percent of income up to $45,000 in 2007. If the employer contribution to the SEP in any year is less than the normal IRA limit applicable for that year as noted in Chapter 12, the employee may contribute the difference up to the allowable applicable annual limit. The employee contribution may be made either to the SEP or to one or more IRAs of the employee's choice.

Contributions made up to the date of the return for the employer's taxable year (including extensions) are treated as being made on account of that year. For example, the XYZ Company has a SEP that provides for a contribution of 25 percent of an employee's compensation during each calendar year. In 2007, employee A earns $20,000 and the maximum permissible contribution under the tax law is $5,000 ($0.25 \times \$20,000$). The XYZ Company makes a $2,500 contribution for employee A on December 31, 2006, and contributes the remaining $2,500 on March 15, 2007. The entire $5,000 contribution is treated as being made on account of the taxable year 2006.

It also should be noted that in the case of self-employed individuals (proprietors and partners), the 25 percent contribution limitation will be on the basis of **earned income** as that term is defined in the law. This means that the contribution will be determined with reference to earned income after having subtracted the amount of the contribution and half the self-employment tax. The result is that the 25 percent contribution limit, as it is applied to these individuals, is 20.00 percent of net income before subtracting the amount of the contribution but after subtracting half the self-employment tax.

A SEP may specify a maximum contribution limit that is lower than required by law. Although this could cause contributions to be discriminatory, they will not discriminate in favor of highly compensated employees because contributions for this group represent a smaller percentage of their earnings.

Deductions

The employer's deduction for a SEP contribution may not exceed the actual contribution made to the SEP to the extent that the contributions for each employee do not exceed the 25 percent and/or Section 415 limit. Although the allowable contribution limit for SEPs was raised from 15 percent of compensation to 25 percent of compensation at the time of EGTRRA's passage, another section of the Internal Revenue Code dealing with the maximum amount an employer could deduct for a SEP was not changed from 15 percent. However, the Job Creation and Worker Assistance Act of 2002 increased this amount to 25 percent as well. If the employer contributes more than the amount deductible, the employer can carry over the excess deduction to succeeding taxable years. A 10 percent excise tax is applied on nondeductible contributions (as discussed in Chapter 6).

Salary Reduction Agreements

In the case of a SEP maintained by an employer with 25 or fewer employees throughout the entire preceding year, an employee may elect (provided the plan allows it) to have the employer make payments as elective contributions to the SEP on behalf of the employee through salary reduction. These plans are known as salary reduction simplified employee pension (SARSEP) plans. The plan may be able to receive an elective contribution if at least 50 percent of the employees elect a salary reduction. The Small Business Job Protection Act of 1996 prohibited the creation of new SARSEP plans after December 31, 1996. These plans were prohibited when SIMPLE plans (described next) were established. Employers who created SARSEPs before January 1, 1997, were permitted to retain these programs and may continue to enroll new hires in the plans according to the pre-1997 rules that govern these plans.

The elective contribution for any employee under a SARSEP may not exceed the allowable elective deferral limits (as set by EGTRRA and indexed for inflation) and the average deferral percentage for *each* highly compensated employee may not exceed 125 percent of the average deferral percentage for all non–highly compensated employees. In any event, elective contributions together with any other employer contributions may not exceed the 25 percent/$45,000 limit in 2007, the Section 415 limits. At the time of EGTRRA's passage in 2001, the limit on elective deferrals was set at $10,500. EGTRRA increased the elective deferral limit for 2002 and scheduled it to increase in subsequent years according to the following schedule:

Year	Elective Deferral Limit
2002	$11,000
2003	$12,000
2004	$13,000
2005	$14,000
2006	$15,000
Years following 2006	Additional amounts are indexed in $500 increments

The Pension Protection Act of 2006 (PPA) made permanent the indexed limit for SARSEPs. As a result of the indexing, the elective deferral limit was $15,500 in 2007.

EGTRRA also provided a type of employee catch-up contribution in years after 2001 for employees who are at least age 50 before the end of the tax year. These employee catch-up contributions allow for increased elective deferrals. At the time EGTRRA was enacted, employee catch-up contributions were scheduled to increase as follows:

Year	Allowable Catch-up
2002	$1,000 additional
2003	$2,000 additional
2004	$3,000 additional
2005	$4,000 additional
2006	$5,000 additional
Years following 2006	Additional amounts are indexed in $500 increments

The PPA of 2006 made permanent the indexed limit for allowable catch-up contributions to SARSEPs. As a result of this schedule and the indexing computation, the allowable catch-up contribution was $5,000 in 2007.

Employee catch-up contributions are not subject to any other contribution limits and are not taken into account in applying other contribution limits to other contributions or benefits under a plan. An employer will not fail the Internal Revenue Code Section 401(a)(4) nondiscrimination rules if the plan allows all eligible plan participants to make the same election regarding catch-up contributions. However, all plans maintained by related employers are treated as one plan if the employers are treated as a single employer. According to the Conference Committee Report, an employer can make matching contributions with respect to catch-up contributions, although these matches would be subject to all the rules typically applicable to matching contributions.

The definition of excess contributions and the rules for their distribution are similar to those described in Chapter 8 for cash or deferred arrangements.

Savings Incentive Match Plans for Employees (SIMPLE Plans)

General Tax Law Requirements

The Small Business Job Protection Act of 1996 instituted **savings incentive match plans for employees (SIMPLE plans)** for years beginning after December 31, 1996. The legislative intent of these plans was to create a retirement savings vehicle for small employers that was not subject to the complex rules associated with qualified plans, such as the nondiscrimination requirements and top-heavy rules. Accordingly, employers with 100 or fewer employees who received at least $5,000 in compensation from the employer in the preceding year could adopt these plans. A SIMPLE plan allows employees to make elective contributions of up to $10,500 per year in 2007 and requires employers to make matching contributions. EGTRRA increased the maximum annual deferral limits for SIMPLE plans according to the following schedule:

Year	Elective Deferral Limit
2002	$7,000
2003	$8,000
2004	$9,000
2005	$10,000
Years following 2005	Additional amounts are indexed in $500 increments

The PPA of 2006 made permanent the indexed limit for SIMPLE plans. As noted earlier, in 2007 the elective deferral limit was $10,500. Also, as a result of EGTRRA, employees age 50 and older are permitted to make catch-up contributions in the following amounts:

Year	Allowable Catch-up
2002	$500 additional
2003	$1,000 additional
2004	$1,500 additional
2005	$2,000 additional
2006	$2,500 additional
Years following 2006	Additional amounts are indexed in $500 increments

The PPA of 2006 made permanent the indexed limit for allowable catch-up contributions to SIMPLE plans. In 2007, the allowable catch-up contribution for SIMPLE plans was $2,500.

A SIMPLE plan may be established either as an individual retirement account or as a 401(k) plan. The required employer matching contribution is either made on a dollar-for-dollar basis (up to 3 percent of an employee's compensation for the year[3]), or the employer can elect to match at a rate lower than 3 percent but not lower than 1 percent (this option to match below 3 percent is available to SIMPLE IRAs but not to SIMPLE 401[k]s). To apply the lower matching percentage, employers must notify employees of their intent to apply the lower match within a reasonable time before the 60-day election period in which employees determine whether they will participate in the plan. Instead of

---

[3] Although employers making a match to a SIMPLE plan are required to match dollar for dollar up to 3 percent of compensation, employers are able to match dollar for dollar up to the full limit permitted in a given year for an employee. SIMPLE IRAs have no limit applicable to employer deductions, whereas SIMPLE 401(k)s are limited to an employer deduction of 25 percent of aggregate gross compensation plus elective deferrals.

making a matching contribution, an employer can opt to make a nonelective contribution of 2 percent of compensation for each eligible employee who earns at least $5,000 during the year. If opting to make nonelective contributions, the employer is again required to advise eligible employees of its intention within a reasonable time before the 60-day election period during which employees decide whether to participate in the plan. Nonelective contributions to a SIMPLE IRA are subject to the $225,000 compensation cap in 2007 (indexed) prescribed by Section 401(a)(17) of the IRC, whereas matching contributions are not subject to this limitation.

An employer electing to create a SIMPLE plan may not maintain another qualified plan in which contributions are made or benefits accrued for service in the period beginning with the year the SIMPLE plan is created. All contributions to a SIMPLE account are fully vested and nonforfeitable. To participate in a SIMPLE plan, an employee must have received at least $5,000 in compensation in any two prior years from the employer, and the employee must be reasonably expected to receive $5,000 in compensation from the employer during the year. There is no stipulation that a certain number of employees participate in a SIMPLE plan in order for an employer to offer such a plan. If an employer ceases to be eligible to offer such a plan because its number of employees earning over $5,000 grows to exceed 100, it may continue to maintain the plan for two years following the last year in which the employer was eligible. Employers eligible to offer SIMPLE plans are determined on a controlled-group basis, taking businesses under common control and affiliated service groups into consideration. Self-employed individuals may participate in a SIMPLE plan. Certain nonresident aliens and employees covered under a collective bargaining agreement may be excluded from participation.

Employee Contributions

Employees elect to participate in a SIMPLE plan within a 60-day period before the beginning of the year. Employees may modify previous years' elections during the 60-day period. Plans also may allow employees to reduce or change their salary reduction agreements during the year. An employee may terminate participation in the plan at any time during the year, but a plan sponsor can prohibit resumed participation until the beginning of the following year. Employee elective contributions are wages for purposes of employment taxes.

Employer Contributions

Employer contributions are deductible for the employer. Nonelective contributions are deductible in the year made, and matching contributions are deductible for the employer's tax year if contributed by the due date—including extensions—for the employer's tax return.

Distribution Issues

Distributions from either a SIMPLE IRA plan or a SIMPLE 401(k) plan generally are taxed according to the rules applicable to these arrangements. Withdrawal limitations restricting early distribution from either type of plan generally apply to SIMPLE accounts. Participants in a SIMPLE IRA who take a distribution before age 59½ are subject to the 10 percent penalty tax for early withdrawals. Employees withdrawing contributions during the two-year period beginning on the date of initial participation are subject to a 25 percent penalty tax.

Plan participants may make rollovers to another SIMPLE account on a tax-free basis. A distribution from a SIMPLE account may be rolled into an IRA without penalty if the individual has participated in the SIMPLE account for two years. After the elapse of the required two-year period, SIMPLE account distributions may be rolled over into another SIMPLE plan, an IRA, a qualified plan, a 403(b) plan, or a governmental 457(b) plan.

Employer Administrative Issues

Employers are required to advise employees of their right to make salary reduction contributions under the plan and of the contribution alternative if elected by the employer. Notification to employees must include a copy of the summary plan description prepared by the plan trustee for the employer. The summary plan description must be provided to the employees before the period in which employees make a plan election. Failure to furnish this information to employees can subject the employer to a penalty of $50 a day until the information is provided. Employers must contribute employee elective deferrals no later than 30 days after the last day of the month for which the contributions have been made. Employer matching contributions are due for deposit by the date that the employer's tax return is due, including extensions. An employer makes contributions on behalf of employees to a designated trustee or issuer. Plan participants must be notified that SIMPLE plan account balances may be transferred to another individual account or annuity.

Employers are not required to file annual reports. A SIMPLE 401(k) plan is not subject to the nondiscrimination and top-heavy rules generally applicable to regular 401(k) plans. This exempts them from the actual deferral percentage (ADP) test and the actual contribution percentage (ACP) test where employer matching contributions are involved. Employers also are relieved of fiduciary liability under the Employee Retirement Income Security Act, once a participant or beneficiary exercises control over account assets. Exercise of control over account assets is deemed to have taken place once an account has been established for a year or earlier if an affirmative election has been made regarding initial investment of contributions or a rollover contribution has been made to another SIMPLE account or IRA.

Trustee Administrative Issues

The SIMPLE plan trustee bears certain administrative responsibilities. Annually, the trustee must provide the employer maintaining the plan with a summary description that contains certain required information. Each individual participant must be supplied with an account statement, detailing account activity and an account balance, within 30 days following the end of the calendar year. Trustees also must file a report with the Secretary of the Treasury. Failure to file any of these documents can result in a $50-a-day penalty until the reporting failure is remedied.

The Solo 401(k) Plan

Another retirement plan for some small employers is the so-called **solo 401(k) plan,** although the applicability of this particular plan is extremely limited. This plan is suggested for a one-person firm, usually a sole proprietorship. The plan may be useful for an individual who has a business with a spouse. In essence, the solo 401(k) plan is simply a 401(k) plan that is offered to a one-person firm, or a two-person firm, usually composed of the owner and her or his spouse. Such a plan must comply with all of the administrative requirements for 401(k) plans explained in Chapter 8. However, the PPA exempts a one-participant plan (and his or her spouse) from filing an annual report (Form 5500) if the plan's assets are $250,000 or less. Historically, 401(k) plans have not made sense for very small employers. However, changes in the law that occurred with the Economic Growth and Tax Relief Reconciliation Act of 2001 made the 401(k) plan much more attractive to a one-person firm or to a firm comprised of an owner and her or his spouse. This is particularly the case when such a firm is highly profitable and the proprietor of such a firm seeks to maximize the amount of money that can be contributed to a plan and sheltered from taxes. Noting the opportunity for tax sheltering with this type of arrangement, some investment companies have sought to offer these arrangements, thus minimizing the administrative tasks and catering to this specialized market niche.

Briefly, the following example details a situation for an individual earning $100,000 in years 2001, 2002, and 2007. The example uses the actual limits applicable in these specific tax years. Prior to the passage of EGTRRA, elective deferrals reduced the payroll base on which nonelective employer contributions could be made. Therefore, if an individual made the maximum elective deferral of $10,500, the payroll base for an employer nonelective deferral was reduced to $89,500. Applying the maximum percentage for an employer contribution to a profit sharing plan in 2001 (15 percent), an individual could contribute an additional $13,425, for a combined total contribution of $23,925. Note that at this point, an individual seeking to make a maximum contribution to qualified plans could have contributed $25,000 by making an employer contribution of $10,000 to a money purchase pension plan and $15,000 to a profit sharing plan. In this way, without using a 401(k) provision, a one-person firm could contribute a greater amount to qualified plans using employer nonelective contributions. When EGTRRA was passed, a number of changes in the law occurred. Specifically,

1. Elective deferrals no longer reduced the payroll base for computing employer nonelective contributions.
2. Profit sharing plans used as the underlying base plan in a 401(k) plan could receive an employer nonelective contribution of 25 percent rather than the prior allowable percentage of 15 percent.
3. Elective deferral limits were increased.
4. Employees age 50 and over could make catch-up elective deferrals to their plans.

The combined effect of these changes in the law can be seen in the example, using the applicable limits in years 2002 and 2007.

Solo 401(k) Example for Select Tax Years

Earnings before elective deferrals through a CODA: $100,000

	2001 Pre-EGTRRA	2002 Post-EGTRRA	2007 Post-EGTRRA
CODA			
Under age 50:	$ 10,500	$ 11,000	$ 15,500
Age 50 or over catch-up	0	1,000	5,000
Payroll base for computing deductible employer contribution	89,500	100,000	100,000
Deductible employer contribution	13,425	25,000	25,000
Combined contribution under age 50:	$ 23,925	$ 36,000	$ 40,500
Age 50 or over:	$ 23,925	$ 37,000	$ 45,500

As can be seen in the example, these changes in the law now result in an individual being able to tax-shelter greater amounts using a solo 401(k) than could occur by using other qualified plan alternatives. In 2002, immediately after enactment of EGTRRA, an individual could have tax-sheltered $36,000 if she or he were under age 50, and $37,000 if she or he were age 50 or older. In 2007, an individual could have tax-sheltered $40,500 if she or he were under age 50, and $45,500 if she or he were age 50 or older. These figures contrast with the ability to shelter $25,000 if an employer nonelective contribution was used. The solo 401(k) allows greater contributions than would occur if a profit sharing plan was used alone without a 401(k) provision. And as was noted in Chapter 6, the combination of offering both a profit sharing plan and a money purchase pension plan no longer allows for greater contributions than the profit sharing plan alone. This is the case since the limit on deductible contributions to a profit sharing plan was increased from 15 percent to 25 percent by EGTRRA.

If a one-person firm was to hire additional employees, this type of plan would likely be viewed as far too expensive because of its generous employer nonelective contributions. Because a 401(k) plan must be nondiscriminatory, such a plan could not be offered to the owner and her or his spouse without including the other employees. If the firm was composed of nonfamily members, it is likely that one of the other alternatives mentioned in this chapter, such as a SEP or a SIMPLE, would be a more appropriate plan alternative. If the firm was to keep a 401(k) plan, the plan would probably be amended, changing the employer contributions to a lower nonelective percentage or to a lower matching percentage. Perhaps a safe-harbor 401(k) would be used.

Incentives for Small Employers to Offer Plans

When EGTRRA was passed in 2001, certain incentives were instituted to encourage small employers to offer retirement plans to their employees. The PPA of 2006 made these incentives permanent. Under these provisions of EGTRRA, small employers with no more than 100 employees receive a tax credit for costs associated with establishing new retirement plans, effective for costs paid or incurred in tax years beginning after December 31, 2001. The credit equals 50 percent of the costs in connection with creation or maintenance of a new plan. The credit is limited to $500 annually and may be claimed for qualified plan costs incurred in each of the three years beginning with the tax year in which the plan first becomes effective. Eligible plans include defined benefit plans, defined contribution plans, SIMPLE plans, and SEPs. In order to qualify for the credit, the plan must cover at least one employee who is not a highly compensated employee. To preclude employers from receiving both a tax credit and a deduction for plan expenses, expenses used for the credit may not be double-counted as a deductible expense. Additionally to encourage the introduction of small employer plans, EGTRRA enacted provisions that exempt a small employer from paying a user fee. The law exempts the small employer from fees for any determination letter request to the Internal Revenue Service with respect to the qualified status of a pension benefit plan that the employer maintains if the request is made before the later of the fifth year that the plan is in existence, or the end of any remedial amendment period beginning within the first five years of the plan. However, sponsors of prototype plans must pay user fees in connection with any requests for letters since the prototype plan does not require a user fee for a determination letter request in order to establish a plan.

Nonrefundable Tax Credits for Certain Retirement Savers

In an effort to encourage lower- and middle-income workers to save for their retirement, EGTRRA provided nonrefundable tax credits to individuals who are 18 years of age or over, unless they are full-time students or claimed as dependents on another taxpayer's tax return beginning in 2002. The credit could be claimed for tax years beginning in 2002 and was to end in 2006. The PPA of 2006 made these credits permanent. The credit is claimed on the taxpayer's tax return and applies to the first $2,000 in retirement plan contributions. Those retirement plan contributions eligible for the credit would include elective contributions to SEPs, SIMPLEs, 401(k)s, 403(b)s, and eligible governmental 457(b) plans, as well as contributions made to traditional and Roth IRAs.

The PPA indexed the adjusted gross income limits needed to qualify for these nonrefundable tax credits beginning in 2007 and allowed taxpayers to direct the Internal Revenue Service after 2006 to deposit any tax refund attributable to the saver's credit into a retirement plan or individual retirement account.

Chapter Summary

- Self-employed individuals may use a Keogh (HR-10) plan to save for retirement. Additionally, simplified employee pension (SEP) plans may be used by all employers to provide retirement plans for their employees using IRAs as funding vehicles.

Savings incentive match plans for employees (SIMPLE plans) can also be used, established as IRAs or 401(k)s.

- Whereas all owner-employees are self-employed individuals, not all self-employed individuals are owner-employees. The distinction is in the amount of proprietary interest held by the individual:
  - An owner-employee is a self-employed individual who owns the entire interest in an unincorporated business (a sole proprietor) or a partner who owns more than 10 percent of the capital or profit interest of the partnership.
  - A partner owning 10 percent or less of the capital or profit interest of a partnership is not an owner-employee even though he or she is a self-employed individual.
- Keogh plans can be established either on a defined benefit or a defined contribution basis. If a defined benefit Keogh plan is used, the same limit applies as for a defined benefit corporate pension plan. For defined contribution Keogh plans, the maximum annual contribution is the same as for a defined contribution corporate plan.
- Sponsoring an individual retirement arrangement or facilitating IRA contributions through payroll deduction is not the same as establishing a simplified employee pension (SEP) plan. A SEP must be a formally adopted program.
- Simplified employee pension (SEP) plans allow an employer to adopt a retirement program with a minimum of paperwork and regulatory compliance. Using individual retirement arrangements as funding vehicles, these plans permit higher contribution limits than those normally associated with IRAs. Contributions for an individual in a SEP are limited to the lesser of 25 percent of compensation or the applicable annual dollar amount permitted under Section 415.
- A SIMPLE plan is available to employers with 100 or fewer employees. SIMPLE plans may be structured either as IRAs or 401(k)-type plans. These plans require employers to make matching contributions under various prescribed formulas. Generally an employer match will take the form of a dollar-for-dollar match up to 3 percent of an employee's compensation, although an employer also can opt for either a match that is lower than 3 percent but not lower than 1 percent (if the plan is an IRA) or alternatively a nonelective contribution of 2 percent of pay.
- Changes in the law that occurred with the Economic Growth and Tax Relief Reconciliation Act (EGTRRA) of 2001 made the 401(k) plan much more attractive to a one-person firm or to a firm comprised of an owner and her or his spouse. This is particularly the case when such a firm is highly profitable and the proprietor of such a firm seeks to maximize the amount of money that can be contributed to a plan and sheltered from taxes. The so-called solo 401(k) plan is suggested for a one-person firm, usually a sole proprietorship. The plan may be useful for an individual who has a business with a spouse. In essence, the solo 401(k) plan is simply a 401(k) plan that is offered to a one-person or two-person firm. Such a plan must comply with all of the administrative requirements for 401(k) plans.
- Effective January 1, 2010 the PPA allows small employers to offer a combined defined benefit and defined contribution plan utilizing a 401(k). This plan is called a "DB/K plan".

Key Terms

earned income, p. *232*
Keogh (HR-10) plans,
   p. *226*
owner-employee, p. *230*

savings incentive match
   plans for employees
   (SIMPLE plans), p. *234*

simplified employee
   pension (SEP) plans,
   p. *230*
solo 401(k) plan p. *238*

Questions for Review

1. Describe the types of tax-favored retirement plans available to self-employed individuals.
2. Distinguish between a self-employed individual and an owner-employee.
3. Describe the contribution deduction limits available for defined benefit and defined contribution Keogh plans.
4. What annual limitations apply to the maximum amount that may be contributed by or on behalf of an employee under a SEP?
5. For whom must employers make contributions under a SEP?
6. Explain how the limitation on compensation that may be taken into account under a SEP can also affect the percentage of pay that must be contributed for non-highly compensated employees.
7. What is the deduction limit for employer contributions made to a SEP?
8. Under what circumstances may a SIMPLE plan be offered by an employer?
9. What are the different types of employer contributions that can be made to SIMPLE plans?
10. Distinguish between employer and trustee administrative responsibilities in operating a SIMPLE plan.
11. Describe the situation in which a solo 401(k) is appropriate and the legal changes that made such plans viable.

Questions for Discussion

1. Discuss how retirement plans for the self-employed compare with qualified corporate retirement plans.
2. Discuss the decision factors in the selection of an appropriate retirement plan for a small employer.
3. Evaluate the relative advantages and disadvantages of a conventional deferred profit sharing plan and a SEP in terms of their application to a self-employed individual as a means of establishing a formal program for accumulating retirement funds.
4. SEPs are, under law, treated as IRAs with higher limits. Likewise, SIMPLE plans established as IRAs allow for higher limits than standard IRAs. What justification exists for permitting higher-limit IRAs for some individuals and not for others?

Resources for Further Study

Bickley, Mary C.; and William H. Rabel. "Individual Retirement Arrangements (IRAs), Simplified Employee Pensions (SEPs), SIMPLE Plans, and HR-10 (Keogh) Plans." In *The Handbook of Employee Benefits*. 6th ed. Jerry S. Rosenbloom, ed. New York: McGraw-Hill 2005.

CCH Editorial Staff. "1996 Tax Legislation: Law and Explanation." *Commerce Clearing House Pension Plan Guide* 1188, no. 1123 (August 1996).

CCH Editorial Staff. "2001 Tax Legislation: Law, Explanation, and Analysis." *Commerce Clearing House Pension Plan Guide* (2001).

CCH Editorial Staff. "Legislation 2006: Pension Protection Act of 2006: Law, Explanation and Analysis." *Commerce Clearing House* (2006).

Damato, Karen. "The One-Man Band Gets a Gift from 401(k) Rules." *The Wall Street Journal,* August 17, 2001.

Kaster, Nicholas. *A Guide to SIMPLE Plans.* Chicago: CCH Incorporated, 1997.

Chapter 14

Executive Retirement Arrangements[1]

After studying this chapter you should be able to:

- Explain the various circumstances under which an executive retirement plan may be appropriate in furthering an employer's business objectives.
- Identify two types of executive retirement plans that receive special treatment under ERISA and Department of Labor regulations.
- Explain the factors an employer should consider in determining eligibility conditions for executive retirement arrangements.
- Discuss how various design features of executive retirement arrangements will differ depending upon the employer objectives in establishing the plan.
- Describe various benefit security techniques that attempt to give an executive some assurance that unfunded benefits will be paid in the future.
- Note the differences in nature and intent between supplemental executive retirement arrangements and deferred compensation agreements.

Up to this point, the discussion in this text has been confined, for the most part, to tax-sheltered qualified retirement plans. Under the Internal Revenue Code (IRC), such plans must be nondiscriminatory in order to maintain their tax-favored status; that is, they must not discriminate in favor of highly compensated employees. Several situations exist when an employer may *wish to* discriminate in favor of a specific executive or group of executives. For these situations, executive retirement arrangements can be used. Generally the limits on qualified plans have resulted in interest in executive retirement arrangements from both employer and employee perspectives.

---

[1] The authors wish to express their thanks to Towers Perrin for its permission to use material and text appearing in *The Handbook of Executive Benefits* (Burr Ridge, IL: Irwin Professional Publishing, 1995). The reader is referred to that handbook for a thorough discussion of all types of executive benefit plans.

ERISA Requirements

The Employee Retirement Income Security Act of 1974 (ERISA) contains a panoply of rules governing employer-sponsored benefit plans. Many executive retirement arrangements are exempt from, or can be designed to avoid the impact of, some or all of these rules. ERISA requirements, as they apply to executive benefits, are discussed briefly in Chapter 27. The following provides a more detailed discussion of these requirements.

Pension Plans

ERISA defines the term *pension plan* broadly to include any plan, fund, or program that provides retirement income or results in the deferral of income until termination of employment or beyond. This definition does not necessarily encompass every plan that defers receipt of compensation or provides retirement income, however. Certain of these plans receive special treatment under the statute and Department of Labor (DOL) regulations.

Two types of executive retirement plans are (1) excess benefit plans and (2) top hat plans.

- **Excess benefit plans** provide benefits that cannot be provided through qualified plans solely because of IRC Section 415 limits on benefits and contributions. If it is unfunded, an excess benefit plan is completely exempt from Title I of ERISA. If it is funded, it is subject to Title I's reporting and disclosure, fiduciary responsibility, and enforcement provisions. A supplemental plan providing benefits that a qualified plan cannot provide for reasons other than Section 415 limits—including the limit on compensation under Section 401(a)(17) and the dollar limit on elective deferrals—would not fall within the excess benefit plan exemption. But such a plan might be considered a top hat plan, as discussed next and would, provided it is unfunded, be exempt from most ERISA requirements.

- **Top hat plans** are plans that are "unfunded and maintained by an employer primarily for the purpose of providing deferred compensation for a select group of management or highly compensated employees." Although they are ERISA Title I pension plans, they are *not* subject to the participation, vesting, funding, or fiduciary responsibility provisions of Title I. However, the enforcement and reporting and disclosure requirements do apply to these top hat plans.[2] Under the enforcement provisions, a top hat plan must comply with ERISA's claims review procedures and provide participants with access to federal courts to pursue a claim for benefits. The reporting and disclosure requirements that apply are simplified; the employer need only file a letter with the DOL setting forth its name, address, and taxpayer identification number; the number of top hat plans it maintains; and the number of employees in each.

Early DOL letters were fairly liberal in interpreting the **"select group" require-ment.** Since issuance of ERISA Proc. 76-1, the DOL has declined to rule on whether

---

[2] Note that "top hat plan" is an informal designation; the term does not appear in ERISA or in any regulations.

a plan is a top hat plan. Despite its failure to issue regulations or a definitive advisory opinion, the DOL clearly has not adopted the IRC definition of highly compensated employees. In a statement on the subject, the DOL expressed the view that the top hat exemption would be available only for those employees who "by virtue of their position or compensation level, have the ability to affect their deferred compensation plan, taking into consideration any risks attendant thereto, and, [who] therefore, would not need the substantive rights and protection of Title I."[3] The DOL also said that the term *primarily,* as used in the phrase "primarily for the purpose of providing deferred compensation for a select group of management or highly compensated employees," refers to the purpose of the plan (i.e., the benefits provided) and not the participant composition of the plan. Thus, if a plan extended coverage beyond a select group, the DOL would not consider it to be a top hat plan.

In addition to limiting participation to a select group, a top hat plan also must be unfunded. The DOL has expressed the view that any determination concerning the funded or unfunded status of a plan must be based on surrounding facts and circumstances, including the status of the arrangement under relevant non-ERISA law. In this regard, the DOL has indicated that, in the absence of pertinent legislative history defining the term *unfunded* for purposes of Title I of ERISA, a significant weight will be accorded to positions adopted by the Internal Revenue Service.

Nonexempt Plans

A plan's ERISA status has important implications for both employers and executives. Proceeding under one of the exemptions to Title I could result in a significant level of unsecured benefits—benefit promises that are not backed with irrevocably committed assets. Further, compliance with the "select group" provision would obviously require that the plan be limited in terms of its coverage. Electing to comply with Title I provisions would provide some level of benefit security, but it also could produce undesirable income tax results (at least for deferred compensation plans) and limit plan design choices. An exemption from Title I requirements gives the employer considerable flexibility in plan design in areas such as participation requirements, vesting, and the forfeiture of otherwise vested benefits under certain conditions.

If a plan comes within the purview of Title I (for example, if it is funded or if it extends beyond a select group of executives), the following provisions of Title I apply:

- *Reporting and disclosure.* Full compliance with all disclosure requirements—summary plan descriptions, annual financial reporting, and so forth—is required.
- *Participation requirements.* The use of minimum age and service requirements must be limited to age 21 and one year of service (unless full and immediate vesting are provided).
- *Vesting.* Use of vesting schedules prescribed by ERISA is required (see Chapter 26 for a description of allowable vesting schedules). In addition, the vesting rules also

---

[3] DOL Opinion Letter 90-14A.

place restrictions on mandatory distributions and cash-outs and forbid noncompete clauses that call for forfeitures.

- *Joint and survivor requirements.* Spousal protection, through the joint and survivor requirements, is applicable.
- *Funding.* Minimum funding requirements must be met.
- *Fiduciary responsibility.* The fiduciary provisions apply in full to nonexempt plans. This includes the requirement that assets of the plan be held in trust for the exclusive benefit of participants.
- *Accrual rules.* Nonexempt plans must meet accrual rules identical to those applicable to qualified plans.

Objectives of Executive Retirement Arrangements

Because the design of an executive retirement arrangement must be responsive to the basic objectives of the plan, it is necessary to establish these objectives before any questions of design, costing, and funding can be considered. The objectives most frequently set forth for implementing a **supplemental executive retirement plan (SERP)** are discussed in the following sections.

Restoring Base Plan Benefits

Most major employers have adopted excess benefit plans to replace retirement benefits that would have been payable under broad-based qualified plans were it not for the Section 415 limits. Many employers also have acted to restore qualified plan benefits lost by reason of other tax law provisions, such as the limit on pay that can be taken into account for qualified plan contributions and benefits under IRC Section 401(a)(17), and the elective deferral limit for 401(k) plans.

Providing More Benefits

Perhaps the simplest and most direct objective of an executive benefit program is to provide a higher level of benefits than that generated by the company's broad-based plans. The relationship between Social Security and employer-sponsored plans is a case in point. Social Security will replace a relatively high percentage of pay—as much as 35 to 40 percent—for lower-paid employees but will replace only 5 to 10 percent of pay, and sometimes even less, for the highly paid. Because of tax law provisions governing the integration of Social Security benefits with broad-based plans, a qualified plan designed to provide reasonable total benefits for the rank-and-file employees probably will provide inadequate benefits for the highly paid. If the broad-based plan is structured to provide what the employer believes to be an adequate pension for the highly paid, combined pension and Social Security benefits for the lower paid could be excessive. One solution to this problem is to design the broad-based plan to meet the needs of the majority of employees and to provide the highly paid with a supplemental plan.

Midcareer Recruiting

An executive who changes jobs in mid- to late career could suffer a significant loss in expected pension benefits because the pension from his or her former employer, although vested, will be frozen at the executive's pay level at the time of change. Even though pension benefits from the new employer will accrue at future pay levels, the total benefit from the two sources could fall substantially short of the benefit that might have been payable had the executive been employed by only one employer for his or her entire career.

While many factors influence an executive's decision to change jobs, the prospect of losing pension benefits can be a major concern. One way for employers to address this problem is to establish a supplemental retirement plan that provides additional benefits to an executive hired in midcareer—by recognizing service with the former employer as though it were service with the current employer, for example, or by granting relatively generous accruals for the first few years of new employment.

Recognizing Incentive Pay

Many broad-based plans provide benefits related to base pay only; other forms of compensation, such as overtime, shift differentials, and bonuses, are not included in the plan's definition of earnings.

Incentive pay normally constitutes a significant part of total compensation for executives, however, and many employers believe that at least some incentive pay should be treated as an element of pay for benefit purposes—in part because an executive's standard of living is based on total compensation, and in part because they believe an executive whose pay is at risk should also reap commensurate rewards.

While employers can base benefits for all employees on total compensation, this approach could generate excessive benefits for some employees and an overall level of higher plan costs. Many companies are more comfortable establishing supplemental plans for executives for the express purpose of providing benefits related to incentive pay.

Executive Transfers

If an organization's benefit programs are not uniform from one operation or location to another, differing to reflect factors such as industry practice, profit margins, local competitive practice, and the like, executives could gain or lose benefits every time they transfer jobs within the organization. A disruption in benefits could present significant problems in individual situations. One solution is a supplemental **umbrella plan** that makes up any difference between the specified umbrella level of benefits and the benefits actually provided at the locations where the executive has been employed.

Other Objectives

Other executive benefit program objectives include the following.

Recognizing Deferred Compensation

It is relatively common for employers to permit executives to defer some part or all of their base salary and/or incentive pay. Some employers may even require that some part of compensation be deferred. Because deferred compensation cannot be considered as pay for determining qualified plan benefits or contributions, employers often establish supplemental arrangements to provide benefits related to deferred amounts.

Golden Handcuffs

Unfunded executive retirement plans need not comply with the vesting rules that apply to broad-based plans. Thus, they can be written so that they include **golden handcuffs.** In these arrangements, a terminating executive will forfeit accrued benefits unless termination occurs under circumstances where the employer is willing to provide these amounts—for example, termination after age 62. Pension benefits accrued under one of these arrangements can be substantial, and the prospect of losing them may deter an executive who is otherwise thinking of leaving the organization. Thus, a supplemental plan with rigorous vesting standards can help retain key executives.

Noncompete Provisions

Broad-based plan benefits cannot be forfeited once they are vested; such is not the case for unfunded supplemental executive benefits, which can be forfeited even after they are in payment status. Making benefits subject to forfeiture if an executive goes to work for a competitor after retirement could be a way of providing some protection in this event.

Golden Handshakes

A number of factors, including human resource needs and deteriorating performance, may make it desirable to encourage certain executives to retire before their normal retirement ages. If benefits available under broad-based plans are not sufficient to meet the financial needs of these executives, supplemental benefits (referred to as **golden handshakes**) can be used to provide incentives to retire early.

Uniform Treatment

Organizations often enter into different deferred compensation and supplemental benefit arrangements with individual executives, usually as a result of negotiated employment agreements or corporate acquisitions. Supplemental executive benefit plans can be used to standardize these arrangements, thus establishing a uniform policy and avoiding the need for special contracts and disclosure.

General Design Considerations

Many factors can influence the structure of an executive benefit program—beginning with the employer's objectives. Before designing or modifying a plan, an employer should articulate those objectives and, if necessary, rank them in order of importance to ensure that they are supported by actual plan provisions.

If the employer wants to facilitate midcareer recruiting, for example, it should probably impose relatively short service requirements for eligibility to participate in its plan and liberal vesting requirements. In addition, it probably will make sense to use a benefit formula that either recognizes service with the prior employer or provides for relatively generous accrual rates during the first few years of the executive's employment. As another example, employers that are interested in golden handcuff retention devices may want to impose stringent vesting requirements.

The employer's basic views on executive compensation and benefits, as well as the environment in which the company operates, also will influence plan design, as will the factors summarized below.

Internal Equity

Many plans provide the same (or close to the same) level of benefits for all executives, while imposing relatively short service requirements. Long-service executives might consider such plans inequitable, since their benefits will not be proportionately greater than those of their shorter-service colleagues. Concern over this issue often prompts employers to include additional service-related benefits—perhaps additional pension accruals at a lower rate for service in excess of some stipulated period such as 20 or 25 years.

Cost and Accounting Considerations

As with any employee benefit plan, the ultimate cost of an executive retirement plan will equal the sum of the benefits paid plus any expenses associated with plan administration. Benefit amounts will, in turn, reflect eligibility requirements, the pay base, service requirements, and other plan design elements. If the benefits are not prefunded, as is typically the case, there is no investment income on plan reserves to offset these costs.

Although employers can and should consider plan costs from a cash flow perspective, they also should consider charges to the company's financial statements (both profit and loss and balance sheet) made in accordance with relevant accounting requirements. Supplemental executive retirement benefits generally fall within the scope of *Financial Accounting Standard 87* (*FAS 87*) and its subsequent refinements with *Financial Accounting Standard 132* (*FAS 132*) and *Financial Accounting Standard 158* (*FAS 158*).

Employers also should take care in selecting the actuarial assumptions used to estimate costs—assumptions that will not necessarily parallel those used in estimating costs under broad-based plans. Assumptions as to future salary growth, turnover, and retirement ages for an executive group might very well differ from those used for rank-and-file employees.

Tax Considerations

Tax results, including the deductibility of employer contributions and the taxation of contributions and benefits, also will differ for broad-based and executive benefit plans. In an unfunded retirement plan, for example, the employer generally is entitled to a deduction only when benefits are paid or become taxable to the executive; by contrast, the employer's contribution to a tax-qualified plan generally is deductible when made.

Also, the employer cost of providing a given amount of supplemental executive retirement benefit could be higher than the cost of providing the benefit under a broad-based plan because investment income under a tax-qualified plan accumulates tax free.

Another important point is that retirement benefits for executives will be treated as ordinary income, with no special treatment for lump-sum distributions. But these benefits will not be subject to penalty taxes for early withdrawals or failures to meet minimum distribution requirements as will be qualified plan payments.

From an executive's standpoint, the employer must make sure that neither the tax doctrine of economic benefit nor the tax doctrine of constructive receipt applies. Under these two doctrines, an employee can be taxed currently on deferred benefits or compensation. The **doctrine of economic benefit** states that if a taxpayer is receiving a current benefit, he or she should be taxed currently on the value of that benefit; the **doctrine of constructive receipt** states that if a taxpayer could receive income at any time but elects to receive it later, he or she is still taxed currently because of having the nonforfeitable right to the income. Revenue Ruling 60-31 states that deferred compensation is not taxed before actual receipt whether it is forfeitable or nonforfeitable, provided the deferral is agreed to before the compensation is earned; the deferral amount is not unconditionally placed in trust or in escrow for the benefit of the employee; and the promise to pay the deferred compensation is merely a contractual obligation not evidenced by notes or secured in any other manner. Thus, while certain assets may be earmarked and informally set aside to give some assurance that benefits will be paid, there must be no formal funding instrument and the executive must not have current access to the benefits if current taxation is to be avoided.

Defined Contribution versus Defined Benefit Plans

While the relative merits of defined benefit and defined contribution plans receive considerable attention when it comes to rank-and-file employees, the differences between these two approaches are less significant in the executive arena. Potential coverage under the plan termination provisions of ERISA often deters a company from establishing a broad-based defined benefit plan, for example, but defined benefit executive plans are not subject to these rules. Similarly, a defined contribution executive benefit plan can be structured to avoid one of the key characteristics of a broad-based plan—the transfer of investment and inflation risks to employees.

Most executive benefit plans have been established on a defined benefit basis, particularly in cases where the plan builds on an underlying broad-based defined benefit plan—for example, by applying the base plan benefit formula to short-term incentive pay.

The defined benefit approach works well when the plan is unfunded because it can accommodate most employer objectives and serves to coordinate benefits from all sources. It also is easy to explain and administer.

With a funded defined benefit executive plan, difficulties may arise when executives have to include the value of their accrued and vested benefits in taxable income, since these values will be based on assumptions as to future pay growth, inflation rates, investment returns, mortality, and the like. If the assumptions prove to be too conservative, the plan may have created more value than is necessary. Because executives will already have been taxed on this value, it cannot be taken away (except on a prospective basis to the extent future accruals and/or compensation can be adjusted). The use of more aggressive assumptions or less-than-full funding to provide a margin can avoid or minimize such problems.

As an alternative, employers can adopt a defined contribution approach to establishing benefit levels and, as a result, funding levels. The defined contribution approach is attractive for a number of reasons, whether or not the plan is funded. For example,

- Executives are accustomed to dealing with the idea of capital accumulation and might feel more comfortable with this approach than with conventional income replacement concepts.
- The defined contribution approach more readily coordinates with the use of company stock and the role of stock in overall executive compensation.
- Any imputed rates of return (where benefits are not funded and otherwise invested) can be tied to company performance measurements such as growth in profits, company stock prices, dividend growth, or return on assets.
- Several design issues are easier to deal with, such as offsets for vested benefits from prior employment, making additional contributions sufficient to attract executives in midcareer, and so forth.

Hybrid approaches also warrant consideration. Under a target benefit plan, for example, the employer uses a defined benefit formula to establish a projected retirement benefit, converts the benefit to a lump sum value, and establishes the annual contribution or credit necessary to fund this value at some assumed interest rate. Once the contribution level has been established, the plan operates like a defined contribution plan.

The cash balance approach is another alternative. A cash balance plan is a defined benefit plan that looks like a defined contribution plan. A participant's account is credited with a specified percentage of pay each year, and the account earns interest at a specified rate; the participant's ultimate benefit equals contributions plus earnings. Annual contributions also may be weighted to reflect age and service. See Chapter 21 for details on hybrid plan designs.

An employer establishing a new executive retirement plan should evaluate the advantages and disadvantages of defined benefit, defined contribution, and hybrid arrangements in light of its specific plan objectives.

Coordination with Broad-Based Plans

By design, an executive benefit plan will have many provisions that differ significantly from corresponding provisions in the employer's broad-based plan—the definitions of pay and service, for example, and benefit accrual rates and early retirement provisions. In other areas, there is little need for different treatment, and consistency is, in fact, desirable.

One such area is the form and manner in which benefits are distributed. The law requires a broad-based plan to provide a joint and survivor benefit as the normal form of distribution for a married employee. The benefit payable to the employee typically will be reduced to reflect the value of the survivor benefit, although this is not always the case. In any event, the executive plan should specify the form in which its payments will be made and whether any offset for base plan benefits will be made before or after any reduction called for by the joint and survivor provision.

Other optional forms of payment also should parallel the broad-based plan, although the executive plan should be structured to avoid constructive receipt by the executive of the entire value of his or her supplemental benefit.

Other provisions where some coordination with base plan provisions might be desirable include the right to make and change beneficiary designations, facility of payment authority (if the payee is mentally or physically incapable of accepting payment), procedures to be followed if a beneficiary cannot be located and which state law will govern plan interpretation, and the right to amend or terminate the plan.

Along these same lines, it may be advisable to coordinate executive and base plan administration and communication, although confidentiality considerations may dictate that the plans be handled separately.

General Plan Features

Eligibility for Participation

Eligibility for participation normally is limited to members of top management who make significant contributions to the organization's success. This definition is subject to wide interpretation, however, and care should be taken to restrict eligibility to those executives for whom the plan is really intended. Eligibility requirements that are too broad or that are established so that they automatically expand the group covered (e.g., a minimum salary requirement that could be eroded by inflationary pressure) can lead to substantial cost increases for an employer.

The most frequently used criterion to establish eligibility for participation is position. For the reason noted earlier, a minimum salary requirement generally is not desirable unless it is tied to some sort of price or wage index. Some organizations determine eligibility by whether the executive is eligible for the company's incentive compensation program.

Some plans avoid the use of specific eligibility requirements and require the executive to be designated for consideration by a group such as the compensation committee of the board of directors of the corporation. Even when specific eligibility requirements are used, it might be desirable to have the flexibility of permitting the designation of individual executives who might not otherwise be eligible but to whom, for unusual reasons, coverage should be extended.

No constraints are imposed by the IRC or ERISA on the selection of eligibility criteria; however, if the group covered is so large that it extends beyond "a select group of management or highly compensated employees," the plan could become a retirement plan as defined under Title I of ERISA and become subject to all of its requirements.[4]

---

[4] In the *Extebank* case, a district court provided support that under the right circumstances potentially 15 percent of the total workforce could be eligible to participate in a top hat plan.

Definition of Compensation

Two factors must be considered in defining the compensation on which benefits will be based: (1) the elements of pay that will be included and (2) the period of time (if any) over which compensation will be averaged.

Elements of Compensation

Base salary and short-term incentives typically are included as compensation elements in executive retirement plans. In fact, providing benefits relating to short-term incentive pay is frequently a key plan objective.

The definition of pay also may include compensation that the executive has deferred for payment at some future time since these amounts cannot be used to determine benefits under a broad-based plan.

While it is possible to include the value of long-term incentive compensation in the pay base, this practice is relatively uncommon. Long-term incentive plans are basically capital accumulation programs that are not considered part of regular, year-to-year compensation and thus need not be replaced when the executive is no longer working. Further, it is extremely difficult to value these plans and arrive at an amount to replace.

Other elements of executive pay, such as perquisites and other forms of imputed income, are typically disregarded in establishing the pay base for executive benefits.

Compensation Averaging Period

Because bonus amounts can vary substantially from year to year, plans that include bonuses in the definition of compensation often use averaging. An executive's year 1 plan compensation might be the sum of his or her year 1 base pay plus an average of bonuses paid during the preceding three years, for example. Longer averaging periods may be appropriate where bonus payments vary significantly over the years.

Current compensation also is appropriate for determining the contributions credited to the executive's account each year under defined contribution or capital accumulation programs. In a conventional defined benefit plan, benefits typically are averaged over a three- or five-year averaging period. Bonuses may be averaged over the same or an even longer period.

Although many executive defined benefit plans use the same averaging period as that used in the broad-based plan, some use a shorter period to produce a relatively higher level of income replacement for the executive group. In fact, some executive plans base pension benefits on the final year's pay without averaging (with the possible exception of bonuses).

Service

An executive's service is relevant for determining initial eligibility to participate, vesting rights, benefit accruals, and eligibility for benefit payments.

In most situations, an executive's service will be defined as the period of employment with the employer, measured from date of hire to date of termination. Like broad-based plans, executive benefit plans should specify whether time on leave (paid or unpaid and/or on account of disability) will be counted as service and whether broken periods of service will be aggregated for various purposes. In the case of plans designed to facilitate midcareer recruiting, service might be defined to include service with the prior employer.

Although it is not common practice, a plan may limit service to the period of time an individual is employed as an executive. It also is possible, although unusual, to limit service to the period of time that the executive participates in the plan.

Retirement Ages

Retirement age is not critical for defined contribution or capital accumulation plans; an executive's benefit equals the account balance at termination—whether for normal, early, or deferred retirement; death; disability; or any other reason. Thus, such a plan can be designed without any specific reference to retirement age. As a practical matter, however, most defined contribution plans do specify normal, early, and deferred retirement ages. One reason for defining normal retirement age is to make it clear when the employer expects executives to retire. Another is to tie the definition to other plans and be consistent in matters such as postretirement health care eligibility.

Normal Retirement Age

Most broad-based plans establish age 65 (or the completion of five years of service, if later) as normal retirement age. Many executive plans do the same, although some employers prefer that executives retire earlier and thus specify an age such as 60 or 62 as normal retirement age under the executive plan.

With one exception, Equal Employment Opportunity Commission (EEOC) requirements prohibit the use of a mandatory retirement age. The exception relates to individuals who have been employed for at least two years as bona fide executives or executives in "high policy-making positions" and whose nonforfeitable employer-provided retirement benefits from all sources are at least $44,000. An employer can force any such individual to retire at or after age 65. Employers need to consider whether they want to take advantage of this limited exception and mandate retirement at age 65 to the extent allowed.

Early Retirement Age

Many executive plans define early retirement eligibility in exactly the same way that it is defined in the underlying broad-based plan—typically, the attainment of age 55 and the completion of at least 10 years of service. Some executive plans are more liberal, particularly when encouraging early retirement as a plan objective. In any case, it is customary for the early retirement service requirement to at least equal the service required for full vesting.

Employers who want to create golden handcuffs may want to be more restrictive, perhaps requiring that executives attain age 62 to be eligible for executive benefits even though the base plan is more liberal. Another approach is to permit early retirement under the executive plan only with employer consent.

Benefits available at early retirement can be designed in a conventional manner— that is, with benefits actuarially reduced if they begin before normal retirement age. Employers also can subsidize the executive plan's early retirement benefits in line with base plan subsidies or to an even greater extent.

Deferred Retirement

Deferred retirement refers to an executive's right to remain employed after his or her normal retirement date. With the noted exception, EEOC regulations apply to executive plans and, as a result, exert significant influence on this plan provision. Thus, individuals who are not bona fide executives or who are not in high policy-making positions must not be discriminated against on account of age. Even those individuals who come within the scope of the exemption must not be discriminated against on account of age if the employer does not use the exemption.

Compliance with EEOC regulations means there can be no mandatory retirement prior to age 65 for bona fide executives and no mandatory retirement at any age for protected executives. Further, benefit accruals must continue until an executive actually retires.

Because defined benefit executive plan accrual rates often are generous, many employers cap recognized service to control benefit levels and costs for employment beyond stipulated periods of time. Such a cap, which is permissible under the law, also can encourage executives to retire early—or at least by the plan's normal retirement age—if that is an employer objective.

Benefit Structure

The benefit structure of an executive retirement plan will vary depending on whether a defined contribution or defined benefit approach is used.

Defined Contribution Plans

The benefit structure of a defined contribution or capital accumulation plan is relatively straightforward. The employer establishes a contribution or credit amount, accumulates the contribution or credit with actual or imputed investment income, and pays out the accumulated amount at some future time—usually upon retirement, death, disability, or other termination of employment. The plan may be unfunded (as is typically the case) or funded. Some employers earmark or conditionally contribute amounts in the executive's name, but these arrangements are usually not considered to be funded as contemplated by ERISA and the tax law, and they do not involve irrevocably committed assets.

Many defined contribution executive plans exist solely to restore benefits lost under broad-based plans due to IRC limitations. In these plans, the amount of employer contribution or credit simply reflects the provisions of the base plan and the tax law.

Other plans go further, providing more substantial employer credits or contributions, sometimes as an alternative to conventional defined benefit arrangements. Employers have several options for establishing contributions, including the target benefit approach. Contributions may be incentive-oriented, reflecting employer profits, or they may represent a fixed percentage of pay. If assistance in midcareer recruiting is a plan objective, additional contributions may be made in the early years of participation to compensate for the potential loss of benefits under a prior employer's plan.

Determining the rate of return on credits or contributions made under a defined contribution executive plan is a key design consideration. If the plan is funded, this rate of return obviously will reflect actual investment results. If the plan is unfunded, the employer must establish some method of imputing investment return. Some companies determine this rate with reference to one or more prime rates; others tie the rate to their own return on capital or their own cost of borrowing. Still others use an external base such as Moody's Bond Index.

Special issues arise if the plan is a restoration plan, because the underlying plan typically will permit several investment choices. Will the rate of return on amounts credited under the executive plan mirror the investment results of the choices the executive made under the base plan, the composite result of all funds under the base plan, the rate of return under a designated fund of the base plan, or something else?

Some observers have suggested that the IRS might consider participants in a nonqualified, unfunded plan to be in constructive receipt of income if participants are given investment authority. Discussions with an IRS official indicate that this does not accurately depict the IRS's attitude in this regard and it appears that a participant may be permitted to direct the investment of his or her account balance in an unfunded plan without being in constructive receipt of the account balance for tax purposes. It may be prudent to include an express provision in the plan stating that the employer is under no obligation to make any investments or to segregate any of its assets in any way in response to a participant's "investment elections" in order to ensure that the plan maintains its status as unfunded for both tax and ERISA purposes. While an employer might actually make investments to match the participant's elections, it should be under no legal obligation to do so.

Defined Benefit Plans

The benefit formula in a defined benefit plan should reflect the employer's income replacement objectives. Key factors include:

- The percentage of pay to be continued in retirement and whether this percentage will vary by income level.
- The definition of what constitutes pay.
- The length of service required for full (or optimal) benefits under the plan.
- The retirement age at which full (or optimal) benefits are provided.
- Sources of income recognized in determining whether income replacement objectives have been met.

The typical broad-based plan replaces a relatively high percentage of preretirement income for lower-paid employees, dropping that percentage as income levels increase. Such a plan typically seeks to replace about 80 to 85 percent of pay for employees at low pay levels, grading down to perhaps 55 to 60 percent for the higher paid.

If the executive plan is strictly a restoration plan, then by definition, it has the same income replacement objectives as the broad-based plan. If the executive plan is to provide benefits over and above those of the broad-based plan, the employer must decide what income replacement percentages to use and whether to use the same percentage for executives at all pay levels. The income replacement target for executives is often 55 to 60 percent of pay, regardless of income level. Higher percentages could provoke shareholder criticism and even raise questions as to reasonableness of compensation from the standpoint of the deductibility of plan costs.

In designing the plan to meet income replacement objectives, the employer must consider how to structure and combine the five components that help design the plan benefit formula: (1) accrual rate, (2) pay base, (3) recognized service, (4) normal retirement age, and (5) any offsets.

1. *Accrual rate.* The rate at which to accrue benefits in the executive plan may be identical to the base plan rate; this would be the case in a restoration plan or in a plan that simply applies the base plan formula to incentive pay. An employer may choose to use a different accrual rate or to front- or backload the formula, depending on its objectives. To facilitate midcareer recruiting, for example, the accrual rate in early years could be quite a bit higher than the rate applied to the later years. Backloaded formulas might be used where an employer objective is to reward long service.

2. *Pay base.* As noted earlier, there are two elements the employer must consider when defining pay: (a) the elements of pay to be included and (b) the period (if any) over which pay is to be averaged. This definition may or may not be the same as that used in the broad-based plan. The most common differences are to include short-term incentive pay in the executive plan and to use a shorter averaging period (e.g., three years or even the executive's pay in his or her final year of employment).

3. *Length of service.* The accrual rate chosen in a broad-based plan usually reflects what the employer believes to be an appropriate period over which to accrue full or optimum plan benefits. Typically, this benefit accrues over a 25- or 30-year period. Often, however, employers want executive benefits to accrue over a shorter period—say, 10 or 15 years. Some employers may want the executive benefit to accrue only over the period of service during which the individual is considered to be an executive. Whatever the decision, the plan should specify the service required before an executive is entitled to full benefits. This, in turn, will help determine the plan's accrual rate.

4. *Normal retirement age.* Broad-based plans typically define normal retirement age as 65. Executive plans, however, often use a younger normal retirement age, such as 62.

5. *Income sources.* Once an employer has established its overall income replacement objectives, it needs to decide which sources of income it will take into account to determine whether those objectives have been met. Obvious sources are the executive plan itself, the underlying broad-based plan, and Social Security. The employer also may want to take the annuity value of any broad-based or supplemental defined contribution plan into account. Another potential offset is the value of any vested benefits the executive might have from prior employment; this type of offset sometimes is found in plans that are designed to facilitate midcareer recruiting and where the executive receives relatively high early year accruals or where service with the prior employer is recognized as service with the current employer.

Vesting

A funded executive plan that is subject to Title I of ERISA must comply with minimum vesting standards similar to those that apply to tax-qualified plans.

No vesting requirements apply to unfunded executive plans. Thus, an employer's options in this regard range from full and immediate vesting to no vesting at all until retirement. Even at retirement, the executive's benefit can be made forfeitable under certain conditions—for example, if he or she goes to work for a competitor.

Vesting in executive benefit plans often parallels the vesting provisions of the underlying broad-based plan. In some cases—for example, in plans designed for midcareer recruiting or to encourage executives to retire early—vesting provisions may be more liberal than those of the broad-based plan. If the executive plan is designed to create golden handcuffs, however, vesting may be restricted and may occur only when the executive qualifies for retirement.

An unfunded plan can provide for forfeiture of benefits that might otherwise have been vested. For example, an executive's benefits might be forfeited if his or her employment is terminated for acts of dishonesty such as fraud or embezzlement. As noted earlier, forfeiture also might occur (even after retirement) if the executive goes to work for a competitor or reveals trade secrets. Such provisions are sometimes difficult to enforce, but many employers believe they provide reasonable and necessary protection.

Disability

Many executive plans treat disability in much the same way it is treated under broad-based plans. A typical provision might continue to accrue service during the period of disability and while disability benefits are being paid to the executive under the firm's long-term disability program.

In some cases, particularly with older individuals, the executive plan may treat disability as early retirement without reducing the benefit for early commencement of payments. The plan might even credit the disabled executive with additional service for the period remaining until normal retirement age—in effect treating him or her as a normal retiree with full service.

Death

Most executive benefit plans provide for some type of death benefit when an executive dies before retirement. In the case of defined contribution plans, the benefit is usually the executive's account balance. A defined benefit plan often provides a lifetime benefit to the spouse equal to part or all of the executive's accrued benefit. This type of benefit also might be payable to dependent children (or parents) in the absence of a spouse. A few defined benefit plans provide for lump sum benefits; however, employers who prefer a lump sum benefit generally find it more effective to provide it through additional amounts of life insurance.

Postretirement death benefits are less common than preretirement benefits, largely because the cost of such benefits is significant.

The design of death benefit provisions in a defined benefit plan requires answers to many of the questions that arise in designing a broad-based plan. Should the plan require a minimum period of marriage (say, one year) before the spouse becomes eligible, for example? If the executive dies before eligibility for early retirement, will the spouse be entitled to immediate payment, or will payments commence only when the executive would have reached early retirement eligibility? Will amounts payable to a joint annuitant be adjusted if he or she is more than a certain number of years younger than the executive?

These are among the issues that employers must address in designing executive death benefit provisions.

Benefit Security Arrangements

Because executive benefits are typically unfunded, an executive's retirement income under the plan is dependent on the solvency of the company and its willingness to pay promised benefits. An additional complicating factor is the length of time over which the benefits accrue and the ultimate payout date. The period could be 25 to 30 years in the future. Consequently, strong interest exists in methods that attempt to give an executive some assurance that these benefits will be paid. Several techniques are now in use to accomplish this purpose.

Probably the most common method is the use of the so-called **rabbi trust.** Under this approach, the company creates an irrevocable trust for the benefit of an executive or a group of participating executives. The terms of the trust limit the use of the assets to providing benefits for the participating executives. Thus, the trust assets cannot be used by current or future management but remain subject to the claims of creditors in the event of the firm's insolvency.

Corporate-owned life insurance (COLI) is another commonly used technique for benefit security. The basic concept under this approach is that the employer is the owner and beneficiary of a life insurance contract designed to accumulate sufficient cash values to pay the benefits promised the executive. The life insurance policy must be carried as a corporate asset and therefore provides only very limited benefit security for the executive since cash values and death benefits are within the employer's control. So-called split dollar life insurance is another mechanism often used in an effort to achieve some level of benefit security.

Other techniques sometimes used to attempt to provide benefit security for executive benefits include employee-owned annuities and irrevocable trusts—sometimes called **secular trusts**—where employer contributions are made on an irrevocable basis for the benefit of participating executives. These are funded plans and are subject to Title I of ERISA, with executives being considered in constructive receipt of the value of their benefits when vested.[5]

Deferred Compensation Agreements

While the main purpose of supplemental executive retirement plans is to provide the executive with an additional layer of retirement benefits over and above those provided by the employer's basic plan, **deferred compensation agreements** deal primarily with earnings deferral, usually to gain tax advantages, with retirement income as a secondary consideration. Postponing the receipt of current income not only reduces executives' current taxable income but puts them in receipt of the funds after retirement, when they may be in a lower tax bracket. However, any deferral of income to a future

[5] G. Victor Hallman and Jerry S. Rosenbloom, *Personal Financial Planning,* 7th ed. (New York: McGraw-Hill, 2003), p. 357.

date must take into consideration the potential effects of increased interest and inflation rates as well as current tax considerations.

Reasons for deferring current income from both the executive's and the employer's viewpoints are (1) extending the executive's income beyond normal working years into retirement, (2) spreading bonuses over a wider span of years, (3) tying the executive to the employer by stipulating conditions on the receipt of deferred amounts, and (4) adding to the executive's retirement income.

The factors to be considered in drawing up the agreement are much the same as those that were discussed for supplemental executive retirement plans. For example, the employer must determine how much compensation will be deferred, whether and how much investment growth will be added to such amounts, whether there will be conditions on receiving the funds, and what the various benefit options will be.

To avoid the possibility of the executives' being judged to be in constructive receipt of the deferred funds, three rules contained in Revenue Ruling 60–31 must be followed in drawing up a deferred compensation agreement. They are that the deferral must be (1) irrevocable, (2) agreed to before the compensation is earned, and (3) for a specified length of time. The agreement also must serve a business purpose.

Effects of Section 409A

Section 409A of the Internal Revenue Code was enacted into law as part of the American Jobs Creation Act of 2004. Section 409A raises several tax issues regarding nonqualified deferred compensation arrangements. A nonqualified deferred compensation arrangement occurs when compensation is earned in a year prior to the year in which payment is made for the services rendered. "Qualified" arrangements are excluded from the application of Section 409A. Qualified arrangements include qualified plan structures such as 401(k) plans. Section 409A generally mandates that income from deferred compensation arrangements may no longer be deferred beyond the year in which such compensation is earned, although there are certain exceptions and allowances when arrangements conform to specific requirements. In addition to the regular taxation that would result from inclusion in income of deferred amounts failing to conform to a stipulated exception under Section 409A, such arrangements would also be subject to an additional 20 percent tax on the amount of deferred compensation that would be imposed on the service provider.

As discussed, certain exceptions allow nonqualified deferred compensation to avoid the requirements of Section 409A. An exception from current inclusion occurs when deferred compensation is subject to a substantial risk of forfeiture. A substantial risk of forfeiture exists if the service performer's entitlement to payment is conditioned on the performance of substantial future services or the occurrence of a condition related to the purpose of the compensation, and the risk of forfeiture is substantial. Similarly, short-term deferrals are not subject to Section 409A. A short-term deferral occurs when payment is made by the later of (1) the 15th day of the third month after the end of the service provider's taxable year in which the amount is free of a substantial risk of forfeiture or (2) the 15th day of the third month after the end of the service recipient's taxable year in which the amount is no longer subject to a substantial risk of forfeiture. Section 409A is not applicable if the service performer utilizes the accrual method of accounting. Section 409A does not require current inclusion if the service performer is an independent contractor who performs "significant" services for two or more unrelated entities and if the service performer is not related to the service recipient.

Except for "performance-based compensation," vested deferred compensation must be included in a service performer's income in the year in which it is earned, unless certain qualifying deferral elections are made. Generally, elections to defer compensation must occur prior to the first day of the calendar year in which the compensation is earned. When new arrangements are made or when individuals first become eligible under existing arrangements, deferral elections may occur within 30 days after the participant becomes eligible for the deferred compensation. When compensation is subject to a substantial risk of forfeiture requiring ongoing service for a period of at least 12 months, the initial deferral election may be made no later than 30 days after the date at which the individual receives a legally binding right to the compensation, as long as the election is made at least 12 months prior to the date on which the forfeiture condition would lapse. Once a qualifying deferral election is made, a change in the election must delay the participant's receipt of the payment for at least five years. Consequently, as a general rule, payments may not be accelerated.

If a deferral election has been made, distributions may only deviate from the election upon the occurrence of the following events: separation from service, disability, death, change in control of the company, or unforeseeable emergencies. The circumstances allowing deviation from the qualifying deferral election are specifically defined under Section 409A.

Generally, equity-based compensation arrangements would be subject to Section 409A, although some of these equity-based compensation arrangements can be exempted from many of the requirements of Section 409A provided the arrangement is not in-the-money at the time of grant. A thorough discussion of equity-based compensation arrangements, including the meaning of an "in-the-money" grant, is provided in Chapter 15.

Although the foregoing description only provides an overview of the requirements of Section 409A, it can be seen that these requirements are detailed and place considerable restrictions on the establishment of nonqualified deferred compensation arrangements. The Section also makes it difficult to modify a qualifying deferral election once made. These stipulations arose in reaction to abusive cases where high-ranking executives were able to terminate deferral arrangements and trigger payments when they foresaw the companies they managed on the verge of financial calamity. These restrictions were enacted into law to prohibit "insiders" from disposing of company stock and accelerating deferred income while rank-and-file workers and members of the general investor population would sustain financial losses.

Overview

Because of their nonqualified status, executive retirement arrangements permit a degree of flexibility unavailable in the more restricted qualified plans. When properly designed and administered, they can serve a number of needs that exist in the relationship between an employer and the executive that do not apply to the rest of the workforce. From

The Employer "Cost" of Deferred Compensation

The employer cost of an unfunded deferred compensation arrangement will be sensitive to the before-tax rate of return credited to deferred amounts relative to the gross rate of return the employer can achieve with respect to these amounts. This is illustrated in the following table, which shows the after-tax cost of deferring a $10,000 payment for 10 and 20 years, respectively, and crediting this amount annually with a 10 percent before-tax return. The table assumes the company has a 35 percent tax rate and that it could earn—before tax—either 10, 15, or 20 percent per year.

| | | Cost to Corporation | | |
| | | Corporate Rate of Return | | |
Deferral Period	Amount Payable to Executive	10%	15%	20%
10 years	$25,937	$ 4,658	$ 379	($ 5,205)
20 years	67,271	20,825	1,945	(31,171)

The higher the corporate rate of return and the longer the period of deferral, the more favorable the results for the corporation. In fact, at very high rates of corporate return, the cost to the corporation is negative.

the employer's point of view, such arrangements can help attract and keep qualified executives, reward such executives for productivity and loyalty, and encourage the early retirement of certain executives. The executive, on the other hand, may look forward to retirement income higher than that provided by the employer's regular plan, or at least to full pension benefits in the case of a short-service executive; certain tax advantages; additional death benefit coverage; early retirement with full benefits; and the extension of income into retirement.

Chapter Summary

- Executive retirement arrangements are established for a variety of reasons. The most common reasons include (1) to replace retirement benefits lost by reason of other tax law provisions, (2) to provide a higher level of benefits than would be generated by a company's broad-based plan, (3) to facilitate midcareer recruiting, (4) to recognize incentive pay excluded from recognition in the company's broad-based plan, and (5) to avoid executives' turning down transfers because of benefit disparities when programs are not uniform throughout an organization. The design features of the executive benefit plan should reflect the objectives for establishing the plan.

- An excess benefit plan provides benefits that cannot be provided through a qualified plan solely because of IRC Section 415 limits on benefits and contributions. If it is unfunded, an excess benefit plan is completely exempt from Title I of ERISA. If it is funded, it is subject to Title I's reporting and disclosure, fiduciary responsibility, and enforcement provisions.

- A top hat plan is a plan that is "unfunded and is maintained by an employer primarily for the purpose of providing deferred compensation for a select group of management or highly compensated employees." It is an ERISA Title I pension plan but is *not* subject to the participation, vesting, funding, or fiduciary responsibility provisions of Title I. However, the enforcement and reporting and disclosure requirements do apply to these top hat plans.

- The differences between defined benefit and defined contribution approaches are less significant with executive retirement plans than they are with broad-based plans. Coverage issues under the plan termination provisions of ERISA, which often deter a company from establishing a broad-based defined benefit plan, do not apply to defined benefit executive plans. In a similar way, a defined contribution executive benefit plan can be designed to avoid the transfer of investment and inflation risks to employees.

- Most executive benefit plans have been established on a defined benefit basis. This is especially true where the plan is structured to build upon an underlying broad-based defined benefit program. Certain characteristics of executive benefit plans should differ from the employer's broad-based plan, while the coordination of other features provides consistency that is desirable.

- While the main purpose of SERPs is to provide the executive with an additional layer of retirement benefits over and above those provided by the employer's basic plan, deferred compensation agreements deal primarily with earnings deferral, usually to gain tax advantages, with retirement income as a secondary consideration. In order to avoid the possibility of the executives' being judged to be in constructive receipt of the deferred funds, three rules must be followed in drawing up a deferred compensation agreement. They are that the deferral must be (1) irrevocable, (2) agreed to before the compensation is earned, and (3) for a specified length of time. The agreement also must serve a business purpose.

- The requirements of Section 409A are detailed and place considerable restrictions on the establishment of nonqualified deferred compensation arrangements. Section 409A also makes it difficult to modify a qualifying election once made or to accelerate payment of compensation previously deferred.

Key Terms

corporate-owned life insurance (COLI), p. *260*

deferred compensation agreements, p. *260*

doctrine of constructive receipt, p. *251*

doctrine of economic benefit, p. *251*

excess benefit plans, p. *245*

golden handcuffs, p. *249*

golden handshakes, p. *249*

rabbi trust, p. *260*

secular trust, p. *260*

"select group" requirement, p. *245*

Section 409A, p. *261*

supplemental executive retirement plan (SERP), p. *247*

top hat plans, p. *245*

umbrella plan, p. *248*

Questions for Review

1. What are the typical objectives of an employer in establishing an executive retirement arrangement? Explain.
2. What is the ultimate cost of an executive retirement plan for an employer? Explain.
3. Describe the eligibility requirements typically used under an executive retirement arrangement.
4. Identify the considerations typically used to establish the level of retirement benefits and the income objectives available under an executive defined benefit retirement plan.
5. Describe how the compensation base applicable to benefits under an executive retirement arrangement usually is established.
6. Explain the reasons for including service requirements in executive retirement arrangements and the types of service requirements used.
7. How can an executive retirement arrangement be used to encourage early retirement? Explain.
8. Are lump sum options normally made available under executive retirement arrangements? Explain.
9. Why are executive retirement arrangements typically not prefunded? Explain.
10. Describe the advantages of deferred compensation arrangements.

Questions for Discussion

1. Discuss the conditions under which an employer may desire to establish an executive retirement arrangement.
2. Compare the similarities and differences in plan design issues between qualified retirement plans and executive retirement arrangements.

Resources for Further Study

Editorial Staff. "Section 409A Compliance: Employment Agreements and Separation Pay Arrangements." Poyner & Spruill, LLP *Employee Benefits*. (December 12, 2005).

Ellerman, Brian G. "The Importance of Nonqualified Benefits during Times of Economic Slowdown." *Compensation & Benefits Management* 17, no. 4 (Autumn 2001).

Goldstein, Michael G.; William A. Drennan; and Christopher E. Erblich. "The Expanding Top Hat: Greater Opportunities with Nonqualified Deferred Compensation." *Journal of Financial Service Professionals* 55, no. 4 (July 2001).

Kirk, Kenneth A.; and William J. Bowden. "Finding and Fixing 'Broken' Nonqualified Plans." *Employee Benefits Journal* 26, no. 4 (December 2001).

Ramagnano, Thomas W.; and David M. Sugar. "Executive Compensation Plans." *The Handbook of Employee Benefits*. 6th ed. Jerry S. Rosenbloom, ed. New York: McGraw-Hill, 2005.

Chapter 15

Employee Stock Compensation Plans[1]

After studying this chapter you should be able to:

- Explain the tax advantages of statutory employee stock plans.
- Discuss the general tax principles that provide advantages to nonstatutory employee stock plans.
- Describe the characteristics and tax treatment of incentive stock options (ISOs).
- Explain the attributes and tax treatment of nonqualified stock options (NQSOs).
- Detail other alternate forms of employee stock compensation and describe the merits of each as a form of executive compensation.
- Discuss important issues regarding stock option plans such as common plan provisions and methods of valuation.

Use of employer stock in compensating employees has grown tremendously in recent years. As a result, many employees have a substantial part of their investment portfolios in employer stock, stock options, and other stock-based compensation.

General Considerations

Employee stock options and other stock plans have been used for many years, and the tax law has had various provisions concerning them.[2] But for most of this time, stock options were granted only, or mainly, to senior executives. However, in recent years some corporations have adopted more broadly based plans covering more levels of management or

[1] This chapter is reprinted from G. Victor Hallman and Jerry S. Rosenbloom, *Personal Financial Planning,* 7th ed. New York, NY: McGraw-Hill, 2003 Minor editorial adaptation has occurred, for example, to refer readers to other chapters in this book.

[2] At various times, tax-favored stock options were called *restricted stock options* and *qualified stock options*. These particular plans have been discontinued. The present tax-favored stock option is called an *incentive stock option* (ISO).

even most of their full-time employees. Of course, many companies also have employee stock purchase plans that are designed to cover virtually all employees.

Types of Plans

In the classification that follows, we have divided employer stock plans into **statutory plans** and **nonstatutory plans.** Statutory plans are those to which the tax law accords special tax advantages but that must meet certain requirements to be eligible for the advantages. On the other hand, nonstatutory plans are not based on any special tax provisions but rather are governed by general tax principles.

Statutory Plans

Incentive Stock Options

Incentive stock options were created by the Economic Recovery Tax Act of 1981 (ERTA) in Section 422 of the IRC. They can be made available at the employer's discretion to only some employees, normally certain highly compensated executives, and hence can be discriminatory.

Requirements for ISOs   A number of requirements must be met before a plan can qualify as an ISO plan. For example, the term (duration) of an option cannot exceed 10 years; the option price must equal or exceed the value of the stock when the option was granted; an employee cannot dispose of the stock within two years from granting the option or within one year of the transfer of the stock to him or her (i.e., after exercise of the option); the option must be nontransferable (except by will or inheritance at death); and the maximum value of stock for which an employee can exercise ISOs for the first time in a calendar year generally cannot exceed $100,000 (valued as of the date of the grant).

Tax Treatment to Employees   The main tax advantage of ISOs is that there is no regular income tax levied at the **grant** or at the **exercise** of the option by the employee. However, the bargain element upon *exercise* of an ISO (i.e., the difference between the fair market value of the stock at exercise and the option price) is an adjustment item for individual alternative minimum tax (AMT) purposes. Aside from this AMT issue, the employee is taxed only when he or she sells the stock purchased under the option plan, and then any gain realized is taxed as a capital gain. The capital gain would be the difference between the option price (the income tax basis of the stock) and the stock's fair market value on the date of sale.

As an example, assume that in 1998 Laura Johnson, who works for Acme Corporation, was granted an ISO to purchase 1,000 shares of her employer's common stock at an option price *(strike price)* of $20 per share, its fair market value at the time. The ISO's term was 10 years. Laura had no gross income for federal income tax purposes at the *grant* of this option. Assume further that in 2003 Laura *exercised* the option with cash and purchased 1,000 shares of Acme common from her employer for $20,000 (1,000 shares × $20 per share = $20,000). At that time, the stock's fair market value was $50 per share, and the bargain element was $30,000 ($50 − $20 = $30 × 1,000 shares = $30,000). Laura had no regular gross income at exercise of the ISO, but she did have an AMT adjustment item of $30,000. Note, however, that if this adjustment item produces an AMT, the AMT may be recouped in future years because of the minimum tax credit (MTC). Laura's regular income tax basis for the 1,000 shares is her cost (purchase price) of $20,000, or $20 per share.

Now assume that in 2005 Laura sells the 1,000 shares for $80 per share. At this point Laura realizes and recognizes long-term capital gain of $60 per share, or $60,000 ($80 − $20 = $60 per share × 1,000 shares = $60,000).[3] Further, if Laura does not sell during her lifetime but holds the Acme stock until her death, it currently would get a stepped-up income tax basis and the gain to that point would never be taxed.

Tax Treatment for the Employer   The general principle is that an employer gets a corporate income tax deduction for compensation expense at the same time and in the same amount as the employee realizes gross compensation income from the stock plan. In the case of an ISO, an employee never realizes compensation income, so the employer never gets a corporate tax deduction.

Employee Stock Purchase Plans

Basic Characteristics   **Employee stock purchase plans** are option arrangements under which all full-time employees meeting certain eligibility requirements are allowed to buy stock in their employer corporation, usually at a discount. The option price cannot be less than the lower of (1) 85 percent of the stock's fair market value when the option was granted or (2) 85 percent of the stock's fair market value when the option was exercised. Many employers use these maximum discounts as the option (strike) prices under their plans.

Employees who participate agree to have an estimated amount withheld from their pay to provide the funds with which to exercise their options at the end of an option period. If an employee decides not to exercise an option, the plan will return the amounts withheld to the employee, usually with interest.

Employee stock purchase plans are nondiscriminatory in that they cannot favor the highly paid executives of a corporation. In fact, no employee who owns 5 percent or more of the stock of a corporation can be granted such an option, and the maximum annual value of stock subject to these plans (determined as of the grant of the option) is $25,000.

Tax Treatment to Employees   If the requirements of Section 423 of the IRC are met, there is no gross income for participating employees at the grant or exercise of options under employee stock purchase plans. However, to get this favorable tax treatment, an employee cannot dispose of the stock within two years from grant of the option and within one year from its exercise. If such a disqualifying disposition were to occur, the employee would be taxed, as ordinary compensation income in the year of disposition, on the difference between the fair market value of the stock and the option strike price when the option was exercised.

---

[3] Note that in this example the holding requirements for an ISO have been met (i.e., two years from grant and one year from exercise). However, if the requirements for an ISO had been violated, the option would be treated as a nonqualified stock option (NQSO) described later in this chapter.

For dispositions (sales) of the stock after the two-year and one-year holding periods (or upon death whenever occurring), when the option price was between 85 percent and 100 percent of the stock's fair market value at grant, the employee (or his or her estate) will be taxed as ordinary compensation income on the lesser of (1) the difference between the fair market value of the stock and the option price at the time of disposition or death or (2) the difference between the fair market value of the stock and the option price as of the time the option was granted. The remainder of any gain at sale during the employee's lifetime would be capital gain. At the employee's death, his or her estate or heirs would get a stepped-up basis for the remainder of any gain, and it would never be taxed.

Many corporations have adopted employee stock purchase plans. While a company's plan may not necessarily be as liberal as permitted by the tax law, a great many are. Therefore, it would seem that eligible employees normally would be well advised to participate in these plans if they are at all financially able to do so. If an employee really does not want to hold the stock, he or she can simply sell it at a profit (assuming the stock price was such that the employee should have exercised the option).

Tax Treatment for the Employer   The employer does not get a corporate income tax deduction at grant or exercise of options under employee stock purchase plans.

Qualified Retirement Plans Invested in Employer Securities

These plans were discussed in Chapters 6 and 7. Stock bonus plans permit investment in employer stock and allow distribution of that stock to participants. Employee stock ownership plans (ESOPs) must invest primarily in employer stock. Qualified savings plans with Section 401(k) options often allow significant portions of employee account balances to be invested in employer stock. These plans were explained in Chapter 8. The planning issue of possible lump-sum distributions of employer securities was explored in Chapter 6.

Nonstatutory Plans

General Tax Law Principles Governing Stock Compensation Plans

General Provisions   Since there are no special provisions governing these plans, they are interpreted under provisions of the Code related to income—Section 61 in general and Section 83 in particular. Section 61 is simply the all-inclusive definition of gross income for federal income tax purposes. The more significant provision is Section 83 which deals with taxation of property transferred in connection with the performance of services.

Section 83 in essence provides that the fair market value of property (less any amount paid for the property) transferred to a person for the performance of services shall be included in that person's gross income in the first taxable year in which the person's rights in the property become transferable or are not subject to a substantial risk of forfeiture, whichever is applicable. A substantial risk of forfeiture might exist, for example, if an employee has to remain with the employer for a certain number of years to receive unfettered ownership or rights to the property. In effect, the property (less any amount paid for it) is taxable to the person rendering the services as soon as all substantial conditions on his or her having it are removed.

Section 83(b) Election   However, an important subsection, **IRC Section 83(b),** provides that a person performing services (e.g., an employee) may elect within 30 days of a transfer to include the fair market value of the transferred property (less any amount paid for the property) in his or her gross income, even though the property then was subject to a substantial risk of forfeiture or was not transferable and hence under Section 83 normally would not have been taxable at that point. This is called a *Section 83(b) election.* It can be an important planning tool.

However, if one makes a Section 83(b) election and the value of transferred property is included in the person's gross income, and the property subsequently is forfeited (because, say, the employee did not remain with the employer for the required period), no tax deduction is allowed for the forfeiture. The election also cannot be revoked without the consent of the Secretary of the Treasury. On the other hand, when the substantial risk of forfeiture expires, there is no tax then.

Normally, of course, one does not want to pay taxes any sooner than necessary. On the other hand, a person receiving property for the performance of services (e.g., an executive receiving restricted employer stock) might want to make a Section 83(b) election and be taxed on the current value of the stock, if the current value is relatively low, the person expects it to rise significantly in the future, and he or she expects to remain with the employer at least through the forfeiture period. These, of course, may be big "ifs." Much depends on the circumstances. But if the stock price currently is low and is expected to do well in the future (as, e.g., in some startup situations), the only real risk the person would seem to be taking is the possible loss of his or her current tax payment.

If an employee makes a Section 83(b) election and is currently taxed, the employer gets a corporate income tax deduction for compensation paid in the amount taxable to the employee. The effects of a Section 83(b) election will be illustrated later in connection with the discussion of restricted stock.

Current Stock Bonus

Some employers pay part of employees' current compensation in unrestricted stock. In this case, the employees receive current compensation equal to the fair market value of the stock. On the other hand, employers often pay part of a current bonus in cash and part in restricted stock (i.e., subject to the condition that the employee stay with the employer for a minimum period). In this case the rules for restricted stock apply.

Nonqualified Stock Options (NQSOs)

Basic Characteristics   **Nonqualified stock options (NQSOs)** are stock options that do not meet the requirements for ISOs and so are taxed on the basis of the general principles just discussed. Correspondingly, NQSOs can have terms decided upon by the parties and are not limited in the amount of stock subject to such options exercisable by an employee in any one year (as are ISOs). Hence, NQSOs can be considerably more flexible for employers and employees. Like ISOs, they can be granted only to certain employees and hence may be discriminatory. NQSOs generally have become more popular than ISOs as a compensation technique. While there are no statutory requirements to do so, NQSOs are often granted with an option price equal to 100 percent of the fair market value of the stock on the date of grant and for option terms of around 10 years.

Tax Treatment to Employees   There normally is no taxable event (gross income) at grant because the tax regulations view their value then as not being readily ascertainable.[4] On the other hand, upon exercise of an option (and transfer of the stock to the employee), the employee will receive ordinary compensation income for regular federal income tax purposes equal to the difference between the fair market value of the stock at exercise and the option price (the bargain element). The employee's income tax basis in the stock is its fair market value at exercise. This is because the employee paid the option price to the employer (a cost basis) and included the remainder of the stock's value (bargain element) in his or her gross income as compensation (basis under the tax benefit principle). Thus, an immediate sale of the stock by the employee (there are no two-year and one-year holding periods for NQSOs) will produce zero capital gain or loss since the amount realized would equal the adjusted basis for the stock.

Let us illustrate these principles by returning to our example involving Laura Johnson. If we assume the same facts except that Laura was granted an NQSO in 1998 instead of an ISO, the tax results would be as follows. Laura would have no gross income at grant of the option. However, when Laura exercised her NQSO in 2003, she would have had ordinary compensation income of $30,000 in that year.[5] Laura's income tax basis for the 1,000 shares is $50,000, or $50 per share ($20 per share of cost basis and $30 per share of basis due to that amount having been taxed).

Now when Laura sells her 1,000 shares of Acme common in 2005 at a price of $80 per share, she will realize and recognize long-term capital gain of $30 per share, or $30,000 ($80 − $50 = $30 per share × 1,000 shares = $30,000). Thus, for the NQSO the total gain on the option stock would still be $60,000, except that $30,000 would be ordinary compensation income and $30,000 long-term capital gain taxable at a maximum 20 percent rate.

Tax Treatment for the Employer   The employer gets a corporate income tax deduction for the amount of compensation income the employee realizes at exercise of the option.

Restricted Stock

Basic Characteristics   **Restricted stock plans** are arrangements by which a corporation grants stock (or stock options) to an employee (or someone rendering services to the corporation), but ownership of the stock is subject to a substantial risk of forfeiture (such as the employee's remaining with the employer for a certain number of years or the corporation's meeting certain profit goals). Such stock may be provided to employees in a variety of circumstances. It can be part of a general compensation package, perhaps

---

[4] Employee stock options, of course, are not traded on organized or over-the-counter markets, may not be transferable, and normally are not vested at grant.

[5] Note that the AMT is not involved here because the $30,000 bargain element is taxable for *regular* income tax purposes.

to entice a candidate to accept an offer of employment. It can be part of a bonus plan as noted earlier. And in some cases, stock issued on exercise of an NQSO can be restricted stock in order to further postpone taxation.

Tax Treatment to Employees and the Section 83(b) Election   As explained earlier, an employee receives ordinary compensation income in the year the employee's rights to the stock are first not subject to the substantial risk of forfeiture or are transferable. The gross income is measured by the fair market value of the stock at that time less any cost to the employee. However, depending on the circumstances, a Section 83(b) election (described earlier) may be considered. A person receiving restricted stock must make a planning decision regarding this election.

Again to illustrate these principles, let us assume that John Venture is a young information technology executive with a large corporation. Recently a former college classmate invited him to join a startup company (XYZ.com) that has some exciting new products in information technology. The offer is for a lower salary, but XYZ.com, which recently went public, will give John a compensation package that includes NQSOs and 10,000 shares of restricted stock (which is conditioned on John's staying with the company for at least three years). John does not have to pay anything for the 10,000 shares. XYZ.com common stock currently is selling at $2 per share.

John accepts the offer in 2003 and makes no Section 83(b) election. He has no gross income from receipt of the 10,000 shares of restricted stock since it is subject to a substantial risk of forfeiture. Let us further assume that at the end of three years (in 2006). John is still with XYZ.com and that its stock has done very well. Its price in 2006 is $20 per share. When the substantial risk of forfeiture ends (in 2006), John will have ordinary compensation income of $200,000 (10,000 shares × $20 per share = $200,000). His income tax basis in the 10,000 shares also will be $200,000, or $20 per share.

Now let us change our facts and assume John made the Section 83(b) election in 2003 within 30 days of receiving the 10,000 shares. He then would be taxed on $20,000 in year 2003 ($2 per share × 10,000 shares = $20,000) as ordinary compensation income, and his basis in the 10,000 shares also would be $20,000, or $2 per share. If John is still with XYZ.com at the end of the three years (in 2006), the substantial risk of forfeiture would end, and he would have unrestricted right to the stock. He would incur no further gross income then. On the other hand, if John should leave XYZ.com after, say, two years, he would forfeit the 10,000 shares and could take no tax deduction for that. In effect, he would lose the tax he paid in 2003 on the $20,000 of ordinary income.

Let us now assume that John stayed with XYZ.com until 2006 and that two years later (in 2008) John sells the 10,000 shares for $30 per share. If he had not made the Section 83(b) election in the year 2003, he would have $100,000 of long-term capital gain ($300,000 amount realized − $200,000 adjusted basis = $100,000 gain realized and recognized). In effect, he would have had $300,000 of total gain on the 10,000 shares of restricted stock ($200,000 of ordinary compensation income and $100,000 of long-term capital gain). On the other hand, if John had made the Section 83(b) election in the year 2003, he would have $280,000 of long-term capital gain ($300,000 amount realized − $20,000 adjusted basis = $280,000 gain realized and recognized). In this situation, he also would have had $300,000 of total gain on the 10,000 shares of restricted stock, but now it is divided as $20,000 of ordinary compensation income and

$280,000 of long-term capital gain. Further, if John does not sell the 10,000 shares (or all of them) during his lifetime, he can still consider other techniques for possibly avoiding capital gains taxation. Finally, if he does not sell or otherwise dispose of his stock, it currently will get a stepped-up basis at death. But if the market price of the stock falls or it becomes worthless, John would have been better off not making the Section 83(b) election.

Tax Treatment for the Employer   Again, the employer gets a corporate income tax deduction when the employee receives gross compensation income. This is either when the substantial risk of forfeiture ends or, when the Section 83(b) election is made.

Other Stock-Based Plans

This is a complex field and only a brief description of some of these plans will be given here.

Stock Appreciation Rights   **Stock appreciation rights (SARs)** are accounts maintained for selected employees that reflect the appreciation in the employer's stock over a certain period. When an executive's rights to an SAR become final, it normally is paid out to him or her in cash and is taxable then.

Phantom Stock   **Phantom stock** accounts also are maintained for selected employees, but they normally reflect the full value of a certain amount of employer stock. The account value varies with the stock's value and normally is paid to the executive in cash at some point. However, there is no actual stock in the account.

Performance Shares or Performance-Based Stock Options   In this case, selected employees are granted stock **performance shares** or options whose vesting is contingent on certain corporate or other performance measures being met.

Provisions of Stock Option Plans

Vesting of Options

This is the period of continuous employment that must elapse after an option is granted and before the employee can exercise the option. There generally are vesting requirements in stock option plans. The periods required for vesting vary but often range from two to four years.

Transferability of Options

Traditionally, employee stock options have not been transferable by the employees receiving the options other than at death. They could not be sold or given away. One of the requirements to be an ISO is that the option by its terms must not be transferable (other than by will or intestate distribution) and must be exercisable during the employee's lifetime only by him or her.

There is no corresponding prohibition for NQSOs. But in the past, corporations in practice have not allowed their NQSOs to be transferable. Recently, however, some corporations have amended their stock option plans to allow NQSOs to be transferred (given) to members of the employee's family, trusts for such members, or possibly family limited partnerships with such members as partners, with the consent of the corporation.

Although nonqualified stock options historically have been nontransferable, there are some notable and innovative exceptions. In 2003, Microsoft permitted employees to transfer certain options to J. P. Morgan based on option exercise price. This 2003 transfer program represented a one-time offering, and it occurred when the company shifted from granting "stock options" to making "stock awards."

Beginning in 2007, Google employees were permitted to auction their vested stock options to qualifying financial institutions. Upon vesting with Google's transferable stock options (TSOs), in addition to holding the options for exercise at a later date, or exercising the stock options and holding or selling the stock acquired, employees had a third alternative—to sell their options to a financial institution through a competitive bidding process.

Among the advantages of allowing employees to auction their options are the following:

1. Increasing the value of granted options.
2. Making option values more tangible for employees.

Since a financial institution purchasing an option would have upside-potential if the underlying stock appreciated, the option would be worth more than the difference between the option exercise price and the current market value of the stock (called intrinsic value). If Google granted an option whose exercise price equaled market price, intrinsic value would be zero, but the bid offering values from the financial institutions would represent a higher and very tangible indicator of value.

Effect of Certain Contingencies on Options

Stock option plans normally have certain forfeiture provisions in the event of termination of employment for various reasons. The option holder (or his or her estate or heirs) usually has a limited period of time to exercise the option after he or she retires (such as three to five years), becomes disabled on a long-term basis (such as three to five years), dies (such as one or two years), voluntarily terminates employment (such as three months), or for other reasons. Some plans also provide that options will be automatically forfeited if the holder becomes employed by or associated with a competitor of his or her former employer. In such a case, if an option holder is planning to change jobs and go with a competing firm, he or she should exercise favorable (i.e., "in the money") vested options before terminating employment.

Exercise of Options

Stock options generally can be exercised in several ways.

Cash Exercise   An option holder can make a **cash exercise** by paying the option price to the employer and having the stock transferred to him or her. In the case of an NQSO, the employer also will require withholding of federal, state, local, and FICA taxes on the taxable amount. The option holder must lay out the option price (and any withholding) in cash.

Stock-for-Stock Exercise   A plan may allow employees to pay the exercise price by delivering shares of the employer's stock that they own that are equal in value to the option price to the employer and having the option stock transferred to them. This may be referred to as a **stock-for-stock exercise.**

As an example, suppose that Ahmed Bastor exercises an NQSO to buy 1,000 shares of ABC Corporation common stock at an option price of $20 per share when the fair market value of the stock is $50 per share. Ahmed already owns ABC common through previous stock option exercises. In a stock-for-stock exercise, Ahmed could deliver 400 shares of his ABC common to the corporation to pay the $20,000 exercise price (1,000 shares × $20 per share = $20,000 exercise price ÷ $50 per share = 400 shares of stock to deliver). Assume that the 400 shares of his stock had an income tax basis to Ahmed of $10 per share. There is no gain recognized on the exchange of his 400 shares for 400 of the option shares and the new shares will have the same holding period for capital gain purposes as the previously owned shares. This is because this is a tax-free exchange of common stock in a corporation for common stock in the same corporation as provided in Section 1036 of the IRC.

The income tax basis of the exchanged shares ($10 per share) will be carried over to 400 of the new option shares. The remainder of the new option shares will be as if it were a cash exercise. The difference between the fair market value of the stock received (600 shares × $50 per share = $30,000) less any cash paid for the stock (0 in this example) would be ordinary compensation income to Ahmed, and his income tax basis in these 600 shares would be $50 per share (or $30,000), which is the amount taken into his gross income for them. The corporation may require cash withholding or allow withholding in the form of stock otherwise issuable to the option holder.

In a stock-for-stock exercise, the option holder is paying for some of the new option stock with existing company stock. This reduces the option holder's overall stock position in the company, as compared with a cash exercise, and is the reason reload options (discussed later) may be granted in this situation.

Cashless Exercise   This type of exercise involves working through a stockbroker who can buy the option stock from the corporation at the exercise price, sell enough stock in the open market to cover the purchase price plus his or her commissions and a small amount of margin loan interest, and then deliver the remaining stock to the option holder. Because of uncertainties concerning employers that arrange loans for executives under the Sarbanes-Oxley Act, as of this writing, employers generally have not been providing for cashless exercises.

Reload Options   These are additional options that may be granted to employees when they pay the exercise price for stock with stock they own in the corporation (a stock-for-stock exercise). The **reload option** normally is for the same number of shares used to pay the exercise price (plus perhaps shares used for federal, state, local, and FICA withholding taxes) and is for the remainder of the option period of the underlying option that was exercised.

A stock-for-stock exercise of an underlying option when there is a reload option can be attractive for an option holder. Using our example of Ahmed Bastor, assume that ABC's plan provides for reload options. In this case, if the underlying option Ahmed exercised originally had a term of 10 years and Ahmed engaged in the stock-for-stock exercise described previously four years after the grant date, he might be granted a reload option for 400 shares (ignoring, for the sake of simplicity, any stock used for tax withholding purposes) at an option price of $50 per share (the current fair market value of the stock) for a term of six years (the remaining term of the exercised underlying option).

Ahmed is now in a better position than he would have been with a cash exercise of a stock-for-stock exercise with no reload option. Under a cash exercise, he would have an exposure to ABC Corporation stock of 1,400 directly owned shares (400 previously owned and 1,000 option shares), but he would have had to come up with the $20,000 needed to exercise the underlying option. Under a stock-for-stock exercise with no reload feature, Ahmed's exposure to ABC stock would be reduced to 1,000 directly owned shares (the option shares). However, under the stock-for-stock exercise with a reload feature, his exposure to ABC stock remains at 1,400 shares (1,000 directly owned option shares and 400 reload option shares), but he does not need to disturb his other assets or cash reserves to exercise the underlying option. This occurs because Ahmed has been given a new option (the reload option), which itself has value.

Valuation of Stock Options

This is a very complex subject. It is made even more so by the fact that employee stock options are different in many ways from publicly traded stock and other options. In essence, however, employee stock options are really call options for the employees on employer stock.

People may be concerned about the **valuation of** employee **stock options** for many reasons. To the extent employers "expense" options when they vest, obviously they must be valued. Employees want to know what they are really worth, since options have become an important part of many compensation arrangements. They also need to be valued for purposes of an employee's asset allocation planning. In some cases, employees may give up cash compensation in exchange for stock options, so they want to have an idea of what the options are worth to evaluate the exchange. Finally, employee stock options may need to be valued for estate planning.

Traded Options

The market prices of publicly traded options are readily available in the financial press and from other sources. Employee stock options, of course, are not publicly traded and have no readily ascertainable market value.

Most traded options are for relatively short durations, such as a few months. However, just to get an idea of how the market values longer-term options relative to the prices of the underlying stocks, it may be instructive to note the market premiums (prices) for leaps. **Leaps** are longer-term publicly traded options. For example, as of this writing, the price of a 21-month call option on one major company's stock with a strike price of $40 when the underlying stock's current market price is $37.35 (i.e., this call option was out of the money) was $5.60 per share, or about 15 percent of the underlying stock's market price.

Naturally, the prices of such publicly traded long-term options will vary with the characteristics of the underlying stocks and market conditions. The only point being made here is that the market itself sets a considerable value on longer-term options, even when they have no intrinsic value (described next) or are out of the money. Clearly then, the market value (as well as the economic value) of long-term options can be substantial.

Intrinsic Value

The intrinsic value of a stock option is the difference between the underlying stock's current market price and the option's strike price. For example, if an employee is granted a 10-year NQSO with an option price of $25 per share when the underlying stock's market price also is $25 per share, the intrinsic value of the option is $0 at grant. As we have just seen for traded options, the intrinsic value does not reflect the fair value or economic worth of an option. In fact, as will be shown in the next section, the economic worth of long-term options can be quite substantial.

Option Pricing Models

A number of models (mathematical systems of analysis) have been developed to compute the fair value or economic worth of options. Probably the best known is the Black-Scholes option pricing model. This model is based on the following six factors to determine the economic value of an option.[6] (Let us say for the following illustration of these factors that we are valuing an employee stock option.)

- Option exercise price (strike price).
- Current market price of the underlying stock.
- Risk-free interest rate during the expected term of the option.
- Expected dividend yield on the stock.
- Expected life of the option. This is the time period for which the employee is actually expected to hold the option before exercising it. It may be shorter than the maximum option period in the plan.
- Expected volatility of the underlying stock's market price. This normally is the most important factor in the model. The greater the expected volatility, the more likely there will be time value gains (see note 6) and the greater the option value will be. Volatility can be estimated from the historical standard deviation of the stock's price changes over past time periods.

To illustrate the *fair value* of an option, let us continue our fact pattern for the NQSO noted earlier with respect to intrinsic value. Using the factors just listed, we assume that this NQSO has an option exercise price of $25 per share, a current market price for the underlying stock is also $25 per share, the assumed risk-free interest rate is 5 percent, the expected dividend yield is 0, the assumed expected life of the option is 10 years, and the expected volatility of the underlying stock's price is 20 percent per month. Under these

---

[6] The concept behind these option pricing models is that the fair value of an option (which, in general, is an instrument that allows, but does not require, a person to buy or sell an asset at a prearranged price during a set time period) consists of two elements: (1) the intrinsic value and (2) a time value, arising because the option holder may benefit from favorable future price movements (volatility) in the asset without having the downside risk of actual ownership of the asset.

assumptions, the Black-Scholes model would produce a fair value of $19.75 per option. This is 79 percent of the underlying stock's current price. Of course, if the assumed expected life of the option were reduced, the fair value would decline. For example, if the expected life were one year, the fair value would be $7.24 per option. Most employee stock options have an expected life of considerably more than one year. Software is available for calculating the fair value of options under option pricing models.

It is clear from this discussion that the *economic value (fair value)* of stock options granted to employees can be substantial. However, it must also be recognized that the *actual value* of such options may never reach the fair value at grant (from an option pricing model), and may even be zero, if the actual market price of the underlying stock fails to rise from the option price or declines.

Sometimes when a stock's price falls and many executive stock options are "under water" (i.e., the stock's market price is below the option price and the option is out of the money), the employer will *reprice the options* to be equal to the stock's current market price (i.e., cancel the old out-of-the-money options and issue new ones at the stock's current market value). However, this tactic is controversial.

Some Caveats Concerning Stock Options and Other Plans

While employee stock options and other stock compensation plans have been a boon for many employees and a bonanza for some, some caveats concerning them are in order.

What Goes Up Can Come Down!

It seems almost trite to say that while employee stock plans can be very attractive when the price of a company's stock is rising, the reverse will be true when the price is falling. However, some employees may not truly understand this. They can overcommit themselves financially on the basis of paper gains in their stock options and other plans.

Some Employees May Not Realize the True Economic Worth of Options

The other side of the coin is that some employees may not truly understand, or may have difficulty in analyzing, the economic value of options or other stock rights granted to them.

Risk of Excessive Concentration in Employer Stock

While employees usually are well advised to take advantage of these plans when they are attractive to them, they also should deal with any issue of overconcentration, assuming they want a reasonably diversified investment portfolio.

Planning Issues Regarding Stock Options and Other Stock Plans

Some of these issues may be summarized as follows:

- Whether to participate in employee stock purchase plan offerings. This depends on the terms of the plan and the employer stock, but in general, these plans are advantageous for employees and are flexible as to whether participating employees will take the stock.

- When to exercise stock options. This can be a complicated issue. Assume an employee simply holds a vested, unexercised option for as long as possible before exercising it. In this case, he or she can benefit if the underlying stock rises in price above the option's exercise price without actually committing any funds and can delay income taxation, in the case of NQSOs until exercise. This can also be attractive if income tax rates on ordinary compensation income (such as will arise from exercising NQSOs) will decline in the future, as under EGTRRA, for example. But if there is a concern that the stock's price may fall and not really ever recover during the remaining option period, it is better to exercise now and sell the stock as soon as possible. Also, if over-concentration in employer stock is an issue, as it often is, the exercise of NQSOs and immediate sale of the stock can be a tax-efficient remedy since compensation income must be realized at some point anyway and there is no capital gain on immediate sale because the basis is equal to fair market value at exercise.
- Whether, in effect, to change an ISO into an NQSO by breaking an ISO require-ment (i.e., making a disqualifying disposition by sale of the stock within one year of exercise). This may be done to avoid an AMT problem or if the stock's price is expected to fall dramatically. A planning technique that may be used in this situation is AMT neutralization. In AMT neutralization, the employee sells enough ISO shares (after exercise) in disqualifying dispositions so that his or her regular tax for the year becomes equal to his or her AMT. Then there is no AMT to pay.
- How to exercise options (including the possible availability of reload options).
- Whether to make a Section 83(b) election with regard to restricted stock or other plans.
- Whether to take option stock as restricted stock, if available. This is done to further delay recognition of income on exercise of NQSOs.
- Whether to take bonuses or other compensation in the form of stock options, if available.
- How to maintain investment diversification in light of favorable terms for acquiring more and more employer stock.
- Any estate planning actions with regard to stock plans. This might include making gifts of NQSOs, if allowed by the plan. However, such gifts should be analyzed carefully. It also may include the exercise of any in-the-money unexercised NQSOs before death (e.g. a "death bed exercise") for estate tax reasons.

Chapter Summary

- Statutory employer stock plans are those plans to which the tax law accords special tax advantages in recognition of their being subject to certain requirements. Nonstatutory employer stock plans are not subject to these requirements, do not receive special tax advantages, but are governed by general tax principles. Among the most com-mon statutory employer stock plans would be incentive stock options, employee stock purchase plans governed by Section 423 of the Internal Revenue Code, and qualified retirement plans invested in employer securities. Among the most common forms of nonstatutory employer stock plans would be current compensation paid as a bonus in unrestricted stock, nonqualified stock options, restricted stock plans, stock appreciation rights, phantom stock, and performance shares or performance-based stock options.

- Incentive stock options require:
  - The term of the option cannot exceed 10 years.
  - The option price must equal or exceed the value of the stock when the option was granted.
  - No disposition can be made of the stock by the person granted the ISO within two years from the granting of the option or within one year of the transfer of the stock to him or her following stock option exercise.
  - The option must be nontransferable except by will or inheritance at death.
  - The maximum value of stock for which an employee can exercise ISOs in any year generally cannot exceed $100,000.

    The main tax advantage of ISOs to employees is that there is no regular income tax levied at the grant or at the exercise of the option by the employee. Since the employer receives a corporate income tax deduction for compensation expense when the employee realizes gross compensation income from a stock plan, in the case of an ISO, the employer never gets a corporate tax deduction.

- Section 423 employee stock purchase plans are structured so that:
  - All full-time employees meeting certain eligibility requirements be permitted to buy stock in their employer corporation.
  - The option price cannot be less than the lower of:
    (1) 85 percent of the stock's fair market value when the option was granted, or
    (2) 85 percent of the stock's fair market value when the option was exercised.
  - If an employee does not exercise an option, the plan returns amounts withheld from the employee's pay, usually with interest.
  - No employee who owns 5 percent or more of the corporation's stock can be granted such an option.
  - The maximum annual value of stock subject to these plans determined as of the grant of the option is $25,000.

    The main tax advantage of a Section 423 plan is that no gross income is attributable to participating employees at either the grant or exercise of the options, provided no disposition of the stock occurs by the employee within two years from grant of the option and within one year from the option's exercise. When dispositions of the stock occur after the requisite holding period, the employee is taxed as having received ordinary compensation income on the lesser of:

    (1) The difference between the fair market value of the stock and the option price at the time of disposition or death, or
    (2) The difference between the fair market value of the stock and the option price as of the time the option was granted.

> The employer does not get a corporate income tax deduction at grant or exercise of options under employee stock purchase plans.

- Nonqualified stock options are stock options that do not meet the tax requirements for ISOs and are taxed on the basis of general tax principles. There normally is no taxable event when the option is granted to the employee. When the option is exercised and stock is transferred to the employee, the employee receives ordinary compensation income equaling the difference between the fair market value of the stock at exercise and the option price of the stock. The basis of the stock at exercise is the stock's fair market value because the employee paid the option price for the stock and reported the difference between fair market value and option price as reportable income. The employer receives a corporate income tax deduction for the amount of compensation income the employee realizes at exercise of the option.

- Internal Revenue Code Section 83 provides that the fair market value of property that is transferred to a person as compensation for the performance of services, less any amount the person pays for the property, is included in the person's gross income in the first taxable year in which the person's rights in the property become transferable or are not subject to a substantial risk of forfeiture. However, subsection (b) of Section 83 allows a person performing services to elect within 30 days of grant to include the fair market value of transferred property, less any amount paid for the property, in his or her gross income immediately. This inclusion occurs even though the property is still subject to a substantial risk of forfeiture or is not transferable and subject to taxation according to Section 83. When the substantial risk of forfeiture subsequently expires, a tax would not be levied on the person at that time because the person already included the fair market value of the property in his or her income with the Subsection 83(b) election. Appreciation in the property would be taxed as a capital gain upon subsequent disposition of the property. An employer takes a corporate income tax deduction when the employee receives gross compensation income—either when the substantial risk of forfeiture expires, or when the Subsection 83(b) election is made.

- Stock options can be exercised in the following ways:
  - *Cash exercise*   The option holder pays the option price to the employer, and the stock is transferred to the option holder.
  - *Stock-for-stock exercise*   The option holder delivers previously owned shares of employer stock to the employer that are equal in value to the option price required for the employer stock under the terms of the option. This transaction is a tax-free exchange as provided in Section 1036 of the IRC.
  - *Cashless exercise*   A stockbroker buys the option stock from the corporation at the exercise price, sells enough stock in the open market to cover the purchase price plus broker's commissions and a small amount of margin interest, and delivers the remaining stock to the option holder. If the option holder wishes to receive cash rather than stock, the option stock is sold and the cash proceeds are remitted to the option holder. Because of uncertainties concerning employers that arrange loans for executives under the Sarbanes-Oxley Act, as of this writing employers generally have not been providing for cashless exercise.

– *Reload options* Additional options are granted to employees when they pay the exercise price for stock with previously owned stock of the corporation. A stock-for-stock exercise with a reload feature allows the option holder to exercise without disturbing other assets or cash reserves and continue to hold an increased option and stock position with upside potential because of the new option which was granted.

Key Terms

cash exercise, p. *274*
employee stock purchase plans, p. *268*
exercise, p. *267*
grant, p. *267*
incentive stock options (ISOs), p. *267*
IRC Section 83(b), p. *270*
leaps, p. *276*

nonqualified stock options (NQSOs), p. *270*
nonstatutory plans, p. *267*
performance shares, p. *273*
phantom stock, p. *273*
reload options, p. *275*
restricted stock plans, p. *271*
statutory plans, p. *267*

stock appreciation rights (SARs), p. *273*
stock-for-stock exercise, p. *275*
valuation of stock options, p. *276*

Questions for Review

1. Distinguish what is meant by both statutory and nonstatutory employer stock plans.
2. Identify common forms of statutory employer stock plans.
3. Identify common forms of nonstatutory employer stock plans.
4. Explain the specific requirements for incentive stock options to receive special tax treatment by employees, and detail what this special tax treatment is.
5. What are the requirements and tax advantages of employee stock purchase plans under Section 423 of the IRC?
6. Discuss the general tax law provisions that govern stock compensation plans.
7. Describe the workings of a Section 83(b) election, its tax ramifications, and its usefulness in the context of tax planning for resticted stock options.
8. Summarize the common provisions needed to be included in stock option plans.
9. Identify and explain the ways in which stock options can be exercised.
10. How are stock options commonly valued?
11. What factors are used to determine the value of an option using the Black-Scholes option pricing model?
12. What caveats or concerns should be recognized by employees eligible for employer stock option plans?
13. List common planning issues for employees eligible for stock options and other employer stock plans.

Questions for Discussion

1. Discuss the advantages and risks involved for an employee who can either accept an employment opportunity with a relatively higher direct compensation package with little or nothing in employer stock plans or, alternatively, a relatively lower direct compensation package with a greater degree of employer stock plan participation.
2. Discuss what personal factors may influence the exposure one might be willing to accept for high concentrations of employer stock beneficially received through employer stock plans.
3. Discuss various financial planning strategies to increase asset diversification when employer stock results in a heavy concentration of employee wealth.

Resources for Further Study

Banham, Russ. "Sunk by Options." *Journal of Accountancy* 192, no. 4 (October 2001).

Editorial Staff. Internal Revenue Service. "IRS Offers Opportunity for Employers to Satisfy Tax Obligations of Rank-and-File Employees with 'Backdated' Stock Options," IR-2007-30. (February 8, 2007).

Hallman, G. Victor; and Jerry S. Rosenbloom. *Personal Financial Planning.* 7th ed. New York: McGraw-Hill, 2003.

Ramagnano, Thomas W.; and David M. Sugar. "Executive Compensation Plans." In *The Handbook of Employee Benefits.* 6th ed. Jerry S. Rosenbloom, ed. New York: McGraw-Hill, 2005.

www.nceo.org—website of the National Center for Employee Ownership.

Chapter 16

Managing Retirement Assets in Multiple Plan Structures

After studying this chapter you should be able to:

- Summarize the reason many workers find their retirement assets spread among multiple retirement savings plans.
- Discuss some of the possible advantages and valid reasons for holding retirement assets in multiple retirement savings plan structures.
- Describe some of the considerations and rationales for consolidating retirement assets in a single or a limited number of retirement savings plans.
- List and describe the two methods for transferring assets between investment companies within an employer's retirement plan and between various types of retirement savings plans.
- Explain the evolution of governmental policy on transferability and portability of assets held within retirement savings plans.
- Summarize the three broad categories of decision items to consider when contemplating the consolidation of retirement plan asset balances.
- Provide detailed explanations of decision items considered when consolidating retirement plan assets.

Introduction

As noted in previous chapters, a wide variety of types of defined contribution plan structures are permissible under the law. Also, the private retirement system has evolved into a system in which defined contribution plans now represent the dominant form of retirement plan for most workers. Defined contribution plans provide accounts that accumulate an asset pool that then provides a retirement income stream for workers. If an individual has worked for several employers during his or her career, as is the case for many workers, it is likely that his or her retirement plan resources will be spread among not only various employers, but also among different types of retirement plan structures. It is possible for some workers to have retirement assets in 401(k) plans, 403(b) plans, 457(b) plans, and other defined contribution structures. Quite possibly, the individual also may have earned a pension benefit payable from an employer-sponsored defined benefit plan. There is nothing intrinsically wrong with having retirement resources spread among a number of different retirement savings vehicles and among the different employers for whom the individual has worked. In fact, it can be argued that some diversification among plan sponsors and differing types of plans may be preferable to having one's retirement assets all in one place. Not only are there diversification effects, but different plans may offer different funds and allow for differing plan features.

Because all rules are not uniform, as of this writing, diversification may allow access to certain plan features that are not allowable in different plan structures. Even if certain features are permissible in different types of plans, not all employers adopt the same features. For instance, not all employers permit participants to access plan loans. Having funds in a plan that allows plan loans may provide access to funds in a way that is desirable to a plan participant. Assuming that an individual has the ability to consolidate plan assets, he or she may choose to keep assets separately segregated in distinct plans for very valid reasons. However, for most people, there should be some consideration of the inefficiencies of having assets spread among various sponsors, and a conscious decision should be made whether it makes sense to keep assets segregated in various plans or to aggregate some of these assets.

Consolidation of assets need not be an all-or-nothing decision. It is possible that some consolidation may make sense without bringing all of the assets into a single plan structure or individual retirement account. The extent to which consolidation should occur can vary. This chapter concerns itself with this issue and discusses the relative merits of holding retirement resources in disparate plans with different employers and the possible merits of consolidating assets in an individual retirement account or other type of plan structure. No single right answer exists on the issue of consolidating plan assets. The determination as to the merits of consolidating assets will depend on the preferences of the individual planning for retirement; that individual's ability to manage assets in different plan structures; and the plan features, including costs and investment options within the individual's array of plan structures. Also, the timing of when consolidation should occur is an individual preference item.

Some individuals may prefer to consolidate their plans throughout their careers as they change jobs and switch employers. Others may decide to wait until transition to the distribution phase at the point of retirement to make this decision. Although there is nothing particularly wrong with waiting, it is preferable that an individual considers this decision throughout her or his career when given the opportunity to make these changes. The reason for considering the viability of consolidation on an ongoing basis when given the opportunity under the law has to do with the available alternatives that an individual has at any point in time. For instance, if an individual had less costly alternatives available and was able to make changes early in her or his career, the effects of compounding could dramatically magnify the accumulation of assets. Delaying the decision could be very costly to the individual. Similarly, if an individual had access to superior funds within a 401(k), 403(b), or 457(b) plan, the foregone opportunity cost associated with remaining in inferior mutual funds again could be very costly. In essence, an individual is not under immediate time pressure in making a decision regarding asset and plan consolidation; however, decisions by default and inertia can be extremely costly and extract a sizable component from the accumulating assets. The remainder of this chapter examines the decision considerations in more detail.

Consolidation of Retirement Assets: An Issue Confronting More Participants

Although individuals have had the ability to consolidate plan assets and make rollover distributions into individual retirement accounts for some time, there were constraints in the past that prohibited certain instances of commingling assets from different types of retirement savings vehicles. One of the reasons for these prohibitions on commingling arose because of differences in the rules applicable to various types of plans. At one time, certain retirement savings vehicles had more stringent rules regarding distributions before retirement than other types of retirement savings structures. Generally, it was not allowable to commingle assets from a type of plan with more stringent rules regarding distribution with assets from a type of plan with less stringent rules regarding distribution. This was the case because one could conceivably bypass the restrictions on distribution by moving the assets from the plan with more stringent rules to the plan with less stringent rules and then subsequently withdraw the funds. This would have provided a means to bypass the constraints prohibiting early distribution from the initial plan.

Over the years, governmental policymakers have come to believe that the retirement system has become much too complex, and an inordinate amount of economic resources are expended in trying to comply with these complicated rules. Although the argument can be made that many of these rules served valid purposes when originally enacted into law, many believe that the layering of successive rules over time has made the system burdensome. A majority of observers seem to favor simplification of the rules. A governmental policy theme has sought simplification, and efforts have been made to seek uniformity across various types of plans. As the rules for various types of plans have converged toward a more uniform set of rules, it has become easier to allow for transferability between various types of plans. **Transferability** relates to the ability of a plan participant to move assets. These assets may be moved from one investment company within an employer's retirement plan offerings to another investment company within the same employer's retirement plan offerings, from one plan to the same type of plan at a different employer, or from one type of plan to a different type of plan at a different employer. Similarly, assets could be transferred to an individual retirement account. In the past when there were more restrictions on moving assets between plans, the term *transferability* usually referred to the ability to move assets from one investment company to another investment company within the same employer's plan. A move from one plan to another plan may have assets moving from one employer's 401(k) plan to another employer's 401(k) plan. An example of assets moving from one type of plan to another type of plan may have assets moving from one employer's 401(k) plan to another employer's 403(b) plan.

Not only has uniformity in the rules between types of plans been sought, but facilitating portability of plan assets has been sought as well. **Uniformity** has to do with a set of rules that are consistent and applicable in the same way to different types of plans. **Portability** involves the ability to move plan assets with the individual plan participant rather than requiring that the assets remain under the control of a given plan sponsor overseeing the assets in the plan where the assets were first contributed. The prevailing theme in many legislative initiatives has been to encourage rather than thwart portability of retirement assets. This view holds that individuals should be able to move assets with them when they move from one employer to another. Very often when individuals terminate employment, they may roll over assets from the employer-sponsored retirement plan into an individual retirement account (IRA). Portability can entail an individual rolling over assets into an individual retirement account, requesting a plan distribution or withdrawal of funds from the retirement plan, or rolling over assets from a previous employer's retirement plan into a new employer's retirement plan.

There are two methods for transferring assets between investment companies within an employer's retirement plan and from one type of retirement savings plan to another type of retirement savings plan. Transfers can occur either as a direct trustee-to-trustee rollover or as a regular or indirect rollover. In a **direct trustee-to-trustee rollover,** the individual instructs the plan trustee or contract issuer to transfer funds directly to the other retirement savings plan. In a **regular or indirect rollover,** the individual receives a check for the eligible rollover distribution from the plan trustee or contract issuer (net of the required 20 percent federal income tax withholding). Then within 60 days of receipt, the individual contributes up to the amount of the **eligible rollover distribution** as a rollover contribution to the receiving retirement savings plan. The benefit of using the direct trustee-to-trustee rollover method is that there is no 20 percent federal income tax withholding. An individual using the regular or indirect rollover method can contribute the 20 percent withholding amount to the receiving retirement savings plan from his or her own personal funds to retain the tax-deferred rollover of the entire amount of the eligible rollover distribution. An eligible rollover distribution that is accomplished either as a direct trustee-to-trustee rollover or as a regular or indirect rollover within 60 days of receipt is not taxable to the individual as a distribution. However, if distributions come out of a traditional IRA or another type of retirement savings plan after January 1, 2008, and are subsequently directed into a Roth IRA, such distributions would constitute a taxable distribution.

The rules allowing plan balances to be consolidated have been liberalized considerably from what they were in the past. For instance, prior to 2002, 403(b) plan assets could only be rolled over into another 403(b) plan or into an individual retirement account. Beginning in 2002 and as a result of changes enacted into law as part of the Economic Growth and Tax Relief Reconciliation Act of 2001 (EGTRRA), rollover distributions were permitted between qualified plans, 403(b) plans, and eligible governmental 457(b) plans. Also, as was permitted previously for qualified plans and 403(b) plans, eligible 457(b) plans could also be rolled over into IRAs. Generally, if an individual terminates employment, he or she often has the option to make an eligible rollover distribution.

Although EGTRRA went a long way to facilitate transferability and portability, there were still some impediments to consolidating certain plan assets following the passage of EGTRRA. The Pension Protection Act of 2006 (PPA) further liberalized rules allowing for greater transfer of assets between various types of plans. Although EGTRRA permitted after-tax contributions to be transferred into a defined contribution plan or an IRA, it did not allow after-tax contributions to be transferred into a defined benefit plan or into a 403(b) plan. The PPA specifically allowed after-tax contributions from qualified retirement plans to be transferred into defined benefit plans or into a 403(b) tax-sheltered annuity as long as the transfer took place through a direct trustee-to-trustee transfer and the transferee plan separately accounted for after-tax contributions and earnings thereon. Prior to enactment of the PPA, a plan participant wanting to transfer assets from a tax-qualified retirement plan, 403(b) plan, or eligible 457(b) plan into a Roth IRA was not able to make a direct transfer into the Roth IRA. An individual desiring to make such a transfer was required to make an interim step of first transferring the plan assets into a traditional IRA and then subsequently move the assets from the traditional IRA into the Roth IRA. Since passage of the PPA, beginning January 1, 2008, distributions from tax-qualified retirement plans, 403(b) plans, or eligible 457(b) plans can be rolled over directly into a Roth IRA, subject to the restrictions that currently apply to rollovers from a traditional IRA into a Roth IRA. For a distribution to be eligible for rollover, it must be an eligible rollover distribution, that is, any distribution of all or a portion of an employee's interest in the plan, but not including (1) any distribution required to be made under the required minimum distribution rules, (2) certain periodic distributions,[1] or (3) any distribution made on account of hardship.

The PPA also changed the law so that distributions from a deceased individual's eligible retirement plan can be rolled over tax free to an IRA of a nonspouse beneficiary using a direct trustee-to-trustee rollover. In this situation, an IRA is established to receive the eligible rollover distribution on behalf of the beneficiary who is not the participant/contract owner's surviving spouse. The transfer is treated as an eligible rollover distribution, and the transferee IRA is treated as an inherited account. Once the funds are transferred into the transferee IRA, the required minimum distribution rules that pertain when a participant/contract owner dies before the receipt of the entire interest in his or her account apply to the transferee IRA.[2] (Note that the special rules applicable to surviving spouse beneficiaries do not apply.)

---

[1] Any distribution that is part of a series of substantially equal periodic payments made at least annually over the life or life expectancy of the individual (or the joint lives or life expectancies of the employee and his or her beneficiary), or for a period of at least 10 years, is not an eligible rollover distribution.

[2] Although the intent of the PPA seemed to allow nonspouse beneficiaries to stretch distributions over their life expectancies, the IRS in January 2007 explained a different interpretation of the law. The IRS position is that if the decedent is under age 70½, the rules of the retirement plan will continue to dictate how fast the money has to be withdrawn. A different rule applies if, at death, the owner of the retirement plan is over age 70½. In this latter case, a nonspouse beneficiary can stretch the withdrawals over his or her own life expectancy (see Gail Buckner, CFP, "IRS Puts a Stingy Spin on Pension Protection Act," *Fox News*, February 4, 2007).

An individual considering consolidation of retirement assets has many issues to consider as she or he contemplates this decision. A number of considerations relevant to this decision are summarized in the next section. Some of these decision factors would equally apply during the accumulation phase, while an individual is still actively working and has switched employers, and during the distribution phase of one's retirement planning, once the individual has actually retired completely or commenced some form of phased retirement. Others of these considerations would have more applicability depending on which stage an individual is in—either the accumulation phase or the distribution phase.

Consolidation Considerations of Relevance During Both the Accumulation and Distribution Phases

The items discussed in the following paragraphs can be segmented into three broad categories: fund and plan expenses, investment choice and performance, and distinctive plan features and supplementary account services. These issues have relevance to the plan participant during both the accumulation phase throughout the worker's career and during the distribution phase when the individual is either fully retired or is working part-time because of some phased retirement arrangement.

Fund and Plan Expenses

Management Fees

The costs that a participant pays for both asset management fees and plan administration expenses reduce the level of assets that will ultimately be available to fund one's retirement. Although the subject of plan expenses is always relevant to a participant, the effect of high fees is especially damaging to the growth in asset values if a participant is many years from retirement. This is the case since the cumulative erosion by fees will have a magnified effect given the nature of compounding over time. Therefore, if an individual is able to move funds from one plan where fees are higher to a plan with a more moderate, or considerably lower fee schedule, substantial value can be added to the retirement compounding mechanism.

Existence of Sales Charges

In addition to the management fees associated with a fund, there can be various sales charges associated with obtaining an investment within a retirement plan. Some mutual funds assess sales charges in the form of loads or commissions. Depending on the particular type of investment product purchased, these fees can be computed in various ways. Sometimes a charge is made when an investment is first purchased. This is known as a *front-end load*. Sometimes a sales charge is made when the individual disposes of the investment. This is known as a *back-end load*, deferred sales charge, or redemption fee. Many times a back-end load will decrease gradually over time and eventually

TABLE 16.1   Effect of Expenses on Retirement Plan Asset Accumulations   The growth of a $10,000 invested lump-sum with various expense charges assuming a 9% rate of return.

The total accumulation after expenses is noted as follows when the:			
Expense Charge is:			
.40%	1.00%	1.50%	2.00%
After a period of:			
5 years	$ 15,106	$ 14,693	$14,356	$14,026
10 years	$ 22,819	$ 21,589	$20,610	$19,672
20 years	$ 52,071	$ 46,610	$42,479	$38,697
30 years	$118,821	$100,627	$87,550	$76,123

disappear if the investment is held for a certain period, for instance if the investment is held in excess of seven years.

Commission Charges

Some investments must pay a commission to a broker or salesperson when they are bought or sold. For instance, if a person wanted to purchase individual stocks in an individual retirement account self-directed brokerage account, he or she would pay commissions when buying or selling the individual stocks. Another investment alternative that has seen tremendous growth in popularity with individual investors is a type of investment called an exchange-traded fund (ETF). An **exchange-traded fund** is a mutual fund whose shares are traded in the secondary markets. The main difference between an exchange-traded fund and a mutual fund is that ETFs can be bought at any time during the trading day and similarly be disposed of any time during the trading day at the current market price. A mutual fund, on the other hand, can only be bought or sold based on the closing net asset value price available at the end of the trading day. ETFs typically have lower expense ratios, or management fees (see earlier discussion) than do mutual funds, but the trading costs or commissions incurred when buying or selling ETFs would be higher than would be the case for mutual funds.

Investment Choice and Performance

Investment Choices

Some plans have a more expansive array of investment choices. Sometimes a fund will close and not accept new monies or allow new investors to enter the fund. However, if an investor works for an employer offering the fund through a retirement plan, he or she often is able to participate with systematic investments or rollovers from other retirement plans. If someone has access to a superior fund in a previous employer's plan, he or she may favor leaving assets in the retirement plan rather than consolidating or moving these plan assets to another investment company. (It should be noted that it is sometimes possible to retain a particular fund and roll the assets into another type of retirement plan, such as an individual retirement account with the same family of funds.) Another consideration can involve fund minimums. A fund may still be generally available outside the employer-sponsored retirement plan. However, a higher minimum contribution may be required for entrance into the fund. The existence of fund minimums can have a bearing on whether an individual wants to move funds. Often an individual can gain access to the fund at a lower minimum when accessing the fund through a retirement savings vehicle such as an individual retirement account.

Investment Performance

As indicated in the previous paragraph, some retirement savings vehicles have superior investment choices. Some actively managed funds claim to have talented managers. While academic studies have tended to put in doubt the ability of active managers to sustain superior performance over long periods of time, there are some managers whose extended period of outperformance in excess of a market benchmark seems to indicate added value beyond indexing. However, investors should cautiously investigate claims of superior investment management talent. On the other hand, an individual may hold retirement assets in a plan with a variety of actively managed funds and choose to roll over funds to an alternative offering a variety of passively managed funds. As can be seen, it is possible to position assets where the asset management strategy is expected to provide superior long-term performance. The pursuit of superior performance can be rooted in active or passive management, alleged talent of investment professionals, lower expense ratios, or specific fund offerings in certain market sectors.

Statutory Considerations on Allowable Investments

Although there has been an attempt to bring uniformity to the rules concerning different types of retirement savings vehicles, the fact remains that as of this writing, substantial differences still exist between allowable investments in various types of retirement planning structures. The existence of these differences can determine whether an individual wants to consolidate assets. For instance, 403(b) plans are restricted to holding either insurance-related types of products such as annuities, or mutual funds through a 403(b)(7) plan. Accordingly, if a participant wanted to self-direct investments by purchasing shares of particular stocks and bonds, this could not be accomplished through a 403(b) plan. This might be a situation where a rollover to an individual retirement account allowing self-direction would be appropriate. Similarly, individual retirement accounts are precluded from holding insurance policies as investments. Keogh plans may hold insurance contracts on account owners. If the holder of a Keogh account possessed an account that contained an individual insurance account on her or his life, the existence of this investment and the desire to retain this investment may very well constrain the choice of consolidating retirement plan investments in another retirement savings vehicle such as an individual retirement account.

Plan-Imposed Restrictions on the Universe of Investments

As indicated in the previous paragraph, some retirement saving structures are actually restricted by statute from offering certain types of investments. Even when there is no statute prohibiting various types of investments, sometimes plan sponsors choose to set boundaries on the allowable universe of investments. Restricting the universe of investments can avoid "choice overload," described in Chapter 11. Although mitigating the effect of choice overload may be helpful to the general employee population, placing limits on choices may adversely affect specific employees who wish to diversify their retirement investments further or find an additional fund choice of particular appeal. When an individual is eligible to consolidate his or her various retirement savings vehicles, the existence of **plan sponsor–imposed restrictions** on allowable investments may determine whether an individual opts to consolidate his or her retirement assets.

Distinctive Plan Features and Supplementary Account Services

Distinctive Plan Features

As mentioned earlier, certain plans may offer plan features that are not present in the other plans that the participant is using or has available to him or her. A loan feature is a good example of a feature that may be of concern to a participant. Availability of a loan feature may allow a plan participant to access funds in his or her account while avoiding taxes that would need to be paid if a taxable distribution was taken from the plan. Certain retirement savings plans such as IRAs prohibit loans. Even when certain plans are permitted to offer loans under the law, a particular employer or plan sponsor may opt not to offer this feature. Some employers believe that a loan feature undermines the basic intent of a retirement savings plan whose aim is to promote long-term savings. Not only could a loan feature be distinctive, but even such details as to how a loan is repaid can be distinctive. Some plans may offer the convenience of payroll deduction to repay plan loans, while other plans may require the mailing of checks. An individual may have preferences involving these types of transactional elements of the plan that influence the decision regarding asset consolidation.

Record Keeping

Although issues regarding fund expenses and investment performance are probably universally viewed as the most important considerations concerning the decision to consolidate retirement assets, other considerations also can affect the decision. Bringing assets under a single umbrella can make record keeping considerably easier for an individual. Although this may at first blush seem like a secondary consideration, if consolidation allows an individual to keep better track of his or her assets, asset allocation and portfolio rebalancing decisions may be facilitated to a greater extent. If this were to occur, it is possible that the retirement assets may actually be better managed and may increase in value to a greater extent over an extended period of time. In terms of improved record keeping, some individuals find it annoying to receive multiple account statements on a quarterly basis. These individuals are often willing to consolidate retirement account holdings to decrease the flow of mail or e-mailed statements they are receiving.

Ability to Manage Account Using Online Tools

Related to record keeping is the availability of online tools. Although some retirement plan custodians dutifully may issue quarterly statements in printed form, online access to those account balances and the ability to self-direct investments using this medium may be less sophisticated and less user-friendly than those offered by other providers. The online capabilities of retirement asset custodians have increasingly become features that distinguish one carrier from another. Although these capabilities may seem less important than investment performance and fund expenses, inability to access information and rebalance accounts in a timely manner can result in investment losses. Individual investors have come to expect an almost instantaneous access to plan information and ability to instantaneously manage plan assets. Any carrier failing to provide these state-of-the-art tools is likely to have a difficult time retaining assets under management and will have difficulty attracting additional clients.

Ease of Account Management

Some asset managers have more streamlined procedures for directing investments and managing an account. If an asset manager is easier to deal with, a participant can better manage her or his account. The ease with which one can manage her or his account is an important consideration whether to consolidate plan assets. Going beyond the online capabilities of a retirement plan provider, other services are important as well. If a retirement plan provider is unable to answer telephone calls expeditiously, respond to inquiries from participants, supply forms when requested, and process these forms quickly once they are submitted, individual plan participants will move assets to other carriers rather than deal with the frustrations of poor service.

Supplementary Online Tools and Financial Planning Services

In addition to the online tools that allow an individual to make fund-to-fund transfers and engage in other plan-related transactions, there are other online tools that are helpful to plan participants. Increasingly, plan participants are interested in planning tools that allow them to engage in modeling that helps determine whether they are saving enough and how their distributions will fair under alternate economic scenarios. Plans are providing modeling software that allows participants to investigate whether their assets are diversified enough, whether their asset allocations seem appropriate given their age and risk tolerances, and whether they will outlive their retirement resources. As the move to defined contribution plans has placed more risk on plan participants, these participants have been placing greater demands on plan custodians to equip them with the tools that will assist in answering questions that will facilitate better decision making when managing retirement accounts.

Financial planning services for a participant-directed plan, such as a 401(k) plan, can be provided. The Pension Protection Act of 2006 (PPA) contains an exemption allowing an adviser, when acting as a fiduciary, to provide participant-level investment advice. The PPA amended both ERISA and the Internal Revenue Code to provide relief from the fiduciary liability and prohibited transaction rules. This relief was effective for advice provided after December 31, 2006 and allows plan sponsors and fiduciaries to appoint qualified fiduciary advisers for individual account plans where participants direct investments. Advice must be given pursuant to an "eligible investment advice arrangement." An **eligible investment advice arrangement** is an arrangement where (1) any fees received by the adviser do not vary on the basis of investment options selected, or (2) the adviser uses a computer model that is certified by an eligible investment expert. An **eligible investment expert** is someone who lacks a material affiliation or contractual relationship with the adviser and who also satisfies any additional requirements promulgated by the U.S. Department of Labor (DOL). Where a computer model is used, the model must apply generally accepted investment theories that use relevant individualized participant characteristics such as expected retirement age, life expectancy, or risk tolerance. The computer model must not be biased in favor of investments offered by the adviser and must take into account all of the investment options offered through the plan. An independent auditor—who is unrelated to the adviser or any other provider of investment options under the plan—must annually certify that the model is appropriate, that the only advice provided is pursuant to use of the computer model, and that all transactions result from the decisions of participants.

Certain notice requirements must be met before investment advice can be provided to plan participants. The information provided in the notice must be written clearly and in a manner that is easily understood by participants and beneficiaries. The DOL has indicated that it will issue a model notice that can be used to conform to these notice requirements. Among the items required for inclusion in the written notice requirements are the following:

- The role of any related party who is involved in developing the computer program.
- The role of any related party who is involved in selecting investment options under the plan.
- The past performance and historical rates of return for each of the investment options made available under the plan.
- Information that the financial adviser is a fiduciary.
- Disclosure of any fees or other compensation received by the fiduciary adviser.
- The manner and circumstances under which any participant information will be used.
- An explanation that the participants have the ability to enter into a separate arrangement with another adviser that has no material affiliation with, and receives no compensation with respect to, the securities or other property offered for investment.

Consolidation Considerations Particularly Relevant During the Distribution Phase

Although the previously discussed items were relevant in deciding whether to reposition or consolidate assets both during the accumulation phase and also during the distribution phase once retired, there are other concerns that become particularly relevant during the distribution phase. Most of these considerations relate to the ability to disburse benefits and then position assets in a way that is favorable should death occur. It is important to determine whether the positioning of assets is consistent with estate-planning preferences. These considerations are discussed in the following paragraphs.

Distribution Alternatives Available through the Plan for Account Owners

Certain plans offer distinct distribution alternatives. For instance, various annuity choices are available from a defined benefit plan. Similarly, a money purchase pension plan must offer annuity distribution options for disbursements from the plan. Many of these direct annuity payments from a plan may be less costly than if one were to attempt to purchase an annuity from an insurance company with a lump-sum distribution from another type of defined contribution plan. Therefore, if an individual knows she or he intends to take distributions in the form of an annuity, that person is well advised to compare the cost of annuity alternatives disbursed through the plan with the costs of annuities available from other providers in the marketplace. This is particularly true when considering early retirement. Many employer plans subsidize early retirement, so an annuity payment available for early retirement often is more attractively priced than comparable annuity options from commercial insurers. If a plan provides for annuity distributions and also allows transfers of account balances into the plan, a participant should consider whether consolidation of more assets through the annuity-providing plan is desirable. Women should be particularly vigilant as to the attractiveness of an annuity form of distribution through a retirement plan because annuities offered through retirement plans are required to use gender-neutral, unisex mortality tables. Women on average tend to have longer life expectancies than do men of the same age, so on average women will receive a larger payment using a unisex mortality table. If the women were to purchase an annuity outside of a retirement plan, insurers are still permitted to use mortality tables based on the annuitant's gender. In addition to annuity options, plans provide distribution options such as fixed periodic payments that may be attractive. Some carriers do not allow flexibility once the periodic distributions are commenced, while other providers allow retirees to modify payments should circumstances change. These options for modification can be very attractive if the individual has outside income from consulting services or part-time employment.

Distribution Options for Beneficiaries

Not only are distribution options important for the original account owner, but the options for continuing payments to beneficiaries are important upon the death of the original account owner. Whether the plan provides for annuity distributions, fixed periodic payments, or lump sums is important. Matching the payment options available from the provider to the account owner's estate-planning needs can influence whether holding the assets with a particular company makes sense.

Opportunities for Tax Planning

Monies can be contributed on either a pretax or after-tax basis, so the assembling of retirement assets in these distinctive tax categories during the accumulation period can position an employee's assets very differently from a tax standpoint when it is time to commence distributions during retirement; after-tax contributions will not be subject to taxation when subsequently distributed. Also, the advent of the ability to contribute monies to a Roth IRA beginning in 1998 and to Roth 401(k) and Roth 403(b) plans beginning in 2006 introduced another opportunity for favorably tax positioning retirement assets. Monies held in Roth-type accounts not only shield contributions from future income taxation, but also shield the accumulating earnings on these contributions from income taxation. Also, distributions from these types of accounts are not counted when determining the taxation of Social Security benefits. Therefore, consolidating plan balances and positioning assets in various types of retirement accounts can have a tax-planning rationale. The accounts a retiree accesses for distributions will determine the retiree's tax liability in a given year.

Consolidation of Payments

In the same way that some individuals find it annoying to receive multiple statements from various providers, it can be inconvenient to receive multiple checks when receiving retirement plan distributions. Some individuals prefer to consolidate the assets from various retirement plans so that they need only receive a single check or wire transfer into their bank account. This simplicity also can make it easier to compute annual income taxes. Other efficiencies may also be possible. For instance, if an employer is providing benefits such as retiree medical coverage and requires that retirees contribute, deductions may be possible if the payment from the employer's plan is sufficient to take the deduction. Retirees often prefer distribution approaches that simplify record keeping and limit the number of other checks they may need to write.

Liquidity Considerations

Often, retirees want access to certain funds that are available should an emergency arise, or if they decide to make a larger one-time purchase such as an automobile or engage in discretionary spending such as travel. Certain conditions that can necessitate increased spending may be far less pleasant and involve such things as medical expenses and funeral expenses should a spouse, dependent, or other family member pass away or become ill. Although some individuals have accumulated an emergency fund to handle some of these contingencies or discretionary purchases, other individuals look to their retirement asset accumulations to fund such spending. In this case, these monies would need to be in a retirement account that is easily accessible and can process payments expeditiously. Certainly retirement accounts that place contractual prohibitions on discretionary distributions, such as would be the case with most annuities, should be avoided.

Estate-Planning Considerations

Planning in terms of the ultimate distribution of assets following death also can affect how assets are positioned in retirement plans. There are many elements related to estate planning that could be of relevance. For instance, whether to place assets in the primary wage earner's individual retirement account or alternatively in a nonworking spouse's individual retirement account could merit consideration. If the assets were placed in the nonworking spouse's account, the estates of the two individuals could be equalized, thus allowing for greater use of the unified credit available upon the death of each individual. Of course, the estate tax laws are constantly in flux, and the merits of such a strategy must be continually monitored as to costs and benefits of alternate approaches. Another example, previously noted, relates to the fact that certain retirement plans such as Keogh plans permit the purchase of life insurance as a plan investment, while other types of plans such as individual retirement accounts prohibit accounts from holding insurance contracts. Because life insurance plays such a vital role in estate planning, the ability to purchase life insurance on a pretax basis through a Keogh plan may present an attractive estate-planning option. Some practitioners have described ways to roll individual retirement account accumulations into a Keogh plan to facilitate the purchase of life insurance policies.[3]

Estate-Planning Assistance and Trust Services

Some investment companies and insurance companies actually facilitate estate planning and provide trust service for their account holders. Access to these services can be extremely helpful particularly for participants with complicated estate-planning needs. Having these services provided may be a pivotal consideration in deciding whether to place retirement assets with a given provider.

All of these described factors should be carefully considered when making decisions regarding the consolidation of retirement plan assets.

Chapter Summary

- Defined contribution plans provide accounts that accumulate an asset pool that provides a retirement income stream for workers. If an individual has worked for several employers during his or her career, as is the case for many workers, it is likely that his or her retirement plan resources will be spread among not only various employers, but also among different types of retirement plan structures.

- There is nothing intrinsically wrong with having retirement resources spread among a number of different retirement savings vehicles and among different employers th individual has worked for. In fact, it can be argued that some diversification amor plan sponsors and differing types of plans may be preferable. Not only are there div sification effects, but different plans may offer different funds and allow for differ plan features. Because all rules are not uniform, as of this writing, diversification r allow access to certain plan features that are not allowable in different plan structi Even if certain features are permissible in different types of plans, not all empl adopt the same features.

- Assuming that an individual has the ability to consolidate plan assets, he or sh choose to keep assets separately segregated in distinct plans for very valid r However, for most people, there should be some consideration of the ineffic of having assets spread among various sponsors, and a conscious decision sh

---

[3] Ed Slott, *The Retirement Savings Time Bomb* (New York: Penguin Putnam, 2003), pp. 16 This reference provides a description of the so-called rollback strategy.

made whether it makes sense to keep assets segregated in various plans or to aggregate some of these assets. Consolidation of assets need not be an all-or-nothing decision. It is possible that some consolidation may make sense without bringing all of the assets into a single plan structure or individual retirement account.

- The determination of the merits of consolidating assets will depend on the preferences of the individual planning for retirement; his or her ability to manage assets in different plan structures; and the plan features, including costs and investment options within the individual's array of plan structures. Also, when consolidation should occur is an individual preference item. Some individuals may prefer to consolidate their plans throughout their careers as they change jobs and switch employers. Other individuals may decide to wait until transition to the distribution phase at the point of retirement to make this decision.

- It is preferable that an individual considers the decision to consolidate plan assets throughout her or his career when given the opportunity to make these changes. The reason for considering the viability of consolidation on an ongoing basis when given the opportunity under the law has to do with the available alternatives that an individual has at any point in time. If an individual had less costly alternatives available and was able to make changes early in her or his career, the effects of compounding could dramatically magnify the individual's accumulation of assets. Delaying the decision could be very costly to the individual. Similarly, if an individual had access to superior funds within a 401(k), 403(b), or 457(b) plan, the foregone opportunity cost associated with remaining in inferior funds again could be very costly. Decisions by default and inertia can be extremely costly and extract a sizable component from an individual's accumulating assets.

- A governmental policy theme has sought simplification, and efforts have been made to seek uniformity across various types of plans. As the regulation of plans has converged toward a more uniform set of rules, it has become easier to allow for transferability. Transferability relates to the ability of a plan participant to move assets. These assets may be moved from one investment company within an employer's retirement plan offerings to another investment company within the same employer's retirement plan offerings, from one plan to the same type of plan at a different employer, or from one type of plan to a different type of plan at a different employer. Similarly, assets can be transferred to an individual retirement account. Not only has uniformity in the rules between types of plans been sought, but facilitating portability of plan assets has been sought as well. Uniformity has to do with a set of rules that are consistent and applicable in the same way to different types of plans. Portability involves the ability to move plan assets with the individual plan participant rather than requiring that the assets remain under the control of a given plan sponsor overseeing the assets in the plan where the assets were first contributed.

wo methods exist for transferring assets between investment companies within an ployer's retirement plan and from one type of retirement savings plan to another e of retirement savings plan. Transfers can occur either as a direct trustee-to-trustee ver or as a regular or indirect rollover. In a direct trustee-to-trustee rollover, the individual instructs the plan trustee or contract issuer to transfer funds directly to the other retirement savings plan. In a regular or indirect rollover, the individual receives a check for the eligible rollover distribution from the plan trustee or contract issuer (net of the required 20 percent federal income tax withholding). Then within 60 days of receipt the individual contributes up to the amount of the eligible rollover distribution as a rollover contribution to the receiving retirement savings plan. The benefit of using the direct trustee-to-trustee rollover method is that there is no 20 percent federal income tax withholding although taxes are still due on subsequent distributions.

- The rules allowing plan balances to be consolidated have been liberalized considerably from what they were in the past. Beginning in 2002 and as a result of changes enacted into law as part of the Economic Growth and Tax Relief Reconciliation Act of 2001, rollover distributions were permitted between qualified plans, 403(b) plans, and eligible governmental 457(b) plans. Also, as was permitted previously for qualified plans and 403(b) plans, eligible 457(b) plans could also be rolled over into IRAs. Generally, if an individual terminates employment, he or she often has the option to make an eligible rollover distribution. Although EGTRRA went a long way to facilitate transferability and portability, there were still some impediments to consolidating certain plan assets following the passage of EGTRRA. The Pension Protection Act of 2006 further liberalized rules allowing for greater transfer of assets between various types of plans.

- There are several decision items to consider when contemplating the consolidation of retirement plan asset balances. These items can be segmented into three broad categories: fund and plan expenses, investment choice and performance, and distinctive plan features and supplementary account services. These issues have relevance to the plan participant's decision on consolidation of retirement plan asset balances both during the accumulation phase throughout the worker's career and during the distribution phase when the individual is either fully retired or is working part-time because of some phased retirement arrangement.

Key Terms

consolidation of assets,
  p. *285*
direct trustee-to-trustee
  rollover, p. *287*
eligible investment advice
  arrangement, p. *294*
eligible investment expert,
  p. *294*

eligible rollover
  distribution, p. *287*
exchange-traded fund,
  p. *290*
plan sponsor–imposed
  restrictions, p. *292*
portability, p. *287*

regular or indirect rollover,
  p. *287*
transferability, p. *286*
uniformity, p. *287*

Questions for Review

1. What advantages are associated with holding assets in a variety of different retirement savings vehicles?

2. When considering the consolidation of assets, must all of the assets be brought into a single plan structure or individual retirement account? Explain.

3. What are the relevant factors for deciding whether to consolidate retirement assets?

4. Why is it preferable for an individual to consider consolidating retirement assets throughout her or his career when given the opportunity to make these changes?

5. What is meant by transferability?

6. Describe the legislative theme relating to uniformity in plan rules and features.

7. Describe the concept of portability of retirement assets.

8. Explain the available methods under the law for transferring assets between investment companies within an employer's retirement plan and from one type of retirement savings plan to another type of retirement savings plan.

9. What is one primary benefit of using the direct trustee-to-trustee rollover method to consolidate retirement assets?

10. How does an individual avoid being taxed on receipt of funds when consolidating retirement assets?

11. How have recent legislative initiatives liberalized the ability to consolidate plan assets?

12. Can a nonspouse beneficiary roll over assets from another type of retirement savings plan into an IRA?

13. How may decision items on consolidation of retirement plan assets be segmented?

14. What is the main difference between an exchange-traded fund and a mutual fund?

15. Explain how the closing of a fund to new investors can influence the decision to consolidate retirement plan assets.

16. What are the sources of superior investment performance?

17. What is an eligible investment advice arrangement?

18. Summarize the notice requirements that must be met before a fiduciary adviser may provide participant-level investment advice.

Questions for Discussion

1. Discuss the ideal design and structure of the retirement savings plan or plans where an individual would ultimately want his or her retirement plan assets upon reaching normal retirement age.

2. Discuss how considerations for positioning assets in retirement savings plans may differ depending on whether the account owner's primary consideration is retirement income or estate planning for the benefit of beneficiaries.

Resources for Further Study

CCH Editorial Staff. "Legislation 2006: Pension Protection Act of 2006: Law, Explanation and Analysis." *Commerce Clearing House* (2006).

Slott, Ed. *The Retirement Savings Time Bomb*. New York: Penguin Putnam, 2003.

Slott, Ed. *Parlay Your IRA into a Family Fortune*. New York: Penguin Group, 2005.

Hallman, G. Victor, and Jerry S. Rosenbloom. *Personal Financial Planning*, 7th ed. New York: McGraw-Hill, 2003.

Knox, Melanie N. Aska, and Joan Gucciardi. *Pension Distribution Answer Book*, 2007 ed. New York: Aspen Publishers, 2007.

Chapter 17

Defined Benefit Plan Features

After studying this chapter you should be able to:

- Describe what the term *normal retirement age* means.
- Explain why reduced benefits are often provided for early retirement.
- Identify the various types of defined benefit formulas used in calculating plan benefits.
- Understand the excess and the offset approaches for integrating benefits under defined benefit plans with Social Security.
- Determine when the overall permitted disparity limits are violated.
- Understand what is meant by an incidental death benefit.

An employer adopting a qualified defined benefit pension plan must make a number of decisions about the basic features to be included in the plan. The employer must, for example, determine what benefits the participants will receive upon retirement, death, or disability; how and when these benefits will be paid; and whether or not employees will contribute toward the cost of these benefits.

This chapter discusses the various factors that bear on an employer's decisions concerning the design of the more prominent features to be included in a defined benefit pension plan. While much of this material applies equally to defined contribution plans, it is oriented specifically toward qualified defined benefit pension plans. The features discussed in this chapter include retirement ages, employee contributions, and retirement, death, and disability benefits. The chapter then discusses the plan design approaches used to counteract the effect of preretirement inflation and approaches used to offset postretirement inflation.

It should be emphasized at this point that the employer's objectives and circumstances covered in Chapter 2, the legal requirements concerning the qualification of a retirement plan covered in Chapters 25 and 26, and the other legal requirements covered in Chapter 27 must be taken into consideration at every phase of the plan design process.

An employer must make sure a plan meets its objectives and does not discriminate in favor of highly compensated employees. Having to remedy either of these problems at a later time can result in considerable expense and administrative complexity for the employer. Consideration of employer objectives and nondiscriminatory requirements will be noted throughout this chapter where they are particularly relevant to the topic under discussion.

Employee Contributions

A major question the employer must resolve is whether employees will be required to make contributions toward the cost of plan benefits. Sound arguments may be presented for both contributory and noncontributory plans, although the ability of the employer or employees to pay is often the controlling factor. In any event, the trend has clearly been in the direction of noncontributory plans, at least in the case of defined benefit plans.

Arguments advanced in favor of contributory plans include the following:

1. From a philosophical viewpoint, employees are responsible for meeting part of their own economic security needs.
2. If employees contribute, it will mean a smaller employer contribution to provide the same overall plan benefits.
3. If an employer does not want to use employee contributions to reduce its own contribution, then by making the plan contributory, the overall plan benefits will be larger.
4. Something for nothing is too often taken for granted, and the deductions from current earnings will continually remind employees that the employer is assuming a large share of providing the plan benefits. (It would seem that this argument could be minimized by an effective method of repeatedly publicizing the plan and its value to employees.)
5. Employees are encouraged to save. The contributory plan also provides an employee with additional funds in the event of termination of employment.

The proponents of a noncontributory plan hold that the contributory plan has the following disadvantages:

1. Employer contributions represent dollars that have not been taxed. On the other hand, dollars received by the employee as earnings that are then contributed under the plan are dollars that have been taxed to the employee.[1] Hence, dollar for dollar, employer contributions provide more than those of an employee.
2. Deductions from earnings are a source of constant irritation to employees.
3. The employer might be forced to increase salaries to compensate for the additional deductions.
4. The number of participants required for a qualified plan might not enroll.

[1] Salary reduction contributions under Section 401(k) of the IRC are not permitted for private employer defined benefit or money purchase pension plans.

5. Some employees may refuse to participate, in which case the employer will still have a problem when these employees reach retirement age.

6. Additional records must be kept by the employer, thereby increasing administrative work and costs.

If the employer decides that employees should make contributions, the next decision will be the amount employees should contribute. While employee contributions may be related to the cost of benefits, generally it is much more satisfactory to relate these contributions to earnings. In this way, employees' contributions are geared to their ability to make them. Furthermore, in most plans it is impossible to predict exactly what the cost of an employee's pension will be until actual retirement. Hence, any contributions made by the employee and related to cost necessarily are estimated and do not have an exact relationship.

Contributory plans usually require that before becoming a participant an employee must sign a request for participation agreeing to make the required contributions and authorizing the employer to withhold contributions from earnings. With passage of the Pension Protection Act of 2006 (PPA), a participant in an individual account plan is deemed to have exercised control over assets in his or her account if a plan's fiduciaries make default investments for a participant in accordance with guidance provided by the Department of Labor. This provision facilitates greater use of automatic enrollment, particularly in defined contribution plans.

Retirement Ages

Normal Retirement Age

The normal retirement age in most plans is 65. The choice of this age was influenced not only by the fact that this was the age at which full Social Security benefits originally commenced but also that retiring employees before age 65 with full benefits could produce prohibitive costs. Federal law defines **normal retirement age** to be the age specified in the plan, but no later than age 65 or the fifth anniversary of the participant's date of initial plan participation, whichever is the last to occur. Occasionally, an earlier age such as 60 will be chosen as the normal retirement age, although, to a great extent, this practice has been confined to public, quasi-public, and charitable institutions. Also, where an employee's occupation is such that his or her working career is shorter than in most other occupations, and when this does not result in prohibited age discrimination, a plan may provide for a normal retirement age lower than 65.

Early Retirement Age

Most plans provide that an employee may choose **early retirement** on a reduced pension, although a few plans limit this feature to cases of total and permanent disability. If an early retirement option is included, it is customary to establish some requirements an employee must fulfill before being allowed to elect early retirement.

A typical requirement for early retirement is that the employee must have attained at least age 55 and completed at least 10 years of service or participation in the plan.

Requirements such as these limit the option to situations where the employee is actually retiring as opposed to changing jobs. They also tend to create a situation in which the employee will receive a reasonable benefit.

The benefit payable at early retirement typically is lower than the normal retirement benefit for two reasons. First, the full benefit will not yet have accrued by the employee's early retirement date. Second, because it is starting several years earlier than anticipated, the benefit will be paid over a longer period of time. Thus, an actuarial reduction factor usually is applied to the value of the employee's accrued benefit to determine the amount of early retirement benefit.

Determining the value of the employee's accrued benefit is relatively simple under an allocated funding instrument.[2] In a pension plan funded entirely by individual insurance policies, for example, the value of the accrued benefit generally is the cash surrender value of the employee's insurance or annuity contract at the time of retirement. In this type of plan, the actuarial reduction is accomplished by the use of the settlement option rates contained in the contract. The employee's benefit is generally that amount that may be provided by applying the cash surrender value under the option at the employee's attained age on his or her retirement date.

In plans using an unallocated funding instrument and where the benefit formula reflects the employee's service, the benefit generally is measured in terms of the employee's accrued benefit to the date of retirement. If the plan uses another type of formula, however, the determination of the value of the employee's accrued benefit is more difficult. One often-used approach is to multiply the value of the employee's projected benefit at normal retirement date by a fraction, the numerator being the years of participation or service the employee has completed at the early retirement date and the denominator being the years of participation or service the employee would have completed at the normal retirement date.

In any event, an employee's accrued benefit at early retirement must meet the accrued benefit requirements of federal tax law that apply to vested benefits (see Chapter 26).

The reduction factor applied to the value of the employee's accrued benefit might be something as simple as a reduction of one-half of 1 percent for each month by which early retirement precedes normal retirement; or, as is sometimes the case, an actuarial reduction factor is determined from a table included in the plan.

There has been a growing interest in recent years in the possibility of retiring earlier than age 65. While some plans actually establish a normal retirement age earlier than age 65, a greater number encourage early retirement by not applying a full actuarial reduction if certain conditions are met. One approach, for example, is to provide for no actuarial reduction at all if the employee retires after attaining some age (such as 60) and after completing some period of service (such as 30 years). A similar approach would be to apply no reduction factor (or a minimum factor) if early retirement occurs when the employee's age and service total to some number such as 90—for example, an employee who is age 62 and who has completed 28 years of service would satisfy this requirement. Still another approach would be to apply some simple factor, such as one-fourth of 1

---

[2] Funding instruments are classified on the basis of whether contributions are allocated to provide benefits to specific employees or whether contributions are accumulated in an unallocated fund to provide benefits collectively for all employees.

percent for each month by which early retirement precedes normal retirement, that is considerably less than the reduction that would otherwise be called for by full actuarial reduction factors. Approaches such as these will, of course, increase the cost of the pension plan; however, employees generally find such a provision to be attractive, and quite frequently the employer finds its overall interests are best served by a provision that encourages early retirement.

Late Retirement Age

Plans also must include a provision allowing an employee to defer retirement. This feature also could be important to the employer, since it permits a greater degree of flexibility in scheduling the actual retirement of a key employee when there is a problem in obtaining or training a replacement.

The federal age discrimination law and state laws protecting employment rights are discussed in Chapter 27. In general, these laws require employees to continue accruing benefits without regard to any maximum age limit.

Retirement Benefits

The formula selected for determining an employee's retirement benefit is a vital provision in a pension plan. The employer's financial capacity and general philosophy concerning the desired level of retirement benefits, as well as the employer's specific objectives as to the distribution of benefits among employees, all play an important role in selecting such a formula.

Many employers believe that a plan should be designed to provide a higher-paid career employee with an income after retirement that, together with primary Social Security benefits, will be about 50 to 55 percent of earnings just before retirement. For lower-paid employees, the percentage generally is set at a higher level—perhaps as much as 80 to 85 percent. For employees considered to be less than career employees (usually those employees with fewer than 25 or 30 years of service with the employer), these percentages would be proportionately smaller. From the employer's viewpoint, the benefit formula selected should in no event result in a plan that produces unacceptable costs so as to endanger the continuation of the plan if corporate earnings are decreased or if current tax advantages are reduced.

Basically, there are two types of benefit formulas for the employer to consider. The first is called a *defined contribution* or a *money purchase formula*. Under this type of formula, contribution rates are fixed, and an employee's benefit varies depending upon factors such as the amount of the contributions made, investment earnings on plan assets, and the employee's entry age and retirement age.[3]

The second type is called a *defined benefit* or an *annuity purchase formula*. Here, a definite benefit is established for each employee, and contributions are determined to be

[3] This chapter is primarily concerned with defined benefit pension plans. Defined contribution plans, such as money purchase pension plans, profit sharing plans, and 401(k) plans, are discussed in more detail in Chapters 6 and 8.

whatever is necessary to produce the desired benefit results. Defined benefit formulas may be subdivided into several different classifications.

Determination of Compensation

Because the amount of benefit under most formulas is based on an employee's compensation, it is important, before discussing specific formulas, to have a clear idea of the various considerations involved in selecting the compensation base to which the benefit formula will be applied. Items such as overtime pay, holiday pay, sick pay, bonuses, and commissions must be specifically excluded or included. The definition chosen must not discriminate in favor of highly compensated employees (HCEs) (i.e., it must satisfy the requirements detailed in Chapter 25).

The question of whether plan benefits should be based on the average of the earnings paid over the entire period of the employee's participation in the plan or on an average of the employee's earnings during some shorter period of time that is near the employee's retirement age is crucial to proper plan design. The latter type of provision, often called a **final-pay provision,** would base benefits on the employee's earnings averaged, for example, over the last three or five years of employment, or over the three or five consecutive years in the 10-year period immediately prior to retirement during which the employee's earnings are the highest.

The advantage of a final-pay plan is that it relates benefits to the employee's earnings and standard of living during a period just preceding retirement. As a result, the employee's initial benefit keeps pace with any preretirement inflationary trends. Moreover, a final-pay plan is more likely to meet employer objectives as to benefit levels than is a **career-pay plan.** This type of plan, however, is usually more expensive than one that bases benefits on career-average earnings. Many employers believe it is best to use a career-average earnings plan and to make periodic adjustments in the benefit formula when economic trends justify such an action.

While a final-pay plan has the disadvantage of committing an employer to increased costs during an extended inflationary period, it should be remembered that in many situations the employer's capacity to absorb these increases also may be increased. Moreover, a final-pay plan generally produces more favorable results for key employees than the career-average approach.

A final point to be noted concerns the requirement of federal tax law that an employee's normal retirement benefit can never be less than the highest early retirement benefit that he or she could have received. Thus, any salary reductions that occur after an employee first becomes eligible to retire early cannot have the effect of reducing the employee's normal retirement benefit.

Defined Benefit Formulas

Broadly speaking, there are four basic defined benefit formulas. They are (1) a flat amount formula, which provides a flat benefit unrelated to an employee's earnings or service; (2) a flat percentage of earnings formula, which provides a benefit related to the employee's earnings but does not reflect service; (3) a flat amount per year of service formula, which reflects an employee's service but not earnings; and (4) a percentage of earnings per year of service formula, which reflects both an employee's earnings and service. Defined benefit formulas also may be integrated with Social Security benefits.

Flat Amount Formula

This type of formula provides for a flat benefit that treats all employees alike, regardless of their service, age, or earnings. For example, the benefit might be $500 or $700 a month. The **flat amount formula,** since it is considered to produce inequitable results, seldom is used by itself. On occasion, this formula is used in conjunction with some other type of formula; for example, a plan may provide a flat benefit of $700 a month for a covered employee, plus a percentage of his or her earnings in excess of the current Social Security taxable wage base. Any such formula, of course, would not be acceptable for qualified plan purposes if it resulted in discriminatory benefits for HCEs.

While the employee's length of service is not reflected directly in this type of formula, service is in effect recognized since most plans require that an employee, upon attaining the normal retirement age specified by the plan, must have been employed for some period of time, such as 25 years. Plans that include such a requirement provide for a proportionately reduced benefit if the employee has accumulated fewer than the required number of years, thus creating, in effect, a formula weighted for service.

Flat Percentage of Earnings Formula

This type of formula is sometimes used today, particularly in plans that cover salaried or clerical employees. Some **flat percentage of earnings,** usually ranging from 25 to 50 percent, is selected as the measure of the pension benefit. It may be used with either career-average or final-average earnings, although it is used most frequently in final-pay plans.

This type of formula does not take an employee's service into account, except in those plans which require that the employee must have completed a minimum period of service by the normal retirement date and which provide for a proportionately reduced benefit if the employee's service is less than the required number of years.

Flat Amount per Year of Service Formula

This type of formula often is found in negotiated plans. It provides a **flat dollar amount per year of service** completed by the employee. Thus, in a plan that provides for a benefit of $40 a month for each year of service, an employee with 27 years of employment would receive a monthly pension of $1,080.

This type of formula frequently requires that an employee must have worked for a minimum number of hours during a plan year to receive a full benefit credit for such year. Minimums often used for this purpose are 1,600 and 1,800 hours. An employee who works fewer than the required number of hours in a given year usually receives some proportionate credit for the actual hours worked. Federal tax law requires that a proportionate credit be given if the employee is credited with at least 1,000 hours of service in the 12-month computation period used by the plan.

Some plans limit benefits to service performed after the plan became effective, although in most cases credit is given for service prior to the inception of the plan. When this is done, credit may or may not be given for service needed to meet any eligibility requirements of the plan. Also, it is not uncommon to include a provision that limits the total service that may be credited for benefit purposes to a period such as 30 years.

Percentage of Earnings per Year of Service Formula

A formula that gives specific recognition for service as well as earnings is considered by many pension practitioners to produce the most equitable results in terms of a benefit formula that provides benefits for employees in relation to their value or contributions to the firm. A formula producing this result often is called a *unit credit* or *past and future service formula.* Under such a formula, an employee receives a benefit credit equal to a **percentage of earnings per year of service** for each year that he or she is a participant under the plan. This benefit credit is called the employee's "future service" or "current service" benefit. The percentage of earnings credited varies from plan to plan, but a typical percentage would be 1 percent or 1.25 percent. It may be used with either career-average or final earnings, and it works particularly well with career-average plans.

Many plans also include a "past service" benefit for employees who enter the plan on its effective date. In a plan that bases future service benefits on career-average earnings, the past service benefit is usually expressed as a fixed percentage of the employee's earnings on the effective date of the plan multiplied by the employee's years of past service. In determining past service benefits, however, it is customary to exclude service that would have been required to join the plan had it always been in effect. It also is possible to limit the total years of past service credited. For example, past service could be limited to a given number of years (such as 10), to service completed after a certain calendar year (such as the year in which the firm was acquired by the current ownership interests), to service completed after attaining a certain age (such as 21), or to a combination of these factors. The percentage applied to earnings to determine past service benefits is usually a lower rate than is applied for future service benefits. The reason for this is that the earnings of an employee on the effective date of the plan generally are higher than the average of the employee's earnings over the period of his or her past service. Rather than determine the employee's actual average earnings during his or her past service, which is often difficult or even impossible because of the lack of records, a rough approximation is made by reducing the percentage applicable to the employee's higher earnings at the time the plan is established.

If the plan bases benefits on final earnings, a distinction usually is not made between past and future service benefits. Here, the employee's total service (subject to any limitations such as a maximum service credit provision or excluding service needed to meet eligibility requirements) is applied to the percentage of final earnings to determine the total retirement benefit.

Variable Benefit Formulas

Variable benefit plans are designed to protect against the effects of inflation on a retired employee's pension benefit. They take either of two general forms: (1) the benefit varies to reflect changes in the value of a specific portfolio of common stocks and similar investments, or (2) the benefit varies to reflect changes in a recognized cost-of-living index such as that published by the Bureau of Labor Statistics. In either case, the plan attempts to adjust benefits to keep an employee's purchasing power on a relatively level basis. These plans are discussed in detail later in this chapter.

Integration with Social Security

For most individuals, retirement income will be derived from both Social Security and private pension plans. Because the employer bears part of the cost of Social Security benefits, it is only logical for the employer to recognize this source of benefits when designing the benefit formula of its retirement plan. Moreover, Social Security favors the lower paid, providing a much higher level of income replacement for individuals at low income levels than it does for those who are highly paid. This difference in the relative value of Social Security benefits by income level is accentuated when replacement ratios are compared on an after-tax basis—Social Security benefits are not taxed at all for individuals with low income; by contrast, up to 85 percent of Social Security benefits are taxable to the highly paid.

For these reasons, many pay-related defined benefit plans are integrated in some fashion with Social Security. This approach is sanctioned by federal tax law, but stringent rules must be followed to prevent the plan from discriminating in favor of the highly paid.

There are, in general, two ways for integrating a benefit plan and Social Security benefits. The first approach—the "excess" method—provides a benefit for pay over a stipulated level (the integration level) that is higher than that provided for pay below this level. The second approach—the "offset" method—provides that the employee's gross plan benefit is reduced by some amount representing all or part of the employer-provided portion of the employee's Social Security benefit.

The following is a very brief summary of how the integration rules affect defined benefit plans. These rules are discussed in greater detail in Chapter 25.[4]

- **Excess plans.** The accrual rate for pay above the plan's integration level cannot be more than two times the accrual rate for pay below this level. In addition, the spread between these accrual rates cannot exceed a "permitted disparity"— three-quarters of 1 percent for each year of participation up to a maximum of 35 years, or a maximum spread of 26¼ percent. The integration level may be any amount up to the Social Security taxable wage base at the beginning of the plan year. The permitted disparity will be reduced, however, if the plan's integration level exceeds the **Social Security–covered compensation level**—the average of the Social Security taxable wage bases for the preceding 35 years. The permitted disparity also is reduced for early retirement (before the Social Security full-benefit retirement age).

- **Offset plans.** The gross plan benefit cannot be reduced by more than 50 percent. Also, the offset cannot exceed three-quarters of 1 percent of final average pay up to the Social Security–covered compensation level, multiplied by years of service up

---

[4] Also, see James G. Durfee, Russell E. Hall, Christian L. Lindgren, Frances G. Sieller, and John Woyke, *A Guide to the Final Nondiscrimination Requirements* (New York: Research Institute of America, January 1994).

to a maximum of 35 years. The three-quarters of 1 percent factor will be reduced if the offset is based on pay above the Social Security-covered compensation level and for early retirement.

A plan that does not meet these integration requirements may still be able to achieve a qualified status by demonstrating that contributions or benefits, or both, do not discriminate in favor of the highly compensated employees under the general nondiscrimination requirements of Section 401(a)(4) of the Internal Revenue Code (IRC) or under a permitted safe harbor plan design.

Minimum Benefits

Closely related to the choice of an adequate benefit formula is the question of whether provision for a minimum pension should be included in the plan.

A minimum pension provision is generally a desirable feature of any pension plan. It is often possible for a benefit formula to produce a very small pension benefit as applied to certain employees. The use of a minimum pension can result in the payment of at least a minimum amount to these employees, while at the same time avoiding the embarrassment and ill will that might otherwise be generated in these situations. Apart from these considerations, if the plan is insured, the insurer may insist on the inclusion of a minimum pension provision as part of its general underwriting requirements—particularly in the case of a plan funded with individual policies.

Death Benefits

An employer-provided death benefit is an optional benefit under a pension plan; however, a great many plans include such a benefit.[5] Broadly speaking, such a death benefit may take one of two forms. The first consists of life insurance provided under some form of individual policy or group life insurance contract issued by an insurer, and the second consists of cash distributions from plan assets. Death benefits also may be classified as being payable in the event of death either before or after retirement.

Death benefits provided under individual policy plans and death benefits provided from plan assets are considered a part of the plan and, as such, are subject to the requirement of the Internal Revenue Service that the death benefit must be "incidental." In a defined benefit plan using life insurance, the incidental test is satisfied if the benefit does not exceed 100 times the expected monthly pension benefit or, if greater, the reserve for the pension benefit. The incidental test is not violated if the death benefit does not exceed the sum of the reserve of the life insurance policy and the amount held for the employee in the conversion fund. Also, as long as less than 50 percent of the employer's contributions for an employee have been used to purchase life insurance, the face amount of the life insurance plus the employee's share of the conversion fund may be paid as the death benefit under a defined benefit plan without violating the incidental death benefits rule.

[5] In the case of a married participant, a qualified retirement plan is required to provide a death benefit to the participant's surviving spouse unless an election and consent to waive such benefits has been made. However, the employer is not required to pay the cost of providing this benefit.

A plan may provide both a lump-sum preretirement death benefit and the qualified preretirement survivor annuity (QPSA) required by law,[6] as long as the incidental death benefits rule is not violated. A plan under which the only preretirement death benefit is a QPSA satisfies the incidental death benefits rule. However, a QPSA is considered an integral part of a preretirement death benefit. Thus, for defined benefit plans, the QPSA must be considered with other preretirement benefits to determine whether the benefits provided are incidental. A plan that provides a lump-sum preretirement death benefit equal to 100 times the monthly annuity amount and a QPSA violates the incidental death benefits rule.[7]

According to Revenue Ruling 85–15, however, there are several amendments that would enable a plan with a lump-sum preretirement death benefit to satisfy the incidental death benefits requirement. For example, the plan could offset the (otherwise) incidental preretirement death benefit by the value of the QPSA. In this regard, if life insurance contracts are purchased by the plan to provide the lump-sum preretirement death benefit, the proceeds could be paid to the plan's trust with the trust providing the QPSA to the surviving spouse and the excess, if any, of the lump-sum preretirement death benefit over the value of the QPSA to the participant's beneficiary (who could also be the surviving spouse).

Disability Benefits

In the pension area, disability benefits, even in insured plans, generally have been provided on a self-insured basis; that is, the benefits are paid in some form directly from plan assets, and the employer's experience in this regard is reflected in the cost level of the plan.

A number of pension plans, particularly those funded with individual policies, provide for full vesting if an employee becomes totally and permanently disabled. Other plans treat such a disability as an early retirement if the employee has completed some minimum period of service or participation in the plan and has attained some minimum age. Unfortunately, the disability benefits provided under such provisions are either nonexistent or inadequate for disabilities occurring at younger ages.

Some group pension and trust fund plans, however—particularly union-negotiated plans—provide for a separate and distinct benefit in the event of total and permanent disability. The benefit provided under such plans sometimes is a specified dollar amount, a specified percentage of earnings, or an amount equal to the employee's accrued or projected pension credits (with or without actuarial reduction). Often, the disability benefit under the plan is integrated with benefits available under government plans such as worker's compensation or Social Security benefits. Sometimes, the plan provides that

---

[6] See Chapter 26 for a discussion of this required benefit.

[7] Rev. Rul. 85–15. The lump-sum preretirement death benefit already equals the maximum amount considered "incidental," so the addition of a preretirement survivor annuity would cause the plan's total preretirement death benefit to violate Internal Revenue Service regulations.

the disability benefit will terminate when the employee reaches normal retirement age, at which time the accrued normal pension benefit will be payable.[8]

Most plans continue to accumulate pension credits during disability and while long-term disability benefits are being paid. If the pension benefit is based on the participant's salary, additional credits often are frozen at the level of the predisability salary.

The Impact of Inflation on Pensioner Income[9]

Everyone, in one way or another, bears the burden of inflation. For many individuals, this burden can be lightened or even eliminated by improvements in pay, investment opportunities, changes in lifestyle, and the like. One segment of the population, however—pensioners who are living on a fixed income—has limited opportunity to counteract the effects of inflation and, as a result, can suffer to a greater extent than those who are still actively employed or those who have accumulated independent wealth.

The rate of inflation has slowed to a considerable extent in recent years. Even so, the general expectations that inflation will continue, at least to some extent, and that the number of years employees will spend in retirement will increase (as a result of recent trends in early retirement and increases in life expectancy), make it important to consider the needs of the retired population. It also is significant that the size of this population is increasing not only in numbers, but also as a percentage of the total population.

Inflation affects pensioners not only in the period following retirement but also during the period of active employment while their pensions are being accrued. The following discusses, first, the plan design approaches used to counteract the effect of preretirement inflation and, second, approaches used to offset postretirement inflation.

Preretirement Inflation

As noted earlier, employer commitments to provide private plan retirement benefits vary from none at all to the replacement of a substantial part of an employee's pay determined at or shortly before retirement.

If an employer's plan provides a specific amount of retirement benefit, the amount of this benefit is expressed either as a dollar amount or in relation to the employee's pay. If pay related, the benefit may be determined as a percentage of pay averaged over the employee's career or over a relatively short period such as three or five years—often the high three-or five-year average during the last 10 years of employment.

Dollar amount plans (e.g., plans that provide a benefit such as $40 per month per year of service) do not directly reflect inflation because they are not pay related. However,

---

[8] It would seem such a provision is consistent with the Age Discrimination in Employment Act, as amended in 1986. However, the Department of Labor and the Equal Employment Opportunity Commission have indicated, in their opinion, such a provision might be in violation of the law concerning disabilities occurring after age 60—where the continuation of some disability income benefit might have to be provided for some period after age 65.

[9] The material in this section is based on material prepared by Towers Perrin. All rights reserved.

these plans are typically union negotiated and, in practice, the dollar amount is increased periodically via the collective bargaining process. Thus, in fact, these plans tend to provide initial retirement benefits that allow for preretirement inflationary trends. Of course, the extent to which this is so for any specific pensioner will depend upon the time of actual retirement and the dollar level then in effect for benefits under the plan.

Those plans that base benefits on final pay provide a retiring employee with an initial benefit that reflects inflation that has taken place prior to retirement. In fact, the majority of the nonnegotiated defined benefit plans in effect today use some form of final-pay base to determine benefits and thus recognize most of the inflation that takes place prior to retirement. The use of a five-year average for this purpose has been quite common. Because most of these plans are noncontributory, the cost of accommodating **preretirement inflation** is being borne primarily by employers. This cost becomes dramatically evident in inflationary periods as total pension plan costs rise, relative to payroll costs, because of pay movement in excess of that anticipated.

Some employers have chosen to develop benefit and cost commitments on the basis of career-pay plans. These plans, of course, reflect some part of the inflation that takes place prior to retirement. However, unless the rates of accrual are set unusually high, or the employer has updated the benefits that have accrued for employees, or the plan also has a minimum benefit formula based on final pay, the initial level of benefit provided for a pensioner will not fully reflect the inflation that has taken place during a working career. In many situations, employers periodically update career-pay plans by recalculating accrued benefits on the basis of then-current pay. Although the career-pay approach, with periodic updates, provides less assurance to employees than the final-pay approach concerning the adequacy of their benefits, there are definite advantages to the employer. First, the employer retains control over the timing and extent to which the cost of inflation is assumed. Second, the employer also receives credit for making periodic benefit improvements.

Postretirement Inflation

The techniques used to adjust benefits for employees who have already retired may be automatic or nonautomatic. The automatic adjustments for **postretirement inflation** provide for increases, at stated intervals, that are related to some form of index such as the Consumer Price Index (CPI) or to rates of return on an investment fund. The nonautomatic increases are provided on an irregular basis, at the employer's discretion, with the amount of increase determined in a variety of ways. The following discusses and evaluates these different techniques.

Automatic Adjustments

Four basic forms of automatic adjustment techniques have been used for making postretirement benefit changes:

1. Equity pensions
2. Cost-of-living formulas
3. Wage-related formulas
4. Specified percentage formulas

Equity Pensions   An **equity pension,** often called a variable annuity, provides retirement income that varies in dollar amounts to reflect the investment results of an underlying fund of common stocks. The equity feature (usually affecting only a portion of the retirement income amount) may operate during the years of active employment as well as during the postretirement payout period. In either case, the assumption is that stock price movement will vary with the movement of all other prices and, hence, reflect the general level of inflation. Proponents of the equity pension approach argue that active employees and pensioners have some assurance their retirement income will fluctuate with the general level of economic activity. Calculations of stock market performance have indicated that only in a few periods would the pensioner have been better off with a fixed-dollar retirement income. Also, from the employer's standpoint, the cost of equity pensions can be predicted beforehand. This is because the risk of potential investment gains and losses has been shifted to plan participants. Another potential advantage to the employer is that equity pensions may eliminate or reduce the need for other pension benefit liberalizations. Finally, an equity pension plan, at least during a rising market, could prove to be popular with employees, particularly where preretirement accruals are geared to stock performance.

Despite these points, equity pensions have some disadvantages:

1. Employees and/or pensioners are required to assume the risk of investment loss as well as the reward of investment gain. It is questionable whether individuals at lower income levels should be asked to assume this risk/reward situation for an item that constitutes an important part of their economic security.

2. The downward fluctuations in pension payments, which invariably occur from time to time, may cause hardship for pensioners. Recognizing this problem, employers may limit the amount of annual downward (or upward) adjustment through the use of a securities fluctuation reserve.

3. Equity pensions are more complicated than fixed-dollar pensions and are often more difficult to explain than other methods of adjusting pensions. This could be particularly important in a situation where the employer's fund fails to perform as well as recognized equity indexes.

4. If the objective is to have an employee's retirement income vary directly with cost- or standard-of-living changes, equity pensions may not be appropriate in the timing and magnitude of the pension fluctuations. At best, equity pensions are only an indirect means of relating retirement income to economic trends. At worst, and particularly over the short term, equity pensions may result in decreasing pension amounts during periods of rampant inflation.

5. From the employer's viewpoint, the equity pension approach may, in fact, produce additional or unnecessary costs. If the value of equities increases faster than the cost of living, benefits will be greater than may be needed to maintain the original income-replacement ratios of pensioners. At the same time, the excess investment return that causes this result will not be available to reduce employer costs. On the other hand, if the cost of living outpaces the performance of the equity market, the employer may very well feel the need to assume the additional cost of providing some form of supplemental benefit for pensioners. Thus, the employer reaps none of the

gain of superior investment performance and might become involved in the cost of underwriting this performance when it falls short of cost-of-living changes.

Cost-of-Living Formulas A direct approach to automatic pension adjustments involves linking retirement income amounts by formula to upward (and in some cases, downward) changes in a cost-of-living or price index such as the CPI. Under these plans, pension amounts increase periodically, subject to limits, if the increase in the price index equals or exceeds a predetermined level. The major advantages of this approach are that employees have advance assurance their retirement income will be adjusted periodically to help preserve their purchasing power and that the CPI, used almost exclusively in such plans, is well known and at least partially understood by most employees. Consequently, the employer has a good chance of avoiding criticism that the pension adjustment technique is faulty.

The following are possible disadvantages:

1. The employer assumes a largely undeterminable future liability tied to a government index over which it has no control. (However, the adjustment formula may be designed to provide ceilings on the amount of the increase in benefits and thus the maximum additional costs that are assumed.)
2. No allowance is made for any rising standard of living that may be experienced by active employees.
3. The CPI may, in fact, overstate rates of inflation and the presumed needs of pensioners, thus resulting in additional and unnecessary costs.
4. The tax law requires that any automatic increases be given to vested terminations—individuals for whom the employer may feel little or no continuing obligation.
5. If the pension plan provides for subsidized early retirement benefits, the cost of this subsidization very possibly will increase because the assurance of protection against inflation will most likely cause an increase in the incidence of early retirement.
6. Providing automatic cost-of-living adjustments for pensioners could create pressure to follow the same approach (i.e., automatic cost-of-living adjustments for wages) for active employees.

The cost implications of providing automatic cost-of-living increases for pensioners can be quite significant. The actual cost increases associated with such a benefit will, of course, vary from plan to plan and can range from about 8 percent to 20 percent for each 1 percent annual increase in benefits. Paradoxically, the greater the degree of funding achieved by a plan, the greater the percentage increase in plan costs when pensioner benefits are increased (as would be true whenever any of the benefits of such a plan are increased). Also, the greater the proportion of females covered by the plan, the greater the actual cost of pensioner increases. Assuming that a plan is approximately 50 percent funded and that the majority of pensioners are male, one rule of thumb is that pension costs will increase by about 10 percent for each 1 percent annual increase in pensioner benefits.[10] Increases in accrued benefit liabilities would generally follow the

[10] This example is illustrative of costs and does not recognize phased-in additional funding requirements mandated by the Pension Protection Act of 2006.

same increase pattern. The extent of the increase in accrued benefit liabilities would be different for each plan and would be most significant where existing pensioner liabilities are small compared with total plan liabilities and where females form a substantial portion of all plan participants.

Cost-of-living formulas frequently are found in the public sector (e.g., the federal civil service and military retirement systems, and various state and municipal plans), but they are still relatively rare in the private sector.

Wage-Related Formulas   This method involves the automatic fluctuation of retirement income payments in response to changes in some designated wage index. This permits pensioners to benefit from standard-of-living improvements enjoyed by active employees. The index could be one of a general nature, such as the Bureau of Labor Statistics' index of the average wage for industrial workers, or a more specialized one, such as the average wage paid by the individual employer. The former alternative normally would seem most appropriate as a measure of general standard-of-living variations, but it might have limited application to a specific employee group. The latter alternative could have a significant impact on pension plan costs if an employer maintains a liberal salary or wage increase policy. Some governmental units sponsor plans with wage-related formulas for pension adjustments; however, this type of plan is relatively uncommon, particularly in the private sector.

Specified Percentage Formulas   Under this approach, a predetermined percentage formula governs the amount of annual increase in retirement income. Unlike cost-of-living or wage-related plans, the company, in a sense, estimates future economic trends and commits itself to a specific increase based on this estimation. For example, the pension may be increased automatically by 1.5 percent a year on the assumption that this increase will offset, at least partially, upward trends in prices. When compared with cost-of-living and wage-related formulas, a specified percentage formula permits a more reliable prediction of plan costs. The primary disadvantage is that no assurance exists that the retirement income increases will actually reflect shifts in the cost of living, particularly over the short run. It is only by coincidence that such a plan would respond precisely to inflation and fulfill employee needs.

Nonautomatic Adjustments

The most popular method of coping with postretirement inflation, and the one that has been adopted by a majority of large, well-known organizations, has been the nonautomatic or discretionary form of adjustment made at irregular intervals and with varying ways of determining the amount of increase provided. Reasons for adopting a discretionary rather than an automatic approach to pension increases include the following:

1. Because the rate of inflation is uncertain, an organization should not commit itself to a predetermined or formula method.
2. Discretionary adjustments have a predictable cost because they remain under the employer's control, in regard to both timing and amount.
3. Both the scope and level of Social Security benefits may eliminate or reduce substantially the need for future retirement income improvements.

4. The employer receives credit for making a plan improvement each time benefits are increased.

One obvious disadvantage of the discretionary approach is the lack of assurance for pensioners that retirement income levels will continue to meet their needs. Another possible disadvantage is that this technique offers no possibility of prefunding the cost of the increases or having employees share in this cost during their active employment.

The discretionary adjustment techniques most frequently used are either fixed-percentage, or flat-dollar formulas, or a combination of the two.

A **fixed-percentage increase** may be applied uniformly to the retirement income of all pensioners. Alternatively, graded percentages may be used with variations based on a pensioner's age group, years of service prior to retirement, or the number of years since retirement date or the last pensioner increase. In a few instances, the pension increase may be limited to a defined "subsistence" income group—that is, a percentage increase may be applied only if a pensioner's total income from the company's plan and Social Security falls below certain dollar amounts. The percentage increase may be at least indirectly contingent on changes in the CPI. Frequently, the increase is subject to a stated dollar minimum and/or maximum; for example, the minimum monthly increase might be $20, with the maximum established at $100 or $125. The usual rationale for having a maximum is that the need for additional income is not as acute for pensioners who are receiving substantial pension payments. However, the higher the level of total pension income, the greater the loss of purchasing power because of inflation. This, of course, is because of the effect of automatic Social Security increases and the significance they have for pensioners at lower income levels.

A **flat-dollar increase** may be applied uniformly or on a variable basis. The latter approach is often used for nonunion, salaried pensioners to provide them with the same level of benefit increases provided for union pensioners.

The choice of formula and the level of percentage or dollar amount chosen depend upon a number of factors, including the cost and funding implications involved; the original level of pension provided; actual CPI movement; changes in Social Security benefits; the timing and form of the last pensioner increase (if any); competitive practices; and the cost and level of other benefits (death and medical expense) being provided.

It also should be noted that nonautomatic adjustments have been negotiated for retired members of a collective bargaining unit. Although these increases are not a mandatory subject of collective bargaining, there is nothing to prevent voluntary negotiations on this issue.

These discretionary adjustments are sometimes made part of the underlying formal plan. At other times, particularly when the formula will not meet Internal Revenue Service requirements for a qualified pension plan, discretionary adjustments are provided as a separate, nonqualified benefit. Even so, such nonqualified benefits are still subject to the labor provisions of ERISA unless they qualify for the exemptions provided.

Although the nonqualified approach has the advantage of permitting flexibility in the design of the formula, it has potential funding disadvantages; for example, the liability for the increase must be funded on a current disbursement basis over the remaining lifetimes of the pensioners, and there is no ability to vary this funding level from year to year without affecting the benefits payable to pensioners. (However, the possibility of some overall funding flexibility is available if the funded position of the underlying formal plan is such that its funding level can be reduced to reflect payments being made under the nonqualified supplement.)

Chapter Summary

- A major question the employer must resolve is whether employees will be required to make contributions toward the cost of plan benefits. Sound arguments may be presented for both contributory and noncontributory plans, although the ability of the employer or employees to pay is often the controlling factor. In any event, the trend is clearly in the direction of noncontributory plans, at least in the case of defined benefit plans.
- The normal retirement age in most plans is 65. The choice of this age was influenced not only by the fact that this was the original age at which full Social Security benefits commenced but also that retiring employees before age 65 with full benefits often produces prohibitive costs. Federal law defines normal retirement age to be the age specified in the plan, but no later than age 65 or the fifth anniversary of the participant's date of initial plan participation, whichever is the last to occur.
- The formula selected for determining an employee's retirement benefit is a vital provision in a pension plan. The employer's financial capacity and general philosophy concerning the desired level of retirement benefits, as well as the employer's specific objectives as to the distribution of benefits among employees, all play an important role in selecting such a formula.
- A plan will not be discriminatory merely because it uses a benefit formula that provides a larger percentage of benefits for earnings in excess of some amount (such as the Social Security taxable wage base) than it does for earnings under this amount. However, if the benefit formula is in any way integrated with Social Security benefits, certain requirements are imposed to prevent discrimination in favor of the highly compensated employees. The basic concept of these requirements is that the benefits from the employer's plan must be dovetailed with Social Security benefits in such a manner that employees earning over the taxable base will not receive combined benefits under the two programs that are proportionately greater than the combined benefits for employees earning under this amount.
- Death benefits provided under individual policy plans and death benefits provided from plan assets are considered a part of the plan and, as such, are subject to the requirement of the Internal Revenue Service that the death benefit be "incidental."
- Plans that base benefits on final pay provide a retiring employee with an initial benefit that reflects inflation that has taken place prior to retirement. In fact, the majority of the nonnegotiated defined benefit plans in effect today use some form of final-pay base to determine benefits and thus recognize most of the inflation that takes place prior to retirement. The use of a five-year average for this purpose has been quite

common. Because most of these plans are noncontributory, the cost of accommodating preretirement inflation is being borne primarily by employers. This cost becomes dramatically evident in inflationary periods as total pension plan costs rise, relative to payroll costs, because of pay movement in excess of that anticipated.

Key Terms

career-pay plan, p. *307*

contributory plans, p. *304*

early retirement, p. *304*

equity pension, p. *315*

excess plans, p. *310*

final-pay provision, p. *307*

fixed percentage increase, p. *318*

flat amount formula, p. *308*

flat dollar amount per year of service formula, p. *308*

flat-dollar increase, p. *318*

flat percentage of earnings formula, p. *308*

normal retirement age, p. *304*

offset plans, p. *310*

percentage of earnings per year of service formula, p. *309*

postretirement inflation, p. *314*

preretirement inflation, p. *314*

Social Security–covered compensation level, p. *310*

Questions for Review

1. Describe the advantages and disadvantages of a final-pay pension plan.
2. Explain the various considerations for an employer in selecting the compensation base that will be used in pension calculations.
3. Explain the four basic defined benefit formulas.
4. Describe how defined benefit pension plans may be integrated with Social Security.
5. Describe how preretirement inflation would be treated in (*a*) dollar amount plans, and (*b*) career-pay plans.
6. From the employer's viewpoint, what advantages are offered by a career-pay approach with periodic updates?
7. Describe the potential advantages and disadvantages of an equity pension.
8. Describe how wage-related formulas may be used to treat the impact of postretirement inflation on pensioner income.
9. Describe the advantages and disadvantages associated with the use of a specified percentage formula.
10. Why might an employer adopt a discretionary rather than an automatic approach to pension increases?

Questions for Discussion

1. Summarize the general theory behind the nondiscrimination requirements for integrated pension plans.

2. Assume that you have been asked to prepare a report to determine if the current system of benefit adjustments for private pension plans could be replaced by automatic benefit increases tied to specific price indicators. What are the major points that need to be covered in such a report?

3. An employer asks you to comment on a new concept of providing pension adjustments for retirees. Under this concept, employees are provided with an option to receive benefits in the form of an increasing annuity. Describe the plan design considerations of such an approach and its relative advantages and limitations.

Resources for Further Study

CCH Editorial Staff. "Legislation 2006: Pension Protection Act of 2006: Law, Explanation, and Analysis." *Commerce Clearing House* (2006).

Krass, Stephen J. *The 2006 Pension Answer Book: 2006 Edition.* New York: Panel Publishers, 2006.

Purcell, Patrick J. "H.R.4: The Pension Protection Act." Journal of Pension Planning & Compliance 32, no. 4 (Winter 2007).

Chapter 18

Cost and Funding Considerations

After studying this chapter you should be able to:

- Explain the difference between the estimated cost and the ultimate cost of a defined benefit (db) retirement plan.
- Identify the factors determining the total benefits paid under a db retirement plan.
- Describe the impact of mortality on the cost of a db retirement plan.
- Describe the impact of turnover on the cost of a db retirement plan.
- Explain the factors that should be considered in setting an interest rate assumption when calculating future db retirement plan benefits.
- Describe the impact of interest rates on the cost of a db retirement plan.

In its simplest form, a db pension plan[1] is a promise by an employer to pay a periodic benefit for life to employees who meet the requirements set forth in the plan. For a given pension benefit, the amount of annual benefit payments under the plan depends upon the number of retired workers. The number of retired workers, in turn, depends upon the rate at which already-retired workers die and the rate at which new employees are added to the retirement rolls. Since the average life expectancy for a 65-year-old person is about 15 years, it is quite likely that for some time after the plan is established, more new members will be added to the retired employee group than will be removed from the group as a result of death. Therefore, under a typical plan, the aggregate annual benefit payout should increase for a substantial number of years after the inception of the plan. The annual benefit payout continues to increase until a point is reached at which the size of the retired employee group tends to stabilize; that is, the point at which the number of retired workers dying is about equal to the number of new additions to the retired group.

However, when the employer prefunds the plan, the pattern of annual contributions under the plan will differ from the benefit payout pattern because, as indicated earlier, the benefit payout pattern for a given level of pension benefit is dependent upon the

---

[1] "Pension plan" as used in this chapter generally refers to the defined benefit form of plan. Also, much of the chapter's discussion centers on using assumptions to estimate pension costs. Since passage of the Pension Protection Act of 2006, there is less flexibility in selecting assumptions for purposes of pension funding although some assumptions may be helpful in better estimating ultimate plan costs.

number of retired workers eligible for benefits during each year and will be the same regardless of the manner in which contributions are made.

The objective of this chapter is to consider some of the important implications of funding a db pension plan and to acquaint the reader with the factors affecting the ultimate cost of a pension plan, apart from specific plan provisions and benefits. Particular reference is made to projecting the costs of a defined benefit plan and the factors that influence these costs.

Estimated Cost versus Ultimate Cost

The only way to determine the true cost of a pension plan would be to wait until the last retired employee dies, add up all the benefit payments and administrative expenses that have been paid since the inception of the plan, and subtract the investment earnings. The **ultimate cost** of the plan could then be stated as the benefits paid plus administrative expenses less investment earnings over the total life of the plan.

However, no business firm would ever establish a pension plan if the cost of the plan were completely uncertain until the plan was terminated at some date in the distant future. The obvious solution is that, although the specific ultimate cost is unknown, actuaries are able to estimate the ultimate cost of the plan with reasonable accuracy and thus arrive at a level of estimated plan contributions. To do this, assumptions must be made regarding the factors that affect the plan's ultimate cost. In subsequent years, adjustments in the estimated amounts of contributions required will have to be made, based on comparisons between the actual experience under the plan and the assumed experience. Experience more favorable than expected permits a reduction in future contributions. Conversely, adverse experience under the plan requires an increase in future contributions.

The point that pension cost projections are estimates and not actual cost figures cannot be overstressed. A moment's reflection regarding the nature of a pension plan should make this point quite clear. Assume, for example, that a pension plan provides employees with a retirement benefit only after attainment of age 65 and completion of a minimum of five years of service with the employer. It is obvious that not all current employees of the firm would be entitled to a retirement benefit under the plan. Some employees may die and others may quit, be laid off, or become disabled prior to age 65. Other employees may defer their retirement beyond age 65. Also, the number of years that retired workers will live cannot be predicted with certainty. Furthermore, in the case of funded plans, the rate of investment income to be earned in the future on accumulated assets in the pension fund can only be estimated.

So how does the pension actuary make an estimate of the ultimate cost of a pension plan? The first step is to make estimates of the various components of the ultimate cost—that is, estimates of the benefits paid, the expenses, and the investment return expected. The estimate of **benefits paid** depends on three things: the benefit provisions of the pension plan, the characteristics of the participants in the plan (age, sex, salary, and length of service), and the actuarial assumptions used to predict the amount of future benefit payments. The benefit provisions and characteristics of plan participants are unique to the plan being valued, while the actuarial assumptions are determined by the pension actuary valuing the plan. Selection of the appropriate actuarial assumptions for predicting future benefit payments along with actuarial assumptions as to expenses and investment return are discussed in the next section of this chapter.

Once an estimate of the ultimate cost of the plan was determined, traditionally the next step was to determine the contributions required to pay for the estimated cost in an orderly manner. One of several actuarial cost methods was used to allocate the costs to the various years. Changes brought about by the Pension Protection Act of 2006 (PPA); however, now place greater emphasis on assuring that db pensions are funded on a termination basis rather than spreading those costs during future years.

Choice of Assumptions

Two important points should be made regarding any choice of assumptions for the calculation of estimated pension costs.

First, the flexibility available in choosing a particular set of actuarial assumptions depends in large part upon the funding instrument involved. The greatest flexibility is available under trust fund plans and under unallocated group pension contracts. If the employer has competent advice, the assumptions used will be reasonable for the type of plan and the characteristics of the employee group covered. Fully insured individual policy plans and group permanent and group deferred annuity instruments offer the employer the least choice in cost assumptions, since the insurance company effectively establishes the assumptions to be used by its premium rates.

Second, the choice of a particular set of assumptions does not normally alter the ultimate cost of the plan. The choice of assumptions may affect the cost allocated to a given year, but the ultimate cost is primarily dependent on actual experience over the life of the pension plan. Obviously, the ages at which employees retire or the rate at which they die or leave their jobs is not necessarily the same as the assumptions in these areas made by the pension actuary. The relative magnitude of actuarial gains and losses under the plan will vary, given different original assumptions, but the end result will be an approximately similar ultimate cost picture except to the extent that investment earnings are affected by the incidence of contributions produced by the funding decisions. This conclusion does not fully apply in the case of plans funded with individual policies. In the case of individual contracts, there is a certain degree of pooling of experience among the whole class of business. For example, the mortality or expense experience under a particular plan is not directly reflected in the insurance company's dividends paid to that group since the dividend scale for individual policies is determined by the experience for that class of business as a whole. There is also an element of pooling in some group plans.

Cost Assumptions

As just discussed, one approach in considering the factors affecting the cost of a pension plan is to relate these factors to the formula for determining the ultimate cost of the plan, that is, benefits paid plus administrative expenses less investment earnings. The Pension Protection Act of 2006 radically changed some of the flexibilities permitted in making actuarial assumptions.

Benefits Paid

Number of Employees Retiring

The amount of benefits paid under a plan depends upon several factors. The first factor is the number of workers who will ultimately be entitled to receive benefits under the plan. The number of employees who will be eligible for benefits will depend on four factors: (1) mortality rates among active employees, (2) rates and duration of disabilities among active employees under a plan that offers a disability benefit, (3) layoffs and voluntary terminations of employment, and (4) rates of retirement at different ages. Let us now turn to a consideration of each of these cost factors.

Mortality   The higher the rate of **mortality** among active employees, the lower will be the cost of retirement benefits under the plan. However, if a participant is entitled to a preretirement death benefit, this will increase the cost of the plan, as additional benefits are being provided.

Mortality among active employees can be an important cost-reducing factor in those plans providing little or no death benefit beyond the mandated death benefits described in Chapter 26. This is particularly true for small plans, where a few deaths can have a significant impact on the cost of the plan.

Actuaries historically have used the same mortality table in projecting mortality among both active and retired employees. Several mortality tables were available in the past for pension cost calculations. For plan years beginning in 1995, plans were required to determine current liability (a concept primarily associated with underfunded plans; see Chapter 22). The prescribed mortality table for calculating current liability was the 1983 Group Annuity Mortality Table (GAM 83). An employer had to use the GAM 83 table and could not adopt a plan-specific mortality table or a table that reflected the increase in life expectancy since 1983. The Internal Revenue Service (IRS) proposed regulations, designed to be effective beginning in 2007 that would have required the use of the RP-2000 Mortality Tables. The RP-2000 Mortality Tables reflect improvements in mortality and project future improvements in mortality. The RP-2000 Mortality Tables provide separate tables for annuitants, nonannuitants, and disabled participants.

When the Pension Protection Act was passed and changed funding rules, it did not require use of the RP-2000 Mortality Tables as did the previously issued IRS proposed regulations. According to the PPA, the Secretary of the Treasury may determine whether the RP-2000 Mortality Tables are adopted. The PPA also permitted plan sponsors to use a plan-specific mortality table, but only with approval of the Secretary of the Treasury and under strictly defined conditions. A plan-specific table will not be approved by the Secretary of the Treasury absent credible information, based on the number of participants and the period of time the plan has been maintained, that is sufficient to allow a determination that the proposed table reflects actual plan experience and projected trends in general mortality experience. Also, the plan-specific table may only be used in determining present value or making other computations for a period of consecutive plan years specified in the request, but not to exceed 10 years. Also, a plan-specific mortality table will cease to be usable, even if the specified period has not elapsed, when a significant change in plan participation occurs as a result of spin-off, merger, or other circumstance.

The use of a plan-specific table must also cease if the table no longer reflects the actual experience of the plan maintained by the sponsor and projected trends in general mortality experience. Mortality gains or losses will develop from year to year, and the actuary can keep abreast of the experience through subsequent modifications of the mortality assumption.

Rate and Duration of Disability   If a pension plan offers a disability benefit, cost projections for that plan should include a disability assumption. The plan actuary must establish two sets of probabilities in evaluating the cost of providing a disability benefit. First, a **rate of occurrence (frequency) of disabilities** of the nature entitling the disabled employee to a benefit under the plan must be estimated. The rates of disability will vary with the plan's definition of disability, the age and sex composition of the covered employee group, the nature of the employment, and the general level of economic activity. At the inception of a plan, the disability experience projected for a particular plan may be based on insurance company data, the actual experience of the employer, or the experience of a large company in the same or a comparable industry. Ultimately, the plan's own experience may be used as a yardstick.

Having determined the probable incidence of disability, the actuary must then project the duration of the disability. The **duration of the disability** will be affected by reemployment opportunities, which in turn will be related to the nature of the employment and general economic conditions. The duration of the benefit period also will be affected by the mortality rates among disabled workers.

It can be seen, then, that the ability to project future disability rates is a difficult task. The actuary must keep a careful check on the actual disability experience evolving under the plan. As noted in the preceding section, the RP-2000 Mortality Tables provide tables for disabled participants.

Turnover   Employees who voluntarily quit or who are laid off represent a cost-reducing factor to a pension fund, assuming the absence of full and immediate vesting. Separate assumptions may be made regarding mortality, disability, and **turnover**; or, as is quite common, the plan actuary may use one set of termination rates covering all causes of termination of employment among nonretired workers.

The illustration in Figure 18.1 shows the effect on costs using different turnover assumptions.

The problems of developing accurate turnover rates for a specific plan are obvious. Future withdrawal rates vary among employers and industries and with changing economic conditions. The age composition of the covered group has a significant impact on turnover rates. It is generally recognized that turnover rates for younger workers are very high. Turnover rates also vary depending on the length of service of employees. Furthermore, working conditions and the personnel policies and benefit programs of a particular employer may affect turnover rates in that firm. Last, economic recessions or periods of prosperity may significantly alter turnover rates. During periods of recession, employees will be less likely to quit, while the rate of layoffs will probably increase. The opposite situation generally prevails during periods of economic prosperity.

The concept of turnover is broader for multiemployer plans than it is for single-employer pension funds. In the former, the employee's coverage is terminated only if he

FIGURE 18.1   Effect of Alternative Termination Rates

Source: Howard E. Winklevoss, *Pension Mathematics,* 2nd ed. (Burr Ridge, IL: Richard D. Irwin, for The Pension Research Council, 1993).

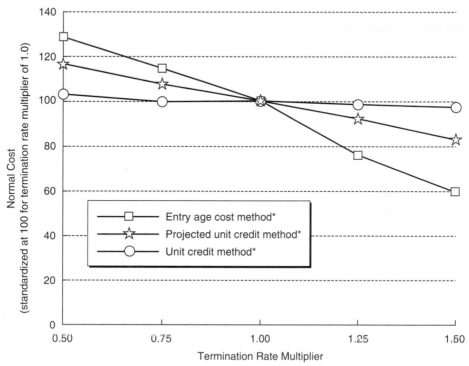

*These actuarial cost methods are described in Chapter 19.

or she fails to be reemployed by a participating employer within a specified time period, usually one or two years. In the skilled trades, withdrawal from the industry is less likely than separation from an individual employer. One of the basic assumptions justifying the existence of a multiemployer pension arrangement is the high degree of job mobility of the covered employees. But it also is assumed that there is a tendency for employees to be reemployed within the scope of coverage of the plan.

It is not surprising, therefore, that two actuaries may recommend considerably different withdrawal rates for the same plan. The choice of turnover assumption must rest, in the final analysis, on the sound judgment of the actuary. This judgment is based on the characteristics of the employee group, the factors discussed earlier, and the actuary's overall experience in pension cost projections. Turnover tables developed to guide pension consultants are of assistance for initial cost calculations, and adjustments in assumed turnover rates can be made as the actual experience under the plan evolves.

The question arises whether a turnover assumption should be used in calculating the plan's costs when the plan covers a relatively small number of employees. The arguments for and against the use of a turnover assumption in these cases are somewhat similar to the arguments regarding the advisability of a mortality assumption under these plans. Turnover is even less predictable than mortality for relatively small groups of employees. However, those pension planners who are in favor of using a turnover assumption say that there will obviously be some turnover in a plan (where there may be no mortality) and to ignore it is to be unrealistic.

Rate of Retirement   In estimating the cost of pension benefits, one must make an assumption regarding the ages at which individuals will retire under the plan.

For those plans that allow retirement at ages other than the normal retirement age, it would be appropriate to make an assumption about the percentage of people retiring at each age (just as the turnover assumption varies by age). However, for practical reasons, most actuaries assume that all employees retire at one age.

The higher the retirement age, the lower will be the cost of a given amount of retirement benefit. For example, if an employee decides to work up to age 65 rather than retiring at age 62, there is an additional three-year period during which the employee may die, with the resulting possibility that the employee will never receive retirement benefits. More important, the requirement of retiring at age 65 will reduce the length of the benefit period. In most plans, offsetting these two factors is the fact that the individual will continue to accrue benefits and hence will be entitled to a larger basic pension.

An actuary generally will use a retirement age assumption lower than the normal retirement age specified in the plan when the plan provides some form of subsidized early retirement benefit (i.e., an early retirement benefit that is greater than the actuarial equivalent of the normal retirement benefit) and when it is expected that many employees will, in fact, retire early.

It is not unusual to find that some employees defer retirement beyond the normal retirement age. Thus, it may be logical to assume in cost estimates that the actual average retirement age is higher than the normal retirement age. This will tend to lower the estimated costs for the plan. However, requirements under age discrimination laws that benefits continue to accrue for service after normal retirement age will tend to offset this automatic reduction in cost. Although not typical, some plans provide actuarially equivalent (larger) benefits to persons deferring retirement beyond normal retirement age. In these plans, no discount should be reflected in the cost calculations for postponed retirements.

Length of Benefit Period

In addition to the number of employees retiring, the amount of benefit paid under the plan is affected by the length of time that retired workers receive their pension benefits (or the length of time payments will be continued under the normal form to a beneficiary of the retired worker after his or her death). The **length of the benefit period** depends on the longevity of retired workers and the normal annuity form. Therefore, an assumption must be made regarding mortality among retired lives. As indicated earlier, the mortality table used for retired lives is generally identical to the table used for active lives, except in the case of individual policy plans.

Benefit Formula

The last factor affecting the total amount paid under the plan is the amount of pension paid to each retired worker. It goes without saying that the higher the benefit level, the greater will be the cost of the plan.

However, projecting benefit levels is more difficult under some benefit formulas than under others. The least difficult formula is one that provides a flat benefit for all retired workers—for example, a $500-a-month benefit. On the other hand, if the benefit formula calls for a pension benefit related to compensation, cost projections may include an assumption regarding expected future increases in the salaries of covered employees. For example, if a plan provides a pension benefit of 1 percent of final five-year average pay per year of covered service, future increases in salary will increase benefit levels and, therefore, the cost of the plan.

The decision regarding the size of the salary progression assumption is an extremely important one because of its dramatic impact on the level of projected costs. Other things being equal, the use of a salary progression assumption substantially increases cost estimates. The substantial impact on a cost estimate that results from use of a salary progression can be illustrated as follows: If a salary progression in the future is at the rate of 5 percent a year, the employee hired at age 20 for $10,000 a year would be receiving about $90,000 a year at age 65.

Also, in the case of negotiated plans providing a flat benefit per year of service, there is generally no advance provision for future increases in the unit benefit amount, and, in fact, current IRS regulations do not allow an assumption of future increases. It generally is recognized that benefit levels will be increased periodically due to inflationary pressures, but recognition is not given to this fact in cost projections until increases actually are negotiated.

Expenses

The expenses of administering the pension plan must be added to the benefits paid in arriving at the ultimate cost of the plan. The expense assumption used depends upon the type of administration and the funding instrument involved. Under individual policy plans and some group pension contracts, the insurance company includes a loading for expenses in the gross premiums charged for purchased benefits. The expense loading is largest under individual policy plans and decreases considerably under group pension contracts. Additionally, some administrative fees necessitated by ERISA may be charged separately from the gross insurance premium.

In the case of trust fund plans, the employer may pay the actuarial, legal, administrative, and investment expenses associated with the plan separately from the contribution payments to the plan. Nevertheless, these expenses must be added to the amount of benefit payment in arriving at the ultimate cost of the plan, even though they may not be included in the actual cost estimates.

Possible differences in the handling of expenses, then, must be recognized in comparisons of cost projections involving different funding instruments.

Investment Return and Interest Rate Assumptions

The investment income earned on the accumulated assets of a funded pension plan reduces the ultimate cost of the plan. Thus, the higher the **investment return** assumption, other things being equal, the lower will be the projected cost of the plan. The illustration in Figure 18.2 demonstrates the difference in the amount initially needed to be invested to provide $1 at age 65 at 6 and 8 percent, respectively. For a given plan, the impact of a change in the investment return assumption on the estimated cost of the plan depends on the age distribution of participants and their relative benefit credits.

The investment return assumption used should recognize the total anticipated rate of return, including investment income, dividends, and realized and unrealized capital appreciation (or depreciation). Therefore, selection of an appropriate investment return assumption should take into account the size of the fund, the anticipated investment policy of the plan trustees, current and projected long-term rates of return, and any other factors that might affect the future pattern of investment earnings of the fund. The choice of an appropriate rate of investment return is particularly difficult if a sizable portion of the assets is invested in common stocks, since these investments are subject to significant fluctuations in value. In addition to having an impact on the selection of an investment return assumption, investments in equities raise the rather difficult issue of when to recognize unrealized capital gains or losses.

FIGURE 18.2 **Amount Initially Invested to Provide $1 at Age 65**

Similar to the constraints on mortality assumptions, underfunded plans had less flexibility in choosing interest rates for determining the current liability following passage of the Retirement Protection Act of 1994. Prior to 1995, plans were required to use an interest rate between 90 and 110 percent of the weighted average of 30-year Treasury securities during the four-year period prior to the beginning of the plan year. The Retirement Protection Act of 1994 lowered the maximum interest rate that could be used for this purpose. (The Job Creation and Worker Assistance Act of 2002 expanded the aforementioned range to between 90 and 120 percent for years after December 31, 2001, and before January 1, 2004, for plans that were adequately funded.) The Pension Funding Equity Act of 2004 (PFEA) replaced the previously applicable 30-year Treasury rate used in funding calculations with the four-year weighted average of the long-term corporate bond rate. Interest rates authorized under the PFEA applied only through 2005. In 2006, current liability was determined pursuant to an interest rate that was 90 percent to 105 percent of the average of interest rates on 30-year Treasury securities for the four-year period ending on the last day before the plan year began. The Pension Protection Act of 2006 retains the blended rate of corporate bonds but introduces a segmented "yield curve" consisting of three different interest rates (based on the unweighted average of interest rates on investment grade corporate bonds) applicable to benefits payable in different time periods.

For a number of reasons, current market values of securities have seldom been used in the past in actuarial valuations. Two of the most important reasons were (1) market values generally would be relatively high in periods of high corporate earnings, thereby reducing the apparent need for contributions (and also the tax-deductible limits) at times when the employer was best able to make large contributions toward the pension fund (in periods of low corporate earnings the reverse would often be true, with required contributions and tax deductible limits increased at a time when the employer's capacity to contribute was at a minimum); and (2) due to market value fluctuations, measuring a plan's unfunded liabilities on any given date by the current market values of the fund's equities could produce a very irregular funding pattern—the antithesis of the orderly procedure, which was viewed as an essential characteristic of a satisfactory pension funding program.[2]

Not withstanding the preceding objections, market values must be used in defined benefit plan asset valuations. Prior to enactment of the PPA of 2006, the law required that asset valuations be computed on the basis of any reasonable actuarial method that took fair market value into account. Subsequent to the passage of the PPA, the value of plan assets must generally be fair market value. As was permissible prior to the enactment of the PPA, a plan may determine the value of plan assets by averaging fair market values over time, and thus "smooth" changes in asset value. However, the PPA requires that the averaging method must (1) comply with regulations that will be issued by the Secretary of the Treasury and (2) may not provide for the averaging of fair market value over more than the period beginning on the last day of the 25th month preceding the month in which the valuation date occurs and ending on the valuation date, or a similar period if

---

[2] William F. Marples, *Actuarial Aspects of Pension Security* (Burr Ridge, IL: Richard D. Irwin, 1965), p. 107.

the valuation date is not the first day of the month. Whereas prior law allowed plan asset values to be smoothed over five years and liabilities over four years, the requirements of the PPA mandate that assets and liabilities be smoothed over a period of a little more than two years. Essentially, this more compressed corridor for smoothing will likely result in greater volatility of plan asset values and consequently result in a more irregular funding pattern. Prior law allowed for smoothing techniques that produced actuarial asset values within a range of 80 percent to 120 percent of current fair market value, whereas the stipulation under the PPA is that plan asset valuation be between 90 percent and 110 percent of the fair market value of assets.

Overview

Historically, pension actuaries have used actuarial assumptions considered reasonable "in the aggregate" while each assumption might not be "individually realistic." For example, when making cost estimates where the benefit is related to final five-year average earnings, a zero percent salary increase assumption might be used, but the corresponding understatement in costs is offset by a conservative (low) investment return assumption.

However, actuaries now are required to use actuarial assumptions that are individually realistic. As can be seen from the preceding discussion, the choice of actuarial assumptions has a significant impact on the estimated costs of a pension plan. It must be repeated, however, that the choice of a particular set of assumptions generally has little effect on the ultimate cost of the plan.

Chapter Summary

- The only way to determine the true cost of a defined benefit pension plan would be to wait until the last retired employee dies, add up all the benefit payments and administrative expenses that have been paid since the inception of the plan, and subtract the investment earnings. The ultimate cost of the plan could then be stated as the benefits paid plus administrative expenses less investment earnings over the total life of the plan.
- The estimate of benefits paid depends on three things: (1) the benefit provisions of the pension plan, (2) the characteristics of the participants in the plan (age, sex, salary, and length of service), and (3) the actuarial assumptions used to predict the amount of future benefit payments. The benefit provisions and characteristics of plan participants are unique to the plan being valued, while the actuarial assumptions are determined by the pension actuary valuing the plan.
- The higher the rate of mortality among active employees, the lower will be the cost of retirement benefits under the plan. However, if a participant is entitled to a preretirement death benefit, this will increase the cost of the plan as additional benefits are being provided.

- In addition to the number of employees retiring, the amount of benefit paid under the plan is affected by the length of time that retired workers receive their pension benefits (or the length of time payments will be continued under the normal form to a beneficiary of the retired worker after his or her death). The length of the benefit period depends upon the longevity of retired workers and the normal annuity form. Therefore, an assumption must be made regarding mortality among retired lives. The mortality table used for retired lives is generally identical to the table used for active lives, except in the case of individual policy plans.

- The investment return assumption used should recognize the total anticipated rate of return, including investment income, dividends, and realized and unrealized capital appreciation (or depreciation). Therefore, selection of an appropriate investment return assumption should take into account the size of the fund, the anticipated investment policy of the plan trustees, current and projected long-term rates of return, and any other factors that might affect the future pattern of investment earnings of the fund. The choice of an appropriate rate of investment return is particularly difficult if a sizable portion of the assets is invested in common stocks, since these investments are subject to significant fluctuations in value. In addition to having an impact on the selection of an investment return assumption, investments in equities raise the rather difficult issue of when to recognize unrealized capital gains or losses.

- Prior to enactment of the Pension Protection Act (PPA) of 2006, the law required that asset valuations be computed on the basis of any reasonable actuarial method that took fair market value into account. Subsequent to the passage of the PPA, the value of plan assets must generally be fair market value. As was permissible prior to the enactment of the PPA, a plan may determine the value of plan assets by averaging fair market values over time, and thus "smooth" changes in asset value. Whereas prior law allowed plan asset values to be smoothed over five years and liabilities over four years, the requirements of the PPA mandate that assets and liabilities be smoothed over a period of a little more than two years. Essentially, this more compressed corridor for smoothing will likely result in greater volatility of plan asset values and consequently result in a more irregular funding pattern. Prior law allowed for smoothing techniques that produced actuarial asset values within a range of 80 percent to 120 percent of current fair market value, whereas the stipulation under the PPA is that plan asset valuation be between 90 percent and 110 percent of the fair market value of assets.

Key Terms

benefits paid, p. *323*
duration of the disability, p. *326*
investment return, p. *330*
length of the benefit period, p. *328*

mortality, p. *325*
rate of occurrence (frequency) of disabilities, p. *326*

turnover, p. *326*
ultimate cost, p. *323*

Questions for Review

1. What factors enter into the determination of the number of employees who will be eligible for benefits under a pension plan?
2. Describe how the type of benefit formula used may present difficulties in projecting the costs of a pension plan.
3. How does administrative expense relate to ultimate pension plan cost? What are some of the major administrative costs?
4. Does the federal law require the use of current market value in the valuation of securities used to fund pension plans? Explain.
5. Describe the approaches to "smooth" current market value in the valuation of pension plan assets held in the form of securities.
6. Does the choice of actuarial assumptions affect the ultimate cost of a pension plan? Explain.
7. Explain how the investment rate assumption affects the ultimate cost of a pension plan.

Questions for Discussion

1. Assume that you are asked to set assumptions for a new defined benefit pension plan. Describe the procedure you would follow.
2. How often should the assumptions established in Question (1) be updated?
3. Comment on how you would expect each of the following to influence retirement age: (*a*) changes in Social Security; (*b*) government regulations, such as the Age Discrimination in Employment Act; (*c*) early retirement incentives; and (*d*) cost-of-living adjustments for retirees.

Resources for Further Study

Amoroso, Vincent; Robert Davis; Timothy Geddes. "Costing and Funding Retirement Benefits." *The Handbook of Employee Benefits.* 6th ed. Jerry S. Rosenbloom, ed. New York: McGraw-Hill, 2005.

CCH Editorial Staff. "2002 Tax Legislation: Law, Explanation, and Analysis. Job Creation and Worker Assistance Act of 2002." *Commerce Clearing House Pension Plan Guide* (2002).

CCH Editorial Staff. "Legislation 2006: Pension Protection Act of 2006: Law, Explanation, and Analysis." *Commerce Clearing House* (2006).

Krass, Stephen J. *The Pension Answer Book: 2007 Edition.* New York: Panel Publishers, 2007.

www.soa.org—website of the Society of Actuaries.

Chapter 19

Budgeting Pension Costs

After studying this chapter you should be able to:

- Distinguish among the three methods of budgeting defined benefit (db) pension costs.
- Describe in general terms the prior paradigm for spreading db pension costs.
- Describe the db pension funding paradigm following passage of the Pension Protection Act of 2006 (PPA).
- Describe the basic elements and calculations to determine db pension funding as required by the PPA.
- Explain the basic requirements for deductibility of employer contributions.

Budgeting Pension Costs

The discussion in Chapter 18 set forth the various factors that affect the ultimate cost of a pension plan and how the choice of actuarial assumptions can significantly affect the estimated costs. In the past, actuaries had a fair degree of flexibility in establishing actuarial assumptions based on long-term data applicable to a particular plan and employer-specific data. The Pension Protection Act of 2006 set restrictions on certain actuarial assumptions and brought more uniformity to this process. Specifically, two very important actuarial assumptions—interest rate and mortality—are no longer left to employer discretion, but are now set by law.

In the past, actuarial techniques were used to determine how the estimated costs of the plan were to be spread over future years. These techniques were referred to as **actuarial cost methods.** More specifically, an actuarial cost method was a particular technique for establishing the amounts and incidence of the normal and supplemental costs pertaining to the benefits (or benefits and expenses) of a pension plan.[1]

---

[1] The terminology pertaining to the actuarial aspects of pension planning reflects, wherever possible, the thinking of the Committee on Pension and Profit Sharing Terminology, sponsored jointly by the American Risk and Insurance Association and the Pension Research Council, University of Pennsylvania.

Two approaches had been used to finance pension plans prior to passage of the Employee Retirement Income Security Act (ERISA) in 1974. Before describing the different actuarial cost methods introduced by ERISA, it might be helpful to review the current disbursement approach and the terminal funding approach. Although these two approaches are basically no longer permitted by the Internal Revenue Code IRC for qualified plans, knowledge of them should provide a better basis for understanding advance funding required by law, which follows.

Current Disbursement Approach

Under the **current disbursement approach,** the employer pays each retired worker's monthly pension as each payment becomes due. There is no accumulation of pension funds in an irrevocable trust or through a contract with an insurance company.

An illustration of the current disbursement approach would be a supplemental executive retirement plan (described in Chapter 14) under which the employer promises all employees with at least 10 years of service a lifetime pension of $1,000 a month beginning at age 65. If no employees are eligible for benefits during the first two years of the plan's existence, the employer does not make any pension plan payments during that period. The employer's pension outlay of $1,000 a month begins with the retirement of the first eligible employee; the outlay increases by that amount as each new retired worker is added to the pension rolls and decreases by $1,000 a month as each retired worker dies. These monthly pension outlays are provided out of current operating income and, in effect, are treated as a part of wage costs.

Terminal Funding

Under the **terminal funding approach,** the employer sets aside for each employee, on the date the latter retires, a lump-sum amount sufficient to provide the monthly pension benefit promised under the plan. The lump-sum amount needed to provide the promised benefit is a function of the amount of benefit assumptions as related to the expected benefit period and the rate of investment return expected to be earned on the investment of this principal sum. For example, assuming mortality rates will occur in accordance with a recent group annuity mortality table and assuming the rate of investment return will be 6 percent, the sum needed to provide $100 a month for life to a male, age 65, is $11,122.[2]

If the mortality and investment return assumptions prove to be accurate, the principal plus investment earnings will be sufficient, on the average, to provide the $100-a-month benefit.

The employer, therefore, sets aside the appropriate single-premium sum as each employee retires. Like the current disbursement approach, terminal funding does not require the employer to make any contributions on behalf of employees who are still actively at work.

---

[2] An expense assumption is ignored in this calculation, because the authors are interested solely in illustrating the concept of terminal funding. In practice, the expenses of administering the benefit would be taken into account in the single-premium rate charged by an insurance company or in determining the amount to be set aside in a trust fund under noninsured plans, if expenses associated with the plan are paid from the trust fund. Normally, the expenses under trust fund plans are paid directly by the employer, and therefore no expense allowance is required.

The benefits can be funded through the purchase of single-premium annuities from insurance companies, or the employer can transfer the estimated single-premium sums to a trust fund.

The reader should not confuse the concept of terminal funding with the practice of split funding that is prevalent in the pension field. The term **split funding,** as it is commonly used in pension planning, refers to the use of two different funding agencies in administering the assets of a pension plan. For example, a plan may provide that contributions on behalf of active employees are to be administered by a corporate trustee. When an employee retires, the trust agreement may require the corporate trustee to withdraw from the trust fund and transfer to an insurance company the single-premium sum needed to purchase a life annuity equal to the monthly pension earned by the employee under the terms of the pension plan. This type of plan is considered to be an advance funded plan unless the employer is paying to the corporate trustee an annual sum that is exactly equal to the amount of single premiums needed to provide the benefits for workers retiring each year—a highly unlikely situation.

Advance Funding

Under **advance funding,** the employer (and the employee, under contributory plans) sets aside funds on some systematic basis prior to the employee's retirement date. Thus, periodic contributions are made on behalf of the group of active employees during their working years. This does not mean that each dollar of contributions is necessarily earmarked for specific employees. As noted in other chapters, contributions are not allocated to specific employees under certain funding instruments (e.g., trust fund and group deposit administration plans). Thus, it is true that in some plans using unallocated funding instruments, contributions in the early years may be sufficient to provide lifetime benefits only to the first group of employees retiring under the plan. However, if contributions are continued on an advance funding basis, the accumulated assets in the pension fund soon will exceed the aggregate single-premium sums needed to provide benefits to those workers who already are retired. This excess of pension assets, then, represents the advance funding of benefits that have been accrued or credited to the active (non retired) employees.

Pension plans operating on an advance funded basis are invariably qualified with the Internal Revenue Service (IRS). An employer generally is not willing to make advance contributions to an irrevocable trust fund unless it receives the tax advantages of a qualified plan.

The relatively even distribution of annual pension outlays under advance funding produces a more equitable allocation of the firm's cash flow over the years. The pension is being provided to employees for the year of service rendered to the firm. Thus, it would seem that the funds available to the owners of the firm (e.g., stockholder dividends) should be reduced by pension contributions in an amount approximately equal to the present value of benefits accruing under the plan. It is true that credit for past service, offered at the inception of the plan, creates a problem. Since the plan was not in existence during those past service years, it is highly improbable that previous generations of owners would be willing to retroactively refund a portion of the funds they received from the firm. The next best solution seemed to be to amortize past service cost in the first

20 or 25 years after the inception of the plan. The Employee Retirement Income Security Act originally required that for new plans, past service costs must be amortized over no more than 30 years. The amortization period was reduced substantially as a result of the Omnibus Budget Reconciliation Act of 1987 and modified by the Retirement Protection Act of 1994.

As will be discussed later, the approach originally instituted by ERISA took a long-term view and attempted to spread costs evenly over the life of the plan. It became clear, however, that a plan could meet the funding requirements mandated under the law but still have insufficient assets to pay benefits if the plan was terminated. Attempts were made to remedy this situation with the deficit reduction contribution (DRC) rules enacted into law in 2004. Even the DRC rules fell short of providing adequate funding when a plan terminated. Because of this issue, the entire approach to pension funding was overhauled with enactment of the Pension Protection Act of 2006. The changes in philosophy for pension funding and elements of this approach are explained later.

The accumulation of assets in a pension fund resulting from the advance funding of benefits serves as a buffer during periods of financial stress. During a period of low earnings or operating losses, an employer may find it advisable to reduce or eliminate pension contributions for a year or for an even longer period. This can be done in those cases where the pension fund is of sufficient size that a temporary reduction of contributions does not violate the minimum funding requirements imposed by ERISA and subsequently modified by the PPA. It should be noted that this financing flexibility does not necessitate any reduction or termination of pension benefits.

Under advance funding, the plan actuary used a set of assumptions and an actuarial cost method in estimating the annual cost of a plan. Annual contribution payments were usually based on these estimated annual costs. However, it should be noted that actual annual contribution payments were not identical to the estimated annual costs generated by a given actuarial cost method, nor was it necessary that they be identical to the accounting expenses described in Chapter 23.[3] As will be noted in later chapters, the employer had some flexibility in the timing of contribution payments under unallocated funding instruments.

ERISA established the foundational framework for pension funding using various actuarial cost methods. When several plans terminated prematurely, it became obvious that although these actuarial cost methods spread costs for the ongoing plan, the plans could still have insufficient funds to pay benefits if the plan terminated. Modifications to the rules were made. Actuarial cost methods, as instituted under ERISA, were still used to determine what was known as a plan's normal cost. With passage of the PPA, the concept of target normal cost was developed. **Target normal cost** is the present value of benefits expected to accrue during the plan year, determined using the same assumptions as for determining the funding target, which will be explained later. Importantly, the target normal cost includes increases in past service benefits because of expected increases in compensation during the year. However, an additional amount called the *shortfall contribution* also must be added to target normal cost to ensure that the plan is able to meet its obligations to participants and beneficiaries if the plan were to terminate.

---

[3] Moreover, the valuation of liabilities described in this chapter will most likely differ from those in Chapter 23 and those used for plan termination insurance purposes (Chapter 22).

This latter requirement to add the shortfall contribution also was instituted by the PPA. The **funding shortfall** is the excess, if any, of the funding target over the value of the plan assets (less any credit balance) as of the valuation date. First, we explain briefly the workings of actuarial cost methods and the methods for the determination of normal costs prior to the enactment of the PPA. Then we describe the changes in the law brought about by the PPA and how these changes affect plan funding.

There were several different actuarial cost methods, each producing different patterns of annual costs under the plan. Having different actuarial cost methods to calculate annual pension costs was analogous to having different methods for determining the annual amount of depreciation of plant and equipment to charge against operations. The depreciation methods that can be used may produce different annual charges, but the total value of the building and equipment to be depreciated is constant regardless of the depreciation formula used. Similarly, the various actuarial cost methods produced different levels of annual cost, but the choice of a particular actuarial cost method would not affect the ultimate cost of the plan. One important exception to the latter conclusion was the fact that if an actuarial cost method was chosen that produced higher initial contributions than other methods, then the asset accumulation would be greater (assuming a positive rate of return) in the early years of the plan, thereby producing greater investment income. An increase in investment income would decrease the ultimate cost of the plan.[4]

If the choice of actuarial cost method usually had little effect on the ultimate cost of a pension plan (after taking into consideration interest and so on), what factors determined which method was used in calculating the amount and incidence of pension contributions? The answer to this question will become more apparent after the following brief discussion of the specific cost methods. However, the reader may find it helpful to keep in mind that the choice of a specific actuarial cost method was significantly influenced by the degree of flexibility desired by the employer in annual contribution payments and the amount of flexibility available under the particular funding instrument used. Much of this flexibility has been minimized since the PPA now requires that pensions be funded so that benefits can be paid if the plan is terminated.

Actuarial Cost Methods

Actuarial cost methods were broadly classified into (1) accrued benefit and (2) projected benefit cost methods.[5]

The class into which a particular cost method fell depended on whether, for cost determination purposes, an employee's benefits under the pension plan were deemed to "accrue" in direct relation to years of service or were viewed as a single "projected" total.

---

[4] More precisely, the timing of contribution payments has additional cost implications if federal income tax rates change, alternative uses of capital vary over time, or investment return rates vary over the life of the plan.

[5] Parts of the material in this section were drawn from Joseph J. Melone, "Actuarial Cost Methods—New Pension Terminology," *Journal of Insurance* 30, no. 3 (September 1963), pp. 456–64.

Most actuarial cost methods broke down the total actuarial cost into the **normal cost** and the **supplemental cost** of the plan. The normal cost of the plan was the amount of annual cost, determined in accordance with a particular actuarial cost method, attributable to the given year of the plan's operation.

Most plans provided credit for service rendered prior to the inception date of the plan. If the normal cost under the particular cost method was calculated on the assumption that annual costs had been paid or accrued from the earliest date of credited service (when in fact they had not), the plan started out with a supplemental liability. At the inception of the plan, the supplemental liability (also known as the actuarial accrued liability, the accrued liability, or the past service liability) arose from the fact that credit for past service was granted, or part of the total benefit was imputed, to years prior to the inception of the plan. The annual contribution prior to the enactment of the PPA was normally equal to the normal cost of the plan plus at least enough of a contribution to **amortize the supplemental liability** over a specified period of time.[6] If it was desired to fund this supplemental liability in a more rapid manner (10 years was generally the minimum period over which it could be funded on a deductible basis), larger annual contributions were required. The portion of the annual cost applied toward the reduction of the supplemental liability was referred to as the plan's supplemental cost. As the plan continued in operation, the size of the supplemental liability normally would change. In addition to normal changes in the supplemental liability that occured as a result of the actuarial method being used, these changes in the size of the supplemental liability could result from variations in benefit formulas, deviations of actual from expected experience, and changes in the actuarial assumptions or in the actuarial cost method used in subsequent normal cost calculations. Offsetting any increase in the supplemental liability would be any unanticipated increase in the size of pension fund assets. The unfunded supplemental liability, then, was the difference between the supplemental liability and any assets that may have accumulated under the plan as a result of prior contributions.

Defined Contribution Plans

The discussion thus far in this chapter has been concerned primarily with the role of actuarial assumptions and actuarial cost methods in calculating the annual cost of a plan. The question arises as to the degree to which this discussion is pertinent in the case of defined contribution (money purchase) plans. In these plans, the employer's contribution commitment was fixed and was usually expressed as a specified percentage of the compensation of covered employees. Thus, it would seem that there was little need for actuarial assumptions and cost methods to determine annual costs under these plans. To allow the employer to estimate future costs or benefits under the plan, projections were required based on appropriate actuarial assumptions and a specific actuarial cost method. In estimating ultimate costs under a defined contribution plan, the actuary could use either the accrued benefit method or a projected benefit cost method, depending on how benefits were defined. Also, under traditional defined contribution plans,

---

[6] The minimum amortization amount depended upon when the supplemental liability was created and also depended on the funding status of the plan.

the annual contribution on behalf of each employee was viewed as a single-premium payment for a unit of deferred annuity to begin upon attainment of normal retirement age. Indeed, some of the defined contribution plans were funded through group deferred annuity contracts. Thus, the age of the employee and mortality and interest assumptions determined the amount of benefit being credited each year. The amount of benefit credited each year for a given employee would vary with the size of the contribution payment and the number of years to retirement age.

A variation of the traditional defined contribution plan was found in some negotiated plans that had both a fixed contribution and a fixed benefit. Negotiated multiemployer plans were established on this basis. The union negotiated a fixed pension contribution rate with all participating employers, and the rate was usually expressed in terms of cents per hour worked or unit of production, or as a percentage of the compensation of covered employees. The contributions were paid into a single trust fund, and a uniform benefit schedule applicable to all covered employees was established. Actuarial assumptions and an actuarial cost method were needed to determine the level of benefits that could be supported by the fixed contribution commitment. In these plans, an additional assumption was made in actuarial computations that was not mentioned earlier in the chapter, that is, the expected level of future contributions. Because the contribution commitment was usually related to compensation or hours worked, changes in levels of economic activity affected the contribution income of the plan. The actuary, therefore, projected the future flow of contribution income to determine an appropriate benefit formula for the plan.

The cost method normally used in actuarial computations for fixed contribution–fixed benefit plans was the projected benefit cost method with a supplemental liability. One reason was that this method tended to produce annual normal costs that were expected to remain fairly stable as a percentage of payroll or in terms of cents per hour if the actuarial assumptions were in fact realized; moreover, this was consistent with the contribution commitment under these plans, which was normally expressed as a percentage of payroll or in cents per hour of work. Another reason was the existence of a supplemental liability, which permitted some flexibility in annual contribution income. Changes in levels of employment would result in fluctuations in the annual aggregate contribution income of the plan, which may not have matched fluctuations in the amount of benefits credited. During periods of prosperity, the excess of actual over expected contribution income could be applied toward amortizing the supplemental liability at a rate faster than anticipated; likewise, periods of recession resulted in extensions of the period over which the supplemental liability was to be amortized. Of course, in both cases, the amortization periods had to be in line with the minimums and maximums permitted under federal law.

Minimum Funding Standards Enacted by the PPA

It is interesting to frame the evolution of funding requirements for single-employer defined benefit plans in an evolutionary context. The rules instituted by ERISA followed foundational actuarial concepts and sought to spread costs of pensions equitably over successive generations of plan contributors. This philosophy had each generation's shareholders and workers (when the plans required employee contributions) bearing their respective share of plan costs for a plan that was seen as having an ongoing continual existence. The plan was perceived as existing for an undetermined period of time. When this long-term perspective was used, the question whether a plan could meet its liabilities if it were to terminate prematurely was not a primary consideration. In this context, actuarial assumptions were based on decades of experience rather than on prevailing current market and situational conditions. Things such as interest rate assumptions changed very slowly and could be considerably different from current conditions and rates in the capital markets. The belief was that these disparities would converge as the financial conditions reverted to a mean over time. Unexpected events were spread out over time because they were considered aberrations. Variations from actuarial assumptions were amortized over 15 to 30 years. All these practices were logical when the funding was being accomplished, assuming the plan had a perpetual existence. However, if a plan terminated because of deteriorating business conditions for the plan sponsor, the funding situation of the plan could be considerably at risk and the plan assets and plan liabilities could be considerably out of alignment.

When a number of businesses experienced adverse conditions resulting in financial difficulties, a number of pension plans needed to seek protection from the Pension Benefit Guaranty Corporation (PBGC), with the PBGC assuming responsibilities for the payment of these pension benefits. The following description is helpful in understanding how the long-term view was incompatible with the realities of a plan termination when a business experienced adverse circumstances:

> A real case illustrates how poorly the ERISA funding rules meshed with a healthy pension insurance system. One fairly large plan that terminated in the mid-1980s was just 3 percent funded at the time of its demise, meaning that virtually all of its benefits wound up being paid from the resources of the PBGC. Yet the employer's contributions had more than met the minimum funding requirements throughout the plan's existence. In fact, the funding standard account had a healthy credit balance.
>
> A number of factors came together to produce this seeming anomaly. During an early period of prosperity, the plan sponsor contributed more than the statutory minimum. When its business began to decline, reductions in force generated large benefit payouts. In some cases, terminated workers were entitled to shutdown benefits, which increased the plan's liabilities. Often, they elected lump sums, which drained assets. This unfavorable experience did generate higher minimum required contributions, but the adjustment was sluggish. In any event, the nominal requirements meant nothing until the abundant funding standard account credits, created by past contributions above the minimum required level, were absorbed.[7]

As this example suggests, assuming pension plans are ongoing enterprises with a perpetual existence was problematic. The PPA discarded this long-standing funding paradigm and instead substituted a totally new funding approach that determines if a plan can meet its payout obligations should the plan be terminated. Essentially, the new

---

[7] Tom Veal, "What a Difference for DB Plan Funding," *The Pension Protection Act of 2006: Essential Insights* (New York: Thompson Publishing Group, 2006), pp. 16–17. This article provides an excellent explanation on the changes to defined benefit plan funding requirements.

system's "ideal is for every plan always to be fully funded, on a termination basis, for all accrued benefits."[8]

Prior to the enactment of the PPA, single-employer defined benefit pension plans were required to make minimum funding contributions equal to the greater of (1) the contributions required under the deficit reduction contribution (DRC) rules or (2) the contributions required under the plan's funding standard account. If the DRC rules applied, sponsors generally needed to contribute a specified percentage of the plan's unfunded liabilities. DRC contribution percentages ranged from 18 percent to just over 30 percent of the differences between the value of plan assets and 100 percent of plan liabilities. These calculations were made using DRC interest rates and mortality assumptions to compute the current liability. Unlike the funding target approach instituted by the PPA, the DRC contributions were required only when a plan fell below 90 percent funding on a current liability basis, or 80 percent for plans that had been 90 percent funded in two consecutive years out of the preceding three years.

For plan years beginning in 2008, the two-tiered system for funding single-employer defined benefit pension plans was replaced with a single-funding approach. The **minimum required funding** for any plan year under the approach instituted by the PPA is the sum of (1) the plan's target normal cost for the plan year and (2) the shortfall contribution necessary to amortize the difference between assets and 100 percent of liabilities over a seven-year period of time. A shortfall contribution is required in the current year and in each of the next six years unless the plan becomes 100 percent funded at an earlier date. For poorly funded plans, considered "at risk," funding requirements are increased so that the shortfall is amortized more quickly until the plan no longer falls within the at-risk category. An **at-risk plan** is one that has a **funding target attainment percentage (FTAP)** (i.e., ratio of the plan assets less any credit balance to the funding target) that is below 80 percent for the preceding year,[9] and has a funding target attainment percentage determined using special at-risk assumptions[10] that is below 70 percent for the preceding year.

Other restrictions for at-risk plans prohibit their sponsors from permitting funding to worsen. These restrictions curtail payment of shutdown benefits, lump-sum distributions, and plan amendments that would increase plan liabilities. An at-risk plan may be required to freeze ongoing benefit accruals. Plan participants must be notified within 30 days after a plan has become subject to any of these restrictions. As previously indicated, target normal cost is defined as all benefits that a plan expects to pay in future

---

[8] Ibid., p. 17.

[9] The 80 percent threshold was phased in over four years—65 percent in 2008, 70 percent in 2009, 75 percent in 2010, and 80 percent thereafter.

[10] At-risk plans utilize special assumptions when computing the funding target and target normal cost. At-risk plans must assume that all participants eligible to retire in the current plan year or the next 10 plan years do indeed retire at the earliest possible date (but not before the end of the current plan year). It is also assumed that these retirees elect the payment form that results in the highest present value of benefits. Additionally, plans that have been in at-risk status in at least two of the preceding four years must add both a loading factor of 4 percent of the not-at-risk amounts and a flat amount of $700 per participant to the funding target. Under no circumstances can the at-risk funding target be less than the not-at-risk funding target, nor can the at-risk target normal cost be less than the not-at-risk target normal cost.

years that accrue during the year. These benefits that accrue during the year include increases in benefits earned in prior years when the increase is related to compensation increases. Under the funding rules instituted by the PPA a funding target is established. The **funding target** is the present value of a plan's accrued benefits similar to the current liability determined using prescribed assumptions. The funding target is used for many purposes, such as for determining funding amounts, benefit restrictions, and PBGC premiums. The funding target requires contributions for a plan year if the sum of the plan's target normal cost for the year and 100 percent of the plan's liability on the valuation date exceeds the value of the plan's assets. As previously indicated, funding shortfall for a year is the excess, if any, of the funding target over the value of plan assets (reduced by all credit balances). A plan is required to make quarterly contributions if, for the preceding plan year, the plan had a funding shortfall. If a plan is required to make quarterly contributions, the quarterly amount is 25 percent of the lesser of 100 percent of the prior year's minimum required contribution or 90 percent of the current year's minimum required contribution. If a quarterly contribution is late, interest is charged at the plan's effective interest rate plus 5 percent.

In terms of effects on actuarial valuations, certain new requirements apply. As previously indicated, actuarial assumptions for interest rates and mortality are no longer left to employer determination. Mortality assumptions are unlikely to have a major impact on the majority of plans. Unless permission is granted by the Treasury Department to use a table that is specific to the employer, the designated mortality assumption is to be prescribed by the Treasury, is to reflect mortality improvements, and is to be revised at least once every 10 years. The Treasury also is specifying separate mortality tables for disabled participants. Changes to interest rate assumptions will have a much more dramatic impact. The special corporate bond rate rules that applied to 2004 and 2005 plan years were extended to 2006 and 2007 plan years. For 2008 and beyond, the funding target is determined using segment rates that apply to benefits paid during three distinct time periods: less than 5 years, between 5 and 20 years, and more than 20 years. These **segment rates** are computed using a corporate bond yield curve developed from a 24-month average of yields on investment-grade corporate bonds in the top three investment quality categories. Alternatively, a plan can use the full yield curve without the 24-month averaging. The option to use the full yield curve without averaging could help minimize contribution volatility for those plan sponsors who have attempted to closely match the duration of plan assets to the underlying plan liabilities. Any elections made with regard to which yield curve to use cannot be changed without approval from the Treasury Department. The Treasury Department is the sole source for segment rates and the underlying yield curves. Contributions made after the valuation date on behalf of the prior plan year must be discounted back to the valuation date using the effective interest rate. The **effective interest rate** is the single rate of interest that, if used instead of the segment rates, would result in the same funding target.

> "Other forward-looking actuarial assumptions have been largely eliminated. Salary scale is not a mandatory assumption, though it can be employed for determining maximum deduction limits. Assumptions concerning early retirement and forms of benefit distribution are required in limited circumstances but ordinarily can be dispensed with."[11]

---

[11] Veal, "What a Difference for DB Plan Funding," p. 18.

Going forward, the contribution pattern for plans will generally look like that resulting from the unprojected unit credit actuarial cost method. This actuarial cost method shifts costs heavily to participants' later years rather than spreading them smoothly. Prior law did not regard unprojected unit credit as a reasonable, much less a favored, actuarial method in most circumstances. The PPA takes the opposite approach because it is uninterested in the pattern of contributions, so long as full or nearly full funding is constantly maintained.[12]

The value of plan assets can be either market value or an average value. If an average value is used, certain requirements apply. Valuing plan assets using any reasonable actuarial method is permissible, but the "smoothing" of asset values that results from actuarial estimates cannot average fair market value over more than a 24-month period. Also the smoothing cannot result in asset values that are lower than 90 percent or greater than 110 percent of the fair market value of such assets at the time of the actuarial valuation. Prior to passage of the PPA, smoothing of asset values could average the fair market value over a period of five years and asset values could range between 80 percent and 120 percent of current fair market value of plan assets.

Phase-In of the Funding Target

The 100 percent funding target instituted by the PPA does not apply until 2011 for plans that are funded up to 92 percent of the funding target in 2008, 94 percent of the funding target in 2009, and 96 percent of the funding target in 2010. Plans subject to the DRC rules for plan years beginning in 2007 do not qualify for this phase-in transition rule for the funding target. "This 'ladder' phase-in is not a traditional phase-in. As a result, many plans (including non-DRC plans) will either have to immediately fund up to the applicable threshold (92% in 2008) or immediately move from a 90% funding target to a 100% funding target in 2008."[13]

Need for Timely Actuarial Valuations

A new feature of the law instituted by the PPA relates to the need for timely actuarial valuations. If a plan was not deemed to be at risk in the prior year, then the funded ratio is presumed to be 10 percent lower in the current year until a new actuarial valuation is done. If the valuation is not done by the beginning of the fourth month of the plan year, then the limitations that would apply with the effect of this 10 percent lower funding level (should it trigger various plan limitations) takes effect as of the beginning of the fourth month. If an actuarial valuation is not done by the beginning of the 10th month of the plan year, then the adjusted funded ratio is presumed to be less than 60 percent as of the beginning of the 10th month, with the relevant limitations taking effect. These limitations relate to plan amendments, lump-sum payments, shutdown benefits, and benefit freezes. Since the most stringent restrictions generally apply once a plan's adjusted funding ratio falls below 60 percent, the implications of a plan failing to complete an actuarial valuation by the 10th month are quite serious.

[12] Ibid.

[13] The Benefits Group of Davis and Harman LLP, "Summary of Provisions of The Pension Protection Act of 2006 Affecting Defined Benefit Plan Funding and Hybrid Plans," October 5, 2006, p. 1.

Prior to passage of the PPA, the valuation date for a plan could be any date within the plan year. Since passage of the PPA for 2008 and beyond, the valuation date is established under the law. For plans with more than 100 participants on a controlled-group basis, the valuation date must be the first day of the plan year. For plans with fewer than 101 participants on a controlled-group basis, the valuation date can be any date within the plan year.

Deductibility of Employer Contributions

Basic Requirements

Apart from the specific provisions of the Internal Revenue Code dealing with the deductibility of employer contributions to a qualified plan, it is first required that if such a contribution is to be deductible, it must otherwise satisfy the conditions of an ordinary and necessary business expense under IRC Sections 162 (relating to trade or business expenses) or 212 (relating to expenses for the production of income). Also, a deduction will not be allowed for any portion of the contribution for any employee that, together with other deductions allowed for compensation for such employee, exceeds a reasonable allowance for services the employee actually has rendered.

The employer's contributions to a qualified plan generally are deductible under Section 404(a) of the IRC. Expenses such as actuarial and trustee fees that are not provided for by contributions under the plan are deductible under Sections 162 or 212 to the extent they are ordinary and necessary expenses.

Employer contributions generally are deductible only in the year in which they are paid. However, an employer will be deemed to have made a contribution during a taxable year if it is in fact paid by the time prescribed for filing the employer's return for such taxable year (including extensions) and if the employer claims the contribution as a deduction for such year. It is important, however, that the plan be in existence by the close of the employer's taxable year in the case of deductions claimed for the first plan year that begins in such taxable year.

Limits on Tax-Deductible Contributions to a Defined Benefit Plan

The PPA dramatically increased the maximum amount that employers can deduct when making contributions to their defined benefit pension plans. For 2006 and 2007, the deduction limitation was equal to 150 percent of the plan's current liability. The plan's **current liability** represents the value of accrued benefits determined using certain specified assumptions minus the value of plan assets. Then, beginning in 2008, the maximum deductible amount generally is equal to the greater of (1) the sum of the plan's funding target, the plan's target normal cost, and a *cushion amount*, minus the plan's unreduced assets for the plan year; or (2) the minimum required contribution for the year. The **cushion amount** generally equals the sum of 50 percent of the plan's funding target for the plan year and the amount by which the funding target would increase based on future compensation increases. For plans that do not base past service benefits on compensation, the addition is based on expected increases in benefits estimated using the average of such benefit increases over the past six years. Also, for plans that are not in the at-risk category, this calculation can be computed assuming that the plan was in at-risk status. If a plan were to terminate during the plan year, the maximum deductible contribution shall not be less than the amount that is required to meet the plan's benefit liabilities.

Deduction limits, by necessity, must exceed required plan contributions because of the differences between the computational methods used to calculate minimum funding standards and those used in Generally Accepted Accounting Principles (GAAP). As a result of changes in the minimum funding standards brought about by the PPA, it is likely that the financial accounting standards, including *Financial Accounting Standard 87 (FAS 87)*, will undergo future revision. As of the publication date of this book, *FAS 87* required the calculation of pension expenses using the projected unit credit method rather than the unprojected method associated with the requirements of the PPA (see Chapter 23 for a more in-depth explanation of accounting standards related to pensions). Pension funding can diverge from pension accounting expenses with funding either exceeding or falling below accounting expenses. Under the rules that applied prior to enactment of the PPA, it was possible to have made an "excess" funding contribution that was not allowable as a deductible expense when made to the plan. An excess funding contribution was to be carried forward to be deducted in a future year. Nondeductible contributions could potentially be subjected to a 10 percent excise tax, although the likelihood of this happening diminished with some legal changes enacted into law in 2001.

The PPA reduces the risk of a funding contribution not being fully deductible because it allows for the deduction of a cushion amount above the minimum funding requirement. For 2006 and 2007, the higher limits representing 150 percent of the plan's current liability allow plans to improve plan funding rapidly before much more severe requirements occur. Employers who had underfunded plans in this time period would want to accelerate deductions, if they possessed the funds to do so, to achieve at least 92 percent funding for 2008 and forestall the large uptick in funding required if the plan were deemed to be at risk. Once plan assets fully fund the maximum benefit specified by the Section 415 limit for defined benefit plans, nothing more generally can be contributed. This is particularly true for small plans, but the PPA makes allowance for plans with more than 100 participants to anticipate future increases in the Section 415 limit, providing them with further ability to accelerate funding. However, for most companies—those neither concerned with an *FAS 87* shortfall nor wanting to increase contributions above the mandatory level—deductions are likely to match their plan contributions.[14]

Overstatement of Pension Liabilities

An excise tax will be imposed on an underpayment of taxes that results from an overstatement of pension liabilities. A 20 percent penalty tax is imposed on the underpayment of tax if the actuarial determination of pension liabilities is between 200 and 399 percent of the amount determined to be correct. If the actuarial determination is 400 percent or more of the correct amount, the penalty tax is increased to 40 percent. If the tax benefit is $1,000 or less, no excise tax will be imposed.

[14] Veal, "What a Difference for DB Plan Funding," p. 20.

Special Limits for Combined Plans

If both a defined benefit pension plan and a defined contribution plan exist, with over-lapping payrolls, the total amount deductible in any taxable year under both plans prior to the enactment of the PPA could not exceed 25 percent of the compensation paid or accrued to covered employees for that year. When excess payments were made in any taxable year, the excess was carried forward to succeeding taxable years, subject to the limitation that the total amount deducted for such succeeding taxable year (including the deduction for the current contribution) could not exceed 25 percent of the compensation paid or accrued for such subsequent year.

The PPA phased in a repeal of the combined defined benefit and defined contribution plan limit, but the repeal only applied if the defined benefit plan was insured by the PBGC. Retaining the combined plan limit for noninsured plans was intended to restrain small businesses, for which qualified plans may serve as tax shelters, from funding defined benefit and defined contribution plans to the maximum possible level simulta-neously.[15] For plan years beginning in 2006, the combined plan deduction limitation did not apply to the extent contributions to one or more defined contribution plans did not exceed 6 percent of compensation of beneficiaries under the plan. Beginning in 2008, the combined plan limit no longer takes into account single-employer defined benefit plans covered by the PBGC insurance program.

Nondeductibility of Contributions to Provide Certain Benefits

No deduction is allowed for the portion of a contribution to a defined benefit plan to fund a benefit for any participant in excess of either the Section 415 annual benefit limita-tion for the year or the Section 401(a)(17) allowable limit on includable compensation (see Chapter 26 for details). In calculating the contribution to a defined benefit plan, anticipated cost-of-living increases in the allowable annual retirement benefit *cannot* be taken into account before the year in which the increase becomes effective. However, as was stated earlier, the PPA makes allowance for plans with more than 100 participants to anticipate future increases in the Section 415 limit, providing them with further ability to accelerate funding.

Chapter Summary

- Under advance funding, the employer (and the employee, under contributory plans) sets aside funds on some systematic basis prior to the employee's retirement date. If contributions are continued on an advance funding basis, the accumulated assets in the pension fund will soon exceed the aggregate single-premium sums needed to pro-vide benefits to those workers who already are retired. This excess of pension assets, then, represents the advance funding of benefits that have been accrued or credited to the active (nonretired) employees.

- The original approach to pension funding as instituted by ERISA took a long-term view and attempted to spread costs evenly over the life of the plan. It became clear,

[15] Ibid., p. 19.

however, that a plan could meet the funding requirements mandated under the law but still have insufficient assets to pay benefits if the plan was terminated. Attempts were made to remedy this situation with the deficit reduction contribution rules enacted into law. Even the DRC rules fell short of providing adequate funding when a plan terminated. Because of this issue, the entire approach to pension funding was overhauled with enactment of the Pension Protection Act of 2006.

- Target normal cost is the present value of benefits expected to accrue during the plan year, determined using the same assumptions as for determining the funding target. Importantly, the target normal cost includes increases in past service benefits due to expected increases in compensation during the year.

- Assuming pension plans are ongoing enterprises with a perpetual existence was problematic, the PPA totally discarded this long-standing funding paradigm and instead substituted a totally new funding approach that determines whether a plan can meet its payout obligations should the plan be terminated. Essentially the new system's ideal is for every plan always to be fully funded, on a termination basis, for all accrued benefits.

- The minimum required funding for any plan year under the approach instituted by the PPA is the sum of the plan's target normal cost for the plan year and the shortfall contribution necessary to amortize the difference between assets and 100 percent of liabilities over a seven-year period of time. A shortfall contribution is required in the current year and in each of the next six years unless the plan becomes 100 percent funded at an earlier date.

- For poorly funded plans, considered at risk, funding requirements are increased so that the shortfall is amortized more quickly until the plan no longer falls within the at-risk category. An at-risk plan is one that has a funding target attainment percentage (i.e., ratio of the plan assets less any credit balance to the funding target) that is below 80 percent for the preceding year and has a funding target attainment percentage determined using special at risk assumptions that is below 70 percent for the preceding year.

- Other restrictions for at-risk plans prohibit sponsors from permitting funding to worsen. These restrictions curtail payment of shutdown benefits, lump-sum distributions, and plan amendments that would increase plan liabilities.

- Under the funding rules instituted by the PPA, a funding target is established. The funding target is the present value of a plan's accrued benefits similar to the current liability determined using prescribed assumptions. The funding target is used for many purposes, such as for determining funding amounts, benefit restrictions, and PBGC premiums. The funding target requires contributions for a plan year if the sum of the the plan's target normal cost for the year and 100 percent of the plan's liability on the valuation date exceeds the value of the plan's assets.

- For 2008 and beyond, the funding target is determined using segment rates that apply to benefits paid during three distinct time periods: less than 5 years, between 5 and 20 years, and more than 20 years. These segment rates are computed using a corporate bond yield curve developed from a 24-month average of yields on investment-grade corporate bonds in the top three investment quality categories. Alternatively, a plan can use the full yield curve without the 24-month averaging. Any elections made with regard to which yield curve to use cannot be changed without approval from the Treasury Department. The Treasury Department is the sole source for the segment rates and underlying yield curves.

- The contribution pattern for pension plans will generally look like that resulting from the unprojected unit credit actuarial cost method. This actuarial cost method shifts costs heavily to participants' later years rather than spreading them smoothly. Prior law did not regard the unprojected unit credit as a reasonable, much less a favored, actuarial method in most circumstances. The PPA takes the opposite approach, because it is uninterested in the pattern of contributions, so long as full or nearly full funding is constantly maintained.

- Valuing plan assets using any reasonable actuarial method is permissible, but the smoothing of asset values that results from actuarial estimates cannot average fair market value over more than a 24-month period. Also the smoothing cannot result in asset values that are lower than 90 percent or greater than 110 percent of the fair market value of such assets at the time of the actuarial valuation.

- The ladder phase-in approach for the funding target is not a traditional phase-in. As a result, many plans (including non-DRC plans) will either have to immediately fund up to the applicable threshold (92 percent in 2008) or immediately move from a 90 percent funding target to a 100 percent funding target in 2008.

- The PPA dramatically increased the maximum amount that employers can deduct when making contributions to their defined benefit pension plans. For 2006 and 2007, the deduction limitation was equal to 150 percent of the plan's current liability. The plan's current liability represents the value of accrued benefits determined using certain specified assumptions minus the value of plan assets. Beginning in 2008, the maximum deductible amount generally is equal to the greater of (1) the sum of the plan's funding target, the plan's target normal cost, and a cushion amount, minus the plan's unreduced assets for the plan year; or (2) the minimum required contribution for the year.

- The cushion amount generally equals the sum of 50 percent of the plan's funding target for the plan year and the amount by which the funding target would increase based on future compensation increases.

- The PPA reduces the risk of a funding contribution not being fully deductible because it allows for the deduction of a cushion amount above the minimum funding requirement.

Key Terms

actuarial cost methods,
  p. *335*
advance funding, p. *337*
amortization of
  supplemental liability,
  p. *340*

at-risk plan, p. *343*
current disbursement
  approach, p. *336*
current liability, p. *346*
cushion amount, p. *346*

effective interest rate,
  p. *344*
funding shortfall, p. *339*
funding target, p. *344*

funding target attainment
  percentage (FTAP),
  p. *343*
minimum required
  funding, p. *343*

normal plan cost, p. *340*
segment rates, p. *344*
split funding, p. *337*
supplemental plan costs,
  p. *340*

target normal cost, p. *338*
terminal funding
  approach, p. *336*

Questions for Review

1. What is the advance funding approach used in connection with making contributions to pension plans?
2. What was problematic about the original approach to pension funding as instituted by ERISA?
3. What is the funding ideal under the approach to pension funding as revamped by the Pension Protection Act of 2006?
4. What is the minimum required funding for any plan not at risk for 2008 and later?
5. What is an at-risk plan?
6. Describe the concept of a funding target.
7. List the three distinct time periods that comprise the segment rates instituted by the PPA.
8. Summarize the actuarial stipulations applicable to valuing plan assets.
9. How is a defined benefit plan's maximum deductible amount of contribution computed for 2008 and later?
10. Since the passage of the PPA, why is it likely that a funding contribution to a defined benefit pension plan will generally be fully deductible?

Questions for Discussion

1. Discuss the merits of using different time bands to value benefit liabilities coming due at different times, as is now done using segment rates.
2. The foundational framework for pension funding was established by ERISA in 1974. As indicated in the chapter, substantial flaws emerged in the original funding approach promulgated by ERISA. A substantial overhaul of these rules occurred with the enactment of the PPA of 2006. Can you foresee any flaws in the funding approach of the PPA that may lead to substantive revisions of its funding rules in the future?

Resources for Further Study

BNA Tax Management Staff, "Pension Bill Makes Sweeping Changes to Plan Funding Rules and Administration," *BNA Tax Management Analysis of PPA '06*, Parts I, II, and III (August 18, 2006).

Buck Consultants, "The Pension Protection Act of 2006—Funding Rules for Single-Employer Defined Benefit Plans," *fyi: for your information Pension Protection Act Analysis*, 29, no. 79 (October 24, 2006).

CCH Editorial Staff. "Legislation 2006: Pension Protection Act of 2006: Law, Explanation and Analysis." *Commerce Clearing House* (2006).

Groom Law Group, "Summary Comparison of Current Law and the Principal Provisions of the Pension Protection Act of 2006: Single-Employer Pension Funding Reforms and Cash Balance Provisions," August 17, 2006.

Hewitt Associates, "The Pension Protection Act of 2006," *Special Report to Clients* (August 2006).

The Benefits Group of Davis and Harman LLP, "Summary of Provisions of The Pension Protection Act of 2006 Affecting Defined Benefit Plan Funding and Hybrid Plans," October 5, 2006.

Veal, Tom. "What a Difference for DB Plan Funding," *The Pension Protection Act of 2006: Essential Insights*, New York: Thompson Publishing Group (2006).

www.actuary.org—website of the American Academy of Actuaries.

www.soa.org—website of the Society of Actuaries.

Chapter 20

Insured Funding Instruments and Trust Fund Plans

After studying this chapter you should be able to:

- Identify various types of funding instruments used to hold and accumulate qualified plan assets.
- Identify the specific guarantees that insurers customarily have provided to plan sponsors under various insured funding instruments.
- Explain the importance of the advent of separate accounts to insurers' ability to compete with trust fund plans in providing flexibility to plan sponsors.
- Discuss the relationship between funding instruments and plan design features and why certain funding instruments are not conducive to certain plan designs.
- Explain the functions, responsibilities, and duties of a trustee under a trust fund plan.
- Discuss the administrative functions commonly carried out by plan trustees for multiemployer and single-employer plans.
- Detail the advantages provided to plan sponsors by using a collective investment fund.
- Address the merits of using more than one type of funding instrument to hold and accumulate plan assets.

A qualified plan must use a **funding instrument** (trusts, custodial accounts, or insurance company contracts) to hold and accumulate plan assets. The trust fund arrangement was the first of the existing funding instruments to be used to fund private pension benefits. In addition to using the oldest of the funding instruments, trust fund plans currently account for the bulk of the employees covered and the assets held by private plans. The trust fund approach is used extensively by multiemployer plans and large single-employer plans, although the increased flexibility now available under group pension contracts has resulted in greater life insurance company competition for multiemployer and large single-employer plan business.

This chapter is concerned with various funding instruments. First, the historical evolution of insured funding instruments will be explained. Next, a more detailed explanation of the operation of trust funds will be provided since these funding instruments generally are more widely used today.

Introduction to Insured Funding Instruments

The prevalence of trusts as the predominant funding instrument has not always been the case. Originally, the majority of pension plan assets were placed with insurance companies and were protected by strong guarantees as to investment and mortality experience. Beginning with group deferred annuity contracts in the early 1920s, insurance products were designed specifically for use in pension plans. These contracts provided that a single premium would be paid to purchase an annuity for each employee promising to pay (at normal retirement age) the equivalent of his or her accrued benefit for that year. Although all investment and mortality risks were transferred from the employer to the insurance company once the annuities were purchased, it was difficult to provide a substantial degree of flexibility in plan design features, such as past-service benefits and supplemental benefits, since the price of funding a dollar's worth of monthly retirement income increases substantially as the employee approaches normal retirement age.

The limited flexibility of this contract eventually led the insurance industry to develop unallocated forms of funding vehicles, such as deposit administration and immediate participation guarantee contracts, which are described in this chapter. Funding instruments generally are classified on the basis of whether contributions are **allocated** to provide benefits to specific employees prior to retirement or whether contributions are accumulated in an **unallocated fund** to provide benefits for employees when they retire.

In time, some sponsors began to question the need for locking up funds for annuity purchases, as is generally the case under deposit administration and immediate participation guarantee contracts, and many were disenchanted with the restrictions or implicit penalties imposed on the withdrawal of funds from such contracts. Many employers used trust fund plans to provide a more flexible funding instrument.[1] The insurance industry responded to the competition from trust fund plans by offering features and products that provided greater flexibility. The introduction of separate accounts permitted sponsors a broader array of investment vehicles, not commonly permitted in the general accounts of insurers. Sponsors also sought investments that had a fixed maturity and did not require an ongoing relationship with the insurer. The insurance industry again responded to this demand by offering guaranteed investment contracts, which offer a unique type of investment guarantee.

---

[1] Trust fund arrangements are discussed later in this chapter.

The major development in the group pension field in the last 20 years has been the substantial increase in flexibility under insurance contracts. Insurers now are in a position to tailor the contract to the specific needs of the employer. Employer demands for greater flexibility in investment policy and the timing of contribution payments have led to a strong preference for the unallocated type of contract in the group pension market. This demand for greater flexibility has extended to the small-employer market, and insurers have accommodated this demand by making unallocated contracts available to relatively small firms. While there are some deposit administration and immediate participation guarantee contracts still active at most insurers, many policyholders have opted to convert their funds into more modern funding vehicles.

Funding Instruments—General History

The **group deferred annuity contract,** unlike individual insurance and group permanent contracts, was devised specifically to meet the funding needs of pension plans, the first such contract being issued in 1921. The volume of these contracts grew very rapidly in the following two decades, and they constituted by far the most prevalent group-insured funding instrument prior to the growth of deposit administration plans in the 1950s. However, they are rarely used today. Group deferred annuity contracts provide for the funding of benefits through the purchase of units of single-premium deferred annuities for each participant.

The **deposit administration contract,** which first appeared in the 1920s, evolved from the basic group deferred annuity contract. The deposit administration contract was developed to overcome certain of the inflexibilities associated with the group deferred annuity contract. Because of the other more flexible funding instruments currently available, group deposit administration contracts are no longer issued as new contracts.

The distinguishing characteristic of deposit administration contracts, as contrasted with group deferred annuity contracts, is that employer contributions are not allocated to specific employees until retirement date. Stated differently, the actual purchase of annuities (which includes a charge for expenses) does not take place until an employee retires.

Contributions are credited to an unallocated fund that, under a conventional deposit administration contract, is variously referred to as the deposit fund, active life fund, deposit account, or purchase payment fund. Contributions credited to the deposit account are invested in the insurer's general investment portfolio or the insurer's separate accounts. **General account investments** principally are fixed-income securities. **Separate accounts** offer a broader choice of investments between fixed-dollar and equity securities. The type of separate account available under the deposit administration contract is primarily one that is invested in common stocks. *Fixed-dollar account* and *equity account* are terms that are used when discussing the features of deposit administration contracts from the policyholder's viewpoint.

The contributions credited to the fixed-dollar account become part of the general assets of the insurance company for investment purposes. The account is credited with the rate of interest guaranteed in the contract. Also, dividends due under the contract are credited to the fixed-dollar account. As pensions become payable to retiring employees, annuities may be provided by allocations from either the fixed-dollar or the equity account, although generally annuities are provided by allocations from the fixed-dollar account. When an annuity is established, a certificate is issued to the retired employee describing the benefits. The contributions credited to the policyholder's equity account are invested in one or more of the insurer's separate accounts provided under the contract.

In the intervening decades since their introduction, group annuity contracts following the basic deposit administration concept have been offered in considerable variety, including immediate participation guarantee (IPG) and guaranteed investment contracts (GICs), varying from product to product in both the degree of insurer guarantee and the degree of contract holder discretion as to contributions, investment, and the mobility of funds. Some such contracts were, in fact, group annuity contracts in name only, functioning solely as investment vehicles, with the purchase of annuities a seldom-used contract holder's option. Most GICs and many separate account contracts are, in practice, investment-only contracts.

Major Insurance Product Developments

Group Immediate Participation Guarantee Contracts

In reaction to employer requests for an immediate reflection of the actual experience under their contracts and their willingness to give up the guarantees of the deposit administration contract to get it, insurance companies developed the **immediate participation guarantee contract,** the first contract of this type being issued in 1950. Under an IPG contract, the employer's account is credited with the contributions received during the contract period plus its share of actual investment income for the year according to the investment year method. The account is charged with all the expenses associated with the particular contract. As issued by many insurance companies, these contracts provide that all benefits, including annuity payments, are charged directly against the account as they are paid. In other words, annuities are not actually purchased for participants at retirement date, as is the practice under deposit administration contracts.

The IPG contract also specifies a schedule of guaranteed annuity gross premium rates. However, since annuities are not actually purchased at retirement date, these guaranteed annuity rates are only of significance if the plan or contract is terminated. IPG contracts as initially developed typically did not provide for a guarantee of principal or a minimum rate of interest.

As IPG contracts developed and grew in popularity, the use of separate accounts, and the types of separate accounts available, grew, enabling insurers to offer group clients a wide range of investment choices. The assets held in separate accounts are not commingled with the general assets of the insurer and are exempt from state statutory investment restrictions normally applied to life insurance companies.

Separate Account Funding

Historically, life insurance companies have invested the bulk of their assets in fixed-dollar investments. The laws in most states restrict the investments of life insurance companies' general account assets in common stocks to some specified percentage (e.g., 5 percent) of the total assets of the company. This restriction is imposed because of the fixed-dollar obligations and contractual guarantees provided in traditional life insurance and annuity contracts and, also, because of the relatively small surplus maintained by life insurance companies.

However, with the advent of separate accounts in 1962, insurers could offer group clients a wide range of investment choices. The assets held in separate accounts are not commingled with the general assets of the insurer and are exempt from state statutory investment restrictions normally applied to life insurance companies.

There is much variety in the manner in which separate accounts are operated by the various insurance companies. Some insurers offer accounts only on a commingled basis; others also offer accounts maintained solely for a single customer. Initially, separate accounts were invested primarily in common stocks, but other forms are now available; further major developments in the nature and form of the separate accounts available can be expected as the types of underlying investments in these accounts are broadened. For example, some insurers have established separate accounts invested primarily in mortgages, including equity participations; others have established commingled separate accounts invested primarily in the ownership of income-producing real property; and other accounts are invested in publicly traded bonds, short-term securities, direct placements, and, most recently, foreign securities. One or more separate accounts may be used under the same group pension contract.

Separate accounts were developed for two reasons: (1) to compete with trust fund plans in making equity investments available to employers for funding fixed-dollar plans and (2) to fund variable annuity plans. In the first case, many employers believe the long-term rate of return on equities will be greater than the return on fixed-income investments and the increased return will serve to reduce their cost of providing the fixed benefits promised under the plan. In the second case, equity-based variable annuities by definition generally require that the assets supporting these annuities be fully invested in equity securities.

The insurer does not guarantee principal or interest for plan assets held in a separate account. The income and gains or losses, realized or unrealized, on separate account investments are credited to or charged against the separate account without regard to the other income, gains, or losses of the insurance company.

Separate accounts are subject to regulation by the Securities and Exchange Commission (SEC). However, exemptions from certain provisions of the acts administered by the SEC have been accorded to qualified retirement plans over the years.[2]

---

[2] First, exemptions under the Securities Act of 1933 and the Investment Company Act of 1940 were provided by Rule 156 and Rule 3(c)3 for noncontributory, qualified plans covering at least 25 lives at the time the contract was issued. Later, Rule 6(e)1 extended the exemption to contributory plans, provided that certain conditions were satisfied regarding employee contributions allocated to separate accounts. Last, the Investment Company Amendments Act of 1970 exempts from the 1940 Act separate accounts used exclusively to fund qualified plans, and from most provisions of the 1933 Act and the Securities Exchange Act of 1934 separate account interests issued in connection with qualified plans (except for HR-10 and individual retirement account plans). Separate accounts also are subject to state regulatory requirements. A 1980 change to the Securities Acts extended the exceptions to plans of governmental units even though not qualified. SEC Rule 180 (December 1981) provides an exception to the registration requirements of the 1933 Act for certain financially sophisticated HR-10 plans.

Annuity Separate Account Contract

In the late 1980s, the annuity separate account contract was developed. This contract provides for the establishment of fixed-dollar annuity guarantees for which underlying reserves are invested, not in the insurer's general account, but in one or more of the insurer's market-valued separate accounts. Annuity separate account contracts have been written primarily on the deposit administration pattern, with unallocated funds and annuities at retirement, but they also have been used for single-premium annuities with both immediate and deferred annuities. Although the participation aspect of an annuity separate account contract is highly comparable to the IPG, with regard to mortality experience, and to separate account unit valuation, with regard to investment results, it is unique in combining the two in a way that allows plan sponsors to direct the investment of assets supporting their already annuitized pensions.

Guaranteed Investment Contracts (GICs)

As defined contribution plans have grown in popularity, funding vehicles intended primarily for such plans have developed. A major vehicle is the **guaranteed investment contract (GIC).**

GICs were first introduced in the 1970s. The basic concept in the early GICs was to offer an "open window," as long as 10 years, during which contributions could be placed in the GIC and credited with interest at a guaranteed rate. By the 1980s, in order to reduce investment risk and cash flow risk of the insurance company, the contribution window was shortened considerably, typically to a period of 3 to 12 months. Many GICs now provide for a one-day "window," whereby a single contribution is made, as opposed to a series of contributions over several months.

Under the typical GIC, the contribution window is followed by a "holding period," during which interest is credited at a rate guaranteed not to change during the life of the contract and during which withdrawals may be made at book value to provide plan benefits. Payment of the accumulated amounts may be made in a single sum at the end of the holding period or in a series of installments over a stated period of months or years. The terms of the GIC are agreed upon between the insurance company and the plan sponsor as part of the negotiation process before the GIC is issued. These terms include the entire length of the contract, the contribution window, the amount of the contribution (or the minimum and maximum amount, if a series of contributions will be made), the payment terms, and the guaranteed interest rate.

GICs also are used as a funding vehicle for defined benefit plans, although to a lesser extent than for defined contribution plans. Under a GIC issued for a defined benefit plan, a single contribution typically is made and held until the scheduled payment date, accumulated with interest at the specified guaranteed rate. It is usually a "nonbenefit responsive" GIC, in that it is not intended that withdrawals will be made from the GIC to meet plan benefit requirements.

The "guarantees" provided by GICs are only guarantees to the extent that the issuing insurance company is able to fulfill the contractual terms that it has "guaranteed" for the purchaser of the investment contract. In the 1980s, this aspect of GICs became problematic to many plan sponsors when certain insurance companies were unable to fulfill their contractual obligations. Accordingly, some plan sponsors have diminished their reliance on GICs for other fixed-income alternatives, while some plan sponsors have sought greater security to ensure guarantees from insurers. The traditional type of GIC described above is part of the insurance company's general account assets. In the late 1980s, insurance companies also began to offer GICs funded in a separate account. By contract, contributions deposited and held in the separate account may be insulated from the other assets and liabilities of the insurer; separate account assets cannot be subject to claim from general creditors or other contract holders. Amounts are invested by the insurance company according to investment guidelines that have been agreed upon between the insurance company and the plan sponsor. A minimum guaranteed interest rate may apply; actual investment returns are credited according to terms specified in the contract.

In the mid-1980s, banks began issuing GICs in competition with the insurance companies. GICs issued by banks commonly are referred to as "BICs." A BIC represents a means of diversification for a plan that has a significant amount of assets held in insurance company vehicles. Another form of diversification is provided by the synthetic GIC, developed in the late 1980s.

Synthetic GICs

A **synthetic GIC** consists of a portfolio of fixed-income securities, "wrapped" with a guarantee (typically by the insurance company or bank) to provide benefit payments according to the plan at book value. The wrap provider guarantees such payments by making up any difference between the book value and the market value of the securities in the portfolio. The synthetic GIC resembles the separate account GIC, except that ownership of the portfolio assets remains with the plan (as opposed to the insurance company separate account) and custody of the assets is with a third party (which manages the investment of the assets). Because the plan owns the assets, if the issuer defaults, the assets will continue to be held by the plan. Investment returns belong to the plan sponsor who holds the contract; the issuer receives only a fee for services in making benefit payments and providing the wrap.

Table 20.1 summarizes the historical introduction of various funding instruments and reviews their primary characteristics. This comparison indicates whether investment risk and mortality risk are transferred to the insurance company. The comparison further examines whether an allocated instrument is used and whether investments are held in an insurer's general account or in separate accounts.

Stable Value Pooled Funds

During the 1990s, GIC pooled funds grew. As these funds include several types of fixed-income investments, they are more generally referred to as **stable value pooled funds.** The investments typically are GICs, BICs, synthetic GICs, money market instruments, and cash. Each participating plan in essence has a pro rata share of each investment. The rate of return for the fund is a blended rate of the actual returns from the fund investments.

The stable value pooled fund provides diversification that plan sponsors, especially those involving plans with smaller asset amounts, might otherwise not be able to obtain

TABLE 20.1 **Funding Instrument Characteristics and Their Development**[a]

Product Name ⇒	Group Deferred Annuity Contracts	Deposit Administration Contracts (DA)	Immediate Participation Guarantee Contracts (IPGs)	
First Introduced ⇒	Early 1920s	1920s	1950s	
Use & Prevalence ⇒	Rapid growth until 1950s when deposit administration contracts introduced. Rarely used today.	Growth in popularity in the early 1950s due to competition from trust fund plans. Not popular today because of more flexible alternatives.	Primary growth occurs in the 1960s. Competition from banks offering diversified forms of investments for pensions, requires a move to a more competitive investment alternative.[b]	
			Original IPGs	Modified IPGs
Investment Risk —Preretirement —Postretirement	Transferred Transferred	Transferred* Transferred	Not transferred* Not transferred[†]	Not transferred* Transferred
Mortality Risk —Preretirement —Postretirement	Transferred Transferred	Not transferred Transferred	Not transferred[†] Not transferred[†]	Not transferred Transferred
Allocated Instrument —Preretirement —Postretirement	Yes Yes	No Yes	No No (Annuities not actually purchased)	No Yes
Insurer Holding Investments in —General account (A/C), or —Separate accounts (A/Cs)	General A/C	Originally general A/Cs; separate accounts introduced in 1962	Originally general A/Cs; separate accounts introduced in 1962	Originally general A/Cs; separate accounts introduced in 1962
Later Developments and Other Modifications			In the late 70s and early 80s, many insurers began offering one-year investment guarantees based on expectations of earnings for new monies.	

* Only if in general account.
[†] Annuity guarantees still provided. Since annuities are not actually purchased at retirement date, guarantees only of significance if plan or contract terminated.
[a] Source: © Dennis F. Mahoney, 1996. *Funding Instrument Characteristics and Their Development,* All rights reserved.
[b] Kenneth L. Walker, *Guaranteed Investment Contracts* (Burr Ridge, IL: Richard D. Irwin, 1989), p. 5.
[c] Ibid., p. 8.

TABLE 20.1   (Continued)

Guaranteed Investment Contracts (GICs)		Trust Fund Plans: Repository for various types of investments, including GICs.
1970s		Predates Insured Products
During the mid-1970s aggressive competition from banks and mutual funds along with stellar performance of the equity markets forced the insurance industry to revise its investment products. . . . The perpetual relationship . . . with the DA and IPG disappeared. The GIC had a known maturity date and constant rate for contract period (akin to a CD).[c]		Though trust fund plans are the oldest and currently the predominant funding instrument used in pension funding, their use has increased over time, eroding market share for insured products that largely were used as the pension marketplace developed.
Original GICs	Synthetic GICs	
Transferred	Transferred	Not transferred
Transferred	Transferred	Not transferred
Not transferred	Not transferred	Not transferred
Not transferred	Not transferred	Not transferred
No	No	No
No	No	No
Predominantly through general A/C, though possible with separate A/C.	Backed by pool of securities placed in separate account controlled by plan sponsor.	Noninsurer arrangement: Assets held as corpus in trust.
Bullet-type receives a single deposit. Extended-guarantee type accepts payments over several-year period.		

directly with issuers of the fund investments. In addition to diversification provided through the types of investments in the fund, diversification is provided by spreading assets among a number of issuers; investment guidelines with respect to a pooled fund typically include a maximum percentage (such as 15 percent) of fund assets that may be placed with any single issuer.

Another feature of a stable value pooled fund is the credit quality required by the terms of the fund. The investment guidelines require that each issuer meet specific credit quality standards by major credit rating agencies (such as Standard & Poor's, Moody's Investors Service, and A.M. Best). Thus, a plan sponsor will know the average quality rating that the fund is intended to meet. An example of an average quality rating is "AA" by Standard & Poor's (or the equivalent from another rating agency), which is the "excellent" category with respect to the claims payment ability of the issuer.

A stable value pooled fund also provides benefit responsiveness. Withdrawals may be made at book value in order to provide the benefits payable to plan participants.

The plan sponsor participating in a stable value pooled fund need deal only with the investment manager of the fund. It is the manager who is responsible for obtaining the investments according to the fund guidelines, reviewing the credit quality of the fund and of each issuer, processing deposits and withdrawals, and reporting returns and fund balances to the plan sponsor.

General Characteristics of Trust Fund Plans

A **trust fund plan** is an arrangement under which employer and employee contributions, if any, are deposited with a **trustee.** The trustee is responsible for the administration and investment of these monies and the income earned on accumulated assets of the fund and normally also is responsible for the direct payment of benefits to eligible participants under the plan.

Increasingly, trustees are no longer responsible for making decisions regarding the investment of a plan's assets. The responsibility for allocating plan assets among investment options is assumed by asset managers hired by the employers who sponsor the pension plans.

Mutual funds also have become a preferred investment custodian used with trust fund plans. Particularly when participant-directed investing is provided, mutual fund families provide a convenient means of supplying a variety of investment choices to plan participants. The mutual fund company selects and monitors the performance of asset managers. The mutual fund company also provides or contracts for the administrative services required for its funds. Therefore, a mutual fund company supplies administrative services, invests plan assets, and serves as the trust's trustee.

If the trust fund arrangement is used in combination with an insured funding instrument, benefit payments to participants generally are made by the insurance company, with transfers from the trust fund made as required. The trustee usually is a corporate trustee (trust company). Individuals also can serve as trustees of the plan, although this practice has become less frequent, except in small single-employer plans, because of the fiduciary requirements of the Employee Retirement Income Security Act of 1974 (ERISA).

Trust Agreement

The duties and responsibilities of the trustee are set forth in a **trust agreement** executed by the employer and the trustee.

In the case of a negotiated multiemployer plan, the trust agreement is executed by individuals representing the unions and individuals representing the employers, and these persons often compose the board of trustees responsible for the administration of the plan. The board of trustees may retain the task of investing plan assets, or it may delegate this duty to an asset management company or a corporate trustee. In the latter case, a trust agreement setting forth the duties and responsibilities of the corporate trustee is executed by the board of trustees and the corporate trustee.

A typical trust agreement between an employer and a corporate trustee contains provisions regarding the irrevocability and nondiversion of trust assets; the investment powers of the trustee, if any; the allocation of fiduciary responsibilities; the payment of legal, trustee, and other fees relative to the plan; periodic reports to the employer to be prepared by the trustee; the records and accounts to be maintained by the trustee; the conditions for removal or resignation of the trustee and the appointment of a new trustee; the payment of benefits under the plan; and the rights and duties of the trustee in case of amendment or termination of the plan.

The trust agreement, then, is concerned primarily with the receipt, investment, and disbursement of funds under a pension plan. The plan provisions may be incorporated in the trust agreement or they can be set forth in a separate plan document. The use of two separate documents is prevalent in trust fund plans and is almost always the approach used in multiemployer plans. The advantage of a separate plan document is that amendments to the plan can be made without the need to involve the trustee in frequent amendments to the trust agreement.

Administrative Duties of a Trustee

The bulk of the record keeping associated with a pension plan normally is performed by the employer under single-employer trust fund plans. If the plan is contributory, the employer generally retains responsibility for maintaining a record of employee contributions. In this case, total contributions are paid to the trustee without reference to any division of employer and employee contributions. The employer normally also assumes responsibility for the maintenance of records of earnings and credited service for each participant. In some cases, the record-keeping function is performed by the consulting actuary for the plan or a third-party administrator.

Most corporate trustees are able to relieve the employer of the burden of maintaining the necessary records associated with the plans. Corporate trustees sometimes maintain records in the case of profit sharing plans or defined contribution pension plans and, to a more limited extent, for multiemployer plans. If the trustee performs any record-keeping function, a service charge, in addition to the trustee's investment fee, is levied on an account basis. The advantages of specialization and economies of scale permit corporate trustees who handle a substantial volume of pension business to perform these services for a reasonable fee. The employer must decide whether it is more economical in its case to maintain these records itself or to have this service provided by the trustee or by a consulting actuary or service organization.

In the case of a negotiated multiemployer plan, the board of trustees, rather than the individual employers, generally is responsible for the maintenance of plan records. The record-keeping function usually is performed by a pension fund office created by the board of trustees. If a corporate trustee is retained to manage the assets of the fund, the plan trustees may delegate the task of record keeping to the corporate trustee. In recent years, there has been a significant increase in the number of professional plan administrators. The function of a professional administrator is to keep all the specific records of service and earnings for individual members of the plan and to handle all routine administrative transactions.

Whether the corporate trustee performs the record-keeping function, it never makes any benefit distributions from the fund without authorization from the employer or retirement committee. In the case of a single-employer trust fund plan, the employer generally appoints a plan or retirement committee, usually composed of officers of the company. It is the responsibility of this committee to determine a participant's eligibility for benefits under the plan, generally based on the recommendations or guidance of a third-party administrator. Under multiemployer plans, authorization of benefit payments is the responsibility of the board of trustees or a committee of its members appointed by the board; however, in some cases, this function is delegated to a professional administrator.

Apart from the administrative aspects of trust fund plans, a corporate trustee is always responsible for maintaining accurate and detailed records of all investments, receipts, disbursements, and other transactions involving the trust assets. In addition, the trustee is required to submit an annual statement regarding these trust transactions to the plan or retirement committee, usually within 90 days of the close of the plan's fiscal year. The trust agreement may require that statements be rendered to the committee more frequently than annually, for example, quarterly or monthly. Also, in some cases, the trustee assumes responsibility for the filing of forms for the trust as required by tax regulations.

Additionally, the trustee must make annual reports under the provisions of ERISA and the basic information must be made available in summary form to all participants and beneficiaries.

Investment Powers of a Trustee

For very large pension plans, it is common to use investment advisors or multiple investment managers with the corporate trustee serving as custodian. For other pension plans, the primary function of a trustee is the investment management of trust assets, although for most relatively small single-employer plans, much of the so-called investment management duties of the trustees are reduced to serving as conduit or to carrying out the investment decisions of the employers. The trustee invests the trust assets (including contributions and investment income) in accordance with the provisions of the trust agreement, the investment policy desired by the employer or retirement committee, and the fiduciary standards imposed by ERISA and by general trust laws. The investment power granted to a trustee by the trust agreement varies among plans; it may range from approval by the investment committee of every action affecting the fund's assets to full discretion in investment affairs. Furthermore, the corporate trustee does maintain personal contact with the employer, and therefore the latter may influence, directly or indirectly, investment decisions. If the trust agreement fails to specify the investment powers of the trustee, the trustee is restricted to investments that are legal for trust funds in the state in which the trust is established and the federal statute governing fiduciary investments.

Before the enactment of ERISA, the trustee could invest all trust assets in the securities of the employer. Essentially, ERISA restricts investment of pension plan assets in an employer's securities to 10 percent of the fund value. The limit does not apply to profit sharing or thrift plans that explicitly permit larger investments in employer securities. Nor does it apply to stock bonus plans or employee stock ownership plans that are invested primarily in employer securities.

The trustee is required to maintain a separate accounting and an actual segregation of the assets of each trust. In other words, the assets of a trust generally cannot be commingled with the assets of other trusts or with the general assets of the trustee. Thus, under these circumstances, there is no pooling of the investment experience of a number of trusts. If the investment experience has been exceptionally favorable for a particular trust, the full benefit of that experience is credited to the trust account. On the other hand, the trust must bear the full impact of adverse investment income and capital loss experience. Therefore, a relatively small trust fund plan would be subject to the danger of inadequate diversification of its investment portfolio. To meet this problem, corporate trustees have established collective investment funds. A **collective investment fund** permits the commingling of assets of all participating trusts. Although originally established to meet the needs of smaller trusts, corporate trustees have obtained permission to allow pension trusts of any size to participate in collective investment funds established specifically for qualified pension plans. A trust participating in a commingled fund for investment purposes buys units or shares of the fund.[3] Dividends are paid on each unit, each dividend being a proportionate share of the total income earned by the commingled fund. These units fluctuate in value as the value of the assets of the commingled fund fluctuates.

The principal advantage of a collective investment fund is that it permits any trust to enjoy the investment advantages normally available to only the very large funds. These potential advantages have been described as follows.[4]

1. *Higher rate of return on fixed-income investments.* Commingled investment permits purchases in amounts large enough to take advantage of private placements and special offerings of securities, which generally carry higher yields than regular market offerings, and in mortgages, leaseback arrangements, or other interests in real property.
2. *Increased growth potential through selective stock holding.* Commingled investment permits such funds to achieve a degree of selective diversification in equities that would be impossible to attain through individual investment, except in sizable funds.

---

[3] Bank of New York, *Trusteed Employee Benefit Plans* (New York: Bank of New York, 1966), p. 10.
[4] Ibid., pp. 10–11.

3. *Maximum liquidity of funds for cash requirements.* Commingled investment permits redemption of units at the end of any month at the current market value of units, so that money required for payouts is made available through use of current cash flow rather than having to sell investments, as might have to be done in a separate fund.

4. *Dollar averaging on investment purchases.* Current cash flow from incoming contributions, spaced as they are at intervals throughout a given year, has the effect of dollar averaging on investment purchases, which generally works to the advantage of all participating trusts.

5. *Lower investment brokerage fees.* A collective investment fund can purchase stocks in round lots and in amounts that entail lower brokerage commissions.[5]

Most corporate trustees believe collective investment funds offer significant advantages to the larger plans as well as to smaller plans. In one large urban bank, approximately 55 percent of all its pension trust accounts participate in the bank's commingled pension trust. However, there is an element of inflexibility in the use of a collective investment fund that should be noted: the inability to transfer specific fund assets to another funding agency. Units can be liquidated, but during a period of depressed security prices, the employer may prefer to transfer trust assets in kind, with the expectation that market prices will be higher at some future date.

Participation in a commingled pension trust is restricted to qualified plans. Participation by a nonqualified trust could result in loss of the qualified tax status of the entire collective investment fund.

Some corporate trustees have established many collective investment funds, with each fund designed to provide an investment medium having certain principal characteristics and objectives. For example, one fund may emphasize investments in bonds, notes, debentures, and other fixed-income obligations. A second fund may be invested principally in private placements, mortgages, or other interests in real property. A third fund may be invested in a selection of quality common stocks with the objective of growth of principal and income over the long term. In addition, a special equity fund may be available for those trusts interested in pursuing a more aggressive investment policy. The multiple collective investment funds offer the employer considerable flexibility in the proportion of trust assets to be invested in each of the classes of investments.

Investment flexibility has been an attractive feature of the trust arrangement for many employers. During the past several decades, many employers have expressed a preference for investment of a relatively large proportion of pension assets in common stocks. Insured plans were not able to offer this investment flexibility until the development of separate account funding.

Retirement Benefit Structure

The trust fund arrangement offers maximum flexibility in the design of a retirement benefit formula. Because funds are not allocated, even for retired employees, any type

---

[5] A small trust fund plan also can obtain the advantages of commingling through investments in mutual fund shares or exchange traded funds (ETFs).

of benefit formula can be used under a trust fund plan. As is true in the case of several of the insurance products described earlier in the chapter (deposit administration and immediate participation guarantee plans), retirement benefits based on final earnings can be provided without difficulty under trust fund plans. Likewise, benefit formulas that provide for the integration of Social Security benefits can be accommodated readily under the trust fund arrangement.

It is true that the more complex the benefit formula, the more difficult is the task of the actuary in projecting costs and calculating contribution payments under the plan. The fact remains, however, that the trust fund instrument does not in itself present any obstacles to the use of the most complex of benefit formulas. For example, even those few plans that have a provision for adjustments of retired employees' benefits in accordance with a designated cost-of-living index can be provided under this funding instrument. The actuary can include in the cost calculations an assumption regarding future price level changes, although these are not readily predictable with a great degree of accuracy. However, actuarial gains and losses because of variations of actual from expected price levels can be reflected in subsequent valuations and determinations of contribution payments. Trust fund plans also can provide a retirement benefit that varies with the market value of the assets supporting the pension benefits of retired workers (variable annuities).

Money purchase defined contribution designs, although less common now, also can be used in trust fund pension plans. A money purchase pension plan generally provides a lifetime annuity benefit to retired employees. The law requires the plan to provide a joint and one-half survivor annuity for an employee and his or her spouse unless there is an election to the contrary. Therefore, under a money purchase pension plan, at some point the accumulations on behalf of each participant must be expressed in terms of a lifetime monthly benefit. The monthly benefit may be calculated as each annual contribution is received, or annual contributions may be accumulated to the retirement date and the determination of the level of monthly benefits made at that time.

In the case of some negotiated plans, particularly multiemployer plans, the employer's financial commitment is expressed as some specified cents-per-hour worked or as a fixed percentage of compensation. However, these plans generally are not traditional defined contribution plans in that they also provide a defined benefit. The trust fund instrument can accommodate these plans without any difficulty.

Early retirement benefits can be, and frequently are, provided under trust fund plans. The amount of early retirement benefit may be the actuarial equivalent of the participant's accrued normal retirement benefit, or, if the employer desires, a more liberal early retirement benefit may be provided. The additional cost under the latter alternative can be anticipated in computations of contribution payments required under the plan.

No guarantees are available under trust fund plans. The trustee cannot guarantee a minimum rate of investment income, nor can it guarantee plan assets against capital losses. Likewise, the mortality risk cannot be transferred to the trustee. The absence of guarantees is consistent with the legal nature of trust arrangements. A trustee's obligation is limited to the management of trust assets in a reasonable and prudent manner and in accordance with the duties set forth in the trust agreement and state and federal law. The adequacy of the fund to provide the benefits promised under the plan is the responsibility of the employer. The high degree of responsibility imposed on the employer under a trust fund plan is consistent with the maximum degree of flexibility available to the employer under this funding instrument. Guarantees must be minimized or eliminated if an employer desires maximum contribution flexibility and complete and immediate reflection of plan experience. Therefore, in choosing a funding instrument, the employer should consider the extent to which guarantees and flexibility are desired.

Under trust fund plans, actuarial valuations are performed annually to determine the adequacy of the fund. If the actual experience evolving under the plan indicates the current level of funding is inadequate, higher levels of contributions are necessary.

Split Funding

The trust fund arrangement can be used in conjunction with individual insurance and annuity contracts as one approach in funding pension benefits. This approach generally is referred to as a **combination plan.** Group pension contracts also can be used in combination with the trust fund arrangement. These latter arrangements usually are referred to as **split-funded plans** (although the term *combination plan* can be applied to describe any plan using two or more funding instruments).

Split-funded plans generally use group deposit administration or immediate participation guarantee or modified immediate participation guarantee contracts. The decision of the employer to split-fund its pension plan usually is motivated by a desire to obtain, at least in part, the advantages of an insurer's guarantees and a possibly favorable investment opportunity. For example, the trust agreement may provide that the trustee administer all assets held on behalf of active employees and that an immediate annuity be purchased as each employee retires. Likewise, an insurer may enjoy relatively high yields on direct placement and mortgage investments, and therefore the employer may decide to invest a portion of plan assets in a deposit administration contract, an immediate participation guarantee contract, or a guaranteed investment contract.

Chapter Summary

- A qualified plan must use a funding instrument such as a trust, custodial account, or insurance company contract to hold and accumulate plan assets.
- The trust fund arrangement, the oldest funding instrument used, currently accounts for the majority of employees covered and assets held by funding instruments. This popularity is largely attributable to the flexibility that this funding instrument affords a plan sponsor. The trust fund plan offers maximum flexibility in the design of a retirement benefit formula, largely because funds are not allocated to the individual accounts of either active or retired employees.

- Funding instruments commonly are classified on the basis of whether contributions are allocated to provide benefits to specific employees prior to retirement or whether contributions are accumulated in an unallocated fund to provide benefits for employees when they retire.

- The major development in the group pension market in the last 20 years is the substantial increase in flexibility under insurance contracts. Insurers can design a contract to meet the particular needs of the employer. Employers seeking flexibility in investment policy and the timing of contribution payments prefer the unallocated type of contract in the group pension market. This demand for greater flexibility has been evident in the small-employer market as well, and insurers have accommodated this demand by making unallocated contracts available to relatively small firms.

- The laws in most states restrict the investment of life insurance companies' general account assets in common stocks to a rather limited percentage—for instance, 5 percent of total company assets. This restriction has been historically common because of the fixed-dollar obligations and contractual guarantees provided in traditional life insurance and annuity products and, also, because of the relatively small surplus maintained by life insurance companies. With the advent of separate accounts, insurers now offer group clients a wide range of investment choices.

- Separate accounts were developed for two reasons: (1) to compete with trust fund plans in making equity investments available to employers for funding fixed-dollar plans and (2) to fund variable annuity plans. In the first case, many employers believe the long-term rate of return on equities will be greater than the return on fixed-income investments and the increased return will serve to reduce their cost of providing the fixed benefits promised under the plan. In the second case, equity-based variable annuities by definition generally require that the assets supporting these annuities be fully invested in equity securities.

- The assets of a trust generally cannot be commingled with the assets of other trusts or with the general assets of the trustee. As a result, no pooling of the investment experience of a number of trusts occurs. If the investment experience has been favorable for a particular trust, that trust fully benefits. Conversely, the trust bears the full impact of adverse investment results. To deal with the issue of inadequate diversification, particularly for smaller trusts, collective investment funds provide a remedy.

- A collective investment fund permits the commingling of assets of all participating trusts. Although collective investment funds were originally developed to benefit smaller trusts, pension trusts of any size can participate in collective investment funds established for qualified plans. Participation in a commingled pension trust is restricted to qualified plans. Participation by a nonqualified trust could result in the loss of the qualified tax status for the entire collective investment fund.

- No guarantees are available under trust fund plans. The trustee cannot guarantee a minimum rate of investment income, nor can it guarantee plan assets against capital losses. Mortality risk cannot be assumed by the trustee. The absence of guarantees is consistent with the legal nature of trust arrangements. A trustee's obligation is limited to the management of trust assets in a reasonable and prudent fashion according to the duties set forth in the trust agreement and specified by state and federal law. The employer is responsible for funding the trust at an adequate level to ensure benefits delineated in the plan can be paid. The high level of employer flexibility available under a trust fund also imposes a high level of responsibility on the employer.

Key Terms

allocated (fund), p. *354*

collective investment fund, p. *365*

combination plan, p. *368*

deposit administration contract, p. *355*

funding instrument, p. *353*

general account investments, p. *355*

group deferred annuity contract, p. *355*

guaranteed investment contract (GIC), p. *358*

immediate participation guarantee (IPG) contract, p. *356*

separate accounts, p. *355*

split-funded plans, p. *368*

stable value pooled funds, p. *359*

synthetic GIC, p. *359*

trust agreement, p. *363*

trust fund plan, p. *362*

trustee, p. *362*

unallocated fund, p. *354*

Questions for Review

1. Explain what guarantees insurers generally provided when insurance products were first used as pension funding instruments.
2. Distinguish between allocated and unallocated funding instruments.
3. Why was the advent of separate accounts important to insurers?
4. Describe the marketplace forces and the time periods when particular funding instruments have been preferred.
5. How does a guaranteed investment contract (GIC) differ from a synthetic GIC?
6. What is a trust fund plan?
7. Describe the provisions that generally are found in a trust agreement.
8. Describe the typical administrative duties and investment powers of a trustee.
9. How does the federal law restrict the trustee's investment powers?
10. What is a collective investment fund?
11. What advantages does a collective investment fund have over an individually managed fund?
12. It has been said that any benefit formula can be used in conjunction with trust fund plans. Explain.

Questions for Discussion

1. Discuss how an employer would decide between an insured funding arrangement and a self-insured, or trust fund, arrangement.
2. Discuss how an employer would decide among the various alternative insured funding arrangements.

3. Discuss how the investment risks assumed under a trust fund plan should be treated by the employer.
4. Discuss how the mortality risks assumed under a trust fund plan should be treated by the employer.

Resources for Further Study

Amoroso, Vincent, Robert Davis; and Timothy Geddes. "Costing and Funding Retirement Benefits." In *The Handbook of Employee Benefits.* 6th ed. Jerry S. Rosenbloom, ed. New York: McGraw-Hill, 2005.

Walker, Kenneth L. *Guaranteed Investment Contracts.* Burr Ridge, IL: Irwin Professional Publishing, 1989.

Chapter 21

Cash Balance and Other Hybrid Retirement Plans[1]

After studying this chapter you should be able to:

- Identify the various types of hybrid benefit plans.
- Note similarities between various hybrid plans and the primary differences that distinguish each of these plans.
- Explain the advantages and disadvantages associated with hybrid plan designs.
- Describe employer characteristics and business conditions that warrant the use of hybrid plan designs.
- Explain the nondiscrimination testing considerations that are important with certain hybrid plan designs.
- Suggest approaches for introducing hybrid plans and explain the challenges that may be encountered in migrating to these newer plan designs from traditional defined benefit or defined contribution plans.

What Is a Hybrid Plan?[2]

Traditional defined benefit and defined contribution plans all have a set of advantages and disadvantages that may or may not meet the needs of employers and workforces.

---

[1] The authors wish to express their appreciation to the International Foundation of Employee Benefit Plans (IFEBP) for permission to use this material. "What's on the Menu Today? Hybrid Retirement Plans" by Peter J. Alles is reprinted with permission from the *Employee Benefits Practices,* 1st Quarter 2000, published by the International Foundation of Employee Benefit Plans, Brookfield, WI. All rights reserved. Statements or opinions expressed in this article are those of the author and do not necessarily represent the views or positions of the International Foundation, its officers, directors, or staff.

[2] Minor editorial modifications have updated this chapter for court rulings and the provisions of the Pension Protection Act of 2006 (PPA), where applicable.

Some plan sponsors, finding it difficult to tweak the design of traditional defined benefit and defined contribution plans to meet the unique needs of their businesses or employees, have responded by offering two separate plans, one a defined benefit and the other a defined contribution plan. Others have begun turning to hybrid retirement plans.

The concept of a hybrid plan is not entirely new. Floor-offset hybrid plans were fairly common before an Internal Revenue Service (IRS) revenue ruling disallowed them in 1969, but have again been allowed since an IRS revenue ruling in 1976.[3] Cash balance hybrid plans made their debut in the mid-1980s,[4] although momentum among employers to adopt cash balance plans did not appear to build significantly until later. In contrast, pension equity plans came of age in the early 1990s, as did age-weighted profit sharing and new comparability plans, which were given a boost by Internal Revenue Code (IRC) Section 404(a)(4) nondiscrimination regulations released in 1993.[5]

Hybrid retirement plans blend attributes of traditional defined benefit pension plans and defined contribution plans in an effort to meet objectives plan sponsors find difficult to achieve with traditional defined benefit or defined contribution plans alone or in pairs. While hybrid plans come in several types and plan designs, each is considered either a defined benefit or a defined contribution plan for the purposes of tax qualification.[6] Within these two categories, the design and purpose of the plans vary significantly. Some defined benefit hybrids are designed to appeal to younger and more mobile workers by providing a portable lump sum benefit option, while maintaining some of the security of a defined benefit structure for older workers. Others use age-weighted formulas that appeal more to older workers. Defined contribution hybrids, on the other hand, are sometimes designed to provide more assurance that income replacement goals will be met while retaining defined contribution flexibility. Others are used to provide a larger allocation of contributions to specific types of workers.

While hybrid plans are often touted as offering flexible options for employers to meet the needs of diverse and changing workforces, the advantages and disadvantages are as varied as the plans and plan designs. In addition, features advantageous to one plan sponsor or participant may not be advantageous to others. As a result, plan sponsors need to review the current benefit package and any possible changes in light of various factors including, but not limited to, workforce demographics and mobility, employee attitudes toward current retirement benefits, relative levels of benefits and rates of benefit accrual, and cost constraints for the plan sponsor. Finally, some hybrid plan types and their sponsors have been criticized for negative effects on the benefit accruals or values of certain groups of plan participants. These criticisms and concerns make awareness

---

[3] Pati Robinson and William Small, "The Floor Offset Retirement Plan: Versatile and Tested, It Merits More Attention," *Compensation & Benefits Review,* May/June 1993, 32, 33.

[4] Raymond J. Lee and William P. Bishop, "Trends in Pensions—Hybrid Pension Plans," *The Pension Actuary,* March–April 1999, 4.

[5] See Michael E. Lloyd and Mark K. Dunbar, "Benefits Testing: The Dawn of a New Day for Defined Contribution Planning," *Journal of Pension Planning & Compliance,* Fall 1993, 49.

[6] An exception is a floor-offset plan, which is really two plans working together. The defined benefit plan funds the difference between the benefit accumulated by a defined contribution plan and a minimum benefit level, or floor benefit.

of the legal, regulatory, and public relations environment of hybrid plans particularly important for plan sponsors considering a hybrid.

Defined Benefit Hybrid Plans

As with traditional defined benefit plans, sponsors of defined benefit hybrid plans promise a specific benefit level and direct investment of plan assets through commingled funds, bear investment risk, and reap investment reward. The plans are relatively easy to integrate with Social Security and establish income replacement targets. Although defined benefit plans must offer distributions in the form of annuities, hybrids also offer lump sums as an option. Defined benefit hybrids also are subject to Employee Retirement Income Security Act of 1974 (ERISA) requirements for defined benefit plans, including minimum standards for eligibility, vesting, and funding. Chapter 26 provides a detailed discussion of eligibility, vesting, and funding requirements. Annual valuations are required, as is payment of Pension Benefit Guaranty Corporation (PBGC) premiums for plan termination insurance. As hybrid plans, however, they have some of the attributes normally associated with defined contribution plans, such as portable benefits and benefits expressed in terms of lump-sum values instead of annuities.

Cash Balance Plans

A cash balance plan is considered a defined benefit plan because the sponsor makes contributions based on a specified formula that provides an annual contribution credit and applies a fixed interest rate credit, making the eventual benefit definitely determinable.[7] **Cash balance plans** take on the appearance of defined contribution plans to participants who receive periodic benefit statements based on hypothetical accounts showing accrued benefit balances. The hypothetical statements are only a communication tool, however, because plan assets are commingled and directed by the plan sponsor. There are no individual accounts, and the amount of benefit shown on the account statement bears no relationship to actual assets held by the plan.

Cash balance plans are career average plans because the contributions credited to participants are typically based on a formula that considers their pay in each year of employment.[8] The portable lump sums and relatively early accrual of benefits under cash balance plans are attractive to employees terminating at younger ages and after fewer years of service, while workers with more years of service are likely to receive more benefits from the traditional defined benefit formula. See Figure 21.1 for a comparison of accrual patterns under traditional defined benefit, cash balance, and pension equity plans.

[7] Some hybrid designs similar to cash balance plans link benefits to an equities index rather than a fixed rate of return. Other cash balance plan sponsors reduce costs by offering a lower level of guaranteed benefits with a cash balance plan, but introduce profit sharing elements that increase contributions in periods of good business performance. See Patricia Rotello and Thomas Osmond, "Part Cash, Part Balancing Act: Why Cash Balance Plans Get So Much Attention," *Journal of Compensation and Benefits,* May/June 1999, 14.

[8] Everett T. Allen et al., *Pension Planning: Pension, Profit Sharing, and Other Deferred Compensation Plans,* 8th ed. (New York: McGraw-Hill, 1997), 328.

FIGURE 21.1 **Comparison of Accrual Patterns: Traditional Defined Benefit, Cash Balance, and Pension Equity Plans**

Source: Gerald E. Cole, Milliman & Robertson, Inc.

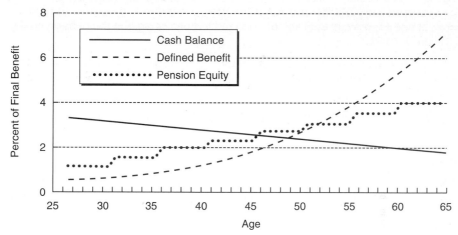

Plan sponsors also may benefit from conversion to a cash balance plan because, as career average plans, they are likely to be less expensive than a final pay defined benefit plan. In addition, the plan sponsor may guarantee an interest rate below what the sponsor expects it can generate on investments, and the higher rate of return reduces the future plan costs for the sponsor.[9]

A disadvantage of cash balance plans is that older participants and those with more years of service have less protection from pre- and postretirement inflation. Their benefits have less direct relation to income replacement needs than under a plan linking benefits to final average pay. Nonetheless, plan sponsors may use flexible formulas that include age or service weights, integration with Social Security, or the ability to use part of plan benefits to pay health insurance premiums after retirement.[10]

Pension Equity Plans

Pension equity plans are based on final average pay and the percentage credits participants receive each year. Upon termination of employment or retirement, the sum of percentage credits is applied to final average pay to determine the lump-sum benefit, which is portable.[11] The percentages upon which credits are based can be relatively flat, but often increase in steps with age or length of service. The age- or service-weighted credits and final average pay formula make pension equity plans appealing to older

---

[9] Dennis R. Coleman, "Cash Balance Pension Plans and Other Evolving Hybrid Pension Plans," in *The Handbook of Employee Benefits: Design, Funding and Administration,* ed. Jerry S. Rosenbloom, 4th ed. (Chicago: Irwin Professional Publishing, 1996), 766.

[10] Rotello and Osmond, 14. Concerning Integration with Social Security, see Gerald E. Cole, "An Explanation of Pension Plans," *Employee Benefits Journal,* June 1999, 8, 9.

[11] Although expressed in a lump sum, participants must have an option to take pension equity benefits as an annuity. Allen et al., 337.

EXAMPLE 21.1 Pension Equity Plan

The year is 2020. Joe Cubicle began working for Company X in 1999, at age 34. His pay has averaged $74,000 for the past five years. He is deciding whether to retire now, at age 55, or work until age 67. His credited percentages in the pension equity plan are as follows.

Age	Annual Percentage Credited	Number of Years	Total Percentage	Factor Applied to Final Average Pay
34–35	3.0%	2	6.0%	
36–40	4.0	5	20.0	
41–45	5.0	5	25.0	51% at age 45
46–50	6.5	5	32.5	
51–55	8.5	5	42.5	126% at age 55
56–60	10.5	5	52.5	
61–67	13.5	7	94.5	273% at age 67
Total			273.0	

What will Joe's lump-sum benefit be?

If he retires at 55, then: $74,000 final average pay × 1.26 = $93,240 lump-sum benefit.

If Joe decides to wait until age 67 and assumes steady 2.5% annual pay increases, then: $104,200 final average pay × 2.73 = $284,466 lump-sum benefit.

If Joe assumes he is moving onto the fast track and will receive steady 5.0% annual pay increases, then $139,000 final average pay × 273 = $379,470 lump-sum benefit.

Alternatively, if Joe leaves to take another job at age 45 with a final average pay of $65,700, then: $65,700 final average pay × 0.51 = $33,507 lump-sum benefit.

Source: Age brackets and percentage credits are from Everett T. Allen et al., *Pension Planning: Pension, Profit Sharing, and Other Deferred Compensation Plans,* 8th ed. (New York: McGraw-Hill, 1997), 339.

---

workers and persons hired in midcareer who have fewer years to accrue benefits. See Example 21.1 for details on how credits often increase by age and/or service in a pension equity plan.

There is not always a strong distinction drawn among pension equity, life cycle, and cash balance plans.[12] The most widely mentioned pension equity plan was adopted by RJR Nabisco when the company determined its cash balance plan did not adequately meet the needs of its workforce.[13] RJR Nabisco determined a pension equity plan would

---

[12] Michael Karlin, "The Life Cycle Pension Plan: A Step Ahead," *Pension World,* May 1992. See also David M. Traverso, "New DB Plan Designs," *The Pension Actuary,* December 1992.

[13] Jeff Barge, "Designing Equitable Pensions," *Crain's New York Business,* 17 June 1996, 33.

more equitably meet the needs of an emerging two-tiered workforce, in which a large number of baby boomers are aging and becoming less mobile while a shrinking number of younger and more mobile workers are joining the workforce each year.[14]

Life Cycle Pension Plans

Similar to pension equity plans, and sometimes considered a pension equity variation, is the **life cycle pension plan.** Life cycle plans make use of hypothetical account balances to communicate benefits to participants.

In addition, **retirement bonus** or mobility bonus **plans** are names sometimes used interchangeably with life cycle plans and are sometimes considered variations of the pension equity plan. Participants in these plans receive, upon retirement, a lump sum based on an accumulation of annual credits multiplied by final average salary.[15] However, adding to the possible confusion, the term *retirement bonus* also appears to be used for some defined contribution plans that allocate contributions on the basis of performance-related pay.[16] See Table 21.1 for a summary of key features of defined benefit hybrid plans.

Benefit Accrual

The relative rates of benefit accrual and methods with which benefits are allocated are central to understanding the purpose of defined benefit hybrid retirement plans and their effect on plan sponsors and participants. Compared with the traditional defined benefit plans they often replace, more benefit accrual typically takes place in earlier years of service for participants of cash balance plans. Expressed in terms of a chart (see Figure 21.1 on page 375), benefit accrual for cash balance plans is flat and steady. Traditional defined benefit plans have rates of accrual that remain relatively low, but jump considerably in later years.

Combining earlier benefit accrual with portability makes the cash balance plan more favorable to younger, mobile workers. Conversion to a cash balance plan from a traditional defined benefit plan could negatively affect the benefits, however, of midcareer or older workers who had begun to accrue sizable benefits in a traditional defined benefit plan (although there were additional provisions plan sponsors could use to hold older workers harmless).

As a result of early cash balance conversions, a considerable amount of litigation resulted. In fact, the Internal Revenue Service stopped issuing determination letters in 1999 because of the uncertainties with age-based discrimination that accompanied conversions from traditional defined benefit plans to cash balance plans. The Pension Protection Act of 2006 clarified the age discrimination and minimum present value rules

---

[14] Gerald Angowitz and Eric Lofgren, "A Pension Plan for Today," *Financial Executive,* January/February 1993, 24.

[15] Allen et al., 338. See also Traverso, 5. Traverso refers to a multivalue pension plan and describes it as a combination of cash balance and traditional defined benefit plan in which a benefit is calculated using both the cash balance and traditional defined benefit formulas, and the participant receives the greater of the two.

[16] See Kevin Fliege's article, "The Qualified Retirement Bonus Plan," *Journal of Pension Benefits,* Fall 1996.

TABLE 21.1 **Key Features of Defined Benefit Hybrid Plans**

	Traditional Defined Benefit	Cash Balance	Pension Equity
Benefit Determination	Can be based on career average or final average pay.	Based on career average pay. May include age or service weights.	Based on final average pay, typically with age or service weights.
Benefit Accrual	Most accrual in later years, favoring employees with long service records.	Age-neutral accrual favors younger employees and midcareer hires.	Age-weighted accrual favors older employees and fast-track employees.
Distribution	Traditionally an annuity with no portability. Alternate designs may offer lump sums.	Annuity or lump sum. Vested lump sums are portable upon termination.	Annuity or lump sum. Vested lump sums are portable upon termination.
Hypothetical Accounts/ Balances	Not used.	Used to communicate lump-sum benefit.	Not generally used, but possible with life cycle plan.

applicable to these types of plans. Specifically, the PPA now requires that a participant's benefit upon conversion be no less than the sum of the participant's old-formula benefit at conversion plus the participant's benefit earned for postconversion service under the new hybrid formula. Previously, it was allowable to set the participant's accrued benefit as the greater of (1) the pre-amendment accrued benefit or (2) the benefit determined by applying the new benefit formula to all of the participant's years of service before and after the amendment creating conversion. When a participant's pre-amendment accrued benefit was greater than the benefit provided under the new formula, there may have been a period during which the participant would not accrue any additional benefits. This was known as "wear away." The PPA now prohibits the use of "wear away" for any conversion occurring after June 29, 2005. The PPA states that no inference is to be drawn with respect to age discrimination for conversions that occurred prior to June 29, 2005. In effect, its language precludes using provisions of the Act to evaluate age discrimination on earlier conversions.

In the case of pension equity plans, benefits build steadily, but in steps, as credit percentages increase as participants move from one age bracket to the next. (Again see Figure 21.1 on page 375.) The age-weighted brackets often used by pension equity plans increase the rate of accrual with age. In contrast to cash balance plans, pension equity plans are more favorable to older workers and persons hired at midcareer who have fewer years to accrue benefits. Yet, the effect of age-weighting is not likely to tilt benefit accrual toward later years as significantly as a traditional defined benefit plan.

Earlier benefit accruals and portability features, in either the cash balance or pension equity plans, may increase plan costs in the short run as mobile employees terminate and take benefits with them.[17] As a result, knowledge of employee turnover rates and the expected effects of plan design on turnover rates may affect a plan sponsor's choice of plans or plan designs. On the other hand, a cash balance plan sponsor reflects only the expense of current pay on financial statements, whereas the sponsor of a final average pay plan must recognize future salary increases.[18]

Benefit Portability and Lump Sums

A key feature of cash balance and pension equity plans is how they combine a defined benefit plan structure with the participant option to roll over a lump sum into another plan or an individual retirement account upon separation. Portability has been recognized as a way to attract younger and more mobile employees who would not normally expect to receive a significant benefit from traditional defined benefit plans. Portability can be advantageous to some midcareer employees who may otherwise feel bound to stay with a company in anticipation of traditional defined benefits. (Some refer to this condition as pension jail because these participants have enough service to have retirement security within sight if they stay, but they are likely to have very limited benefits from the plan if they leave. The result is that separating participants need to start rebuilding their retirement benefits, but with fewer working years left.) With a cash balance or pension equity plan, midcareer employees can take their account balances and move their careers in a new direction. At the same time, portability serves as a release valve for some companies because employees who are unhappy are able to leave.

There are several possible disadvantages of portability. First, some plan sponsors may find the portable account balances make it too easy for employees to leave for other employment too quickly. Second, the meaningfulness of portability is driven, in part, by rates of benefit accrual. If benefits do not accrue quickly enough, younger and more mobile participants may not view the portable benefit as sufficient and may not perceive the plan as attractive. For example, benefit portability would not be as meaningful with the accrual rates of a traditional defined benefit plan as with the accrual rates in cash balance plans because the lump sums are likely to be very small comparatively until the very later years of a career. Midcareer workers seeking a new employer will view the pension equity accrual rates more favorably than under a cash balance plan because benefits accrue more rapidly in higher age categories under the age-weighted approach. (Cash balance plan sponsors may also add age weights to the benefit plan formula.)

Third, if the overriding purpose of the plan sponsor is to provide retirement benefits, then the option to take a lump-sum distribution upon retirement or termination may defeat this purpose. Participants may choose not to roll over their distributions to new plans or to individual retirement accounts, jeopardizing their retirement security. Some

[17] Elayne Robertson Demby, "Cash Balance Converts," *Plan Sponsor,* June 1999, 24.
[18] Ibid., 30.

surveys indicate a much higher percentage of 401(k) plan participants with smaller account balances take their lump sums in cash and do not roll over balances to other plans or individual retirement accounts.[19] Although the survey shows a higher percentage of participants with larger account balances roll over their lump sum payments to other plans or individual retirement accounts, the concern remains that the smaller account balances taken as cash are accounts that could have grown to help build retirement security in later years. The small accounts could also represent the bulk of retirement funds for some low-wage earners who are likely to find it more difficult to "catch up" with retirement saving as they age.

In addition to the portability of funds, proponents of some hybrid plans assert that benefits expressed in terms of lump sums, such as the hypothetical account balances in cash balance plans, are more easily understood by participants and more appreciated. Whether this is true may be a point of debate and may depend on individual participants and their circumstances. A portable lump-sum dollar amount is easily understood and appreciated in present terms for participants deciding whether to depart for other employment. On the other hand, it is possible for sponsors of traditional defined benefit plans to provide participants with summaries of projected and accrued benefits.[20] In addition, hypothetical account balances can cause some confusion. For example, if the interest credits of a cash balance plan are indexed rather than fixed, the amount of benefit shown by the hypothetical account balance may be different from the actual payout because the balance changes with interest fluctuations. When interest credits increase, it may actually appear to the participants that benefits have been cut.[21]

Investment Risk and Reward

Traditional defined benefit plans and defined benefit hybrid plans place investment decisions and the resulting risk and reward in the hands of plan sponsors, who guarantee a defined benefit. But the entire allocation of risk and reward does not always have to fall upon plan sponsors. Defined benefit hybrid plans can include design features that shift investment risk and reward opportunities to participants in whole or in part. In some instances, some shared risk and reward may be appreciated by plan participants, some of whom are familiar with investing. They may want some of the opportunities, and may be willing to bear some of the risks associated with investing in equities.

Some varieties of cash balance and other defined benefit hybrids are creative in how they assign risk and reward. For example, a **minimum balance pension plan** is a cash balance variant that offers participants the greater benefit of either a traditional defined benefit pension plan (often final average pay) or the benefit accumulated by the cash balance method.[22] Other cash balance variations give employees the option of linking the growth rate of their accounts with an equities index, introducing the prospect of both higher returns and more risk to participants.[23]

[19] Survey results by Hewitt Associates LLC.

[20] Thomas O'Conner and William F. Noyes, "Ten Issues to Consider with a Cash Balance Retirement Plan," *Benefits & Compensation Solutions,* September 1999, 59.

[21] Ibid.

[22] Allen et al., 333 and 334.

[23] Ibid.

Outside of plan design variations, plan sponsors may be able to help with preretirement inflation and the possibility of lagging income replacement needs on an ad hoc basis. Several multiemployer funds with cash balance plans have made it a practice to periodically share positive investment experience in excess of the guaranteed interest rate by making adjustments to accrued benefits that are reflected in the account balance statements participants receive.[24] Not only do participants see a very direct additional benefit and some protection against preretirement inflation (which can be troublesome for cash balance plans because they are based on career average pay), but the plan sponsor gets direct credit for the increase. Regardless, the opportunity to grant ad hoc benefit adjustments to share good investment experience is not unique to cash balance plans and has been used with traditional defined benefit retirement plans.

The Transition to Defined Benefit Hybrid Plans

Many defined benefit hybrid plans begin with conversion from a traditional defined benefit plan. Plan conversions can be a sensitive issue regardless of the types of plans involved. Since different plans have different rates of accrual or allocation methods, some plan participants will fare better than in the previous plan, and others will see a less favorable situation with the new plan. Furthermore, regardless of how individuals or groups of participants actually fare in the new plan compared with the old (which they may not be able to determine without help from the plan sponsor), attitudes toward change and feelings about employer motives are important to consider. Some plan participants may be wary of any type of change. And, in some cases, employers have been criticized for using plan conversions as a way to recoup large amounts of surplus pension plan assets. Other possible reasons for differing levels of acceptance among participants in some plans include the relative levels of interest or indifference to benefit changes, differences in the amount of participant knowledge of the changes and their effects, and the relative success of some participants in publicizing views concerning changes.

Much of the negative attention concerning conversions has been focused on cash balance plans. The conversion of a traditional defined benefit plan to a cash balance plan often caused a condition some call **pension wear away** for participants with longer service records because of the difference in benefit accrual patterns between plans. Employees who had reached or were nearing the final stage of a traditional defined benefit plan, generally the later years of a career when the benefit accrual rate increases rapidly, would experience a sudden decrease in accrual rates and expected benefit under a cash balance plan with less of the overall benefit accrual taking place in later years.[25]

As stated earlier, the PPA prohibited wear away in conversions occurring after June 29, 2005. However, if a plan had already converted and existed on June 29, 2005, new interest crediting rules did not apply until plan years beginning after 2007, unless the employer elected to have those rules apply as of June 29, 2005.

---

[24] Joseph Moynihan, "Introduction to Cash Balance Plans," presentation at the 44th Annual Employee Benefits Conference of the International Foundation of Employee Benefit Plans, Las Vegas, 13 and 14 October 1998, cassette. For information on how to order this cassette or other cassettes, contact IFEBP Audiovisual Department at (888) 33-IFEBP, option 6.

[25] Rotello and Osmond, 19, suggest the effect on older workers' benefits may be an advantage to some plan sponsors because it will help the sponsor retain older workers.

Another concern is that some companies convert from traditional defined benefit plans to cash balance plans to take advantage of the reduced rates of accrual. Reduced rates of accrual may result in a larger surplus for the new plan, and a larger surplus can translate into lesser future costs for the plan sponsor.[26] In addition, plan sponsors can report surplus assets on their income statements and pension income can constitute as much as 3 percent of annual corporate operating income for large companies.[27] Regardless, a strong motivation for conversion can be plan design changes, and some conversions appear to have been positively received by employers and employees alike. Reasons for the more favorable reception toward some conversions can be attributed in some cases to provisions to hold employees harmless. Methods for holding employees harmless from adverse effects of a conversion have included:

- Allowing all employees to choose between the old plan and the new plan.
- Allowing employees whose benefits were adversely affected by the conversion the choice to remain in the old plan.
- Making an adjustment to initial account balances of the new plan for adversely affected employees.
- Making additional contributions to other plans sponsored by the employer and within which the adversely affected employees are participating.

Plan sponsors need to carefully consider the cost of these types of **"grandfather" provisions** and adjustments. For example, when one company announced the addition of a pension equity formula to its defined benefit plan, the company also enhanced the match on its 401(k) plan. The company also created retirement planning software and held workshops to assist plan participants in understanding the combined impact of the pension equity formula and the new 401(k) plan options.[28] Other companies have enhanced or started stock option programs.[29]

Although a number of companies have already converted traditional defined benefit plans to cash balance plans, uncertainty surrounding future conversions of traditional defined benefit plans to cash balance plans has been a political and regulatory issue for hybrid plans. In light of the conversion controversy, and as was stated earlier, the IRS stopped issuing letters of determination for new cash balance plans. In addition, the federal Equal Employment Opportunity Commission (EEOC) established a "National Cash-Balance Pension Team" to investigate the effects of plan conversions to determine whether they unlawfully discriminated against older plan participants covered by the Age Discrimination in Employment Act (ADEA).[30]

---

[26] In the case of a sufficiently large surplus, plan sponsors may make their future contributions from surplus assets rather than from the operating income of the company. Plan sponsors then have more operating income available to meet other goals and objectives.

[27] Mike Barry, "Who Gets the Surplus: No One," *Pensions & Investments,* 4 October 1999, 16.

[28] Arleen Jacobius, "Motorola Adds PEP to Its Defined Benefit Plan," *Pensions & Investments,* 12 July 1999, 3.

[29] Robertson Demby, 27.

[30] U.S. Equal Employment Opportunity Commission, "EEOC Creates National Cash-Balance Pension Team," Press Release, http://www.eeoc.gov/press/9–20–99.html.

Two key events have since occurred that should serve to quell the controversy surrounding conversions from traditional defined benefit plans to various types of hybrid plans. The first, as indicated earlier, was passage of the PPA with its various clarifications related to age discrimination in hybrid plans. The second was the decision by an appellate court in the case of *Cooper* v. *IBM* that reversed a lower court ruling on the issue of "accrued benefits" and, at the appellate court level, determined that cash balance plans generally are and always have been legal. The PPA amended the Internal Revenue Code, ERISA, and the ADEA to provide that defined benefit plans are not age discriminatory if, as of any date, a participant's accrued benefit is at least equal to the accrued benefit of any similarly situated, younger individual. Accordingly, cash balance plans are not age discriminatory as long as pay and annual interest credits for older workers are not less than pay and annual interest credits for younger workers. Note that this provision does not apply unless interest credits are not greater than a market rate of return and cumulative interest credits are not negative.

Although legal clarifications appear to have paved the way for more employers to convert from traditional defined benefit plans to hybrid plans, many employers may feel the controversy surrounding cash balance plans is still too recent of an event to embark on such a plan change. In other words, there may be a reticence to convert plans until a period of time elapses. Accordingly, plan sponsors should continue to assess marketplace conditions and watch for further legislative and judicial activity.

Defined Contribution Hybrid Plans

Defined contribution hybrid plans combine a defined contribution plan structure with attributes of a defined benefit plan, such as the ability to allocate benefits in favor of specific participant groups or plan sponsor contributions that are determined actuarially and are fixed obligations. Defined contribution hybrid plans include target benefit plans, age-weighted profit sharing plans, and new comparability plans. Table 21.2 compares key features of defined contribution hybrid plans.

Target Benefit Plans

Although **target benefit plans** are considered defined contribution plans, the plan sponsor's required contributions are determined actuarially in order to meet income replacement targets established in the plan and expressed in terms of a percentage of salary near the time of retirement. Once an initial contribution formula is established, subsequent adjustments to actuarial assumptions are not made.[31] Despite using actuarially determined contributions, target benefit plans are defined contribution plans because the targets are not guaranteed, individual participant account values reflect the gains and losses from investments, and the investments of most target benefit plans are participant directed.[32] While the exact benefit to be received is less certain than in a

---

[31] Michael J. Canan, *Qualified Retirement and Other Employee Benefit Plans,* 1998 Practitioner Edition, vol. 1 (St. Paul: West Publishing, 1997), 190.

[32] Sharyn Campbell, "Hybrid Retirement Plans: The Retirement Income System Continues to Evolve," EBRI Special Report SR-32/Issue Brief Number 171, March 1996, 22.

TABLE 21.2 **Key Features of Defined Contribution Hybrid Plans**

	Target Benefit Plans	Age-Weighted Profit Sharing Plans	New Comparability Plans
Contribution Flexibility	Contributions are a fixed annual obligation of plan sponsor.	Contributions are discretionary.	Contributions are discretionary.
Contribution Determination/ Allocation	Contributions are determined actuarially to meet targeted income replacement.	Contributions are allocated on an age-weighted basis favoring older, highly compensated participants.	Contributions are allocated among separate and distinct allocation groups keyed to criteria such as ownership or position. This plan favors specific employees.
Contribution Targets	Specific income replacement levels are targeted for all participants, but not guaranteed.	Contributions are skewed toward older, highly compensated participants.	Contributions are skewed toward a narrow, select group of participants.
Investment Direction	Most often participant directed.	Most often participant directed.	Most often participant directed.
Accounts and Accumulation	Individual account balances reflect contributions, investment gains and losses. Participants bear risk and receive rewards.	Individual account balances reflect contributions, investment gains and losses. Participants bear risk and receive rewards.	Individual account balances reflect contributions, investment gains and losses. Participants bear risk and receive rewards.

defined benefit plan, employer contributions are more certain than in a typical profit sharing plan. Contributions in target benefit plans tend to be heavily weighted by age to favor older participants.[33]

Age-weighted profit sharing and new comparability plans take a different approach. Both are considered vehicles through which the owners of a company and select individuals, or a relatively narrow select group, can receive a disproportionate share of annual contributions to a profit sharing plan. In addition, the plans maximize contribution flexibility to the owner.

[33] Norman Gerber, "Age Weighted Profit Sharing vs. Target Benefit Plans," *The Tax Adviser*, August 1991, 510.

Age-Weighted Profit Sharing Plans

Age-weighted plans are very similar to traditional profit sharing plans except they apply age factors to allocate contributions more heavily to older participants, much like traditional defined benefit plan benefits favor workers with more years of service (who are typically older participants).[34] Age-weighted plans tend to appeal to smaller employers with older executive staff and younger rank-and-file employees. Plan sponsors with a goal of allocating as much benefit as possible to higher level employees (who tend to be older) may see some unintended effects if some higher level employees are relatively young and receive less benefit than some lower level employees who are at an advanced age. Furthermore, two participants with the same years of service and pay levels may receive different annual allocations because they fall within different age categories, creating potential for dissatisfaction and misunderstanding among some participants.

New Comparability Plans

New comparability is a term used for a set of plan types that are similar to the age-weighted plans, but take a further step in directing allocations by dividing participants into separate **allocation groups** (or rate groups) to provide larger percentage contributions to select participants. Plan sponsors have wide latitude in the criteria used to establish allocation groups, such as job descriptions, ownership interest, age, and length of service.[35]

Just as there are multiple options for categorizing participants for the purpose of allocation, new comparability plan sponsors also have flexibility in determining how the allocation process will work. "Super-integrated [new comparability] plans use formulas similar to normal safe harbor integrated formulas, but ignore the limitations to the formulas since the plans are being generally tested. These plans may use a contribution formula such as 3 percent of pay plus 50 percent of pay in excess of $100,000."[36] Allocations are often arranged in several stages. For example, the first-stage allocation may consist of 3 percent of pay allocated to all employees, followed by second- and third-stage allocations based on formulas designed to favor a select few. Alternatively, a first-stage allocation can be the maximum contribution allowed for one key employee ($45,000 in 2007), followed by minimum top-heavy contributions for all non-highly compensated employees, and possibly followed by another round of contributions with remaining funds to highly compensated employees who have not yet received the maximum contribution.[37]

Nondiscrimination Requirements

In contrast to the defined benefit hybrids, which directly alter rates of accrual, the age-weighted and new comparability plans use their defined contribution features to provide larger contribution allocation to certain types or specific groups of workers. Both

---

[34] It is possible to have age-weighted money purchase plans or stock bonus plans; however, profit sharing plans are much more common. Lloyd and Dunbar, 57.

[35] Campbell, 21.

[36] Fliege, 21.

[37] See Lloyd and Dunbar, 60–67, for examples. See also Jeffrey D. Poland, "New Comparability—A New Concept in Profit Sharing Plan Design," *Journal of Compensation and Benefits,* July/August 1996, 55.

age-weighted and new comparability plans must satisfy the requirements of IRC Section 401(a)(4) that benefits not discriminate in favor of highly compensated employees. They satisfy the nondiscrimination requirements using a process called **cross-testing** (also referred to as benefits testing because nondiscrimination is tested on the basis of projected benefits rather than current contributions). Under one method of cross-testing, the annual profit sharing contribution for a participant is projected with interest to age 65, then converted to an annuity. The annuity is expressed as a percent of each participant's pay and then the percentages for highly compensated employees are compared with percentages for non–highly compensated employees. The testing approach makes it possible to allocate more to highly compensated and older participants because, when compound interest assumptions are used to project benefits, lesser amounts of annual contribution are needed to provide younger and lower-paid participants with a projected benefit that is a substantial percentage of pay.[38] In addition, the age-weighted and new comparability plans can be integrated with Social Security.

Floor-Offset Plans: Two Plans Working as One

The **floor-offset plan** differs from other hybrids because it is actually two separate plans, a defined benefit plan and a defined contribution plan, working to complement one another. The structure coincides with the floor-offset plan's somewhat unique purpose of protecting participants from potential negative effects of market risk or unfortunate investment decisions, while allowing them to direct their own investments in some plans. The defined benefit plan establishes a minimum level (floor) of benefit participants will receive if the defined contribution benefit does not exceed the minimum (floor) benefit. Upon retirement, the benefit of a given participant is the amount accumulated in the defined contribution plan, if that amount meets or exceeds the minimum (floor) benefit. If the benefit accumulated in the defined contribution plan is less than the minimum (floor) benefit, the difference between the defined contribution account balance and the minimum (floor) is paid by the defined benefit floor plan.[39] Floor-offset plans are most useful for employers seeking to balance the goals of providing meaningful benefit accumulation and portability for younger and shorter-term workers, and providing income and security for older and longer-term employees.[40]

Although floor-offset plans offer flexibility of plan design, plan sponsors are responsible for administering two separate plans. In terms of administrative work and cost, the existence of the defined benefit plan means the plan sponsor must pay termination insurance premiums to the PBGC, file two separate 5500 forms, and include Schedule B as an attachment for the defined benefit plan. However, there are some efficiencies because much 5500 information is the same for both plans.[41] Plan sponsors must also

---

[38] Poland, 55.

[39] The defined benefit formula is usually offset by 100 percent of the defined contribution plan balance, but it may be offset by only a specified part of the balance. See Allen et al., 340, endnote 9.

[40] Robinson and Small, 29.

[41] Ibid., 32.

comply with Section 404 deduction limits and the Section 416 top-heavy test for both plans combined. They are also responsible for all the usual administrative duties of a defined contribution plan, including record-keeping functions, selection and monitoring of investment options, and providing participants with adequate information and opportunities to make investment decisions (if participant direction is allowed). Explaining the interaction of the defined contribution plan with the defined benefit plan and their effects on benefits can be difficult. Nonetheless, during times of low investment returns or losses, reminding participants of the floor plan guarantee can calm nerves and enhance appreciation. Establishing a reasonable floor benefit level, however, is a balancing act. If the floor benefit guaranteed by the defined benefit plan is not high enough, it may encourage excessively risky investment behavior by participants. On the other hand, a reasonable floor may help encourage some risk averse participant investors to accept more of the risk required to generate the returns necessary for retirement security.

Conclusion

Variety in retirement plan design is nothing new. The relatively recent development and growing popularity of some additional hybrid plan designs, however, offer more choices for plan sponsors seeking to achieve an optimal balance between providing adequately for participant retirement needs and working within financial and administrative business constraints. The introduction of more choices does not necessarily make choices any easier for sponsors. Sponsors need to be aware of the effects of, and likely reaction to, various plan and design options on various participant groups and individuals in today's workforce and the workforce of tomorrow. They also need to keep an ear to the ground to listen for changes in the sometimes dynamic regulatory and legislative landscape in which hybrid plans exist. At the same time, some plan sponsors may be able to accomplish the same allocation, accrual, and portability goals for various segments of the workforce by offering separate defined contribution and defined benefit plans in tandem.

Chapter Summary

- Hybrid retirement plans combine attributes of both traditional defined benefit and defined contribution plans. Although there are various types and plan designs associated with hybrids, for the purposes of tax qualification, a hybrid is either considered to be a defined benefit or a defined contribution plan.
- Sponsors of defined benefit hybrid plans promise a specific benefit level, direct the investment of plan assets through commingled funds, bear investment risk, and reap investment reward. Defined benefit hybrids are subject to ERISA requirements for defined benefit plans, including minimum standards for eligibility, vesting, and funding. Annual actuarial valuations are needed, and plan termination insurance premiums must be paid to the PBGC.
- Cash balance plans are career average defined benefit hybrids. Although qualified as defined benefit plans, these hybrids take on the appearance of defined contribution

plans to participants. Typically contributions are credited to participants based on a formula that considers pay in each year of employment. Portable lump sums and earlier accrual of benefits appeal to employees terminating at younger ages with fewer years of service. Workers with more years of service are likely to receive more benefits from a traditional defined benefit plan.

- Pension equity plans are final average defined benefit hybrids. When employees terminate employment or retire, the sum of percentage credits that have accrued is applied to final average pay to determine a lump-sum benefit which is portable. Age- or service-weighted credits and a final average pay formula make pension equity plans appealing to older workers and persons hired in midcareer who have fewer years to accrue benefits.

- Life cycle pension plans, sometimes considered a pension equity plan variation, use hypothetical account balances to communicate plan benefits to participants. These plans provide a lump sum based on an accumulation of annual credits multiplied by final average salary. Life cycle plans are also referred to using such terms as retirement bonus plans or mobility bonus plans.

- A minimum balance pension plan is a cash balance plan variant offering plan participants the greater benefit of either a traditional defined benefit pension plan (often based on final average pay) or the benefit accumulated on a career average basis through the cash balance method.

- Defined contribution hybrid plans combine a defined contribution plan structure with certain attributes of a defined benefit plan. Defined contribution hybrid plans include target benefit plans, age-weighted profit sharing plans, and new comparability plans.

- Target benefit plans are a defined contribution hybrid where the plan sponsor's required contributions are determined actuarially to meet income replacement targets expressed in terms of a percentage of salary near the time of retirement. However, these targets are not guaranteed once initially set and the ultimate pension benefits depend on account values reflecting the actual gains and losses from plan investments. Typically target benefit plans permit participant-directed investments, and contributions tend to be heavily weighted by age to favor older participants.

- Age-weighted profit sharing plans are similar to traditional profit sharing plans except they apply age factors to allocate contributions more heavily to older participants. These plans tend to appeal to smaller employers with older executive staff and younger rank and file employees.

- New comparability plans are similar to age-weighted plans but have plan contributions provided to separate allocation groups in order to provide larger percentage contributions to select plan participants. Allocation groups are determined using certain business criteria, such as job descriptions, ownership interest, age, and length of service.

- A floor-offset plan is a hybrid plan involving two separate plans, a defined benefit and a defined contribution plan. The defined benefit plan establishes a minimum level (floor) of benefit participants will receive if the defined contribution benefit does not exceed the minimum (floor) benefit.

Key Terms

age-weighted (profit
   sharing) plans, p. *385*
allocation groups, p. *385*
cash balance plan, p. *374*
cross-testing, p. *386*
floor-offset plan, p. *386*
"grandfather" provisions,
   p. *382*

hybrid retirement plans,
   p. *373*
life cycle pension plan,
   p. *377*
minimum balance pension
   plan, p. *380*
new comparability (plans),
   p. *385*

pension equity plans,
   p. *375*
pension wear away, p. *381*
retirement bonus plans,
   p. *377*
target benefit plans, p. *383*

Questions for Review

1. What is a hybrid retirement plan?
2. What are the features of a defined benefit hybrid plan?
3. Describe the characteristics of a cash balance plan.
4. What is a pension equity plan?
5. Note the similarities between cash balance plans and pension equity plans and the key characteristic differentiating these two plan types.
6. Compare and contrast pension equity and retirement bonus plans.
7. What is a life cycle pension plan?
8. Explain the operation of a minimum balance pension plan.
9. List the various types of defined contribution hybrid retirement plans.
10. Describe the characteristics of a target benefit plan.
11. What is an age-weighted profit sharing plan?
12. Describe the use of "allocation groups" and "rate groups" in connection with a new comparability plan.
13. Describe the employer conditions under which a new comparability plan may have the most appeal.
14. When are floor-offset plans most useful?
15. What are some of the disadvantages of a floor-offset plan?

Questions for Discussion

1. Discuss the issues an employer would face in migrating from a more traditional retirement plan design to one of the hybrid plans described in the chapter. Describe employer characteristics, business conditions, and specific hybrid designs that would allow such a change.
2. Select a specific hybrid plan design and discuss its advantages over a more traditional retirement plan. Discuss how these advantages could be communicated to a large employer's workforce, particularly one where there is a diversity of educational backgrounds, age demographics, and geographical work locations.

3. An employer is looking at a merger with a company with an equivalent workforce size. The employer offers a traditional defined benefit plan, but the merger candidate has recently converted from a defined benefit plan to a cash balance plan. Describe the considerations involved in offering a recommendation whether to retain both pension forms or consolidate into one unified program.

Resources for Further Study

Bureau of National Affairs, Inc. "IRS Issues Guidance on Qualification Requirements for Cash Balance Plans." *Daily Tax Report,* January 19, 1996, pp. G-5, L-2, L-6.

CCH Editorial Staff. "Legislation 2006: Pension Protection Act of 2006: Law, Explanation and Analysis." *Commerce Clearing House* (2006).

Charles D. Spencer & Associates, Inc. "Company Continues Target Benefit Plan after Growing from 200 to 4,000 Employees." *Spencer's Research Reports on Employee Benefits.* Chicago, IL: Charles D. Spencer & Associates, 1993.

Charles D. Spencer & Associates, Inc. "Pension Equity Plans: Comparison of Plan Features Reveals Ability to Satisfy Mid-Career Hires." *Spencer's Research Reports on Employee Benefits.* Chicago, IL: Charles D. Spencer & Associates, Inc., July 8, 1994.

Edlund, Taina; and Ira Kastrinsky. "Cash Balance Plans: Finding the Proper Perspective." *The Handbook of Employee Benefits.* 6th ed. Jerry S. Rosenbloom, ed. New York: McGraw-Hill, 2005.

Edwards, J. Robert. "An Overview of Age-Based Profit Sharing Plans." *BookeMarks.* Winston-Salem, NC: Booke & Company, February 1992.

McKeon, David. "New Opportunities with Age-Weighted Profit Sharing Plans." *Pension World,* October 1993.

Robinson, Patti; and William S. Small. "The Floor-Offset Retirement Plan: Versatile and Tested, It Merits More Attention." *Compensation & Benefits Review,* May/June 1993.

Silva, Chris. "Landmark Ruling, New Bill Validates Legality of Hybrids." *Employee Benefit News.* Thomson Financial, October 2006.

"Summary of Provisions of the Pension Protection Act of 2006 Affecting Defined Benefit Plan Funding and Hybrid Plans." The Benefits Group of Davis and Harman LLP, October 5, 2006.

Chapter 22

Plan Termination Insurance for Single-Employer Pension Plans

After studying this chapter you should be able to:

- Identify the different types of voluntary plan terminations.
- Describe the relevance of an involuntary plan termination.
- Explain the importance of reportable events.
- Analyze the types of benefits guaranteed by the PBGC.
- Describe what happens to residual assets after a plan termination.
- Explain the premium system currently in place to finance the PBGC.

The **Pension Benefit Guaranty Corporation (PBGC)** is a federal government agency created under Title IV of the Employee Retirement Income Security Act (ERISA). In general, the purposes of the PBGC are to encourage the continuation and maintenance of voluntary private pension plans for the benefit of their participants, provide for the timely and uninterrupted payment of pension benefits to the participants and beneficiaries under all insured plans, and maintain premiums at the lowest level consistent with carrying out the PBGC's statutory obligations. The PBGC administers two insurance programs: one for single-employer pension plans and one for multiemployer pension plans. This chapter deals exclusively with single-employer plans.[1]

[1] ERISA, and more significantly the Multiemployer Pension Plan Amendments Act (MEPPAA) of 1980, had a major effect upon the PBGC's jurisdiction over multiemployer plans, employer liabilities, and the administrative practices of trustees. The MEPPAA has many implications for almost all aspects of multiemployer plans, especially concerning plan termination insurance and employer liabilities.

In 1974, ERISA established a plan termination insurance program for the majority of defined benefit pension plans in the United States to ensure that pensioner benefit rights would be protected (up to a maximum amount per month) in the event of a pension plan's terminating with unfunded liabilities. In 1986, one of the major defects associated with the original design was corrected when the Single Employer Pension Plan Amendments Act (SEPPAA) changed the insured event from that of, in essence, any plan termination to a termination accompanied by a specified event for the plan sponsor.

This change effectively limited the insurable event to an insufficient termination due to bankruptcy by the sponsor, thereby virtually eliminating the opportunity for an ongoing sponsor to exchange the unfunded vested liabilities of the plan for 30 percent of its net worth (an option existing under the original provisions of ERISA). However, it did nothing to change the premium structure from a flat dollar amount per participant. Congress redressed this shortcoming in part by enacting a variable-rate premium structure in 1987 that relates the sponsor's annual premium to the plan's underfunding (as measured on a termination basis). Although this change factors the plan's potential severity into the determination of the annual premium, it falls short of a risk-related premium structure that would characterize the insurance if it were written in the private sector. Such a structure would base annual premiums not only on the potential severity but also on the probability of an insured event's taking place (i.e., bankruptcy of a sponsor with an underfunded plan). The new premium system also differs from a free market approach in that it specifies a maximum charge per participant.

Another perceived problem with the change in the premium structure in 1987 was that it provided a maximum per-participant cap on the level of the premium. The Retirement Protection Act of 1994 increased premiums for plans with the largest exposure by phasing out the per-participant cap over three years. The 1994 legislation also included provisions designed to strengthen and accelerate funding for underfunded pension plans as well as improve information for workers and retirees in underfunded plans.

The Pension Protection Act of 2006 (PPA) involved major overhaul of the funding rules for defined benefit plans and also contained numerous provisions related to the PBGC. One of the many objectives of the PPA was to improve funding of the PBGC in the wake of substantial and projected deficits caused by inadequate funding for defined benefit plans that have been terminated or are likely to terminate in the future. The PPA provides for premium rate adjustments, a directive for the PBGC to study multiemployer funding rules, limits on the PBGC guarantee of benefits due to plant shutdowns and other similar events, and a provision to relax certain funding requirements for PBGC-approved benefits.

Another major change brought about by the PPA regards the appointment of the PBGC Director. The PPA now requires that the Director of the PBGC be appointed by the President of the United States, rather than by the Secretary of Labor, and the appointment is then subject to joint confirmation by the Senate Committee on Finance and the Senate Committee on Health, Education, Labor and Pensions. Making the PBGC Director subject to Senate confirmation reflected the view of legislators that the position was too important not to be subject to Senate review.

The PPA also extends the PBGC's missing participant program to defined contribution plans and other plans not subject to the PBGC termination insurance program. Under the existing missing participant program, defined benefit plan administrators must either buy an annuity or transfer a missing participant's designated benefit to the PBGC. The PPA extends this program to multiemployer plans following the issuance of final regulations. The PPA will allow, but not require, plan administrators of other pension plans (specifically defined contribution plans, defined benefit plans with fewer than 25 active participants and maintained by professional service employers, and the portion of defined benefit plans providing benefits based on separate accounts of participants) not subject to the missing participant program and not subject to the termination insurance program to elect to transfer missing participant benefits to the PBGC upon plan termination.

Plans Covered

The PBGC's single-employer plan termination insurance provisions apply to virtually all defined benefit pension plans. The following material examines the specific plans covered and then describes the type of pension benefits protected by the PBGC's insurance program.

Subject to specific exceptions, ERISA Section 4021(a) requires mandatory coverage of employee pension benefit plans that either affect interstate commerce (and, in the case of nonqualified plans, have for five years met the standards for qualified plans) or are qualified under the Internal Revenue Code (IRC). The following plans are specifically excluded from coverage:

1. Individual account plans (e.g., money purchase pension plans, profit sharing plans, thrift and savings plans, and stock bonus plans).
2. Government plans.
3. Certain church plans other than those that have voluntarily opted for coverage.
4. Certain plans established by fraternal societies to which no employer contributions are made.
5. Plans that do not provide for employer contributions after September 2, 1974.
6. Nonqualified deferred compensation plans established for select groups of management or highly compensated employees.
7. Plans established outside of the United States for nonresident aliens.
8. So-called excess benefit plans established and maintained primarily to pay benefits or accrue contributions for a limited group of highly paid employees in excess of the Section 415 limits.
9. Plans established and maintained exclusively for "substantial owners," meaning proprietors, partners with a greater than 10 percent interest in the capital profits of a partnership, or shareholders of a corporation owning—directly or indirectly—more than 10 percent in value of either the voting stock or all the stock of the corporation.

10. Plans of international organizations exempt from tax under the International Organization Immunities Act.

11. Plans maintained only to comply with workers' compensation, unemployment compensation, or disability insurance laws.

12. Plans established and maintained by labor organizations as described in Section 501(c)(5) of the IRC that do not provide for employer contributions after September 2, 1974.

13. Plans that are defined benefit plans to the extent that they are treated as individual account plans.[2]

14. Any plan established and maintained by professional service employers, provided that there are not, at any time after September 2, 1974, more than 25 active participants in the plan.

For purposes of the last category, a professional service employer means any proprietorship, partnership, corporation, or other association or organization owned or controlled by professional individuals or by executors or administrators of professional individuals, the principal business of which is the performance of professional services.

Plan Termination Defined

The termination of a pension plan should be a clearly identifiable event. Otherwise, it may be difficult to assess if a termination has occurred and, if so, when. Establishing the exact date of termination is important to all parties concerned—the plan sponsor, the plan participants, their beneficiaries, and the PBGC. A plan termination can be voluntary or involuntary. However, the PBGC will not proceed with the voluntary termination of a plan if it violates the terms and conditions of an existing collective bargaining agreement.[3]

During the first 10 years of PBGC coverage, the insured event for single-employer plan termination insurance was simply the termination of the defined benefit pension plan. Because this event is generally within the control of the sponsor, coupled with the fact that the sponsor's liability to the PBGC was at that time limited to 30 percent of its net worth, several underfunded plans were terminated even though the sponsors continued in existence and in some cases even attempted to establish new pension plans immediately after the original plans were terminated. As the financial condition of the PBGC continued to deteriorate in the first half of the 1980s, several attempts were made to legislatively amend the definition of the insured event. The SEPPAA radically changed these provisions in an attempt to preserve the financial integrity of the system.

---

[2] However, if the assets under a terminating cash balance plan (see Chapter 21) are insufficient to meet the benefit obligation under the plan, the PBGC will assume the unfunded benefits on the same terms as those applicable to traditional defined benefit plans.

[3] It should be noted that this does not limit the PBGC's authority to proceed with an involuntary termination as described later in this chapter.

The following section describes the circumstances under which the single-employer **plan termination insurance** applies.

Voluntary Plan Termination

A single-employer plan may be terminated voluntarily only in a standard termination or a distress termination. Disclosure of the appropriate information is provided through a series of PBGC forms known as the Standard Termination Filing and Distress Termination Filing forms.

Standard Termination

A single-employer plan may terminate under a standard termination if, among other things, the plan is sufficiently funded for benefit liabilities[4] (determined as of the termination date) when the final distribution of assets occurs.

Provided the PBGC has not issued a notice of noncompliance and the plan's assets are sufficient for benefit liabilities when the final distribution occurs, the plan administrator must distribute the plan's assets in accordance with the requirements for allocation of assets under ERISA Section 4044 (described later).

Distress Termination

After receiving the appropriate information, the PBGC must determine whether the necessary distress criteria have been satisfied. Basically, these criteria are met if each person who is a contributing sponsor or a member of the sponsor's controlled group meets the requirements of any of the following:

1. Liquidation in bankruptcy or insolvency proceedings.
2. Reorganization in bankruptcy or insolvency proceedings.[5]
3. Termination required to enable payment of debts while staying in business or to avoid unreasonably burdensome pension costs caused by a declining workforce.

If the PBGC determines that the requirements for a distress termination are met, it will either determine that (1) the plan is sufficient for guaranteed benefits (or that such a determination cannot be made on the basis of the available information) or (2) the plan is sufficient for benefit liabilities (or that such a determination cannot be made on the basis of the available information). The plan administrator will be notified of the decision, and one of the following types of terminations will then be carried out:[6]

1. In any case in which the PBGC determines that the plan is sufficient for benefit liabilities, the plan administrator must distribute the plan's assets in the same manner as described for a standard termination.

---

[4] Benefit liabilities are equal to the benefits of employees and their beneficiaries under the plan (within the meaning of Section 401(a)(2) of the Internal Revenue Code of 1986).

[5] For this requirement to be met, a bankruptcy court must determine that, unless the plan is terminated, the sponsor will be unable to pay all its debts pursuant to a plan of reorganization and will be unable to continue in business outside the Chapter 11 reorganization process.

[6] ERISA Section 4041(c)(3).

2. In any case in which the PBGC determines that the plan is sufficient for guaranteed benefits but is unable to determine that the plan is sufficient for benefit liabilities, the plan administrator must distribute the plan's assets in the same manner as described for a standard termination.

3. In any case in which the PBGC determines that it is unable to determine that the plan is sufficient for guaranteed benefits, the PBGC will commence proceedings as though an involuntary termination (described later) were taking place.

The plan administrator must meet certain requirements during the interim period from the time the PBGC is notified to the time a sufficiency determination is made. Essentially, the administrator must:

1. Refrain from distributing assets or taking any other actions to carry out the proposed termination.

2. Pay benefits attributable to employer contributions, other than death benefits, only in the form of an annuity.

3. Not use plan assets to purchase from an insurer irrevocable commitments to provide benefits.

4. Continue to pay all benefit liabilities under the plan but, commencing on the proposed termination date, limit the payment of benefits under the plan to those benefits guaranteed by the PBGC or required to be allocated under ERISA Section 4044 (described below).

When two organizations merge, the resulting single plan does not result in a termination if the new, merged organization assumes responsibility for the plan. Also, under ERISA, a pension plan may not be merged or consolidated with another pension plan or have its assets transferred to another plan unless each participant in the prior plan is credited in the successor plan with a benefit at least as great as that which he or she would have received had the old plan been terminated.[7]

Involuntary Plan Termination

The PBGC may institute termination proceedings in a U.S. district court in the jurisdiction where the employer does business if it finds that (1) the plan does not comply with the minimum funding standards of the IRC; (2) the plan is unable to pay benefits when due; (3) within the preceding 24 months, and for a reason other than death, a distribution of $10,000 or more has been made to a participant who is the substantial owner of the sponsoring firm and following the distribution there are unfunded liabilities; or (4) the eventual loss to the PBGC for the plan may be expected to increase unreasonably if the plan is not terminated. Moreover, the PBGC is required to institute proceedings to terminate a single-employer plan whenever it determines that the plan does not have assets available to pay benefits currently due under the terms of the plan. The PBGC may decide not to seek **involuntary plan termination,** even if one of the conditions

---

[7] IRC Section 401(a)(12).

for such action has occurred, if it deems that it would be in the best interests of those involved not to force termination of the plan.

Reportable Events

Within 30 days after the plan administrator or the contributing sponsor knows or has reason to know that a **reportable event** (described below) has occurred, he or she shall notify the PBGC that such event has occurred. The PBGC is authorized to waive the requirement with respect to any or all reportable events with respect to any plan and to require the notification to be made by including the event in the annual report made by the plan.

A reportable event is said to occur under any of the following conditions:

1. When the Secretary of the Treasury issues notice that a plan has ceased to be a plan described in Section 4021(a)(2), or when the Secretary of Labor determines the plan is not in compliance with Title I of ERISA.

2. When an amendment of the plan is adopted whereby, under the amendment, the benefit payable from employer contributions with respect to any participant may be decreased.

3. When the number of active participants is less than 80 percent of the number of such participants at the beginning of the plan year, or is less than 75 percent of the number of such participants at the beginning of the previous plan year. This reduction is tested on a plan-by-plan basis.

4. When the Secretary of the Treasury determines that there has been a termination or partial termination of the plan within the meaning of Section 411(d)(3) of the Internal Revenue Code of 1986 but the occurrence of such a termination or partial termination does not, by itself, constitute or require a termination of a plan under this Title.

5. When the plan fails to meet funding standards or applies for a minimum funding waiver under Section 412 of the IRC (without regard to whether the plan is a plan described in Section 4021(a)(2) of ERISA) or under Section 302 of ERISA.

6. When the plan is unable or projects an inability to pay benefits thereunder when due. A projected inability to pay benefits exists when as of the last day of any quarter of the plan year the plan's liquid assets are less than two times the amount of the disbursement from the plan for such quarter.

7. When there is a distribution under the plan to a participant who is a substantial owner as defined in Section 4022(b)(5) if *(a)* the total of all distributions made to the substantial owner within the one-year period ending with the date of such distribution exceeds $10,000; *(b)* such distribution is not made by reason of the death of the owner; and *(c)* immediately after the distribution, the plan has nonforfeitable benefits that are not funded.

8. When a plan merges, consolidates, or transfers its assets under Section 208 of ERISA or Section 414(1) of the Code.

9. When, as a result of a transaction, any person(s) ceases to be a member of the plan's controlled group.

10. When a contributing sponsor or a member of a contributing sponsor's controlled group liquidates, institutes a proceeding to be dissolved, or liquidates in a case under Bankruptcy Code or under any similar law.

11. When a contributing sponsor or a member of a contributing sponsor's controlled group declares an extraordinary dividend or redeems its own stock, reporting responsibilities vary if the resulting distribution is a reportable cash, non-cash, or combined distribution. For cash, an aggregate distribution for the fiscal year (or the three prior fiscal years) is reportable if it exceeds the adjusted net income of the person making the distribution for the preceding fiscal year (or the four preceding fiscal years). For non-cash, an aggregate distribution is reportable if it exceeds 10 percent of the total net assets of the person making the distribution. If both cash and non-cash distributions to shareholders are made during a fiscal year, a distribution is reportable when the sum of the cash distribution percentage and the non-cash distribution percentage for the fiscal year exceeds 100 percent.

12. When, in a 12-month period ending with the date of the transfer, an aggregate of 3 percent or more of the benefits liabilities of a plan covered by this Title and maintained by a contributing sponsor or a member of its controlled group are transferred to a person who is not a member of the controlled group or to a plan or plans maintained by a person or persons that are not such a contributing sponsor or a member of its controlled group.

13. When a member of a plan's controlled group defaults on a loan of $10 million or more.

14. When there is the commencement of a bankruptcy case or any other type of insolvency proceeding by any member of a controlled group.

15. When any other event occurs that may be indicative of a need to terminate the plan and that is prescribed by the PBGC in its regulations.

In some situations certain contributing sponsors must notify the PBGC no later than 30 days before the effective date of a reportable event. A contributing sponsor is subject to this advance notice requirement if both of the following conditions apply:

- Neither the contributing sponsor nor any member of the controlled group to which the reportable event relates is a public company.

- The contributing sponsor's controlled group has one or more plans that, when combined have unfunded vested benefits of more than $50 million, and have a funded vested benefit percentage of less than 90 percent. (Unfunded vested benefits for this purpose entail participant and beneficiary vested benefits in excess of the actuarial value of plan assets.)

Provided the aforementioned conditions are met, the following type of events are subject to advance reporting:

1. Controlled group change.
2. Liquidation.
3. Extraordinary dividend or stock redemption.
4. Transfer of benefit liabilities.
5. Application for a minimum funding waiver.
6. Loan defaults.
7. Bankruptcy or similar settlement.

In terms of the method of notification to the PBGC for reportable events, the final regulations on reportable events provide detailed information on prescribed notification methods. If a commercial delivery service—such as FedEx—is used, the PBGC considers the filing date to be the date it is deposited with the delivery service, provided it is received by the PBGC within two business days. Notices submitted by fax or electronic mail are considered timely if certain minimal information is submitted electronically by the due date and the remaining information is received by the PBGC within a day after the due date for advance notices and within two days after the due date for postevent notices.

Failure to provide a required notice or other required information may result in the PBGC assessing a penalty of up to $1,000 per day against each person required to provide the notice.[8]

Date of Termination

For purposes of Title IV of ERISA, the **termination date** of a single-employer plan is one of the following:

1. In the case of a plan terminated in a standard termination, the termination date proposed in the notice of intent to terminate.
2. In the case of a plan terminated in a distress termination, the date established by the plan administrator and agreed to by the PBGC.
3. In the case of an involuntary termination, the date established by the PBGC and agreed to by the plan administrator.
4. In the case of distress or involuntary termination in any case in which no agreement is reached between the plan administrator and the PBGC, the date established by the court.

It should be noted that the PPA of 2006 amended prior law so that if a plan terminates after an employer enters bankruptcy, the date of the bankruptcy filing is substituted for the termination date for purposes of determining the maximum PBGC benefit guarantee and for purposes of determining the asset allocation for retirees or those who could have retired three years prior to the termination date. Effectively, this provision of the

[8] Andrew D. Eisner, "PBGC Issues Final Regulations on Reportable Events," *Journal of Compensation & Benefits* (May/June 1997), pp. 13–14.

PPA serves to freeze the amount of PBGC-guaranteed benefits when a contributing plan sponsor enters bankruptcy. This is important because, during the time a sponsor is in bankruptcy, payment of lump sums and annuity purchases may drain plan assets, which may reduce assets available for payment of nonguaranteed benefits to other participants. Benefits may also continue to accrue during bankruptcy and the PBGC limits on guarantees may continue to increase as a result of inflation adjustments, which may further increase unfunded benefits and the liability of the pension insurance system.[9]

In the latter three cases previously mentioned, the date on which the termination of a plan becomes effective is significant for a number of reasons. It not only establishes the date the PBGC assumes legal obligation for the plan's benefits, but it also establishes the date for the determination of the employer's possible contingent liability for unfunded benefits (described later). The effective termination date also is important to the participant. It fixes the date on which benefit accruals cease, the vesting schedule position is determined, and the phase-in of insurance coverage stops.

Restoration of Plan

If it appears that the pension plan could be continued even though plan termination proceedings have begun, the PBGC may halt the proceedings and take whatever action is necessary to restore the plan.[10]

Benefits Guaranteed

Even though a plan is covered by the PBGC's single-employer plan termination insurance, there is no assurance that all a participant's accrued pension benefit will be paid after the plan's termination. The individual participant (or beneficiary) must first meet three prerequisites before the benefit is guaranteed by the PBGC, and, even if the prerequisites are met, the individual still may be subject to specific limitations on the amount of the benefit covered.

Prerequisites for PBGC Guarantees

Subject to the various limits described later, the PBGC guarantees the payment of all nonforfeitable benefits that qualify as a pension benefit other than those accelerated by plan termination. A benefit that becomes nonforfeitable solely because of plan termination is not subject to ERISA benefit guarantees; however, a benefit won't fail to satisfy the PBGC requirement merely because a participant is required to submit a written application, retire, or complete a mandatory waiting period as a condition for receiving pension payments.

There are two additional exceptions to the general rule on forfeitability. First, guaranteed benefits paid to survivor beneficiaries are not deemed to be forfeitable for purposes of the PBGC guarantee merely because the plan provides for termination of benefit payments should the beneficiary remarry or attain a specific age. Second, disability benefits are not deemed forfeitable solely because they end on a participant's recovery.

---

[9] CCH Editorial Staff. "Legislation 2006: Pension Protection Act of 2006: Law, Explanation and Analysis." *Commerce Clearing House* (2006), 210–211.

[10] ERISA Section 4047.

For a payment to qualify as a pension benefit, it must be payable as an annuity or as one or more payments related to an annuity. Further, the benefit must be payable either to a participant who permanently leaves—or has left covered employment—or to a surviving beneficiary. It also is necessary that the pension benefit payment provide a substantially level income to the recipient, although the leveling could be accomplished in conjunction with Social Security payments. Under certain circumstances, the PBGC also guarantees annuities payable for total disability[11] and benefits payable in a single installment.[12]

The final requirement for protection under the PBGC guarantee is that the participant or beneficiary be entitled to the benefit. This prerequisite is met if any one of the following is satisfied:

1. The benefit was in pay status on the date of plan termination.
2. The benefit payable at normal retirement age is an optional benefit under the plan, and the participant elected the optional form of payment before the plan termination date.
3. The participant actually is eligible to receive benefits and could have received them before the plan terminated.
4. The benefit would be payable on the participant's retirement absent a contrary election.
5. The PBGC determines the participant is entitled to the benefit based on the particular circumstances.

Limitation on Amount of Monthly Benefits

There is a limit on the amount of monthly guaranteed benefits insured by the PBGC. The amount is adjusted annually to reflect changes in the Social Security taxable wage base. The original limit was $750 per month, but for plans terminated in 2007 the limit increased to $4,125.00 per month. The limit is in terms of a single-life annuity commencing at age 65 and without a refund feature. If the benefit is payable at a lower age, it is reduced by actuarial factors denoted by the PBGC. The benefit is not actuarially increased when the participant retires at an age later than 65. Table 22.1 provides PBGC maximum monthly guarantees at various ages.

The guaranteed monthly benefit of a participant cannot be greater than his or her average gross monthly income during the five consecutive years of highest earnings (or, if the period is shorter, the time during which he or she was an active participant in the plan).

New or Amended Plans and Benefits

To prevent possible abuses, the insurance covers guaranteed benefits provided those benefits have been in effect under the provisions of the plan for 60 months or longer at the time of plan termination.[13]

---

[11] PBGC Regulation Section 2613.7.

[12] The benefit will not be paid in a single installment, but the PBGC will guarantee the alternative benefit, if any, in the plan that provides for the payment of equal periodic installments for the life of the recipient. PBGC Regulation Section 2613.8.

[13] ERISA Section 4022(b)(8).

TABLE 22.1   **Illustration of PBGC Single-Life Annuity Maximum Monthly Guarantees**

Year Plan Terminated	Monthly Guarantee Limit at Age 65	Monthly Guarantee Limit at Age 62	Monthly Guarantee Limit at Age 60	Monthly Guarantee Limit at Age 55
2007	4,125.00	3,258.75	2,681.25	1,856.25
2006	3,971.59	3,137.56	2,581.53	1,787.22
2005	3,801.14	3,002.90	2,470.74	1,710.51
2004	3,698.86	2,922.10	2,404.26	1,664.49
2003	3,664.77	2,895.17	2,382.10	1,649.15

If benefits are attributable to a plan amendment or to a newly adopted plan, the benefits attributable to that amendment or new plan are guaranteed only to the extent of the greater of 20 percent of the amount of such increase or new benefit multiplied by the number of years (up to five) that the plan or amendment has been in effect, or $20 per month multiplied by the number of years (up to five) that the plan or amendment has been in effect.

The effect of this rule guaranteeing 20 percent of the amount of such increased or new benefit multiplied by the number of years (up to five) results in a phase-in of PBGC pension protection coverage over a five-year period of time. It should be noted that although rank-and-file participants received coverage over a five-year period, substantial owners were held to a more stringent phase-in for their coverage. Prior to the passage of the PPA, coverage for PBGC guarantees was phased in over a 30-year period for those holding an ownership interest exceeding 10 percent. This disparity in phase-in rules resulted in a business owner having a smaller PBGC guaranteed benefit than a similarly-situated nonowner. Some experts argued that this lack of comparable coverage, coupled with perceived high administrative costs associated with defined benefit plans, served as a disincentive for small employers to sponsor defined benefit plans. Accordingly the PPA changed this rule, allowing business owners to qualify for PBGC guaranteed benefits sooner. Now the application of the phase-in rule depends on ownership interest. For "substantial owners," the same 60-month phase-in rule applies as it would with nonowners. For "majority owners," (those with an entire interest of an unincorporated business, or a 50 percent interest in a partnership or corporation), the amount of benefits guaranteed is determined by multiplying:

- A fraction (which may not exceed 1), where the numerator is the number of years from *(a)* the later of the effective date of the amendment or the plan adoption date and *(b)* the termination date, and the denominator is 10; by the
- Amount of benefits that would be guaranteed under the phase-in rules for participants who are not majority owners.

Thus, the phase-in for majority owners occurs over a 10-year period and depends on the number of years the plan has been in effect. Additionally, the majority owner's guaranteed benefit cannot be more than the amount phased in over 60 months for other participants.[14]

[14] CCH Editorial Staff, *"Legislation 2006: Pension Protection Act of 2006: Law, Explanation and Analysis,"* (New York: Commerce Clearing House, 2006), p. 213.

Limitation for Shutdown and Other Benefits

The PBGC guarantee for benefits for plant shutdown and other unpredictable, contingent events will be calculated using a phase-in over a five-year period, generally at a rate of 20 percent of the guaranteed benefit per year, as enacted into law by the PPA of 2006.

Payments in Excess of Unfunded Guaranteed Benefits

Participants, beneficiaries, and alternate payees under qualified domestic relations orders (QDROs) under a single-employer plan will be paid a percentage of the plan's unfunded benefit liabilities in excess of PBGC-guaranteed benefits equal to a percentage recovered by the PBGC on the total claim.[15] Amounts will be allocated to participants in accordance with the ERISA Section 4044 asset allocation rules. Generally, the recovery percentage will be determined from past PBGC experience. In the case of large amounts (i.e., unfunded benefit liabilities in excess of guaranteed benefits of at least $20 million), data from the particular termination will be used in determining the recovery percentage.

Specifically, the amount is determined by multiplying (1) the "outstanding amount of benefit liabilities" by (2) the applicable "recovery ratio." The outstanding amount of benefit liabilities is the value of the benefit liabilities under the plan less the value of the benefit liabilities that would be so determined by taking into account only benefits that are guaranteed or to which assets of the plan are allocated under ERISA Section 4044(1).[16]

In the case of a terminated plan in which the outstanding amount of benefit liabilities is less than $20 million, the recovery ratio is the average ratio, with respect to prior plan terminations under the plan sponsor liability rules, of the following:[17]

$$\frac{\text{The value of the recovery of the PBGC under the plan}}{\text{sponsor liability rules for the prior plan terminations}}$$
$$\frac{}{\text{The amount of unfunded benefit liabilities under the plan}}$$
as of the termination date of the prior plan terminations

For these plans with outstanding benefit liabilities below $20 million, the PPA created a separate recovery ratio for determining amounts recovered for unpaid employer contributions owed to the plan. This recovery ratio uses the same PPA-amended five-year period. The PBGC determines the amount by multiplying (1) the amount of liability

---

[15] ERISA Section 4022(c).

[16] It should be noted that this does not limit the PBGC's authority to proceed with an involuntary termination as described later in this chapter.

[17] A prior plan termination was a termination of which (1) the PBGC had determined the value of recoveries under the plan sponsor liability rules; and (2) notices of intent to terminate were provided after December 31, 1987, and within the five fiscal years of the federal government ending before the year in which the date of the notice of intent to terminate the plan of which the recovery ratio was being determined was provided. The PPA of 2006 changed this computation so the determination period will be based on the five–federal fiscal year period that ends with the third fiscal year preceding the fiscal year in which occurs the date of notice of intent to terminate the plan.

under ERISA Sec. 4062(c) as of the date of plan termination by (2) the ERISA Sec. 4062(c) recovery ratio. Prior to the passage of the PPA, amounts recovered from terminated plans attributable to unpaid employer contributions were determined based on a specific plan, rather than on the PBGC experience.[18]

In the case of a terminated plan for which the outstanding benefit liabilities exceed $20 million, the recovery ratio is:

$$\frac{\text{The value of the recovery of the PBGC under the plan sponsor liability rules for the terminated plan}}{\text{The amount of unfunded benefit liabilities under the plan as of the termination date}}$$

For purposes of these ratios, the amount of unfunded benefit liabilities is (1) the value of benefit liabilities under the plan less (2) the current value of the assets of the plan.

Determinations under these rules are to be made by the PBGC. A determination will be binding unless shown by clear and convincing evidence to be unreasonable.

Allocation of Assets on Plan Termination

Priority Categories

Plan assets must be allocated to the benefit categories applicable on plan termination under ERISA Section 4044. This prevents employers from establishing new benefit levels, terminating plans, and allocating existing plan assets to such benefits resulting in the subordination of insured to uninsured benefits. On termination, the assets of a plan must be allocated in the following order of priority:[19]

1. Employees' voluntary contributions.
2. Employees' mandatory contributions.
3. Annuity payments in pay status at least three years before the termination of the plan (including annuity payments that would have been in pay status for at least three years if the employee had retired then) based on the provisions of the plan in effect during the five years before termination of the plan under which the benefit would be the least.
4. All other insured benefits (this includes benefits that would be insured except for the special limitation with respect to a substantial owner; also, the aggregate benefit limitation for individuals does not apply).
5. All other vested, but uninsured, benefits.
6. All other benefits under the plan.

An allocation within a **priority category** that cannot be covered in full is settled on a pro rata basis, except that subpriorities within a priority category may be provided for by the plan. If there are any assets remaining after satisfaction of all liabilities for accrued benefits, they may be paid to the employer if provided for by the plan provisions.

---

[18] CCH Editorial Staff, *"Legislation 2006: Pension Protection Act of 2006: Law, Explanation and Analysis,"* (New York: Commerce Clearing House, 2006), p. 216.

[19] ERISA Section 4044.

Chevron and Gulf Oil announced a merger in 1984, and the merger was completed two years later. In July 1986, Gulf Oil's main pension plan and several subordinate plans, as well as a smaller Chevron plan, were merged into the Chevron Retirement Plan. The merger involved the transfer of approximately $700 million that had accumulated in the plans since their establishment. Chevron used the plans' assets for various corporate purposes.

In November 1986, a class action suit was filed on behalf of 40,000 former participants in the Gulf Oil plans, contending that the transfer of assets violated ERISA Section 208. That section requires that each participant in a plan must receive a benefit immediately after a merger or transfer of assets that is equal to or greater than the benefit the participant would have been entitled to receive immediately before the merger or transfer. The former participants further argued that the Gulf Oil plans had undergone a partial termination.

In 1991, the U.S. District Court ruled ERISA Section 208 affords protection only to *accrued* benefits, that an entitlement to an actuarial surplus is not an accrued benefit, and thus that the participants in the class action suit were not entitled to the $550 million in excess assets under the main Gulf Oil plan.

The court went on to find that the Gulf Oil plans had undergone a partial termination and ordered that all participants in the plans who were employed by Chevron on the date of the merger be vested in benefits accrued under those plans as of that date.

The former participants appealed. Although the appellate court agreed that the Gulf Oil plans had undergone a partial termination, it rejected the participants' argument that they were entitled to a pro rata share of the plans' excess assets.

According to the court, if the participants had any such right, it had to be found in the plans' language (and) . . . since the plans did not discuss what happened after plan liabilities were fully satisfied, the plan language created at least an implied right to reversion in Gulf Oil.

Source: "Chevron to Retain Excess Assets from Gulf Oil Merger," *Employee Benefit Plan Review,* February 1995, pp. 46–47. Reprinted with permission of the *Employee Benefit Plan Review* magazine, Charles D. Spencer & Associates, Inc., publishers, Chicago, IL.

Reversion of Residual Assets to the Employer

In general, the funds in a qualified pension plan may not be used for purposes other than the exclusive benefit of employees or their beneficiaries prior to the termination of the plan and the satisfaction of all liabilities. However, with the exception of pension plan assets attributable to employee contributions, employers may recapture any residual assets of a terminated single-employer defined benefit pension plan if the following conditions are satisfied:

1. All liabilities of the plan to participants and their beneficiaries have been satisfied.
2. The distribution does not contravene any provision of law.
3. The plan provides for such a distribution in these circumstances.

Residual assets are equal to the plan funds remaining after satisfaction of all liabilities.[20]

The PBGC, Treasury Department, and Department of Labor have issued the following joint implementation guidelines on asset reversions:

1. An employer may not recover any surplus assets until it has fully vested all participants' benefits and has purchased and distributed annuity contracts.

2. If employees are offered lump-sum payments in lieu of future pensions, the amount of the lump-sum distribution must fairly reflect the value of the pension to the individual.

3. An employer that terminates a sufficiently funded defined benefit pension plan may establish a new defined benefit plan covering the same group of employees, granting past-service credit for the period during which an employee was covered by the terminated plan. This is known as a termination/reestablishment, and the successor plan is exempt from the five year phase-in of benefit guarantees that applies to newly established plans.

4. Spinoff/terminations[21] will not be recognized, and any attempt to recover surplus assets will be treated as a diversion of assets for a purpose other than the exclusive benefit of employees and beneficiaries unless the employees receive timely notice of the event and the following conditions are satisfied:

    a. The benefits of all employees must be fully vested and nonforfeitable as of the date of the termination. This also applies to the benefits covered by the ongoing plan.

    b. All accrued benefits must be provided for by the purchase of annuity contracts.

5. In the case of a spinoff/termination and a termination/reestablishment, attempts to recover surplus assets will be treated as a diversion of assets for a purpose other than the exclusive benefit of employees and beneficiaries unless the funding method for the ongoing plans is to be changed by modifying the amortization basis.[22]

6. An employer may not engage in either a termination/reestablishment or spinoff/ termination transaction involving reversion of assets any earlier than 15 years following any such transaction.

Amounts recovered under a reversion are subject to a 50 percent excise tax.[23] This penalty is reduced to 20 percent if (1) 25 percent of the otherwise recoverable reversion

---

[20] Restrictions on reversions from recently amended plans are specified in ERISA Section 4044(d)(2). The allocation of residual assets attributable to employee contributions is described in ERISA Section 4044(d)(3).

[21] Under a spinoff/termination, the active participants (and their liabilities) are spun off from the original defined benefit plan. Assets are then transferred from the original plan to the new plan in an amount at least equal to the active participants' liabilities. The original plan, which at this point covers only retired and terminated employees, is then terminated, and annuities are used to satisfy the plan's obligations.

[22] The modification must be in accordance with IRC Section 412(b)(4). Details of the modification are provided in PBGC News Release 84–23.

[23] Prior to the Omnibus Budget Reconciliation Act of 1990, the tax rate had been 15 percent. In addition to the increased penalty, this legislation allowed employers to use surplus pension assets to prefund retiree health plans through 401(h) accounts.

is transferred to another qualified retirement plan that covers at least 95 percent of the active participants of the terminated plan, (2) 20 percent of the otherwise recoverable reversion is used to provide pro rata increases in the benefits accrued by participants under the terminated plan, or (3) the employer is in Chapter 7 bankruptcy liquidation.

If the employer adopts a plan amendment increasing terminated defined benefit plan benefits, the 25 percent cushion is reduced dollar for dollar by the present value of the increase. These benefit increases must satisfy the generally applicable qualification requirements, such as the nondiscrimination rules described in Chapter 25.

Compliance with the 20 percent pro rata increase option requires that increased benefits must be provided to all qualified participants. This includes active participants, participants and beneficiaries receiving benefits on the termination date, and other participants who retain rights under the plan and who terminate employment (or plan eligibility) during a period starting three years before the termination date and ending on the final asset distribution date.[24] Beneficiaries of this last group also are eligible if they have a vested plan benefit. Employees who stop working before the plan termination date and receive a lump-sum distribution are not entitled to benefit increases.

Liabilities on Plan Termination

Distributee Liability-Recapture

When a plan terminates, the termination trustee is authorized to recover for the benefit of the pension plan certain payments received by a participant within the three-year period prior to plan termination. The recoverable amount is the sum of all payments made to the participant in excess of $10,000 made during any consecutive 12-month period within three years before termination or, if less, the amount he or she would have received as a monthly benefit under a single-life annuity commencing at age 65.[25] Payments to a disabled participant and payments made after or on account of the death of a participant are not subject to recovery. The PBGC can totally or partially waive any amount otherwise entitled to be recaptured whenever recapture would result in substantial economic hardship to a participant or his or her beneficiaries.

Employer Liability

During the legislative process leading up to the enactment of ERISA, concern was expressed that in the absence of appropriate safeguards under an insurance system, an employer might establish or amend a plan to provide substantial benefits with the realization that its funding might be inadequate to pay the benefits called for. Such an employer might, it was argued, rely on the insurance as a backup, enabling it to be more generous in promised pension benefits to meet labor demands than would be the case if it knew that the benefit would have to be paid for entirely out of the assets of the employer. On the other hand, it was clear that the imposition of heavy obligations on employers would discourage provisions for adequate pension plans.

---

[24] The assets allocated to increase the benefit of nonactive participants cannot exceed 40 percent of the total.

[25] ERISA Section 4045.

To deal with these competing considerations, the decision was made to impose on the employer a limited liability to reimburse the insurance system for a portion of the payment that must be made by the PBGC in satisfaction of its obligation if the employer plan fails. Unfortunately, the limited liability was much smaller than the amount of unfunded benefit for many sponsors, and several plans in this category were terminated to take advantage of this "pension put."

The SEPPAA substantially modified the computation of the sponsor's liability on termination, and the Omnibus Budget Reconciliation Act of 1987 made further modifications the following year. Currently, in any case in which a single-employer plan is terminated in a distress termination or an involuntary termination is instituted by the PBGC, any person who is, on the termination date, a contributing sponsor of the plan or a member of such a contributing sponsor's controlled group will incur a liability under Section 4062 of ERISA. This liability consists of two components:

1. The liability to the PBGC.
2. The liability to the Section 4042 trustee (described later).

Although special rules pertain to a case in which it is discovered that the plan is unable to pay guaranteed benefits after the authorized commencement of termination,[26] the following section defines the rules generally applying to the two components of the sponsor's liability and the required means of payment.

Liability to the PBGC

The liability to the PBGC consists of the total amount of the unfunded benefit liabilities[27] (as of the termination date) to all participants and beneficiaries under the plan, together with interest (at a reasonable rate) calculated from the termination date in accordance with regulations prescribed by the PBGC.

The total amount of the liability is paid to the PBGC, which, as described earlier in this chapter, pays out a portion of unfunded benefit liabilities in excess of the unfunded guaranteed benefits based on the total value of the PBGC's recovery with respect to the total liability of the employer. Amounts paid to participants are allocated in accordance with Section 4044 as described earlier in this chapter.

The liability to the PBGC is generally due as of the termination date. The PBGC and any person liable for payment also may agree to alternative arrangements for the satisfaction of the liability.

Liability to the Section 4042 Trustee

The liability to a Section 4042 trustee for the sponsoring employer and each member of its controlled group consists of the outstanding balance (accumulated with interest from the termination date) of the following:

1. The accumulated funding deficiency of the plan, modified to include the amount of any increase that would result if all pending applications for waivers of the minimum funding standard and for extensions of the amortization period were denied and if no additional contributions were made.

---

[26] ERISA Section 4062(b)(1)(B).
[27] Benefit liabilities are defined in the Standard Termination section of this chapter.

2. The amount of waived funding deficiencies.

3. The amount of decreases in the minimum funding standard account.

Determination of Net Worth

In general, the collective net worth for purposes of determining the liability to the PBGC consists of the sum of the individual net worths of all persons who have individual net worths greater than zero and who are contributing sponsors of the terminated plan or members of their controlled groups. The net worth of a person is determined on whatever basis best reflects, in the determination of the PBGC, the current status of the person's operations and prospects at the time chosen for determining the net worth of the person. The net worth is increased by the amount of any transfers of assets made by the pension that are determined by the PBGC to be improper under the circumstances. Determinations of net worth are made as of a day chosen by the PBGC during the 120-day period ending with the termination date. Net worth is computed without regard to termination liabilities.

Liability of Substantial and Multiple Employers

A liability applies to all employers, other than multiemployer plans terminating after April 29, 1980, who maintain a plan under which more than one employer makes contributions. The liability also attaches to all employers who, at any time within the five plan years preceding the date of plan termination, made contributions under the plan. The liability is allocated among the employers in the ratio of their required contributions for the last five years prior to termination.

If the withdrawing employer prefers, a bond may be furnished to the PBGC in an amount not exceeding 150 percent of its liability. The bond must be issued by a corporate surety acceptable on federal bonds under the authority granted by the Secretary of the Treasury.

PBGC Lien for Employer Liability

To the extent an employer liability is not satisfied and the amount does not exceed 30 percent of the collective net worth of the sponsor and its controlled group, the amount of the liability (including interest) is a lien in favor of the PBGC upon all property and rights to property, whether real or personal, belonging to the employer.

Premiums

Although Congress corrected several of the major design flaws in the single-employer plan termination insurance system with the passage of SEPPAA, there were still lingering doubts concerning the equity of a premium structure based solely on a flat-rate premium per participant. Therefore, Congress mandated that the PBGC prepare a study on several issues relating to the premium structure. On the basis of its findings, the PBGC proposed a variable-rate **premium structure** that added an additional premium charge based on the difference between the plan liabilities and the plan assets. This basic concept was incorporated into the Omnibus Budget Reconciliation Act of 1987 and later modified by the Omnibus Budget Reconciliation Act of 1990.

For plan years beginning after 1990, the single-employer flat-rate premium per participant was $19. An additional premium of $9 per $1,000 of unfunded vested benefits also was required of underfunded plans. Subsequently, the flat rate premium was increased from $19 to $30 by the Deficit Reduction Act of 2005, effective for plan years beginning on or after January 1, 2006. Also, single-employer plans that are terminated through a distress termination procedure, where the PBGC becomes trustee of the terminated plan, are subject to a termination premium of $1,250 per participant calculated using the number of plan participants in the plan immediately before the termination date. To compute the variable rate premium on "unfunded vested benefits," beginning in 2008 the calculation is modified to conform to the funding rule changes contained in the PPA of 2006.

Newly implemented with the PPA was a limit on the allowable variable rate premium for small-employer plans. For small-employer plans, defined as those with 25 or fewer employees on the first day of the plan year, the PBGC variable rate premium payments for each participant cannot exceed $5 multiplied by the number of participants in the plan as of the close of the preceding plan year.

The contributing sponsor or plan administrator must pay the premiums imposed by the PBGC. If the contributing sponsor of any plan is a member of a controlled group, each member is jointly and severally liable for any premiums.

Chapter Summary

- A single-employer plan may be terminated voluntarily only in a standard termination or a distress termination. A single-employer plan may terminate under a standard termination if, among other things, the plan is sufficiently funded for benefit liabilities (determined as of the termination date) when the final distribution of assets occurs.

- The PBGC must determine whether the necessary distress criteria have been satisfied. Basically, these criteria are met if each person who is a contributing sponsor or a member of the sponsor's controlled group meets the requirements of any of the following:
  1. Liquidation in bankruptcy or insolvency proceedings.
  2. Reorganization in bankruptcy or insolvency proceedings.
  3. Termination required to enable payment of debts while staying in business or to avoid unreasonably burdensome pension costs caused by a declining workforce.

- Subject to various limits, the PBGC guarantees the payment of all nonforfeitable benefits that qualify as a pension benefit other than those accelerated by plan termination. A benefit that becomes nonforfeitable solely because of plan termination is not subject to ERISA benefit guarantees; however, a benefit won't fail to satisfy the PBGC requirement merely because a participant is required to submit a written application, retire, or complete a mandatory waiting period as a condition for receiving pension payments.

- There is a limit on the amount of monthly guaranteed benefits insured by the PBGC. The amount is adjusted annually to reflect changes in the Social Security taxable wage base. The original limit was $750 per month, but for plans terminated in 2007 the limit increased to $4,125.00 per month. The limit is in terms of a single-life annuity commencing at age 65 and without a refund feature. If the benefit is payable at a lower age, it is reduced by actuarial factors denoted by the PBGC. The benefit is not actuarially increased when the participant retires at an age later than 65.

- Plan assets must be allocated to the benefit categories applicable on plan termination under ERISA Section 4044. This prevents employers from establishing new benefit levels, terminating plans, and allocating existing plan assets to such benefits resulting in the subordination of insured to uninsured benefits. On termination, the assets of a plan must be allocated in the following order of priorities:

  1. Employees' voluntary contributions.
  2. Employees' mandatory contributions.
  3. Annuity payments in pay status at least three years before the termination of the plan (including annuity payments that would have been in pay status for at least three years if the employee had retired then), based on the provisions of the plan in effect during the five years before termination of the plan under which the benefit would be the least.
  4. All other insured benefits (this includes benefits that would be insured except for the special limitation with respect to a "substantial owner"; also, the aggregate benefit limitation for individuals does not apply).
  5. All other vested, but uninsured, benefits.
  6. All other benefits under the plan.

- In general, the funds in a qualified pension plan may not be used for purposes other than the exclusive benefit of employees or their beneficiaries prior to the termination of the plan and the satisfaction of all liabilities. However, with the exception of pension plan assets attributable to employee contributions, employers may recapture any residual assets of a terminated single-employer defined benefit pension plan if the following conditions are satisfied:

  1. All liabilities of the plan to participants and their beneficiaries have been satisfied.
  2. The distribution does not contravene any provision of law.
  3. The plan provides for such a distribution in these circumstances.

- For plan years beginning after 1990, the single-employer flat-rate premium per participant was $19. An additional premium of $9 per $1,000 of unfunded vested benefits also was required of underfunded plans. Subsequently, the flat rate premium was increased from $19 to $30 by the Deficit Reduction Act of 2005, effective for plan years beginning on or after January 1, 2006. Also, single-employer plans that are terminated through a distress termination procedure, where the PBGC becomes trustee of the terminated plan, are subject to a termination premium of $1,250 per participant calculated using the number of plan participants in the plan immediately before the termination date. To compute the variable rate premium on "unfunded vested benefits," beginning in 2008 the calculation is modified to conform to the funding rule changes contained in the PPA of 2006.

- Newly implemented with the PPA was a limit on the allowable variable rate premium for small-employer plans. For small-employer plans, defined as those with 25 or fewer employees on the first day of the plan year, the PBGC variable rate premium payments for each participant cannot exceed $5 multiplied by the number of participants in the plan as of the close of the preceding plan year.
- The contributing sponsor or plan administrator must pay the premiums imposed by the PBGC. If the contributing sponsor of any plan is a member of a controlled group, each member is jointly and severally liable for any premiums.

Key Terms

involuntary plan
    termination, p. *396*
Pension Benefit Guaranty
    Corporation (PBGC),
    p. *391*

plan termination
    insurance, p. *395*
premium structure, p. *409*
priority category, p. *404*

reportable event, p. *397*
termination date, p. *399*

Questions for Review

1. In general, what types of pension plans are covered by plan termination insurance?
2. What classes of pension plans are specifically excluded from plan termination insurance coverage?
3. How is the PBGC kept apprised of events affecting plan solvency or operations that may justify an involuntary termination?
4. Explain the significance of the date of termination for a pension plan.
5. Explain the definition of a basic benefit with respect to *(a)* early retirement incentives and *(b)* death and disability benefits.
6. Explain how insurance coverage is phased in for benefits that have been in effect for less than five years.
7. Why is it necessary to establish priority classes for pension benefits at the time of termination?
8. Is the trustee authorized to recapture benefit payments already made prior to the occurrence of the plan termination? Explain.
9. Must the sponsor of a terminated plan reimburse the PBGC for any loss that it incurs in meeting the benefit obligations of the terminated plan?
10. What condition must be satisfied before a plan sponsor is able to recapture excess assets from a pension plan?

Questions for Discussion

1. Discuss the public policy issues involved in the termination of overfunded defined benefit pension plans.

2. In 1987, the PBGC adopted a new variable rate premium structure that included a premium component based on the amount of a defined benefit pension plan's unfunded vested benefits. Discuss the relative merits of this approach.

3. Many people have suggested that the PBGC should switch to a risk-related premium structure in which the premium a sponsor pays for plan termination insurance is based on *(a)* the relative likelihood that the plan will terminate and *(b)* the potential magnitude of the claim. Discuss the relative merits of this approach.

Resources for Further Study

Buckley, Allen; and George Prothro. "Accrued Benefits of Missing Participants in Nonterminating Retirement Plans." *Journal of Pension Benefits* 8, no. 3 (Spring 2001).

CCH Editorial Staff. "2002 Tax Legislation: Law, Explanation, and Analysis: Job Creation and Worker Assistance Act of 2002." *Commerce Clearing House Pension Plan Guide* (2002).

CCH Editorial Staff. "Legislation 2006: Pension Protection Act of 2006: Law, Explanation and Analysis." *Commerce Clearing House* (2006).

Eisner, Andrew D. "PBGC Issues Final Regulations on Reportable Events." *Journal of Compensation & Benefits* 12, no. 6 (May/June 1997).

www.pbgc.gov—website of the Pension Benefit Guaranty Corporation.

Chapter 23

Employers' Accounting for Pensions

After studying this chapter you should be able to:

- Chronicle the rationale for the development of pension accounting standards by the accounting profession.
- Contrast differences between actuarial funding methods and pension accounting standards.
- Describe the calculation of net periodic pension cost under FAS 87.
- Explain the required disclosures that an employer sponsoring a defined benefit pension plan must make as amended by FAS 132(r).
- Discuss limitations on interest rate assumptions used in calculating both the assumed rates at which the pension benefit obligations may be settled and the assumed rates for the return on plan assets.
- Summarize the major provisions of both FAS 87 and FAS 88 as amended by FAS 132.
- Summarize the major provisions of FAS 158.

Accounting procedures for pension plans consist of various components, each of which is controlled by a separate Financial Accounting Standards Board (FASB) statement. FAS Statement No. 35, *Accounting and Reporting by Defined Benefit Pension Plans* (FAS 35), establishes standards for financial accounting and reporting for the annual financial statement of a defined benefit pension plan. FAS Statement No. 87, *Employers' Accounting for Pensions* (FAS 87), establishes standards for financial reporting and accounting for an employer that offers pension benefits to its employees.[1] Closely related to FAS 87, FAS Statement No. 88, *Employers' Accounting for Settlements and Curtailment of Defined Benefit Pension Plans and for Termination Benefits* (FAS 88),

[1] In FAS parlance, pension benefits are defined as periodic (usually monthly) payments made pursuant to the terms of the pension plan to a person who has retired from employment or to that person's beneficiary.

414

establishes standards for an employer's accounting for settlement of defined benefit pension obligations, for curtailment of a defined benefit pension plan, and for termination benefits.

In February of 1998, the FASB issued Statement No. 132, *Employers' Disclosures about Pensions and Other Postretirement Benefits* (FAS 132). FAS 132 superseded the disclosure requirements in FAS Nos. 87, 88, and 106 for fiscal years beginning after December 15, 1997. FAS 132 dealt only with disclosure requirements for pensions and other postretirement benefits, but did not alter measurement and recognition procedures outlined in the earlier FAS statements. FAS 132 required organizations to disclose additional information previously not required and eliminated some disclosure requirements no longer considered to be useful.

On September 29, 2006, the FASB issued FAS 158, *Employers' Accounting for Defined Benefit Pension and Other Postretirement Benefit Plans*. This accounting standard was issued to respond to growing concerns regarding the lack of transparency in employers' accounting for pensions and other postretirement benefits. FAS 158 required employers to place the funded status of their pension and other retiree benefit plans on corporate balance sheets. Publicly traded companies were required to state the underfunded or overfunded status of their plans on financial statements at the end of fiscal years occurring after December 15, 2006. All other entities were required to report underfunded or overfunded status at the end of fiscal years occurring after June 15, 2007.

FAS 158 was the result of the completion of the first of a two-step process engaged in by the FASB to reconsider the rules governing the accounting for pensions and other postretirement benefits. The second phase of this project was expected to take some three to five years to complete and would encompass a comprehensive reexamination of all aspects of employers' accounting for their pension and other postretirement benefits.

This chapter focuses primarily on the consequences of sponsoring a single-employer pension plan on the employer's financial statements. Therefore, the major emphasis is on FAS 87[2] and 88 [as updated by FAS 132 and FAS 158(r)]. A brief discussion of the evolution of pension accounting standards is presented first, and then the FAS statements are described in detail and their impact on pension plan sponsors is analyzed.

The Evolution of Pension Accounting Standards

Although various accounting conventions were applied to pension plans prior to 1966,[3] this was an era in which the accounting profession exercised little control over pension accounting while the government exercised considerable control over pension funding. As a result, pension accounting during this time has been characterized as essentially a

---

[2] Although they are beyond the scope of this chapter, FAS 87 also contains provisions treating multiemployer plans, non–U.S. pension plans, and business combinations.

[3] For an interesting historical analysis of the evolving relationship between the employer contributions and the charge for pension expense, see E. L. Hicks and C. L. Trowbridge, *Employer Accounting for Pensions: An Analysis of the Financial Accounting Standards Board's Preliminary Views and Exposure Draft* (Burr Ridge, IL: Richard D. Irwin for the Pension Research Council, 1985), pp. 16–18.

discretionary system that typically resulted in the amount of pension expense recorded for a year being equal to the employer's pension contribution.

Since 1966, employer pension accounting has been governed by Accounting Principles Board Opinion No. 8, *Accounting for the Cost of Pension Plans* (APB 8). This pronouncement eliminated the previous discretionary method of accounting for pension costs and replaced it with a methodology that established a range of minimum and maximum annual costs based on a number of approved actuarial cost methods. For a variety of reasons, however, the appropriateness of this standard has been questioned since the passage of the Employee Retirement Income Security Act in 1974 (ERISA). In that year, the FASB added two pension projects to its agenda: one to cover accounting principles for the pension plan itself and another to cover accounting by employers for pensions.

As a result of these projects, FAS 35 and FAS Statement No. 36, *Disclosure of Pension Information* (FAS 36), were issued in 1980. FAS 35 established rules governing the measurement and reporting of plan assets and plan obligations by the plan itself. Under this pronouncement, plan assets typically must be measured at market value, while plan liabilities (both vested and nonvested) must be measured on a basis that ignores future salary progression. FAS 36, which established rules governing how the employing firm must disclose plan assets and liabilities on its financial statements, required a measurement procedure compatible with FAS 35. Although FAS 36 was heralded by some financial analysts as a significant improvement in disclosure, it was intended to serve only as a stopgap measure until the more contentious issues raised in response to the perceived limitations for APB 8 could be resolved.

FAS 87

Even with the modifications imposed by FAS 36, the APB 8 approach to pension accounting was criticized for the following reasons:

1. Pension costs were not comparable from one company to another.
2. Pension costs were not consistent from period to period for the same company.
3. Significant pension obligations and assets were not recognized in the body of the financial statements (although FAS 36 did require footnote disclosure in the balance sheet).

The board had four basic objectives in the preparation of FAS 87. The first objective was to provide a measure of pension cost that better reflects the terms of the plan and recognizes the cost of the employee's pension over his or her service with the employer. As shown in Chapter 19, many of the actuarial cost methods historically chosen for funding purposes allocated pension contributions as a percentage of payroll. Of the actuarial cost methods acceptable for minimum funding purposes, only the accrued benefit cost method determined an amount that was based directly upon benefits accrued to the valuation date. Second, the board wanted to provide a more comparable measure of pension cost. Not only were pension plan sponsors able to choose from a number of acceptable actuarial cost methods, but, prior to 1987, they were also given a degree of flexibility in choosing the amortization period for supplemental liabilities (in essence, anywhere from

10 to 30 years). Third, it desired to have disclosures that would allow users to understand the effect of the employer's undertaking. Previous pension accounting standards allowed the sponsor to record one net amount for the pension expense. It was believed that disclosure of the individual components of this amount would significantly assist users in understanding the economic events that occurred. In theory, those disclosures also would make it easier to understand why the reported amount changed from period to period, especially when a large cost was offset by a large revenue to produce a relatively small net reported amount. Finally, as mentioned earlier, there was a desire to improve reporting of financial position. This relates primarily to the inclusion of underfunded pension liabilities on the balance sheet of the sponsor.

The new accounting requirements mandated by FAS 87 were phased in with a two-step process. The income statement (expense) provisions were applied for years beginning after December 15, 1986, while the balance sheet (liability) provisions were applied for years beginning after December 15, 1988.

Scope

FAS 87 definitely excludes postretirement health care and life insurance benefits. Although these benefits were originally part of the board's project on accounting for pension benefits, it has since been spun off into a separate endeavor and is currently controlled by FAS Statement No. 106, *Employers' Accounting for Postretirement Benefits Other Than Pensions.*

Use of Reasonable Approximations

FAS 87 was intended to specify accounting objectives and results, rather than specific computational means of obtaining those results. Pension plan sponsors are allowed to use shortcuts if they will not result in material differences from the results of a detailed application.

Single-Employer Defined Benefit Pension Plans

The most significant elements of FAS 87 involve an employer's accounting for a single-employer defined benefit pension plan. After describing the basic elements of pension accounting, this section explains the recognition procedures for the net periodic pension cost and the pension liabilities and assets. Certain details concerning measurement procedures are demonstrated, and modifications to disclosure requirements are discussed. Finally, certain miscellaneous provisions are presented.

Basic Elements of Pension Accounting

It is important to note that FAS 87 did not apply to the government constraints on minimum or maximum (deductible) funding. Although the accrued benefit cost method (or projected unit credit method in FAS parlance) mandated for use in computing the net periodic pension cost was one of the acceptable actuarial cost methods under Internal Revenue Code Section 412, it is highly likely that the FAS 87 net periodic pension cost differed substantially from the ERISA funding amount. Furthermore, it is important to understand that FAS 87 incorporated two different definitions of the sponsor's pension liability. The **projected benefit obligation** is the amount used to measure pension cost and is defined as the actuarial present value of all benefits attributed by the plan's benefit formula to employee service rendered prior to that date, assuming future salary levels if the formula is based on future compensation.[4] In contrast, the **accumulated benefit obligation** was used for balance sheet recognition prior to the adoption of FAS 158. It was determined in the same manner as the projected benefit obligation but without salary assumptions. Therefore, for those plans with nonpay-related pension benefit formulas, the projected benefit obligation and the accumulated benefit obligation were the same.

FAS 132(r) eliminated the prior disclosure requirement that there be separate identification of the accumulated and vested benefit obligation components of the projected benefit obligation. FAS 132(r) also eliminated the prior requirement that portions of the accumulated benefit obligation attributable to retirees, other fully eligible participants, and other active plan participants be separately identified.

FAS 158 requires employers to place the funded status of their defined benefit pensions and other retiree benefit plan obligations on balance sheets rather than in notes to financial statements. Prior accounting standards allowed employers to delay recognition of certain changes in plan assets and obligations that affected the costs of providing such benefits. Employers previously were only required to disclose the complete funded status of their plans in the notes to financial statements. Accordingly, employers reported an asset or liability that almost always differed from the plan's funded status. The overfunded or underfunded status of a defined benefit postretirement plan is measured as the difference between the fair value of plan assets and the benefit obligation. For a pension plan, the benefit obligation would be the projected benefit obligation; for any other postretirement benefit plan, such as a retiree health care plan, the benefit obligation would be the accumulated postretirement benefit obligation. The projected benefit obligation includes estimates of employee salary increases and other costs far into the future. According to the standard, an employer reports a postretirement benefit asset for all of its plans that are overfunded and a postretirement benefit liability for all of its plans that are underfunded. The two cannot be offset against each other.

Deferred plan costs and income—such as any remaining unamortized transition obligation or asset, unrecognized losses and gains, and unrecognized prior service costs and credits—are required to be reported in **accumulated other comprehensive income (AOCI),** net of tax effects, until they are amortized. Essentially this provision of the standard recognizes as a component of other comprehensive income, net of tax, the actuarial gains and losses and the prior service costs and credits that arise during the period but, pursuant to FAS 87 and FAS 106, are not recognized as components of net periodic benefit cost as described in the next section. Amounts recognized in AOCI would then be adjusted as they are subsequently recognized as components of net periodic benefit cost pursuant to the recognition and amortization provisions of FAS 87 and FAS 106.

FAS 158 also made some other changes to the pension accounting rules. Previously, employers could report plan assets and net periodic cost at a date prior to the fiscal year-end date. This was referred to as an "early measurement date." For fiscal years ending after December 15, 2008, this practice of using an "early measurement date"

---

[4] Turnover and mortality also are assumed.

is prohibited. FAS 158 also required some additional disclosures from plan sponsors. Additional information must be supplied regarding the current and noncurrent division of the postretirement benefit liability. Also there must be additional disclosures about the deferred costs and income in AOCI and how they changed during the year and the expected amortization of those deferred amounts in the coming year's net periodic cost.

Recognition of Net Periodic Pension Cost

Under FAS 87, the net periodic pension cost is made up of six components:

1. Service cost.
2. Interest cost.
3. Actual return on plan assets, if any.
4. Amortization of unrecognized prior service cost, if any.
5. Gain or loss to the extent recognized.
6. Amortization of the unrecognized net asset or obligation existing at the date of the initial application of FAS 87.

Service cost is the actuarial present value of benefits attributed by the pension benefit formula to employee service during that period.[5] **Interest cost** is the increase in the projected benefit obligation due to the passage of time. This can be thought of as simply the accrual of interest on a present value or discounted amount. The actual return on plan assets is based on the fair value of plan assets at the beginning and the end of the period, adjusted for contributions and benefit payments.[6]

The prior service cost component for accounting purposes is conceptually similar to the amortization of supplemental liability described in Chapter 19; however, the allocation procedure does not result in a level dollar amount assigned to each year in the amortization period. Under FAS 87, the cost of retroactive benefits is the increase in the projected benefit obligation at the date of the amendment. This cost is then amortized by assigning an equal amount to each future period of service for each employee active at the date of the amendment who is expected to receive benefits under the plan. Once determined, the amortization period does not change for that amendment.

The basic notion represented by this amortization procedure can be illustrated by the following simple example. Assume that a defined benefit pension plan is amended on January 1, 2007, generating an unrecognized prior service cost of $100,000. At that time, the employer has three employees who are expected to receive benefits under the plan. Employee A is expected to leave after one year, employee B after two years, and employee C after three years. The expected years of service from this employee population in 2007 would be equal to three (one year from all three employees); in 2008 there

---

[5] There are obvious similarities between this component of net periodic pension cost under FAS 87 and the normal cost under the accrued benefit cost method described in Chapter 19.

[6] While the return is titled "actual" for disclosure purposes, FAS 87 states that the difference between the actual and expected return on plan assets must be accounted for as a part of the gain or loss component of pension expense. The net result of this treatment is that the expected return on plan assets is used to calculate pension cost for the period.

would be only two expected years of service (since employee A would already have left); and in 2009 there would be only one expected year of service. Summing these figures gives an aggregate expected years of future service of six (three from 2007, plus two from 2008, plus one from 2009).

The amortization rate for each year is determined by taking the ratio of expected years of service for that year and dividing it by the aggregate expected years of service (six). The amortization rate for the year is then multiplied by the increase in the projected benefit obligation resulting from the plan amendment to determine the amortization for the year. In this example, the 2007 amortization amount would be $100,000 \times (3 \div 6)$ = $50,000. The amount in 2008 would be $100,000 \times (2 \div 6) = \$33,333$; in 2009, the amount would be $100,000 \times (1 \div 6) = \$16,667$.

In certain cases, the amortization of prior service cost must be accelerated. A history of regular plan amendments may indicate that the period during which the employer expects to realize benefits (through employee goodwill, etc.) for an amendment is shorter than the remaining service period. This is likely to transpire in collective bargaining agreements with flat dollar plans in which the dollar amount is renegotiated upward every several years.[7]

The fifth component of net periodic pension cost (gain or loss) results from changes in either the projected benefit obligation or the plan assets. These changes result either from experience different from that assumed or from changes in assumptions. Gains and losses include both realized and unrealized gains and losses. Asset gains and losses are equal to the difference between the actual return on assets during a period and the expected return on assets for that period. The expected return on plan assets is determined from the expected long-term rate of return on plan assets and the market-related value of plan assets.[8] Amortization of unrecognized net gain or loss is included as a component of net pension cost if, at the beginning of the year, the unrecognized net gain or loss (excluding asset gains and losses not yet reflected in market-related value) exceeds a so-called corridor amount. This corridor was designed to minimize the volatility in pension expense that otherwise would result from application of the new accounting convention and is defined as 10 percent of the greater of the projected benefit obligation or the market-related value of plan assets. The amortization for the year will be equal to the amount of unrecognized gain or loss in excess of the corridor divided by the average remaining service period of active employees expected to receive benefits under the plan.

In addition to the amortization of the unrecognized net gain or loss from previous periods, the overall gain or loss component of net periodic pension cost also consists of the difference between the actual return on plan assets and the expected return on plan assets.

The final component of net periodic pension cost is the amortization of the unrecognized net asset or obligation existing at the date of initial application of FAS 87. At

---

[7] It also is possible for a plan amendment to decrease the projected benefit obligation. In that case, the reduction must be used to reduce any existing unrecognized prior service cost, and the excess, if any, must be amortized on the same basis as the cost of benefit increases.

[8] The market-related value of assets must be either fair value or a calculated value that recognizes change in fair value in a systematic and rational manner over not more than five years.

the time the plan sponsor first applies FAS 87, the projected benefit obligation and the fair market value of plan assets must be determined.[9] The difference between these two amounts is then amortized on a straight-line basis over the average remaining service period of employees expected to receive benefits under the plan. There are two exceptions to this general rule, though. First, if the average remaining service period is less than 15 years, the employer may elect to use a 15-year period. Second, if all, or almost all, of a plan's participants are inactive, the employer must use the inactive participant's average remaining life expectancy period instead.

Recognition of Liabilities and Assets Under FAS 87

Under FAS 87, a balance sheet entry is made if there is a discrepancy between net periodic pension cost and employer contributions. Specifically, a liability (unfunded accrued pension cost) is recognized if net periodic pension cost exceeds employer contributions, and an asset (prepaid pension cost) is recognized if net periodic pension cost is less than employer contributions. Moreover, a balance sheet entry is made if the firm sponsors an "underfunded" plan. If the accumulated benefit obligation is greater than plan assets, employers must recognize a liability (including unfunded accrued pension cost) equal to the unfunded accumulated benefit obligation. It should be noted, however, that the treatment is not symmetrical: FAS 87 does not permit recognition of a net asset if plan assets are greater than the accumulated benefit obligation.

If an additional liability is recognized, an equal amount is recognized on the balance sheet as an intangible asset, provided that the asset recognized does not exceed the amount of unrecognized prior service cost. In the case in which the additional liability is greater than the unrecognized prior service cost, the excess is reported as a reduction of equity, net of any tax benefits.

Measurement of Cost and Obligations

FAS 87 provides much more guidance than its predecessors with respect to the interest rate assumptions chosen by the plan sponsor. In essence, the interest rate assumption used for funding calculations actually has two separate elements in the pension accounting context. The first is the assumed discount rate, which must reflect the rates at which the pension benefit could be settled effectively. FAS 87 states that it is appropriate to consider rates used to price annuity contracts in settling the pension obligation (including the rates used by the Pension Benefit Guaranty Corporation to value the liabilities of terminating pension plans). Rates of return on high-quality, fixed-income investments currently available and expected to be available during the period to maturity of the pension benefits also may be considered.

The second assumption deals with the expected long-term rate of return on plan assets and is not necessarily equal to the discount rate assumption. FAS 87 states that this assumption must reflect the average rate of earnings expected on the funds invested or to be invested to provide for the benefits included in the projected benefit obligation.

---

[9] Technically, this amount will be increased by any previously recognized unfunded accrued pension cost and reduced by any previously recognized prepaid pension cost. These terms are defined in the next paragraph.

This will necessitate an assumption as to the rate of return available both for reinvestment and for the current assets.

Disclosures

An employer sponsoring a defined benefit pension plan must disclose the following:[10]

1. A reporting of the beginning of period and ending of period balances for the benefit obligation. This reporting must detail service cost, interest cost, actuarial gains and losses, participant contributions, benefits paid, plan amendments, and impacts of special items such as the effects of business combinations and divestitures, foreign currency exchange rate fluctuations, and any settlements, curtailments, or special termination benefits.
2. The amount of net periodic pension cost for the period, showing separately prior service cost, recognized gains and losses, any unrecognized transition obligation, and any gain or loss because of a settlement or curtailment.
3. A schedule reconciling the beginning of period and ending of period balances for the fair value of plan assets. This reporting must detail employer contributions, participant contributions, benefits paid, actual return on plan assets, effects of business combinations and divestitures, effects of foreign currency exchange rate fluctuations, and settlements.
4. A schedule reconciling the funded status of the plan with financial statement reporting. This schedule must detail any unamortized prior service cost, any unrecognized gain or loss, any unamortized net obligation or net asset existing at the initial adoption of FAS 87, the net pension prepaid asset or accrued liability, and any intangible asset and the amount of accumulated other comprehensive income.
5. The weighted-average assumed discount rate and rate of compensation increase (if applicable) used to measure the projected benefit obligation and the weighted-average expected long-term rate of return on plan assets.
6. The amount included in other comprehensive income resulting from a change in the minimum pension liability.
7. Amounts resulting from any significant transactions between the plan, the employer, and any related parties. If applicable, the amounts and types of securities of the employer and related parties included in plan assets and the approximate amount of annual benefits for employees and retirees covered by annuity contracts issued by the employer and related parties. Also, if applicable, the alternative amortization methods used to amortize prior service cost and gains or losses and the existence and nature of commitment beyond the written terms of the plan.
8. A past practice or history of regular benefit increases.
9. Amounts resulting from termination benefits.

An explanation of any changes in the benefit obligation or plan assets that is not made evident by any of the other disclosures required by FAS 87 as amended by FAS 132(r) and FAS 158.

---

[10] Requirements as amended by FAS 132(r) and FAS 158.

Employers with Two or More Plans

If an employer sponsored more than one defined benefit pension plan, all provisions of FAS 87 applied to each plan separately. Moreover, unless an employer had a right to use the assets of one plan to pay the benefits of another plan, the excess assets of an over-funded plan could not offset the additional liability for unfunded accumulated benefit obligations of another plan sponsored by the same company.

FAS 132(r) revised disclosure requirements and permitted combined disclosures for plans with assets in excess of the accumulated benefit obligation and those with accumulated benefit obligations in excess of plan assets. However, separate disclosure must be made of the benefit obligations and fair value of plan assets for plans with benefit obligations in excess of plan assets. Also, foreign plans may not be combined with U.S. plans when the benefit obligations of the foreign plans are significant relative to the total benefit obligation and those plans use significantly different plan assumptions. Also, prepaid benefit costs and accrued benefit obligations must be separately disclosed in the balance sheet.

Contracts with Insurance Companies

Benefits covered by annuity contracts are excluded from the projected benefit obligation and the accumulated benefit obligation. If the benefits are covered by nonparticipating annuity contracts, the cost of the contract determines the service cost component of net periodic pension cost for that period. If participating annuity contracts are used, the excess premium (over that available from a nonparticipating annuity contract) must be recognized as an asset and amortized systematically over the expected dividend period under the contract.

Defined Contribution Plans

Under FAS 87, the net periodic pension cost for the typical defined contribution plan is the contribution called for in that period. However, if a plan calls for contributions for periods after an individual retires or terminates, the estimated costs must be accrued during the employee's service period. An employer that sponsors one or more defined contribution plans must disclose the following separately from its defined benefit plan disclosures:

1. The nature and effect of significant matters affecting comparability of information for all periods presented. [FAS 132(r) amended this requirement for the description of the nature and effect of any significant changes during the period affecting comparability, noting such items as a change in the rate of employer contributions, a business combination, or a divestiture.]
2. The amount of cost recognized during the period.

FAS 88

FAS 88 defines one event (a settlement) that requires immediate recognition of previously unrecognized gains and losses and another event (a curtailment) that requires immediate recognition of previously unrecognized prior service cost. It also changes the method of computing gains or losses recognized on asset reversions and specifies special transition rules for companies that have undergone previous asset reversions. Companies were required to adopt FAS 87 and 88 simultaneously.

Definitions

Before discussing the mechanics behind these accounting procedures, it is important to note the board's interpretation of the following terms.

Settlement

A **settlement** is defined as a transaction that is an irrevocable action, relieves the employer of primary responsibility for a projected benefit obligation, and eliminates significant risks related to the obligation and the assets used to effect the settlement. Examples of settlements include making lump-sum cash payments to plan participants in exchange for their rights to receive specified pension benefits and purchasing non-participating annuity contracts to cover vested benefits. For an example of a transaction that would *not* qualify as a settlement, assume that a sponsor invests in a portfolio of high-quality, fixed-income securities with principal and interest payment dates similar to the estimated payment dates of benefits. Note that in this case, the decision can be reversed, and such a strategy does not relieve the employer of primary responsibility for an obligation, nor does it eliminate significant risks related to the obligation.

Annuity Contract

If the substance of a participating annuity contract is such that the employer remains subject to most of the risks and rewards associated with the obligation covered or the assets transferred to the insurance company, the purchase of the contract does not constitute a settlement.

Curtailment

A **curtailment** is an event that significantly reduces the expected years of future service of present employees or eliminates for a significant number of employees the accrual of defined benefits for some or all of their future services. Examples of a curtailment include the termination of employees' services earlier than expected (e.g., closing a facility) and termination or suspension of a plan so that employees do not earn additional defined benefits for future services.

Accounting for Settlement of the Pension Obligation

The maximum gain or loss in this case is the unrecognized net gain or loss plus any remaining unrecognized net asset existing at the date of initial application of FAS 87.[11] The entire maximum amount is recognized in earnings only if the entire projected benefit obligation is settled. However, if only part of the projected benefit obligation

---

[11] This will include any net gain or loss first measured at the time of settlement. This may happen if the insurance company uses an interest rate assumption for determining the annuity purchase price that differs from the discount rate assumed by the employer.

is settled, the employer will recognize in earnings a pro rata portion of the maximum amount equal to the percentage reduction in the projected benefit obligation.

If a participating annuity contract is purchased, the maximum gain is reduced by the cost of the participation right. Also, a provision is included to allow flexibility for employers who annually purchase annuities as a funding vehicle. If the cost of all settlements in a year is less than or equal to the sum of the service cost and interest cost components of the net periodic pension cost for the plan for the year, gain or loss recognition is permitted but not required for those settlements. However, the accounting policy adopted must be applied consistently from year to year.

Accounting for a Plan Curtailment

Under FAS 88, the unrecognized prior service cost associated with years of service no longer expected to be rendered as the result of a curtailment is treated as a loss. This includes the cost of retroactive plan amendments and any remaining unrecognized net obligation existing at the date of initial application of FAS 87.

It should be noted that the projected benefit obligation may be decreased or increased by a curtailment. To the extent that such a gain exceeds any unrecognized net loss (or the entire gain, if an unrecognized net gain exists), it is a curtailment gain. To the extent that such a loss exceeds any unrecognized net gain (or the entire loss, if any unrecognized net loss exists), it is a curtailment loss. Any remaining unrecognized net asset existing at the date of initial application of FAS 87 is treated as an unrecognized net gain and is combined with the unrecognized net gain or loss arising subsequent to transition to FAS 87.

Special Transition Rules for a Reversion

Employers that entered into a reversion before the effective date of FAS 88 must recognize a gain as the cumulative effect of a change in accounting principle at the time of initial application of FAS 87. The amount of gain recognized is the lesser of:

1. The unamortized amount related to the asset reversion.
2. Any unrecognized net asset for the plan (or the successor plan) existing at the time of transition.

Chapter Summary

- Accounting procedures for pension plans consist of various components, each of which is controlled by a separate Financial Accounting Standards Board (FASB) statement. FAS Statement No. 35, *Accounting and Reporting by Defined Benefit Pension Plans* (FAS 35), establishes standards for financial accounting and reporting for the annual financial statement of a defined benefit pension plan. FAS Statement No. 87, *Employers' Accounting for Pensions* (FAS 87), establishes standards for financial reporting and accounting for an employer that offers pension benefits to its employees. Closely related to FAS 87, FAS Statement No. 88, *Employers' Accounting for Settlements and Curtailment of Defined Benefit Pension Plans and for Termination*

Benefits (FAS 88), establishes standards for an employer's accounting for settlement of defined benefit pension obligations, for curtailment of a defined benefit pension plan, and for termination benefits.

- In February of 1998, the FASB issued Statement No. 132(r), *Employers' Disclosures About Pensions and Other Postretirement Benefits* [FAS 132(r)]. FAS 132(r) supersedes the disclosure requirements in FAS Nos. 87, 88, and 106 for fiscal years beginning after December 15, 1997. FAS 132(r) deals only with disclosure requirements for pensions and other postretirement benefits, but does not alter measurement and recognition procedures outlined in the earlier FAS statements. FAS 132(r) required organizations to disclose additional information previously not required and eliminated some disclosure requirements no longer considered to be useful.

- On September 29, 2006, the FASB issued FAS 158, *Employers' Accounting for Defined Benefit Pension and Other Postretirement Benefit Plans.* This accounting standard was issued to respond to growing concerns regarding the lack of transparency in employers' accounting for pensions and other postretirement benefits. FAS 158 required employers to place the funded status of their pension and other retiree benefit plans on corporate balance sheets.

- FAS 158 was the result of the completion of the first of a two-step process engaged in by the FASB to reconsider the rules governing the accounting for pensions and other postretirement benefits. The second phase of this project was expected to take some three to five years to complete and would encompass a comprehensive reexamination of all aspects of employers' accounting for their pension and other postretirement benefits.

- The standards board had four basic objectives in the preparation of FAS 87. The first objective was to provide a measure of pension cost that better reflects the terms of the plan and recognizes the cost of the employee's pension over his or her service with the employer. Second, the board wanted to provide a more comparable measure of pension cost. Third, it desired to have disclosures that would allow users to understand the effect of the employer's undertaking. This resulted in the disclosure of the individual component parts of net periodic pension cost. Finally, as mentioned earlier, there was a desire to improve reporting of financial position. This relates primarily to the inclusion of underfunded pension liabilities on the balance sheet of the sponsor.

- It is important to note that FAS 87 did not apply to the government constraints on minimum or maximum (deductible) funding. Although the accrued benefit cost method (or projected unit credit method in FAS parlance) mandated for use in computing the net periodic pension cost was one of the acceptable actuarial cost methods under IRC Section 412, it is highly likely that the FAS 87 net periodic pension cost differed substantially from the ERISA funding amount.

- It is important to understand that FAS 87 incorporates two different definitions of the sponsor's pension liability. The projected benefit obligation is the amount used to measure pension cost and is defined as the actuarial present value of all benefits attributed by the plan's benefit formula to employee service rendered prior to that date, assuming future salary levels if the formula is based on future compensation. In contrast, the accumulated benefit obligation was used for balance sheet recognition prior to the adoption of FAS 158. It was determined in the same manner as the projected benefit obligation but without salary assumptions. Therefore, for those plans with nonpay-related pension benefit formulas, the projected benefit obligation and the accumulated benefit obligation were the same.

- Under FAS 87, the net periodic pension cost is made up of six components: (1) service cost; (2) interest cost; (3) actual return on plan assets, if any; (4) amortization of unrecognized prior service cost, if any; (5) gain or loss to the extent recognized; and (6) amortization of the unrecognized net asset or obligation existing at the date of the initial application of FAS 87.

- Service cost is the actuarial present value of benefits attributed by the pension benefit formula to employee service during that period.

- Interest cost is the increase in the projected benefit obligation due to the passage of time. This can be thought of as simply the accrual of interest on a present value or discounted amount. The actual return on plan assets is based on the fair value of plan assets at the beginning and the end of the period, adjusted for contributions and benefit payments.

- The prior service cost component for accounting purposes is conceptually similar to the amortization of supplemental liability described in Chapter 19; however, the allocation procedure does not result in a level dollar amount assigned to each year in the amortization period. Under FAS 87, the cost of retroactive benefits is the increase in the projected benefit obligation at the date of the amendment. This cost is then amortized by assigning an equal amount to each future period of service for each employee active at the date of the amendment who is expected to receive benefits under the plan. Once determined, the amortization period does not change for that amendment.

- The fifth component of net periodic pension cost (gain or loss) results from changes in either the projected benefit obligation or plan assets. These changes result either from experience different from that assumed or from changes in assumptions. Gains and losses include both realized and unrealized gains and losses. Asset gains and losses are equal to the difference between the actual return on assets during a period and the expected return on assets for that period. The expected return on plan assets is determined from the expected long-term rate of return on plan assets and the market-related value of plan assets.

- FAS 87 provides much more guidance than its predecessors with respect to the interest rate assumptions chosen by the plan sponsor. In essence, the interest rate assumption used for funding calculations actually has two separate elements in the pension accounting context. The first is the assumed discount rate, which must reflect the rates at which the pension benefit could be settled effectively. FAS 87 states that it is appropriate to consider rates used to price annuity contracts to settle the pension obligation (including the rates used by the PBGC to value the liabilities of terminating pension plans). Rates of return on high-quality, fixed-income investments currently available and expected to be available during the period to maturity of the pension benefits also may be considered. The second assumption deals with the expected long-term rate of return on plan assets and is not necessarily equal to the discount rate assumption. FAS 87 states that this assumption must reflect the average rate of earnings expected on the funds invested or to be invested to provide for the benefits included in the projected benefit obligation. This will necessitate an assumption as to the rate of return available both for reinvestment and for the current assets.

Key Terms

accumulated benefit
  obligation, p. *418*
accumulated other
  comprehensive income
  (AOCI), p. *418*

curtailment, p. *424*
interest cost, p. *419*
projected benefit
  obligation, p. *417*

service cost, p. *419*
settlement, p. *424*

Questions for Review

1. Describe the accounting conventions used for pension plans prior to FAS 87.
2. What were the limitations of the pre-FAS 87 accounting conventions for pension plans?
3. Explain the scope of FAS 87 as subsequently amended by FAS 132.
4. Explain the difference between accumulated benefit obligation and projected benefit obligation.
5. Identify the six components of pension expense under FAS 87.
6. Under what circumstances must a pension plan sponsor recognize a pension liability on its balance sheet?
7. What types of interest rate assumptions are required under FAS 87?
8. Describe how contracts with insurance companies are handled under FAS 87.
9. Describe the FAS 88 accounting treatment for settlement of pension obligations.
10. Describe the FAS 88 accounting treatment for plan curtailments.
11. Summarize the modifications to pension accounting resulting from FAS 158.

Questions for Discussion

1. Discuss the likely impact of FAS 87 on funding levels for defined benefit pension plans.
2. Discuss the likely impact of FAS 87 on asset allocation decisions for defined benefit pension plans.
3. Assume an employer has an overfunded defined benefit pension plan and is currently considering the merits of terminating the plan and replacing it with a defined contribution pension plan. Discuss how FAS 88 might influence the employer's decision.

Resources for Further Study

Decker, William E.; and Kenneth E. Dakdduk. "Employers' Accounting for Pension Costs." In *The Handbook of Employee Benefits.* 6th ed. Jerry S. Rosenbloom, ed. New York: McGraw-Hill, 2005.

Katz, David M. "FASB Rule Puts Pensions on Balance Sheet." CFO.com, CFO Publishing Corporation (September 29, 2006).

Towers Perrin HR Services. "Adopting FAS 158—Practical Implications and Next Steps for Plan Sponsors," Towers Perrin, October 2006.

Verrekia, JulieAnn. "Employee Benefit Plan Accounting and Reporting." In *The Handbook of Employee Benefits.* 6th ed. Jerry S. Rosenbloom, ed. New York: McGraw-Hill, 2005.

http://accounting.rutgers.edu/raw/fasb—website of the Financial Accounting Standards Board (FASB).

www.aicpa.org—website of the American Institute of Certified Public Accountants.

Chapter 24

Defined Benefit Plan Investment Management

After studying this chapter you should be able to:

- Determine how the characteristics of various investments affect their suitability for use in a defined benefit pension plan.
- Understand the importance of a guideline statement for investment managers.
- Illustrate how risk-adjusted performance may be calculated.
- Identify the major classes of assets for defined benefit plans.
- Explain the process used to select an investment manager.
- Explain the relative advantages and limitations of passive and active investing.

Although the investment of pension plan assets is important in individual account plans (i.e., money purchase, profit sharing, thrift and savings, and cash or deferred arrangements [CODAs]), a fundamental difference exists between these plans and defined benefit pension plans. Namely, the investment risk is borne directly by the employees covered by individual account plans. As a result of this difference, sponsors of individual account plans typically provide participants with a choice of investment vehicles. Alternative funds provided under individual account plans generally include company stock, diversified funds, equity funds, fixed-income funds, guaranteed investment contracts (GICs), and a money market fund. These plans are discussed in some detail in Chapter 29.

By contrast, the investment risk under a defined benefit pension plan is borne almost entirely by the plan sponsor. It should be noted that active and retired employees may have at least an indirect interest in the performance of the plan assets, however. Many defined benefit pension plans grant ad hoc increases every few years to counter the effects of inflation. To the extent that these increases depend on a particular "cushion" of plan assets, the sponsor's investment performance may indeed have an impact on the participants. The participants also may have a stake in the adequacy of plan assets if a plan is terminated with unfunded liabilities.

This chapter provides a broad overview of basic investment issues. These fundamental principles of investing are relevant to both defined benefit and defined contribution plans. The chapter also explores those investment issues that are of particular importance to defined benefit plans.

Investment Policy

An investment policy prescribes an acceptable course of action to the fund's investment managers. It communicates a risk policy in that it states the degree of investment risk that the sponsor is willing to assume.

Determining Investment Objectives

In contrast to an investment policy, an investment objective is a desired result of the investment process. Before such objectives can be established, the various risk-return characteristics of the alternative investments must be recognized.

Types of Risk

Modern portfolio theory (described later in this chapter) defines *risk* in terms of the volatility of an investment (or portfolio of investments) in relation to the market. However, it is useful to consider the individual components of this aggregate concept:[1]

1. Purchasing power risk.
2. Business risk.
3. Interest rate risk.
4. Market risk.
5. Specific risk.

Purchasing power risk reflects the relationship between the nominal rate of return on an investment and the increase in the rate of inflation. **Business risk** involves the prospect that the corporation issuing the security may suffer a decline in earnings power that would adversely affect its ability to pay interest, principal, or dividends. **Interest rate risk** comprises the well-known inverse relationship between interest rates and (long-term) bond prices; that is, when interest rates increase, the value of long-term bonds falls.

The final two types of risk are usually used exclusively to explain stock price behavior. **Market risk** can be thought of as an individual stock's reaction to a change in the market. In general, most stock prices will increase if the stock market increases appreciably and decrease if the market decreases appreciably; however, the price of one stock may change half as fast as the market, on average, while another may change twice as fast. This relationship is quantified later in the chapter by a measure known as *beta*.

Obviously, market risk cannot account for the entire fluctuation of a stock's price. For example, if a biotechnology firm suddenly patents an unexpected cure for cancer, there would most likely be a rapid increase in its stock price in expectation of the future profit

---

[1] Jerome B. Cohen, Edward D. Zinbarg, and Arthur Zeikel, *Investment Analysis and Portfolio Management,* 5th ed. (Burr Ridge, IL: Richard D. Irwin, 1987), pp. 6–11.

stream. In contrast, if the product developed by this firm later resulted in a massive product liability award for which the firm was not adequately insured, the stock price would most likely fall. These factors, intrinsic to the firm, are known as **specific risks.**

Characteristics of Investments

There are four primary characteristics of pension plan investments that need to be considered:

1. Tax advantages.
2. Liquidity.
3. Stability in value.
4. Ability to preserve purchasing power.

The tax aspect of the investment is important because of the tax-exempt status of the pension fund. Because the investment income of qualified pension plans is tax-exempt, certain types of investments may not be as attractive to pension funds as they would be for other types of funds. For example, the price of municipal bonds is likely to be bid up by individual investors in the highest marginal tax rates until they reach a point where their before-tax rates of return are below those that can be realized on corporate bonds or U.S. government bonds of a similar maturity.

Liquidity refers to the ability to convert an investment to cash within a short time period with little, if any, loss in principal. This may be an important attribute for at least a portion of the pension plan assets in case the plan has to weather a short period of time when the plan sponsor is unable to make contributions (or contributions are less than the amount of the benefit payments for the year) and at the same time the securities markets are depressed. If the plan does not possess an adequate degree of liquidity, the sponsor might have to sell securities at an inopportune time, perhaps resulting in the realization of capital losses.

Stability in value is closely akin to liquidity in that it emphasizes investments with minimal fluctuations in value. Achieving maximum stability in value is not particularly difficult—one need only limit investments to U.S. Treasury bills and money market instruments. However, the opportunity cost of foregone higher investment returns in riskier assets may be prohibitive. Instead, the objective of the sponsor should be to construct a portfolio that will maximize investment income for the desired level of risk.

The ability to preserve purchasing power is important because many defined benefit pension plans attempt to provide at least a partial offset against inflation for their retirees.

Historical Returns Achieved by the Various Classes of Investments

Although there have been several empirical studies of the historical risk-return trade-off exhibited by the major classes of investments, the seminal work is that of Ibbotson and Sinquefield.[2] More recently, Ibbotson Associates Inc. has statistically analyzed an 80-year time series of the major classes of investments and found, as expected, that the

[2] Roger G. Ibbotson and Rex A. Sinquefield, *Stocks, Bonds, Bills and Inflation: Historical Returns 1926–1978* (Charlottesville, VA: The Financial Analysts Research Foundation, 1979).

riskiest investments also generated the highest yields.[3] Common stocks provided the highest annual return with small-company stocks having a compound annual growth rate of 12.6 percent and large-company stocks having a compound annual growth rate of 10.4 percent.[4] However, investors purchasing common stocks paid a price in terms of the volatility of their investment. Over the past several decades, the large-company stocks experienced one-year losses of as high as 26.47 percent (in 1974). Long-term bonds issued by the government had a significantly lower return (5.5 percent). U.S. Treasury bills were obviously the safest investment in terms of annual volatility; however, they generated a return of only 3.7 percent.

These figures cannot be viewed in isolation, and it is important to consider how they fared after the effects of inflation had been removed. According to Ibbotson during this period, the compound inflation rate was 3.0 percent, an amount that should be subtracted from the nominal rate of return to find the real rate of return produced by an investment.

Guidelines for Investment Managers

After the investment objectives have been developed, they need to be expressed in a manner that is useful to the investment manager. Often, this expression takes the form of a guideline statement. The guideline statement should cover questions such as:[5]

1. How much risk is the plan sponsor prepared to take to achieve a specific benchmark rate of return?
2. What is the time period for measurement of performance relative to objectives?
3. What is the sponsor's preference in terms of asset mix, especially as it relates to stocks?
4. What is the liability outlook for the plan and what should the fund's investment strategy be in light of this outlook?
5. What are the sponsor's cash flow or liquidity requirements?
6. How much discretion is the manager permitted regarding foreign investment, private placements, options, financial futures, and so on?

Another matter that needs to be discussed at an early stage is exactly what constitutes an acceptable level of turnover. If the sponsor has decided that extensive turnover activity does not add value to the portfolio performance, guidelines to limit this activity should be established. If the sponsor has come to the conclusion that turnover expenses should be virtually eliminated, a tactic known as passive investment should be considered.[6]

[3] Ibbotson & Associates, Inc., *Stocks, Bonds, Bills, and Inflation 2006 Yearbook*, pp. 23–28.

[4] Technically, the returns reported in this chapter are geometric average returns (sometimes referred to as compound annual returns). The figure can be obtained by multiplying (1 + rate of return) for each of the *n* years in the time series and then taking the *n*th root of the product. It should be noted that this is not the same as computing an arithmetic average, which is obtained by simply adding the rates of return for each of the *n* years in the time series and then dividing by *n*. Unless the rate of return is constant over the *n*-year time series, the geometric average will be less than the arithmetic average.

[5] Martin D. Sass, "How (Not) to Manage Your Pension Fund Manager," *FE Manual*, August 1985, pp. 38–39.

[6] See the latter part of this chapter for a more-detailed discussion of this topic.

Performance Measurement

The primary purpose of **performance measurement** is to "obtain information on which to base decisions in regard to investment objectives, portfolio strategy, and manager selection. In addition, performance measurement should improve communications with managers by creating a standard format for discussion."[7]

Effective performance measurement requires four steps:[8]

1. *Definition.*   The establishment of investment objectives and, to the extent practical, a clearly formulated portfolio strategy.
2. *Input.*   The availability of reliable and timely data. Incorrect and tardy data will render the most sophisticated system ineffective.
3. *Processing.*   The use of appropriate statistical methods to produce relevant measurements. The complex interaction of objectives, strategies, and managers' tactics cannot be understood if inappropriate statistical methods are used. A meaningful summary will make possible analysis of the investment process at the necessary depth.
4. *Output.*   The analysis of the process and results presented in a useful format. Presentation should relate realized performance to objectives and pre-established standards. Enough material should be available to understand and analyze the process. Exhibits should be designed to highlight weaknesses in the investment process and to suggest possible improvements.

Four important caveats must be kept in mind in choosing a performance measurement system:[9]

1. There is a danger that a hastily chosen system, poorly related to real needs, can rapidly degenerate into a mechanistic, pointless exercise.
2. The system should fit the investment objectives and not the reverse.
3. Measuring the process may alter it.
4. To save time and cost, it is important that overmeasurement be avoided.

Performance Measurement Methodology

Before any performance is measured, it is necessary to agree upon the correct definition for the return that is being measured. Two alternative definitions, internal rate of return and time-weighted rate of return, have been used in the investment community for more than 35 years. It is quite likely that the two rates of return will vary considerably. Therefore, it is critical that the sponsor understand the differences.

The **internal rate of return** (or dollar-weighted rate of return) is the rate that accumulates all of the cash flows of a portfolio, including all outlays, to exactly the market value of the ending balance.

---

[7] Sidney Cottle, "Pension Asset Management—Measuring Performance," *Financial Executive,* September 1981, p. 24.

[8] Ibid, p. 25.

[9] Ibid.

The internal rate of return is valuable in that it allows the sponsor to determine whether the investment is achieving the rate of return assumed for actuarial calculations; however, it is largely ineffective as a means of evaluating investment managers because it is contaminated by the effects of the timing of investments and withdrawals—a factor over which the investment manager presumably has no control. In response to this limitation of the internal rate of return approach, the Bank Administration Institute published a study in 1968 suggesting a different performance measurement technique known as the **time-weighted rate of return.** This value is computed by

> ... dividing the interval under study into subintervals whose boundaries are the dates of cash flows into and out of the fund and by computing the internal rate of return for each subinterval. The time-weighted rate of return is the [geometric] average for the rates for these subintervals, with each rate having a weight proportional to the length of time in its corresponding subinterval.[10]

Assessing Risk

Having correctly measured the time-weighted returns, it is necessary to evaluate the risk-adjusted performance of investment managers. Although some investment managers still report their performance by comparing their equity portfolio return with a common stock index (such as the Standard & Poor's 500 Stock Average) and their bond portfolio results with a bond index (such as the Lehman Brothers aggregate bond index) without any adjustment for their portfolio's risk, there is a growing realization that return cannot be meaningfully evaluated without simultaneously considering the risk of the investment. Portfolio risks are commonly measured in one or more of the following three ways:[11]

1. Total variability in absolute terms.
2. Total variability in relative terms.
3. Market-related variability.

Absolute risk can be measured in one of two ways. The most common is to compute the standard deviation of the periodic returns. Another method is to rank the returns in order over a particular period and to divide the distribution into percentiles. The range from the 25th to the 75th percentile, referred to as the semi-interquartile range in several measurement systems, is then used as a measure of the portfolio's absolute risk.

Relative risk measurements start with one of the two absolute risk measurements for the portfolio in question and then divide it by a similar measure for the market during the same time period. For example, if the absolute risk measure for an equity portfolio was its standard deviation based on quarterly returns for the last five years, the denominator for the relative risk measure might be the standard deviation of the S&P 500 based on quarterly returns for the last five years.

---

[10] *Measuring the Investment Performance of Pension Funds for the Purpose of Inter-Fund Comparison* (Park Ridge, IL: Bank Administration Institute, 1968).

[11] Cottle, "Pension Asset Management," p. 28.

For investment managers trying to secure new clientele in the lucrative pension industry, "putting your best foot forward" was a saying that took on a new meaning. Providers in the industry recognized there was a need for a level playing field where plan sponsors could compare apples to apples without fear of any hidden bruises. Instrumental in bringing about these changes was the Association of Investment Management and Research (AIMR), which formed a committee in 1987 to investigate and suggest methods for standardizing the presentation of data by investment managers. Its Performance Presentation Standards, which describe the minimum guidelines managers must follow when presenting performance to existing and potential clients, finally were implemented officially in 1992. ...

Although AIMR task force members could not make compliance with the standards mandatory, they nonetheless felt the marketplace would force investment managers to do so. To a large extent, this has happened.

According to Greenwich Associates research, more money managers are presenting their performance results according to AIMR standards. More important, an increasing number of plan sponsors are insisting that they do so ...

An ancillary benefit of AIMR's standards is that other groups have adopted their own performance-reporting standards. In particular, the Investment Management Consultants Association (IMCA) has implemented its own set of performance measurement standards based on AIMR's procedures.

Source: Steve Bergsman, "Comparing Apples to Apples." Reprinted with permission, from the December 1994 issue of *Pension Management* magazine, pp. 12–13. © Intertec Publishing Corp.

Although relative risk measurement is an improvement over absolute risk measurement in that it factors in the activity of the market over the measurement period, at present the state of the art for adjusting returns for risk is to use the **capital asset pricing model (CAPM)**.[12] The CAPM uses standard statistical techniques (simple linear regression) to analyze the relationship between the periodic returns of the portfolio and those of the market (e.g., the S&P 500). Although several modifications of the basic regression analysis exist, most applications will begin by subtracting out a risk-free rate of return (e.g., the Treasury bill rate) from both the portfolio and market returns.

For those not familiar with regression analysis, this technique can be thought of as simply plotting the periodic returns of the portfolio (on the vertical axis) against the periodic returns of the market (on the horizontal axis). A minimum number of data points are required for the statistical procedure to operate with the desired degree of

---

[12] It should be noted that this theory is based on a number of very restrictive assumptions: investors are risk-averse individuals who maximize the expected utility of their end-of-period wealth; investors make their investment decisions based on a single-period horizon; transaction costs are low enough to ignore; taxes do not affect the choice of buying one asset versus another; all individuals can borrow and lend unlimited amounts of money at a single-period riskless rate of interest; and all individuals agree on the nature of the return and risk associated with each investment. However, extensions of the CAPM have solved many of these problems.

confidence. The number of observations plotted depends upon the type of returns measured—five years of data are typically used in the case of quarterly returns, while three years of data are typically considered to be sufficient if monthly information is used. The straight line that provides the "best fit" for the observations is drawn on the graph, and two features of this line are noted. The first is the point at which the line crosses the vertical axis and zero on the horizontal axis. This is referred to as the portfolio's **alpha value** and can be thought of as the amount of return produced by the portfolio, on average, independent of the return on the market. The second feature is the slope of the line measured as the change in vertical movement per unit of change in the horizontal movement. This is referred to as the portfolio's **beta value** and represents the average return on the portfolio per 1 percent return on the market. For example, if the portfolio's beta is 1.25, then a 2 percent increase (decrease) in the market would be expected to be associated with a 2.5 percent (1.25×2) increase (decrease) in the portfolio, on average.

Assessing Performance

Once the portfolio's beta has been computed, it is possible to use the CAPM to provide a risk-adjusted measure of the portfolio's performance. The CAPM asserts that the predicted **risk-adjusted rate of return** for the portfolio (R_p) will be equal to the risk-free rate (R_f) plus a risk premium that is equal to the amount of risk, beta (β), times a market risk premium that is equal to the difference between the market rate of return (R_m) and the risk-free rate:

$$R_p = R_f + (R_m - R_f) \times \beta$$

To illustrate this concept, assume that an investment manager's portfolio has a beta of 1.25, the risk-free rate of return is 6 percent, and the market rate of return is 10 percent. If the portfolio yielded a rate of return of 11.5 percent, what would be the risk-adjusted rate of return? The answer is found by first finding the predicted risk-adjusted rate of return for the portfolio. This is accomplished by simply substituting the values in the equation above:

$$R_p = 0.06 + (0.1 - 0.06) \times 1.25 = 0.11$$

This predicted value is then subtracted from the portfolio's actual value to produce a risk-adjusted rate of return of a positive 0.5 percent ($11.5 - 11$). The risk-adjusted rate of return can be used to measure risk-adjusted performance and to compare portfolios with different risk levels developed by actual portfolio decisions.

Allocation of Fund Assets

The asset allocation decision is a process that determines the best portfolio composition among the various major types of assets (stocks, bonds, etc.). This decision takes into account the sponsor's investment objective and, as a result, reflects the level of risk desired by the sponsor.

Major Factors to Be Considered

In addition to the type of plan (i.e., defined benefit versus individual account), there are three considerations that must be assessed in setting investment objectives:

1. Characteristics of the sponsor and its industry.
2. Demographics of the workforce and maturity of the plan.
3. Possibility of plan termination.

Characteristics of the sponsor and its industry must be considered in determining policy. For example, a sponsor with thin profit margins and high labor costs in a highly cyclical industry has less tolerance for variability in pension costs than does a company with relatively large profit margins, low labor costs, and a less-cyclical earnings pattern. Whether the industry as a whole is growing, stagnant, or declining also will affect the degree of conservatism built into the investment strategy.

Demographics also are important because a rapidly growing company with a young workforce has less concern for cash flow and investment liquidity than does a company with a more mature workforce and many pensioners. A sponsor in the first category would be more likely to be able to withstand several years of capital losses on the pension plan portfolio without impeding benefit payments.[13]

The possibility of plan termination is important for companies with some risk of plant shutdown, merger, acquisition, or other corporate reorganization because the investment policy must take into account the possibility that the PBGC will take over the plan. If a plan termination occurs during a business recession and the PBGC steps in, the claim against the sponsoring company will be larger.

Classes of Assets

Retirement plan assets are estimated to be more than $6.5 trillion for the 1,000 largest U.S. plans. The largest 1,000 defined benefit and defined contribution funds held the following assets in their portfolios in 2006:[14]

Asset Category	Defined Benefit	Defined Contribution
Stocks	60.5%	57.9%
Fixed income	26.6	8.2
Cash	1.6	7.9
Real estate equity	3.9	n/a
Private equity	3.6	n/a
Stable value	n/a	13.5
Mortgages	0.3	n/a
Other	3.5	12.5

[13] This statement only considers the cash flow aspects of the plan.

[14] "The P&I 1000," *Pensions & Investments,* January 22, 2007, pp. 1, 13, 46.

The major asset classes, as well as mutual funds and financial futures, are discussed later.

Money Market Instruments

As discussed earlier, pension plans typically will have a need to retain at least a portion of their assets in vehicles that will be readily convertible to cash. The exact portion will depend on the specifics of the plan design (e.g., loan features and employees' ability to select lump-sum distributions) and the demographics of the plan participants. This portion of the portfolio should be invested in assets that have a low default risk, have a short maturity, and are readily marketable. There are five major categories of this type of investment alternative: U.S. Treasury bills and notes, federal agency issues, certificates of deposit, commercial paper, and money market mutual funds.

U.S. Treasury Bills and Notes

Treasury bills have maturities at issue ranging from 91 to 360 days, while Treasury notes have initial maturities ranging from one to five years. There is almost no default risk on these investments. In other words, the probability that either interest or principal payments will be skipped is nearly zero.

Federal Agency Issues

The Treasury is not the only federal agency to issue marketable obligations. Other agencies issue short-term obligations that range in maturity from one month to more than 10 years. These instruments typically will yield slightly more than Treasury obligations with a similar maturity.

Certificates of Deposit

These certificates are issued by commercial banks and have a fixed maturity, generally in the range of 90 days to one year. The ability to sell a certificate of deposit prior to maturity usually depends upon its denomination. If it is over $100,000, it usually can be sold in a secondary market; if it is under that amount, banks usually will assess a penalty if they buy it back early. The default risk for these certificates depends on the issuing bank, but it is usually quite small. Therefore, their yield is generally only slightly higher than similar maturities in the previous two categories.

Commercial Paper

This is typically an unsecured short-term note of a large corporation. This investment offers maturities that range up to 270 days, but the marketability is somewhat limited if an early sale is required. The default risk depends on the credit standing of the issuer, but commensurately higher yield is available.

Money Market Mutual Funds

These funds invest in the money market instruments described earlier. As a result, investors achieve a yield almost as high as that paid by the direct investments themselves and at the same time benefit from the diversification of any default risk over a much larger population of investments. In addition, these funds allow the pension plan to maintain complete liquidity with respect to this portion of its portfolio.

Bonds

The use of bonds in pension plan portfolios typically can be attributed to one of two reasons. First, if the sponsor realizes that (to a large extent) the pension plan's obligations are fixed-dollar obligations that will be paid out several years in the future, there may be a desire to purchase assets that will generate a cash flow similar to the benefit payments. This technique is referred to as dedication or immunization and is described in detail later in this chapter. Second, the investment manager may be willing to purchase assets with a longer maturity than the money market instruments described above. This assumption of interest rate risk is presumably compensated for by a higher yield than that available from shorter maturities.

Bonds are simply long-term debt claims entitling the holder to periodic interest and full repayment of principal by the issuer. For purposes of this discussion, the universe of bonds will be dichotomized into corporate bonds and government bonds.

Corporate Bonds

There are several characteristics of corporate bonds that are important to pension plan investment managers. For example, there are different degrees by which the promises of future cash flow are secured. Under a **mortgage bond,** a corporation pledges certain real assets as security for the bond. In contrast, a **debenture** is a long-term bond that is not secured by a pledge of any specific property. However, it is secured by any property not otherwise pledged.

The ability of the issuing corporation to call in the bond for redemption prior to the stated maturity date is known as a **call provision.** Although the issuer typically must pay some type of penalty (known as a *call premium*) for exercising this right, the holder of a bond with a call provision must be cognizant of the fact that the amount received (call premium plus principal) may be less than the value of the bond if the call had not been exercised. This typically will be the case in times of declining interest rates.

The marketability of corporate bonds usually is not an issue. However, if the investment manager sells them prior to the maturity date, the price received will be subject to both the business risk and interest rate risk described earlier. Investment managers also must be concerned with business risk, even if there is an intention to hold the bonds until maturity.

Government Bonds

Pension plans will limit their investments in government bonds to those that generate taxable investment income. Hence, municipal bonds are not candidates for inclusion in a pension plan portfolio. Federal government bonds are possible candidates and they are evaluated in a manner similar to corporate bonds. The major exception is that the default risk is nearly nonexistent and, as a result, the yield would be expected to be lower than that available on corporate bonds of similar maturities.

The field of government bonds has expanded to include mortgage-related securities. Government National Mortgage Association (GNMA) pass-through certificates have an interest in a pool of single-family residential mortgages that are insured by the Federal Housing Authority or the Veteran's Administration. The timely payment of principal and interest on these securities is guaranteed by the U.S. government. The Federal Home

Loan Mortgage Corporation (FHLMC) issues another mortgage-backed security, known as Freddie Mac. Although this instrument is not guaranteed by the U.S. government, it is unconditionally guaranteed by the FHLMC.

Common Stocks

Although there is no definitive manner of categorizing common stocks, it is customary to speak of them in the following terms:[15]

1. *Blue chip stocks.* These are stocks issued by major companies with long and unbroken records of earnings and dividend payments. They should appeal primarily to pension plans seeking safety and stability.
2. *Growth stocks.* These are stocks issued by companies whose sales, earnings, and share of the market are expanding faster than either the general economy or the industry average. They represent a higher risk, but the prospects for capital appreciation should produce a correspondingly higher total return. Because they pay relatively small dividends, they may not be attractive to pension plans needing cash flow.
3. *Income stocks.* These are stocks that pay higher-than-average dividend returns. They have been attractive to pension plans that purchase stock for current income.
4. *Cyclical stocks.* These are stocks issued by companies whose earnings fluctuate with and are accentuated by the business cycle.
5. *Defensive stocks.* These are stocks issued by recession-resistant companies. This may be an important consideration for pension plans that cannot afford major capital losses.
6. *Interest-sensitive stocks.* These are stocks whose prices tend to drop when interest rates rise, and vice versa.

Mutual Funds

For plans with assets too small to be handled by an investment manager, mutual funds may be the only choice other than a common trust fund. Larger plans also may choose mutual funds as a relatively inexpensive way of diversifying their portfolios.[16]

Pension plans choose mutual funds to invest in for the following reasons:[17]

1. Greater liquidity through ease of entry and exit.
2. Greater degree of diversification.
3. Easier means of portfolio specialization.
4. Daily update of holdings through Internet listings.
5. Ease of meeting asset allocation or market timing goals.
6. Ease of checking past performance through published studies and indexes.

---

[15] Jerome B. Cohen, Edward D. Zinbarg, and Arthur Zeikel, *Investment Analysis and Portfolio Management,* 5th ed. (Burr Ridge, IL: Richard D. Irwin, 1987), pp. 21–29.

[16] See the Passive versus Active Management section later in this chapter for more detail.

[17] Jay M. Dade, "Mutual Funds Today: Strength through Diversity," *Pension World,* December 1986, pp. 34–36.

Real Estate

The enormous number of real estate investments available in today's market makes a comprehensive treatment of this topic beyond the scope of this book.[18] However, certain basic characteristics of this market provide insight as to its overall place in a pension plan portfolio. First, real estate investments (particularly ownership interests) appear to offer an adequate inflation hedge under most scenarios. Second, real estate investing does not operate in the same efficient market as stocks and bonds. Instead of having several thousand individuals bidding on the price of a homogeneous asset each day, a real estate property may be on the market for months before any offer is made. A third point, closely related to the second, is the relative lack of marketability for many real estate investments. This feature alone would prevent most pension plans from investing the preponderance of their assets in real estate. A final point deals with the volatility of real estate investments. Although it is difficult to develop reliable estimates in the absence of an active market, the consensus opinion appears to be that the volatility of real estate investments has been significantly below that of common stocks.

Futures

A futures contract is an agreement to make or take delivery of a specified commodity (e.g., the S&P 500 index) at a specified date at an agreed-upon price. No money changes hands until the delivery date; however, a deposit is required that may be invested in Treasury securities in the interim. The account is settled each day. This means that if a pension plan made a contract to sell the S&P 500 in the future and the index declined that day, money would be deposited into the pension plan's account; however, money would be withdrawn from the account if the index had increased.

Although this may appear to be a highly speculative investment when viewed in isolation, many pension plans have used this technique in conjunction with an existing portfolio of equities. This may serve as a useful hedge against losses in the equity portfolio.

Selecting an Investment Manager

The process of selecting an investment manager obviously differs from sponsor to sponsor; however, the following five steps are typical of the procedure employed by many sponsors.[19]

Review Investment Firms

The first step in selecting an investment manager is to initiate a search to screen initial candidates. This procedure generally is conducted by an individual within the plan sponsor's firm, perhaps with the aid of outside consultants. Plan sponsors can obtain outside consulting services from a number of sources, including brokerage firms, actuarial and accounting organizations, and pension consulting firms.

[18] For an excellent discussion of this topic, see *Investment Policy Guidebook for Corporate Pension Plan Trustees,* Appendix A (Brookfield, WI: International Foundation of Employee Benefit Plans, 1984).

[19] Ibid., pp. 103–106.

Although many sponsors may be inclined to perform the investment firm review solely on an in-house basis, there are several potential advantages to using a consultant that should be considered. First, since the consultants have continuing exposure to the investment firms, they probably will have a better understanding of which investment firms could best serve the sponsor's objectives. Second, consultants have much more experience in the evaluation process. They are more likely to ask the investment firms pertinent investment questions, and they are less inclined to have their decisions swayed by the marketing aspects of client presentations. On a more positive side, they can pinpoint the specific information needed from investment management candidates, frame the questionnaire, and help organize the subsequent interviews. Third, consultants can help construct the initial list, so that firms may be screened efficiently without the search team having to waste time and effort.

Regardless of whether the plan sponsor is being aided by a consultant, there is an obvious need to obtain information on investment firms at this stage. Fortunately, several sources exist for this purpose. Included among these are top management and members of the board of directors, counterparts at other companies, pension fund actuaries, accountants and attorneys, specialized magazines, and senior officers of brokerage companies.

Send Detailed Questionnaires

After the original list has been reduced to a manageable size (perhaps with the aid of a consultant), a detailed questionnaire should be sent to the remaining investment firms. The questionnaire should be carefully designed to elicit specific information on several topics, including:

1. Portfolio strategies and tactics.
2. Ownership as well as employee compensation.
3. Decision-making procedures.
4. List of current clients and specific people to contact for references.
5. Names of accounts lost as well as those gained in recent years.
6. Historic performance of each class of assets managed.
7. Explanation of exactly how the firm's performance statistics have been computed.

Conduct Interviews

After the questionnaires have been reviewed and the references have been thoroughly checked, interviews should be conducted (in the presence of the sponsor's consultant, if one is used). Whether it is better to hold the initial interview at the sponsor's location or to visit the offices of candidates is debatable; however, it is argued that the latter produces a more realistic impression of the investment firm.

It is important that specific guidelines for the presentations be formulated in advance. For example, the "canned presentations" should be limited within some specific time frame. Moreover, questions should be designed to elicit specific information on:

- Research procedures.
- Decision-making routine.

- Strategies and tactics employed.
- Control disciplines.
- Transaction guidelines.
- Levels of salaries and other incentives for employees.
- Key personnel.
- Investment performance statistics and the degree of performance variation among accounts.

Final Evaluation

Before an attempt is made to analyze the information obtained from the interviews, it may be useful to review sample portfolios of the investment firms to assess whether a firm actually uses the methods described by its literature and representatives. At this time, the written questionnaires often are reviewed to check for inconsistencies with oral statements made during the interviews. Using the assembled information, the list of investment firms is condensed to a small group of finalists (i.e., less than five) and the information is given to the sponsor's top management.

The management of the sponsor will then meet with senior officers and relevant portfolio personnel of the finalist firms, and the decision regarding which firm(s) shall be retained to manage the pension assets will be made.

Postselection Activity

A substantial amount of activity remains after the decision has been made. For example, legal agreements should be reviewed, all fees and other costs should be determined, and the initiation date for performance measurement should be established.

The selection of the investment firm is not the final step in this process. Indeed, it is just the first iteration of a continuing operation. Portfolio review and evaluation using the performance measurement techniques described earlier must be performed periodically. This will be facilitated by having the mechanics of fund and reporting systems worked out as soon as possible.

Passive versus Active Management

A passive investment strategy is characterized by a broadly diversified buy-and-hold portfolio aimed at replicating the return on some broad market index at minimum cost. The costs of highly trained professionals can be minimized and the transaction costs kept relatively low due to the reduced amount of trading. In contrast, active investment strategies attempt to outperform the market either by selecting assets whose returns, on average, exceed those of the market, or by timing the movement of funds into and out of the market in an attempt to capitalize on swings in the prices of the assets.

Proponents of the passive strategy argue that as the stock market becomes increasingly efficient, it is more difficult for investment managers to consistently outperform the market. If actively managed funds do indeed encounter difficulties producing a gross rate of return superior to that of the market, it will obviously be even more difficult to produce a superior return on a net basis (after the effects of fees and transaction costs have been accounted for).

There are various degrees to which passive investing may be implemented. The two most popular forms—index funds and dedication and immunization techniques—are described next.

Index Funds

Index funds represent the ultimate form of passive investing. An equity index fund replicates a particular index such as the S&P 500 and is designed to generate a beta of 1.0 (i.e., the rate of return on the fund is expected to be equal to that of the S&P 500). These funds are based on the efficient market hypothesis (EMH), which states that the securities markets are efficient in the processing of information. In other words, the prices of securities observed at any time are based on a correct evaluation of all information available at the time.

If this hypothesis were true, the value of an investment manager's services would be far less than the current level of compensation enjoyed by these professionals. However, a number of published studies have reported contrary evidence indicating at least a lack of complete efficiency in the market. Anomalous results have been found in the so-called weekend, small-firm, and January effects.[20]

Some sponsors will use index funds as an investment for the core of their portfolio and allow active management of the remaining amount of the assets. This tactic possesses the advantage of freeing the investment managers from having to deal with the core portfolio and, instead, allowing them to focus their time on their specialty areas. Moreover, given a relative sense of security for the core investment, investment managers are able to pursue a higher-risk strategy on their subset of the plan's assets in hopes of above-average returns.

Dedication and Immunization Techniques

Another form of passive investment of pension plan assets makes use of the bond market and has been variously referred to as dedication, immunization, and contingent immunization.[21] This technique attempts to construct a bond portfolio such that its cash flow can be used to fund specific plan liabilities—for example, to pay benefits to a group of retirees.

The typical **dedication program** will start by modeling the expected schedule of liabilities under a particular subset of the plan. The benefits related to the retired population often are chosen due to the fact that the benefits are already determined (i.e., there is no uncertainty regarding career- or final-average salary) and the time horizon will be shorter than the liabilities associated with the active employee population. The model will produce a monotonically decreasing payout schedule over time, most likely reaching a negligible amount by the end of 30 years (the maximum maturity for most types of bonds). A computer program will then search for an optimal combination of

---

[20] Jeremy J. Siegel, *Stocks for the Long Run* (New York: McGraw-Hill, 1998), pp. 253–259, 260–266.

[21] Martin L. Leibowitz, "The Dedicated Bond Portfolio in Pension Funds—Part I: Motivations and Basics," *Financial Analysts Journal,* January–February 1986, pp. 68–75.

acceptable bonds that will produce a cash flow over this period to meet the liability payout schedule.

Perhaps the easiest way to visualize this is to assume that all payouts will be met through principal payments (when the bonds mature) or coupon payments. This would certainly minimize the administrative complexity of the program since, if principal and coupon payments are exactly equal to the payouts each year, there would be no need to reinvest the proceeds. However, this may not produce the optimal combination of bonds in that another combination of maturities (one that assumes some proceeds need to be reinvested for a period of time before they are used to satisfy plan liabilities) may produce a lower total cost to the sponsor. It should be realized that this is a riskier undertaking, however, since the eventual cost to the sponsor may increase if the assumed rates at which these proceeds may be reinvested prove to be too optimistic.[22]

In contrast to the cash-matching nature of dedication, an **immunization program** attempts to construct a portfolio of bonds whose market value equals the present value of the selected subset of liabilities and whose value, even if the interest rate changes, will always be at least as great as the value of the liabilities.[23] Although the feasibility of this approach may not be intuitively obvious, it depends on the capital gains on the assets offsetting the decrease in reinvestment income when interest rates fall. This balancing is accomplished through a concept known as "duration," which provides a measure of the portfolio's sensitivity to interest rate changes.[24]

As opposed to the relatively simple administrative requirements involved in a dedicated portfolio, an immunized portfolio will require subsequent rebalancing. Moreover, although immunization provides more flexibility in constructing the bond portfolio (and should therefore result in a lower cost to the sponsor), it is possible for the assumptions used in the immunization model to be violated and, as a result, the sponsor may experience a shortfall from this approach.

Largely in response to the limitations of the immunization approach, a hybrid technique known as **horizon matching** has been introduced. In essence, this approach splits the liabilities into two portions. The first portion consists of all liabilities that occur up to a certain horizon (three to five years) and is handled through a dedicated portfolio. The second portion consists of liabilities beyond the horizon and is treated through immunization. Although this tactic will give up some of the cost savings of a full immunization approach, the restructuring will mitigate the effects of failing to satisfy the assumptions of the immunization approach.[25]

[22] Other risks that may exist in either type of dedication include call vulnerability, quality, type of issue, and diversification across type and individual issues. See Leibowitz, "The Dedicated Bond Portfolio in Pension Funds—Part I," pp. 73–74.

[23] Martin L. Leibowitz, "The Dedicated Bond Portfolio in Pension Funds—Part II: Immunization, Horizon Matching and Contingent Procedures," *Financial Analysts Journal,* March–April 1986, pp. 47–57.

[24] The duration measure can be thought of as the average life of the liabilities when weighted by the present value of their respective cash flows. Technically, the duration match of assets and liabilities is not a sufficient condition for an "immunized" portfolio. In addition, certain second-order conditions must be satisfied. See Michael R. Granito, *Bond Portfolio Immunization* (Lexington, MA: Lexington Books, 1984) for more detail.

[25] Specifically, this is designed to dampen the effect of yield curve reshaping.

A major disadvantage of the immunization approaches is that the sponsor gives up the opportunity to produce additional income through active management of the bond portfolio. This is overcome, to a certain extent, through a device known as **contingent immunization.** Basically, this approach assumes the sponsor is willing to accept a minimum rate of return on the bond portfolio a percentage point or two below the current market rate. This differential provides a safety margin for the investment manager to adopt an active management strategy. If the safety margin is exhausted through market losses, the portfolio will be in a position such that it can be immunized at the minimum rate of return.

Chapter Summary

- An investment policy prescribes an acceptable course of action to the fund's investment managers. It communicates a risk policy in that it states the degree of investment risk that the sponsor is willing to assume.

- The primary purpose of performance measurement is to "obtain information on which to base decisions in regard to investment objectives, portfolio strategy, and manager selection. In addition, performance measurement should improve communications with managers by creating a standard format for discussion."

- The asset allocation decision is a process that determines the best portfolio composition among the various major types of assets (stocks, bonds, etc.). This decision takes into account the sponsor's investment objectives and, as a result, reflects the level of risk desired by the sponsor.

- A passive investment strategy is characterized by a broadly diversified buy-and-hold portfolio aimed at replicating the return on some broad market index at minimum cost. The costs of highly trained professionals can be minimized and the transaction costs kept relatively low due to the reduced amount of trading. In contrast, active investment strategies attempt to outperform the market either by selecting assets whose returns, on average, exceed those of the market, or by timing the movement of funds into and out of the market in an attempt to capitalize on swings in the prices of the assets.

- Another form of passive investment of pension plan assets makes use of the bond market and has been variously referred to as dedication, immunization, and contingent immunization. This technique attempts to construct a bond portfolio such that its cash flow can be used to fund specific plan liabilities—for example, to pay benefits to a group of retirees.

Key Terms

alpha value, p. *437*
beta value, p. *437*
business risk, p. *431*
call provision, p. *440*
capital asset pricing model (CAPM), p. *436*
contingent immunization, p. *447*
debenture, p. *440*
dedication program, p. *445*
horizon matching, p. *446*

immunization program,
   p. *446*
index funds, p. *445*
interest rate risk, p. *431*
internal rate of return,
   p. *431*

market risk, p. *431*
mortgage bond, p. *440*
performance
   measurement, p. *434*
purchasing power risk,
   p. *431*

risk-adjusted rate of
   return, p. *437*
specific risks, p. *432*
time-weighted rate of
   return, p. *435*

Questions for Review

1. Describe the major types of investment risk.
2. Describe why an investment's relative liquidity may be important to a pension plan's investment manager.
3. What have historical studies demonstrated with respect to the risk-return characteristics of the major classes of investments?
4. What types of questions should the investment manager's guideline statement cover?
5. Describe the steps involved in effective performance measurement.
6. Explain how the internal rate of return and the time-weighted rate of return are calculated.
7. Which of the two rates of return mentioned in the previous question should be used for performance measurement? Explain.
8. Explain the importance of the alpha and beta values produced by the capital asset pricing model (CAPM).
9. Explain the importance of the risk-adjusted rate of return.
10. Explain the factors that should be considered in the allocation of pension fund assets.
11. Describe the various forms of money market instruments.
12. Explain why a pension plan investment manager might invest pension assets in bonds instead of money market instruments. What are the additional risks associated with this decision?
13. What type of information should be elicited in questionnaires sent to prospective investment managers?
14. Explain why a passive investment strategy may be attractive to a pension plan sponsor.
15. Describe the basic objectives behind the use of dedication or immunization techniques for pension plan portfolios.

Questions for Discussion

1. If common stocks are assumed to produce a higher long-term rate of return than bonds, discuss why many defined benefit pension plan portfolios contain a significant percentage of bonds.

2. Discuss how the beta value produced by the capital asset pricing model could be used to construct an investment portfolio suited to the employer's objectives.
3. Discuss why performance measurement based exclusively on rate of return may lead to nonoptimal investment strategies.
4. Discuss how an employer might decide between active and passive investment strategies.

Resources for Further Study

Bodie, Zvi; P. Brett Hammond; and Olivia S. Mitchell. "New Approaches to Analyzing and Managing Retirement Risks." *Benefits Quarterly* 17, no. 4 (Fourth Quarter 2001).

Burroughs, Eugene B. "Funding Retirement Plans—Investment Objectives." In *The Handbook of Employee Benefits.* 6th ed. Jerry S. Rosenbloom, ed. New York: McGraw-Hill, 2005.

Pension & Investments Editorial Staff. "The P & I 1000." *Pension & Investments,* January 22, 2007.

Chapter 25

Tax Qualification Requirements

After studying this chapter you should be able to:

- Summarize the various requirements for a plan to be qualified under the Internal Revenue Code (IRC).
- Determine which plan participants are highly compensated employees.
- Explain the concepts of nondiversion, exclusive benefit, and plan permanency.
- Distinguish among the alternate methods that may be used to satisfy the minimum coverage tests.
- Explain the alternate methods and limitations for integrating a plan with Social Security.
- Explain the remaining tests that need to be passed in order to comply with the Section 401(a)(4) nondiscrimination requirements.

While an employer may choose to use a nonqualified approach to providing retirement benefits for certain highly paid employees, the requirements of the law are such that a qualified plan is the only tax-effective way to provide these benefits for a large group of employees. Moreover, the tax advantages provided under the Internal Revenue Code (IRC) for qualified plans are most significant—both to the employer and its employees. The principal tax advantages of such plans are as follows:

- Contributions made by the employer, within the limitations prescribed, are deductible as a business expense.
- Investment income on these contributions normally is not subject to federal income tax until paid out in the form of benefits.
- An employee is not considered to be in receipt of taxable income until benefits are distributed—even though the employee may be fully vested and even though the employee has the right to receive the amounts involved without restriction.[1]

[1] Until the year 1999 (and thereafter for individuals born before January 1, 1936), certain lump-sum distributions also may qualify for favorable tax treatment.

To obtain these tax benefits, the plan must achieve a qualified status by meeting the requirements of the IRC and appropriate regulations and rulings issued by the Internal Revenue Service (IRS). Many of these provisions are quite complex, and a detailed review of these requirements is beyond the scope of this text.[2] The purpose of this chapter and Chapter 26 is only to provide an overview of these requirements and to give the reader a sense of the general concepts involved. This chapter covers nondiscrimination requirements relating to coverage, benefits and contributions, and other rights and features. Other tax law requirements are discussed in Chapter 26.

Summary of Major Tax Law Provisions

To achieve a tax-qualified status, a plan must conform with the provisions of Section 401(a) and related sections of the IRC. The following is a brief summary of the requirements that must be met in order for a plan to be qualified under the IRC:

- The plan must be created and maintained exclusively for the benefit of employees and their beneficiaries.
- Plan assets cannot be diverted or used other than for the exclusive benefit of employees and their beneficiaries prior to the satisfaction of all plan liabilities.
- Plan coverage must not discriminate in favor of highly compensated employees.
- Defined benefit plans must cover a specified minimum number of employees.
- The plan must not discriminate in favor of highly compensated employees in terms of contributions, benefits, rights, or other features; within limits, however, a plan may integrate its benefits with those of Social Security, thus providing a measure of additional benefits for the highly compensated.
- Limits are imposed on the amount of benefits paid to an employee and/or annual additions made to his or her account, and on the amount of contributions an employee may make on a before-tax basis (elective contributions).
- Employee compensation in excess of a stipulated amount cannot be taken into account for plan purposes.
- Age and service requirements for participation in the plan cannot be more stringent than specified minimums.
- An employee's service must be determined in accordance with specific rules.
- Benefits must vest after an employee completes the prescribed period of service.
- Special vesting and benefit requirements apply to top-heavy plans—those that benefit key employees to a significant extent.
- Distributions must be made according to rules that specify the time by which payments must commence and the period over which they may be paid.
- Qualified joint and survivor annuity (QJSA) rules and qualified preretirement survivor annuity (QPSA) rules must be met for married employees.

[2] For a comprehensive discussion of nondiscrimination requirements, see James G. Durfee et al., *A Guide to the Final Nondiscrimination Requirements* (New York: Research Institute of America, January 1994).

- There are limits on the assignment or alienation of benefits other than pursuant to qualified domestic relations orders (QDROs).
- Accrued benefits, to the extent funded, must be protected in case of a plan merger or consolidation or a transfer of plan assets.
- Individual accounts must be maintained for participants under defined contribution plans.

Most of these requirements are discussed in this chapter and Chapter 26. It should be noted, however, that there are still other requirements that apply to specific types of plans—for example, profit sharing and employee stock ownership plans (ESOPs). Additional requirements also apply to plans that include cash or deferred arrangements (CODAs) and plans that include matching employer contributions or after-tax employee contributions. Requirements for these plans are discussed separately in Chapters 6 through 10.

Key Concepts

There are a number of key concepts that must be understood before proceeding to a discussion of specific qualification requirements. These involve the definitions of "compensation" and "highly compensated employees," and the concepts of "controlled groups" and "qualified separate lines of business."

Compensation

Compensation generally determines the amount of an employee's benefits or contributions under a plan. For this purpose, an employer can use any definition of compensation it chooses, provided the definition does not discriminate in favor of highly compensated employees. Thus, for example, a plan definition that uses base pay only would generally be acceptable, while a definition that is limited to base pay plus bonuses would probably be found to be discriminatory since, in most situations, only the highly paid receive bonuses.

Quite apart from what the plan might use as its definition of compensation, the IRC has specific definitions that must be used for limiting benefits and/or contributions and for nondiscrimination testing.

Section 415 Compensation

IRC Section 415 limits the amount of benefits that can be paid to an individual employee under a defined benefit plan and the annual additions that can be made to an employee's account under a defined contribution plan.[3] Limits for both types of plans are restricted to the lesser of a dollar amount or a percentage of compensation. In general, compensation used for purposes of these limits is W-2 compensation less income realized from the exercise of a nonqualified stock option or when restricted stock either becomes freely transferrable or is no longer subject to substantial risk of forfeiture, or from the sale of stock acquired under a qualified stock option or the disqualifying disposition of an

---

[3] These limits are discussed at greater length in Chapter 26.

incentive stock option. After 1997, Section 415 compensation includes salary reductions under flexible benefit plans, a qualified transportation fringe benefit plan, and elective deferrals under CODAs, simplified employee pension arrangements, savings incentive match plans for employees (SIMPLE plans), and tax-sheltered annuities.

Definition of Highly Compensated Employee

For this purpose, the IRC defines compensation as that used for Section 415 purposes inclusive of salary reductions under flexible benefit plans, a qualified transportation fringe benefit plan, and elective deferrals under CODAs, simplified employee pension plans (SEPs), savings incentive match plans for employees (SIMPLE plans), and tax-sheltered annuities. (Although these items were included in Section 415 compensation beginning in 1998, they were not previously part of this compensation definition.)

Nondiscrimination Testing

The basic **definition of compensation** used for purposes of nondiscrimination testing relates back to the Section 415 definition. An employer can select from among four definitions that are automatically deemed to meet the Section 415 definition. These four safe harbors are:

> *Traditional 415 Compensation.* This is the basic Section 415 definition described previously.

> *Modified 415 Compensation.* This is sometimes referred to as the short-list definition because it includes only some of the items included in the traditional definition. For example, deductible moving expenses are not included.

> *W-2 Wages.* This is the amount reported in Box 1 on Form W-2.

> *Wages Subject to Withholding.* This is compensation on which an employer must withhold federal income tax.

Employers may modify the four safe harbor definitions for nondiscrimination testing to include or exclude certain elements of compensation. Items that could be included for years prior to 1998 were elective deferrals under CODAs and tax-sheltered annuities and salary reductions under flexible benefits plans. Items that now may be excluded are expense reimbursements or allowances, cash or *noncash fringe benefits*, moving expenses, deferred compensation, and welfare benefits.

An employer also can use an alternative definition of compensation for nondiscrimination testing if it meets three criteria: (1) it must be reasonable; (2) it must not, by design, favor highly compensated employees; and (3) it must meet an objective nondiscrimination test. This test is satisfied if the ratio of the alternative definition of compensation to total compensation for the highly paid group does not exceed, by more than a *de minimis* amount, the same ratio for the lower-paid employees.

Highly Compensated Employee (HCE)

For years prior to 1997, the tax law contained extremely complicated provisions defining who was to be considered a **highly compensated employee (HCE)** for purposes of various nondiscrimination requirements. These provisions were greatly simplified by the

Small Business Job Protection Act of 1996. In 2007, an employee is deemed a highly compensated employee if he or she (1) is a 5 percent owner of the employer during the current or preceding year, or (2) had compensation in the preceding year of $100,000 (indexed for inflation) and (at the election of the employer) was in the top 20 percent of employees in terms of compensation for that year.

If the employer makes this election, the determination of who falls into the top 20 percent of employees is a two-step process. The first step is determining how many employees constitute 20 percent. In making this determination, employers may exclude employees who have not completed six months of service or who have not attained age 21 by year-end, and employees who normally work less than 17½ hours per week or less than six months during any year. Nonresident aliens who have no U.S.-source income also may be excluded as well as employees included in a collective bargaining agreement that does not provide for participation in the plan (but only if 90 percent or more of all employees of the company are covered under such an agreement).

The next step is identifying the specific members of the top 20 percent. To do this, the employer must subtract excludable employees (except for union employees) and then multiply the remaining number by 20 percent. The excluded employees are then added back in to determine which specific employees are in the top-paid group.

Some key points to keep in mind when determining who is an HCE include the following:

- The compensation used must meet the definition set forth in the preceding section.
- The $100,000 dollar amount is adjusted for increases in the consumer price index (CPI); after the new dollar amount is determined, it is rounded down to the next lower multiple of $5,000.
- Family aggregation rules ceased to apply when determining who was an HCE, beginning in 1997. However, family attribution rules under IRC Section 318 apply to the determination of HCEs. Lineal ascendants and descendants of an HCE (who is an HCE by way of ownership) also are considered to be HCEs.
- The determination of HCEs is made on a "controlled group" basis, as described in the following section.

Controlled Groups

The nondiscrimination requirements of the IRC could be easily circumvented if employers were given complete flexibility in splitting employees among a number of subsidiaries. For example, one subsidiary could contain all the HCEs and cover the entire group while the second subsidiary could contain the vast majority of non-highly compensated employees (NHCEs) and provide no coverage at all. If the subsidiaries could be tested separately, the plan of the subsidiary covering the HCEs would be acceptable since it would exclude no one and would provide benefits that do not discriminate within the group covered.

To eliminate this potential for abuse, the IRC provides that, for nondiscrimination purposes, employees of all corporations who are members of a controlled group of corporations are to be treated as if they were employees of a single employer.

The most common **controlled group** consists of a parent and subsidiary, where one entity owns at least 80 percent of the other entity. A second type is the brother–sister controlled group, where five or fewer "persons" (individuals, estates, or trusts) own (1) at least 80 percent of the entities being examined and (2) more than 50 percent of the entities being examined, taking into account "identical interests" only (an identical interest meaning the lowest level of ownership he or she has in the entities being examined).

Two or more entities also may be treated as a single entity if they are deemed to be an affiliated service group. However, these rules apply only to service organizations and organizations performing management functions for one organization (or a group of related organizations). The affiliated service group rules look at a combination of very low ownership interests and services between entities.

Qualified Separate Lines of Business (QSLOBs)

The controlled group rules can result in the aggregation of employee groups for qualification testing purposes that would otherwise be considered separate. However, an employer may be able to test a plan in a controlled group separately if it can show that the employees covered by the plan are in a **qualified separate line of business (QSLOB).** These rules are designed to allow employers to structure benefit programs to meet the competitive needs of separate business operations or operating units in separate geographic locations.

The QSLOB regulations issued by the IRS establish stringent requirements that make it difficult for most employers to establish separate lines for testing purposes. In brief, employers must:

- Identify their lines of business.
- Establish that the lines are separate—that is, formally organized as separate units with separate profit centers and separate profit and loss reporting, separate workforces, and separate management.
- Demonstrate that the separate lines are qualified.
- Allocate each employee to a qualified separate line.
- Test plans covering employees of separate lines: first, under the nondiscriminatory classification test on a controlled group basis, and then again under the coverage and nondiscrimination rules on a QSLOB basis.

Tax Qualification Requirements

With the foregoing concepts in mind, the following section discusses the major requirements a plan must meet if it is to achieve and maintain a tax-qualified status.

Nondiversion/Exclusive Benefit Requirements

The plan must specifically provide that it is impossible for the employer to divert or recapture contributions before the satisfaction of all plan liabilities. With certain exceptions, funds contributed must be used for the **exclusive benefit** of employees or their beneficiaries. One exception to this rule may occur at termination of a pension plan when, after all fixed and contingent obligations of the plan have been satisfied, funds remain because of "actuarial error." In this event, such excess funds may be returned to the employer. A second exception makes it possible to establish or amend a plan on a conditional basis so that employer contributions are returnable within one year from the denial of qualification if the plan is not approved by the IRS. It is also possible for an employer to make a contribution on the basis that it will be allowed as a deduction; if this is done, the contribution, to the extent disallowed, may be returned within one year from the disallowance. Further, contributions made on the basis of a mistake in fact can be returned to the employer within one year from the time they were made.

Permanency

The plan must be a **permanent** one. While the employer may reserve the right to amend or terminate the plan at any time, it is expected that the plan will be established on a permanent basis. Thus, if a plan is terminated for any reason other than business necessity within a few years after it is established, this will be considered as evidence that the plan, from its inception, was not a bona fide plan designed for the benefit of employees. This, of course, could result in adverse tax consequences.

In the profit sharing area, it is not necessary that the employer make contributions in accordance with a definite predetermined formula. However, merely making a single or an occasional contribution will not be sufficient to create a permanent and continuing plan. The regulations require that "substantial and recurring" contributions be made when a predetermined contribution formula is not used.

Nondiscrimination in Coverage

A qualified plan must meet specific nondiscriminatory requirements as to employees covered under the plan. This requirement is set forth in Section 410(b) of the IRC, and the tests required by this section often are called the "410(b)" or **coverage tests.** A plan will be considered nondiscriminatory as to coverage if it meets one of the following two tests: (1) the ratio percentage test or (2) the average benefit test.

Ratio Percentage Test

To perform this test, the employer must divide its universe of employees into two groups—HCEs and NHCEs. In doing this, certain employees may be excluded—for example, those who have not met the plan's minimum age and service requirements, certain nonresident aliens, and so forth. The percentage of HCEs benefiting under the plan is then determined by dividing the HCEs who are benefiting by the total number of HCEs in the controlled group. The same procedure is followed for NHCEs. The plan will pass the **ratio percentage test** if the percentage of NHCEs benefiting under the plan is at least 70 percent of the percentage of HCEs who so benefit.

Average Benefit Test

If a plan fails to pass the ratio percentage test, it must pass the **average benefit test.** This test has two parts: the nondiscriminatory classification test and the average benefit percentage test.

Nondiscriminatory Classification Test   To meet the **nondiscriminatory classification test,** a plan must cover a classification of employees that is reasonable and nondiscriminatory under an objective test. To be reasonable, the classification must be established under objective business criteria that identify the category of employees who benefit under the plan—for example, a classification of salaried or hourly employees only. The objective test works like the ratio percentage test described above, but it uses different percentages. The regulations specify both safe and unsafe harbors. A plan is in the safe harbor if the percentage of NHCEs who benefit is at least 50 percent of the percentage of HCEs who benefit. A plan is in the unsafe harbor if the percentage of NHCEs who benefit is 40 percent or less of the percentage of HCEs who benefit. A plan that lies somewhere in between will be subject to a facts and circumstances test. Both the safe and unsafe harbor percentages are reduced if NHCEs make up more than 60 percent of the employer's workforce. The safe and unsafe harbor percentages are shown in Table 25.1. To select the safe and unsafe harbor percentages, first compute the NHCE concentration percentage by dividing the number of NHCEs by the total number of employees.

TABLE 25.1   Safe Harbor and Unsafe Harbor Percentages

NHCE Concentration Percentage	Safe Harbor Percentage	Unsafe Harbor Percentage	NHCE Concentration Percentage	Safe Harbor Percentage	Unsafe Harbor Percentage
0–60	50.00	40.00	80	35.00	25.00
61	49.25	39.25	81	34.25	24.25
62	48.50	38.50	82	33.50	23.50
63	47.75	37.75	83	32.75	22.75
64	47.00	37.00	84	32.00	22.00
65	46.25	36.25	85	31.25	21.25
66	45.50	35.50	86	30.50	20.50
67	44.75	34.75	87	29.75	20.00
68	44.00	34.00	88	29.00	20.00
69	43.25	33.25	89	28.25	20.00
70	42.50	32.50	90	27.50	20.00
71	41.75	31.75	91	26.75	20.00
72	41.00	31.00	92	26.00	20.00
73	40.25	30.25	93	25.25	20.00
74	39.50	29.50	94	24.50	20.00
75	38.75	28.75	95	23.75	20.00
76	38.00	28.00	96	23.00	20.00
77	37.25	27.25	97	22.25	20.00
78	36.50	26.50	98	21.50	20.00
79	35.75	25.75	99	20.75	20.00

Average Benefit Percentage Test   Once a plan has satisfied the classification test, it then must satisfy the **average benefit percentage (ABP) test.** This part of the average benefit test is satisfied if the average benefit percentage (ABP) for NHCEs (determined as described below) is at least 70 percent of the ABP for HCEs. To perform this test, the employer must determine a benefit percentage for each nonunion employee, and all qualified plans—including 401(k) plans and ESOPs—must be tested together.[4] Also, only employer-provided benefits are tested. In simple terms, the ABP test works as follows:

1. The employer determines an annual contribution or accrual rate for each employee covered under the plan.
2. This rate is then divided by the employee's compensation to determine a percentage.
3. If the plan is integrated with Social Security, the percentage so determined may be increased by an amount representing the employer-provided portion of Social Security. The resulting percentage is added to the percentage for plans that cannot be integrated with Social Security (for example, CODAs and ESOPs), and the result is the benefit percentage for each employee.
4. These percentages are then averaged for both HCEs and NHCEs to determine whether the average benefit percentage for NHCEs is at least 70 percent of the ABP for HCEs.

ABP calculations are performed under each of three tests: contribution rate, annual benefit basis, and accrued-to-date basis. All tests are performed with and without permitted disparity; a plan need only pass one of these tests.

Other Provisions of the Coverage Test

The coverage requirements must be satisfied on each day of the calendar year. However, a quarterly testing option is available, taking into account individuals who are employees on the day being tested. An annual testing option also is available, but this requires taking into account all individuals who are or were employees at any time during the year.[5] Annual testing is the most common due to the expense of more frequent testing options.

NHCEs are not affected when a plan fails to meet the coverage test. HCEs, however, will be taxed on the present value of vested employer-derived benefits and on income earned on any contributions, to the extent that such amounts have not been previously taxed. In practice, however, the plan document often will contain a "fail-safe" provision to bring employees into the plan in order to pass the ratio test. Alternatively, a preliminary test will be performed *before* the contribution level is finalized to ensure the plan will pass coverage testing.

Minimum Participation Test

In addition to passing the general coverage test, a defined benefit plan also must benefit at least 50 employees or, in companies with fewer employees, the greater of 40 percent

---

[4] Plans covering union employees are deemed to satisfy the coverage requirements and are thus excluded when performing this test.

[5] Employers must use the annual testing option when testing a plan subject to Sections 401(k) and 401(m) and when performing the average benefit test.

of all employees of the employer or two employees (one employee if the employer has only one employee). As with the general coverage tests, certain employees may be excluded when performing this **minimum participation test**—those who have not met the plan's minimum age and service requirements, nonresident aliens, and so forth. Beginning in 1997, this test no longer applied to defined contribution plans.

Nondiscrimination in Benefits or Contributions

A plan cannot be qualified if it provides benefits or contributions in amounts that discriminate in favor of HCEs. Further, every optional form of benefit, subsidy, or other right or feature under the plan must be available to a nondiscriminatory group of employees. These requirements are found in Section 401(a)(4) of the IRC. Only nonelective contributions are tested under 401(a)(4).

Amount Testing

The regulations provide a limited number of **safe harbors**—formulas that allow a plan to qualify under the amount test without detailed numerical testing. Plans that do not meet a safe harbor must proceed to numerical participant-by-participant testing.

If a plan must be tested numerically, it can be tested on either a benefits or a contributions basis. If a safe harbor is to be used, however, this choice is not available; a defined contribution plan must use a defined contribution safe harbor, and a defined benefit plan must use a defined benefit safe harbor.[6] A plan using a nondiscriminatory definition of compensation that satisfies the integration rules (discussed later in this chapter) will almost invariably meet one of the safe harbor rules.

Defined Contribution Safe Harbors   The reader is reminded to distinguish between Section 401(a)(4) testing and the actual deferral percentage (ADP) test described in Chapter 8. The 401(k) deferrals and matching contributions are never tested under 401(a)(4). By way of review, under the ADP test, the portion of a plan that consists of a CODA is considered to be nondiscriminatory with respect to contribution amounts if it satisfies the actual deferral percentage (ADP) test under Section 401(k) of the IRC. In addition, the portion of a plan that represents after-tax employee contributions and matching employer contributions not used in passing the ADP test is considered to be nondiscriminatory if it satisfies the actual contribution percentage (ACP) test of Section 401(m). Beginning in 1999, safe harbors were available with respect to the ADP test and the ACP test in regard to matching employer contributions.[7] The Pension Protection Act of 2006 instituted a provision whereby a 401(k) plan that contains an automatic enrollment feature and conforms to certain other requirements will satisfy the nondiscrimination rules for deferrals and matching contributions and will not be subject to the top-heavy rules described in Chapter 26.

Other defined contribution plans are deemed to provide nondiscriminatory contributions if they meet one of two design-based safe harbors: (1) a uniform formula or (2) an age- or service-weighted formula.

---

[6] Exceptions to this rule are provided for hybrid plans. For example, cash balance plans may be tested on a contributions basis and target benefit plans may be tested on a benefits basis, if certain rules are met.

[7] A detailed description of these tests and safe harbors is set forth in Chapter 8.

A uniform formula is one that allocates contributions using the same percentage of compensation, the same dollar amount, or the same dollar amount per uniform unit of service (not to exceed one week) for every participant. If forfeitures are reallocated among participants, they must be allocated under the same formula. The permitted disparity allowed under the integration regulations may be ignored in determining whether a plan meets this safe harbor.

The safe harbor for plans that use age or service weighting is not really a *safe* harbor—rather, it is closer to a simplified numerical test. Employee-by-employee calculations are required, but testing is performed on an averaging basis. To meet this safe harbor, the plan formula must allocate contributions (and forfeitures, if applicable) based on the relative number of points credited to a participant. Points must be provided on a uniform basis for age or service or both. In addition, points may (but need not) be provided for units of compensation. The unit of compensation used must be a single dollar amount not exceeding $200. Also, the average allocation rate for HCEs must not exceed the average for NHCEs. This safe harbor is *not* available for integrated plans.

Defined Benefit Safe Harbors   There are three safe harbors for defined benefit plans. To qualify for safe harbor treatment, however, a plan must meet some general uniformity requirements. These requirements are as follows:

1. All safe harbor defined benefit plans must provide a uniform normal retirement benefit—that is, the annual benefit under the plan must be the same percentage of annual compensation or the same dollar amount (unrelated to compensation) for all participants with the same number of years of service at normal retirement age. The permitted disparity allowed under integration regulations may be ignored for this purpose.

2. A uniform normal retirement age must apply to all participants under the plan.

3. The plan also must provide uniform post-normal retirement benefits—that is, the annual benefit for a post-normal-retirement-age employee with a given number of years of service must be the same dollar amount or percentage of average annual compensation as would be payable at normal retirement age to an employee with the same number of years of service.

4. Each subsidized optional form of benefit under the plan must be currently available to essentially all participants.

5. A safe harbor plan that bases benefits on compensation must generally use average annual compensation—averaged over a period of at least three consecutive 12-month periods—and this average must be the highest average determined with respect to the employee's compensation history. The "consecutive" requirement does not apply to a nonintegrated plan that uses nonconsecutive pay in determining benefits.

6. A plan must use the same definition of years of service for purposes of applying the benefit formula and meeting backloading requirements.[8]

In addition to the defined contribution and defined benefit safe harbors described above, there is a unit credit safe harbor, a fractional accrual rule safe harbor, and a safe harbor for certain insurance contract plans.

[8] See the discussion of backloading requirements in Chapter 26.

Unit Credit Safe Harbor   A unit credit safe harbor plan is one under which an employee's accrued benefit is determined by multiplying the benefit formula by the years of service and, if applicable, an employee's compensation. All employees with the same number of years of service will have an accrued benefit that is the same percentage of compensation or the same dollar amount. The plan must satisfy the 133⅓ percent rule in meeting the backloading requirements.

Fractional Accrual Rule Safe Harbor   A unit credit plan that uses the fractional accrual rule to meet the backloading requirements can meet this safe harbor if no employee accrues normal retirement benefits at a rate that is more than 133⅓ percent of the rate of any other actual or potential employee, ignoring employees with more than 33 years of projected service at normal retirement age. All participants with the same entry age and the same number of years of service as of any plan year must have an accrued benefit at normal retirement age that is the same percentage of compensation or the same dollar amount.

Insurance Contract Safe Harbor   Plans funded exclusively through the use of insurance contracts are provided with a safe harbor if the benefit formula does not recognize service before an employee commences participation.[9] The plan's benefit formula must satisfy the fractional accrual rule safe harbor. Scheduled premiums must be paid as level annual payments to normal retirement age; premiums after normal retirement age must equal the amount necessary to fund the additional benefits that accrue each year under the plan's formula.

The General Test

A plan that does not meet one of the safe harbors must use the general test to determine whether it is discriminatory as to the amount of contributions or benefits it provides. The general test is structurally like the ABP test in IRC Section 410(b) except only nonelective contributions/allocations are used, and this testing is conducted within rate groups. This is one of the more complicated areas of nondiscrimination testing, and the following discussion provides only highlights of the general concepts involved.

The basic goal of the general test is to ensure that, at each benefit level, employees at that level and above constitute a nondiscriminatory coverage group. This test can be done on either a benefits or a contributions basis, at the employer's discretion. Thus, for example, a defined contribution plan can be tested on the basis of the benefits provided, rather than the contributions allocated to employees, and vice versa.

The first step in testing is to determine an accrual rate (or allocation rate if testing is done on a contribution basis) for each individual covered under the plan. After accrual or allocation rates have been established, they are tested against the general nondiscrimination rule. A plan meets this general rule if, for every possible grouping of accrual or allocation rates in the plan, all participants in that grouping or above constitute a nondiscriminatory group under the 410(b) coverage rules.

This grouping of employees is accomplished through the concept of rate groups. A **rate group** for defined benefit testing consists of a highly compensated employee and all employees (highly compensated or not) who have both "normal" and "most valuable" accrual rates equal to or higher than that employee. The normal accrual rate is based

[9] This restriction does not apply if the plan was in effect on September 19, 1991.

on the accrued benefit—that is, the benefit accrued at any point in time, payable as of normal retirement age. The most valuable accrual rate is determined based on the qualified joint and survivor annuity that may be paid at any time under the plan, which, in turn, depends on the accrued benefit. Qualified Social Security supplements that meet accrual, vesting, and joint and survivor rules also are taken into account.

Defined contribution testing groups are formed only using normal allocation or accrual rates. For a defined contribution plan, a rate group consists of an HCE and every other HCE and NHCE that have rates equal to or exceeding the HCE's rate that created the rate group.

If you apply the discretionary 5 percent rule while testing, then employees are placed in rate groups that are determined in bands. The range of each band may not be wider than either (1) 0.05 of a percentage point above or below a midpoint or (2) from 95 to 105 percent of a midpoint for normal accrual rates or 85 to 115 percent for most-valuable accrual rates. All employees within the band are treated as having identical accrual rates.

The general rule states that a plan qualifies if, and only if, every rate group constitutes a nondiscriminatory group under the 410(b) coverage rules.

Other Rights, Options, and Features

The second part of the Section 401(a)(4) test applies to all optional forms of benefits, ancillary benefits, and all other rights and features and requires that these be offered to employees on a nondiscriminatory basis. To meet this test, each benefit, right, or feature must be "currently available" and "effectively available" to a nondiscriminatory group of employees. Actual use of benefits, rights, and features is irrelevant.

Benefits, rights, or features must be currently available to a group of employees that need satisfy only the nondiscriminatory classification test under Section 410(b). It is not necessary that the plan satisfy the ABP test for this purpose; the employer may rely on the nondiscriminatory classification test even if the plan otherwise meets the coverage requirements under the 70 percent ratio test. Generally, age and service conditions may be disregarded for optional forms of benefit; they may not be disregarded in the cases of ancillary benefits or other rights and features. Employers also may ignore certain other conditions, including the attainment of a certain vesting percentage; termination of employment; death; satisfaction of (or failure to satisfy) a specified health condition; disability; hardship; family status; default on a plan loan; execution of a covenant not to compete; application for benefits or election of a benefit form; the application for benefits and other administrative or mechanical acts; absences from service; and the execution of a waiver under the Age Discrimination in Employment Act (ADEA) or other federal or state law.

The effectively available requirement is applied on the basis of all the facts and circumstances. This provision is intended to thwart abusive situations where it is predominantly the highly paid who meet the criteria for a benefit, right, or feature that is nominally available to all participants. This does not require, however, that those who actually use the benefit, right, or feature constitute a nondiscriminatory group.

Integration Rules

The tax law in effect allows a limited form of discrimination by permitting employers to provide additional contributions or benefits for higher-paid employees under a qualified plan so as to compensate for the fact that the relative value of Social Security decreases as pay levels go up. The extent to which additional benefits can be provided for the highly paid is limited by the integration rules of Section 401(l) of the IRC and the general nondiscrimination requirements of Section 401(a)(4). The basic concept of these limitations is that benefits from the employer's plan must be dovetailed with Social Security benefits in a manner such that employees earning above the Social Security taxable wage base will not receive combined benefits under both programs that are proportionately greater than the combined benefits for employees earning under this amount.

Later in this section, an overview of the integration rules is presented. Before beginning this overview, however, the following should be noted:

- An employee stock ownership plan cannot be integrated.
- The CODA portion of a plan cannot be integrated.
- Total integration is available only once. For example, if an employer has a defined benefit plan that takes Social Security benefits into account to the fullest extent permitted by law, it has no more capacity to integrate a defined contribution plan covering the same employees.
- A plan that does not meet the integration rules set forth in Section 401(l) (which are discussed later) may still achieve a qualified status if it can meet the general nondiscrimination tests of Section 401(a)(4); in a sense, the integration rules of Section 401(l) are safe harbors for compliance purposes.

It also will be helpful, before discussing the integration rules, to define some terms that will be used:

- **Excess plan.** This type of integrated plan is one where a higher level of contribution or benefit is provided for a certain level of compensation than is provided for compensation below that level. Both defined benefit and defined contribution plans can be established on an **excess plan** basis.
- **Offset plan.** This type of plan subtracts, or offsets, some amount from a gross plan benefit. Only defined benefit plans use the **offset plan** approach.
- **Social Security taxable wage base.** This is the amount of compensation on which both the employer and the employees pay taxes for old-age, disability, and survivor benefits under the Federal Insurance Contributions Act (FICA). This amount is adjusted annually for changes in the CPI; for 2007, it was $97,500.
- **Integration level.** This is the dollar amount of compensation specified in an excess plan that is the breakpoint at which the contribution or accrual rate is increased. For example, in a plan that provides for a contribution of 5 percent of pay up to $20,000 of compensation plus 8 percent of pay over this amount, $20,000 is the plan's integration level. In general, a plan's **integration level** may be any amount up to the Social Security taxable wage base.
- **Covered compensation.** This is the average (without indexing) of the Social Security taxable wage base amounts in effect for an employee for each year during the 35-year period that ends with the year in which his or her Social Security full benefit retirement age is attained.

The following sections first discuss the integration rules for defined contribution plans and then those that apply to defined benefit plans.

Defined Contribution Plans

When a plan's integration level equals the Social Security taxable wage base, the contribution percentage for pay above this amount (the excess percentage) may exceed the contribution percentage for pay below this amount (the base percentage) by the lesser of (1) 5.7 percent and (2) the percentage applicable to pay below the integration level. This rule also can be stated as follows:

- When the base percentage is equal to or less than 5.7 percent, the excess percentage cannot be more than twice the base percentage.
- When the base percentage is more than 5.7 percent, the excess percentage cannot be more than the base percentage plus 5.7 percent.

The amount of additional percentage contribution permitted under this rule is called the **permitted disparity.**

This rule applies only if the plan's integration level is set either at the Social Security taxable wage base or at or below an amount equal to 20 percent of the Social Security taxable wage base ($19,500 for 2007). If the integration level falls between these two amounts, the 5.7 percent standard in determining the plan's permitted disparity is reduced. If the plan's integration level is more than 80 percent of the Social Security taxable wage base, it is reduced to 5.4 percent; if the integration level falls between 20 percent and 80 percent of the wage base, it is reduced to 4.3 percent.

Defined Benefit Plans

Excess Plans The integration rules for defined benefit excess plans work in much the same fashion as they do for defined contribution plans. If the plan's integration level is set at or below covered compensation, the benefit accrual percentage for pay above the integration level—the permitted disparity—is the lesser of (1) 0.75 percent or (2) the benefit accrual percentage applicable to pay below the integration level. Again, the rule for determining a plan's permitted disparity can be restated as follows:

- When the base percentage is equal to or less than 0.75 percent, the excess percentage cannot be more than twice the base percentage.
- When the base percentage is more than 0.75 percent, the excess percentage cannot be more than the base percentage plus 0.75 percent.

Offset Plans The rules for offset plans are mathematically equivalent to those that apply to excess plans. These rules establish the maximum offset allowance that may be used as the lesser of (1) 0.75 percent or (2) 50 percent of the gross benefit accrual percentage, multiplied by a fraction (not to exceed one) equal to the employee's average annual compensation divided by the employee's final average compensation up to the offset level. To understand this rule, three terms need to be defined: (1) an employee's "average annual compensation" is based on an averaging period of at least three consecutive years during a period that ends with the current year; (2) an employee's "final average compensation" is calculated as an average over the last three years of service; and (3) the plan's "offset level" is covered compensation.

Other Rules for Defined Benefit Plans   There are additional requirements for defined benefit plans that do not apply to defined contribution plans. For example, the 0.75 percent factor must be reduced if the plan's integration or offset level exceeds covered compensation; it also must be reduced for benefits payable prior to the employee's having attained age 62.[10] Further, the disparity between percentages must be uniform for all participants with the same years of service.

There is an aggregate maximum on the use of permitted disparities for employees. This is accomplished by determining an annual permitted disparity fraction for each employee. This fraction is the ratio of the plan's actual disparity to its maximum allowance. The cumulative disparity fraction is equal to the sum of the total annual disparity fractions for each year of service over an employee's entire career and may not exceed 35.

Chapter Summary

- A qualified plan is the only tax-effective way to provide benefits for a large group of employees. The tax advantages provided under the Internal Revenue Code (IRC) for qualified plans are most significant—both to an employer and to its employees. The principal tax advantages of such plans are as follows:
  - Contributions made by the employer, within the limitations prescribed, are deductible as a business expense.
  - Investment income on these contributions normally is not subject to federal income tax until paid in the form of benefits.
  - An employee is not considered to be in receipt of taxable income until benefits are distributed—even though the employee may be fully vested and even though the employee has the right to receive the amounts involved without restriction.
- An employer can use any definition of compensation it chooses, provided the definition does not discriminate in favor of highly compensated employees (HCEs). Despite what the plan might use as its definition of compensation, however, the IRC has specific definitions that must be used for limiting benefits and/or contributions and for nondiscrimination testing.
- In 2007, an employee is a highly compensated employee if he or she (1) is a 5 percent owner of the employer during the current or preceding year or (2) had compensation in the preceding year of $100,000 (indexed for inflation) and (at the election of the employer) was in the top 20 percent of employees in terms of compensation for that year.
- One of the most important requirements of a qualified plan is that it must be for the exclusive benefit of employees or their beneficiaries. A plan cannot be structured so that it discriminates in any fashion in favor of highly compensated employees.
- A qualified plan must meet specific nondiscriminatory requirements as to employees covered under the plan. This requirement is set forth in Section 410(b) of the IRC,

[10] It also may be increased for benefits that commence after the employee's Social Security full benefit retirement age.

and the tests required by this section often are called the 410(b) or coverage tests. A plan will be considered nondiscriminatory as to coverage if it meets one of the following two tests: (1) the ratio percentage test or (2) the average benefit test.

• In addition to passing the general coverage test, a defined benefit plan also must benefit at least 50 employees or, in companies with fewer employees, the greater of 40 percent of all employees of the employer or two employees (one employee if the employer has only one employee). Beginning in 1997, this test no longer applied to defined contribution plans.

• If an employer is treated as operating qualified separate lines of business, the minimum coverage requirements (including the nondiscrimination requirements) and the minimum participation requirements may be applied separately with respect to the employees of each qualified separate line of business.

• Section 401(a)(4) of the IRC requires that a plan cannot be qualified if it provides benefits or contributions in amounts that discriminate in favor of HCEs. Further, every optional form of benefit, subsidy, or other right or feature under the plan must be available to a nondiscriminatory group of employees.

• The tax law in effect allows a limited form of discrimination by permitting employers to provide additional contributions or benefits for higher paid employees under a qualified plan so as to compensate for the fact that the relative value of Social Security decreases as pay levels go up. The basic concept of integration with Social Security is that benefits from the employer's plan must be dovetailed with Social Security benefits in a manner such that employees earning above the Social Security taxable wage base will not receive combined benefits under both programs that are proportionately greater than the combined benefits for employees earning under this amount.

Key Terms

average benefit percentage (ABP) test, p. *458*
average benefit test, p. *456*
controlled group, p. *454*
coverage tests, p. *456*
definition of compensation, p. *453*
excess plan, p. *463*
exclusive benefit (requirements), p. *455*

highly compensated employee (HCE), p. *453*
integration level, p. *463*
minimum participation test, p. *459*
nondiscriminatory classification test, p. *456*
offset plan, p. *463*

permanent (plan), p. *456*
permitted disparity, p. *464*
qualified separate line of business (QSLOB), p. *455*
rate group, p. *461*
ratio percentage test, p. *456*
safe harbors, p. *459*

Questions for Review

1. Summarize the major tax law provisions necessary for a retirement plan to qualify under the Internal Revenue Code.

2. Who is a highly compensated employee? Explain.

3. Describe when common ownership results in a controlled group of corporations or businesses.

4. Explain the importance of a qualified separate line of business in testing for plan qualification.

5. How does a profit sharing plan demonstrate compliance with the requirement for plan permanency?

6. Explain the minimum participation requirements.

7. Describe the ways a plan administrator can demonstrate that a plan is nondiscriminatory in coverage.

8. Explain the alternate approaches in demonstrating that a plan is nondiscriminatory in benefits or contributions.

9. Are employers allowed to adopt any definition of compensation for purposes of defining benefits and/or contributions for a qualified retirement plan? Explain.

10. What is meant by integration with Social Security?

11. Explain the difference between an excess plan and an offset plan.

Questions for Discussion

1. Explain why it is important to identify the highly compensated employees for purposes of pension plan qualification.

2. What plan design recommendations would you make to an employer initially designing a pension or profit sharing plan who seeks simplicity in meeting nondiscrimination testing requirements as an administrative objective?

3. Explain the economic rationale behind permitting employers to integrate retirement plans with Social Security.

Resources for Further Study

Allen, Everett T., Jr.; and Dennis F. Mahoney. "Retirement Plan Design." *The Handbook of Employee Benefits.* 6th ed. Jerry S. Rosenbloom, ed. New York: McGraw-Hill, 2005.

CCH Editorial Staff. "Legislation 2006: Pension Protection Act of 2006: Law, Explanation, and Analysis." *Commerce Clearing House* (2006).

Donovan, Kevin J. "Proposed New Comparability Regulations Add More Complexity." *Journal of Pension Benefits* 8, no. 2 (Winter 2001).

Durfee, James G.; Russell E. Hall; Christian L. Lindgren; Frances G. Sieller; and John F. Woyke. *A Guide to the Final Nondiscrimination Requirements.* New York: Research Institute of America, January 1994.

26

Tax Qualification Requirements (Continued)

After studying this chapter you should be able to:

- Summarize the requirements for determining and counting service for plan qualification purposes.
- Describe the minimum vesting standards set by law.
- Explain the significance of the Section 401(a)(17) compensation cap for both defined contribution and defined benefit plans.
- Determine how much a company may contribute to a defined contribution plan on behalf of a participant.
- Determine the maximum annual retirement benefit that a defined benefit plan may provide.
- Explain the legal rights that spouses have to qualified plan benefits.
- Describe the special qualification requirements that apply to top-heavy plans.

There are many requirements, other than those relating to coverage, contributions, and benefits, that a plan must meet if it is to achieve a qualified status under the Internal Revenue Code (IRC). These additional requirements are discussed in this chapter.

Determination of Service

The law establishes specific requirements for the determination of an employee's service in three key areas: (1) initial eligibility to participate, (2) vesting, and (3) the right to a benefit accrual. The law does not mandate how service is to be determined for other purposes (e.g., the right to retire early). Any method chosen for these other purposes, however, must not discriminate in favor of highly compensated employees (HCEs).

The basic concept of the law is that an employee must be given credit for a year of service for any "computation period" during which the employee is credited with 1,000 hours of service. A **computation period** is a 12-month period and may be established as a plan year, calendar year, or employment year; however, for eligibility service, the initial 12-month period must begin with the date of employment. The employee also must be given a ratable benefit accrual, if participation has commenced, for any computation period in which he or she is credited with at least 1,000 hours of service.

If an employee is credited with fewer than 1,000 hours of service within a computation period, credit need not be given for a year of service and the employee need not be given any benefit accrual for the period in question. However, if the employee has been credited with at least 501 hours of service in the computation period, this will prevent the employee from incurring a **break-in-service.** Whether the employee has incurred a break-in-service is significant in terms of eligibility and vesting of benefits.

Additional requirements for the determination of service are as follows:

- Service must be determined on a controlled-group basis.
- Service with a predecessor company must be taken into account for eligibility and vesting purposes if the employer maintains the plan of the predecessor. If the employer maintains a plan that is not the plan of the predecessor, service with the predecessor will have to be determined to the extent prescribed in regulations.
- Although an employee's initial computation period for determining eligibility service must begin with his or her employment date, the employer can convert to using another type of computation period after the first 12 months of employment, provided the beginning of the new computation period overlaps with the first employment year.
- Certain service may be excluded for vesting purposes—for example, service prior to the year in which the employee attains age 18, service for any period during which the employee did not elect to contribute under a plan requiring employee contributions, and service prior to the adoption of the plan.
- Years of service before a break-in-service also may be excluded but only if the number of consecutive one-year breaks in service equal or exceed the greater of (1) five or (2) the number of prebreak years of service, and the participant did not have any nonforfeitable right to any part of his or her accrued benefit attributable to employer contributions. Thus, pre- and postbreak service will be aggregated if the employee had any degree of vesting in employer-provided benefits or if his or her break-in-service was shorter than five years.
- A special rule for maternity or paternity absences exists. This rule applies to an individual who is absent from work by reason of the pregnancy of the individual, the birth of a child of the individual, the placement of a child with an individual in connection with adoption, or for purposes of caring for such a child for a period beginning immediately following birth or placement. The law requires that, for purposes of determining whether a one-year break-in-service has occurred, the

plan treat as hours of service the lesser of the hours that otherwise would have been credited to the individual, or 501 hours. If the participant would be prevented from incurring a one-year break-in-service solely because the period of absence is treated as hours of service, these hours would be credited only in the year in which the absence began; otherwise, they would be credited in the year immediately following.

Hour of Service

The first step involved in calculating service is to determine what constitutes an hour of service. Depending on the compliance method selected, all or some of these hours of service will have to be taken into account.[1] The regulations define an **hour of service** as an hour for which:

- An employee is paid, or entitled to payment, for the performance of duties for the employer.
- An employee is paid, or entitled to payment, by the employer for a period of time during which no duties are performed (irrespective of whether the employment relationship has terminated) due to vacation, holiday, illness, incapacity (including disability), layoff, jury duty, military duty, or leave of absence.
- Back pay, irrespective of damages, is either awarded or agreed to by the employer.

However, a plan need not credit an employee with more than 501 hours of service for any single, continuous period during which the employee performs no duties, or for any period of nonworking service for which payment is made under workers' compensation, unemployment compensation, or state disability laws.

Compliance Methods

An employer has three methods to choose from in crediting employees with service. The same method may be used for all purposes or, under the decoupling provisions of the regulations, a different compliance method may be used within the same plan for eligibility, vesting, and benefit accrual purposes. Also, if discrimination does not result, a different method may be used for different classes of employees (a particularly helpful factor when distinguishing between part-time and full-time employees). Finally, the regulations permit the use of one compliance method for pre-ERISA service and another for post-ERISA service (again, an important factor in view of the lack, in many instances, of adequate pre-ERISA employment records).

The first method is the **standard hours–counting method,** under which all hours of service must be taken into account. While this method is, in one sense, the simplest to describe, many employers find it difficult to administer—particularly in the case of exempt employees who often do not keep a record of actual hours worked.

The second method involves the use of equivalencies. Under this method, four alternatives exist. The first determines service on the basis of actual hours worked, including overtime and excluding all other nonworked hours for which compensation is paid, such

---

[1] Under the elapsed-time method of compliance, the hours of service concept is not relevant since total service is measured from date of employment to date of severance.

as vacations, holidays, and so forth. The second alternative involves only regular hours worked and excludes overtime hours, along with nonworked hours for which compensation is paid. The third alternative relates service to a time period established by the plan. This time period can be a day, a week, a half-month, a month, or a shift. Under this third alternative, an employee is credited with an imputed number of hours for the time period involved as long as he or she is credited with at least one hour of service during such time period. The fourth alternative involves the employee's earnings, and here hours of service are related to the earnings received by the employee during the period involved.

The third method is the **elapsed-time method.** Under this method, service is measured from the employee's date of employment to date of severance, and the concept of counting hours is not relevant.

An employer who wishes to use an equivalency in lieu of counting hours must pay a "premium." In the case of time-period equivalencies, this premium is measured in terms of the number of hours that must be credited for the time period selected. In essence, the hours credited will exceed a normal work schedule for the period involved to build in a credit for overtime or additional hours that might have been worked. This means that under the time-period equivalencies, an employee will be credited with 1,000 hours of service in a much shorter period of time (in the average situation) than would be the case under the actual standard hours-counting method. The hours that must be credited under each time-period equivalency are as follows:

- One day—10 hours
- One week—45 hours
- Half-month—95 hours
- Month—190 hours
- Shift—actual hours included in the shift

The premium for using the other equivalencies is measured by reducing the 1,000-hour standard for a full year of service and the 501-hour standard for applying the break-in-service rules. The reductions for the different equivalencies are shown in Table 26.1.

Under the elapsed-time method, service credit for eligibility and vesting must begin with the employee's date of hire (except for permissible statutory exclusions, such as service prior to the effective date of the plan). For benefit accrual purposes, service must

TABLE 26.1   **Adjustments in Hours of Service Required for Crediting a Year of Service and for Break-in-Service Rules under Certain Equivalencies**

Equivalency	Year of Service	Break-in-Service
Hours worked	870	435
Regular hours worked	750	375
Earnings		
Hourly rated employees	870	435
Other employees	750	375

be credited starting with the date the employee begins participating in the plan. Service must continue to be credited, for all purposes for which the method is used, until the employee's date of severance. In the case of quitting, discharge, retirement, or death, the employee's severance date is immediate. In the case of absence from employment for other reasons such as layoff, leave of absence, or disability, the employee's severance date will be 12 months after the beginning of the absence. After the employee's severance date, the plan need not credit service. However, there are two exceptions to this rule. The first exception is if the employee is reemployed within 12 months after quitting, discharge, or retirement, the plan must grant service credit (but only for eligibility and vesting purposes, not for benefit accruals) for the period of absence. The second exception is if an employee quits, is discharged, or retires during a layoff, disability, or leave of absence and is reemployed within 12 months after the absence began, the plan must grant service credit for the period of severance (again, for eligibility and vesting, but not for benefit accruals). Also, under the elapsed-time method, a one-year period of severance is treated the same as a one-year break-in-service.

Eligibility Requirements

As a general rule, a qualified plan cannot require, as a condition of eligibility, that an employee complete more than one year of service. However, a two-year service requirement is acceptable if a plan provides for full and immediate vesting and is not a cash or deferred arrangement (CODA). In addition, a qualified plan cannot require that an employee be older than 21 to participate.[2] A maximum age cannot be used.

The use of entry dates is permissible, but they cannot delay an employee's participation by more than six months. Thus, if it is desirable to use the most stringent minimum age and service requirements possible, the plan should permit entry at least every six months. The use of an annual entry date is permissible only when the minimum age and/or service requirements are at least six months less than those permissible under the law (e.g., age 20½ or six months of service).

Other eligibility requirements, such as employment classifications, may be used provided the plan can pass the nondiscrimination tests discussed in Chapter 25.

Vesting Requirements

A qualified plan must provide that employees will have a vested right to their benefits under specific rules. The value of after-tax and elective (before-tax) employee contributions must be fully vested at all times.[3] The value of employer contributions must be vested

[2] Tax-exempt educational institutions may use age 26 as a minimum age in a plan that provides full and immediate vesting.

[3] This does not necessarily require a minimum benefit equal to the amount the employee has contributed. In a defined contribution plan, for example, there may have been investment losses that have resulted in the value of the employee's contributions being less than the amount actually contributed by the employee. In this situation, the plan would not have to return to the employee an amount greater than the value of the employee contributions after taking investment losses into account.

when the employee reaches the plan's normal retirement age, regardless of the employee's service at that time. Otherwise, the value of employer contributions must be vested at least as rapidly as provided under the minimum vesting schedules described here:

For a defined contribution plan:

- Since passage of the Pension Protection Act of 2006 (PPA), after December 31, 2006:
    - 100 percent vesting after three years of service.
    - Graded vesting, with 20 percent vesting after two years of service, increasing by 20 percent multiples for each year until 100 percent vesting is achieved after six years.

For a defined benefit plan:

- Since passage of the Tax Reform Act of 1986, after December 31, 1986:
    - 100 percent vesting after five years of service.
    - Graded vesting, with 20 percent vesting after three years of service, increasing by 20 percent multiples for each year until 100 percent vesting is achieved after seven years.

As can be seen from the vesting requirements listed, there is a difference in these requirements for defined contribution and defined benefit plans. Originally, the vesting requirements that were revised with the passage of the Tax Reform Act of 1986 applied to both defined contribution and defined benefit plans equally.

With passage of the Economic Growth and Tax Relief Reconciliation Act of 2001 (EGTRRA), the minimum vesting schedules were shortened beginning generally in 2002 for employer matching contributions in defined contribution plans to:

- 100 percent vesting after three years of service.
- Graded vesting, with 20 percent vesting after two years of service, increasing by 20 percent multiples for each year until 100 percent vesting is achieved after six years.

These accelerated vesting schedules applied only to employer matching contributions that matched voluntary before- or after-tax employee contributions from 2002 through 2006 (as opposed to involuntary contributions made as a condition of employment). Employer contributions made to noncontributory, employer-pay-all type plans were subject to the previously mentioned five-year cliff and seven-year graded schedules from 2002 through 2006.[4] However, the rule applicable to employer-matching contributions was generally made applicable to all employer contributions in defined contribution plans for plan years beginning after December 31, 2006, by the PPA of 2006.

Backloading Rules

The IRC also stipulates minimum standards to be followed in determining an employee's accrued benefit for purposes of applying a vesting schedule under defined benefit plans; these rules are not applicable to defined contribution plans.

---

[4] TIAA-CREF, *"Benefit Plan Counselor Special Report"* (July 2001), pp. 2–3.

A plan will be acceptable if it meets any one of the three following rules:

- **The 3 percent rule.** The employee's accrued benefit must be at least equal to 3 percent of the projected normal retirement benefit for each year of participation, to a maximum of 100 percent after 33⅓ years of participation.
- **The 133⅓ percent rule.** The accrued benefit may be the employee's actual benefit earned to date under the plan, provided any future rate of benefit accrual is not more than 133⅓ percent of any prior year's benefit accrual rate.
- **The fractional rule.** The employee's accrued benefit may not be less than the projected normal retirement benefit prorated for years of plan participation.

Most plans are expected to be able to satisfy either or both the 133⅓ percent rule and the fractional rule. Any plan that permits the accrual of benefits for more than 33⅓ years will not be able to satisfy the 3 percent rule.

If a defined benefit plan requires employee contributions, the accrued benefit attributable to employer contributions is determined by subtracting the life annuity value of the employee's contributions.

Other Vesting Requirements

The tax law also establishes a number of other requirements concerning the vesting and payment of an employee's benefits.

1. Vested amounts of less than $5,000 may be paid in a lump sum at termination of employment without employee consent; otherwise, an employee must consent to a lump-sum payment and must have the right to leave his or her accrued benefit in the plan until the later of age 62 or normal retirement age. A plan may not impose a significant detriment on a participant who does not consent to a distribution.[5] EGTRRA made a direct rollover the default option for involuntary distributions that exceed $1,000 when the qualified retirement plan provides that nonforfeitable accrued benefits which do not exceed $5,000 must be distributed immediately.

2. If an employee receives payment for his or her accrued benefit and is later reemployed, the service for which the employee received payment may be disregarded in determining his or her accrued benefit after reemployment. The employee, however, must be permitted to "buy back" the accrued benefit attributable to such service by repaying the cash payment with compound interest. (In the case of a defined contribution plan, such a buyback is required only before the employee has incurred five consecutive one-year breaks in service, and interest need not be paid.)

3. Once vested, no forfeitures are permitted—even if termination of employment is due to dishonesty. If a plan has more liberal vesting provisions than the law requires,

---

[5] EGTRRA clarified that a plan may disregard rollovers to the plan in determining the involuntary cash-out threshold. Therefore, if a newly hired employee had accrued a benefit below the cash-out threshold and subsequently terminated her or his new employment, she or he could be cashed out. This could occur even if she or he had transferred retirement benefits from another source, such as an individual retirement account or a plan sponsored by a previous employer. This could be especially troubling to an employee who has secured a loan from the plan because the loan would immediately become due for payment.

however, forfeitures are possible up to the time the employee would have to be vested under the law.

4. Any employee who terminates employment must be given written notification of his or her rights, the amount of his or her accrued benefits, the portion (if any) that is vested, and the applicable payment provisions.

5. A terminated employee's vested benefit cannot be decreased by reason of increases in Social Security benefits that take place after the date of termination of employment.

6. If the plan allows an active employee to elect early retirement after attaining a stated age and completing a specified period of service, a terminated employee who has completed the service requirement must have the right to receive vested benefits after reaching the early retirement age specified. However, the benefit for the terminated employee can be reduced actuarially even though the active employee might have the advantage of subsidized early retirement benefits.

7. Any plan amendment cannot decrease the vested percentage of an employee's accrued benefit. Also, if the vesting schedule is changed, any participant with at least three years of service must be given the election to remain under the preamendment vesting schedule (for both pre- and postamendment benefit accruals).

8. The accrued benefit of a participant may not be decreased by an amendment of the plan. This includes plan amendments that have the effect of eliminating or reducing an early retirement benefit or a retirement-type subsidy or eliminating or reducing the value of an optional form of benefit with respect to benefits attributable to service before the amendment. In the case of a retirement-type subsidy, this applies only with respect to a participant who satisfies the preamendment condition for the subsidy, either before or after the amendment. EGTRRA directed the Internal Revenue Service (IRS) to issue regulations providing that the prohibitions against eliminating or reducing an early retirement benefit, a retirement-type subsidy, or optional form of benefit did not apply to "any plan amendment which reduces or eliminates benefits or subsidies which create significant burdens or complexities for the plan and plan participants, and does not adversely affect the rights of any plan participant in a more than *de minimis* manner." The intent of these regulations was to eliminate duplicative benefit options following plan mergers and consolidations while ensuring that meaningful benefit options and subsidies are not eliminated.[6]

Individual Limits

To achieve a tax-qualified status, a plan must observe two statutory limits on contributions and/or benefits.[7] The first is a limit on the amount of an employee's compensation that may be taken into account when determining the contributions or benefits made on his or her behalf. The second is a limit on the annual additions that may be made to an

[6] CCH, "2001 Tax Legislation: Law, Explanation, and Analysis," *Commerce Clearing House Pension Plan Guide,* 2001, pp. 271–72.

[7] There is also a limit on the amount an employee may electively defer (contribute on a before-tax basis) under a CODA. This limit was discussed in Chapter 8.

employee's account in the case of a defined contribution plan, or on the benefits payable to an employee in the case of a defined benefit plan. Moreover, there is a combined limit on annual additions and/or benefits that applies for years through 1999 in the case of employees who participate in both types of plans.

Limit on Compensation

The Tax Reform Act of 1986 added **Section 401(a)(17)** to the **IRC,** limiting the amount of an employee's compensation that can be taken into account in determining contributions or benefits under a qualified plan. This limit was originally set at $200,000 and was increased for changes in the Consumer Price Index (CPI). By 1993, it had increased to $235,840. However, beginning in 1994, it was rolled back to $150,000. This revised limit also increased with changes in the CPI, but only when the cumulative changes increased the then-effective limit by at least $10,000. For 2001, the limit was $170,000. EGTRRA increased the includable compensation limit to $200,000 in 2002 with indexing in future years in $5,000 increments rather than $10,000 increments. In 2007 the includable compensation limit was $225,000.

Limits on Annual Additions and Benefits

As already mentioned, limits on annual additions and benefits are found in Section 415 of the IRC and are often referred to as the **Section 415 limits.** In general, there is one limit for the annual additions that can be made under a defined contribution plan and one limit for the annual benefit that can be paid from a defined benefit plan.[8]

Annual Additions Limit

This limit applies to the total employer and employee contributions that may be added to an employee's account each year under a defined contribution plan. This includes all employee contributions, whether made on a before- or after-tax basis.[9] Any forfeitures that might be reallocated to an employee's account when other employees terminate without full vesting are also included under this limit. If an employer maintains a contributory defined benefit plan, the after-tax employee contributions made under that plan are considered to be part of his or her annual addition and will be added to contributions (employer and employee) made to any defined contribution plan.

The basic limit is that the amount added to an employee's account each year cannot exceed the smaller of (1) 100 percent of the employee's compensation and (2) $45,000. This $45,000 amount (in 2007) is adjusted for changes in the CPI. The adjusted amount will then be rounded down to the next lower multiple of $1,000. For 2007, the limit was

[8] In addition, there was a combined plan limit that applied for years through 1999 when an individual participated in both a defined contribution and a defined benefit plan. It should be noted that these limits were applied on a controlled-group basis; for this purpose, however, the controlled-group concept is applied to a parent/subsidiary group on the basis of more than 50 percent ownership or control, rather than 80 percent.

[9] For years beginning before January 1, 1987, the term *annual additions* meant the sum of employer contributions, after-tax employee contributions in excess of 6 percent of compensation (or 50 percent of after-tax contributions if less), and forfeitures. This distinction was important for purposes of the combined limit (described later) because of its cumulative nature.

$45,000. For this purpose, the percentage limit applies to compensation in a limitation year—the calendar year unless the employer elects otherwise.

For limitation years beginning before 1998, an employee's elective (before-tax) deferrals under a CODA or a tax-sheltered annuity or salary reduction contributions to a flexible benefits plan lowered his or her annual additions limit. For example, if an employee with gross compensation of $50,000 deferred $5,000 to a CODA, his or her annual additions limit was calculated on $45,000. For years beginning after 1997, however, these deferrals or salary reduction contributions do not reduce an employee's compensation for purposes of determining the annual addition limit.

Annual Benefit Limit

The maximum annual benefit that can be paid to a participant under a defined benefit plan is the lesser of (1) 100 percent of the participant's high three-year average compensation and (2) $180,000 (in 2007 and subsequently adjusted for inflation). The limit for 2007 was $180,000. The following should be kept in mind when considering this limit:

- The participant's high three-year average compensation is determined over the three consecutive calendar years during which his or her compensation was the highest.
- The compensation taken into account must meet one of the acceptable definitions of compensation described in Chapter 25.
- The compensation taken into account also must be limited to $225,000 (in 2007) adjusted for inflation.
- The limits apply only to employer-provided benefits; any after-tax employee contributions, as previously noted, will be subject to the annual additions limit, even though they are made to a defined benefit plan.
- The limits are reduced if the participant retires before age 62. Retirement prior to age 62 will be considered an early retirement for purposes of these limits, even though the retirement may be at the plan's normal retirement age.
- The limits are increased if a participant retires after his or her Social Security full benefit retirement age.
- After the dollar limits have been recalculated for changes in the CPI, the resulting figure will be rounded down to the next lower multiple of $5,000, and this rounded amount will become the current limit.
- The benefits are reduced if the participant has less than 10 years of participation or service. The dollar limit is reduced if he or she has less than 10 years of participation; the percentage limit is reduced if he or she has less than 10 years of service.
- There will be no reduction in the limits if benefits are paid in the form of a qualified joint and survivor annuity to the participant's spouse. The limits will be reduced, however, for any other optional form of payment.
- Many employers maintain both a defined benefit and a defined contribution plan. A special combined plan limit applied for years through 1999. The pension simplification provisions of the Small Business Job Protection Act of 1996 repealed this combined plan limit for years after 1999.

Joint and Survivor Annuities

The two death benefits required by law prior to passage of the PPA were (1) in the case of a vested participant who retires under the plan, the accrued benefit must be provided in the form of a **qualified joint and survivor annuity (QJSA)**; and (2) in the case of a vested participant who dies before the annuity starting date and who has a surviving spouse, a **qualified preretirement survivor annuity (QPSA)** must be provided to the surviving spouse. The plan (or the employer) is not required to absorb the cost for either benefit; this cost may be passed on to the employee, typically in the form of a reduction in the retirement benefit otherwise payable.

These joint and survivor annuity requirements apply to all defined benefit plans and to money purchase plans.[10] They also apply to other defined contribution plans unless (1) the participant's vested account balance is paid in full upon his or her death to the participant's surviving spouse, (2) the participant has not elected benefits in the form of a life annuity contract, and (3) all or any portion of the participant's account balance has not been transferred from a plan subject to the joint and survivor rules.

The law defines a QJSA as an annuity for the life of the participant with a survivor annuity for the life of the participant's spouse that is not less than 50 percent or more than 100 percent of the amount of the annuity payable to the participant. The joint and survivor annuity must be the actuarial equivalent of a single life annuity for the life of the participant.

In general, the QPSA provides a survivor annuity for the life of the spouse in an amount not less than the amount that would be payable as a survivor annuity under the QJSA. In the case of a participant who dies after attaining the earliest retirement age, it is assumed that he or she has retired with an immediate QJSA on the day before the date of death. For a participant who dies before retirement eligibility, it is assumed that he or she has separated from service on the date of death, survived to the earliest retirement age, retired with an immediate QJSA at the earliest retirement age, and died the next day.[11] The benefit, however, need not be paid until the date the participant would have attained the earliest retirement age.

Following passage of the PPA, the minimum survivor annuity requirements were revised to provide, at the election of a participant, to pay benefits in the form of a **qualified optional survivor annuity (QOSA)** for plan years beginning after December 31, 2007. A qualified optional survivor annuity is defined under the law as: (1) an annuity for the life of the participant with a survivor annuity for the life of the spouse that is equal to the applicable percentage of the amount of the annuity that is payable during the joint lives of the participant and the spouse; and (2) the actuarial equivalent to a single annuity for the life of the participant. When the survivor annuity under the plan's qualified joint and survivor annuity is less than 75 percent of the annuity payable during the joint lives of the participant and spouse, the applicable percentage is 75 percent. If the

---

[10] If the money purchase plan is part of an employee stock ownership plan (ESOP), the joint and survivor rules will not apply if the plan otherwise meets the conditions that exempt defined contribution plans from compliance.

[11] Note that if the plan requires a service period for early retirement that is greater than the service the participant has completed at the time of death, the earliest retirement age will be the participant's normal retirement age.

survivor annuity under the plan's qualified joint and survivor annuity is greater than or equal to 75 percent of the annuity payable during the joint lives of the participant and spouse, the applicable percentage is 50 percent. The written explanation of a qualified joint and survivor annuity provided to participants also must include the terms and conditions of the qualified optional survivor annuity. This provision will allow some couples to opt for a smaller initial payment while they are alive with a larger subsequent benefit to the surviving spouse.

In the case of a defined contribution plan, a QJSA means an annuity for the life of the surviving spouse, the actuarial equivalent of which is not less than 50 percent of the account balance of the participant on the date of death.

A participant may elect at any time during the applicable election period to waive the QJSA form of benefit, the QOSA form of benefit or the QPSA form of benefit, or all three, and may revoke any such election at any time during the applicable election period. However, the spouse must consent to the election. This requirement is satisfied if (1) the spouse of the participant consents in writing to such election, and the spouse's consent acknowledges the effect of the election and is witnessed by a plan representative or a notary public; or (2) it is established to the satisfaction of a plan representative that this consent cannot be obtained because there is no spouse or because the spouse cannot be located. It should be noted, however, that this notice is not required where the plan fully subsidizes the cost of the benefit, provided the plan does not permit a participant or beneficiary to select a form of benefit that does not satisfy the QJSA, QOSA, and QPSA requirements. The law defines this as a situation under which the failure to waive the benefit by a participant will not result in a decrease in any plan benefit for the participant and will not result in increased contributions for the participant.

These annuities need not be provided if the participant and spouse have been married less than one year. In general, QJSAs, QOSAs, and QPSAs will not be required to be provided unless the participant and spouse have been married through the one-year period ending on the earliest of the participant's annuity starting date or the date of the participant's death. However, if a participant marries within one year before the annuity starting date, and the participant and the participant's spouse have been married for at least a one-year period ending on or before the date of the participant's death, the participant and spouse must be treated as having been married throughout the one-year period ending on the participant's annuity starting date.

The law also provides detailed notification requirements for QJSAs, QOSAs, and QPSAs. The rules for QJSAs and QOSAs require that each plan provide to each participant a written explanation of:

- The terms and conditions of the QJSA or QOSA.
- The participant's right to waive the QJSA or QOSA and the effect of this election.
- The rights of the participant's spouse.
- The right to revoke an election and the effect of this election.

The explanation must be provided within a reasonable period of time before the annuity starting date.

The rules for QPSAs require the plan to provide to each participant a written explanation that is comparable to that required for QJSAs. This explanation must be provided within the applicable period defined as the later of:

- The period beginning with the first day of the plan year in which the participant attains age 32 and ending with the close of the plan year in which the participant attains age 35.
- A reasonable period after the individual becomes a participant.
- A reasonable period after the plan ceases to fully subsidize the cost of the benefit.
- A reasonable period after the survivor benefit requirements become applicable with respect to the participant.
- A reasonable period after separation from service in the case of a participant who separates before attaining age 35.

Distribution Rules

Unless otherwise requested by the participant, benefit payments must commence within 60 days of the latest of the following three events: (1) the plan year in which the participant terminates employment, (2) the completion of 10 years of participation, or (3) attainment of age 65 or the normal retirement age specified in the plan.

Minimum distribution rules are found in Section 401(a)(9) of the IRC. There are two distinct elements to these rules. The first is that distributions, either to an employee or a beneficiary, must commence within stated periods of time. The second is that distributions must be made in minimum amounts.[12]

The basic requirement is that distributions to a participant must commence by April 1 of the year following the later of (1) the year in which the participant retires or (2) the year in which he or she attains age 70½. In addition, distributions must be made by December 31 of each year thereafter.[13] For years prior to 1996, the rule was different—distribution had to commence by April 1 of the year following the year in which the participant attained age 70½, even though the participant was still working. While this old rule no longer applies to most employees, it still applies to 5 percent owners who must commence distribution when they reach age 70½, regardless of their employment status. The payments must be made over a period not exceeding the employee's life (or life expectancy) or the joint lifetimes (or joint life expectancy) of the employee and his or her beneficiary.

If the participant dies before payments have begun, a designated beneficiary was named, and the plan so allows; the participant's interest payable to or for the benefit of the designated beneficiary must commence within one year of the employee's death, and be distrubuted over the life of such beneficiary, or over the period not extending beyond the life expectancy of such beneficiary. This is known as the life expectancy rule. If this

---

[12] Failure to make distributions in accordance with these rules may result in the imposition of a penalty tax on the recipient of 50 percent of the amount by which the distribution falls short of the required amount. See Chapter 31 for a more detailed discussion on distribution issues.

[13] If an employee, other than a 5 percent owner, continues to work after age 70½, his or her accrued benefit under a defined benefit plan must be actuarially increased to take into account the period after age 70½ during which benefits are not being paid.

life expectancy rule is not used, or if the proper designated beneficiary is not named, the five-year rule requires that the entire interest of the employee be distributed within five years of the employee's death regardless of who or what entity receives the distribution. An exception to these rules is that if the beneficiary is the employee's spouse, distribution can be deferred until the employee would have reached age 70½.

Top-Heavy Plans

If a plan is considered to be **top-heavy** (as defined in the following), it must:

- Meet one of two accelerated vesting schedules.
- Provide for minimum contributions or benefits for nonkey employees.

Top-Heavy Plans Defined

A defined contribution plan is top-heavy in a plan year if, as of the determination date (generally the last day of the preceding plan year), either (1) the sum of account balances of all key employees participating in the plan is more than 60 percent of the sum of the account balances for all covered employees, or (2) the plan is part of a top-heavy group, as explained next.

A defined benefit plan is top-heavy in a plan year if, as of the determination date, either (1) the present value of the accumulated accrued benefits of all key employees participating in the plan is more than 60 percent of the present value of the accumulated accrued benefits for all covered employees, or (2) the plan is part of a top-heavy group.

A top-heavy group is the combination of two or more plans and, under the law, it may be required or permissible to aggregate two or more plans to determine top-heaviness. It is required to aggregate into a group (1) all plans covering key employees and (2) any plan upon which a key-employee plan depends for qualification under the coverage and nondiscrimination requirements of the IRC. It is permissible for an employer to expand the group by aggregating other plans as long as the resulting group continues to satisfy the coverage and nondiscrimination rules.

The 60 percent test applies to the top-heavy group. If the group is top-heavy, then each plan also is deemed to be top-heavy. However, a plan included solely at the employer's election is not necessarily considered top-heavy. In applying the top-heavy group rules, all plans of all employers who are part of the same controlled group are treated as a single plan.

In determining the present value of accrued benefits and account balances, the employer may count both employer and employee contributions. Accumulated deductible employee contributions, however, must be disregarded.[14] Also, in the past the employer counted any amount distributed to or for a participant under the plan within the five-year period ending on the current determination date. Under provisions enacted with EGTRRA, the five-year rule continues to apply with respect to in-service distributions; however, for distributions due to termination of service, death, or disability, only distributions during the year in which the determination is being made are taken into account.

---

[14] A federal income tax deduction was available for qualified voluntary employee contributions prior to 1987.

Rollover and similar transfers to a plan made after 1983 will not be part of the top-heavy plan computation, unless they are made to a plan maintained by the same, or an affiliated, employer.

Key Employees Defined

Key employees are defined as (1) all officers[15] (up to a maximum of 50) with annual compensation in excess of $145,000 (in 2007); (indexed for cost-of-living adjustments in $5,000 increments), (2) an employee who owns a 5 percent or greater interest in the employer, and (3) an employee who owns a 1 percent or greater interest in the employer and whose annual compensation is more than $150,000.

The following should be considered when applying this definition:

- An employee who falls into more than one category need only be counted once.
- If an employer has more officers than are required to be counted, the officers to be considered are those with the highest compensation.
- An employee is considered to be a key employee only if he or she qualifies as a key employee during the plan year containing the determination date.
- In determining stock ownership, an employee is treated as owning stock even if it is owned by other members of his or her family or certain partnerships, estates, trusts, or corporations in which the employee has an interest. The rules for establishing ownership in noncorporate entities are similar to those for determining corporate ownership.

Top-Heavy Qualification Requirements

A top-heavy plan must meet certain additional requirements if it is to be qualified under the IRC. Moreover, the Internal Revenue Service (IRS) currently requires all plans (except governmental plans and certain plans covering only employees who are members of a collective bargaining unit), even if they are not top-heavy, to include provisions that will automatically take effect if that event should occur. These additional requirements are discussed in the sections that follow.

Vesting

A top-heavy plan must meet one of two alternative "fast" vesting schedules for all accrued benefits: (1) 100 percent vesting after three years of service; or (2) graded vesting of at least 20 percent after two years of service, 40 percent after three, 60 percent after four, 80 percent after five, and 100 percent after six years.[16]

---

[15] If the employer has between 30 and 500 employees, the number of officers included will never have to be greater than 10 percent of all employees. Also, the regulations state that the determination of whether a person is an officer will be based on all the facts and circumstances. Thus, not all individuals with the title of officer will be deemed officers for this purpose.

[16] Since the provisions of EGTRRA compressed the minimum vesting schedules for voluntary employee-matched contributions from five-year cliff and seven-year graded to three-year cliff and six-year graded vesting, respectively, the vesting schedules imposed on top-heavy plans were not more onerous than normal vesting requirements if the plan involved voluntary employee-matched contributions through 2006. Subsequently the Pension Protection Act of 2006 further extended these compressed vesting schedules to all defined contribution plans beginning in 2007.

Minimum Benefits for Nonkey Employees

A top-heavy plan must provide a minimum benefit or contribution for all nonkey employee participants. Social Security benefits or contributions may not be applied toward these minimums.

For each year (maximum of 10) in which a defined benefit plan is top heavy, each nonkey employee must accrue an employer-provided benefit of at least 2 percent of compensation (generally defined as the average of the five consecutive highest years of pay). For each year in which a defined contribution plan is top heavy, an employer must contribute at least 3 percent of compensation for each nonkey participant; however, in no case does an employer have to contribute more than the percentage contributed for key employees. Reallocated forfeitures are counted as employer contributions under a defined contribution plan. When a nonkey employee participates in both a defined benefit and a defined contribution plan, the employer does not have to provide minimum benefits under both plans. Since passage of EGTRRA, employer matching contributions are now taken into account in determining whether the minimum benefit requirement is satisfied for a defined contribution plan.

EGTRRA created a safe harbor for cash or deferred arrangements (i.e., 401[k] plans) that meet the safe harbor requirements for the actual deferral percentage (ADP) nondiscrimination test and meet the requirements for matching contributions under Internal Revenue Code Section 401 (m)(11). The impact of this provision was to expand the 401(k) ADP nondiscrimination safe harbor into a top-heavy safe harbor as well. Effectively, this provision eased the top-heavy requirements allowing smaller employers using a 401(k) safe harbor plan design to avoid the complexity of the top-heavy rules. The Pension Protection Act of 2006 also provided that a 401(k) plan that contained an automatic enrollment feature that satisfied certain requirements was treated as satisfying the nondiscrimination rules for deferrals and matching contributions for 401(k) plans and was not subject to the top-heavy rules.[17]

Other Tax Law Requirements

There are many other requirements that a plan must meet if it is to achieve and maintain a qualified status. Some of the more important ones are discussed in the following.

Must Be in Writing

A qualified plan must be in writing and must set forth all the provisions necessary for qualification. This is normally accomplished by means of a trust agreement, a plan document, or both.

A trust agreement generally is required for trust fund plans and for plans using individual insurance or annuity contracts along with a conversion fund.[18] This allows the employer to make irrevocable contributions on a basis that permits the employee to defer

---

[17] The EGTRRA and PPA safe harbor requirements are explained in Chapter 8.

[18] A trust agreement is not necessary for plan assets held in insurance policies or nontransferable annuities, assets held by insurance companies, or funds held in custodial accounts. However, a plan instrument of some type is still required so that plan provisions can be set forth in writing.

amounts including these contributions as taxable income until they are distributed. If a group pension contract is employed, an intervening trust usually is not necessary, since the same results can be achieved through the group contract itself.

Communication to Employees

The plan also must be communicated to employees. An announcement letter or booklet is frequently used for this purpose.[19] If employees are not given a copy of the actual plan, they should be told that a copy is available for inspection at convenient locations.

U.S. Trust

If a trust is used, it must be one organized or created in the United States and maintained at all times as a domestic trust. The earnings of a trust created outside of the United States will be taxable, although if the trust otherwise qualifies, the employer will be allowed to take appropriate deductions for its contributions.

Definitely Determinable Benefits

A qualified pension plan must provide definitely determinable benefits. A money purchase pension plan meets this requirement since the employer's contribution formula is definite and, for this reason, benefits are considered actuarially determinable. Also, variable annuity plans or plans under which the benefit varies with a cost-of-living index are acceptable.

Because of the definitely determinable benefit requirement, any amounts forfeited by a terminating employee may not be used to increase benefits for the remaining participants under a defined benefit plan. Instead, these forfeitures must be used to reduce employer contributions next due. Moreover, a defined benefit plan will not be considered to provide definitely determinable benefits unless actuarial assumptions are specified in the plan whenever any benefit under the plan is to be determined using those assumptions. The assumptions must be specified in the plan in a way that precludes employer discretion. For defined contribution plans, forfeitures can be used to increase benefits or reduce employer contributions.

The definitely determinable benefit requirement does not apply to profit sharing plans. While it is not required that there be a definite formula for determining the amount to be contributed to the profit sharing plan, it is required that there be a definite formula for allocating contributions among participants and distributing funds after a fixed number of years, upon the attainment of a stated age, or upon the happening of some event such as layoff, illness, disability, retirement, death, or severance of employment.

Anti-Cutback Rules

Because of the **anti-cutback rules,** a qualified plan may not be amended to eliminate or reduce a benefit that has already accrued unless the Internal Revenue Service approves a request to amend the plan or the elimination or reduction satisfies certain requirements. However, a plan (subject to certain notice requirements) may be amended to eliminate or reduce benefits yet to be accrued.

---

[19] For a discussion of employee communications using electronic means, see "Final Rules Relating to Use of Electronic Communication and Record Keeping Technologies by Employee Pension and Welfare Benefit Plans"; Final Rule, 29 CFR Part 2520 issued on April 9, 2002.

Mergers and Consolidations

A plan must provide that the value of an employee's accrued benefit cannot be diminished in any way by any merger or consolidation with, or transfer of assets or liabilities to or from, any other plan.

Rollovers and Transfers

A plan must provide, as a condition of qualification, that recipients of distributions eligible for rollover treatment may make direct rollovers or transfers of the amounts to an individual retirement account (IRA) or another qualified plan. While plans are required to make such rollovers or transfers for distributees, they are not required to accept them on behalf of new employees.

EGTRRA expanded the flexibility associated with rollovers by permitting an employee to roll over after-tax contributions to an employee plan, an individual retirement account (IRA), or another defined contribution plan. EGTRRA also made a direct rollover the default option for involuntary distributions that exceed $1,000 when the qualified retirement plan provides that nonforfeitable accrued benefits which do not exceed $5,000 must be distributed immediately.

The PPA of 2006 further expanded rollover capabilities by allowing that after-tax contributions from a qualified plan may be rolled over to a defined contribution plan, defined benefit plan, 403(b) plan, or an individual retirement account for plan years beginning after December 31, 2006. Such a rollover to a defined benefit plan or a 403(b) plan must occur through a trustee-to-trustee transfer.

Assignments/Qualified Domestic Relations Orders (QDROs)

The law requires that a plan prohibit the assignment or alienation of benefits, with three exceptions: (1) an employee may be permitted to assign up to 10 percent of any benefit payment, (2) an employee may use his or her vested interest as collateral for a loan from the plan (if such loan is not a prohibited transaction and meets certain requirements),[20] and (3) a payment may be made to an alternate payee pursuant to a **qualified domestic relations order (QDRO).**

A QDRO is a domestic relations order that satisfies all of the following requirements:

1. It must create or recognize the existence of an alternate payee's right to, or assign to an alternate payee the right to, receive all or a portion of the benefit payable with respect to a participant under the plan. An alternate payee is a spouse, former spouse, child, or other dependent of a participant who is recognized by a domestic relations order as having a right to receive all, or a part of, the benefits payable under the plan.

2. It must clearly specify certain facts about the participant's benefits. The order must clearly specify the name and the last known mailing address of the participant and the name and mailing address of each alternate payee covered by the order; the amount or percentage of the participant's benefit to be paid by the plan to each such alternate payee, or the manner in which such amount or percentage is to be determined; the number of payments or periods to which such an order applies; and each plan to which such an order applies.

---

[20] See the discussion of loans in Chapter 6.

3. It must not alter the amount or form of benefits. The QDRO may not require the plan to provide (a) any type or form of benefit, or any option, not otherwise provided under the plan; (b) (actuarially) increased benefits; or (c) the payment of benefits to an alternate payee when such benefits are already required to be paid to another alternate payee under another order previously determined to be a QDRO.

In the case of any payment before a participant has separated from service, a QDRO may require that payment be made to an alternate payee on or after the date on which the participant attains the earliest retirement age[21] as if the participant had retired on the date on which payment is to begin under the order. In this case, the amount of the payment is determined by taking into account the present value of the benefits actually accrued, rather than the present value of an employer subsidy for early retirement. The QDRO must be limited to a form that may be paid under the plan to the participant.

ERISA-Required Provisions

In addition to some of the provisions already mentioned, ERISA requires that several other items be covered in the plan. For example, the plan must provide for named fiduciaries and must set forth a procedure for establishing and carrying out the plan's funding policy. The plan also should describe clearly any procedure for the allocation of fiduciary and administrative duties and responsibilities, and it should stipulate the basis on which payments will be made to and from the plan. The plan also should spell out the procedure for making claims and for appealing claim decisions.

Chapter Summary

- The law establishes specific requirements for the determination of an employee's service in three key areas: (1) initial eligibility to participate, (2) vesting, and (3) the right to a benefit accrual. The law does not mandate how service is to be determined for other purposes (for example, the right to retire early).

- The Internal Revenue Code requires that the employee's rights to that portion of his or her accrued benefit attributable to his or her own contributions be fully vested at all times. In any event, accrued benefits attributable to employer contributions must vest when the employee reaches normal retirement age. Otherwise, they must vest at least as rapidly as provided by one of the following standards. The first standard required that all accrued benefits must be 100 percent vested after five years of service. The second standard permitted graded vesting, with 20 percent of accrued benefits vesting after three years of service and that percentage increasing in 20 percent multiples each year until 100 percent vesting is achieved after seven years. With passage of the Economic Growth and Tax Relief Reconciliation Act of 2001 (EGTRRA), the minimum vesting schedules were shortened beginning generally in 2002 for employer matching contributions in defined contribution plans to:

[21] This has been defined as the earlier of (1) the earliest date benefits are payable under the plan or (2) the later of the date the participant attains age 50 or the date on which the participant could obtain a distribution from the plan if the participant separated from service.

- 100 percent vesting after three years of service.
- Graded vesting, with 20 percent vesting after two years of service, increasing by 20 percent multiples for each year until 100 percent vesting is achieved after six years.

These accelerated vesting schedules applied only to employer matching contributions that matched voluntary before- or after-tax employee contributions (as opposed to involuntary contributions made as a condition of employment). Similarly, employer contributions made to noncontributory, employer-pay-all type plans were subject to the previously mentioned five-year cliff and seven-year graded schedules. This was the case following the passage of EGTRRA through 2007. Beginning in 2007 the PPA of 2006 made these compressed vesting schedules applicable to all defined contribution plans.

- To achieve a tax-qualified status, a plan must observe two statutory limits on contributions and/or benefits. The first is a limit on the amount of an employee's compensation that may be taken into account when determining the contributions or benefits made on his or her behalf. The second is a limit on the annual additions that may be made to an employee's account in the case of a defined contribution plan, or on the benefits payable to an employee in the case of a defined benefit plan. Through 1999 there was a combined limit in the case of an employee who participated in both types of plans.
- The Tax Reform Act of 1986 added Section 401(a)(17) to the IRC, limiting the amount of an employee's compensation that can be taken into account in determining contributions or benefits under a qualified plan. For 2007, the limit was $225,000.
- In the case of a defined contribution plan, the basic limit is that the amount added to an employee's account each year cannot exceed the smaller of (1) 100 percent of the employee's compensation or (2) $45,000. This $45,000 amount (in 2007) is adjusted for changes in the CPI. The adjusted amount will then be rounded down to the next lower multiple of $1,000.
- In the case of a defined benefit plan, the maximum annual benefit that can be paid to a participant is the lesser of (1) 100 percent of the participant's high three-year average compensation and (2) $180,000 (in 2007 and subsequently adjusted for inflation).
- The three death benefits required by law are (1) in the case of a vested participant who retires under the plan, the accrued benefit must be provided in the form of a qualified joint and survivor annuity (QJSA), or (2) in the form of a qualified optional survivor annuity (QOSA), and (3) in the case of a vested participant who dies before the annuity starting date and who has a surviving spouse, a qualified preretirement survivor annuity (QPSA) must be provided to the surviving spouse. These joint and survivor annuity requirements apply to all defined benefit plans and to money purchase plans. They also apply to other defined contribution plans unless (1) the participant's vested account balance is paid in full upon his or her death to the participant's surviving spouse, (2) the participant has not elected benefits in the form of a life annuity contract, and (3) all or any portion of the participant's account balance has not been transferred from a plan subject to the joint and survivor rules.
- Unless otherwise requested by the participant, benefit payments must commence within 60 days of the latest of the following three events: (1) the plan year in which the

participant terminates employment, (2) the completion of 10 years of participation, or (3) the attainment of age 65 or the normal retirement age specified in the plan.

- If a plan is considered to be top-heavy, it must:
  - Meet one of two accelerated vesting schedules for all employer contributions.
  - Provide for minimum contributions or benefits for nonkey employees.
- Cash-or-deferred arrangements (i.e., 401[k] plans) meeting the safe harbor requirements for the actual deferral percentage (ADP) nondiscrimination test effectively comply with the top-heavy rules. Similarly a 401(k) plan that contains an automatic enrollment feature meeting certain requirements instituted by the PPA of 2006 will satisfy nondiscrimination rules and will not be subject to the top-heavy rules.

Key Terms

anti-cutback rules, p. *484*
break-in-service, p. *469*
computation period, p. *469*
elapsed-time method,
  p. *471*
hour of service, p. *470*
key employees, p. *482*
minimum distribution
  rules, p. *480*

qualified domestic
  relations order
  (QDRO), p. *485*
qualified joint and
  survivor annuity
  (QJSA), p. *478*
qualified optional survivor
  annuity (QOSA),
  p. *478*

qualified preretirement
  survivor annuity
  (QPSA), p. *478*
Section 401(a)(17) of the
  IRC, p. *476*
Section 415 limits, p. *476*
standard hours–counting
  method, p. *470*
top heavy (plan), p. *481*

Questions for Review

1. The law establishes specific regulations for the determination of service in what key areas?
2. When will an employee incur a break-in-service? Why is this significant?
3. Explain (*a*) how hours of service are generally related to the calculation of service for plan participants; (*b*) the break-in-service rules for maternity or paternity absences; and (*c*) the compliance methods available for counting hours of service.
4. Describe the vesting requirements for accrued benefits attributable to (*a*) the employee's contributions, (*b*) the employer's nonelective contributions, (*c*) the employer's matching contributions for employee voluntary contributions.
5. Does an employer have complete flexibility in determining the minimum benefit amount that must be credited to a participant who terminates from the plan in a vested status? Explain.
6. Describe the dollar limits for defined benefit and defined contribution pension plans.
7. Describe a qualified joint and survivor annuity (QJSA) and qualified optional survivor annuity (QOSA).
8. Describe the payments that must be provided under a qualified preretirement survivor annuity (QPSA) if (*a*) a participant dies after reaching the earliest retirement age and (*b*) a participant dies on or before the date of attaining the earliest retirement age.

9. When must a qualified plan start distributing plan benefits?
10. How is top heaviness determined for a qualified pension plan? What are the consequences of such a status?
11. What are the three exceptions to a qualified plan's prohibition on the assignment and alienation of benefits?

Questions for Discussion

1. What public policy objectives are served by establishing specific requirements in connection with (*a*) service and vesting, (*b*) limits on plan contributions and/or benefits, (*c*) joint and survivor annuities, and (*d*) top-heavy rules?
2. An employer maintains two plans. Plan A covers key employees, while plan B covers nonkey employees. Both plans independently satisfy the coverage and nondiscrimination requirements of the IRC. (*a*) *Must* the employer aggregate the two plans to determine top heaviness? (*b*) *May* the employer aggregate the two plans to determine top heaviness? (*c*) Why would an employer want to aggregate the two plans if this option were available?

Resources for Further Study

Allen, Everett T., Jr.; and Dennis F. Mahoney. "Retirement Plan Design." *The Handbook of Employee Benefits.* 6th ed. Jerry S. Rosenbloom, ed. New York: McGraw-Hill, 2005.

Bloss, Julie L. *QDROs: A Guide for Plan Administration.* 2nd ed. Brookfield, WI: International Foundation of Employee Benefit Plans, 1997.

CCH Editorial Staff. "Legislation 2006: Pension Protection Act of 2006: Law, Explanation, and Analysis." Commerce Clearing House (2006).

CCH Editorial Staff. "2001 Tax Legislation: Law, Explanation, and Analysis." *Commerce Clearing House Pension Plan Guide* (2001).

Salisbury, Dallas L. "Regulatory Environment of Employee Benefit Plans." *The Handbook of Employee Benefits.* 6th ed. Jerry S. Rosenbloom, ed. New York: McGraw-Hill, 2005.

Chapter **27**

Other Legal Requirements

After studying this chapter you should be able to:

- Identify disclosure items that must be automatically filed with the government under Title I of the Employee Retirement Income Security Act (ERISA).
- Describe the information that must be included in a summary plan description (SPD).
- Explain the claim denial procedure that a plan sponsor must include in an employee benefit plan.
- Describe what is meant by fiduciary responsibility under ERISA and who qualifies as a fiduciary.
- Distinguish ERISA exemptions for nonqualified plans and explain how these plans are treated differently from qualified employee benefit plans.
- Discuss other legislative requirements that affect employee benefit plans.

While tax law is clearly the most important law affecting qualified retirement plans, employers also must be concerned about the effects of other laws. This chapter briefly reviews some of the major laws that need to be considered in this regard.

The chapter first discusses the provisions of **Title I of ERISA**—the labor law provisions dealing with reporting, disclosure, and fiduciary responsibilities. This coverage of labor law provisions also discusses the potential application of other Title I requirements to executive benefit arrangements that do not meet the tax law standards for a qualified plan.[1] The chapter next treats prohibitions against age and sex discrimination. Securities and Exchange Commission (SEC) requirements also are covered in this chapter because of their relevance for plans that permit employees to invest in employer

---

[1] The provisions of Title IV of ERISA deal with plan termination insurance and the Pension Benefit Guaranty Corporation (PBGC). Due to their complexity and the fact that they are applicable to defined benefit plans only, these provisions are treated separately in Chapter 22.

stock. The chapter also includes a limited discussion of collective bargaining issues as well as a brief discussion of military leaves and unrelated business income.

ERISA—Title I

The labor law provisions of ERISA contained in Title I of the act include many provisions that are virtually identical to the tax law provisions passed at the same time. Thus, for example, Title I has minimum participation, funding, and vesting requirements, as well as joint and survivor protection for the spouses of employees. For the most part, however, jurisdiction and administration of these provisions has been assigned to the Internal Revenue Service (IRS) under the tax provisions—a notable exception being that the Department of Labor (DOL) was given jurisdiction over the determination of service for eligibility, vesting, and benefit accrual.

Title I, however, contains important provisions concerning two key areas: (1) reporting and disclosure and (2) fiduciary responsibilities. Except for some restrictions on prohibited transactions, there is no counterpart for these provisions in the tax law.

The following first discusses reporting and disclosure and then provides an overview of the fiduciary provisions of the law. There also is discussion of executive benefit plans that are not tax-qualified and which could come within the purview of other Title I provisions if certain conditions are not observed.

Reporting and Disclosure

A major aspect of Title I concerns the disclosure of information—to participants and their beneficiaries and to the government. These requirements generally apply to most tax-qualified plans regardless of the number of participants involved. There are, however, a limited number of exemptions. They do not, for example, apply to **unfunded excess benefit plans,** which are maintained to provide employees with benefits they would otherwise have received but that were not provided under the qualified plan because of Section 415 limitations. It should be noted that this exemption is limited in scope and does not, for example, apply to so-called excess benefit plans that restore benefits lost because of the maximum limit on pay that can be taken into account when calculating plan benefits or contributions. Also, if an unfunded plan is maintained for the exclusive benefit of a "select group of management or highly compensated employees," the only disclosure requirement is that the DOL be notified of the existence of the plan and the number of employees that it covers.

Otherwise, the disclosure and reporting provisions require that certain items be automatically filed with the government, others automatically given to employees, and still others made reasonably available to employees upon request. The following items are important disclosure documents:

- The plan's **summary plan description (SPD)**—that is, the booklet, folder, or binder that describes the plan and is given to employees.

- Any **summary of material modifications (SMM)**—a summary of any plan amendment or change in information that is required to be included in the SPD after the initial SPD has been issued.[2]
- The plan's annual financial report (filed using **Form 5500**). The Pension Protection Act (PPA) of 2006 requires that certain annual report information be filed in an electronic format for Internet display by the DOL. The DOL must post the information to the Internet website within 90 days of the filing. This information must also be displayed on any intranet website for employees maintained by the plan sponsor.

  Items that must be automatically distributed to employees include:
- The plan's SPD.
- Any SMMs.
- A **summary annual report (SAR)**—a summary of the plan's annual financial report. The PPA requires that a defined benefit plan no longer provide an SAR or a Section 4011 Notice of Funding Status beginning in 2008, but annual notices currently sent to participants by multiemployer defined benefit plans also will be required for single-employer defined benefit plans. These annual plan funding notices provide expansive detail on plan funding and asset values and need to be furnished in written or electronic form within 120 days after the end of the plan year to the Pension Benefit Guaranty Corporation (PBGC), plan participants and beneficiaries, and unions (if applicable).
- A statement of benefits for all employees who terminate employment.
- A written explanation to any employee or beneficiary whose claim for benefits is denied.[3]
- Benefit statements—As noted later, a plan sponsor must supply a benefit statement to a participant or beneficiary upon request, although the employer need not provide more than one statement in every 12-month period. The Pension Protection Act of 2006 (PPA) modified the requirements for benefit statements, expanding the need for issuance beyond the need to fulfill a plan member's request in any 12-month period beginning after December 31, 2006. Under the PPA rules:
  - If a participant in a defined contribution plan is entitled to direct plan investments, he or she must receive a benefit statement once per quarter.
  - If a participant in a defined contribution plan is not entitled to direct plan investments, he or she must receive a benefit statement once per year.
  - For an active, vested participant in a defined benefit plan, the plan sponsor must provide either (1) a benefit statement once every three years or (2) an annual

---

[2] Although previously an employer was required to automatically submit plan SPDs and SMMs to the Department of Labor, as of August 5, 1997, with passage of the Taxpayer Relief Act of 1997, plan administrators subject to the Employee Retirement Income Security Act were no longer required to file SPDs and SMMs or updated SPDs with the Labor Department. A plan sponsor must supply these documents to the DOL if requested. Civil penalties of up to $100 per day (not to exceed $1,000 per request) may be assessed against administrators who fail to furnish the requested information to the Department within 30 days.

[3] There are many other items that also must be automatically furnished to employees under other provisions of the law (e.g., employees must be notified of rollover opportunities and related tax treatment).

notice describing the availability of a benefit statement and the manner in which the participant can obtain a benefit statement.

There are other items that must be given to employees upon request and/or made available for examination at the principal office of the plan administrator and at other locations convenient for participants. These items include:

- Supporting plan documents.
- The complete application made to the IRS for determination of the plan's tax-qualified status.
- A complete copy of the plan's annual financial report.
- A personal benefits statement (on written request only and required to be furnished only once a year). See information on the preceding page explaining how this requirement has been modified.
- A plan termination report (IRS Form 5310) should the plan be terminated.

The locations at which documents must be made available include any distinct physical location where business is performed and in which at least 50 participants work. Plan materials need not be kept at each location as long as they can be provided there within 10 working days after a request for disclosure. The employer may charge for reproduction of all materials requested unless the material falls in a category where it must be automatically furnished. Any item automatically distributed by mail must be sent by a class of mail that ensures timely delivery.

Summary Plan Description (SPD)

The SPD must be given to new employees within 90 days after they become participants and to beneficiaries within 90 days after they start receiving benefits. For new plans, the initial SPD must be given to participants within 120 days after establishment of the plan. New, complete SPDs must be filed and distributed at least every 10 years. If there have been material changes since the last SPD was issued, however, the employer must file and distribute a new SPD every five years.

The SPD must be in permanent form and must be current regarding all aspects of the plan and the information required by Title I of ERISA. It must include the following information:

- The plan name and the type of plan (e.g., profit sharing).
- The type of plan administration (e.g., trusteed).
- The name (or position title) and address of the person designated as agent for the service of legal process, as well as a statement that legal process also may be served on a plan trustee or the plan administrator.
- The name, address, and telephone number of the plan administrator.
- The name and address of the employer (or employee organization) that maintains the plan.
- The name and/or title and business address of each trustee.
- The employer's identification number assigned by the IRS and the plan number assigned by the plan sponsor.

- In the case of a collectively bargained plan maintained by at least one employer and one employee organization, or, in the case of a plan maintained by two or more employers, the name and address of the most significant employer or organization plus either of the following: (1) a statement that a complete list of sponsors may be obtained on written request and is available for review or (2) a statement that, on written request, participants may receive information about whether a particular employer or organization is a sponsor and, if so, the sponsor's address.
- If a collective bargaining agreement controls any duties, rights, or benefits under a plan, a statement that the plan is maintained in accordance with the agreement and that a copy of the agreement may be obtained on written request and is available for examination.
- Plan requirements as to eligibility for participation and benefits (e.g., age, service, retirement age, and so forth).
- A description of the provisions for nonforfeitable benefits.
- Information about vesting, forfeiture of benefits, credited service, breaks-in-service, and so forth.
- A description of any joint and survivor benefits and any action necessary to elect or reject them.
- Circumstances that may result in disqualification, ineligibility, denial, loss, forfeiture, or suspension of benefits.
- A statement of the extent to which a pension plan is insured by the PBGC; where more information about this insurance is available (usually from the administrator); and the name and address of the PBGC. A summary of the pension benefit guaranty provisions of Title IV of ERISA is included in the SPD content regulations. An SPD incorporating this language will be in compliance. In addition, SPDs for any pension plans that are not insured (e.g., profit sharing plans) must note the reason for lack of insurance.
- The source of contributions to the plan, the method by which contributions are determined, and the identity of any organization through which the plan is funded or benefits are provided.
- A description and explanation of plan benefits.
- The date of the end of the plan year for purposes of maintaining the plan's fiscal records.
- The procedures to be followed in presenting claims for benefits under the plan and the remedies available under the plan for the redress of claims that are denied in whole or in part.
- A statement of the participants' rights under Title I of ERISA. This must appear as a consolidated statement; no information may be omitted. (The regulations contain suggested language which, if used, will ensure compliance.)

When different classes of participants are covered with different benefits under the same plan, prominent notice must appear on the first page of the text listing the various classes for whom different SPDs have been prepared.

All this information must be "written in a manner calculated to be understood by the average plan participant" and should be "sufficiently accurate and comprehensive" to inform employees and beneficiaries of their rights and obligations under the plan. The explanations provided by legal plan texts and insurance contracts ordinarily will not meet these standards. The DOL regulations recommend the use of simple sentences, clarifying examples, clear and liberal cross-references, and a table of contents in the SPD. The use of type is important; varying sizes and styles of type may not be used when they may mislead employees.

If a plan covers 500 or more people who are literate only in a language other than English, or if 10 percent or more of the participants working at a "distinct physical place of business" are literate only in a non-English language (25 percent or more where the plan covers fewer than 100 participants), the SPD must include a prominent notice in the familiar language offering assistance—which may be oral—in understanding the plan.

Retired and terminated vested participants, as well as beneficiaries receiving benefits, come under Title I's definition of participants. Thus, they must be furnished automatically with copies of SPDs and SMMs; irrelevant plan amendments, however, need not be communicated, although copies must be available upon request.

Annual Report

A plan's annual financial report is filed on Form 5500. This form must be filed with the DOL[4] within seven months after the close of each plan year. For employers who have received extensions from the IRS for income tax filings, identical extensions are automatically granted for the plan's annual financial report.

The annual report is designed to require a complete disclosure of all financial information relevant to the operation of the plan. Thus, for example, it includes items such as a statement of assets and liabilities presented by category and valued at current market prices; changes in assets and liabilities during the year; and a statement of receipts and disbursements. It requests details, where applicable, for transactions with parties in interest, loans and leases in default or uncollectible, and certain reportable transactions (e.g., transactions involving in excess of 3 percent of the current value of plan assets). The report also requires information on plan changes made during the reporting period and on employees included or excluded from participation.

Certain financial statements in the report have to be certified by an independent qualified public accountant. Insurance companies and banks are required, within 120 days after the end of the plan year, to furnish any information necessary for the plan administrator to complete the annual report.

Plans that are fully insured are granted limited exemptions. These plans do not have to complete the financial information sections of the form, nor need they engage an

[4] Traditionally, Form 5500 was filed with the Internal Revenue Service. When Form 5500 was revised for 1999 and subsequent plan-year filings, completed forms and any required attachments could be filed electronically through the "EFAST" system. The Internal Revenue Service contracts the processing for Forms 5500 to the Department of Labor. However, should a plan sponsor file for an extension of time to file Form 5500, this is done by directly filing the application for extension (Form 5558) with the Internal Revenue Service.

accountant for audit or include an accountant's opinion. Plans with fewer than 100 participants have less complex filing requirements for their Form 5500.

Summary Annual Report (SAR)

An SAR must be automatically distributed to plan participants within two months after the filing date for Form 5500. The SAR is a simplified summary of the full annual report and may use language prescribed in current DOL regulations.

Summary of Material Modification (SMM)

When a material modification is made to a plan, a summary description of that change, written in clear language, must be distributed automatically to all affected participants and beneficiaries. The SMM must be furnished within 210 days after the end of the plan year in which the change is adopted.

Plan Documents

Plan documents include the text of the actual plan itself and any collective bargaining agreement, trust agreement, contract, or other document under which the plan is established or operated. Plan participants and beneficiaries are entitled to receive copies of these documents within 30 days of making a written request. The DOL may request copies of these documents at any time.

Benefit Statements for Terminating Employees

Each **terminated vested participant**—that is, a participant who terminates service with a vested right in his or her plan benefits—should receive a clear statement of these benefits and the percentage that is vested. The statement should include the nature, amount, and form of the benefit. Any participant who has had a break-in-service of one year is automatically entitled to receive a benefits statement. Statements must be given to vested participants within 210 days after the end of the plan year in which they terminate service.

A statement also should be given to employees who terminate or incur a one-year break-in-service without a vested interest, thus clearly communicating that any such individual is not entitled to receive benefits under the plan.

Personal Benefits Statement

Traditionally, plan participants and beneficiaries could request in writing a statement of their own benefits, but not more often than once in any 12-month period. The statement would include the total benefits accrued and the portion, if any, that was vested or, if benefits were not vested, the earliest date on which they would become vested. While still retaining the right to request a benefit statement within any 12-month period, the PPA expanded issuance requirements as described earlier. Additionally, the PPA added a number of substantive requirements for the content of personal benefit statements. If a participant can direct plan investments, the benefit statement must provide the following:

- Information explaining any restrictions on the right to direct investments.
- An explanation on the importance of diversifying investments.

- A statement cautioning participants on the risk of holding more than 20 percent of a portfolio in the securities of any single entity, such as employer securities.

For a defined benefit plan, the benefit statement must include an explanation of any permitted disparity under Section 401(l) or of a floor-offset arrangement.

Claim Denials

Anyone denied a claim under any plan is entitled to a written statement giving the reasons for the denial, usually within 90 days. This explanation should be a clear, comprehensible statement of the specific reasons for the denial of the claim. The explanation also must include a description of any material or information necessary for the claimant to improve the claim and the reasons this additional material is needed. Also in the explanation should be a full description of the plan's appeal procedure. The claimant must be given at least 60 days thereafter in which to appeal the claim and is entitled to a final decision in writing within 60 days of the appeal (120 days in special circumstances).

Joint and Survivor Notifications

Under defined benefit pension plans and some defined contribution plans, each participant must be informed, individually and in writing, of the right to elect or reject both pre- and postretirement survivor benefits.

Timing for **notification as to postretirement survivor benefits** is nine months before the earliest retirement date under the plan. **Notification** for **preretirement survivor benefits** must be provided between the first day of the plan year in which the participant becomes age 32 and the end of the plan year in which he or she becomes 35. If an employee is over age 32 when hired, notification must be provided within three years after that employee becomes a plan participant. If a vested participant terminates employment before age 32, notice must be provided within one year after the termination date.

The notifications must include enough information about the potential financial impact on the individual's own benefit for the participant to make an informed decision. Contents of the notification are specified by regulations.

Rollover Notifications

When a distribution from a qualified plan is eligible to be rolled over into an individual retirement account (IRA) or another employer's qualified plan, the plan administrator, within a reasonable period of time before making the distribution, must send a **rollover notification** to the participant or beneficiary explaining the rollover and direct transfer rules, the tax withholding requirements on distributions that are not directly transferred, and how taxes can be reduced or deferred (e.g., rollover). In general, the timing of the notice must meet the same requirements that apply to notifying participants of their rights as to the qualified joint and survivor annuity rules under a defined benefit plan.

The Economic Growth and Tax Relief Reconciliation Act of 2001 (EGTRRA) expanded notice requirements for eligible rollover distributions by requiring that the written explanation being provided to recipients of eligible plan rollover distributions include a discussion of the potential restrictions and tax consequences that may apply to distributions from the new plan to which the distribution is rolled over that are different from those applicable to the distributing plan.

EGTRRA also made a direct rollover the default option for involuntary distributions that exceed $1,000 when the qualified retirement plan provides that nonforfeitable accrued benefits which do not exceed $5,000 must be distributed immediately.

Enforcement

ERISA provides for a number of penalties for violation of the disclosure requirements. Among the penalties are the following:

- If a plan administrator does not fill a participant's or beneficiary's request for information to which he or she is entitled under the plan within 30 days, the plan administrator may be personally liable to the individual who made the request, for a fine of up to $110 per day.
- Willful violation of any of the reporting and disclosure provisions may incur a criminal penalty of up to a $5,000 fine and/or one year in prison for an individual, and up to a $100,000 fine for a corporation.
- Civil actions may be brought against the plan administrator by participants or beneficiaries to obtain information to which they are entitled under their plan, to enforce their rights under the plan, or to clarify their rights to future benefits under the plan.
- Civil action also may be brought by the Secretary of Labor, a participant, a beneficiary, or another fiduciary against an individual who breaches his or her fiduciary duty.

It is expected that random audits will be performed continually and that a team of investigators will follow up on all discrepancies found and all complaints filed by plan participants or beneficiaries. Records now are required to be kept for a period of six years after the documents are due for filing, even for those plans that are exempt from filing.

Disclosure of Plan Information Using Electronic Media[5]

On April 9, 2002, the DOL issued final regulations on disclosing plan information using electronic media. Previously, safe harbors were only provided when issuing SPDs, SMMs, and SARs. The final regualtions expanded the scope of safe harbors to all ERISA Title I disclosures. Such items as pension plan investment information, material on pension plan loans, responses to written requests from plan participants and beneficiaries, and notices relating to qualified domestic relations orders may now be conveyed in electronic form. Compliance with the regulation meets ERISA's general requirement that disclosure be "reasonably calculated to insure actual receipt." The regulation was effective October 9, 2002, regardless of plan year.

Electronic delivery may be used if the employee has access to the employer's computer system where the employee is reasonably expected to perform his or her duties.

---

[5] Neal S. Schelberg, Craig A. Bitman, and Steven D. Weinstein, "Paperless Benefit Plan Administration," *Compensation & Benefits Review* (July/August 2000), pp. 59–61. Reprinted with Permission of Sage Publications, Inc. Copyright © Sage Publications, Inc., Thousand Oaks, CA.

Access to the computer system must be an integral part of the employee's duties. Providing access to electronic documents using the computer kiosk in a common area would not meet this requirement. Use of electronic media is permitted for disclosure to nonemployees as long as these individuals provide an address for electronic delivery of documents and affirmatively consent to the electronic disclosure in a manner that reasonably demonstrates the individual's ability to access information in electronic form. Nonemployees must give this consent after receiving a statement from the plan sponsor explaining the electronic delivery system and the hardware and software needed to use it. Additionally, all of the following conditions must be met:

- The administrator must take appropriate and necessary measures to ensure that the system for furnishing the document results in actual receipt by participants of the transmitted information and documents.
- Each participant must be provided with notice, through electronic means or in writing, apprising the participant of the document to be furnished electronically, the significance of the document, and the participant's right to request and receive a paper copy of the document.
- On request, the plan administrator must provide the document in paper form to a participant.
- The electronically furnished version of the document must be the same in all material respects as the paper version.
- The electronically furnished document must satisfy all other requirements with respect to the substance and presentation required to be in the paper version of such a document.
- When a disclosure includes personal information relating to an individual's accounts or benefits, the plan administrator must take reasonable and appropriate steps to safeguard the confidentiality of the information.

The Internal Revenue Service has stated in Notice 99–1 that where the Code or regulations do not specify how a particular transaction is to be conducted (e.g., in writing), then a plan may perform the transaction electronically without jeopardizing the plan's qualified status under the Code. The IRS provided various examples of activities that can be performed with the assistance of electronic media. The enumerated actions include the following:

- Enrolling participants in a plan.
- Designating employee contribution rates.
- Designating beneficiaries (except where spousal consent is required).
- Designating investment allocation of future contributions and currently held assets.
- Receiving and responding to participant information requests.
- Electing direct rollovers.

With respect to those plan activities for which the IRS has detailed a specific means of execution, electronic media may not be used unless the IRS has issued specific guidance permitting such use.

According to the IRS, functions may be performed through the use of electronic media if the following conditions are satisfied:

- The electronic media must be reasonably accessible to the participant.
- The electronic form of the notice must be as understandable as the paper version.
- The participant must be advised that he or she has the right to request and receive the notice or consent forms in paper version at no charge.
- The system must be reasonably designed to preclude someone other than the appropriate party from giving consent (e.g., by using passwords).
- The system must give the participant a reasonable opportunity to review, modify, or rescind his or her consent before an election becomes effective.
- The participant must be given confirmation of his or her consent and the terms thereof either through paper or electronic media.

Fiduciary Requirements

Fiduciary provisions are set forth in Part Four of Title I of ERISA, although the definition of fiduciary is found in Part One of ERISA, Section 3(21). The following provides a brief overview of these provisions.

Definition of Fiduciary

A person (or corporation) is considered a **fiduciary** under ERISA if that person exercises any discretionary authority or control over the management of the plan, exercises any authority or control over assets held under the plan or the disposition of plan assets, renders investment advice for direct or indirect compensation (or has any authority or responsibility to do so), or has any discretionary authority or responsibility in the administration of the plan.

Clearly, the trustee of a plan is a fiduciary. So also are officers and directors of a corporation who have responsibility for certain fiduciary functions—for example, the appointment and retention of trustees or investment managers or the appointment and monitoring of an investment advice provider. On the other hand, individuals whose duties are purely ministerial (e.g., applying rules of eligibility and vesting) are clearly not fiduciaries.

Fiduciary Responsibilities

A fiduciary is required to discharge all duties solely in the interest of participants and beneficiaries and for the exclusive purpose of providing plan benefits and defraying reasonable administrative expenses. In addition, a fiduciary is charged with using the care, skill, prudence, and diligence that a prudent person who is familiar with such matters would use under the circumstances then prevailing—a standard that has come to be called the **prudent expert rule.** A fiduciary also is responsible for diversifying investments so as to minimize the risk of large losses unless it is clearly prudent not to diversify.[6] Finally, the fiduciary must conform with the documents governing the plan and must

---

[6] Investments in employer securities in accordance with the prohibited transaction rules also are permitted under the diversity requirement; however, they must comply with the prudence and "exclusive benefit of employees" standards.

invest only in assets subject to the jurisdiction of U.S. courts. This latter requirement does not preclude investing in international securities; it simply requires that the assets be held in a manner such that they are subject to the jurisdiction of U.S. courts.

Prohibited Transactions

Both labor law (Title I of ERISA) and the IRC prohibit certain transactions between the plan and "disqualified persons."[7] A disqualified person is broadly defined to include any plan fiduciary; a person providing service to the plan; any employer or employee organization whose employees or members are covered by the plan; a direct or indirect owner of 50 percent or more of the business interest of the employer; a relative of any of the above; an officer, director, and certain HCEs; or a person having 10 percent or more of the ownership interest in any of the preceding. Under ERISA, an employee also is considered to be a party in interest; an employee, however, is not considered to be a disqualified person.

The following transactions between the plan and a party in interest or a disqualified person are prohibited:

- The sale, exchange, or leasing of property.
- Lending money or extending credit (including funding the plan by contributing debt securities).
- Furnishing goods, services, or facilities.
- A transfer or use of plan assets.
- The acquisition of qualifying employer securities and real property in excess of allowable limits

These prohibitions apply even to "arm's length" transactions and even though the plan is fully protected.

Under ERISA, a fiduciary will be personally liable for any breach or violation of responsibilities and will be liable to restore any profits made through the use of plan assets. Under the IRC, an excise tax of a percentage of the amount involved in a prohibited transaction may be levied on the disqualified person who engages in the transaction. For prohibited transactions occurring after August 5, 1997, the initial excise tax is 15 percent of the amount involved. If the situation is not corrected within the time allowed (90 days unless extended by the IRS), a further excise tax of 100 percent of the amount involved may be imposed. However, engaging in a prohibited transaction will not cause the plan to be disqualified.

As noted earlier, the prohibited transaction rules limit the investment of plan assets in qualifying employer securities and real property. Qualifying employer securities include stock. Marketable obligations (e.g., bonds and notes) also are considered to be qualifying employer securities if certain requirements are met. Qualifying employer real property includes real property that is dispersed geographically, is suitable for more than one use, and has been leased to the employer.

[7] The IRC refers to transactions between the plan and "disqualified persons." ERISA refers to transactions between the plan and "parties in interest." For the most part, IRC and ERISA provisions are similar, although the penalties for engaging in a prohibited transaction differ.

In general, defined benefit and money purchase plans cannot invest more than 10 percent of the fair market value of plan assets in employer securities. Deferred profit sharing plans that specifically so provide may invest without limit in employer securities or real property; if the plan does not so specify, however, a 10 percent limit will apply. Of course, stock bonus plans are primarily invested in employer securities.

Even though investment in employer securities and real property is permitted under the prohibited transaction rules (and under the fiduciary requirements for diversity), investments of this type must still satisfy the overriding requirement that they be for the exclusive benefit of employees. Moreover, they also must satisfy the fiduciary requirement of prudence. Since the passage of the PPA, participants are now permitted to diversity their holdings in employer securities as described in Chapter 29.

Fiduciary Liabilities

Apart from excise taxes that might be imposed because of a prohibited transaction under the tax law, a fiduciary will be personally liable for any breach or violation of responsibilities and will be liable to restore any profits made through the use of plan assets.

In addition, the DOL may impose a 20 percent penalty on any fiduciary who is found liable for a breach of fiduciary rules. The penalty is applied to the recovery amount—that is, the amount recovered from the fiduciary on behalf of the plan or its participants pursuant to either an out-of-court settlement with the DOL or a court order under a judicial proceeding instituted by the DOL. The DOL may waive or reduce the penalty in cases where the fiduciary acted reasonably and in good faith or where the fiduciary will not be able to restore all losses to the plan absent the waiver or reduction. The penalty is automatically reduced for prohibited transactions by the 15 percent excise tax imposed in those cases.

A fiduciary also may be liable for the violations of a cofiduciary if the fiduciary knowingly participates in or conceals a violation, has knowledge of a violation, or by the fiduciary's own violation enables the cofiduciary to commit a violation. If a plan uses separate trusts, however, a trustee of one trust is not responsible for the actions of the other trustees. Also, a fiduciary will not be responsible for the acts of a duly appointed investment manager (except to the extent that the fiduciary did not act prudently in selecting or continuing the use of the investment manager). A trustee also is not responsible for following the direction of named fiduciaries in making investment decisions if the plan so provides.

The PPA increased the penalty for coercively interfering with participants' exercise of their rights under ERISA. Any party coercively interfering with participants' exercise of their ERISA rights can be fined up to $100,000 and can be subject to the maximum prison term, which is 10 years.

Delegation of Authority

Noninvestment activities can be delegated by a fiduciary if the plan so permits and the procedure for doing so is clearly spelled out; however, fiduciaries remain responsible, under the prudent expert rule, for persons delegated those responsibilities. Similarly, they remain responsible for the acts of their agents in performing ministerial duties.

Fiduciary standards mandated by the Employee Retirement Income Security Act of 1974 (ERISA) are intended to provide protection for plan participants and beneficiaries. ERISA makes clear that fiduciaries must discharge their plan duties solely in the interest of plan participants and beneficiaries. Plan fiduciaries must also act for the exclusive purpose of providing benefits to the participants and beneficiaries and take actions to keep plan administration expenses at reasonable levels. In handling their responsibilities, plan fiduciaries must use the care, skill, prudence, and diligence that a prudent person would use under the applicable prevailing circumstances. Not only must plan fiduciaries do this while assets are being accumulated, but these responsibilities also apply during the distribution phase. The selection of an annuity provider, like the selection of an investment manager, whether it occurs upon the separation or retirement of a participant or upon the termination of a plan, is a fiduciary decision. Previously fiduciaries were expected to attempt to ascertain the "safest annuity available" unless, under the prevailing circumstances, it would be prudent to do otherwise.

This concept of procuring the "safest annuity available" has been seen as a problematic concept. Questions have arisen, such as should a more costly annuity be purchased because it is deemed to be safer? How much more safety justifies higher costs? Because of these difficult questions, the Pension Protection Act of 2006 changed the standard for annuity purchases. Annuity purchases are no longer subject to the "safest annuity available" standard, though they must still meet other fiduciary standards.

Earmarked Investments—Section 404(c)

The law permits a defined contribution plan to be established on a basis that allows **earmarked investments**—that is, employees are allowed to direct the investment of their own accounts. Under these plans, sponsors and other plan fiduciaries might be exempt from liability for investment returns that result from participant choices, provided that participants are given the opportunity to exercise control over the assets in their individual accounts and can choose from a broad range of categories.

The DOL has issued regulations that provide statutory relief from fiduciary liability under these plans if certain requirements are met. Failure to comply with these requirements does not necessarily mean that the fiduciaries will be liable for investment performance; it simply means that this regulatory protection is not available.

To ensure that participants have both control over their assets and the opportunity to diversify their holdings, the regulations:

• Require the plan to provide participants with reasonable opportunities to give investment instructions to the plan fiduciary, who is obligated to comply with these instructions.

- Require that a plan offer at least three "diversified categories of investment"— with materially different risk and return characteristics—that collectively allow participants to construct a portfolio with risk and return characteristics within the full range normally appropriate for a plan participant.
- Establish specific rules regarding participant transfer elections; sponsors must allow at least quarterly elections for transfers in or out of the three diversified investment options that must, as a minimum, be offered under the plan, and more frequent transfers may be required if appropriate in light of the volatility of a particular investment.

Look-through investment vehicles, such as mutual funds or bank commingled funds and guaranteed investment contracts, qualify as diversified categories of investment because the underlying assets are diversified. Employer stock, however, does not qualify as a diversified category of investment, although some liability protection is provided if the stock is publicly traded and if certain other conditions are met.

Each participant must be provided with or have the opportunity to obtain sufficient information to make informed decisions as to investment alternatives under the plan, as well as financial information concerning these alternatives. This includes, among other things:

- A general description of the investment objectives and risk and return characteristics of each investment alternative.
- An explanation of how to give investment instructions and any limitations on such instructions.
- An identification of investment managers.
- An explanation of voting, tender, and similar rights.
- A description of transaction fees and expenses that could affect the participant's account balance.
- The name, address, and phone number of the plan fiduciary.
- Where appropriate for the investment alternative, any applicable prospectus.
- A notice that the plan is intended to comply with ERISA Section 404(c) and that fiduciaries' liability is thereby limited.
- If a plan utilizes automatic enrollment and default investment alternatives, these must be specified as described in Chapter 11.

Employee Investment Education

The majority of defined contribution plans let participants direct how their account balances will be invested. While employers recognize the need to encourage employees to save, historically they had been reluctant to provide extensive education about investing these savings. This reluctance had been due, in part, to the fiduciary provisions of ERISA, which impose both responsibility and liability on those who provide investment advice for a fee or other compensation. The concern for these employers had been to distinguish between investment education and investment advice, recognizing that some efforts to provide only education may end up being interpreted as advice. This situation has undergone some change. Now that the PPA has provided guidelines on a plan sponsor's ability to appoint a fiduciary investment adviser, it is expected that more plans will make use of these services and be less concerned about prohibited transactions related to paying fees for investment advice. The requirements for appointing and monitoring a fiduciary investment adviser are explained in Chapter 29.

Previously the DOL had issued an interpretive bulletin to enable employers and providers to distinguish between education and advice. The bulletin specifies four types of investment-related information that employers could provide without fear of exposing themselves to fiduciary liability in the view of the DOL.[8] These safe harbors were:

- *General plan provisions.* This includes information about plan features and operations, the benefits of participating in the plan, and descriptions of the plan's investment alternatives, including investment objectives, risk and return characteristics, and historical information—as long as such information does not address the appropriateness of particular investment options for a given participant or beneficiary.
- *General financial and investment information.* Information about general investment concepts may be provided—for example, risk and return, diversification, dollar-cost averaging, and the advantages of tax-favored savings. It also is acceptable to provide information as to historical differences in rates of return between different asset classifications, investment time horizons, and estimates of future retirement income needs.
- *Asset allocation models.* Participants and beneficiaries can be provided with asset allocation models illustrating the projected performance of hypothetical asset allocations using varying time horizons and risk profiles.
- *Interactive investment material.* Acceptable material here includes items such as questionnaires, worksheets, computer software, and other materials that employees can use to estimate their retirement income needs and the potential impact of various investment strategies on their ability to meet those needs.

To qualify for safe harbor treatment, asset allocation models and interactive materials must be based on generally accepted investment theories and their underlying assumptions must be disclosed (or, in the case of interactive materials, selected by the participant). And, if allocation models or interactive materials identify a specific investment option under the plan, they should indicate that other investment alternatives having similar risk and return characteristics may be available under the plan and must identify where information on these alternatives may be obtained. Further, models and interactive materials must be accompanied by a statement explaining that participants should consider all of their other income, assets, and investments in applying the model or using the interactive tool.

---

[8] The Securities and Exchange Commission (SEC) has indicated that *employers* whose educational efforts conform to these four "safe harbors" will not be subject to registration or regulation under the Investment Advisors Act of 1940 (unless, of course, they hold themselves out as investment advisors or otherwise meet the definition of advisors in the 1940 law).

It is interesting that the Pension Protection Act is now requiring that plan sponsors display certain plan information electronically for plan years beginning after December 31, 2007. Previously plans were permitted to provide plan information electronically, but such display of plan information was not specifically required to be in an electronic form. The PPA now requires employers to provide identification, basic plan information, and actuarial information from the Form 5500 annual report to the Secretary of Labor in an electronic format that facilitates Internet display. The Secretary of Labor then is making this information available on an Internet website maintained by the Department of Labor. Additionally, this same information must be made accessible on any intranet website that the plan sponsor or the plan administrator maintains.

The DOL's bulletin also pointed out that employers may be able to provide investment education that falls outside these safe harbors without automatically being viewed as providing investment advice.

EGTRRA provided that employer-provided qualified retirement planning services are excludable from employees' gross wages. The exclusion applies to qualified retirement planning services offered to both employees and their spouses by employers sponsoring qualified retirement plans for years beginning after December 31, 2001. For this exclusion to apply to highly compensated employees, it must be available on substantially the same terms to rank-and-file employees. The provision allows for overall retirement income planning such as how the employer's plan fits into an employee's overall retirement income plan. The provision does not allow for related services such as tax preparation, accounting, legal, or brokerage services.

Since passage of the PPA, beginning in 2007 retirement plans' fiduciaries could provide investment advice to participants and be paid an additional fee for providing this advice. Prior to 2007, providing investment advice for an additional advisory fee by a plan fiduciary would result in a prohibited transaction under ERISA and the Internal Revenue Code. Now that the PPA allows plan sponsors to offer investment advice services, it is important to note the fiduciary responsibilities that apply to these services. Plan sponsors are not required to offer investment advice services. However, if plan sponsors offer such services to their participants, there are certain fiduciary responsibilities. Plan sponsors must prudently select the advice provider. Subsequently, the plan sponsor also must monitor the investment advice provider. The specific fiduciary requirements for plan sponsors offering these investment advice provider services to their plan participants are more fully explained in Chapter 29.

Remittance of Employee Contributions

The DOL has taken the position that participant contributions become plan assets as of the date they can be segregated from the employer's general assets but no later than 90 days after withholding. However, the DOL issued final regulations in August 1996 that shorten this outside deadline to the 15th business day following the month in which the employee contribution is received or withheld. A procedure is set forth under which an employer can obtain an additional 10 business days if certain conditions are met. This rule was generally effective February 3, 1997, although for collectively bargained plans, the effective date was extended to the first day of the plan year after the latest bargaining agreement in effect on August 7, 1996, had expired.

Miscellaneous Requirements

Plan provisions that purport to relieve a fiduciary of responsibilities are void and of no effect. However, a plan, employer, union, or fiduciary may purchase insurance to cover the fiduciary's liability, but if the plan purchases this insurance, the insurer must have subrogation rights against the fiduciary. An employer or union also may agree to indemnify a fiduciary against personal liability.

If convicted of certain specified crimes, a person cannot serve as a plan administrator, fiduciary, officer, trustee, custodian, counsel, agent, employee, or consultant for five years after conviction (or the end of imprisonment, if later). This prohibition will not apply if citizenship rights have been restored or if approved by the United States Board of Parole.

All fiduciaries and persons who handle plan funds or other plan assets are to be bonded for 10 percent of the aggregate amount handled, with minimum and maximum dollar amounts specified, as described in Chapter 28.

A plan must be established and maintained pursuant to a written instrument that specifically provides for one or more named fiduciaries. Each plan must provide a procedure for establishing and carrying out a funding policy and method to achieve plan objectives, and it must describe any procedure for allocating operational and administrative responsibilities. There also must be a provision that sets forth the amendment procedure and identifies the persons who have authority to amend the plan. The plan also must specify the basis on which payments are made to and from the plan.

Nonqualified Plans

As noted earlier, Title I of ERISA contains a number of labor law provisions that parallel the tax law requirements for qualified plans. For the most part, these provisions do not come into play insofar as qualified plans are concerned and—with the exception of determining service for eligibility to participate, vesting, and benefit accruals—the tax law provisions are controlling.

It must be remembered, however, that ERISA defines **pension plan** in very broad terms—on a basis that encompasses any plan, fund, or program maintained by an employer to the extent that, by its express terms or as a result of surrounding circumstances, it provides retirement income to employees or results in a deferral of income for periods extending to termination of employment or beyond.

Thus, any plan of deferred compensation, to the extent that it does not meet the tax law requirements for a qualified plan, comes under the purview of Title I and, unless exempted, must comply with various requirements such as minimum participation, funding and vesting, joint and survivor provisions, and the like. If a plan is not tax-qualified, and if it must be funded and vested, the tax consequences could be undesirable—with employees being in constructive receipt of the value of vested benefits. Thus, most employers prefer to design programs that qualify for one of the available exemptions.

One specific exemption is granted for **excess benefit plans**—plans that provide employees with contributions and/or benefits that would otherwise have been provided to them under the qualified plan were it not for the limitations of Section 415. This exemption is total for excess benefit plans that are unfunded; if funded, the exemption is partial and compliance only is required for reporting, disclosure, and fiduciary rules.[9]

Another exemption applies to plans that are "unfunded and . . . maintained by an employer primarily for the purpose of providing deferred compensation for a select group of management or highly compensated employees." However, these plans are still subject to the reporting and disclosure requirements of Title I.[10] Although ERISA has been in effect since the mid-1970s, this phrase has never been clarified by the DOL. Thus, there is some uncertainty as to how it may be applied. The concern, of course, is that if the group covered does not come within this exemption, the entire plan could become subject to all Title I provisions.

Despite this uncertainty, many employers have established supplemental executive benefit programs that rely on this exemption. Many of them are limited to **restoration plans** that simply restore benefits lost under qualified plans because of restrictions other than Section 415—for example, the limitation on pay that can be used to determine contributions and benefits or the annual limit on elective deferrals. Other plans are much broader in scope, encompassing all forms of deferred compensation and providing benefits for executives that are clearly in addition to those contemplated by broad-based programs. Executive benefit programs are covered at length in Chapter 14.

Rules imposed as part of the PPA now link the ability of a plan sponsor to pay non-qualified plan benefits to executives to the funded status of the organization's qualified defined benefit plan if the organization offers such a plan. If the sponsor of the defined benefit plan sets aside assets in a trust or other arrangement to pay nonqualified benefits to certain executives described in the law, during a "restricted period," then (1) the transferred assets will be taxed at the time of vesting under IRC Section 83 and (2) the 20 percent tax and interest penalties in effect under IRC Section 409A (as described in Chapter 14) will apply to the amounts taxed under IRC Section 83. A restricted period includes any period in which the qualified plan is deemed to be in "at-risk" status, any period of time when the plan sponsor is in bankruptcy, and any 12-month period beginning 6 months before the termination of an underfunded qualified plan. Essentially, this provision prevents companies with underfunded pension plans from setting aside or reserving assets to pay nonqualified plan benefits for individuals subject to insider trading rules under the Securities Exchange Act of 1934.

Unrelated Business Income

While the investment income of a qualified trust established in conjunction with a qualified plan is generally exempt from tax, all or part of this income could be subject to tax if it is considered to be **unrelated business income.**

---

[9] A partial exemption from disclosure and reporting has been provided by the DOL for these plans. In essence, all that is required is that the DOL be notified of the existence of any such plan and the number of individuals it covers.

[10] The partial exemption from disclosure and reporting also applies to these plans.

Unrelated business income is the gross income derived from any unrelated trade or business regularly carried on by the trust, less allowable deductions directly connected with the carrying on of such trade or business, with certain exclusions.

Only income resulting from the *direct* operation of the unrelated trade or business is subject to tax. Thus, for example, if the trust owns all of the stock of a corporation but the corporation directly operates the business, the stock dividends received by the trust will not be subject to tax.

The following income is not considered to be unrelated business income: dividends, interest, annuities, royalties, most rents from real property, and gains from the sale or exchange of noninventory property, except if such income is attributable to debt-financed property.

Age/Sex Discrimination

Discrimination on the basis of age is prohibited by the **Age Discrimination in Employment Act (ADEA),** as amended; discrimination on the basis of sex (or sex-related conditions, such as pregnancy) is prohibited by Title VII of the Civil Rights Act of 1964, as amended.

In the case of age discrimination (which protects employees age 40 and older), the major requirements for retirement-type plans are as follows:

- An employee cannot be excluded from participation because of age. Use of a minimum age of up to 21, as permitted under ERISA and the tax law, is acceptable; use of any maximum age is prohibited.

- An employee cannot be required to contribute more or at higher levels because of having attained an age that is 40 or more, nor can employer contributions and/or employer-provided benefits be increased or decreased by reason of age. It is permissible, however, for both employee and employer contributions and for employer-provided benefits to change with respect to length of service where this is clearly not age-related.[11]

- An employee cannot be made to retire upon attaining any specified age, such as the plan's normal retirement age.[12]

- As long as a participating employee remains employed, he or she must be eligible to continue full participation in the plan. In the case of a defined contribution plan, this means that the employee must continue to share in employer contributions (assuming the employee makes any mandatory contributions or elective deferrals that are required as a condition of receiving such contributions). In the case of a defined benefit plan, the employee must continue to accrue benefits for actual pay

---

[11] In the case of a defined benefit pension plan, any increase in employer-provided benefits on account of length of service would have to comply with the benefit accrual rules that limit the extent to which a plan can be "backloaded."

[12] There is a limited exception for "bona fide" executives whose annual employer-provided benefit from all sources is $44,000 or more. For these individuals, an employer can enforce mandatory retirement at age 65.

changes up to the time of retirement; the employee also must continue to accrue benefits for service until the plan maximum on service, if any, has been reached.

The prohibitions against sex discrimination are similar:

- Different employee and/or employer contributions cannot be made or required on account of the employee's sex.
- Benefits provided cannot be different by reason of the employee's sex.
- There can be no distinction in any plan eligibility requirements—for initial participation, rights to certain options or benefits, treatment of leaves of absence, and so forth—on account of sex.
- If annuity or lifetime installment benefits are offered by the plan, there can be no distinction in annuity or installment costs and/or benefits on account of sex; these costs and benefits must be based on unisex mortality tables.

Military Leaves

Although prior law required employers to give vesting and eligibility credits for periods of military service under all types of retirement plans, benefit accruals were clearly required only under defined benefit plans. Legislation passed in 1996 broadened veterans' pension rights by requiring employers to also make retroactive contributions for periods of military service to defined contribution plans upon the employees' return to work.

For a cash or deferred arrangement (CODA) or a plan permitting after-tax contributions, the returning employee must be allowed to make up missed deferrals or contributions over a period equal to three times the period of military service—up to a maximum of five years. If the employee does this, the employer must make up any missed matching contributions. Employers also are required to contribute any missed profit sharing allocations. However, employers are not required to make up earnings and forfeitures with respect to missed contributions.

Amounts credited to employees under pay-based plans must be based on the compensation rate the employee would have received had he or she not taken military leave. If the pay that would have been paid is not "reasonably certain," the credit could be based on the employee's pay for the 12-month period preceding military service.

Securities and Exchange Commission (SEC) Requirements

Various securities law requirements affect employee benefit and executive compensation plans. The following is a brief discussion of registration requirements and insider trading restrictions.

Offering Registration

In general, an offer to sell securities must either be registered with the SEC or conform to an available exemption from registration. If an offering must be registered with the SEC, a prospectus generally must be prepared for distribution to potential purchasers.

For purposes of this registration requirement, employee benefit plans can be divided into two groups: (1) those under which *employee* contributions are invested in employer stock and (2) all other plans. After-tax contributions always are considered employee contributions for this purpose. Elective deferrals, however, are treated differently, depending on whether they are made by way of salary reduction or by foregoing a year-end profit sharing contribution or bonus. The former type of elective deferral is considered to be an employee contribution, notwithstanding the fact that for tax purposes, it is considered to be an employer contribution. The latter type is treated by the SEC, as well as by tax law, as an employer contribution.

A plan that does not involve the investment of employee contributions in employer stock does not have to be registered with the SEC (e.g., an employee stock ownership plan [ESOP] funded entirely with employer contributions). However, any employee benefit plan in which employee contributions may be invested in employer stock is considered an offering to sell securities. Thus, such a plan must be registered with the SEC (and a prospectus prepared) or it must fit within an exemption. In many cases, no exemption is available for plans of publicly traded companies and such plans must be registered. A special type of registration, using the format of Form S-8, is available.[13]

In lieu of using a prospectus, an employer can meet its disclosure requirements through a variety of documents, including SPDs; however, the typical SPD will not be sufficient, by itself, to meet the SEC disclosure requirements (e.g., that there be a three-year history of financial data on investment alternatives).

It also should be noted that a prospectus (or equivalent information) must be given to employees before they are eligible to participate in the plan.

Plans that are registered with the SEC must file annual reports with the commission, using Form 11-K; this requirement, however, does not apply (except for the initial filing) to plans with fewer than 300 participants.

Insider Trading Restrictions

Section 16(b) of the Securities Exchange Act prohibits an insider from buying and selling, or selling and buying, company stock within a six-month period. Insiders who violate this six-month trading restriction are required to return all short-swing profits made on such a transaction to the company.

These insider trading rules are not relevant to a variety of broad-based retirement and allied make-up plans covering insiders—for example, defined benefit plans. However, they must be considered for any such plans that are individual account plans and provide for investments in actual or phantom employer stock by insiders. In this case, transactions that increase the amount of stock allocated to an insider are "purchases," and transactions that decrease the amount of stock allocated to an insider are "sales."

---

[13] Plans of private companies may be exempt under Rule 701. This rule permits an employer to grant up to $5 million worth of stock annually to employees without registration. This rule also requires that employees be given a copy of the plan document and that they receive adequate disclosure of material information. Further, the SEC must be notified within 30 days after sales total $100,000 and annually thereafter.

The SEC completely revised the insider trading rules with respect to broad-based plans in 1996. The revised rules, and their application to defined contribution and other plans, are discussed next.

Blanket Exemption

Nearly all transactions under broad-based plans are now exempt without any conditions—other than that the plan involved must satisfy one of the definitions so as to be a "qualified plan," an "excess benefit plan," or a "stock purchase plan"—or unless they constitute a discretionary transaction (described in the next section).

- To be a qualified plan, the plan must satisfy the coverage and participation requirements of Section 410 of the IRC.[14]

- An excess benefit plan is defined as one that is operated in conjunction with a qualified plan and that provides *only* the benefits or contributions that cannot be provided under the qualified plan because of the limitations of Section 401(a)(17),[15] Section 415, and any other applicable contribution or benefit limit set forth in the IRC.[16]

- A stock purchase plan is defined as a plan that meets the coverage and participation requirements of Sections 423(b)(3) or 423(b)(5), or, in the alternative, Section 410 of the IRC. The purpose of including this alternative is to make the exemption available to plans that do not satisfy Section 423 but nonetheless cover a broad base of employees. For example, a plan that is limited to nonunion employees and that does not qualify under Section 423 could still qualify for the exemption if the minimum coverage requirements of Section 410 were satisfied. Consistent with the broad exemptive relief provided to tax-conditioned plans, all purchases under a stock purchase plan are exempt and will not be matched with any other sale during the preceding or succeeding six-month period for purposes of determining any short-swing profit. However, an open market sale of stock acquired in an exempt purchase under a stock purchase plan is matchable with any nonexempt purchase (e.g., an open-market purchase during the relevant six-month periods).

Because of this **blanket exemption,** a variety of purchases and sales of stock that may occur under a qualified plan are now unconditionally exempt. For example, insiders can enroll, receive stock distributions, change the level of their contributions, cease contributions, or change the amount of future contributions invested in employer stock

---

[14] See the discussion of these requirements in Chapter 25. Note that a plan does not have to meet all of the tax-qualification requirements—just those relating to coverage and participation.

[15] Note the SEC regulations use the term "excess benefit plan" in a broader context than does ERISA.

[16] Excess benefit plans would appear to include nonqualified plans that permit 401(k) deferrals in excess of the elective deferral limit as adjusted ($15,500 in 2007) or allow contributions to make up for limitations resulting from actual deferral percentage (ADP) or actual contribution percentage (ACP) nondiscrimination tests. However, many types of deferred compensation plans (e.g., a plan permitting an executive to defer a percentage of base pay or bonus) would not be included. Also, deferred compensation plans for outside directors could never qualify as excess plans under this definition because a company cannot sponsor a qualified plan for its outside directors.

without any special restrictions. Only transactions that are defined as "discretionary transactions" must satisfy added conditions to be exempt—even under a tax-conditioned plan.

The regulations also provide a separate, unconditional exemption for purchases and sales of employer stock made pursuant to domestic relations orders (DROs), as defined under ERISA and the IRC. This exemption applies both for purposes of the short-swing profit restriction and for reporting purposes. It should be noted that DROs do not have to meet the more stringent requirements of QDROs imposed under the tax law. This means that potentially more transactions could be exempted—for example, those under nonqualified plans.

Discretionary Transactions

For qualified, excess benefit, and stock purchase plans, the only types of transactions that must satisfy an extra condition in order to be exempt are so-called discretionary transactions. These are defined as involving either:

- An intraplan transfer (i.e., a transfer of an existing account balance from one plan fund to another where one of the funds involves actual or phantom employer stock).
- A cash distribution funded by a sale of such employer stock.

These transactions are only subject to this extra condition if they are made at the election of an insider. Hence, an involuntary distribution from an employer stock fund triggered by an actual deferral percentage (ADP), actual contribution percentage (ACP), or Section 415 limit failure is not subject to this special rule. Also, transactions are exempt from the extra condition if made "in connection with" the insider's death, disability, retirement, or termination of employment or if they are required to be made available to the insider pursuant to the IRC.[17]

Even for discretionary transactions, the condition for exemption is relatively easy to satisfy and administer. All that is required is for every election of a discretionary transaction to occur at least six months after the most recent preceding election of a discretionary transaction that is the "opposite way." As long as six months have elapsed between the elections by the insider to make such transactions, they will be exempt. It should be noted that the focus is on the date of the elections, not the transactions themselves.

Reporting Requirements

Insiders generally are required to file periodic reports and annual reports (on Forms 4 and 5, respectively) with the SEC concerning their transactions in employer stock. The aforementioned regulations liberalize the scheme for reporting transactions in tax-conditioned plans. Most transactions under qualified, excess benefit, and stock purchase plans—those covered by the blanket exemption—will be completely exempt from reporting. Only intraplan transactions and cash distributions would be subject to annual reporting on Form 5. An executive can choose, however, to voluntarily report discretionary transactions on an earlier Form 4 (within 10 days after the close of the calendar

---

[17] Examples within this last category of transactions include an ESOP diversification election or an age 70½ minimum required distribution.

month in which the transaction occurs) rather than at year-end on Form 5. Discretionary transactions must be reported even though they qualify for the conditional exemption.

Collective Bargaining Requirements

It has long been recognized that employee benefits are mandatory subjects of collective bargaining under the National Labor Relations Act (NLRA). Thus, employers may not refuse to discuss providing employee benefits to employees who are represented by a collective bargaining unit, and they must negotiate in good faith concerning their demands.

In many situations, plans negotiated for union employees are unilateral plans that cover only individuals who work for the employer. Typically, the negotiation process involves design issues, such as eligibility, contribution levels, vesting provisions, and so forth, with funding of the benefits being left under employer control. On occasion, however, a union's proposal may be for coverage under a joint labor–management trust fund—a multiemployer or Taft-Hartley plan—as this is sometimes called. The law requires that these plans have equal labor and management representation on the board of trustees. For the most part, multiemployer plans have been limited to defined benefit pension plans and health and welfare programs.

Chapter Summary

- There are a number of legal requirements that plan sponsors must recognize in the administration of pension plans beyond the tax law qualification requirements. These requirements include
  - Title I of ERISA labor law provisions.
  - Title I of ERISA requirements for nonqualified executive benefit arrangements.
  - Prohibitions against age and sex discrimination.
  - Unrelated business income requirements when such income is earned within benefit plans.
- Securities and Exchange Commission (SEC) requirements apply to defined contribution plans investing in employer securities.
- Title I of ERISA contains labor law provisions dealing with the reporting, disclosure, and fiduciary responsibilities of plan sponsors. The intent of the reporting and disclosure requirements is to clearly inform plan participants and their beneficiaries regarding the benefit provisions and financial operation of their plans. Title I stipulates that certain documents must be filed with the government, certain documents must be automatically distributed to employees, and other items must be given to participants upon request and/or made available for examination.
- ERISA defines a fiduciary and requires that fiduciaries discharge all duties solely in the interest of plan participants and their beneficiaries and for the exclusive purpose of providing plan benefits and defraying reasonable administrative expenses. ERISA prohibits certain transactions between a plan and "parties in interest."

- According to the prudent expert rule, a fiduciary is charged with using the care, skill, prudence, and diligence that a prudent person who is familiar with such matters would use under the circumstances then prevailing.
- ERISA provides limited exemptions from its requirements for certain types of plans. Any plan of deferred compensation, to the extent that it does not meet the tax law requirements for a qualified plan, comes under Title I and, unless exempted, must comply with various requirements, such as the minimum participation, funding and vesting, and joint and survivor provisions. Plans qualifying for exemptions include:
  - Excess benefit plans.
  - Plans that are "unfunded and maintained by an employer primarily for the purpose of providing deferred compensation for a select group of management or highly compensated employees."
- The investment income of a qualified trust established in conjunction with a qualified plan is generally exempt from tax, although all or part of this income could be subject to tax if it is deemed to be unrelated business income.
- Various securities law requirements affect employee benefit and executive compensation plans.

Key Terms

Age Discrimination in Employment Act (ADEA), p. *509*

blanket exemption, p. *512*

earmarked investments, p. *503*

excess benefit plans, p. *508*

fiduciary, p. *500*

Form 5500, p. *492*

look-through investment vehicles, p. *504*

notification(s) as to pre- and postretirement survivor benefits, p. *497*

pension plan, p. *507*

prudent expert rule, p. *500*

restoration plans, p. *508*

rollover notification, p. *497*

Section 16(b) of the Securities Exchange Act, p. *511*

summary annual report (SAR), p. *492*

summary of material modifications (SMM), p. *492*

summary plan description (SPD), p. *491*

terminated vested participant, p. *496*

Title I of ERISA, p. *490*

unfunded excess benefit plans, p. *491*

unrelated business income, p. *508*

Questions for Review

1. List the disclosure items that must be either automatically furnished to the government or supplied to the government upon request under Title I of ERISA.
2. What information must be included in an SPD?
3. Describe the claim denial procedure that must be included in an employee benefit plan.
4. Are the directors of a corporation fiduciaries under Title I of ERISA? Why or why not?

5. Under what circumstances do the provisions of Title I of ERISA apply to nonqualified plans maintained for executives?

6. Describe the requirements of the ADEA that apply under defined benefit plans when an employee continues employment beyond his or her normal retirement date.

7. Under what circumstances do SEC requirements apply to qualified profit sharing and savings plans?

Questions for Discussion

1. An employee can become fully vested in his or her accrued benefits after three years of service and well before he or she has attained age 32. Once vested, the employee automatically must be protected by the joint and survivor provisions of the law. Nevertheless, the law does not require that the employee be notified of the joint and survivor benefits and rights until he or she has attained age 32. Explain why notification is not required before age 32 even though the employee could be entitled to the benefit.

2. Explain the rationale for the DOL's position concerning the granting of safe harbors for plans that permit earmarked investments (where employees choose the funds in which their contributions will be invested), and describe the conditions under which these safe harbors apply.

3. Do SEC requirements concerning the disclosure of information to eligible employees (when employee contributions may be used to purchase employer stock) supplant the SPD disclosure requirements of Title I of ERISA? Why or why not?

Resources for Further Study

CCH Editorial Staff. "2001 Tax Legislation: Law, Explanation, and Analysis." *Commerce Clearing House Pension Plan Guide* (2001).

Cleveland, Alan P. "Fiduciary Liability Issues under ERISA." *The Handbook of Employee Benefits.* 6th ed. Jerry S. Rosenbloom, ed. New York: McGraw-Hill, 2005.

Geller, Sheldon M. "Compliance Audits Can Protect Plan Sponsors." *Journal of Compensation and Benefits* 17, no. 2 (March/April 2001).

Mahoney, Dennis F. "Employee Benefit Plan Management." *The Handbook of Employee Benefits.* 6th ed. Jerry S. Rosenbloom, ed. New York: McGraw-Hill, 2005.

Maniaci, Serafina. "Communicating Employee Benefits Programs." *The Handbook of Employee Benefits.* 6th ed. Jerry S. Rosenbloom, ed. New York: McGraw-Hill, 2005.

Munson, Arlene; and David Leach. "SEC Liberalizes Insider Trading Rules." *Journal of Compensation and Benefits* 17, no. 2 (March/April 2001).

Reish, C. Frederick; Bruce Ashton; and Gail Reich. "Revised Form 5500 and ERISA 404(c) Compliance." *Journal of Pension Benefits* 8, no. 2 (Winter 2001).

Vitiello, James. "Internet/Web-Based Administration of Benefits." *Employee Benefits Journal* 26, no. 3 (September 2001).

Chapter 28

Fiduciary Oversight and Plan Governance[1]

After studying this chapter you should be able to:

- Describe the composition and workings of a formal retirement plan committee.
- Discuss issues a retirement plan committee should monitor when it delegates responsibilities to external service providers.
- Explain the purpose of a qualified retirement plan's fidelity bond.
- Summarize the purposes and the typical issues addressed in an investment policy, a loan policy, and a hardship distribution policy.
- Distinguish between the purposes of a policy document and an actual plan document.
- List the advantages and disadvantages of utilizing a bundled service provider.
- Explain the purpose of using a request for proposal (RFP) when selecting external service providers.
- Describe different types of fees charged to retirement plans and the fiduciary responsibilities in monitoring fee arrangements.
- Discuss the fiduciary issues involving retirement plans when companies merge or acquire other companies.

Background and Historical Setting

When companies first started offering retirement plans to their employees in the early twentieth century, there were few rules and regulations regarding how these plans should be managed internally. It was not until these plans had become fairly common and more meaningful to employees that there grew an expectation that there should

[1] The authors gratefully acknowledge the contribution of Mary Komornicka, CEBS, ChFC, PMP, of WNK Consulting Ltd., who wrote this chapter.

be more structure and controls around these plans. With the passage of the Employee Retirement Income Security Act (ERISA) in 1974, the fiduciary responsibilities relative to pension plans were significantly clarified and increased. The discussion regarding fiduciary requirements that is provided in Chapter 27 explains these plan sponsor responsibilities. Over time, as the legal and accounting regulations concerning pension plans increased and as pension plans grew in asset size, number of covered participants, and prevalence throughout all industries, proper plan governance became an important aspect in the successful operation of a plan.

The plan governance functions cover many of the elements that have been discussed in other chapters throughout this book. This chapter primarily focuses on how a plan sponsor ensures that (1) all the elements of fiduciary responsibility are properly executed in a manner so the plan operates as intended, (2) there is clarity concerning party is responsible for which fiduciary functions, and (3) the oversight necessary to ensure proper administration of the retirement plan is occurring. The actual manner a plan sponsor might decide to fulfill the various aspects discussed here may differ depending on the nature of the corporation or other organizational entity, its size and internal structure, as well as the precise requirements described in the plan document. Therefore, each retirement plan will have a different manner of handling these functions, but if some of these aspects of plan governance are neglected, the likelihood of improper plan administration resulting in failure to meet a legal requirement or the occurrence of a participant lawsuit is increased.

Retirement Plan Committee

A plan sponsor should establish a formal **retirement plan committee** that has responsibility regarding the governance and administration of the plan. While this committee may not be responsible for actually performing any of the administrative functions or handling actual participant communication relative to the plan, the committee does delegate that responsibility to an appropriate party and provides oversight to ensure that the proper actions are happening in a timely fashion. The membership of this committee is generally fairly small: three to five individuals often is sufficient, and membership consists of key senior leaders of the organization. In a small company, it may consist of the company president and the senior financial and human resources officers. In a larger company, the membership may be the chief financial officer, the human resources vice president, the corporate counsel, plus two other organizational members from senior management.

This committee should be authorized by the corporation to make all decisions necessary regarding the administration of the retirement plan. This committee determines the plan design; selects the service providers; meets with legal counsel; and reviews the overall status of the plan. As a committee, they meet at least annually but probably no more than quarterly—unless addressing some current, pressing issue. As an ongoing committee, the agenda focuses on investment performance review and administrative service provider review as well as address any legal or regulatory change that affects the retirement plan. In some companies, the retirement plan committee also may review and approve any written polices and procedures that are developed to assist in the day-to-day administration of the plan. Other companies permit the human resources or benefits department to develop and implement those policies and procedures without formal approval by the committee.

A key function of the retirement plan committee is the delegation of responsibilities to other parties. This includes internal corporate delegation as well as the delegation of certain plan functions to **external service providers** such as a plan trustee, record keeper, actuary, investment manager, and plan consultant. Although a corporation may hire external entities to provide these services, this does not relieve the plan sponsor of fiduciary responsibility for these functions. Therefore, it is essential that the retirement plan committee understand clearly what these external service providers will and will not be doing relative to the administration of the plan.

The corporation is depending on the retirement plan committee to ensure that key fiduciary aspects of the plan are satisfied, including avoiding any party-in-interest violations. As senior leaders in the corporation, these committee members are in a better position than a benefits manager to know if some anticipated corporate event might trigger a party-in-interest conflict and determine how to avoid the actual occurrence of such a conflict. The retirement plan committee also should have the responsibility to maintain proper fiduciary bonding for the plan. A **fidelity bond** is a form of protection that covers policyholders for losses that are incurred as a result of fraudulent acts by individuals specified in the bond's contract. All qualified retirement plans are required to have a fidelity bond that covers at least 10 percent of the plan assets in case of loss to the plan because of criminal acts or embezzlement by any of the plan fiduciaries or other plan officials. The maximum required amount for the fidelity bond is $500,000 unless the plan holds employer securities, in which case the maximum is increased to $1,000,000. It often is possible to have this fidelity bond added to the corporation's existing fidelity bond but care should be taken to ensure that the fidelity bond fully complies with ERISA requirements.

Plan Document

The actual decision regarding the plan design is typically a key responsibility of the retirement plan committee. While this decision should be made with advice supplied from consultants and legal advisers, it is important for the committee to determine the fit between the choice of various plan features and the unique benefit goals and human resource issues of the corporation. The initial design of the plan is important, but today often more time is spent regarding ongoing amendments to the plan. An **amendment** is a change or modification to the plan document that alters the operation of the plan. Such amendments are often driven by changes in the laws that happen on a continuing basis. Most companies will use the opportunity presented when amendments are needed to comply with new legal requirements to reevaluate the current features in the plan to determine if other amendments should be implemented. Drafting, reviewing, implementing, and communicating amendments is a costly process. It not only involves legal costs, but also adds the expense of distributing information to plan participants and changing other employee communications such as policy manuals and company websites. Sometimes a plan amendment necessitates changes to payroll systems and company procedures. Often an amendment is communicated through issuance of a "Summary of Material Modification," as described in Chapter 27. It is critical that the benefits staff understands how corporate systems such as payroll, procedures, policies, and corporate communications interrelate to properly manage the changes that must be implemented when amendments occur.

Often, the effective date for any required change because of new legislation is the start of the following plan year after the legislation is passed by Congress, even though the plan document is not required to be amended for a period of up to two or three years. For example, the Pension Protection Act of 2006 (PPA) had several provisions that became effective on the first day of the plan year that began on or after January 1, 2007. Even though these changes were expeditiously implemented as directed by the PPA, the plan documents affected were not required to be formally amended until the last day of the plan year that begins in 2009. Therefore, a plan sponsor needs to operate in compliance with the terms of the PPA for up to three years before the plan document will actually be amended to reflect these changes. This creates two distinct challenges for a plan sponsor: First, the plan sponsor must determine what elements of the plan will be altered due to this legislation. Second, the plan must be consistently administered according to the altered terms of the plan, as it will be after the amendment process has occurred. A plan that ignores operating in a manner as directed by the legislation until the formal amendment deadline would be found to be out of compliance with the law. Failure to make these plan changes in a timely manner places the plan at risk of being penalized by the Internal Revenue Service or the Department of Labor. Therefore, a procedure should be established that clearly identifies how the plan will operate during this interim period until the plan document has been formally amended.

Policies and Procedures

While the plan document provides the formal legal structure and general operating policies of the plan, numerous other procedural elements require more in-depth plan features that need to be addressed that are not detailed in the plan document. A well-managed plan will have a set of policies and procedures that guide the daily operation of the plan. There are some policies that every plan should have and that should be formally prepared, reviewed, and maintained. These include an investment policy; policies regarding participant loans and hardship distributions, if applicable; and a policy regarding qualified domestic relation orders (QDROs). Some of these policies can be anticipated at the plan's inception and should be in place at the start of plan operations, such as the investment policy. Other policies may be determined when a question or unique situation arises, for example, how to handle the enrollment of an individual who is returning after an absence from the workplace (do they reenter the plan on the first of the month or with the start of the next payroll period). The critical aspect about these policy determinations is that they must be consistently applied to all similarly situated employees. **Similarly situated employees** are workers who share the same status as employees. Therefore, similarly situated employees may be full-time versus part-time workers, have the same job class, etc. Care needs to be taken to ensure when a policy is being established for what appears to be a unique situation, it is a policy that will be acceptable should a similar situation happen to another participant. Failure to follow the same approach for all participants can result in employee relations issues with disgruntled participants and can even lead to lawsuits asserting a breach of fiduciary duty.

An investment policy is needed for every type of plan, including a plan that permits participants to direct the investments in their own accounts. The **investment policy** is the written document outlining the guidelines for the structure, operation, and decision making for the investments held by the retirement plan. The investment policy would include such things as the selection criteria for the investment managers or mutual funds offered in the plan, the benchmarks that will be used to measure the performance of the investments, the process and criteria used to change an investment or fund offering, the frequency that the investments will be reviewed (quarterly or annually), and how the investment fees are to be paid. If the plan investments are not participant-directed, then the policy should include the targeted asset allocation and the frequency of rebalancing. If the investments are participant-directed, the policy should include the number of fund options permitted, the range of investment options allowed, and the default investment option. (Chapter 11 contains detailed information on an exemption from fiduciary liability provided by the PPA when selecting default investment options if certain requirements are met.) Particular care should be given to whether the plan will permit investments in more exotic or risky investments such as hedge funds. It also is important to specify if any restrictions exist on certain types of investments, such as establishing that are no investments permitted in mutual funds that have a front-end load. While it is possible to make future changes in the investment policy, the purpose of the policy document is to establish a thoughtful, comprehensive investment structure that matches the goals of the retirement plan. Such an approach will serve to provide a long-term statement of the guiding principles that will be applied as the investment structure of the plan is reviewed.

The investment policy for a plan that has $3 million in assets will look significantly different from one with $300 million in assets. A smaller plan would more likely have investments in mutual funds, while a larger plan might have an investment manager who selects actual stocks. Thus, the policy needs to reflect the appropriate investment approach that matches the size of the plan; whether the plan participants direct the investments in their accounts; and the plan features, such as the particular payout structures within a defined benefit plan.

The **loan policy** is the guiding document that provides answers to many of the administrative issues that arise for plan loans. In addition to stating the statutory limits or plan limits (if different) regarding participant loans, this policy also provides guidance regarding how certain events will be handled. For example, if a participant has an outstanding loan and then is terminated, what will happen? Will the plan permit the participant to continue making payments on the loan, or will the participant be required to repay the loan at that time or have the loan amount deemed to have been distributed (a taxable event)? If the participant is permitted to continue making loan payments, by what date must the monthly payments be received, and what is the consequence of a late payment? Is a participant who has been laid off allowed to continue making payments? What happens if a participant has too few hours of work in a particular pay period for the loan payment to be made, given that there are other required deductions such as FICA tax, income tax, and medical premiums? The loan policy also should address the required period of time between the repayment of a loan and the issuance of a new loan. By establishing these policies in advance of any situations, the staff administering the plan is able to provide consistent answers to questions from plan participants. This minimizes the risk that unfair treatment to one participant over another will occur. Participant loans continue to be an area of scrutiny by the IRS during audits, so proper administration is very important.

A policy regarding hardship distributions if the plan permits these types of distributions should be in place. While the plan document will establish the minimum requirements regarding what qualifies as a "hardship," the policy should include the following elements:

• How frequently are hardship distributions processed (monthly, quarterly, or on an ad hoc basis)?
• Is there a minimum loan amount requirement (e.g., $1,000)?
• What will be acceptable proof to establish the hardship, and/or who will make the determination that there is in fact a hardship?
• What other sources of funds must a participant have used or attempted to use prior to applying for a hardship distribution?

The difference between what is contained in the plan document regarding plan features like loans or hardships and what is contained in the policy often is confusing. Generally, the elements within the policy are items that may change over time because of changing aspects of the business, internal procedures, or even government regulations. While it is important to have a consistent policy applied evenly to all participants, it also is important that a plan administrator be able to respond to changing conditions without having to amend the formal plan document frequently. The **policy document** serves as the guide for the day-to-day functions of the plan. Of course, the actual plan document is the controlling instrument and any policy or procedure developed must agree with the terms of the plan document.

Plan Administration

In other chapters the various rules regarding eligibility, service, and other plan requirements were discussed. At this time, we are not focusing on the specific limitations but on the various administrative elements that are tied to these requirements, in particular:

1. Who performs the various testing required.
2. Who determines whether an employee has satisfied the eligibility requirements.
3. Who is responsible for the communications to the employee.
4. Who is responsible for the filing of the Form 5500 and any other governmental required forms.

Service Providers

In today's world, few retirement plans are administered and managed solely by the company itself and its employees. Almost every plan hires one or more external service providers to fulfill one or more functions for the plan. Doing this does not change the fact that the company remains the **plan administrator** for the legal purposes of the plan document. The company is responsible for the actions of these service providers, so it is important that the company makes the selection carefully and monitors how the services are provided. The first step is to determine what elements should be performed by internal staff and which are better completed by external providers. Depending on the size and nature of a company or organization, certain functions may be completed more easily by the plan sponsor. For example, some companies prefer to have the participant communication functions done by the human resources (HR) department while others hire a record keeper to provide this service. Over time, the particular mix of who is responsible for which pieces of the plan administration may change. It is important, however, that the plan sponsor knows who is providing which services, what the key aspects of those services are, who is paying for those services, and how the fee for services is being assessed. It also is important to monitor if the services promised are being delivered in the timely and high-quality manner expected by the plan sponsor. In general, a company will consider using an external record keeper, investment manager, and/or corporate trustee.

Another fundamental decision the plan sponsor must make is whether to have the various services provided by one provider (often called a **bundled service-provider**) or whether to select different providers for various services. Several advantages exist for the bundled service-provider approach, including efficiencies in communication for the plan sponsor; increased coordination between the various elements of record keeping, investments, participant communications, and trustee functions; and potential fee savings. The disadvantage of this approach is that the plan sponsor may be forced to accept certain features or limitations in one aspect of the plan in order to have all these services bundled together. The provider may be excellent in several administrative functions but not all; if the plan sponsor is dissatisfied with the provider, the plan sponsor may be forced to change all elements of the plan administration including plan investments.

Selection and Oversight

Having determined what services will be performed within the company and which will be done by a service provider, the plan sponsor must then select the provider or providers that will be hired. The first step in the selection process usually is the development of a **request for proposal (RFP).** An RFP is a formal written document distributed to vendors inviting them to present their capabilities and place a bid with their pricing to become a service provider to the plan. The RFP generally identifies the key items that will be critical to the decision to select one provider over another. Thus, each RFP differs, depending on the particular needs of the organization drafting the RFP. The following list identifies many common elements that would be found in an RFP being issued by a company seeking 401(k) plan administrative services:

- *Experience*: How many years has the company been in business? What is the experience and training of key personnel? How much staff turnover occurs?
- *Client size*: What is the average size relative to both participants and assets? Is there any minimum size requirement?
- *Investment options available*: Is there a specific family of funds that must be included? Are there some funds that are not permitted? Must a certain percentage of assets be invested in a particular family of funds? Is there the ability to handle company stock? Are default investment options available? What are the maximum number of investments? What is the availability and cost of self-directed accounts? What is the availability of lifestyle funds and the structure of those investments?
- *Investment management*: What is the company's management style, experience level, and performance level? What are the total assets under management per fund?
- *Statements*: What is the format and timing of the statements? Do they have the flexibility to include company-specific information?
- *Management reports*: What is the frequency and format of the reports? What information is provided?
- *Compliance testing*: When are tests performed? Which tests are performed?
- *Service standards*: What are the timing standards for processing loans, distributions, and statements? Are there any performance guarantees?
- *Fees*: What are the specific fees? How are they calculated? When are they assessed?
- *Participant materials*: What is the range of materials available? Is customization available, and, if so, are there extra costs or are these costs included in the base?
- *Website*: What is the functionality of the website for participants and for benefits staff? What is the look and feel? Is it customizable to the specific company?
- *Employee meetings*: What is the frequency of employee meetings? Who conducts the meetings? What is the format of the meetings? What locations can the provider service?
- *Participant telephone support*: What are the hours of service? What is the staff experience? Which topics or issues can be handled by the phone support staff?
- *Interactive participant tools*: What is the function of the tools? How do participants access the tools? Are the participants' personal data preloaded into the projection software?
- *Data transfer*: What are the format requirements or limitations? What security controls govern the electronic transfer of information?
- *Government reporting*: Who will complete Form 5500 and other government reports?

The plan sponsor should identify and indicate in the RFP if there are specific elements in any of these items that are required. It is not uncommon for the service providers to have questions regarding elements in the RFP. Therefore, a process should be established to answer the questions that vendors replying to the RFP will have. Some common queries regarding questions are such things as: Will only written questions be received, and will the answers be shared with all bidders?

Having selected the service provider or providers, the awarding of a contract is the start of a partnership between the plan sponsor and the vendor. The success of the partnership depends on the ongoing communication among the various parties involved in the partnership as well as the quality and timeliness of the services being provided. The plan sponsor retains ultimate responsibility regarding the legal compliance of the plan as well as ensuring that the participants' needs are being met by the plan service providers. Therefore, the plan sponsor needs to carefully monitor the actions of the service providers to ensure that the plan is being administered according to the terms of the plan document as well as adhering to the agreed-upon levels of service. Many companies establish a practice of formally assessing the service providers on a regular basis, such as every three to five years. In some cases, this may only be an internal review while in other cases the plan sponsor may proceed with a full RFP process each time. In either case, a predetermined schedule of review provides assurance that the plan sponsor remains in control of the plan and is aware of the quality of service being provided to the participants.

Fees

In recent years, the importance of how fees are calculated and charged to retirement plans has gained increased attention by both plan sponsors and plan participants. It also has become an area of concern for the Department of Labor as well as the subject of several class action lawsuits. Therefore, it is critical the plan sponsor be keenly aware of the true costs of the plan and how the fees are structured. For defined benefit plans, the impact of any fees is borne by the plan sponsor as they are either paid directly by the plan sponsor from assets outside the plan or paid from plan assets. If paid from plan assets, this effectively results in increased contribution requirements for the plan sponsor. However, for defined contribution plans, if the fees are paid from plan assets, the net effect is to reduce participant benefits. Therefore, the actual structure of the fees for defined contribution plans becomes a fiduciary issue. The rest of this discussion is focused on the fees for a 401(k) plan, although many of these fees also may apply to other defined contribution plans.

The challenge for most plan sponsors is to understand exactly what the fees are and how they are being assessed. While it is obvious that no service provider works for free, it is not uncommon for fees to be computed and charged so that there are no direct costs to the plan sponsor, which makes it appear to be a no-cost service. However, the fees may be buried within the management expenses of the investment fund or paid by **revenue-sharing agreements** between the record keeper and the investment manager. It is important that the plan sponsor understands the fees and how these fees are shared or split among the various service providers. This is necessary so that it can be determined if the overall fee structure is reasonable and appropriate. In addition,

Assume you are an employee with 35 years until retirement and a current 401(k) account balance of $25,000. If returns on investments in your account over the next 35 years average 7 percent, and fees and expenses reduce your average returns by 0.5 percent, your account balance will grow to $227,000 at retirement, even if there are no further contributions to your account. If fees and expenses are 1.5 percent, however, your account balance will grow to only $163,000. The 1 percent difference in fees and expenses would reduce your account balance at retirement by 28 percent.

Source: U.S. Department of Labor, http://www.dol.gov/ebsa/publications/401k_employee.html.

because most fees are charged as a percentage of assets, as the plan grows the fee also increases. This presents an opportunity for the plan sponsor to discuss a possible reduction in the rate being charged when assets under management increase. A plan sponsor also should inquire as to an enhancement in services as plan assets increase.

Mutual Fund Fees

- *Sales charges* (also known as loads or commissions). These are basically transaction costs for the buying and selling of shares. They may be computed in different ways depending on the particular investment product.
- *Management fees* (also known as investment advisory fees or account maintenance fees). These are ongoing charges for managing the assets of the investment fund. They generally are stated as a percentage of the amount of assets invested in the fund. Sometimes management fees may be used to cover administrative expenses. The level of management fees can vary widely, depending on the investment manager and the nature of the investment product. Investment products that require significant management, research, and monitoring services generally will have higher fees.
- *Other fees.* This category covers services such as record keeping, furnishing of statements, toll-free telephone numbers, and investment advice. It also covers costs involved in the day-to-day management of investment products. This expense category may be stated either as a flat fee or as a percentage of the amount of assets invested in the fund.
- Some mutual funds assess sales charges (see the first bullet item for a discussion of sales charges). These charges may be paid when an individual invests in a fund (known as a front-end load) or when he or she sells shares (known as a back-end load, deferred sales charges, or redemption fees). A front-end load is deducted upfront and, therefore, reduces the amount of a participant's initial investment. A back-end load is determined by how long a person keeps the investment. Various types of back-end loads exist, including some that decrease and eventually disappear over time. A back-end load is paid when the shares are sold (i.e., if the participant decides to sell a fund share when a back-end load is in effect, he or she will be charged the load).
- Mutual funds also may charge what are known as **Rule 12b-1 fees,** which are ongoing fees paid out of fund assets. Rule 12b-1 fees may be used to pay commissions to brokers and other salespersons, to pay for advertising and other costs of

Department of Labor's Statement Regarding Fees   2

ERISA requires employers to follow certain rules in managing 401(k) plans. Employers are held to a high standard of care and diligence and must discharge their duties solely in the interest of the plan participants and their beneficiaries. Among other things, this means that employers must:

- Establish a prudent process for selecting investment alternatives and service providers.
- Ensure that fees paid to service providers and other expenses of the plan are reasonable in light of the level and quality of services provided.
- Select investment alternatives that are prudent and adequately diversified.
- Monitor investment alternatives and service providers once selected to see that they continue to be appropriate choices.

Source: U.S. Department of Labor, http://www.dol.gov/ebsa/publications/401k_employee.html.

promoting the fund to investors, and to pay various service providers to a 401(k) plan pursuant to a bundled service arrangement. They usually range between 0.25 percent and 1.00 percent of assets annually.

- Some mutual funds may be advertised as "no-load" funds. This can mean that there is no front- or back-end load. However, there still may be an incremental 12b-1 fee.

Collective Investment Funds

A collective investment fund is a trust fund managed by a bank or trust company that pools investments of 401(k) plans and other similar investors. Each investor has a proportionate interest in the trust fund assets. For example, if a collective investment fund holds $10 million in assets and a participant's investment in the fund is $10,000, the individual has a 0.1 percent interest in the fund. Like mutual funds, collective investment funds may have different investment objectives. There are no front- or back-end fees associated with a collective investment fund, but there are investment management and administrative fees.

Fee-Sharing Arrangements

There are a variety of ways that the fees charged to the investments are shared with other service providers. As a fiduciary, the plan sponsor has a responsibility to understand the fees that are being charged to the plan—the reasonableness of those fees as well as knowing who receives any fees from the plan. Underlying this issue is the responsibility to ensure the fees are used for services that benefit the participants.

Soft-Dollar Arrangements

Use of soft-dollar arrangements is one of the most common ways to share revenue generated by a plan. **Soft-dollar arrangements** occur when the standard fee charged for a service is greater than the actual cost incurred. For example, if it cost a brokerage firm 4 cents to execute a trade but the standard charge is 10 cents, the brokerage firm could make the difference (6 cents) available to the broker initiating the trade for use against the cost of various services. This might be used for services such as access to the brokerage firm's security analysis system. This practice is permitted under Securities and Exchange Commission (SEC) regulation 28(e). In the retirement plan world, this arrangement may provide services to the investment consultant used by the plan.

Subtransfer Agent Fees

Subtransfer agent fees are typically found in a participant-directed account plan, such as a 401(k) plan. The fees may be structured as a flat dollar amount per participant ($5) or as a small percentage of assets (10 basis points). Two potential issues arise with this fee. First, if it is charged as a percentage of assets, the fee will increase as the plan assets grow—even though there has been no corresponding increase in services provided to either the plan or the participant. The second issue relates to who receives this payment and what services have been provided for this fee. This arrangement often is used to cover the cost of the record-keeping services. However, because different mutual funds provide different levels of subtransfer fees to the record keeper, this may cause the record keeper to encourage the use of one fund over another. Therefore, it is important the plan sponsor know what subtransfer fees are being received and the extent used to offset the overall cost of the services provided to the plan.

The underlying fiduciary requirement that plan sponsors must remember is that ERISA requires that plan assets must be used for the exclusive benefit of the plan participants and their beneficiaries. The fact a fee-sharing arrangement exists does not mean there is a problem or that any party is engaged in improper actions. The plan sponsor, as the plan fiduciary, does have the responsibility to understand the range of fees, how they are charged, who receives the fees, and for what services these fees apply. The various service providers should supply this information upon request to the plan sponsor.

Mergers and Acquisitions

When a company decides to merge with another firm or to acquire another firm, close attention must be given to the impact of the merger or acquisition on the retirement plans of the two respective companies. Only in rare situations would the status of the retirement plans control the decision on whether to merge with or acquire another firm, but there will be important consequences to the retirement plans that the corporate managers need to evaluate and address. If the firm being acquired has a defined benefit pension plan, the funding status of that plan must be carefully evaluated early in the process. The decision may be made to terminate the plan prior to the formal acquisition of the company so that the liability for the plan may be determined before the merger is finalized.

Where both companies have defined contribution plans, issues exist that need to be addressed early in the merger process. A primary decision must be made if the two plans will be combined or whether both plans will continue to be maintained separately. While it may be easier initially to maintain two plans, in the long term this generally is feasible only if there will be an overall separation of the two workforces rather than the creation of an integrated company. If the decision is made to maintain two separate plans, it will be necessary to make sure that both plans properly address the treatment of employees who transfer between the two divisions, ensuring that the plans give credit for service with either company for vesting purposes. The plans also need to specify which employees are considered participants in which plans, and if a participant who transfers between the divisions can transfer her or his account from one plan to the other.

The following is a partial list of issues that should be addressed prior to a merger assuming the decision has been made to maintain only one plan long term:

1. Compare the plan documents relative to the following items to determine if there are any differences and determine how the feature will be handled in the future plan:

   Participation requirements.

   Entry dates.

   Definition of compensation, hours of service, etc.

   Vesting schedules.

   Matching contributions.

   Participant loans.

   Hardship distributions.

   In-service distributions.

   Distributions at retirement.

2. Review the plan document, SPD, SMM, and Form 5500s. These formal documents should be reviewed to ensure that they are current with all laws and regulations. The last plan audit also should be reviewed for any potential problems or outstanding issues.

3. Evaluate the investment options available in the two plans, and determine if there are any investment options that will be eliminated. Frequently, there are similar investment options in the two plans, and a determination should be made as to which investment option is the better one to retain. Of greater concern is when the plan of the firm being merged contains investment options deemed to be inappropriate. This will create a significant participant communication challenge to explain why the investment option will no longer be available to the participants and what options are available that can address that investment objective. It is recommended that the plan sponsor follow the investment policy for the plan in the process of making these decisions.

4. Evaluate the differences in participant communications, investment education, record keeping, and participant services such as websites and telephone services. Even when there are no fundamental differences in the plan features, participants may perceive a loss of plan benefits when there are changes in the communication features of the plan. At a time of plan merger, participants often are anxious regarding the future and security of the retirement plan. Therefore, attention to these aspects early in the process can alleviate these concerns.

5. Plan the consolidation of the two plans by working closely with the various service providers (record keeper, trustee, investment manager). The combination of the plan assets and records require careful planning to ensure that everything happens in a smooth manner. It is reasonable to anticipate that it will take 60 to 90 days to plan for the actual transfer. Most of this time will be spent in preparation for the transfer, with the actual change occurring over a few days, sometimes even overnight.

6. An extensive communication plan should be developed that will let participants know what elements of the plan will be changing, when the change will occur, what action is required on their part, and what will happen if they fail to take that action.

The key to a successful integration of plans following a merger or acquisition is early involvement of the benefits staff and ERISA counsel in the evaluation of the plans and the alternatives.

Chapter Summary

- A plan sponsor should establish a formal retirement plan committee that has responsibility regarding the governance and administration of the plan.

- A key function of the retirement plan committee is the delegation of responsibilities to other parties. This includes internal corporate delegation as well as the delegation of certain plan functions to external service providers such as a plan trustee, record keeper, actuary, investment manager, and plan consultant. Although a corporation may hire external entities to provide various services, this does not relieve the plan sponsor of fiduciary responsibility for these functions.

- All qualified retirement plans are required to have a fidelity bond that covers at least 10 percent of the plan assets in case of loss to the plan due to criminal acts or embezzlement by any of the plan fiduciaries or other plan officials. The maximum required amount for the fidelity bond is $500,000 unless the plan holds employer securities, in which case the maximum is increased to $1,000,000.

- While a decision on plan design should be made with advice supplied from consultants and legal advisers, it is important for the retirement plan committee to determine the fit between the choice of various plan features and the unique benefit goals and human resource issues of the corporation.

- A well-managed plan will have a set of policies and procedures that guide the daily operation of the plan.

- An investment policy is needed for every type of plan, including a plan that permits participants to direct the investments in their own accounts. The purpose of the policy document is to establish a thoughtful, comprehensive investment structure that matches the goals of the retirement plan. Such an approach will serve to provide a long-term statement of the guiding principles that will be applied as the investment structure of the plan is reviewed.

- The policy document serves as the guide for the day-to-day functions of the plan. Of course, the actual plan document is the controlling instrument, and any policy or procedure that is developed must agree with the terms of the plan document.

- The request for proposal (RFP) generally identifies the key items that will be critical to the decision to select one external service provider over another. Thus, each RFP differs, depending on the particular needs of the organization drafting the RFP.

- Many organizations establish a practice of formally assessing their external service providers on a regular basis, such as every three to five years. In some cases this may only be an internal review, while in other cases the plan sponsor may proceed with a full RFP process each time.

- Fees may be buried within the management expenses of an investment fund or paid by revenue-sharing agreements between the record keeper and the investment manager. It is important that the plan sponsor understands the fees and how these fees are shared or split among the various service providers. This is necessary so that it can be determined whether the overall fee structure is reasonable and appropriate.

- When a company decides to merge with another firm or to acquire another firm, close attention must be given to the impact of the merger or acquisition on the retirement plans of the two respective companies. There will be important consequences to the retirement plans that the corporate managers need to evaluate and address.

Key Terms

amendment, p. *519*
bundled service provider, p. *523*
external service providers, p. *519*
fidelity bond, p. *519*
investment policy, p. *521*
loan policy, p. *521*

plan administrator, p. *523*
policy document, p. *522*
request for proposal (RFP), p. *523*
retirement plan committee, p. *518*
revenue-sharing agreements, p. *525*

rule 12b-1 fees, p. *526*
similarly situated employees, p. *520*
soft-dollar arrangements, p. *527*
subtransfer agent fees, p. *528*

Questions for Review

1. What are the responsibilities of a retirement plan committee?
2. What is the purpose of a fidelity bond?
3. Can a plan make changes effective prior to the plan document being formally amended? Explain.
4. What is the purpose of policies and procedures that supplement the actual plan document?
5. Why must a plan consistently apply policies to similarly situated employees?
6. What types of issues are addressed in a retirement plan investment policy?
7. What is the purpose of the investment policy document?

8. Distinguish between the purposes of a policy document for a retirement plan and the actual plan document.

9. What are the advantages of using a bundled service provider to assist in administering a retirement plan?

10. What are the disadvantages of utilizing a bundled service provider to assist in administering a retirement plan?

11. When looking to hire an external service provider, what is the purpose of a request for proposal issued by a retirement plan committee?

12. How do companies and other organizational entities assess service providers on a regular basis?

13. Distinguish the different ways fees to external service providers are paid for defined benefit and defined contribution plans.

14. Explain why defined contribution fee payments become a fiduciary issue.

15. Can a no-load fund charge a rule 12b-1 fee? Explain.

16. What are soft-dollar arrangements?

17. What are subtransfer agent fees, and how can these fees bias a record keeper?

18. What condition generally must be present if two companies merging decide to separately maintain their two preexisting defined contribution plans?

Questions for Discussion

1. Discuss the advantages and disadvantages of an organization not having an investment policy document.

2. Assume that an organization issues an RFP and receives two proposals from external service providers. Their responses are nearly identical except in the area of fees. Although both fees are about the same in the aggregate, one assesses a flat dollar amount per participant while the other charges as a percentage of assets. Discuss which fee arrangement you favor and why. What organizational considerations would influence which provider you would select?

Resources for Further Study

Cleveland, Alan P. "Fiduciary Liability Issues Under ERISA," *The Handbook of Employee Benefits*, 6th ed. Jerry S. Rosenbloom, ed. New York: McGraw-Hill, 2005.

Trone, Donald B. "Developing an Implementation Matrix: Lessons to be Learned from Defined Contribution Plans," *Journal of Financial Planning* (2000).

Trone, Donald B. *Procedural Prudence: The Fiduciary's Handbook for Management of Retirement Plan Assets*. New York: Veale & Associates, 1997.

Chapter 29

Facilitating Investment of Defined Contribution Plan Assets[1]

After studying this chapter you should be able to:

- Identify employer responsibilities in administering a defined contribution plan.
- Specify employee responsibilities as stakeholders in a defined contribution plan.
- Analyze the workplace and market trends that have contributed to the popularity of defined contribution plans.
- Explain the fiduciary duties of an employer sponsoring a defined contribution plan.
- Discuss the legal and communications considerations of a plan sponsor developing an investment education program for defined contribution plan participants.
- Describe the ongoing nature of employer responsibilities in the design, implementation, and monitoring of a defined contribution plan.

Chapter 24 examined many investment concepts applicable to both defined benefit and defined contribution plans. This chapter examines the particular investment issues relevant to defined contribution plans where employees bear the risk associated with plan asset investment choices. Both employers and employees have a vital stake in the plan investment provisions of a defined contribution plan. The employer is responsible for structuring appropriate investment programs, selecting suitable investment managers, monitoring investment performance, and communicating critical investment provisions to employees. In the typical plan, employees are responsible for deciding how to invest their account balances, and they assume all of the risks associated with

---

[1] The authors wish to express their appreciation to Towers Perrin for permission to use historical material—much of which was originally contained in *The Handbook of 401(k) Plan Management* (Burr Ridge, IL: Irwin Professional Publishing, 1996).

investment performance. Both employers and employees must have a sound understanding of basic investment principles if they are to succeed in fulfilling their respective responsibilities.

For the employer, the benefits of a successful investment program include low cost fees, ease of administration, flexibility to make needed changes in investment arrangements, and improved recognition of the company as a source of valuable benefits. For employees, a well-executed investment program maximizes capital accumulation through increased participation, improved returns, and lower costs.

Although written in the context of defined benefit plans, most of the material in Chapter 24 regarding matters such as asset classes, asset allocation strategies, types of investment risk, investment objectives, and investment manager selection is equally applicable to defined contribution plans. For this reason, the following discussion relates primarily to fiduciary responsibilities and design features that are unique to defined contribution plans.

Historical Development

The initial era of defined contribution investing was driven, to a large extent, by expediency. Ease of administration—particularly record keeping—often dictated the number and types of investment choices that were made available. Some plans provided no choice at all, simply investing plan assets in a single fund. Others offered two investment funds: one a fixed income fund such as a guaranteed investment contract (GIC), in which all employee contributions were invested, and the other an employer stock fund in which all employer contributions were invested. Still others allowed a relatively limited choice, such as a choice between a fixed-income and an equity fund.

Another factor that tended to limit investment options was employer concern about potential legal liability for giving employees any kind of financial advice. Restricting investment choice obviously limited the need for such counsel. As described later, the Pension Protection Act of 2006 (PPA) made changes in the law mitigating this concern. Since passage of the PPA, beginning in 2007 retirement plans' fiduciaries could provide investment advice to participants and be paid an additional fee for providing this advice. Prior to 2007, providing investment advice for an additional advisory fee by a plan fiduciary would have resulted in a prohibited transaction under ERISA and the Internal Revenue Code.

Most important, however, was the fact that few employers had articulated specific investment objectives for their defined contribution plans. In many situations, this reflected the fact that investment results in these plans do not affect the employer's financial statements; thus, pressure from this source to improve financial results does not exist. Most employers designed their defined benefit plans to replace specified levels of preretirement income and viewed their defined contribution plans as simply providing supplemental benefits. Thus, little thought was given to defined contribution plan investment choices or investment performance. For example, while the need to diversify is a staple of modern investment theory, many plans gave employees little or no opportunity to diversify, either among or within various investment classes. Further, employers tended to do little in the way of providing useful investment information to their employees—either about the options available to them or about basic principles of investing. In short, the early age of defined contribution plan asset management was characterized by limited employee choice and a lack of well-defined plan and investment objectives.

The past 25 years have seen a definite shift—at least in terms of the investment opportunities made available to employees. Many factors have contributed to this change, including a growing public awareness of the role of defined contribution plans in providing economic security and the importance of saving and investing wisely; an increased recognition on the part of employers of the need to provide flexibility of choice and investment education; improved and more-efficient administrative capabilities; and the aggressive marketing efforts of the leading mutual funds.

Most of today's plans provide a wide variety of investment funds for their participants, and the number of choices available in these plans underscores the need for educating employees to become better investors. The fact that employees have more investment choices does not mean they are making the most of what their plans have to offer. Overall, billions of dollars in defined contribution plan assets are still being invested very conservatively and with insufficient diversification. While this reflects the fact that employees need to know more about investments and financial planning, it also reflects the fact that many employers still have not focused on managing their plans as effectively as possible.

The situation is changing, however. To a much greater extent, employers look more closely at plan objectives and plan performance and are recognizing that more effective plan management can improve plan values with no additional company contributions to the plan. Not only are employers changing their perspectives on these plans, but governmental policy has adapted to the more significant role defined contribution plans play in the financial well-being of countless workers. In fact, many of the provisions of the PPA were perceived as recognizing the need for enhanced governmental protection for plan participants. In addition to the provisions facilitating the ability to provide investment advice, the diversification requirements for defined contribution plans, and the fiduciary exemption associated with automatic enrollment, are examples of public policy measures to protect the retirement savings of plan participants. The components of effective plan management—including the design of investment structures and overall investment operations—are discussed in the following sections.

Plan Design Considerations

The investment provisions of a defined contribution plan should be compatible with the plan sponsor's objectives. Three major areas to be considered are (1) fiduciary responsibilities, (2) the role employer stock will play, and (3) administrative issues.

Fiduciary Considerations

As noted in Chapter 27, a fiduciary must discharge its duties solely in the interests of plan participants and their beneficiaries and for the exclusive purpose of providing plan

How Long Must a Plan Sponsor Contract with an Investment Advisor?   1

Securities and Exchange Commission (SEC) "no-action" letters and Department of Labor (DOL) regulations prohibit advisory contracts from binding plans for unreasonable lengths of time (e.g., one year or more) or from imposing a penalty upon a plan's termination. Both of these practices are deemed to violate the advisor's fiduciary duties.

Reasonable cancelation provisions could be included, for example, setting forth a certain number of days or months that advance written notice must be given to the advisor and, if appropriate, the reimbursement by the advisor of any reasonable expenses caused by such cancelation.

Source: Robert B. Van Grover, "Advisory Agreements: A Guide to Advisors and Trustees of Benefit Plans." Reprinted with permission, from the August 1993 issue of *Pension Management* magazine, p. 36. © Intertec Publishing Corp.

benefits and meeting administrative expenses. Further, a fiduciary is held to a prudent expert standard in the discharge of its duties.[2]

It is not uncommon for plans to be structured so that trustees and external investment managers, rather than the employer, are responsible for the investment of plan assets. In these plans, the plan sponsor has delegated specific investment authority to outside professionals, thus limiting its own fiduciary liabilities. It is important to emphasize, however, that delegating responsibilities to outside professionals does not relieve the employer of all fiduciary responsibilities; the employer is still responsible, as a fiduciary, for the proper selection and retention of these external fiduciaries.

A plan sponsor can further limit its fiduciary liability by permitting employees to make their own allocations among the various investment options, provided a certain minimum number of options spanning a range of investment classes are offered and employees are permitted to make changes to their allocations no less frequently than quarterly. The employer also must provide employees with information sufficient for them to make an informed choice among the various options available. These requirements are covered in more detail in Chapter 27 and are commonly referred to as the Section 404(c) safe harbor provisions. In general, these safe harbor provisions require that a plan offer at least three diversified categories of investment with materially different risk and return characteristics. Compliance with these guidelines does not relieve the employer of the responsibility of ensuring that the investment options offered under the plan are prudent and properly diversified and does not relieve the employer of fiduciary responsibility for investments over which the employee has no control, such as employer contributions that are automatically directed to one of the investment options.

Now that the PPA has allowed plan sponsors to offer investment advice services, it is important to note the fiduciary responsibilities that apply to these services. Plan sponsors

[2] It should be noted that fiduciary responsibilities, in the context of an ERISA plan, apply the concept of portfolio diversification to the total portfolio and not on an asset-by-asset basis.

are not required to offer investment advice services. However if plan sponsors decide to offer such services to their participants, there are certain fiduciary responsibilities. Plan sponsors must prudently select the advice provider. Subsequently, the plan sponsor must monitor the investment advice provider. Therefore, fiduciary responsibilities relate both to the **appointment of the investment advice provider** and the **ongoing monitoring process of the investment advice provider.** The Department of Labor has specified the following criteria as important when appointing an investment advice provider:

• The plan sponsor must review and assess the provider's qualifications, quality of services offered, and reasonableness of fees charged.

• The plan sponsor's review process must avoid self-dealing, conflicts of interest, or improper influence.

• The plan sponsor's review process must assess the adviser's experience and qualifications, the adviser's compliance with registration requirements and other relevant securities laws, the adviser's assumption of fiduciary responsibility under ERISA, and whether the advice is based on generally accepted investment theories.

With regard to monitoring the investment advice provider, the DOL has prescribed the following responsibilities for plan sponsors:

• The plan sponsor must note any changes in the information that served as the basis for the initial selection of the investment adviser. This information includes continuing compliance with securities laws and whether the advice is based on generally accepted investment theories.

• The plan sponsor must also note whether the investment adviser complies with the terms of its agreement with the plan sponsor, the use of advice services by participants relative to the cost of these services, and any comments and complaints about the service.

• A plan sponsor needs to investigate any complaints, and to the extent that complaints raise issues regarding the actual advice provided, the plan sponsor may need to review the specific advice with the advisor.[3]

Employer Stock as an Investment Option

The Section 404(c) safe harbor provisions permit a company to offer employer stock as one of the investment options, provided the plan also offers the three required options and the employer's shares are publicly traded in a recognized market. In addition, all purchases, sales, voting, and related share activities must be implemented on a confidential basis. If the employer stock option meets these criteria, the fiduciary liability protection afforded plan sponsors under Section 404(c) is extended to the employer stock option.

Employer stock is a common investment option in many defined contribution plans. Some employers believe that stock ownership strengthens the link between employee

---

[3] Robert J. Lowe, "New Retirement Plan Investment Advisor Rules Put More Obligations on Plan Sponsors," *BNA Tax Management Insights and Commentary*, (February 26, 2007), pp. 1–5.

and corporate interests. Others seek to create or expand a friendly group of shareholders as a barrier to hostile takeover attempts.

However, there are several potential disadvantages to the use of employer stock as an investment option:

- Employer stock is a completely undiversified investment option and may be inappropriate from a financial perspective.
- Employer contributions invested in company stock at the employer's direction are not eligible for the Section 404(c) safe harbor provisions.
- Plan sponsors who permit employee contributions to be invested in company stock must comply with Securities and Exchange Commission (SEC) registration and reporting requirements.[4]
- Employee relations problems may surface if the value of the employer stock declines.
- If significant balances are built up in the company stock fund, employees have not only their livelihood but also a sizable block of their savings tied to the well-being of the company.
- Any investment in employer stock, must be shown to satisfy the requirement that plan assets be "expended for the exclusive benefit of employees" and must satisfy the **fiduciary requirement for prudence.**

If employer stock is offered as one of the investment options, the employer also must consider what opportunities an employee will be offered to diversify out of the employer stock as he or she approaches retirement.

Although certain diversification requirements were already prescribed for ESOPs, the PPA expanded diversification requirements for other types of defined contribution plans. These diversification rules were phased in over a three-year period with regard to employer contributions beginning in 2007. However, the three-year phase-in rules for employer contributions did not apply to individuals who attained age 55 and had completed at least three years of service before the first plan year beginning after December 31, 2005. Specifically, an applicable defined contribution plan will not be treated as a qualified trust unless the plan meets the diversification requirements prescribed by law. The plan must allow an "applicable individual" to direct the plan to divest any employer securities where a portion of employee contributions and elective deferrals are invested. The individual must then be permitted to reinvest an equivalent amount in other investment options. A participant in a plan who has completed at least three years of service, or a beneficiary of a participant or of a deceased participant, must be allowed to divest that portion of an account that contains employer securities or employer property. The individual must then be permitted to reinvest an equivalent amount in other investment options. A plan must provide no less than three investment options other than employer securities in which an applicable individual may direct the proceeds from the divestment of employer securities. Each of these offerings must be diversified and have materially different risk and return characteristics. A plan is permitted to place limits on the

[4] See Chapter 27.

time periods for divestment and reinvestment but may not restrict them to occur less frequently than quarterly. These rules that apply to defined contribution plans generally, do not apply to employee stock ownership plan (ESOPs). ESOPs have their own specific diversification requirements as explained in Chapter 7.

If the plan is an ESOP or if the employer stock fund has been designed as an ESOP, yet another issue to be considered is whether dividends will be passed through to employees and, if so, how frequently (e.g., quarterly or annually). Paying such dividends might be attractive to some employers since the dividends paid will be tax deductible; however, paying them in cash might be viewed as being inconsistent with a major plan objective—that of accumulating assets for the purpose of providing an additional measure of retirement security. Employers whose stock is not publicly traded also must deal with issues such as the inclusion of rights of first refusal and put options.

Administrative Issues

There are several administrative issues that need to be addressed in structuring the investment provisions of a defined contribution plan.

Frequency of Valuation

How often will plan assets and account balances be valued for purposes of processing loans, distributions, withdrawals, and investment election changes? If monthly or daily valuations are preferred to quarterly valuations, what will be the additional expense? How long will it take to process a requested transaction subsequent to the valuation date? How does the choice of valuation frequency affect other plan provisions such as the availability and repayment of loans?

Frequency of Change

How often will employees be permitted to change their investment elections? The **Section 404(c) safe harbor provisions** require that employees must be permitted to make changes at least quarterly, and more often for more-volatile investment options. (An employer, of course, may choose not to comply with these safe harbor provisions.) Plans generally permit employees to make changes to the investment elections on either a quarterly, monthly, or daily basis.

Allowing employees to change their investment elections frequently—for example, on a daily basis—may send them mixed signals. The primary focus in educating employees to save wisely for their futures requires an emphasis on setting and achieving long-term goals. Permitting frequent changes to investment elections may appear to be inconsistent and may potentially thwart the long-term focus of defined contribution plan investing.

Default Provisions

Employers must provide some sort of **default option** in the event an employee fails to make an investment election for contributions. As explained in Chapter 11, the PPA has clarified standards for default options and exempted plan sponsors from fiduciary liability when they abide by the Act's requirements.

Negative Elections

Instead of following the usual method of requiring an employee to elect to participate in a defined contribution plan such as a 401(k), some employers redesigned their plans to automatically enroll eligible employees. Under this enrollment method, employees are deemed to have elected to defer a certain percentage, say 1 percent or 2 percent, of their eligible compensation unless they affirmatively elect not to participate in the plan, or elect a different deferral amount. These assumed automatic plan enrollments are referred to as **negative elections.** When employers first started implementing negative elections in their retirement plans, there was some concern specifically regarding 401(k) plan contributions. Because participants had not made an affirmative election between receiving cash and having compensation deferred as a plan contribution, it was thought that these contributions might not be considered elective deferrals under Regs. Sec. 1.401(k)-1(g)(3). However, the Internal Revenue Service clarified this issue with Revenue Ruling 98–30 in which it concluded that if employees have the opportunity to elect out of a plan's automatic deferral provisions, contributions made under a negative election will not fail to be considered elective deferrals.

There are several advantages that make negative elections attractive to both plan sponsors and employees. First, negative elections encourage employees to start saving for retirement sooner. More employees are brought into the plan and the plan enjoys greater overall participation. Also, negative elections often help a plan to pass the actual deferral percentage (ADP) test by ensuring this higher participation in the plan. Greater plan participation from a broad cross section of employees with a certain predetermined level of contribution also may be beneficial to highly compensated employees already participating in the plan. Participation by non-highly compensated employees at a certain level of contribution may permit highly compensated employees to increase their plan contributions, thus enhancing the retirement security of the higher-paid employees.

The PPA instituted another method by which plan sponsors using an automatic enrollment feature can ensure passing of nondiscrimination tests. Automatic enrollment plans can avoid nondiscrimination testing entirely if they design their automatic enrollment feature to conform to a safe harbor that exempts the plan from nondiscrimination testing. For the plan to be deemed to have a qualified automatic enrollment feature, the participant's deferrals must be at least 3 percent of compensation in the participant's first year, and they must subsequently increase by 1 percentage point each year up to 6 percent in the fourth year and remain at 6 percent into the future. The automatic deduction cannot exceed 10 percent of compensation, and the percentages must be applied uniformly to all employees who have been automatically enrolled. For non-highly compensated employees (NHCEs), the employer also must provide either a nonelective contribution equal to at least 3 percent of the employee's compensation or a matching contribution of 100 percent of at least 1 percent of the participant's compensation and 50 percent of the employee's deferrals between 2 and 6 percent of compensation. The match provided for highly compensated employees (HCEs) cannot exceed the match provided to NHCEs. Also, plans using the automatic enrollment safe harbor must vest employer contributions 100 percent within two years.

Employee Communications

Employee communication is a critical link in the long-term success of defined contribution plans. The DOL now requires that the employer offer participants sufficient information to enable them to make an intelligent choice among the investment options available to them. Among other things, this information should encompass investment basics such as the importance of diversification, the relationship between risk and reward, and the influence of the investment time horizon on the potential outcome of plan investments. With the additional guidance furnished by the DOL in terms of distinguishing between investment education and investment advice, many employers go beyond these minimum requirements in providing employees with investment education.

The Economic Growth and Tax Relief Reconciliation Act of 2001 (EGTRRA) contained a provision that excludes employer-provided qualified retirement planning services from employees' gross wages. The exclusion not only applies to such services offered to employees, but also to services offered to spouses of employees. According to the law, qualified retirement planning services involve any retirement planning advice or information provided to an employee and his or her spouse by an employer maintaining a qualified employer plan. Reference to a qualified employer plan, as it is used here, is not in the usual restrictive sense. Such services can be provided by an employer offering a qualified plan under IRC 401(a), governmental plans, 403(b) plans, annuity plans, simplified employee pensions (SEPs), SIMPLE plans, and certain employee-only trusts established prior to June 25, 1959. The exclusion extends to services provided to highly compensated employees only if the qualified retirement planning services are available on substantially the same terms to all employees who normally receive education and information regarding the plan. Qualified retirement planning services do not include such items as accounting services, tax preparation, legal services, or brokerage services.

The PPA provided a new prohibited transaction exemption allowing qualified fiduciary advisers to provide personally developed professional investment advice to assist plan participants in managing their retirement plan investments. Fiduciary advisers may provide investment advice pursuant to an eligible investment advice arrangement whereby either portfolio recommendations are supplied to the participant based on an unbiased computer model that has been certified and audited by an independent third party, or investment advice services are provided charging a flat fee that does not vary depending on the investments selected.

Design, Implementation, and Monitoring of Plan Investments

There are three continuing stages in the development of plan investment provisions: design, implementation, and monitoring.

Design

In the design phase, the employer must make a series of decisions about plan assets. The first is to consider what asset classes will be offered. This decision will be influenced by administrative costs, risk and return characteristics, plan objectives, and participant needs. The range of asset classes to be considered includes cash equivalents, guaranteed investment contracts (GICs), bank investment contracts (BICs), bonds, large-capitalization stocks, small-capitalization stocks, international stocks and bonds, emerging markets, and employer stock. Some employers also may wish to consider the use of real estate, energy, and private equity (venture capital) investments. However, these asset classes are somewhat more cumbersome to include given the private nature of the markets in which they exist and the liquidity constraints this imposes.

The next issue in the design phase is whether to offer these asset classes as distinct investment options from which the employees will choose their own mix or to combine them into predetermined sets of diversified portfolios reflecting different risk and return characteristics.

Each asset class in and of itself also can be diversified, combining different management styles such as growth and value in the equity portfolio, long-term and short-term fixed-income strategies, and a stable of GIC providers in a GIC portfolio. Employers who offer company stock as an investment option may want to consider an alternative equity option specifically designed to complement the company stock. For example, an energy company, whose economic fortune is closely tied to the rise and fall of the energy markets, may want to ensure that at least one plan equity option involves less market exposure to energy stocks.

Combining Asset Classes into Predetermined Portfolios

Different employees will have different degrees of risk tolerance, depending not only on their investment horizons but also on their own psychological preferences. It is quite difficult for a professional investor to gauge the relative risk and return trade-offs of the various potential combinations of assets, even with the benefit of years of education and experience. If plan participants are to make an intelligent allocation of their investment dollars, then substantial guidance is required from the plan sponsor.

One approach is to combine the asset classes in varying degrees into a series of portfolios lying across the efficient frontier to express successively higher risk/reward expectations. Another approach previously described in Chapter 11 is the creation of a series of life cycle funds. In a sense, the use of a life cycle fund builds on the approach of combining asset classes lying across the efficient frontier for risk/reward expectations:

> The efficient frontier provides a good starting point for building an investment portfolio: balancing the trade-off between the risks and potential returns of various asset classes. But it remains a two-dimensional look at portfolio construction. Integrating an investor's time horizon gives a richer, three-dimensional sense—a feeling for whether the risk an investor is assuming is appropriate for his or her stage of the lifecycle.[5]

[5] Boyce Greer, "The Case for Age-Based Lifecycle Investing," *Fidelity Investments Viewpoint Investment Concepts White Paper* (2006), p. 12.

Implementation

Once the asset classes or portfolios to be offered have been determined, appropriate investment objectives for each asset class must be established. This is essential in order to ascertain that the right investment managers are selected. The objectives should clearly articulate the employer's expectations as to risk and return, any investment style preferences, and the time horizon over which the assets will be managed. For example, an employer may wish to introduce an equity option intended to replicate the broad market averages without taking undue amounts of risk. Another equity option may be offered with the objective of substantially outperforming the market averages but with a higher degree of risk.

The relevant time horizon also is critical for guidance in selecting the appropriate manager. In a balanced fund targeted toward employees within five years of retirement, aggressive equity options are probably inappropriate. Where corporate circumstances are such that it is known that the plan will terminate within a certain time frame—for example, upon an anticipated merger or divestiture—it is equally inappropriate to offer investment options whose success is dependent on long-term investment horizons.

Within each asset class, the employer also must decide whether to pursue an **active** or **passive investment management style.** Passive styles are designed to replicate their respective markets. They have the advantage of being easy to communicate to employees and tend to be significantly less expensive than active investment management options. If, however, the employer believes it can be successful in choosing active managers who will outperform the markets in the long run, then the range of options broadens considerably. It may be appropriate to combine both active and passive management styles, either within or across asset classes.

The next major task in the implementation process is the selection of investment managers. Some employers have chosen the route of selecting a single provider of investment and administrative services (e.g., a mutual fund) in an attempt to simplify administration and communication responsibilities. However, this results in considerably less flexibility in structuring investment options and the potential of suboptimal performance for one or more of the funds made available, and it may not necessarily result in lower fees. In addition, use of a single, brand-name provider may have the unintended result of identifying that provider, rather than the employer, as the source of benefits.

Selecting appropriate investment managers requires consideration of a number of factors, including the goals and objectives of the portfolio and the employer, past performance, and fees. In general, it is essential to develop an understanding of the factors that have led to the manager's historical investment performance and gain some level of assurance that those same factors will be brought to bear on future investments.[6]

The bottom line for any investment manager is how well it has performed in the asset class for which it is being considered. **Performance evaluation** is more than a

---

[6] The process of selecting investment managers is discussed at length in Chapter 24. Although that chapter relates primarily to defined benefit plan investing, the comments there concerning manager selection are equally applicable to defined contribution plans.

Performance fees, fees based on capital appreciation of plan assets, generally are prohibited under the Investment Advisors Act of 1940 (the '40 Act) and the Employee Retirement Income Security Act (ERISA), although fees may be based on a percentage of assets under management. Certain exceptions to this prohibition have been permitted by regulation under the '40 Act and by the Department of Labor (DOL) opinions under ERISA, but parties must be careful to structure such arrangements in conformity with such approved standards or be prepared to request interpretive advice from the DOL (and possibly the Securities and Exchange Commission if guidance is needed for '40 Act compliance).

Source: Robert B. Van Grover, "Advisory Agreements: A Guide to Advisors and Trustees of Benefit Plans." Reprinted with permission, from the August 1993 issue of *Pension Management* magazine, p. 36. © Intertec Publishing Corp.

simple comparison of the past one, three, or five years against a market index, however. Both long-term and short-term performance and trends in performance over these time frames and over market cycles need to be evaluated against a universe of other money managers with similar investment objectives as well as against appropriate market benchmarks. It is commonly recognized that certain investment styles go in and out of favor on an unpredictable basis. Thus, to compare a growth manager against the broad market indexes over a period when growth has been out of favor does little to inform the observer as to how well the growth manager fulfilled its assignment. Instead, it is more appropriate to compare the manager's performance against both a passive portfolio of growth stocks (such as the Russell 1000-Growth if it is a large-capitalization growth manager) and a universe of managers with comparable investment styles and objectives. In addition to evaluating the return characteristics of the firm, it also is important to understand the risks that the manager assumed in generating the historical performance record. It is the **risk-adjusted return** that truly distinguishes good management.

Monitoring Performance

Both the structure of plan investments and the performance of the investment manager must be monitored on an ongoing basis. Performance must be monitored in the context of the objectives that were established at the outset. Key matters to be covered in the review process include the following:

- Returns for the last quarter and the last one- and two-year periods.
- A comparison of these returns with agreed-upon benchmarks and objectives.
- A comparison of these returns with the results of other managers with similar objectives.
- An analysis of whether these returns are meeting expectations over the long run.
- An analysis of any trends of consistent underperformance that have emerged.
- A determination of whether the manager's investment policy is still sound in light of any changing capital market conditions.

- A review of whether there have been any substantive changes in the manager's investment policies, procedures, or personnel.

Replacement of investment managers can be expected, from time to time, either because of changes in the plan itself or because of unsatisfactory investment performance. Questions to be asked periodically in evaluating the overall structure of plan investments include:

- Have the original goals and objectives changed?
- Are the number and type of investment options offered sufficient?
- Is employee usage of the available options appropriate given their demographics?
- Are investment and administrative expenses at an acceptable level?

An Investment Management Checklist

The following checklist summarizes some of the key questions that employers should address in structuring and managing their defined contribution investment programs.

Design

- Do the investment choices span the appropriate spectrum of risk and reward choices given plan objectives and participant demographics?
- Are employer contributions and employee contributions invested in appropriate asset classes?
- Is the ability to change investment mix decisions appropriate given the choices available, plan objectives, and participant demographics?
- Is the plan designed to take advantage of the Section 404(c) safe harbor provisions?
- Is each investment option prudently diversified?
- How often and when will participants be able to change their investment choices?
- Is useful investment information communicated to participants for each investment option, including accurate, meaningful descriptions; qualified risk and return expectations; investment objectives; and frequent, consistent, and understandable investment reports?
- Are participants provided with sufficient information to enable them to make informed allocations among the investment options offered?
- Will employees be provided with educational materials (brochures, seminars, interactive software, etc.) to make them more proficient investors?

Implementation

- Has an explicit active/passive investment decision been made for each investment alternative?
- Has a prudent manager selection process been documented and applied to each manager selected?
- Is there a written statement of investment policies and objectives for each investment manager?

Monitoring

- Is a review of manager performance undertaken quarterly, with a more formal, in-depth review conducted at least annually?
- Have clear criteria been established for use in determining whether to retain and/or replace an investment manager?
- Are plan investment policies, procedures, and objectives formally reviewed and verified at least annually?
- Are the investment options offered evaluated at least annually?

Chapter Summary

- Both employers and employees have a vital stake in the plan investment provisions of a defined contribution plan. The employer is responsible for structuring appropriate investment programs, selecting suitable investment managers, monitoring investment performance, and communicating critical investment provisions to employees. In the typical plan, employees are responsible for deciding how to invest their account balances and they assume all of the risks associated with investment performance. Both employers and employees must have a sound understanding of basic investment principles if they are to succeed in fulfilling their respective responsibilities.

- The benefits of a successful investment program include, for the employer, low cost fees, ease of administration, flexibility to make needed changes in investment arrangements, and improved recognition of the company as a source of valuable benefits. For employees, a well-executed investment program maximizes capital accumulation through increased participation, improved returns, and lower costs.

- Historically, most employers designed their defined benefit plans to replace specified levels of preretirement income and viewed their defined contribution plans as simply providing supplemental benefits. This perspective of defined contribution plans as supplemental savings vehicles may partially account for the little attention some employers have paid to managing their plans as effectively as possible.

- The past 25 years has seen a movement toward increased investment opportunities being made available to employees. Many factors have contributed to this change, including a growing public awareness of the role of defined contribution plans in providing economic security and the importance of saving and investing wisely; an increased recognition on the part of employers of the need to provide flexibility of choice and investment education; improved and more-efficient administrative capabilities; and the aggressive marketing efforts of the leading mutual funds.

- The investment provisions of a defined contribution plan should be compatible with the plan sponsor's objectives. Three major areas to be considered are (1) fiduciary responsibilities, (2) the role employer stock will play, and (3) administrative issues.

- There are several administrative issues that need to be addressed in structuring the investment provisions of a defined contribution plan. These include, frequency of change in investment elections, default provisions, employee communications (including investment education), and rights regarding diversification when employer securities are involved.

- There are three continuing stages in the development of plan investment provisions: design, implementation, and monitoring. Design issues require the employer to make a series of decisions about plan assets, including what asset classes to offer and whether these asset classes will be offered as distinct investment options or combined into predetermined sets of diversified portfolios. Implementation involves explicitly deciding how these assets will be managed. Decisions must be made regarding active or passive investment styles, and manager selection must occur. Likewise, a drafting of investment policies and objectives should occur. Monitoring involves the ongoing review of manager performance, the development of a predetermined schedule for performance review, and the establishment of criteria for use in determining whether to retain and/or replace an investment manager.

Key Terms

active versus passive
  investment
  management styles,
  p. *543*
appointment of the
  investment advice
  provider, p. *537*
default option, p. *539*

fiduciary requirement for
  prudence, p. *538*
negative elections, p. *540*
ongoing monitoring
  process of the
  investment advice
  provider, p. *537*

performance evaluation,
  p. *543*
risk-adjusted return, p. *544*
Section 404(c) safe harbor
  provisions, p. *539*

Questions for Review

1. Explain the reasons for limited investment options in early defined contribution plans.
2. Describe the factors in the past 25 years that have contributed to an expansion in employee investment options in defined contribution plans.
3. Discuss employer motivations to look more closely at plan objectives and plan performance.
4. Identify three major areas where plan investment provisions should be compatible with plan sponsor objectives.
5. How can a plan sponsor limit its fiduciary liability regarding the investment of plan assets?
6. What are the Section 404(c) safe harbor provisions?
7. What are the disadvantages to using employer stock as an investment option in a defined contribution plan?
8. What administrative issues need to be addressed in structuring the investment provisions of a defined contribution plan?
9. What does Section 404(c) require regarding the frequency of change of investment elections?

10. What are the three continuing stages in the development of plan investment provisions?
11. What decisions must be made in the design phase of developing plan investment provisions?
12. What types of questions should the plan sponsor ask during the design, implementation, and monitoring phases of the development of plan investment provisions?
13. Describe the difference between active and passive investment management styles.
14. Identify key matters to be addressed in the review process of investment management performance.
15. What is meant by risk-adjusted return?

Questions for Discussion

1. Discuss alternative approaches to investment education and what techniques may be particularly effective in instructing employee participants on retirement planning issues.
2. Discuss employer situations where the selection of predetermined sets of diversified portfolios may be preferred to distinct investment options in certain asset classes.
3. Discuss the criteria that you would use to make a change in plan investment managers.

Resources for Further Study

CCH Editorial Staff. "2001 Tax Legislation: Law, Explanation, and Analysis." *Commerce Clearing House Pension Plan Guide* (2001).

CCH Editorial Staff. "Legislation 2006: Pension Protection Act of 2006: Law, Explanation, and Analysis." *Commerce Clearing House* (2006).

Gordon, Catherine D., and Stephen P. Utkus. "The Investment of Retirement Plan Assets." In *The Handbook of Employee Benefits*. 6th ed. Jerry S. Rosenbloom, ed. New York: McGraw-Hill, 2005.

Gordon, Catherine D., and Kimberly A. Stockton. "Funds for Retirement: The Life-Cycle Approach," Vanguard Investment Counseling and Research. Malvern: Vanguard Group, 2006.

Greer, Boyce. "The Case for Age-Based Lifecycle Investing," Fidelity Investments Viewpoint Investment Concepts White Paper. Boston: FMR Corp., 2006

Siegel, Jeremy J. *Stocks for the Long Run*. New York: McGraw-Hill, 2002.

Towers Perrin. *The Handbook of 401(k) Plan Management*. Burr Ridge, IL: Irwin Professional Publishing, 1996.

Van Derhei, Jack, and Sarah Holden. "Investment of Defined Contribution Plan Assets." In *The Handbook of Employee Benefits*. 6th ed. Jerry S. Rosenbloom, ed. New York: McGraw-Hill, 2005.

Chapter 30

Retirement Asset Wealth Management

After studying this chapter you should be able to:

- Explain what is meant by the concept of wealth management.
- Describe how retirement planning in a wealth management context is both possible and desirable in today's complex financial environment.
- Explain why wealth management retirement planning is a relatively new approach that has not been utilized traditionally by individuals planning for retirement.
- Discuss the types of retirement plan decisions individuals can make in a wealth management context.
- Explain specific wealth management strategies and tactical approaches.
- Describe the link between retirement planning and estate planning in a wealth management context.

Introduction

Throughout this book it has been noted that the transformation of the private retirement system from one where defined benefit plans historically dominated to one in which defined contribution plans have grown to be the more prominent retirement funding sources places more responsibility on the individual participant. This added responsibility means the individual participant bears more risk. However, another aspect of moving this additional risk to the participant is that most plans also allow the participant greater flexibility and control over his or her retirement account. Participants can select investments, make decisions concerning their savings levels, and, in some plans, determine whether savings occur on a pre- or after-tax basis. As indicated in Chapter 16, when an individual works for different employers throughout his or her career, certain actions can be taken to consolidate retirement savings plans of past employers. Often when an individual terminates employment, he or she is permitted to withdraw assets from the plan either by taking a cash disbursement or by rolling over assets into an individual retirement account (IRA) or into a subsequent employer's plan. In essence, decisions can be made whether to roll over assets into an individual retirement account or consolidate assets in a single or a few employer plans, assuming these employer plans will accept transferred assets. With the availability of these decisions, the individual participant is much more empowered to manage these accumulating assets and position them in the most favorable way that will best serve his or her specific, longer-term financial goals and objectives.

This chapter explores the emerging concept of managing an employee's personal portfolio and integrating the management of retirement plan assets with other holdings in the individual's portfolio of investable assets. The idea of managing retirement assets using a wealth management approach involves holistic decision making to achieve better overall results for an individual's total accumulated wealth rather than making retirement plan decisions in isolation. This is probably best understood by looking at a decision about an individual's choice concerning asset allocation. If a plan participant only makes asset allocation decisions by examining the assets held in the employer-sponsored retirement plan, those decisions may under- or over-allocate assets to specific asset classes when the individual's total investment holdings are considered. If that individual were to examine total investable assets, looking at assets held within the retirement plan *and* assets held outside the retirement plan, the targeted asset allocation occurring in the retirement plan is likely to be quite different. Other decisions concerning the management of retirement plan assets also can be made using this wealth management approach. This chapter explores making retirement planning decisions by examining broader wealth management considerations.

Retirement Planning in a Wealth Management Context

To explore the concept of retirement planning within a wealth management context, it is necessary to first examine what is meant by the concept of wealth management. **Wealth management** is a process for managing resources that seeks to meet an individual's needs and achieve his or her objectives by integrating a diverse range of services. Typically, the process of wealth management utilizes a holistic approach involving investment management, financial planning, retirement planning, estate planning, tax planning, asset protection, risk management, and cash flow and debt management.[1] As such, retirement planning necessitates being placed in this overall wealth management context to be more effectively implemented and tactically executed.

---

[1] American Institute of Certified Public Accountants, "The Wealth Management Solution," *Journal of Accountancy,* May 2004. p. 1. This definition as presented in the article is slightly adapted to include the function of risk management that was not included in the original version. The risk management process is perceived as an important component of wealth management by most practitioners.

If conducted effectively and executed successfully, retirement planning in a wealth management context should yield a number of advantages for the individual engaged in such planning. Wealth management retirement planning should result in greater asset accumulation, less overall financial risk, reductions in tax liabilities, cost reductions related to the management of resources, and efficiencies in managing cash flow and reducing debt.

> A growing body of research is pointing to the importance of financial education and planning as key ingredients to a financially secure retirement.[2]

> Ameriks, Caplin and Leahy are starting to develop evidence that certain types of human behavior indicate a propensity to plan, and that those with a higher propensity to plan actually do more planning, and thus accumulate more wealth.[3]

Wealth management retirement planning should also position retirement resources so they conform during the accumulation phase leading up to retirement, thus, these assets are thoughtfully configured to produce retirement income when the distribution phase of retirement commences. This does not necessarily mean that there will be no reallocation of assets when retirement income distributions commence. However, while assets are being accumulated, there is thought and planning concerning the transition necessary to strategically move into the distribution phase at retirement. Focus on strategic planning is a hallmark of the wealth management process.

> According to Stuart Lucas, chairman of the Wealth Strategist Network and heir to the Carnation fortune, "Wealth management requires constant thinking about strategic issues, not tactical moves."[4]

Given the risk transfer that has occurred with the transformation in the private pension system, today's individual participant is, in most cases, more empowered than ever before to strategically manage his or her retirement assets. This trend toward more empowerment and control in managing retirement assets is one that is likely to continue. This trend has been supported both by marketplace forces and governmental policy initiatives. An individual should make the most of this empowerment. This is true both during the accumulation phase, while assets are being built up within retirement savings plans, and during the distribution phase, when the assets are being drawn upon to generate retirement income. Because individuals have the ability to select investments and, in some plans, determine whether their contributions occur on a pre- or after-tax basis, individuals can control both asset allocation and tax status of their accumulating retirement resources. An individual also can determine what type of retirement savings vehicle to use to accumulate assets. Many individuals covered by an employer-sponsored retirement plan also opt to save for retirement outside the employer-sponsored plan utilizing an IRA, so decisions can be made on whether to use the employer's plan for

---

[2] Mimi Lord, "Financial Planning and Wealth Accumulation: Identifying Individuals' Propensity to Plan," *Retirement Planning,* July/August 2002, p. 34

[3] Ibid., p. 32.

[4] Shelley A. Lee, "Stuart Lucas on Being Wealthy, Sharing Wealth, and the KISS Principle of Wealth Management," *Journal of Financial Planning,* March 2007, p. 17.

supplemental saving or to choose an alternative retirement savings vehicle outside the employer's plan.

Within a family unit, family members can choose to position assets within various members' control, such as rights of survival should one family member predecease another. This positioning of assets can occur in various ways. For instance, a retirement saver could segment an IRA with different beneficiaries. Alternatively, an individual with a spouse may choose to contribute to a spousal IRA up to the maximum limit rather than to increase savings within his or her own IRA. The ability to make these decisions provides many opportunities to craft the individual's retirement program and simultaneously develop an estate plan to coordinate with other holdings and, in such a way, to pursue various longer term objectives and goals.

Various tax efficiencies may be captured during the retirement asset accumulation period with proper planning. The very buildup of tax-deferred assets within a retirement savings plan captures tax efficiencies. If the plan were not used, taxes would need to be paid. The deferral of taxes allows plan participants to generate investment income on resources that would have been lost to taxes earlier. Tax efficiencies may be extended into the ensuing retirement distribution phase as well. Estate planning objectives also may be realized. For instance, an individual could opt to move holdings contributed on a pretax basis in a 401(k) plan into a Roth IRA, paying taxes but eliminating the need to pay federal income taxes in future years. This strategy could be especially potent if the conversion occurs when an asset class is undervalued in the market and it is anticipated that asset values will considerably appreciate in future years. Unfortunately, too many individuals view their retirement programs as compartmentalized employer-controlled plans and fail to strategically manage their retirement holdings with a focused strategy aimed at enhancing their overall wealth. Understanding the features of these plans and making some key decisions can optimally position the plan holdings within this overall wealth-creating context. Many individuals simply fail to integrate their retirement plans in a meaningful way with their other assets through financial strategies that are within their personal control.

Why do so few individuals use a wealth management context to manage and integrate their retirement plans within their broader family financial planning? Although no single definitive answer to this question exists, there are several reasons that readily can be identified. First, until rather recently, many aspects of private retirement plans were indeed controlled to a much greater extent by employers. Going back to a time when defined benefit plans were the primary form of employer-sponsored plan, there were few decision factors within an individual's control. For most individuals, the only decision available was what type of annuity to select and whether payments would continue to a spouse upon the individual's death.[5] Looking at the relatively limited choice in the past and comparing the choices of the past to the expanded variety of choices available today, the opportunity for introducing strategic planning to enhance wealth creation has greatly expanded. Considerably more alternatives and

---

[5] Although this particular decision was very limited, an individual still could have made this decision within a wealth management context based on whether he or she had life insurance or other assets and his or her anticipation of life span based on such factors as family history, present health status, etc.

choices are available to the individual who is willing and able to plan. There also is much more complexity in today's retirement planning arena. Although the marketplace and legal structures supporting these alternatives have evolved over time, it is notable that the breadth of choices is relatively new when viewed from a historical perspective. With this empowerment, employees also incur risk when they act to integrate their retirement plans with their other assets and financial strategies. Certain changes in philosophy and the retirement planning paradigm have allowed participants to embark on this more strategic, risk-laden, and empowered wealth management activity. For the most part, this paradigm shift also has been evolutionary in nature, rather than abrupt and revolutionary. The rest of this section describes some of the forces that have supported this paradigm shift.

Change in the Employer–Employee Employment Contract

The employer–employee employment contract has changed over time. In the past, many employers perceived the **employer–employee employment contract** as a longer-term, enduring relationship. Once an employer hired an employee, within many industries and established enterprises, it was common for the employee to make a career with a single employer. This long-term nature of the employer-employee working relationship affected the nature and the design of the retirement plan sponsored by the employer. Most often in the past, the retirement plan of choice was a defined benefit plan, and the intended result was to continue a percentage of final pay determined by using specific income replacement ratios targeted at the pension plan's inception. In today's labor markets, such long-term, enduring employment relationships are far less common. Consequently, the design and features of retirement plans are very different from the plans that popularized this prior era. Rapid technological change and the globalization of markets have made for a more competitive and changing environment. With this continuous change, whole industries have been reshaped very quickly. Increasingly, employers have been less able to guarantee long-term employment or career ladders to their employees. Employers offer their employees a challenging work environment, and employees offer their employers the state-of-the-art skills that they continually seek to improve and develop. Consequently, employers have substituted defined contribution plans and leave the future management of plan assets to the individuals who have received plan contributions from their employers.

Change in Governmental Policy

Changes in governmental and tax policy have allowed employees to exercise greater authority over plan selections. Not only has the employer-employee employment contract undergone revision, but governmental policy has changed to support these marketplace shifts. Realizing that employees spend shorter tenures with their employers, the government has reduced vesting standards as described in Chapter 25. Public policy has moderated to bring more uniformity to plan structures, and increased portability has allowed plan participants to aggregate assets from these multiple plans in an employer-sponsored plan or an individual retirement account. Governmental policy has supported a system that allows the individual participant to play a larger role in controlling his or her personal assets accumulated from a variety of employers during a career.

Marketplace Forces and Competition by Market Participants

Entrance of new participants into various market sectors has brought the introduction of new products and services in the retirement planning area. The presence of insurance companies, mutual funds, trust companies, other asset managers, and record keepers has meant innovation in the plan offerings for employers and increased competition to provide administrative services to employer-sponsored retirement plans. Employee benefit consultants also have been influential in assisting employers in ensuring plan compliance and innovating plans to capitalize on the latest options and features permitted by law. With many changes in the law requiring compliance, employers found it difficult to stay current with legally required modifications to their plans. As more employee benefit consulting firms and asset managers moved to provide outsourced administrative services to plans, more employers have seen that employee benefit plan administration most often is not an organizational core competency. This recognition along with the expertise, high-quality services, and cost savings resulting from economies of scale provided by these vendors, have resulted in a movement of plan administration to external vendors. The providing of these specialized administrative services has increased the pace in which innovation has moved into employer-sponsored retirement plans.

Enhancements in Technology and Record-Keeping Services

All the administrative change affecting retirement plans could not have occurred without advances in technology. Improved technology and innovations in record-keeping services have facilitated this more flexible and portable system. The aforementioned marketplace forces coupled with product innovations and improved record-keeping services have supported this change. The paradigm shift in retirement planning has occurred as the marketplace has matured, with tax rules and regulations governing plans being recrafted to support this paradigm shift. However, it is unlikely that the marketplace changes could have occurred without the technological infrastructure to support doing business in this manner.

With a basic understanding of the forces that have shaped the current environment, we can now examine how the individual plan participant can conduct his or her retirement planning using a wealth management approach.

Principles of Strategic Wealth Management

The process of wealth management is, at its very core, a management activity. As with the general management approach utilized in directing the workings of an organizational enterprise, an effective wealth management process is an activity that involves planning, execution, ongoing monitoring, measurement of outcomes, accountability, and, at times, creative new approaches. It also involves team activities, gathering together the expertise of different disciplines, combining the contributions of various specialties, employing project management skills, and demonstrating leadership in achieving results. It is as much art as it is science. However, an important hallmark of a wealth management process is its integrative nature, that is, ensuring that goals and objectives are developed that lead to overall wealth enhancement and security. An integrative approach is necessary rather than attempting to pursue isolated goals. For example, the pursuit of superior investment returns while failing to consider tax impacts may achieve high pre-tax returns but result in reduced after-tax returns that contribute less to overall wealth creation.

Although taking an integrated approach is easily appreciated from a theoretical or strategic perspective, creating an effective strategy is difficult given the complexity of the wealth management process. It is equally difficult to translate the strategy into action and implement it at a tactical level because of the complexity of personal financial affairs, the uncertainty of the investment environment, the unknowns related to personal risks, and the challenges in aligning disparate financial products and services. Similarly, the complex nature of the tax environment, which has a significant impact on the viability of certain strategies, is difficult to anticipate. The tax law has become so complicated—involving phase-outs of deductions and exemptions and the applicability of the alternative minimum tax—that projecting the tax consequences of various tactical actions frequently is not easy to evaluate. Couple this fact with the propensity of legislators to enact provisions of the law that subsequently "sunset" and the ever-present danger that major portions of the tax law are frequently amended, and the difficulty in truly effective integrated planning is obvious.

Integrated planning can be difficult to achieve; however, complete disregard for an integrated approach can have extremely costly and problematic consequences. Failure to employ holistic strategies can result in additional costs and unintended impediments that seriously compromise the long-term goals being pursued. The difficulty of employing holistic strategies necessitates that individuals take charge of the wealth management process. Many researchers suggest that individuals take charge of the wealth management process and do it early.[6] This is particularly relevant in retirement planning wealth management because the complexity of personal finances and tax factors necessitate that the individual be in control of the process to ensure a strategic focus on the most meaningful goals. Leadership is necessary, and a culture of accountability should be created.[7] Reliance on advisers without oversight often leads to suboptimal results and an absence of accountability for the overall strategic goals. As indicated earlier, performance metrics should be established and performance measured.

Retirement Planning Wealth Management Decision Elements

Several decision elements are involved in accumulating wealth for retirement income purposes. Important decision elements also are present when subsequently

---

[6] "Eight Principles of Strategic Wealth Management," *Knowledge at Wharton*, August 9, 2006, p. 1.
[7] Ibid., p. 1.

distributing that wealth to support income needs during retirement. Decisions must be made concerning the following issues:

1. Developing the retirement resource target.
2. Assessing the efficiencies of funding structures.
3. Examining the funding structures in relation to other factors, participant needs, or the broader environment.
4. Investment selection, risk management, and strategic allocation of resources within the retirement saving structures and the impact of these decisions on an overall portfolio of wealth.
5. Distribution planning and execution.
6. Monitoring excesses or deficiencies relative to retirement income needs.
7. Final disposition of excesses or deficiencies when retirement income is no longer needed.

Developing the Retirement Resource Target

To plan for retirement income needs, it is necessary to have some understanding of the required resources needed to fund the retirement years. A **retirement resource target** is the projected asset base that will provide adequate funds through either income generation or use of principal to meet the income needs of an individual in his or her anticipated period of retirement. The anticipated retirement can be the time that an individual completely removes him- or herself from the workforce, or it can involve a transition period where phased retirement occurs. If phased retirement occurs, the income needs should be lessened and the retirement resource target can be reduced. Retirement savers during their working careers should be accumulating the necessary resources that will either meet or exceed their retirement resource target. Nevertheless, adequately assessing this target is an elusive exercise. As outlined in Chapter 4, the multiple and overlapping risks, some of which are dependent upon each other, make it difficult to assess the true resource needs that an individual will have in retirement. Nevertheless, financial advisers attempt to target retirement resource needs using various types of models. These models may be helpful but have limitations. Retirement planning software models may be segmented into the following three model types according to Still River Retirement Planning Software Inc.[8]

1. **Deterministic models** use a set of "fixed" assumptions. The assumptions are determined by the model developer, the model user, or some combination of the two. Purely deterministic models do not possess effective means for measuring risk. They can illustrate risks in two ways: (*a*) the model can be run multiple times illustrating different scenarios or (*b*) assumptions can be varied indicating sensitivity to various assumptions (i.e., investment return, mortality, inflation, etc.) An example of a deterministic model would be one that projects asset accumulations based on current holdings and an assumed savings rate given assumptions

---

[8] Still River Retirement Planning Software, Inc., "Retirement Income Planning, Part 10: Risk Analysis and Calculation Methods," May 2006, pp. 1–5.

Financial planners have used models for many years to assist their clients. These models are helpful in retirement planning to project future asset accumulations given savings patterns with assumptions regarding future investment returns. Models also are used to gauge the likelihood that the asset accumulations of plan participants will be able to withstand market downturns and still provide sufficient purchasing power to meet retirement income needs. The Pension Protection Act (PPA) of 2006 permits plan sponsors to provide individualized investment advice to plan participants without engaging in a prohibited transaction when this advice occurs under an "eligible investment advice agreement." One allowable arrangement requires that investment advice be provided using an *unbiased computer model* that has been certified and audited by an independent third party. Given the potential for fiduciary liability, it is important that computer models used for this purpose undergo careful scrutiny and review. Failure to adequately monitor the assumptions utilized in models or their operation and use could lead to the assertion of a fiduciary breach by a plan sponsor. According to Field Assistance Bulletin 2007-01, the Department of Labor anticipates that the process utilized by a responsible fiduciary to select an investment adviser "will take into account the extent to which advice to be furnished to participants and beneficiaries will be based upon generally accepted investment theories."

about investment return and salary increases. This type of model provides a single, expected, future asset accumulation based on the inputs of beginning balance, years to retirement, investment return, ongoing savings amount, and salary increases.

2. **Stochastic models** do not use fixed assumptions, but rather vary assumptions and yield probabilities of success or failure depending on repeated iterations of the model. These models employ statistical techniques to introduce variability into the parameters of the model. Pure stochastic models do not really exist because all of these models need to employ certain fixed assumptions. Although the models allow for the variation of some assumptions, there are some elements that remain fixed, even though these elements of the environment actually can and do undergo change.

3. **Mixed models** use a combination of fixed (deterministic) assumptions and variable assumptions. These models allow a certain set of assumptions to vary; thus these types of models attempt to gauge probabilities of success or failure. Monte Carlo techniques are examples of these mixed models. A simulation is an analytical method meant to imitate a real-life system, especially systems that are too mathematically complex or too difficult to reproduce. A **Monte Carlo simulation** selects variable values randomly, and the model is run multiple times to assess outcomes. For each uncertain variable that can have a range of possible values, the possible values are defined with a probability distribution. The type of distribution selected is based on the conditions that surround this variable.

It is fruitless to think that financial projection or risk assessment models can adequately depict the environmental complexity that is inherent in the retirement planning process. Nevertheless, these models can be helpful in depicting certain parameters when assessing retirement preparedness and the savings and investing strategies to accumulate sufficient resources. The models often are particularly useful to portray the influence of environmental variation on plans to achieve targeted outcomes.

Assessing the Efficiencies of Funding Structures

After attempting to gauge a retirement resource target, an individual should make a decision concerning the retirement savings structures in which to accumulate retirement resources. The selected structures include plan types allowed under current law as well as particular fund families; the asset managers offered through these plans; distinct asset classes; and in some cases, specific investments. In making decisions in this area, an individual is assessing the tax efficiencies of the retirement savings vehicle, the costs associated with the investment products, and the risks of either asset classes or specific investments. The risks of asset classes should not be assessed in isolation but should include consideration of other asset classes held, both in retirement savings vehicles and in other savings vehicles outside the retirement plans. These other holdings combined with the assets held within retirement savings plans comprise the individual's master portfolio. The **master portfolio** includes the entire set of assets held by the individual. The individual may decide to exclude certain master portfolio holdings from consideration in building a diversified total portfolio for retirement funding purposes. Some of the assets excluded may be such items as educational savings or an emergency fund as these particular savings may be earmarked for specific goals and may possess markedly different planning horizons. Generally assets earmarked for specific purposes such as these would be unavailable to meet retirement resource needs. Therefore, it is appropriate to exclude these savings in making wealth management asset allocation decisions.

Poterba examined implicit after-tax rates of return on retirement savings and how they differ depending on the type of account in which the assets are held. The **implicit after-tax return** is the compound annual return that an individual needs to earn on a given amount of pre-tax earnings to achieve a certain after-tax balance at the time of withdrawal.[9] Not only does the type of plan holding the asset determine the implicit after-tax return, but other factors influence this rate of return as well. Among these factors are the holding period for the asset when held in a taxable account (i.e., short-term [less than one year] or long-term [one year or more]), type of investment return earned (i.e., dividend, interest payment or capital gain), the individual's tax rate that can either decrease or increase over time, etc. Table 30.1 portrays differences in the tax characteristics of different types of accounts under the current law.

Judgments about the optimal positioning of assets within these accounts to optimize implicit after-tax return are not easily determinable. Combining these factors in different ways and the uncertainty of their occurrences can change the implicit after-tax return and cause deviation from expected outcomes. Even if an individual had the capacity to plan his or her personal circumstances so there was no

---

[9] James M. Poterba, "Saving for Retirement: Taxes Matter," *An Issue in Brief,* 17 (May 2004), p. 2.

TABLE 30.1   Characteristics of Common Asset Funding Structures

Investment or Account Type	Treatment of Initial Capital	Treatment of Earnings	Treatment on Liquidation
Investments in Taxable Accounts			
Fixed-income investments	No tax benefit (source: after-tax income)	Ordinary income tax	Repayment of principal (capital gain on appreciation)
Common stocks dividends	No tax benefit (source: after-tax income)	Ordinary income tax	Capital gains tax applicable (capital gain on appreciation)
Shelters Provided in Retirement Savings Vehicles			
Tax-qualified plans [401(k)s, 403(b)s, 457(b)s]	Contributions are not taxed on entry	Earnings tax deferred	Taxed as ordinary income on distribution
IRAs	Contributions made from after-tax income, although some taxpayers receive a tax deduction because of income level	Earnings tax deferred	Taxed as ordinary income on distribution
Roth-type accounts [Roth 401(k)s, Roth 403(b)s, Roth IRAs]	Contributions made from after-tax income	Earnings initially tax deferred, but tax free if taken as a qualified distribution	Contributions received tax free since tax already paid; earnings are tax free if taken as a qualified distribution

deviation from what was expected, the structure of the tax relationships among various types of retirement savings plans and nonretirement savings vehicles can change. This change would render an outcome different from the expected outcome. In short, the tax characteristics of these accounts can change as tax law is modified.

> The Job Growth and Taxpayer Relief Reconciliation Act of 2003 (JGTRRA) reduced both the dividend tax rate and the capital gains tax rate. These changes raised the after-tax rate of return that investors could earn on equities held outside their retirement accounts. The 2003 reform therefore increased both the after-tax rate of return and the amount of retirement wealth that could be generated by a given equity investment held in a taxable account, relative to the same asset in a tax-deferred account.[10]

[10] Ibid., p. 2.

Nevertheless, certain observations are worth noting. The provision of an employer match through some type of qualified plan usually makes this type of plan the most advantageous from a wealth accumulation perspective. Retirement savings plans are most often advantageous because they allow the account owner to accumulate resources on which additional monies can be earned that would have been paid as taxes in the absence of contributions into such a plan. Whether a tax-deferred plan or a Roth plan is preferable depends on timing issues when monies are withdrawn as well as the differential in marginal tax rates applicable to contributions and withdrawals. A mere comparison of marginal tax rates, however, will not immediately determine which is the preferred alternative. Often, monies being contributed into a tax-deferred savings plan will come off the top and thus provide tax savings upon contribution at the top marginal tax rate. When monies are distributed from the plan, if the plan is the sole source of retirement income, they will be distributed at a variety of tax rates. This fact usually tilts the advantage to the tax-deferred plan over the tax-free Roth type account, all other factors being equal. However, with many tax practitioners expecting tax rates to increase in future years, paying taxes now by using a Roth account may in some cases be preferable. As can be seen from these considerations, making the determination of which funding structure to use in accumulating retirement resources to optimally build wealth is not easy.

Examining the Funding Structures in Relation to Other Factors, Participant Needs, or the Broader Environment

Before beginning to save within a retirement savings vehicle, an individual should assess the compatibility of the savings structure with his or her needs. For instance, does the retirement savings vehicle allow participant loans if the individual thinks such access may be important within the planning horizon? What are the costs associated with the array of asset classes available within the retirement savings plan? If there is turbulence in capital markets and a person needs to switch from one fund to another, is it easy to process such a transaction? Does the array of alternate funds offer the mix that the person would want if he or she were to switch in the future? What would be the tax consequences or commissions incurred in removing assets from the retirement savings plan? Are these costs imposed by statute, or are these costs imposed by the custodian who is managing the assets? All of the economic and administrative characteristics of a given structure for accumulating resources can ultimately affect the capacity of the assets held within the structure to accumulate wealth. Particular needs of the account owner can trigger transactions that can potentially incur additional costs or subject the investments to regular taxation or additional penalty taxes. Therefore, the utmost care should be taken in assessing whether a given structure for holding accumulating assets is the appropriate selection for an individual's personal circumstances. Not only should the individual's planned needs and the characteristics of the saving structure be examined for a compatible match, but circumstances in the broader environment should be assessed as well. For instance, if the eligibility of a transaction for special tax treatment is dubious, environmental factors, such as governmental audit and disallowance, can render a particular financial strategy within a certain structure counterproductive. Occurrences in the capital markets and a decrease in value for an entire asset class should also be considered.

Investment Selection, Risk Management, and Strategic Allocation of Resources within the Retirement Saving Structures and the Impact of These Decisions on an Overall Portfolio of Wealth

Investment decisions must be made within the retirement savings structures, and the decisions must be made within a larger context in relation to other savings held by the individual. Some individuals look to the assistance of professionals to assist them in the wealth management function, particularly with the investment management function.

> Wealth managers combine, for the benefit of their clients, knowledge of the process of financial planning with the intellectual capital of the pioneers of modern finance. In particular, many wealth managers have incorporated a number of key concepts of modern investment theory (Graham, Markowitz, Sharpe, and Brinson) into investment planning for their clients. These concepts, such as mean variance optimization, efficient frontiers, and extensive diversification, have been accepted as "gospel" by most of the planning profession . . . Not only has today's wealth manager been taught that the professionally correct process for portfolio design is the development of a sound and well diversified investment policy, modern law (ERISA, the Third Restatement of Trusts, Uniform Prudent Investor Act) mandates adherence to this process.[11]

Because of these underlying investment theories and the nature of the law, many wealth managers implement investment strategies using a prescribed methodology:

> The investment process wealth managers currently use for designing and implementing portfolio strategies for their clients has been modeled after investment policy design and implementation strategies developed for large tax-exempt institutional clients. This has led to the design of multi-asset-class/style portfolios, implemented by selecting style-consistent active managers. In selecting an asset class and style universe, wealth managers tend to mimic the universe reflected in the Morningstar style boxes and categories. Although it is unlikely that a wealth manager will use all, or even most, of these class/styles for a single client, a policy will typically include at least six and rarely less than four asset classes/styles.[12]

Although this methodology of investment management using multiple asset managers is widely practiced by professional wealth managers, it is being questioned because of the potentially higher expenses that can occur with such an approach. Using several actively managed portfolios means higher costs associated with active versus passive management as well as costs for the professional wealth manager making investment recommendations at the overall portfolio level. In a low return environment, the effect of these cumulative investment management expenses can have an adverse effect on the total return of the portfolio. A similar overall approach to portfolio construction can be attempted using a collection of passively managed no-load mutual funds. Although a similar approach using no-load, passively managed mutual funds is possible, some wealth managers may avoid such a strategy if it does not yield sufficient fees for their services.

---

[11] Harold Evensky, "Changing Equity Premium Implications for Wealth Management Portfolio Design and Implementation," *FPA Journal,* June 2002, p. 1.

[12] Ibid., pp. 1, 6.

Distribution Planning and Execution

The considerations mentioned in the preceding sections often apply during the distribution phase of the wealth management process as well. So, considerations related to asset allocation and diversification, appropriate type of retirement savings plan and its features, and plan expenses would still apply. Additionally, other considerations related to the actual distribution features need to be examined. For instance, should a certain amount of income be distributed through an annuity, or should a system of periodic distributions occur funded through income generated from underlying investments? Should asset allocation be geared more toward income maintenance than future growth? Will a certain portion of the portfolio need to be liquidated to fund income needs? If assets need to be liquidated, should this occur in taxable accounts or in retirement savings plans where taxes can be deferred? All these issues are important considerations for the retiree managing his or her retirement plans and other taxable assets using a wealth management approach. Chapter 31 examines in further detail the issues that an individual should consider when contemplating retirement plan distribution options. Tax issues are vitally important when retirement plan distributions occur. Chapter 31 also discusses the tax implications of various types of retirement plan distributions occurring under a variety of circumstances.

Monitoring Excesses or Deficiencies Relative to Retirement Income Needs

Although a retirement resource target was initially computed when establishing a plan for systematic savings, this issue should be revisited both during the period of asset accumulation and during the period of asset distribution to determine if the retirement plan resources are sufficient to fund expected living expenses. Deviation can occur either because investment returns or savings are not conforming to initial plans or because personal circumstances have changed and the resource needs require revision. Monitoring progress toward the retirement resource target and ongoing assessment on whether the target is realistic and genuinely appropriate is a continuing function in the wealth management process. Even among professional economists considerable debate exists on the resources relative to final income that need to be accumulated to provide reasonable retirement income security. In fact, some economists have suggested that a substantial cohort of the working population may be saving in excess of their retirement income needs.[13] This view contrasts markedly with the many studies that have asserted that Americans are saving insufficient amounts to fund their retirements. Although this debate will no doubt continue, it seems appropriate to err somewhat on the side of oversaving rather than undersaving.

Final Disposition of Excesses or Deficiencies When Retirement Income Is No Longer Needed

To the extent that individuals experience a mismatch between their retirement income needs and their retirement resources, there either will be an excess or deficiency created.

---

[13] Paul B. Farrell, "You Are Being Tricked into Saving Too Much for Retirement," *Marketwatch*, March 7, 2007, p. 1.

To the extent that there is a deficiency, individuals need to revise their strategy to fill the gap created by this shortfall during the retirement years. Most often this deficiency necessitates some lifestyle change or liquidating assets whose use was not expected to fund retirement income needs. A likely asset may be the equity in a home through a reverse mortgage. Alternatively, individuals may seek part-time employment. Or they may move in with relatives or make other lifestyle changes to decrease living expenses. To the extent there are excess resources that exceed retirement income needs, individuals can engage in estate planning to make a disposition of the excess resources. Some attention is given to estate planning in Chapter 31 as part of the discussion of retirement plan distribution strategies.

Universal Retirement Wealth Management Principles

Certain basic wealth management principles should be universally employed by all retirement plan participants accumulating their retirement resources. These universal wealth management principles should also be considered during the distribution phase of retirement.

When the time comes to commence distributions to fund living expenses in retirement, considerable planning must take place. Generally, participants are faced with numerous choices and are interested in obtaining reassurance that the decisions they are making are both rational and optimal. Oftentimes, reassurance can be provided regarding the rationality of a given course of action. Unfortunately, under most circumstances, it is more difficult to provide reassurance whether the decisions being made are, in fact, optimal. Whether a retirement planning decision is optimal is usually only ascertainable in retrospect, depending whether the individuals planning their retirement live a long time or a short time. Whether the decision is optimal also depends on the performance of the capital markets. Sometimes this factor can become readily apparent if the markets make a dramatic and sustained movement either in a positive or negative direction. It is quite unsettling and painfully apparent for some individuals that they have made a less than optimal choice.

Nevertheless, the following guiding principles should be considered in managing retirement wealth both during the accumulation phase and throughout the subsequent distribution phase.

Comprehensive Diversification

As stated earlier, a comprehensive and holistic approach generally should be utilized when conducting asset allocation. Individuals should diversify and look at the entire set of investments along the same investment time horizon; in addition, asset allocation should use a comprehensive perspective. Failing to use this comprehensive approach could result in under- or over-allocating to specific asset classes. This assumes, however, that all of the assets being considered are being accumulated to support the retirement resource needs of the individual. This may not be the case in many situations. For instance, compartmentalization of assets often occurs when individuals are saving for specific goals, such as educational savings or the creation of an emergency fund. If an individual is earmarking certain assets for college funding for his or her children, these assets must be accessed within a targeted time period when those children are obtaining their educations. Consequently, it would be problematic to use a comprehensive approach since these assets have been segregated with a specific purpose for their use. Also, the investment horizon for accessing these funds would not match the investment horizon for commencing retirement plan distributions. Similarly, an emergency fund needs to be fairly liquid because it needs to be accessed on short notice for unexpected occurrences. An emergency fund may be able to be accessed in retirement, but it is generally held for other unexpected purposes. However, apart from earmarked funds for specific financial goals, other assets accumulating for general investment purposes and additional resources for retirement should be allocated to asset classes using a comprehensive approach.

Attainable Efficiencies Should Be Sought

When accumulating resources for retirement, an individual can capture certain efficiencies during the accumulation process. These efficiencies can occur from different sources. For instance, the very nature of retirement savings vehicles confers tax savings through tax deferral when accumulating retirement resources within a tax-qualified plan. In addition to tax savings, certain retirement savings vehicles offer lower costs to retirement savers. Sometimes these costs are further reduced when individuals achieve a certain asset size within their accounts. Additionally, a family of mutual funds may offer access to a high-performing fund that is no longer available to new investors in the general public but still offers access to members of the employer group. An individual who has access to more efficient or cost-effective alternatives generally should avail him- or herself of these efficiencies. This would be the case for lower investment management expenses associated with plan choices. If an individual can access similar funds at a lower cost within the same tax-favored plans, it would make sense to move assets to the less costly alternative unless there are significant considerations to the contrary. When managing assets in a wealth management context, an individual remains vigilant for opportunities to capture these efficiencies. When an individual is starting his or her retirement savings program, vigilance for these savings and the effect of compounding on the individual's savings can appreciably enhance wealth accumulation.

Duplication of Benefits Should Be Eliminated

Traditionally, plan sponsors have attempted to use an integrated approach when selecting plan offerings for their employees. The **functional approach to employee benefits**[14] entails the use of this integrated approach, where employers look for overlap in plan offerings and attempt to eliminate duplication of coverage so as to better utilize limited resources in providing a broad scope of benefit protections addressing the diverse needs of their workforce. As employees have become more

[14] G. Victor Hallman, "Functional Approach to Designing and Evaluating Employee Benefits," *The Handbook of Employee Benefits,* 6th ed. (New York: McGraw-Hill, pp. 15–37).

empowered in the selection and management of their retirement resources, this same exercise is relevant from an individual perspective. An individual should compare his or her benefit needs and the sources available to address these needs. For instance, an individual may determine that various survivorship needs are applicable because of family circumstances. An individual with a nonworking spouse and several children in all likelihood needs resources to provide income for his or her dependents should he or she die prematurely. In many cases, this need is addressed with the purchase of life insurance. However, an individual with this need should examine all sources that potentially address this need. Some of this need is addressed through social insurance sources. Specifically, Social Security provides survivor benefits to a worker's family. Given the age of dependents and the expected time horizon until retirement, an individual may find that a significant portion of this need is addressed by Social Security. Therefore, an individual who determines the adequacy of social insurance may be able to channel more resources into retirement savings, rather than spending these funds on the purchase of additional life insurance. Therefore, the elimination of redundant or duplicated coverage can be a source of funds for retirement wealth creation.

Traditional Assumptions Warrant Questioning

Although many fundamental principles of financial planning exist that contribute to wealth enhancement, sometimes individual circumstances warrant deviation from the traditional wisdom. For instance, it is generally preferable to use tax-deferred vehicles to save for retirement. Individuals routinely are counseled to opt for deferring taxes until a later date and use the growth and income-generating capability of the saved taxes to enhance wealth creation. This is generally the preferred wealth creation strategy in most circumstances. However, there can be situations when deviation from this strategy results in greater wealth building. An individual with large tax deductions related to such things as mortgage expense may actually be in a lower marginal tax bracket than they will experience in retirement. If the individual were to have access to investment options within a retirement savings plan where asset values are deeply undervalued or discounted, it may be advisable to pay taxes currently. This is especially true if asset prices within a retirement planning savings vehicle are expected to dramatically appreciate in the future. Under these conditions it may be preferable to purchase these assets as investments through a Roth IRA, Roth 401(k), or Roth 403(b). Because the Roth retirement savings vehicles mean future appreciation can be disbursed as qualified distributions that are tax-free, the foregone tax saving when contributing to the account may result in even greater tax savings when the future distributions occur.

Strategic Retirement Wealth-Building Decisions

In the pursuit of managing retirement plan wealth, the following decisions are typically required. The descriptions of these strategic decisions briefly explain the opportunity presented to enhance wealth creation.

Possible Wealth-Building Strategies

- *Means to diversification.* Diversification is an important component in managing investment risk. This is true for retirement plan portfolios in the same way that it is true for other investment portfolios. However, because retirement plan assets need not be accessed for distributions until a distant date in the future, diversification need not be continuously maintained throughout the entire period of accumulation. If certain asset classes are thought to be undervalued in the market, a higher weighting can be given to these asset classes, and some degree of portfolio concentration can be tolerated in the short run to enhance longer-term rewards. Of course, as an individual approaches the distribution phase of retirement planning, most fiduciary advisers suggest carefully examining portfolio risk and how to reduce it by lessening the percentage of plan assets dedicated to equities and other volatile asset classes.

- *Dollar cost averaging.* **Dollar cost averaging** is a method of regular, systematic investing in which an individual invests the same dollar value on a periodic basis, usually monthly, in equity investments regardless of whether the valuation of these equities is considered to be undervalued, overvalued, or fairly valued. The dollar cost averaging approach is appealing because it avoids some of the emotional pitfalls that individuals can succumb to (see Chapter 11). Typically, an individual purchases more shares when the market is cheaper and buys fewer shares when the market is more expensive. This method of systematic investing can be conducive to wealth building and is recommended quite often in investment literature. It is particularly easy to apply to retirement plan investing because of the regularity of investment that accompanies the payroll cycle. Although widely recommended, recent studies suggest some other investment approaches may be superior to this traditional investment method.[15]

- *Risk transfer at favorable pricing.* Given the retirement risks described in Chapter 4, it is sometimes a preferable risk management strategy to transfer some of these risks. For the individual planning for retirement, this is often accomplished through the purchase of insurance. Risk transfer can occur by using life insurance, health insurance, and long-term care insurance. Retirement income risks and investment risks can be transferred by purchasing an annuity or by opting for a retirement distribution in an annuity form. When these products are priced favorably, they should be considered. Some discussion of the merits of an annuity payout from a retirement savings plan is provided in Chapter 31.

- *Strategic asset positioning.* Sometimes the selection of specific assets within certain retirement savings plans can enhance wealth creation. For example, a corporate stock paying a substantial dividend would normally be subject to ordinary income taxation on the dividend. The purchase of this same stock within a self-directed Roth IRA would mean a high tax-free yield if withdrawals met the

[15] Haiwei Chen, and Jim Estes, "Value Averaging for 401(k) Plans Makes More 'Cents' Than Dollar Cost Averaging, *FPA Journal*, February 2007, p. 1.

stipulations for a qualified distribution. Positioning assets strategically can assist individuals in meeting their financial income and wealth-building objectives.

- *Preemptive tax planning.* Anticipating the tax consequences of strategic actions can result in individuals selecting the optimal alternative. Tax consequences have such important impacts on retirement planning strategies that they should always be considered. This is especially true concerning the distribution of income from retirement savings plans.

- *Beneficiary planning.* The assets held in retirement plans typically represent a substantial component of a decedent's net worth. Because of the substantive size of retirement accumulations and the importance of these assets for the maintenance of living standards for spouses and other designated beneficiaries, the designation of the beneficiary for these resources should be carefully considered. Retirement plan assets give rise to **income in respect of a decedent (IRD).** IRD occurs when a deceased person was entitled to items that would have created gross income for federal income tax purposes but that were not includable in the decedent's gross income for the year of his or her death. IRD items are generally treated as gross income to whoever receives them after the decedent's death. They do not receive a step-up in basis following the decedent's death, as do capital assets at present.[16] Accordingly, these assets can be subject to substantial taxation. Also, because of the ability of assets within these plans to compound on a tax-deferred basis (or on a tax-free basis for Roth plans), these plans can create substantial wealth. Selection of a beneficiary whose life expectancy extends or stretches the period of favorable tax treatment can result in substantial wealth-building possibilities.

- *Balance between active and passive management.* Selecting the investment approach for the assets within retirement savings plans is an important decision. The merit of active versus passive management of assets has been the subject of considerable academic research. Selecting an appropriate and effective investment strategy for retirement plan assets is a very important strategic consideration with long-term consequences to wealth accumulation. Given the ability to compound investment earnings within retirement savings vehicles by deferring taxes (or avoiding taxes with Roth accounts), these types of plans become a "high-performance engine" for wealth creation. A cost-effective investment strategy yielding positive and competitive performance will increase wealth.

In summary, there are many strategic decisions and tactical actions that can be made in pursuit of retirement planning goals. Today's environment places a substantial amount of risk on the individual plan participant. However, this same environment has created substantial opportunities for the individual to take control of retirement planning utilizing a wealth management approach. When managing assets and risks from such a perspective, the individual often is empowered to increase his or her financial security and well-being by creating and enhancing wealth.

[16] G. Victor Hallman, and Jerry S. Rosenbloom, *Personal Financial Planning,* 7th ed. (New York: McGraw-Hill, 2003), p. 263.

Chapter Summary

- Wealth management is a process for managing resources that seeks to meet an individual's needs and achieve his or her objectives by integrating a diverse range of services. Typically, the process of wealth management utilizes a holistic approach involving investment management, financial planning, retirement planning, estate planning, tax planning, asset protection, risk management, and cash flow and debt management.
- If conducted effectively and executed successfully, retirement planning in a wealth management context should yield a number of advantages for the individual engaged in such planning. Wealth management retirement planning should result in greater asset accumulation, less overall financial risk, reductions in tax liabilities, cost reductions related to the management of resources, and efficiencies in managing cash flow and reducing debt. Wealth management retirement planning also should position retirement resources to conform assets during the accumulation phase leading up to retirement so that these assets are thoughtfully configured to produce retirement income when the distribution phase of retirement commences.
- The process of wealth management is, at its very core, a management activity. Effective wealth management involves planning, execution, ongoing monitoring, measurement of outcomes, accountability, and creative new approaches. It also involves team activities, gathering together the expertise of different disciplines, combining the contributions of various specialties, employing project management skills, and demonstrating leadership in achieving results. It is as much art as it is science.
- Several decision elements are involved in accumulating wealth for retirement income purposes and then subsequently distributing that wealth to support income needs. Decisions must be made concerning the following issues:
  - Developing the retirement resource target.
  - Assessing the efficiencies of funding structures.
  - Examining the funding structures in relation to other factors, participant needs, or the broader environment.
  - Investment selection, risk management, and strategic allocation of resources within the retirement saving structures and the impact of these decisions on an overall portfolio of wealth.
  - Distribution planning and execution.
  - Monitoring excesses or deficiencies relative to retirement income needs.
  - Final disposition of excesses or deficiencies when retirement income is no longer needed.
- Financial projection or risk assessment models cannot adequately depict the environmental complexity that is inherent in the retirement planning process. Nevertheless, these models can be helpful in depicting certain parameters when assessing retirement preparedness and the savings and investing strategies to accumulate sufficient resources. The models are particularly useful to portray the influence of environmental variation on plans to achieve targeted outcomes.

- Apart from earmarked funds for specific financial goals, other assets that are accumulating for general investment purposes plus additional resources for retirement should be allocated to asset classes using a comprehensive approach.
- When the time comes to commence distributions to fund living expenses in retirement, considerable planning must occur.
- Retirement plan assets give rise to income in respect of a decedent (IRD). IRD occurs when a deceased person was entitled to items that would have created gross income for federal income tax purposes, but that were not includable in the decedent's gross income for the year of his or her death. IRD items generally are treated as gross income to whoever receives them after the decedent's death. They do not receive a step-up in basis following the decedent's death, as do capital assets at present. Accordingly, these assets can be subject to substantial taxation.
- Today's environment places a substantial amount of risk on the individual plan participant. However, this same environment has created substantial opportunities for the individual to take control of retirement planning utilizing a wealth management approach. When managing assets and risks from such a perspective, the individual often is empowered to increase his or her financial security and well-being by creating and enhancing wealth.

Key Terms

deterministic models, p. 556

dollar cost averaging, p. 566

employer-employee employment contract, p. 553

functional approach to employee benefits, p. 564

income in respect of a decedent (IRD), p. 567

implicit after-tax return, p. 558

master portfolio, p. 558

mixed models, p. 557

Monte Carlo simulation, p. 557

retirement resource target, p. 556

stochastic models, p. 557

wealth management, p. 550

Questions for Review

1. What is wealth management?
2. Why should retirement planning be conducted in a wealth management context?
3. What are some of the advantages an individual can secure by conducting retirement planning in a wealth management context?
4. Why do many individuals view the management of their retirement assets using a compartmentalized perspective rather than the more holistic wealth management approach?
5. What environmental changes have occurred to make retirement planning in a wealth management context a viable approach?

6. Summarize the managerial tasks involved in wealth management.
7. What impediments hamper the use of wealth management practices at the tactical level?
8. Describe retirement planning wealth management decision elements.
9. Describe the types of models used in retirement planning.
10. What is meant by implicit after-tax return?
11. Why is it difficult to determine the optimal positioning of assets within retirement savings plans?
12. What is the typical approach used by professional wealth managers in managing investments for clients?
13. What is the functional approach to employee benefits, and how does it apply to individuals planning for retirement?
14. What is income in respect of a decedent (IRD)?

Questions for Discussion

1. Discuss methods for fostering a team approach among various professionals and ways to align financial products and strategies to best serve an individual seeking to use a wealth management approach in retirement planning.
2. Discuss how employers can encourage employees to use a wealth management approach in planning for retirement.

Resources for Further Study

Chen, Haiwei, and Jim Estes, "Value Averaging for 401(k) Plans Makes More 'Cents' than Dollar Cost Averaging," *FPA Journal* (February 2007).

Evensky, Harold, "Changing Equity Premium Implications for Wealth Management Portfolio Design and Implementation," *FPA Journal* (June 2002).

Gardner, Randy, and Julie A. Welch, "Recent Developments Help Avoid the Double Tax on IRD Property," *Journal of Financial Planning* (February 2007).

Hallman, G. Victor, and Jerry S. Rosenbloom, *Personal Financial Planning,* 7th ed. New York: McGraw-Hill, 2003.

Lucas, Stuart E., "Eight Principles of Strategic Wealth Management," *Knowledge at Wharton* (August 9, 2006).

Poterba, James M., "Saving for Retirement: Taxes Matter," *An Issue in Brief,* 17, May 2004.

Chapter 31

Retirement Asset Distribution Planning

After studying this chapter you should be able to:

- Provide an overview of the various distribution options available to participants in qualified plans and to owners of other retirement savings vehicles.
- Discuss the merits of annuity payments relative to other forms of retirement account distributions.
- Describe the option of accessing multiple types of distribution options as a strategy for providing retirement income.
- Summarize how the Pension Protection Act of 2006 has affected retirement distribution planning.
- Explain how retirement plan distributions are taxed depending on the contingency that triggers a distribution.

Introduction

This chapter examines the important considerations in determining how distributions from a retirement savings plan should be taken. Individuals in today's workforce can spend a lifetime accumulating resources within a defined contribution plan (DCP) for their retirement. Although many retirement planning strategies primarily direct their focus on the accumulation of assets and on enhancing asset values, the distribution function is equally important. Employers often encourage their workers to increase savings and attempt to instruct workers through investment education to become better investors. As important as the savings and investment functions are, it also is extremely important to develop distribution strategies for the assets accumulated in DCPs. Failure to adequately design effective distribution strategies can result in withdrawals that do not align with participant needs, waste resources, and are inefficient from a tax standpoint.

The chapter primarily is concerned with decisions related to accumulations held within participant-directed defined contribution plans. The chapter begins by providing an overview of plan distribution options. Next it discusses the merits of taking distributions in the form of an annuity. It then covers considerations in designing a distribution strategy. The chapter expands upon the idea of strategy by considering the idea of a strategy that uses multiple types of distributions. Since the passage of the Pension Protection Act of 2006 (PPA), certain changes have occurred that allow for other considerations in designing a distribution strategy. These elements are considered. The balance of the chapter provides a detailed analysis of tax factors that apply to retirement plan distributions.

Overview of Distribution Options

There are multiple ways in which funds held in participant-directed defined contribution plans may be accessed. On a short-term basis, many plans allow for the withdrawal of funds through plan loans. Short of withdrawing funds using a loan with the expectation of repayment later, withdrawals can be made in a variety of other ways. Distributions can occur as a one-time transaction, or as a series of systematic distributions that will continue on a recurring basis. Some plans allow for distributions in an **annuity form,** where the plan sponsor guarantees that the participant cannot outlive the stream of payments and provides a guarantee through the plan or through an insurance company as to continued payments until death. If a plan allows for an annuity payment option, there are usually various types of annuities with various guarantee periods and continuing distributions to co-annuitants or beneficiaries. Some of these continuing annuity payments may continue for a lifetime or a stipulated guaranteed time period. Another option is to move funds from one type of retirement savings plan into another type of retirement savings plan through a tax-free rollover and then to commence distributions either immediately or at a future point from the second retirement savings plan. Distributions can be made in certain years directly to charities for those who have charitable gifting objectives. All these distribution options have varied tax consequences, and the preferred form of distribution for one plan participant may be inappropriate for another plan participant. Therefore, individuals need to assess their personal circumstances when considering distribution options.

At the same time that a plan distribution decision is being made, an intrinsic investment decision also may accompany the distribution decision. This occurs because some forms of distribution may restrict the ability to make certain investment decisions in the future. Many times this is the case in a plan offering purchase of an annuity. For instance, if a plan allows for an annuity pay-out, an individual may be restricted from changing the investment mix in the account once a contractual annuity guarantee occurs. In addition to an intrinsic investment decision with distribution, the decision also can have ramifications for flexibility associated with estate planning. Continuing the annuity payment example, an annuity usually guarantees income distributions for a period of time but requires some surrender of the investment principal when the account owner dies. This surrender of principal would mean the account owner would forego the opportunity to distribute these resources through his or her estate in the event of death before having received all these resources. Another estate planning consideration involves the potential for different types of payments to beneficiaries following the death of the primary account owner. Some types of retirement savings vehicles may permit beneficiaries to withdraw plan funds over an extended period of time, while other plans may restrict such options. Therefore, the development of a retirement plan distribution strategy involves at least the following key considerations:

- Enumerating possible distribution alternatives and developing a means to evaluate which single distribution option or combination of distribution options meet the individual's retirement income needs and other objectives.
- Determining the adequacy of the expected income stream provided by a single or combination of distribution options to meet expected living expenses.
- Assessing the flexibility and risks related to various distribution methods.
- Making relevant investment decisions before the initiation of distributions and planning for future investment decisions, if available, with distribution choices.
- Planning for estate considerations should excess resources exist and distributions occur to charities or beneficiaries.

Specific Distribution Options

Annuity Payment Options

The distinguishing characteristic of an annuity payment option is the guarantee of lifetime income by the plan or the insurer. The reason that an insurer can guarantee lifetime income to a contract owner is because of the law of large numbers and the operational fact that some payments from the annuity contract will be terminated when a plan participant dies. Given a large enough population, some individuals in the pool will live beyond their anticipated life expectancy, while some individuals will die prematurely. Because of the averaging that occurs across the entire pool, the insurance company can guarantee lifetime income and, with its loading factor, earn a profit on the pool of lives receiving annuity payments.

Annuity options are attractive as retirement plan distribution arrangements because the individual opting for this form of payment cannot outlive the income source. **Immediate life annuities** are insurance products that convert a single sum of money or an accumulated balance of plan assets into a series of income payments that continue as long as the contract owner(s) (annuitant, or co-annuitants, if there are more than one person receiving guaranteed payments) remain living. A **deferred life annuity** involves making payments into an insurance product that contractually promises to provide a series of payments in the future. There are different types of immediate and deferred annuities. A **fixed annuity,** usually backed by a portfolio of fixed income investments, guarantees a series of fixed payments. Most fixed annuities provide a stable lifetime income once they are established. Some fixed annuities possess both a guaranteed contractual payment, plus an incremental portion that can vary to some degree. The nonguaranteed payment from some fixed annuities may change gradually from the initial payment depending on interest rate movements. A **variable annuity** provides a periodic lifetime income to annuitants. However, the amount of the annuity payments is not guaranteed. The income provided by a variable annuity varies depending on the performance of the underlying investments in the portfolio. Usually this portfolio consists primarily of equity investments. The initial payment is generally established assuming a relatively modest return, such as 4 percent. Then on the annual anniversary date, the payment will be adjusted upward or downward based on the portfolio's return. The advantage of a variable annuity is that it may tend to keep pace with inflation over longer time horizons. However, the variability associated with this kind of annuity may be a disadvantage, particularly in the short run, if poor performance means a downward adjustment in income payments to annuity owners.

With both fixed and variable annuities, an individual can opt for various payment options depending on whether income is guaranteed to a single annuitant only or to both a first and a second annuitant. Many insurers also allow individuals to opt for income to continue for a fixed number of years to beneficiaries in the event that the annuitant(s) dies prematurely. In these situations, the payments would continue to a designated beneficiary if both first and second annuitants died prematurely (assuming an annuity guaranteeing payments to two annuitants) and the guaranteed payment period had not elapsed. For example, suppose Mr. Robertson purchases an annuity for him and his wife, Mrs. Robertson, that will pay them $1,000 monthly as long as both live, but with a guaranteed payment period of 20 years. In this case if Mr. Robertson died in year 7, the $1,000 would continue to be paid to Mrs. Robertson. If Mrs. Robertson subsequently died in year 13, the $1,000 monthly payment would be paid for an additional 7 years, until the 20th year, to a beneficiary.

If an insurer assumes the risk of an annuity, a charge is levied and paid by annuity policy owners. A common assertion is that many annuities are expensive in terms of fees and charges. These costs, if excessive, would be a disadvantage in opting for an annuity form of distribution.

Periodic Payments

Rather than opt for an annuity, an individual may opt for some form of periodic payment. A person may select payments for a fixed-dollar amount or perhaps for a fixed number of years. If an individual opted for the fixed-dollar amount, the same dollar amount would be distributed until the total amount held in the account is exhausted. If the fixed number of years approach was selected, the trustee holding the assets might adjust the payment amount at certain times to attempt to ensure the account is totally distributed by the anticipated end date. The periodic payment approach would avoid the expenses associated with annuities that compensate an insurer for assumption of longevity risk. A disadvantage of fixed periodic payments is that an individual can exhaust his or her asset base at a future time. If this asset base is the sole or primary means for funding living expenses and the period of disbursement elapses before death, the individual could become indigent. However, if the return on the asset base exceeds that which originally was projected, the individual will either be able to adjust the payment upward or have excess assets to distribute in his or her estate.

Intermittent (Nonperiodic) Payments

Unlike the periodic payment option, an individual may opt to withdraw assets from his or her account, but on an intermittent or irregular basis. Both with the previously described periodic payments and the intermittent payments, investment decisions must be made. If the assets held in the retirement savings plan are generating income, as in the case of bonds, the income routinely may be distributed. If the assets in the account are not generating an income stream or if the income stream is insufficient to meet the individual's living expenses, decisions must be made concerning the liquidation of assets. The **liquidation decision** involves formulating a strategy concerning the systematic conversion of investments into cash for distribution to support living needs. It also involves establishing priorities for which assets will be liquidated and which assets will be held until a future period for later liquidation. Given that assets are held in various types of taxable and nontaxable accounts and that market conditions are constantly in flux, assigning priorities and then executing liquidation decisions becomes very complicated. Preferably assets are liquidated when they are richly valued rather than when they are poorly valued. The liquidation strategy is another important component of a wealth enhancing strategy described in Chapter 30.

On the fixed income side, one approach often suggested is a **laddered bond portfolio.** Here, bonds of different maturities are purchased so that the interest and maturing repayment of the principal amounts create an ongoing flow of income. This approach allows the individual to avoid the loss of principal should interest rates increase. An individual need not liquidate his or her bond holdings at an inopportune time when laddering is implemented effectively. Costs associated with the liquidation of investments should also be considered as part of the distribution strategy. An example will clarify this issue. Suppose a retirement plan investor could either hold a low-cost index fund or the exact same index, but in the form of an exchange-traded fund (ETF). Recall that ETFs often own a collection of stocks, with many ETFs holding the stocks that comprise well-known market indexes, such as the Standard & Poor's 500 Index. Many of these ETFs have even lower management fees than low-cost mutual funds containing the same stocks. However, the investor pays a commission when he or she buys or sells an ETF. Therefore, for the buy-and-hold investor, it may be more cost effective to hold the index in an ETF during the accumulation phase of his or her career to shift a substantial accumulation into an index at one time. However, if at a later date the investor entered the distribution phase, it may be more cost effective to hold the same basket of stocks in a mutual fund. This would be the case if an individual were selling shares of the ETF on a regular, recurrent basis and would, thus, continually have to pay commissions on these small sales of the ETF.

An intermittent payment approach is probably not feasible if the retirement savings account being used is the only source of funding for living expenses. However, if an individual has a sufficient income stream coming from other sources, then, in combination with these other sources, the intermittent approach may make sense. These other sources could include a defined benefit pension, an annuity, Social Security, or perhaps a spouse's pension.

Lump-Sum Distribution

A qualifying lump-sum distribution is a distribution from a qualified retirement plan of the balance to the credit of an employee after age 59½ and within one taxable year of the recipient. The distribution must be made on account of the employee's death, attainment of age 59½, or separation from service. It should be noted that a distribution to the employee in the form of annuity payments after retirement will not prevent the employee's beneficiary from receiving a qualifying lump-sum distribution.

Sometimes an employee holds employer securities in a qualified plan. These securities may offer an opportunity for favorable tax treatment that should be considered. When a qualified plan distributes employer securities as part of a lump-sum distribution to employees or their beneficiaries, the net unrealized appreciation (NUA) on any employer securities included as part of the lump-sum distribution qualifies for special tax treatment. The NUA is the difference between the fair market value of the employer securities at distribution and their cost or other basis to the plan. The employee can elect to include either the market value of the employer securities or their cost basis to the trust as taxable income at the time of distribution. The employee, if choosing the cost basis when acquired, is deferring taxation on the unrealized appreciation until the securities are sold in the future. If and when the employee subsequently sells the securities, the net unrealized appreciation, plus any future increase in the value of these securities, is taxed as a capital gain. If the employer securities are held until the employee's death, under current estate tax rules, the employee's heirs would have a cost basis in the securities equal to their market value at the time of death. This would mean the appreciation in value unrealized at the time of death would not be taxed as income. If the employer securities were included in a distribution that failed to meet qualifying conditions, only the portion of securities attributable to employee contributions could be valued on the basis of cost to the trust.

Lump Sum with Rollover into IRA

Oftentimes, rather than subject a rollover to immediate taxation, an individual will roll over qualifying plan assets into an individual retirement account (IRA) and subsequently take distributions from the IRA. The rollover to the IRA can be motivated by favorable investment alternatives available within the IRA, an ability to access funds at a lower expense, or the desire simply to consolidate assets through a single retirement savings vehicle to facilitate easier management of the assets. These motivations for consolidation within an IRA were described in Chapter 16. Sometimes this centralization of assets can be motivated by the desire to position assets in a single funding vehicle to simplify estate planning.

Combining Various Payment Options

Individuals often will examine distinct distribution options and think of them separately without giving adequate consideration to the merits of combining various payment options. It often is preferable to combine various payment options to arrive at a distribution strategy that merges the advantages of these distinct options so as to arrive at a more integrated solution for providing retirement income. For instance, an individual may budget expected living expenses. Assuming the individual possesses adequate retirement resources, the individual may utilize a fixed annuity to have a base amount of income that covers his or her basic living expenses. The individual may decide to supplement the fixed annuity with a variable annuity or periodic or intermittent distributions from the plan. Similarly, these other sources of income need not be started immediately upon retirement. For an individual deriving income from part-time work or consulting income, distributions may be subsequently commenced when these activities diminish or end. Although there are various ways in which these payment options can be integrated, the essential point to understand is that the variety of payment options permit an enormous number of permutations and combinations that can be tailored to the unique circumstances of the individual retiree. Sometimes, an individual may base distribution decisions on contingent events. For instance, if a spouse is in poor health, a delay on certain decisions may be warranted in the event that when death occurs, life circumstances and needs change dramatically.

Merits of Annuity Pay-Out Methods

In the past with the popularity of defined benefit plans, annuity distribution options were much more popular. With the migration from defined benefit plans (DBPs) to defined contribution plans, fewer people have direct access to annuity distributions directly through their retirement plans.

> Once the norm, annuity options are now offered in fewer than one-third of defined contribution plans, and many of those plans offering annuities experience extremely low utilization by plan participants.[1]

Certain types of plans, such as money purchase pension plans and traditional 403(b) plans, provide annuity distribution options directly through the plan. However, many 401(k) plans do not provide such an option. Therefore, individuals would need to move monies to an insurance product if they sought the guarantees provided by annuities.

A key difference exists between annuities offered directly through a retirement plan and annuities offered through an insurer outside a retirement plan. This difference involves the mortality table used to compute lifetime income payments. Retirement plan annuities must use unisex mortality tables, where the payments are the same for men and women who have attained the same age. This has been required ever since the Supreme Court so ruled in the case of *Arizona Governing Committee* v. *Norris* in 1983. Annuities sold by insurers outside a retirement plan may use different annuity tables for men and women because women's life expectancies exceed those of men. Using such gender-specific tables provides higher income for men compared with women who have attained the same age.

There is considerable debate on the merits of using annuities. As stated previously, much of the controversy involves the costs associated with annuity products. Many times

---

[1] Bill McClain, "The Annuity Alternative: Answering the Need in DC Plans," *Benefits Quarterly,* First Quarter 2007, p. 18.

in the past these charges have been excessive, exacting a heavy financial expense on such distribution options.

> Annuities fell out of favor within defined contribution plans due to their track record of high fees, poor investment performance, and limited flexibility. In addition, administrative burdens, fiduciary concerns, and limited participant understanding constrained their usage. Now, a combination of demographic and marketplace trends is causing plan sponsors to revisit the role of annuities in defined contribution plans, thanks to promising new approaches such as **third-party annuity placement services.**[2]

Under such an arrangement, plan participants receive quotes from a number of different insurance companies, compare pricing and other features, and ultimately purchase an annuity. This information can be readily reported on the Internet. The purchase of annuities occurs outside the plan, and some insurers can structure the arrangement so the plan participant rolls over his or her plan balance into an IRA with the insurer. The subsequent annuity distributions are generated from the IRA.

The economics of annuities are such that they can offer a higher rate of return with the potential to enhance income distributions. Life annuities are useful for managing longevity risk because of the economics of risk pooling. At least some payments in the annuity contract are **life contingent;** that is, these payments are discontinued at death.

> This contingency allows the annuity provider to offer living annuitants an implicit per-period total rate of return above that attainable from similar investments outside of the immediate annuity arrangement. Because the assets backing the annuity are pooled and payments are at least in part life-contingent, a portion of the assets contributed by early decedents can be used to finance higher payments to those that live longer. Contrary to a widely held misperception, it is the pooling of assets and risk that enables providers of fixed immediate annuities to support implicit rates of return significantly higher than a risk-free rate. This has nothing to do with the investment acumen of the annuity provider; it's simply basic principles of insurance.[3]

One of the plan sponsors' concerns involved the previous Employee Retirement Income Security Act (ERISA) standard that an annuity must be the "safest available." As previously described in Chapter 27, the Pension Protection Act of 2006 (PPA) no longer requires that defined contribution plans select the "safest available" annuity. The fact that individuals can move their balances out of the plan to an IRA to make the annuity purchase distances the plan sponsor from having to deal with some fiduciary concerns related to annuity issuers. However, there could still be fiduciary issues if the plan has selected a service allowing plan participants to compare the annuities offered by various insurers.

Individuals may purchase an annuity from an insurance company if they want a contractual assurance from an insurance company that they will not outlive their income stream. However, even when an individual purchases an annuity, there are

---

[2] Ibid., p. 16.
[3] John Ameriks, and Paul Yakoboski, "Reducing Retirement Income Risks: The Role of Annuitization," *Benefits Quarterly,* Fourth Quarter 2003, p. 14.

uncertainties regarding the sufficiency of the future income stream. First, the guarantee of lifetime income is only as good as the solvency of the insurance company making the contractual commitment. If the insurer were to become insolvent, there is the possibility of bail-out from state guaranty funds, but the insured may still not receive the entire assumed income stream. Apart from the concerns of insurer solvency, an annuity income stream can still have its purchasing power eroded if inflation increases or persists. Therefore, even with so-called guaranteed income streams, uncertainties persist.

Developing a Retirement Plan Distribution Strategy

Developing a retirement income strategy involves several important considerations. First, an individual must assess retirement income needs and have some idea of the ongoing expenses he or she will incur during retirement. Additionally, an individual should assess the risks described in Chapter 4 and the possibility of additional expenses related to the occurrence of such risks. Costs and tax implications of various approaches should be considered. Integrated planning is essential when distributing retirement income from the assets that have been accumulated for this purpose. To achieve the level of income necessary to meet income objectives, some repositioning of assets is necessary. Making changes to existing asset allocations is often easier to implement if all of the required asset shifts can occur within tax-favored retirement planning structures. If this is the case, the changes can occur without an immediate tax consequence. On the other hand, if asset reallocations must occur among taxable assets, the level of tax planning that must accompany the asset reallocation is greater because the disposition of assets can generate immediate tax consequences.

Apart from the tax consequences, individuals are making decisions regarding which income-generating options will supply the resources needed to provide income sufficiency for an extended period of time. This is not an easy exercise. Although several innovative techniques using Monte Carlo simulation exist to address the question of asset sufficiency, uncertainty accompanies the decision, and individuals often find this uncertainty unsettling.

For the participant who possesses both a defined benefit and defined contribution plan, the income options selected under the DCP should be made, supplementing the stream of income that will be generated from the DBP. Similarly, the income stream generated by Social Security, which is almost universally available to workers, should also be considered when deciding on the form and level of resources distributed from the DCP. Comparisons should be made of the budgeted resource needs of the individual and the extent to which distributions from guaranteed sources will meet the minimum income needs in retirement. For those possessing defined contribution assets only, it is critical that the plan to convert assets into income be well conceived, considering risks inherent in the capital markets.

Utilizing Multiple Distribution Forms in a Retirement Income Strategy

As indicated earlier, an individual may opt to combine various distribution options as part of a retirement income strategy. If an individual possesses sufficient resources and has charitable giving or estate-planning objectives in addition to retirement income objectives, it is even more likely that a single distribution option alone will fail to meet all of the individual's needs. Therefore, many individuals planning for retirement distributions evaluate multiple distribution forms as components of their overall retirement income strategy. In addition to blending multiple income distribution forms, the timing when these distributions commence also can be varied. As such, a phased approach can produce income enhancements at select prearranged times or when circumstances dictate additional resource needs. Distribution forms can affect taxes and risks. Utilizing multiple distribution forms and varying their use at select times can contribute to an overall wealth-building strategy that reduces taxes and risks.

Reducing Taxes

Affecting taxes can be easily demonstrated. For example, suppose an individual decides to move assets from a traditional IRA to a Roth IRA, either because he or she expects tax rates to increase in the future or because he or she wishes to position assets in a tax-free distribution vehicle for the future. Immediate conversion of an entire balance held in a traditional IRA may be very costly from a tax perspective. A full, immediate conversion may cause a significant portion of the accumulation in the traditional IRA to be taxed at a higher marginal tax rate when converted. Full conversion also may cause an individual to lose various tax credits, exemptions, and deductions because tax preferences are phased out at higher income levels. An individual who converts a portion of the traditional IRA to the Roth over a period of years could cause the conversion to occur at lower marginal tax rates and eliminate the phase-out of beneficial credits, exemptions, and deductions.

This same principle of subjecting income to higher marginal tax rates and the loss of tax credits and deductions also applies if an individual holds assets in qualified plans on a tax-deferred basis and also holds balances in a Roth IRA or other Roth-type account such as a Roth 401(k) or a Roth 403(b). Varying distributions from these retirement savings plans that receive different tax treatments can reduce taxes and increase disposable income. A more detailed explanation of the tax consequences for various retirement plan distributions is provided at the end of this chapter.

Reducing Risks

Distribution options affect risk retention. Previously, it was shown that annuity distribution options are effective in managing longevity risk. Other distribution options increase and decrease risks as well. One research paper noted differential impacts on risk depending on the way distributions occur.[4] The paper indicated a spending strategy

---

[4] Keith Marbach, "A Choice of Risks When Spending in Retirement: Optimizing the Plan for Each Retiree," Zunna Research website, 2002, p. 12.

could involve withdrawals to maintain an individual's standard of living and another in which withdrawals are a fixed percentage of the value of the account. In the first case, the ultimate risk is insolvency with the account being exhausted, whereas the second alternative risks a sustained and persistent reduced standard of living below what is really necessary.

Combining distribution options also can have an impact on risk because of correlations between risks similar to the correlation between individual securities in an overall portfolio. Researchers have shown that the inclusion of an annuity distribution option with other distribution methods can have a beneficial impact on reducing risk. The impact of immediate life annuities on the sustainability of retirement plan distributions was studied. The study noted,

> . . . the 4.5 percent withdrawal factor can be sustained with more certainty, for longer time periods, by adding the risk-pooling characteristics of an immediate annuity to the overall retirement portfolio. In much the same way as asset classes are used to hedge financial risks, immediate annuities can be used to hedge longevity risk."[5]

Even though various risks can be reduced with a combination of distribution forms, trade-offs exist with the selection of different distribution methods. The study noting the reduction in longevity risk cautions,

> . . . that the pooling of longevity risk has consequences other than portfolio withdrawal stability. If the retiree dies early in the retirement years, after having purchased an immediate annuity, then the investment in the pool continues to pay other annuity holders rather than the retiree's heirs. This opportunity cost should be assessed before any decision is reached regarding the structure of retirement portfolios.[6]

Additional Distribution Options with Passage of the Pension Protection Act of 2006

The Pension Protection Act of 2006 made some changes in the law affecting plan distributions and rollovers from various retirement plans. Some of these changes affect defined benefit plans while others affect defined contribution plans.

The PPA made changes to the mortality table and interest rate that is used to compute the minimum value of a lump-sum distribution paid from a DBP. The effect of these changes (effective for plan years beginning after December 31, 2007) generally is to reduce the value of the lump sum that would be paid under prior law. The law requires use of the mortality table under minimum funding standard rules for single-employer DBPs. The applicable interest rate is the adjusted first, second, and third segment rates applied under the minimum funding rules.

In the past, distributions to plan participants from a qualified plan before severance of employment were problematic. This issue caused difficulties in facilitating phased

---

[5] John Ameriks, Robert Veres, and Mark J. Warshawsky, "Making Retirement Income Last a Lifetime," *FPA Journal*, December 2001, p. 12.

[6] Ibid., p. 12.

retirement arrangements for workers nearing retirement. The PPA made clear that a qualified plan may provide distributions to an employee who attains the age of 62 even though the employee has not separated from service.

The PPA directed the Secretary of the Treasury to change regulations regarding hardship withdrawals from qualified plans, tax-sheltered annuities, nonqualified deferred compensation plans, and deferred compensation plans of state and local governments and tax-exempt organizations. With the adjustment in these regulations, distributions for hardships and unforeseen financial emergencies that were previously allowed for conditions affecting spouses and dependents of plan participants would now be extended to a participant's beneficiary under the plan. This provision would be especially helpful in situations involving hardship withdrawals for the payment of medical expenses.

The PPA waived the 10 percent early withdrawal penalty tax on qualified public safety employees who separate from service at their employers and take distributions from government pension plans after having attained the age of 50. The definition of a qualified public safety employee applies to any employee who provides police protection, firefighting services, or emergency medical services for any area within the jurisdiction of a state or political subdivision. Similarly, the PPA waived the 10 percent early withdrawal penalty tax on distributions to qualified reservists taking distributions from an IRA or from elective deferrals made under a 401(k) plan, a 403(b) plan, or certain similar types of plans. To qualify for this exception, the qualified reservist needed to be called to active duty for a period in excess of 179 days. Additionally, the qualified reservist needed to be called to active duty after September 11, 2001, and before December 31, 2007.

Rollovers from various types of retirement savings plans beginning January 1, 2008, may be directly placed into Roth IRAs rather than having to first be moved into a traditional IRA as was the case previously. A comprehensive discussion of IRAs is provided in Chapter 12. The PPA also permitted the rollover of after-tax contributions through a trustee-to-trustee transfer from a qualified retirement plan to a DBP or a 403(b) plan. After-tax rollovers, although previously allowable into DCPs and IRAs, had not been permitted into DBPs or 403(b) plans prior to January 1, 2007. Another rule change related to rollovers involves nonspouse beneficiaries. Beginning January 1, 2007, a nonspouse beneficiary can receive a distribution from an eligible retirement plan previously held by a deceased participant or account owner. Such a distribution must occur through a direct trustee-to-trustee transfer into an IRA created to receive the distribution on behalf of the beneficiary. When such a distribution occurs, the transfer is considered an eligible rollover distribution. The IRA that received the distribution is treated as an inherited account, and the required minimum distribution rules applicable where the participant or account owner dies before the entire interest is distributed apply. At time of publication of this book, the Internal Revenue Service issued guidance explaining that if the decedent was under age 70½, the rules of the retirement plan would continue to dictate how fast money needed to be withdrawn from the IRA. If the decedent was over age 70½, a nonspouse beneficiary could stretch the withdrawals over his or her own life expectancy. This guidance has substantial implications on the time limit in which tax-deferred (or tax-free for a Roth) compounding occurs, dramatically affecting wealth accumulation within a nonspouse IRA.

In tax years 2006 and 2007, IRA owners who are at least age 70½ are allowed to make tax-free distributions of up to $100,000 per year from their IRAs to public charities.

Taxation of Retirement Plan Distributions

Unquestionably, a major advantage of a qualified pension or profit sharing plan is that an employer's contributions, although currently deductible, will not be considered as taxable income to an employee until they are distributed. Moreover, when a distribution does represent taxable income to the employee or a beneficiary, it may be received under favorable tax circumstances.

Broadly speaking, distributions from a qualified plan are taxable in accordance with the annuity rules of Section 72 of the Internal Revenue Code. Lump-sum distributions made to individuals born before January 1, 1936, may qualify for special income-averaging treatment if certain conditions are met. Although these general principles apply regardless of the contingency that gives rise to the distribution, the remaining sections of this chapter discuss the tax aspects of a distribution in terms of the contingency that has brought it about. Thus, this chapter briefly explores the tax situation of an employee during employment (including in-service distributions of the employee's account), as well as the tax situation when distributions are made because of the employee's retirement, death, severance of employment, or disability.

With a view toward achieving some degree of simplicity, the discussion has been confined to the federal taxation of typical forms of distribution under plans that have a qualified status when the distributions are made. In certain instances, penalty taxes are imposed in addition to federal income taxes on distributions that

- Commence too early.
- Commence too late.

The last three sections of this chapter provide a discussion of these penalty taxes.

For a complete treatment of the taxation of distributions from a qualified retirement plan, the discussion of tax-free rollovers to an individual retirement account or another qualified retirement plan, Chapter 12 should be consulted. In addition, Chapter 6 discusses the requirements that must be met to prevent a loan from a qualified pension plan from being treated as a taxable distribution.

Taxation during Employment

Even though employer contributions may be vested fully in an employee under a qualified plan, the employee will not have to report these contributions as taxable income until such time as they are distributed. Thus, employer contributions made on behalf of an employee generally will not be considered as taxable income to the employee during the period of employment.

If the plan includes a life insurance benefit for employees, however, the employee is considered to have received a distribution each year equal to the portion of the employer's contribution (or the portion of the trust earnings) that has been applied during such year to provide the pure insurance in force on the employee's life.[7] The pure insurance is considered to be the excess, if any, of the face amount of the employee's life insurance contract over its cash value. The amount that the employee must include as taxable income for each year is the one-year term insurance rate for the employee's attained age multiplied by the amount of pure insurance involved. This insurance cost often is called the **PS 58 cost** because the original Treasury Department ruling on the subject was so numbered.

If the death benefit is being provided outside the qualified plan by a nondiscriminatory group term life insurance contract issued to the employer rather than to the trustee of the pension trust, the employee is not required to consider any part of the premium paid by the employer as taxable income, except to the extent that the employee's coverage exceeds $50,000. However, if the trustee of a qualified trust purchases the group term life insurance instead of the employer, the value of the insurance attributable to employer contributions will be considered as taxable income to the covered employees, regardless of the amounts of coverage involved.

Determination of Cost Basis

Before discussing the taxation of benefits, it is important to have a clear idea of the elements that constitute an employee's cost basis (or **investment in contract**), if any, since the employee's cost basis is an important factor in the taxation of distributions under the plan.

Briefly, **Section 72 of the IRC** provides that an employee's cost basis includes the following:

1. The aggregate of any amounts the employee contributed on an after-tax basis while employed.

2. The aggregate of the prior insurance costs the employee has reported as taxable income, but only for distributions made under that policy. (If the employee has made contributions and the plan provides that employee contributions will first be used to pay any cost of insurance, the employee's reportable income for any year is the excess, if any, of the insurance cost of protection over the amount of the employee's contribution for the year, and not the full cost of insurance protection.)

3. Other contributions made by the employer that already have been taxed to the employee. An example could be where the employer has maintained a nonqualified plan that later was qualified.

---

[7] Note that the amount applied during any year to provide life insurance often covers a period extending into the following year. The employee, however, is not permitted to apportion this insurance cost between the two years and is required to include this amount as taxable income in the year in which it is applied, even though the period of protection extends into the subsequent year.

4. Loans from the qualified retirement plan to the participant that were treated as taxable distributions.

There also is provision for the inclusion of other items in an employee's cost basis, such as contributions made by the employer after 1950 but before 1963 while the employee was a resident of a foreign country. For the most part, however, the items listed above will constitute an employee's cost basis in the typical situation.

Taxation of In-Service Distributions

When an employee receives an in-service cash distribution of the entire value of his or her account, the amount of the distribution that exceeds the employee's cost basis will be taxable in the year of distribution as ordinary income. In addition, it may be subject to the early distribution tax discussed later in this chapter. A distribution that occurs after age 59½ may be eligible for special averaging treatment in very limited circumstances, if it meets the requirements for a qualifying lump-sum distribution and if made to an individual born before January 1, 1936.

If the in-service distribution represents only a part of the employee's account, it still will be taxed as ordinary income, with a pro rata tax-free recovery of the employee's cost basis. The amount of the distribution that is considered a recovery of cost basis is determined by multiplying the distribution amount by a fraction. The numerator is the employee's total cost basis; the denominator is the present value of the employee's vested account balance. For example, if the value of the employee's total vested account balance is $100,000 and the corresponding cost basis is $30,000, the fraction is 3/10. If the employee's partial distribution is $10,000, 3/10 of this amount, or $3,000, would be considered as a tax-free recovery of cost basis and $7,000 would be taxed as ordinary income. It should be noted that this result occurs no matter how the plan describes the withdrawal. Thus, even though the plan permits only a withdrawal of after-tax employee contributions and an employee perceives that only his own money is being returned, the distribution will be taxed in this manner.

The Tax Reform Act of 1986 (TRA '86) mandated the pro rata recovery of an employee's cost basis. The basis recovery rules of prior law treated all distributions as a return of cost basis until that basis was fully recovered; all distributions thereafter were taxable. In plans that permitted in-service withdrawals on May 5, 1986, and had separate accounting for employee contributions, pre-1987 employee contributions can be withdrawn under the old rules until exhausted; thereafter, the updated rules apply.

TRA '86 also provided some relief for defined contribution plans (and some defined benefit plans)[8] by permitting them to categorize the portion of the employee's account balance attributable to after-tax contributions as a separate account for purposes of the

---

[8] A defined benefit plan is to be treated as a defined contribution plan for this purpose to the extent that a separate account is maintained for employee contributions to which is credited actual earnings and losses. Crediting employee contributions with a specified rate of earnings will not be sufficient to create a separate account. Notice 87-13, Q&A-14, except for plans permitting unmatched voluntary contributions allocated to a separate account, it is unlikely that most contributory defined benefit plans will satisfy this requirement.

basis recovery rules.[9] In effect, this permits employers to make distributions only from the account or separate contract that consists solely of after-tax employee contributions plus earnings. Thus, while the pro rata distribution rule still applies, calculations are based on the ratio of after-tax employee contributions to the value of the separate contract that consists of these contributions and earnings thereon. To use this approach, the plan must maintain adequate separate accounts by keeping separate records of after-tax contributions and earnings and by allocating earnings, gains, losses, and other credits between the separate account and other portions of the plan on a reasonable and consistent basis.

As a result, plan sponsors have three general options for establishing contracts in a plan:

1. *One contract.* There is no separate contract for employee contributions; the plan consists of only a single contract in which all contributions and associated earnings are held.
2. *Two contracts.* Pre-1987 and post-1986 employee after-tax contributions and associated earnings are held in a separate contract; all other plan contributions and earnings are held in the other contract.
3. *Two contracts.* There is a separate contract only for post-1986 after-tax employee contributions and earnings; the other contract contains all other plan contributions and earnings, including pre-1987 employee contributions and earnings. This option often has been called the "fresh start" approach.[10]

Taxation of Retirement Benefits

This section examines the taxation of retirement benefits received in the form of lump-sum distributions as well as distributions in the form of periodic payments.

Distributions to a Retired Employee

If an employee's benefit is paid from a qualified plan in the form of a qualifying lump-sum benefit at retirement, the employee's cost basis will be recovered free of income tax. The excess of the qualifying distribution over the employee's cost basis will qualify for favorable tax treatment if paid to an individual born before January 1, 1936.

It should be noted, however, that even though a provision exists for the favorable taxation of some lump-sum distributions, a qualified retirement plan may not make distributions to an employee prior to his or her severance of employment.

A special transition rule exists for individuals born before January 1, 1936. Qualifying lump-sum distributions made to these individuals, regardless of when made, could continue to use the capital gains provisions in effect prior to the Tax Reform Act of 1986 and have the pre-1974 portion of the lump-sum distribution taxed as a

---

[9] Internal Revenue Code Section 72(d).

[10] For examples of these options and how they differ in results, see Towers Perrin, *The Handbook of 401(k) Plan Management* (Burr Ridge, IL: Irwin Professional Publishing, 1996), pp. 166–68.

long-term capital gain with a maximum rate of 20 percent. An eligible individual also could elect to choose 10-year averaging for all or the remaining portion of the distribution. If 10-year averaging was chosen, however, the individual would have to use the tax rates in effect for the 1986 tax year.

For purposes of determining whether there has been a qualifying lump-sum distribution, all plans of the same type (e.g., defined benefit or defined contribution) and all plans within a given category (pension, profit sharing, or stock bonus) are aggregated and treated as a single plan. Because only similar types of plans are required to be aggregated for this purpose, it is possible to have a distribution from a profit sharing plan qualify as a lump-sum distribution even though the employee has an interest in a pension plan sponsored by the employer.

If a distribution includes an annuity contract and/or employer securities, some part of the distribution may not be currently taxable. The value of the annuity will not be taxed when distributed, and the employee will be taxed only on annuity payments when actually received. Similarly, any unrealized appreciation on employer securities will not be taxable in the year of distribution unless the employee so elects.

Distributions to an Alternate Payee

Any **alternate payee** who is the spouse or former spouse of the participant is treated as the distributee of any distribution or payment made to him or her under a qualified domestic relations order (QDRO). For purposes of computing the tax on lump-sum distributions, the balance to the credit of an employee does not include any amount payable under a QDRO.

Distributions in the Form of Periodic Payments

Distributions to a Retired Employee

If a retiring employee receives the distribution in the form of **periodic payments,** these payments will be taxed to the employee as ordinary income in accordance with the annuity rules of Section 72 of the Internal Revenue Code.

If the employee has no cost basis, all payments will be taxable as ordinary income when received. If the employee has a cost basis, part of each distribution will be considered a tax-free recovery of that cost basis. If payments are being made on a non-lifetime basis, each payment will be multiplied by an exclusion ratio or fraction to determine the amount that is tax free and the amount that is taxable. The numerator of the fraction is the total cost basis; the denominator is the employee's expected return under the payment arrangement. Thus, for example, if the employee is to receive payments of $12,000 for 10 years, his or her expected return is $120,000 (10 × $12,000). If the employee's cost basis is $10,000, his tax-free recovery each year will be $1,000, or 1/12th ($10,000/$120,000) of $12,000.

This concept of determining an exclusion ratio also was applicable to life income arrangements with an annuity starting date before November 19, 1996. For life income arrangements with an annuity starting date of November 19, 1996, or later, a simplified method is used to determine the portion of each payment that is a tax-free return of cost basis. The nontaxable portion received each month will be the employee's cost basis, divided by the following number of anticipated payments:

Age on Annuity Starting Date	Number of Payments
Up to 55	360
Over 55, up to 60	310
Over 60, up to 65	260
Over 65, up to 70	210
Over 70	160

If payments are made to the employee for a period certain or with a refund feature, the cost basis will be adjusted, when determining the employee's exclusion ratio, to reflect the value of the refund or period-certain feature.

Distributions to an Alternate Payee

Any alternate payee who is the spouse or former spouse of the participant is treated as the distributee of any distribution or payment made under a QDRO.[11] The investment in the contract must be allocated on a pro rata basis between the present value of such distribution or payment and the present value of all other benefits payable with respect to the participant to which the QDRO relates.

Taxation of Death Benefits

Lump-Sum Distributions

A lump-sum distribution to the employee's beneficiary from a qualified plan made on account of the employee's death after age 59½ (either before or after severance of employment) will entitle the beneficiary to the favorable tax treatment previously described. The favorable tax treatment is granted if the distribution represents the full amount then credited to the employee's account and if it is received within one taxable year of the beneficiary. This applies, however, only to distributions made with respect to individuals born before January 1, 1936.

In determining the net amount of gain subject to tax, the beneficiary's cost basis will be the same as the employee's (i.e., the aggregate of the employee's contributions and any amounts, such as insurance costs, on which the employee previously has been taxed).

If any portion of the distribution consists of life insurance proceeds and the employee either paid the insurance cost or reported this cost as taxable income, the pure insurance—that is, the difference between the face amount of the contract and its cash value—will pass to the beneficiary free of income tax under Section 101(a) of the

---

[11] For payments prior to October 22, 1986, this treatment also applied to alternate payees other than a spouse or former spouse.

Internal Revenue Code. The beneficiary will have to treat only the cash value of the contract, plus any other cash distributions from the plan, as income subject to tax.

The following example illustrates how the death benefit under a typical retirement income contract would be taxed if the employee died before retirement and the face amount of the contract was paid to the beneficiary in a lump sum.

Face amount of contract	$25,000
Cash value of contract	−11,000
Amount of pure insurance excludable under Section 101(a)	$14,000
Cash value of contract	$11,000
Amount subject to income tax	$11,000
Beneficiary's cost basis (aggregate of prior insurance costs that employee reported as taxable income)	−940
Balance taxable to beneficiary	$10,060

The beneficiary would, therefore, receive $14,940 of the total distribution free of income tax, and only $10,060 would be considered as being taxable.

The regulations provide that if the employee has not paid the insurance cost of his or her contract or has not reported the cost of insurance as taxable income, the portion of the insurance proceeds consisting of pure insurance will be considered as taxable income to the beneficiary.

When an employee dies after retirement and after having received periodic payments, a lump-sum death payment to the employee's beneficiary, if it meets the requirements previously noted, could qualify for the favorable tax treatment described. The beneficiary's cost basis, however, will be reduced by any amount that the employee had recovered free from income tax.

Distribution in the Form of Periodic Payments

Death before Retirement

If death occurs before retirement and the plan provides for the distribution of the employee's death benefit over a period of years (including payments based on the life expectancy of the beneficiary), these payments will be taxed in accordance with the annuity rules of Section 72 of the Internal Revenue Code.

The beneficiary's cost basis will consist of the amount that would have been the employee's cost basis had the employee lived and received the payments.

If any part of the periodic payments arises from pure life insurance, the proceeds are divided into two parts:

1. The cash value of the contract immediately before death.
2. The pure insurance (the excess of the face amount of the contract over its cash value).

That portion of each periodic payment attributable to the cash value of the contract will be taxed to the beneficiary under the annuity rules. The balance of each payment that is attributable to the pure insurance element will be treated as insurance proceeds under Section 101(d) of the Internal Revenue Code.

Death after Retirement

The taxation of payments to the beneficiary of an employee who dies after retirement and after periodic payments have begun depends on whether the employee had a cost basis (and if so, whether it had been recovered by the employee) as well as on the method of payment involved. If the employee had no cost basis, each payment would be considered as taxable income to the beneficiary as received. However, where the payments are being continued under a joint and survivor annuity form, the exclusion ratio established when the annuity became effective shall apply until the unrecovered investment in the contract is eliminated.

Taxation of Severance-of-Employment Benefits

For the most part, the discussion in this chapter on the taxation of distributions at retirement is equally applicable to the taxation of distributions on severance of employment. If the distribution is in the form of periodic payments, the taxation of payments to the employee will be governed by the annuity rules after taking the employee's cost basis, if any, into account. However, a penalty tax on early distributions may apply as explained later in this chapter.

If the distribution is in the form of a life insurance contract, its cash value less the employee's cost basis, if any, will be considered as taxable income in the year in which the employee receives the contract, even though the contract is not then surrendered for its cash value. The distribution may qualify for favorable tax treatment if all necessary conditions are met. On the other hand, the employee may avoid any current tax liability by transferring this amount, within 60 days, to a qualified individual retirement savings plan (described in Chapter 12) or to another employer's qualified plan. The employee also may avoid any current tax liability by making an irrevocable election, within 60 days of the distribution, to convert the contract to a nontransferable annuity that contains no element of life insurance.[12]

If the employee would otherwise receive a cash distribution but has the option under the plan of electing, within 60 days, to receive a nontransferable annuity in lieu of the

---

[12] The regulations spell out what is meant by nontransferable, and the language of the regulations has been used as a guide by many insurers in endorsing their contracts. Such an endorsement might read approximately as follows:

> This contract is not transferable except to the ABC Insurance Company. It may not be sold, assigned, discounted, or pledged as collateral for a loan or as security for the performance of an obligation or for any other purposes to any person other than this Company.
> However, notwithstanding the foregoing, the owner may designate a beneficiary to receive the proceeds payable upon death and may elect a joint and survivor annuity.

cash payment, he or she may also avoid current tax liability by making a timely exercise of this option. It should be noted that if the employee receives a direct payment from the plan and then rolls over or transfers the gross amount to an individual retirement savings plan or another employer's plan, automatic withholding of 20 percent will be made on the distribution—even though it is rendered not currently taxable by the roll-over or transfer. Any excess withholding that results can then be recaptured when the employee files his or her tax return for the year in question. Alternatively, the employee may direct the plan to transfer the amount involved directly to the individual retirement savings plan or another employer's qualified plan. In this event, the automatic 20 percent withholding will be avoided.

If current tax liability is avoided by such an election, the employee will not pay any tax until payments are made from the annuity contract. At that time, the payments will be considered ordinary income under the annuity rules.

If the distribution is in the form of an annuity contract, the tax situation is governed by the date of issue of the contract. If issued after December 31, 1962, the distribution will be treated exactly the same as the distribution of a life insurance contract unless the annuity is endorsed or rewritten on a nontransferable basis within the 60 days allowed. If issued before January 1, 1963, the employee would not have had to include any amount as taxable income until payments were actually received. At that time, payments would have been considered ordinary income under the annuity rules.

Taxation of Disability Benefits

Many qualified pension plans provide for a monthly benefit if an employee becomes totally and permanently disabled. Typically, the benefit is payable for life (subject to the continuance of the disability), but this is true only for a disability that occurs after the employee has attained some minimum age, such as 50 or 55, or has completed some minimum period of service, such as 10 years. The benefit may or may not be related to the employee's accrued or projected pension. Frequently, the amount of the benefit will be adjusted if disability continues until the employee attains the normal retirement age specified in the plan.

Generally speaking, disability benefits of this type will be taxed to the employee in accordance with the annuity rules of Section 72 of the Internal Revenue Code.

Tax on Early Distributions

TRA '86 added an additional 10 percent tax on any taxable amounts received before age 59½ from a qualified retirement plan. This additional tax on **early distributions** does not apply in the case of death, disability, or termination of employment after age 55. Exceptions also are granted for:

1. Distributions that are part of a series of substantially equal periodic payments made for the life (or life expectancy) of the employee or the joint lives (or joint life expectancies) of the employee and his or her beneficiary.

2. Distributions used to pay medical expenses to the extent the expenses exceed 7.5 percent of adjusted gross income. Also, distributions used to pay health insurance premiums after separation from employment.

3. Certain dividend distributions made from an employee stock ownership plan (ESOP).

4. Payments to alternate payees pursuant to a qualified domestic relations order.

5. Distributions used to pay qualified education expenses of the tax payor or his or her spouse, child, or grandchild.

6. Distributions for the purchase of a first home (limited to $10,000).

7. Certain other distributions, such as those to pay an IRS tax levy or a timely corrective distribution from the plan.

8. The exceptions described earlier in the chapter as enacted by the PPA.

Tax on Late Distributions

Chapter 26 described the requirement that participants must commence benefit payments by April 1 of the calendar year following the calendar year in which they reach age 70½ after terminating employment.

If the participant's benefit is determined from an individual account, the minimum amount that must be paid each year is determined by dividing the account balance[13] by the applicable life expectancy. The applicable life expectancy is the life expectancy of the employee or the joint life expectancies of the employee and the employee's designated beneficiary, if any.

If the participant's benefit is determined by the annuity distribution from a defined benefit plan, the annuity must be paid for in one of the following durations:

• The life of the participant.

• The lives of the participant and the participant's designated beneficiary.

• A period certain not extending beyond the life expectancy of the participant or the joint life expectancies of the participant and the participant's designated beneficiary.

The penalty for failure to make a required distribution of (at least) the correct amount is a nondeductible excise tax of 50 percent of the difference between the minimum required amount and the actual distribution. This tax is imposed on the payee.

Chapter Summary

• Individuals in today's workforce can spend a lifetime accumulating resources within a defined contribution plan for their retirement. Employers often encourage their

[13] Technically this is the account balance as of the plan's last valuation date in the calendar year immediately preceding the calendar year for which the distribution is made.

workers to increase savings and attempt to instruct workers through investment education to become better investors. As important as the savings and investment functions are, it also is extremely important to develop distribution strategies for the assets accumulated in defined contribution plans.

- Failure to adequately design effective distribution strategies can result in withdrawals that do not align with participant needs, waste resources, and are inefficient from a tax standpoint.

- Distributions can occur as a one-time transaction or as a series of systematic distributions that will continue on a recurring basis. Some plans allow distributions in an annuity form, where the participant cannot outlive the stream of payments. If a plan allows for an annuity payment option, there are usually various types of annuities with various guarantee periods and continuing distributions to co-annuitants or beneficiaries.

- Rather than opt for an annuity, an individual may opt for some form of periodic payment.

- If the assets held in the retirement savings plan are generating income, the income routinely may be distributed. If the assets in the account are not generating income or if the income stream is insufficient to meet the individual's living expenses, decisions must be made concerning the liquidation of assets. The liquidation decision involves formulating a strategy concerning the systematic conversion of investments into cash. It also involves establishing priorities for which assets will be liquidated and which assets will be held until a future period for later liquidation.

- When a qualified plan distributes employer securities as part of a lump-sum distribution to employees or their beneficiaries, the net unrealized appreciation on any employer securities included as part of the lump-sum distribution qualifies for special tax treatment. The NUA is the difference between the fair market value of the employer securities at distribution and their cost or other basis to the plan.

- For those possessing defined contribution assets only, it is critical that the plan to convert assets into income be well conceived, considering risks inherent in the capital markets.

- An individual may opt to combine various distribution options as part of a retirement income strategy. Many individuals planning for retirement distributions evaluate multiple distribution forms as components of their overall retirement income strategy. In addition to blending multiple income distribution forms, the timing as to when these distributions commence also can be varied.

- The Pension Protection Act of 2006 made some changes in the law affecting plan distributions and rollovers from various retirement plans.

- Distributions from a qualified plan generally are taxable in accordance with the annuity rules of Section 72 of the Internal Revenue Code.

- Even though employer contributions may be vested fully in an employee under a qualified plan, the employee will not have to report these contributions as taxable income until such time as they are distributed. Employer contributions made on behalf of an employee generally will not be considered as taxable income to the employee during the period of employment.

- When an employee receives an in-service cash distribution of the entire value of his or her account, the amount of the distribution that exceeds the employee's cost basis will be taxable in the year of distribution as ordinary income. In addition, it may be subject to the early distribution tax.

- Participants must commence benefit payments by April 1 of the calendar year following the calendar year in which they reach age 70½ after terminating employment and over a stipulated period of time. The penalty for failure to make a required distribution of (at least) the correct amount is a nondeductible excise tax of 50 percent of the difference between the minimum required amount and the actual distribution.

Key Terms

alternate payee, p. *587*
annuity form, p. *572*
deferred life annuity,
 p. *573*
early distributions, p. *591*
fixed annuity, p. *573*
immediate life annuities,
 p. *573*

investment in contract,
 p. *584*
laddered bond portfolio,
 p. *575*
life contingent, p. *578*
liquidation decision,
 p. *575*
periodic payments, p. *587*

PS 58 cost, p. *584*
Section 72 of the IRC,
 p. *584*
third-party annuity
 placement services,
 p. *578*
variable annuity, p. *573*

Questions for Review

1. Summarize the key considerations in the development of a retirement plan distribution strategy.
2. Describe various types of annuities.
3. Compare and contrast a periodic payment option with an annuity distribution option.
4. What challenges are present when liquidating assets in a defined contribution plan?
5. How does a laddered bond portfolio protect a fixed-income portfolio against liquidation risk?
6. Describe the favorable tax treatment afforded to net unrealized appreciation on employer securities held in a qualified plan.
7. Can various payment options be combined? Explain.
8. How can a third-party annuity placement service be used by a qualified plan?
9. Explain some of the changes to distribution options resulting with passage of the PPA.
10. What factors are included in determining an employee's cost basis in a pension plan?
11. How are the pension distributions in the form of periodic payments taxed when the employee has no cost basis in the plan?

12. How will the answer to the previous question change if the employee has a cost basis in the plan?
13. How are severance-of-employment benefits taxed?
14. Explain the taxation of disability benefits.

Questions for Discussion

1. Discuss how different individual objectives influence a retirement plan distribution strategy.
2. Discuss the likely effect of the early distribution penalty tax on plan design.

Resources for Further Study

Ameriks, John, Robert Veres, and Mark J. Warshawsky. "Making Retirement Income Last a Lifetime," *FPA Journal* (December 2001).

CCH Editorial Staff. "Legislation 2006: Pension Protection Act of 2006: Law, Explanation and Analysis." *Commerce Clearing House* (2006).

Department of Labor Employee Benefits Security Administration. "Default Investment Alternatives Under Participant Directed Individual Account Plans; Proposed Rule," 29 CFR Part 2550 (September 27, 2006).

Hallman, G. Victor, and Jerry S. Rosenbloom. *Personal Financial Planning,* 7th ed. New York: McGraw-Hill, 2003.

Knox, Melanie N. Aska, and Joan Gucciardi. *Pension Distribution Answer Book.* 2007 ed. New York: Aspen Publishers, 2007.

Lucas, Stuart E. "Eight Principles of Strategic Wealth Management," *Knowledge at Wharton* (August 9, 2006).

Poterba, James M. "Saving for Retirement: Taxes Matter," *An Issue in Brief* 17 (May 2004).

Slott, Ed. *The Retirement Savings Time Bomb.* New York: Penguin Putnam, 2003.

Slott, Ed. *Parlay Your IRA into a Family Fortune.* New York: Penguin Group, 2005.

Appendix 1

Social Security and Medicare

Robert J. Myers

Economic security for retired workers, disabled workers, and survivors of deceased workers in the United States is, in the vast majority of cases, provided through the multiple means of Social Security, private pensions, and individual savings. This is sometimes referred to as a *three-legged stool* or the *three pillars of economic-security protection*. It also can be seen as a layered arrangement, with Social Security providing the floor of protection, private-sector activities building on top of it, and public assistance programs, such as Supplemental Security Income (SSI), providing a net of protection for those whose total retirement income does not attain certain levels or meet minimum subsistence needs.

Although some people may view the Social Security program as one that should provide complete protection, over the years it generally has been agreed that it should only be the foundation of protection.

As described elsewhere, private pension plans have, to a significant extent, been developed to supplement Social Security. This is done in a number of ways, both directly and indirectly. The net result, however, is a broad network of retirement protection.

This appendix discusses in detail the retirement, disability, and survivor provisions of the Social Security program—not only their historical development and present structure but also a summary of the financial crises of the late 1970s and early 1980s (and what was done to solve them) and possible future changes. Following this, the Medicare program is described. Also, descriptions of the two public assistance programs (Supplemental Security Income and Medicaid) that supplement Old-Age, Survivors, and Disability Insurance (OASDI) and Medicare are given.

The term *Social Security* is used here with the meaning generally accepted in the United States, namely, the cash benefits provisions of the OASDI program. International usage of the term *social security* is much broader than this and includes all other types of governmental programs protecting individuals against the economic risks of a modern industrial system, such as unemployment, short-term sickness, work-connected accidents and diseases, and medical care costs.

Old-Age, Survivors, and Disability Insurance Program

Persons Covered under OASDI

OASDI coverage—for both taxes and earnings credits toward benefit rights—currently applies to somewhat more than 90 percent of the total workforce of the United States. About half of those not covered have protection through a special government employee retirement system, while the remaining half are either very low-paid intermittent workers or unpaid family workers.

The vast majority of persons covered under OASDI are so affected on a mandatory or compulsory basis. Several categories, however, have optional or semi-optional coverage. It is important to note that OASDI coverage applies not only to employees, both salaried and wage earner, but also to self-employed persons. Some individuals who are essentially employees are nonetheless classified as self-employed for the sake of convenience in applying coverage.

Compulsory coverage is applicable to all employees in commerce and industry (interpreting these classifications very broadly) except railroad workers, who are covered under a separate program, the Railroad Retirement system. However, financial and other coordinating provisions exist between these two programs, so that, in reality, railroad workers are covered under OASDI. Members of the armed forces are covered compulsorily, as are federal civilian employees hired after 1983. Compulsory coverage also applies to lay employees of churches (with certain minor exceptions), to employees of nonprofit charitable and educational institutions, to employees of state and local governments that do not have retirement systems (first effective after July 1, 1991; before then, coverage was elective, on a group basis, by the employing entity), and to American residents who work abroad for American corporations. Self-employed persons of all types (except ministers) also are covered compulsorily unless their earnings are minimal (i.e., less than $400 a year); beginning in 1990, covered self-employment is taken as 92.35 percent of the self-employment net income (such figure being 100 percent minus the OASDI–Hospital Insurance tax rate applicable to employees).

From a geographical standpoint, OASDI applies not only in the 50 states and the District of Columbia but also in all outlying areas (American Samoa, Guam, the Northern Mariana Islands, Puerto Rico, and the Virgin Islands).

Elective coverage applies to a number of categories. Employees of state and local governments who are under a retirement system can have coverage at the option of the employing entity and only when the current employees vote in favor of coverage. Similar provisions are available for American employees of foreign subsidiaries of American corporations, the latter having the right to opt for coverage. Once that coverage has been elected by a state or local government, it cannot be terminated. Approximately

70 percent of state and local government employees are now covered as a result of this election basis and the compulsory coverage applicable when the entity does not have a retirement plan.

Because of the principle of separation of church and state, ministers are covered on the self-employed basis, regardless of their actual status. Furthermore, they have the right to opt out of the system within a limited time after ordination on grounds of religious principles or conscience. Americans employed in the United States by a foreign government or by an international organization are covered compulsorily on the self-employed basis.

Historical Development of Retirement Provisions

When what is now the OASDI program was developed in 1934–1935, it was confined entirely to retirement benefits plus lump-sum refund payments to represent the difference, if any, between employee taxes paid, plus an allowance for interest, and retirement benefits received. It was not until the 1939 act that auxiliary (or dependents') and survivors' benefits were added, and not until the 1956 act that disability benefits were made available. The likely reason that only retirement benefits were instituted initially is that such type of protection was the most familiar to the general public, especially in light of the relatively few private pension plans then in existence.

The *normal retirement age* (NRA), also called the full retirement age, was originally established at 65. This figure was selected in a purely empirical manner; it was a middle figure between two perceived extremes. Age 70 seemed too high, because of the common belief that relatively so few people reached that age, while 60 seemed too low, because of the large costs that would be involved if that age had been selected. Many of the existing private pension plans at that time had a retirement age of 65, although some in the railroad industry used age 70. Furthermore, labor force participation data showed that a relatively high proportion of workers continued employment after age 60. A widely cited, but erroneous, explanation of why age 65 was selected is that Bismarck chose this age when he established the German national pension program in the 1880s; the age used originally in Germany actually was 70 (the plan was primarily a disability benefits one). The 1983 act provided for the NRA to increase from age 65 to age 67 in a deferred, gradual manner. Specifically, the NRA is 65 for those attaining this age before 2003 and first becomes 67 for those attaining this age in 2027.

The original program applied only to workers in commerce and industry. It was not until the 1950s that coverage was extended to additional categories of workers. Now, almost all are covered, including the self-employed.

The initial legislation passed by the House of Representatives did not require eligible persons to retire at age 65 or over to receive benefits, although it was recognized that inclusion of a retirement requirement would be essential in the final legislation. The Senate inserted a requirement of a general nature that benefits would be payable only upon retirement, and this was included in the final legislation. Over the years, this retirement earnings test, or work clause, has been the subject of much controversy, and it has been considerably liberalized and made more flexible over the years.

Beginning in the 1950s, pressure developed to provide early-retirement benefits, first for spouses and then for insured workers. The minimum early-retirement age was set at 62, again a pragmatic political compromise, rather than a number based on any completely logical reason. The three-year differential, however, did represent the approximate average difference in age between men and their wives; but, of course, as with any averages, the difference actually is larger in many cases. The benefit amounts are reduced when claimed before the NRA is reached, and are increased, although currently to not as great an extent, when the claim for benefits is delayed beyond the NRA. As the NRA increases beyond age 65, the reduction for claiming benefits at age 62 becomes larger.

Eligibility Conditions for Retirement Benefits

To be eligible for OASDI retirement benefits, individuals must have a certain amount of covered employment. In general, these conditions were designed to be relatively easy to meet in the early years of operation, thus bringing the program into effectiveness quickly. Eligibility for retirement benefits—termed *fully insured status*—depends on having a certain number of *quarters of coverage* (QCs), sometimes referred to as *credits*, varying with the year of birth or, expressed in another manner, depending on the year of an individual's attainment of age 62.

Before 1978, a QC was defined simply as a calendar quarter during which the individual was paid $50 or more in wages from covered employment; the self-employed ordinarily received four QCs for each year of coverage at $400 or more of earnings. Beginning in 1978, the number of QCs acquired for each year depends on the total earnings in the year. For 1978, each full unit of $250 of earnings produced a QC, up to a maximum of four QCs for the year. In subsequent years the requirement has increased, and it will continue to increase in the future, in accordance with changes in the general wage level; for 2007, it is $1,000.

The number of QCs required for fully insured status is determined from the number of years in the period beginning in 1951, or with the year of attainment of age 22, if later, and the year before the year of attainment of age 62, with a minimum requirement of six QCs. As a result, an individual who attained age 62 before 1958 needed only six QCs to be fully insured. A person attaining age 62 in 1990 has a requirement of 39 QCs, while a person attaining age 65 in 1990 needs 36 QCs. The maximum number of QCs that will ever be required for fully insured status is 40, applicable to persons attaining age 62 after 1990. It is important to note that, although the requirement for the number of QCs is determined from 1951, or from year of attainment of age 22, and before attainment of age 62, the QCs to meet the requirement can be obtained at any time (e.g., before 1951, before age 22, and after age 61).

Beneficiary Categories for Retirement Benefits

Insured workers can receive unreduced retirement benefits in the amount of the primary insurance amount (PIA), the derivation of which will be discussed next, beginning at the NRA, or actuarially reduced benefits beginning at earlier ages, down to age 62. For retirement at age 62 before 2000, the benefit was 80 percent of the PIA, while for retirement at age 62 in 2000, it is 79⅙ percent. As the NRA increases beyond 65, the reduction will become larger (eventually being 30 percent).

Retired workers can also receive supplementary payments for spouses and eligible children. The spouse receives a benefit at the rate of 50 percent of the PIA if claim is first made at the NRA or over, and at a reduced rate if claimed at ages down to 62 (before 2000, a 25 percent reduction at age 62—i.e., to 37.5 percent of the PIA); as the NRA increases beyond 65, the reduction for age 62 will be larger, eventually being 35 percent, 25% percent in 2000). However, if a child under age 16 (or a child aged 16 or over who was disabled before age 22) is present, the spouse receives benefits regardless of age, in an unreduced amount. Divorced spouses, when the marriage had lasted at least 10 years, are eligible for benefits under the same conditions as undivorced spouses.

Children under age 18 (and children aged 18 or over and disabled before age 22, plus children attending elementary or high school full-time at age 18) also are eligible for benefits, at a rate of 50 percent of the PIA; prior to legislation in 1981, post-secondary-school students aged 18 to 21 were eligible for benefits, and spouses with children in their care could receive benefits as long as a child under age 18 was present. Grandchildren and great-grandchildren can qualify as "children" if they are dependent on the grandparent and if both parents of the child are disabled or deceased.

An overall maximum on total family benefits is applicable, as is discussed later. If a person is eligible for more than one type of benefit (e.g., both as a worker and as a spouse), in essence only the largest benefit is payable.

Computation Procedures for Retirement Benefits

As indicated in the previous section, OASDI benefits are based on the PIA. The method of computing the PIA is quite complicated, especially because several different methods are available. The only method dealt with here in any detail is the one generally applicable to people who reach age 65 after 1981.

Persons who attained age 65 before 1982 use a method based on the average monthly wage (AMW). This is based essentially on a career average, involving the consideration of all earnings back through 1951. To take into account the general inflation in earnings that occurred in the past, automatic adjustment procedures were involved in the benefit computations. However, these turned out to be faulty, because they did not—and would not in the future—produce stable benefit results (as to the relationships of initial benefits to final earnings). Accordingly, in the 1977 amendments, a new procedure applicable to those attaining age 62 after 1978 was adopted, but the old procedure was retained for earlier attainments of age 62. The result has been to give unusually and inequitably large benefits to those who attained age 62 before 1979 and who worked well beyond age 62, as against similar people who attained age 62 after 1978, thus creating a "notch" situation.

Persons who attained age 62 in 1979 to 1983 can use an alternative method somewhat similar to the AMW method (but with certain restrictions) if this produces a larger PIA than the new, permanent method. In actual practice, however, this modified AMW method generally produces more favorable results only for persons attaining age 62 in 1979 to 1981 and not continuing in employment after that age.

Still another method is available for all individuals who have earnings before 1951. In the vast majority of such cases, however, the new start methods based on earnings after 1950 produce more favorable results.

The first step in the ongoing permanent method of computing the PIA applicable to persons attaining age 65 in 1982 or after is to calculate the average indexed monthly earnings (AIME). The AIME is on a career-average earnings basis. For persons who attain age 62 in 1991 or after, the AIME is based on the highest 35 years of indexed earnings after 1950. Actual earnings are indexed (i.e., increased) to reflect nationwide wage inflation from the particular year up to the year of attaining age 60. Details on the computation of the AIME are given in Appendix 1A.

Now, having obtained the AIME, the PIA is computed from a benefit formula. A different formula applies for each annual cohort of persons attaining age 62. For example, for those who reached age 62 in 1979, the formula was 90 percent of the first $180 of AIME, plus 32 percent of the next $905 of AIME, plus 15 percent of the AIME in excess of $1,085. For the 2001 cohort, the corresponding dollar bands are $561, $2,820, and $3,381. These bands are adjusted automatically annually, according to changes in nationwide average wages.

A different (and less favorable) method of computing the PIA for retirement benefits (and also for disability benefits, but not for survivor benefits) is applicable for certain persons who receive pensions based in whole or in part on earnings from employment not covered by OASDI or Railroad Retirement (in the past or in the future, and in other countries as well as in the United States). This is done to eliminate the windfall benefits (due to the weighted nature of the benefit formula) that would otherwise arise. Appendix 1A gives details on the application of the windfall elimination provision.

Prior to legislation in 1981, if the PIA benefit formula produced an amount smaller than $122 in the initial benefit computation, then this amount was nonetheless payable. However, for persons first becoming eligible after 1981, no such minimum is applicable.

A special minimum applies to the PIA for individuals who have a long period of covered work, but with low earnings. As of December 2000, this minimum is approximately $30 times the "years of coverage" (see Appendix 1A for definition) in excess of 10, but not in excess of 30; thus, for 30 or more years of coverage, the minimum benefit is $600.90. In practice, this procedure rarely applies for current retirees.

The resulting PIAs then are increased for any automatic adjustments applicable, because of annual increases in the consumer price index (CPI-W) that occur in or after the year of attaining age 62, even though actual retirement is much later. These automatic adjustments are made for benefits for each December. Such CPI increases were as high as 14.3 percent for 1980 and 11.2 percent for 1981, but have been much lower in recent years (3.5 percent in 2000).

The resulting PIA then is reduced, in the manner described earlier, for those who first claim benefits before the NRA. Conversely, retired workers who do not receive benefits for any months after they attain the NRA, essentially because they elect not to receive them (usually because they have high earnings and do not need them currently), receive increases that are termed delayed retirement credits (DRCs). Such credits for those who attained age 65 in 1982 to 1989 are at the rate of 3 percent per year of delay (actually 0.25 percent per month) for the period between ages 65 and 70. For those who attained age 65 before 1982, the DRC is at a rate of only 1 percent per year. For those who attain the NRA after 1989, such credit is gradually increased from 3.5 percent for the 1990 to 1991 cases to 4 percent for the 1992 to 1993 cases, 4.5 percent for the 1994 to 1995 cases, 5.0 percent for the 1996 to 1997 cases, 5.5 percent for the 1998 to 1999 cases, and

6 percent for the 2000 to 2001 cases, until it is 8 percent for those attaining the NRA (then 66) in 2009. The DRC applies only to the worker's benefit and not to that for spouses or children (but it does apply to any subsequent widow(er)'s benefits).

A maximum family benefit (MFB) is applicable when there are more than two beneficiaries receiving benefits on the same earnings record (i.e., the retired worker and two or more auxiliary beneficiaries). Not considered within the limit established by the MFB are the additional benefits arising from delayed retirement credits and the benefits payable to divorced spouses. The MFB is determined prior to any reductions made because of claiming benefits before the NRA, but after the effect of the earnings test as it applies to any auxiliary beneficiary (e.g., if the spouse has high earnings, any potential benefit payable to her or him would not be considered for purposes of the MFB of the other spouse).

The MFB is determined from the PIA by a complex formula. This formula varies for each annual cohort of persons attaining age 62. The resulting MFB is adjusted for increases in the CPI in the future (in the same manner as is the PIA). For the 2007 cohort, the MFB formula is 150 percent of the first $869 of PIA, plus 272 percent of the next $386 of PIA, plus 134 percent of the next $381 of PIA, plus 175 percent of PIA in excess of $1636. For future cohorts, the dollar figures are changed according to changes in nationwide average wages. The result of this formula is to produce MFBs that are 150 percent of the PIA for the lowest PIAs, with this proportion rising to a peak of 188 percent for middle-range PIAs, and then falling off to 175 percent—and leveling there—for higher PIAs.

Earnings Test and Other Restrictions on Retirement Benefits

From the inception of the OASDI program, there has been some form of restriction on the payment of benefits to persons who have substantial earnings from employment. This provision is referred to as the retirement earnings test. It does not apply to non-earned income, such as from investments or pensions. The general underlying principle of this test is that retirement benefits should be paid only to persons who are substantially retired.

The basic feature of the earnings test is that an annual exempt amount applies, so full benefits are paid if earnings, including those from both covered and noncovered employment, are not in excess thereof. Then, for persons under the NRA (which is age 65 until 2003), for each $2 of excess earnings, $1 in benefits is withheld; the reduction was on a "$1 for $3" basis for those at and above the NRA in 1990 to 1999. Legislation in 2000 eliminated the test for the month of attaining the NRA and later months; the test still applies for earlier months in the year of attaining the NRA, but applicable only to earnings in such months. For persons aged 65 to 69 (at any time in the year), the annual exempt amount is $17,000 for 2000, $25,000 for 2001, and $30,000 for 2002, with the amounts for subsequent years being automatically determined by the increases in nation-wide wages. Beginning with the month of attainment of age 65, the test no longer applies (this limiting age was 70 before 2000). For persons under full retirement age, the exempt amount is $12,960 in 2007, with automatic adjustment thereafter.

An alternative test applies for the initial year of retirement, or claim, if it results in more benefits being payable. Under this, full benefits are payable for all months in which the individual did not have substantial services in self-employment and had wages of one-twelfth of the annual exempt amount or less. This provision properly takes care of the situation where an individual fully retires during a year, but had sizable earnings in the first part of the year, and thus would have most or all of the benefits withheld if only the annual test had been applicable.

Earnings of the "retired" worker affect, under the earnings test, the total family benefits payable. However, if an auxiliary beneficiary (spouse or child) has earnings, and these are sizable enough to affect the earnings test, any reduction in benefits is applicable only to such individual's benefits.

If an individual receives a pension from service under a government-employee pension plan under which the members were not covered under OASDI on the last day of her or his employment, the OASDI spouse benefit is reduced by two-thirds of the amount of such pension. This provision, however, is not applicable to women—or to men who are dependent on their wives—who become eligible for such a pension before December 1982, while for December 1982 through June 1983 the provision applies only to those (both men and women) who cannot prove dependency on their spouse. This general provision results in roughly the same treatment as occurs when both spouses have OASDI benefits based on their own earnings records; and then each receives such benefit, plus the excess, if any, of the spouse's benefit arising from the other spouse's earnings over the benefit based on their own earnings, rather than the full amount of the spouse's benefit.

Benefits are not payable to prisoners convicted of crimes involving confinement that lasts for at least 30 days (except for prisoners who are in an approved rehabilitation program) although payable to auxiliary beneficiaries of such prisoners—also applies to disability and survivor benefits.

Historical Development of Disability Provisions

It was not until the 1956 act that monthly disability benefits were added to the OASDI program, although the "disability freeze" provision (in essence, a waiver-of-premium provision), described later, was added in the 1952 act.[1] It may well be said that long-term disability is merely premature old-age retirement.

The monthly disability benefits initially were available only at age 50 and over—that is, deferred to that age for those disabled earlier—with no auxiliary benefits for the spouse and dependent children. These limitations were quickly removed, by the 1958 and 1960 acts.

Eligibility Conditions for Disability Benefits

To be eligible for disability benefits, individuals must be both fully insured and disability insured.[2] Disability insured status requires 20 QCs earned in the 40-quarter period ending with the quarter of disability, except that persons disabled before age 31 also can

---

[1] Actually, it was so written in the 1952 legislation as to be inoperative, but then was reenacted in 1954 to be on a permanent, ongoing basis.

[2] Blind persons need be only fully insured.

qualify if they have QCs in half of the quarters after age 21.[3] The definition of disability is relatively strict. The disability must be so severe that the individual is unable to engage in any substantial gainful activity, and the impairment must be a medically determinable physical or mental condition that is expected to continue for at least 12 months or to result in prior death. Benefits are first payable after completion of six full calendar months of disability. For persons with alcoholism or drug abuse, disability benefits are not payable unless they have another severe disabling condition which, by itself, would be qualifying.

Beneficiary Categories for Disability Benefits

In addition to the disabled worker, dependents in the same categories that apply to old-age retirement benefits can receive monthly benefits.

Benefit Computation Procedures for Disability Benefits

In all cases, the benefits are based on the PIA, computed in the same manner as for retirement benefits, except that fewer dropout years than five are allowed in the computation of the AIME for persons disabled before age 47.[4] The disabled worker receives a benefit equal to 100 percent of the PIA, and the auxiliary beneficiaries each receive 50 percent of the PIA, subject to the maximum family benefit.

An overall maximum on total family benefits is applicable, which is lower than that for survivor and retirement benefits—namely, no more than the smaller of 150 percent of the PIA, or 85 percent of AIME (but not less than the PIA).

Eligibility Test for Disability Benefits and Other Restrictions on Benefits

The earnings or retirement test applies to the auxiliary beneficiaries of disabled workers, but not to the disabled worker beneficiary. However, the earnings of one beneficiary (e.g., the spouse of the disabled worker) do not affect the benefits of the other beneficiaries in the family (e.g., the disabled worker or the children). The test does not apply to disabled worker beneficiaries, because any earnings are considered in connection with whether recovery has occurred, except those during trial work periods (which earnings may possibly lead to removal from the benefit roll later).

OASDI disability benefits are coordinated with disability benefits payable under other governmental programs (including programs of state and local governments), except for needs-tested ones, benefits payable by the Department of Veterans Affairs, and government employee plans coordinated with OASDI. The most important of such coordinations is with workers' compensation (WC) programs, whose benefits are taken into account in determining the amount of the OASDI disability benefit (except in a few states that provide for their WC benefits to be reduced when OASDI disability benefits are payable—possible only for states that did this before February 19, 1981). The total of the OASDI disability benefit (including any auxiliary benefits payable) and the other disability benefit recognized cannot exceed 80 percent of "average current earnings"

---

[3] For those disabled before age 24, the requirement is six QCs in the last 12 quarters.

[4] Specifically, four such quarters for ages 42 to 46, grading down to none for ages 26 and under.

(generally based on the highest year of earnings in covered employment in the last six years, but indexed for changes in wage levels following the worker's disablement).

Disability Freeze

In the event that a disability beneficiary recovers, the so-called disability freeze provision applies. Under this, the period of disability is "blanked out" in the computation of insured status and benefit amounts for subsequent retirement, disability, and survivor benefits.

Historical Development of Survivor Provisions

When what is now the OASDI program was developed in 1934–1935, it was confined entirely to retirement benefits (plus lump-sum refund payments to represent the difference, if any, between employee taxes paid, plus an allowance for interest, and retirement benefits received). It was not until the 1939 act that monthly survivor benefits were added with respect to deaths of both active workers and retirees, in lieu of the refund benefit.

The term *widow* is used here to include also widowers. Until 1983, the latter did not receive OASDI benefits on the same basis as widows, either being required to prove dependence on the deceased female worker or not being eligible at all. Now, because of legislative changes and court decisions, complete equality of treatment by sex prevails for OASDI survivor benefits.

The minimum eligibility age for aged widows was initially established at age 65. This figure was selected in a purely empirical manner because it was a round figure (see the earlier discussion about retirement benefits on why this was selected as the minimum retirement age).

Beginning in the 1950s, pressure developed to provide early retirement benefits, first for widows and spouses and then for insured workers themselves. The minimum early retirement age was set at 62, again a pragmatic political compromise, rather than a completely logical choice and was later lowered to 60 for widows. The three-year differential, however, did represent about the average difference in age between men and their wives (but, of course, as with any averages, in many cases the actual difference is larger). The benefit amounts were not reduced for widows when they claimed before age 65 under the original amendatory legislation, but this is no longer the case.

Eligibility Conditions for Survivor Benefits

To be eligible for OASDI survivor benefits, individuals must have either fully insured status or currently insured status. The latter requires only six QCs earned in the 13-quarter period ending with the quarter of death.

Survivor Beneficiary Categories

Two general categories of survivors of insured workers can receive monthly benefits. Aged survivors are widows aged 60 or over (or at ages 50 to 59 if disabled) and dependent parents aged 62 or over. Young survivors are children under age 18 (or at any age if disabled before age 22), children aged 18 who are full-time students in elementary or high school (i.e., defined just the same as in the case of retirement and disability beneficiaries), and the widowed parent of such children who are under age 16 or disabled before age 22. In addition, a death benefit of $255 is payable to widows or, in the absence of a widow, to children eligible for immediate monthly benefits.

The disabled widow receives a benefit at the rate of 71.5 percent of the deceased worker's PIA if claim is first made at ages 50 to 59. The benefit rate for other widows grades up from 71.5 percent of the PIA if claimed at age 60 to 100 percent if claimed at the NRA, which is age 65 for those attaining age 60 before 2000, grading up to 67 for those attaining age 60 in 2022 and after. Any DRCs that the deceased worker had earned also are applicable to the widow's benefit. Widows, regardless of age, caring for an eligible child (under age 16 or disabled before age 22) have a benefit of 75 percent of the PIA. Divorced spouses, when the marriage lasted at least 10 years, are eligible for benefits under the same conditions as undivorced spouses.

The benefit rate for eligible children is 75 percent of the PIA. The benefit rate for dependent parents is 82.5 percent of the PIA, unless two parents are eligible, in which case it is 75 percent for each one.

The same overall maximum on total family benefits is applicable as is the case for retirement benefits. If a person is eligible for more than one type of benefit (e.g., both as a worker and as a surviving spouse), in essence, only the largest benefit is payable.

Benefit Computation Procedures for Survivor Benefits

In all cases, the monthly survivor benefits are based on the PIA, and then are adjusted to reflect the maximum family benefit, both of which are computed in essentially the same manner as is the case for retirement benefits.[5]

Eligibility Test for Survivor Benefits and Other Restrictions

Marriage (or remarriage) of the survivor beneficiary generally terminates benefit rights. The only exceptions are remarriage of widows after age 60 (or after age 50 for disabled widows) and marriage to another OASDI beneficiary (other than one who is under age 18).

From the inception of the OASDI program, there has been some form of restriction on the payment of benefits to persons who have substantial earnings from employment, the earnings or retirement test. The same test applies to survivor beneficiaries as to retirement benefits for retirees who are under NRA. However, the earnings of one beneficiary (e.g., the widowed mother) do not affect the benefits of the other beneficiaries in the family (e.g., the orphaned children).

If a widow receives a pension from service under a government employee pension plan under which the members were not covered under OASDI on the last day of her employment, the OASDI widow's benefit is reduced by two-thirds of the amount of such pension. This provision, however, is not applicable to women (or to men who were dependent on their wives) who became eligible for such a pension before December

---

[5] For individuals who die before age 62, the computation is made as though the individual had attained age 62 in the year of death. In addition, for deferred widow's benefits, an alternative computation based on indexing the deceased's earnings record up to the earlier of age 60 of the worker or age 60 of the widow is used if this produces a more favorable result.

1982 or to individuals who became first so eligible from December 1982 through June 1983 and who were dependent on their spouses.

Financing Provisions of OASDI Program

From its inception until the 1983 act, the OASDI program has been financed entirely by payroll taxes (and interest earnings on the assets of the trust funds), with only minor exceptions, such as the special benefits at a subminimum level for certain persons without insured status who attained age 72 before 1972. Thus, on a permanent ongoing basis, no payments from general revenues were available to the OASDI system; the contributions for covered federal civilian employees and members of the armed forces are properly considered as "employer" taxes.

The 1983 act introduced two instances of general-revenues financing of the OASDI program. As a one-time matter, the tax rate in 1984 was increased to what had been previously scheduled for 1985 (i.e., for both the employer and employee, from 5.4 percent to 5.7 percent), but the increase for employees was, in essence, rescinded, and the General Fund of the Treasury made up the difference to the OASDI Trust Funds. On an ongoing basis, the General Fund passes on to the trust funds the proceeds of the income taxation of 50 percent of OASDI benefits for upper-middle income and high-income persons (first effective for 1984), and, in fact, does so somewhat in advance of actual receipt of such moneys.[6]

The payroll taxes for the retirement and survivors benefits go into the OASI Trust Fund, while those for the disability benefits go into the DI Trust Fund, and all benefit payments and administrative expenses for these provisions are paid therefrom. The balances in the trust fund are invested in federal government obligations of various types, with interest rates at the current market values for long-term securities. The federal government does not guarantee the payments of benefits. If the trust fund were to be depleted, it could not obtain grants, or even loans, from the General Fund of the Treasury. However, a temporary provision (effective only in 1982) permitted the OASI Trust Fund to borrow, repayable with interest, from the DI and HI Trust Funds. A total of $17.5 billion was borrowed ($12.4 billion from HI). The last of such loans was repaid in 1986. Payroll taxes are levied on earnings up to only a certain annual limit, which is termed the earnings base. This base is applicable to the earnings of an individual from each employer in the year, but the person can obtain a refund (on the income tax form) for all employee taxes paid in excess of those on the earnings base. The self-employed pay OASDI taxes on their self-employment income on no more than the excess of the earnings base over any wages they may have had.

Since 1975, the earnings base for OASDI has been determined by the automatic-adjustment procedure, on the basis of increases in the nationwide average wage. However, for 1979 to 1981, ad hoc increases of a higher amount were legislated; the 1981 base was established at $29,700. The 1982 and subsequent bases were determined under the automatic adjustment provision. The 2000 base was $76,200, while that for 2007 is $97,500.

---

[6] The income taxes on the next 35 percent of benefits (first effective in 1994) anomalously go to the Hospital Insurance Trust Fund.

The payroll tax rate is a combined one for OASI, DI, and HI, but it is allocated among the three trust funds. The employer and employee rates are equal. The self-employed pay the combined employer–employee rate. In 1984 to 1989, they had an allowance for the reduction in income taxes as if half of the OASDI-HI tax were to be considered as a business expense (as it is for incorporated employers); such allowance was a uniform reduction in the tax rate—2.7 percentage points in 1984, 2.2 percentage points in 1985, and 2.0 percentage points in 1986 to 1989. After 1989, the direct procedure of considering half of the OASDI-HI taxes as a deduction from income is done for the self-employed. Also, until 1991, the earnings base was the same for OASDI and HI, but in 1991, the base for HI was raised to $125,000, and it was $130,200 in 1992 and was eliminated for 1994 and after.

The employer and employee rates were 1 percent each in 1937 to 1949, but have gradually increased over the years, until being 7.15 percent in 1986 to 1987 (the latter subdivided 5.2 percent for OASI, 0.5 percent for DI, and 1.45 percent for HI). These rates increased to 7.51 percent in 1988, and then to 7.65 percent in 1990 (and after), the latter being subdivided 5.3 percent for OASI, 0.9 percent for DI, and 1.45 percent for HI for 2000 and after.

Past Financing Crises of OASDI Program

In the mid-1970s, the OASI and DI trust funds were projected to have serious financing problems over both the long range and the short range. The short-range problem was thought to be remedied by the 1977 act, which raised taxes (both the rates and the earnings bases). At the same time, the long-range problem was partially solved by phased-in significant benefit reductions, by lowering the general benefit level, by freezing the minimum benefit, and by the "spouse government pension" offset, although an estimated deficit situation was still present for the period beginning after about 30 years.

The short-range problem was not really solved. The actuarial cost estimates assumed that earnings would rise at a somewhat more rapid rate than prices in the short range; but the reverse occurred—and to a significant extent—in 1979 to 1981. Because increases in tax income depend on earnings and because increases in benefit outgo depend on prices, the financial result for the OASI Trust Fund was catastrophic. It would have been exhausted in late 1982 if not for legislation enacted in 1981. The DI Trust Fund did not have this problem, because the disability experience, which had worsened significantly in 1970 to 1976, turned around and became relatively favorable—more than offsetting the unfavorable economic experience.

The 1981 act significantly reduced benefit outgo in the short range by a number of relatively small changes, shown in detail in Appendix 1B.

Further action beyond the 1981 amendments was essential to restore both the short-range and long-range solvency of the OASDI program. Because of the difficult political situation, President Reagan established The National Commission on Social Security Reform—a bipartisan group whose members were appointed both by President Reagan and the congressional leadership—to study the problem and make recommendations for its solution. Such recommendations were adopted almost in their entirety in the 1983 act. The most significant changes made by this legislation are described in Appendix 1B.

The changes made by the 1983 act were eminently successful over the short run. In the following years, the assets of the OASDI Trust Funds grew steadily from their very low level then and were about $1 trillion at the end of September 2000. Further, they are estimated to increase rapidly for the next two decades and reach a height of $6 trillion in 2024. However, thereafter a decline is estimated, and the balance will be exhausted in 2040 unless changes are made before then (which will most certainly occur). Ideally, the fund balance should be at least equal to one year's outgo at all times during the 75-year valuation period.

Possible Future OASDI Developments

Advisory groups have, over the years, advocated so-called universal coverage. Following the 1983 amendments, relatively little remains to be done in this area, except perhaps to cover compulsorily all new hires in state and local government employment (as was done in the federal area).

The NRA was increased from the present 65 to age 67, phased in over a period of years, by the 1983 act. This was done in recognition of the significant increase in life expectancy that has occurred in the last 40 years, as well as likely future increases. If life expectancy increases even more rapidly than currently projected, a further increase in such age would reduce the higher long-range future cost of the program resulting from such increase.

The earnings test has always been subject to criticism by many people, who argue that it is a disincentive to continued employment and that "the benefits have been bought and paid for, and therefore should be available at age 65." The 1983 act, by increasing ultimately (beginning with those who attain age 66 in 2009) the size of the delayed retirement credits (to 8 percent per year) to approximately the actuarial-equivalent level, virtually eliminated the earnings test after the NRA insofar as the cost aspects thereof are concerned. In other words, when the DRC is at an 8 percent level, the individual receives benefits for delayed retirement having approximately the same value as if benefits were paid without regard to the earnings test, beginning at the NRA. Some persons have advocated that the DRC should be at the 8 percent rate as soon as possible. As mentioned earlier, the earnings test was eliminated in 2000 for the month of attaining NRA, although insured workers can waive receipt of benefits and receive DRCs.

As to disability benefits, the definition might be tightened, such as by using "medical only" factors (and not vocational ones). Conversely, the definition could be liberalized so as to be on an occupational basis at age 50 and over. Also, the five-month waiting period could be shortened. The general benefit level was significantly increased in 1969 to 1972 (by about 23 percent in real terms), but financial problems caused this increase to be partially reversed in subsequent legislation (1974 and 1977). Nonetheless, there will be efforts by many persons to reverse the situation and expand the benefit level.

Over the years, the composition of the OASDI benefit structure—between individual-equity aspects and social-adequacy ones—tended to shift more toward social adequacy. The 1981 amendments, however, moved in the other direction (e.g., by phasing out student benefits and the minimum-benefit provision). There may well be efforts in the future to inject more social adequacy into the program—or, conversely, more individual equity.

It frequently has been advocated that people should be allowed to opt out of the OASDI system and provide their own economic security through private-sector mechanisms, using both their own taxes and those of their employer. Although this approach has certain appealing aspects, it has some significant drawbacks. First, it is not possible to duplicate to any close extent the various features of OASDI, most notably the automatic adjustment of benefits for increases in the CPI.

Second, because the low-cost individuals (young, high-earnings ones) would be the most likely to opt out, there is the question of how the resulting financing shortfalls of the OASDI program would be covered. Those who make such proposals (or even the more extreme ones, which involve terminating OASDI for all except those currently covered who are near retirement age) do not answer this question. The only source of financing would be from general revenues, and this means more general taxes, which would be paid to a considerable extent by those who have opted out.

Many have argued that part of the cost of OASDI should be met from general revenues. At times, an indirect manner of implementing such a funding method has been advocated, such as by moving part of the HI tax rate to OASDI and then partially financing HI from general revenues. The difficulty with this procedure is that no large amounts of general-revenues moneys are available for all future years to come; the General Fund of the Treasury is now estimated to have relatively small surpluses for the next 10 to 15 years or so, but not thereafter. In turn, this would mean either that additional taxes of other types would have to be raised or that any budget deficit would become larger, and inflation would be fueled. Those opposed to general-revenues financing of OASDI, and of HI as well, believe that the financing, instead, should be entirely from direct, visible payroll taxes. Nonetheless, it is likely that pressure for general-revenues financing of OASDI will continue.

According to the latest intermediate-cost estimate for present law, the OASDI Trust Funds are adequately financed over the next 10 years. Under current budgetary procedures, annual excesses in the OASDI Trust Funds are often considered as meeting the budget-deficit targets, and thus they hide the extent of titanic general-budget deficits.

Supplemental Security Income Program

The Supplemental Security Income (SSI) program replaced the federal/state public assistance programs of aid to the aged, blind, and disabled, except in Guam, Puerto Rico, and the Virgin Islands. Persons must be at least age 65 or be blind or disabled to qualify for SSI payments.

The basic payment amount, before reduction for other income, for 2007 is $623 per month for one recipient and 50 percent more for an eligible couple. An automatic-adjustment provision closely paralleling that used under OASDI is applicable.

A number of "income disregards" are present. The most important is the disregard of $20 of income per month per family from such sources as OASDI, other pensions, earnings, and investments. The first $65 per month of earned income is disregarded, plus 50 percent of the remainder.

SSI has certain resource exemptions. To receive SSI, for 2007, resources cannot exceed $2,000 for an individual and $3,000 for a couple. However, in the calculation of resources, certain items are excluded—the home, household goods, and personal effects (depending on value), an automobile with value of $4,500 or less, burial plots, and property needed for self-support—if these are found to be reasonable. Also, if life insurance policies have a face amount of $1,500 or less for an individual, their cash values are not counted as assets.

Some states pay supplements to SSI.

In addition to SSI, a public assistance program provides payments for widowed mothers (and fathers) with children. This is on a state-by-state basis, with part of the cost borne by the federal government.

Medicare Program

Health (or medical care) benefits for active and retired workers and their dependents in the United States is, in the vast majority of cases, provided through the multiple means of the Medicare portion of Social Security for persons age 65 and over and for long-term disabled persons, private employer-sponsored plans, and individual savings. As mentioned earlier, this is sometimes referred to as a "three-legged stool" or the three pillars of economic security protection. Another view of the situation for persons age 65 and over and for long-term disabled persons is of Medicare providing the floor of protection for certain categories, or, in other cases, providing the basic protection. Supplementing this, private insurance is present, with public assistance programs such as Medicaid, providing a safety net of protection for those whose income is not sufficient to purchase the needed medical care not provided through some form of prepaid insurance.

Private health benefit plans supplement Medicare to some extent. In other instances—essentially for active workers and their families—health benefit protection is provided by the private sector. The net result, however, is a broad network of health benefit protection.

Historical Development of Provisions

Beginning in the early 1950s, efforts were made to provide medical care benefits (primarily for hospitalization) for beneficiaries under the OASDI program. In 1965, such efforts succeeded, and the resulting program is called Medicare.

Initially, Medicare applied only to persons age 65 and over. In 1972, disabled Social Security beneficiaries who had been on the benefit rolls for at least two years were made eligible, as were virtually all persons in the country who have end-stage renal disease (i.e., chronic kidney disease). Since 1972, relatively few changes in coverage or benefit provisions have been made, other than the enactment of prescription drug benefits in 2003 (described later). In 1988, legislation that provided catastrophic coverage benefits—to be financed largely through a surtax on the income tax of eligible beneficiaries—was enacted. However, as a result of massive protests from those who would be required to pay the surtax, these provisions were repealed in 1989.

Medicare is really three separate programs. One part, Hospital Insurance (HI),[7] is financed primarily from payroll taxes on workers covered under OASDI, including those under the Railroad Retirement system. Beginning in 1983, all civilian employees of the federal government were covered under HI, even though, in general, not covered by OASDI. Also, beginning in April 1986, all newly hired state and local government employees are covered compulsorily (and, at the election of the governmental entity, all employees in service on March 31, 1986, who were not covered under OASDI can be covered for HI). The second part, Supplementary Medical Insurance (SMI), is on an individual voluntary basis and is financed partially by enrollee premiums, with the remainder, currently about 75 percent, coming from general revenues. The third part, prescription drug benefits, is financed by a mixture of payments by the insured person, the SMI program, and general revenues.

As an alternative to "traditional" Medicare, persons eligible under both HI and SMI (except those previously diagnosed with end-stage renal disease) can elect to participate in a Medicare + Choice plan. There are several types of such plans, but generally they must provide at least the same benefits as Medicare (usually, they provide more, such as some drug benefits and lower cost-sharing payments). These plans receive per capita payments from Medicare (the participant continues paying the SMI premium to Medicare), which hopefully are equitable reimbursement. In theory, these plans are supposed to provide better health care at a lower cost (through managed-care principles), but some critics believe that they do not always provide adequate care, especially because they usually do not allow free choice of physicians to provide the services (and generally little or no choice at all).

Persons Protected by HI

All individuals age 65 and over who are eligible for monthly benefits under OASDI or the Railroad Retirement program also are eligible for HI benefits (as are federal employees and state and local employees who have sufficient earnings credit from their special HI coverage). Persons are "eligible" for OASDI benefits if they could receive them when the person on whose earnings record they are eligible is deceased or receiving disability or retirement benefits, or could be receiving retirement benefits except for having substantial earnings. Thus, the HI eligibles include not only insured workers, but also spouses, disabled children (in the rare cases where they are at least age 65), and survivors, such as widowed spouses and dependent parents. As a specific illustration, HI protection is available for an insured worker and spouse, both at least age 65, even though the worker has such high earnings that OASDI cash benefits are not currently payable because of election to defer receipt of benefits.

In addition, HI eligibility is available for disabled beneficiaries who have been on the benefit roll for at least two years (beyond a five-month waiting period). Such disabled eligibles include not only insured workers but also disabled child beneficiaries aged 18 and over who were disabled before age 22, and disabled widowed spouses aged 50 to 64.

---

[7] Sometimes referred to as Part A. Supplementary Medical Insurance is Part B.

Further, persons under age 65 with end-stage renal disease (ESRD) who require dialysis or renal transplant are eligible for HI benefits if they meet one of a number of requirements. Such requirements for ESRD benefits include being fully or currently insured, being a spouse or a dependent child of an insured worker or of a monthly beneficiary, or being a monthly beneficiary.

Individuals aged 65 and over who are not eligible for HI as a result of their own or some other person's earnings can elect coverage, and then must make premium payments, whereas OASDI eligibles do not. The standard monthly premium rate is $410 for 2007 (but only $226 if they have at least 30 quarters of coverage).

Benefits Provided under HI

The principal benefit provided by the HI program is for hospital services. The full cost for all such services, other than luxury items, is paid by HI during a so-called spell of illness, after an initial deductible has been paid and with daily coinsurance for all hospital days after the 60th one, but with an upper limit on the number of days covered. A spell of illness is a period beginning with the first day of hospitalization and ending when the individual has been out of both hospitals and skilled nursing facilities for 60 consecutive days. The initial deductible is $992 for 2007. The daily coinsurance is $248 in 2007 for the 61st to 90th days of hospitalization. A nonrenewable lifetime reserve of 60 days is available after the regular 90 days have been used; these lifetime reserve days are subject to daily coinsurance of $496 for 2007. The deductible and coinsurance amounts are adjusted automatically each year after 2007 to reflect past changes in hospital costs.

Benefits also are available for care provided in skilled nursing facilities, following at least three days of hospitalization. Such care is provided only when it is for convalescent or recuperative care and not for custodial care. The first 20 days of such care in a spell of illness are provided without cost to the individual. The next 80 days, however, are subject to a daily coinsurance payment, which is $124 in 2007, and it will be adjusted automatically in the future in the same manner as the hospital cost-sharing amounts. No benefits are available after 100 days of care in a skilled nursing facility for a particular spell of illness.

In addition, an unlimited number of home health service benefits are provided by HI and/or SMI without any payment being required from the beneficiary. Also, hospice care for terminally ill persons is covered if all Medicare benefits, other than physician services, are waived; certain cost restrictions and coinsurance requirements apply with respect to prescription drugs.

HI benefit protection is provided only within the United States, with the exception of certain emergency services available when in or near Canada. Not covered by HI are those cases where services are performed in a Department of Veterans Affairs hospital or where the person is eligible for medical services under a workers' compensation program. Furthermore, Medicare is the secondary payor in cases when (1) medical care is payable under any liability policy, especially automobile ones; (2) during the first 30 months of treatment for ESRD cases when private group health insurance provides coverage; (3) for persons aged 65 and over (employees and spouses) who are under employer-sponsored group health insurance plans (which is required for all plans of employers with at least 20 employees) unless the employee opts out of it; and (4) for disability beneficiaries under the plan of an employer with at least 100 employees when the beneficiary is either an "active individual" or a family member of an employee.

Financing of HI

With the exception of the small group of persons who voluntarily elect coverage, the HI program is financed by payroll taxes on workers in employment covered by OASDI. This payroll tax rate is combined with that for OASDI. The HI tax rate is the same for employers and employees; self-employed persons pay the combined employer–employee tax rate, but have an offset to allow for the effect of business expenses on income taxes (as described earlier in connection with OASDI taxes). Such HI tax rate for employees was 1.45 percent in 1990 (and in all future years). The maximum taxable earnings base for HI was the same as that for OASDI for all years before 1991, but thereafter was a higher amount, and, beginning in 1994, no limit is applicable. Also, beginning in 1994, part of the income taxes on OASDI benefits is diverted to finance HI. It should be noted that the HI Trust Fund is inadequately funded over the next decade, with trust fund assets projected to fall short of 100 percent expenditures in 2012.

The vast majority of persons who attained age 65 before 1968, and who were not eligible for HI benefit protection on the basis of an earnings record, were nonetheless given full eligibility for benefits without any charge. The cost for this closed blanketed-in group is met from general revenues, rather than from HI payroll taxes.

The HI Trust Fund receives the income of the program from the various sources and makes the required disbursements for benefits and administrative expenses. The assets are invested and earn interest in the same manner as the OASDI Trust Funds.

Although the federal government is responsible for the administration of the HI program, the actual dealing with the various medical facilities is through fiscal intermediaries, such as Blue Cross and insurance companies, which are reimbursed for their expenses on a cost basis. Beginning in 1988, reimbursement for inpatient hospital services is based on uniform sums for each type of case for about 490 diagnosis-related groups.

Persons Protected under Supplementary Medical Insurance

Individuals aged 65 or over can elect SMI coverage on an individual basis regardless of whether they have OASDI insured status. In addition, disabled OASDI and Railroad Retirement beneficiaries eligible for HI and persons with ESRD eligibility under HI can elect SMI coverage. In general, coverage election must be made at about the time of initial eligibility; that is, attainment of age 65 or at the end of the disability-benefit waiting period. Subsequent election during general enrollment periods is possible but with higher premium rates being applicable. Similarly, individuals can terminate coverage and cease premium payment of their own volition.

Benefits Provided under SMI

The principal SMI benefit is partial reimbursement for the cost of physician services, although other medical services, such as diagnostic tests, ambulance services, prosthetic devices, physical therapy, medical equipment, home health services, and drugs not self-administerable are covered. Not covered are out-of-hospital drugs, most dental services, most chiropractic services, routine physical and eye examinations, eyeglasses and hearing aids, and services outside of the United States, except those in connection with HI services that are covered in Canada. Just as for HI, there are limits on SMI coverage in workers' compensation cases, medical care under liability policies, private group health insurance applicable to ESRD, and employers-sponsored group health insurance for employees and their spouses.

SMI pays 80 percent of "recognized" charges, under a complicated determination basis that usually produces a lower charge than the reasonable and prevailing one, after the individual has paid a calendar-year deductible of $100 for 1991 and after. Special limits apply on out-of-hospital mental health care costs and on the services of independent physical and occupational therapists. The cost-sharing payments ($100 deductible and 20 percent coinsurance) are waived for certain services (e.g., home health services, pneumococcal vaccine, and influenza shots, and certain clinical diagnostic laboratory tests). Beginning in 1993, physicians cannot charge Medicare patients more than 115 percent of Medicare "recognized" charges.

Financing of SMI

The standard monthly premium rate is $93.50 for 2007. (For the first time, in 2007 Americans with higher income will pay a higher Part B premium.) The premium is higher for those who fail to enroll as early as they possibly can, with an increase of 10 percent for each full 12 months of delay. The premium is deducted from the OASDI or Railroad Retirement benefits of persons currently receiving them, or is paid by direct submittal in other cases.

The remainder of the cost of the program is met by general revenues. In the aggregate, persons aged 65 and over pay only about 25 percent of the cost, while for disabled persons such proportion is only about 20 percent. As a result, enrollment in SMI is very attractive, and about 95 percent of those eligible to do so actually enroll.

The enrollee premium rate will be changed every year after 2007, effective for January. According to "permanent" law, the rate of increase in the premium rate is determined by the percentage rise in the level of OASDI cash benefits in the previous year under the automatic adjustment provisions, and in part by the percentage rises in the per capita cost of the program. However, for the premium years 1996 to 1998, the premium rate was set at 25 percent of the cost for persons aged 65 or over. (The premium rates for 1992 to 1995 were established by legislation.)

The SMI Trust Fund was established to receive the enrollee premiums and the payments from general revenues. From this fund are paid the benefits and the accompanying administrative expenses. Although the program is under the general supervision of the federal government, most of the administration is accomplished through "carriers," such as Blue Shield or insurance companies, on an actual cost basis for their administrative expenses.

Prescription-Drug Benefits Insurance

Beginning in January 2006, comprehensive drug benefits became available to Medicare beneficiaries. In 2007, a premium rate of about $22 per month applies if this coverage is elected, and an annual initial deductible applies, as does 25 percent cost-sharing until there has been $2,400 of drug costs in excess of the initial deductible, with 5 percent cost-sharing after $5,451 out-of-pocket expenses.

Possible Future Development of Medicare

Over the years, numerous proposals have been made to modify the Medicare program. Some of these would expand it significantly, while others would curtail it to some extent.

Among the proposals that would expand the program are those to establish some type of national health insurance program, having very comprehensive coverage of medical services applicable to the entire population. Somewhat less broadly, other proposals would extend Medicare coverage to additional categories of OASDI beneficiaries beyond old-age beneficiaries aged 65 and over and disabled beneficiaries on the roll for at least two years—such as to early-retirement cases at ages 62 to 64 and to all disability beneficiaries.

In another direction, liberalizing proposals have been made to add further services, such as physical examinations and dental services. Still other proposals have been made in the direction of reducing the extent of cost-sharing on the part of the beneficiary by lowering or eliminating the deductible and coinsurance provisions and by eliminating the duration-of-stay limits on HI benefit eligibility.

Proposals have been made to reduce the cost of the Medicare program by increasing the cost-sharing payments made by the beneficiary. For example, the cost-sharing in the first 60 days of hospitalization could be changed from a one-time payment of the initial deductible to some type of daily coinsurance that would foster the incentive to shorten hospital stays. Also, it has been proposed that the minimum age for nondisabled persons should rise above 65 when the NRA for OASDI does so.

A major risk for persons aged 65 and over that is not covered by Medicare is the cost of long-term custodial nursing home care and homemaker services for disabled or frail persons. Although many persons recognize the serious nature of this problem, it is currently being met only on a means-test basis by the Medicaid program. Some people believe that the problem should be met on an "insurance" basis under a new part of Medicare, but others think that it is not an "insurable" risk and must be handled on a means-test basis (possibly liberalized somewhat).

Proposals have been enacted to lower the cost of the HI programs as far as reimbursement of hospitals and skilled nursing facilities is concerned, although this would have no effect on the Medicare beneficiary directly.

Medicaid

Over the years, the cost of medical care for recipients of public assistance and for other low-income persons has been met in a variety of ways. Some years ago, these provisions were rather haphazard, and the medical care costs were met by inclusion with the public assistance payments. In 1960, a separate public assistance program in this area was enacted—namely, Medical Assistance for the Aged (MAA), which applied to persons aged 65 and over, both those receiving Old-Age Assistance and other persons not having sufficient resources to meet large medical expenses. Then in 1965, the MAA program and the federal matching for medical vendor payments for other public assistance categories than MAA were combined into the Medicaid program. This new program covered not only public assistance recipients but also persons of similar demographic characteristics who were medically indigent.

The Medicaid program is operated by the states, with significant federal financing available. Some states cover only public assistance recipients.

Medicaid programs are required to furnish certain services, to receive federal financial participation. These services include those for physicians, hospitals (both inpatient and outpatient), laboratory and X-ray tests, home health visits, and nursing home care. Most other medical services, such as drugs, dental care, and eyeglasses, can be included at the option of the state, and then federal matching will be made available. Also, as a result of legislation enacted in 1988, states must pay the SMI premiums and the HI and SMI cost-sharing payments for persons who are eligible for Medicare and who have incomes below the poverty level and have resources of no more than twice the standard under the Supplemental Security Income program. Thus, the states have the advantage of the relatively large general-revenues financing in the Medicaid program.

The federal government pays a proportion of the total cost of the Medicaid expenditures for medical care that varies inversely with the average per capita income of the state. This proportion is 55 percent for a state with the same average per capita income as the nation as a whole. States with above-average income have a lower matching proportion, but never less than 50 percent. Conversely, states with below-average income have a higher federal matching percentage, which can be as much as 83 percent. The federal government also pays part of the administrative costs of the Medicaid programs; generally, this is 50 percent, although for certain types of expenses that are expected to control costs the federal percentage is higher.

Appendix 1A

Detailed Descriptions of Several Social Security Benefit Elements

This appendix describes the features of three complex elements involved in the computation of OASDI benefits.

Computation of Average Indexed Monthly Earnings

The AIME is a career-average earnings basis, but it is determined in such a manner as to closely approximate a final-average basis. In a national social insurance plan, it would be inadvisable to use solely an average of the last few years of employment, because that could involve serious manipulation through the cooperation of both the employee and the employer; whereas in a private pension plan, the employer has a close financial interest not to do so. Furthermore, OASDI benefit computation is not proportionate to years of coverage or proportion of worklife in covered employment, as is the case for private pension plans generally.

The first step in computing the AIME is to determine the number of years over which it must be computed. On the whole, the number depends solely on the year in which the individual attains age 62. The general rule is that the computation period equals the number of years beginning with 1951, or with the year of attaining age 22, if later, up through the year before attainment of age 62, minus the so-called five dropout years. The latter is provided so the very lowest five years of earnings can be eliminated. Also, years of high earnings in or after the year of attaining age 62 can be substituted for earlier, lower years.

As an example, persons attaining age 62 in 1990 have a computation period of 34 years (the 39 years in 1951 to 1989, minus five). The maximum period is 35 years for those attaining age 62 after 1990. For the infrequent case of an individual who had qualified for OASDI disability benefits and who recovered from the disability, the number of computation years for the AIME for retirement benefits is reduced by the number of full years after age 21 and before age 62 during any part of which the person was under a disability.

The AIME is not computed from the actual covered earnings, but rather after indexing them, to make them more current as compared with the wage level at the time of retirement. Specifically, covered earnings for each year before attainment of age 60 are indexed to that age, while all subsequent covered earnings are used in their actual amount. No earnings before 1951 can be utilized, but all earnings subsequently, even before age 22 or after age 61, are considered.

The indexing of the earnings record is accomplished by multiplying the actual earnings of each year before the year that age 60 was attained by the increase in earnings from the particular year to the age-60 year. For example, for persons attaining age 62 in 1990 (i.e., age 60 in 1988), any earnings in 1951 would be converted to indexed earnings by multiplying them by 6.90709, which is the ratio of the nationwide average wage in 1988 to that in 1951. Similarly, the multiplying factor for 1952 earnings is 6.50251, and so on. Once the earnings record for each year in the past has been indexed, the earnings for the number of years required to be averaged are selected to include the highest ones possible; if there are not sufficient years with earnings, then zeroes must be used. Then, the AIME is obtained by dividing the total indexed earnings for such years by 12 times such number of years.

Application of Windfall Elimination Provision

Excluded from the operation of this provision are the following categories: (1) persons who attain age 62 before 1986; (2) persons who were *eligible* for a pension from noncovered employment before 1986; (3) disabled-worker beneficiaries who became disabled before 1986 (and were entitled to such benefits in at least one month in the year before attaining age 62); (4) persons who have at least 30 "years of coverage" (as defined hereafter); (5) persons who were employed by the federal government on January 1, 1984, and were then brought into coverage by the 1983 amendments; and (6) persons who were employed on January 1, 1984, by a nonprofit organization that was not covered on December 31, 1983, and had not been so covered at any time in the past.

Under this method of computation of the PIA, beginning with the 1990 cohort of eligibles, the percentage factor applicable to the lowest band of earnings is 40 percent, instead of 90 percent. As a transitional measure, those who became first eligible for OASDI benefits in 1986 have an 80 percent factor, while it is 70 percent for the 1987 cohort, 60 percent for the 1988 cohort, and 50 percent for the 1989 cohort.

For persons who have 21 to 29 years of coverage, an alternative phase-in procedure is used (if it produces a larger PIA). The percentage factor applicable to the lowest band of earnings in the PIA formula is 85 percent for 29 years of coverage, 80 percent for 28 years, down to 45 percent for 21 years.

In any event, under any of the foregoing procedures, the PIA as computed in the regular manner will never be reduced by more than 50 percent of the pension based on noncovered employment (or the pro rata portion thereof based on noncovered employment after 1956 if it is based on both covered and noncovered employment).

Determination of Years of Coverage for Special Minimum Benefit and for Windfall Elimination Provision

For purposes of the special minimum benefit, for periods before 1991, a *year of coverage* is defined as a year in which earnings are at least 25 percent of the maximum taxable earnings base; while after 1990, a factor of 15 percent is used. However, for 1979 and after, the maximum taxable earnings base is taken to be what would have prevailed if the ad hoc increases in the base provided by the 1977 act had not been applicable, but, instead, the automatic annual increases had occurred.

For the purposes of the windfall elimination provision, a year of coverage is defined in the same way, except that the 25 percent factor continues after 1990.

In 2007, a year of coverage is $10,890 for purposes of the special minimum benefit and $18,150 for the windfall elimination provision.

Appendix 1B

Changes in Social Security Program Made by Amendments in 1981 and 1983

This appendix describes the most important changes that were made in the OASDI program in 1981 and 1983, when it experienced a significant financial problem, of both a short-range and a long-range nature. The 1981 amendments were of a stop-gap nature, while the 1983 amendments were intended to provide a complete solution to the problem.

The 1981 act significantly reduced benefit outgo in the short range by the following actions:

1. The regular minimum benefit (an initial PIA of $122) was eliminated for all new eligibles after 1981, except for certain covered members of religious orders under a vow of poverty.

2. Child school attendance benefits at ages 18 to 21 were eliminated by a gradual phase-out, except for high school students aged 18.

3. Mother's and father's benefits with respect to nondisabled children terminate when the youngest child is aged 16 (formerly 18).

4. Lump-sum death payments were eliminated, except when a surviving spouse who was living with the deceased worker is present, or when a spouse or child is eligible for immediate monthly benefits.

5. Sick pay in the first six months of illness is considered to be covered wages.

6. Lowering of the exempt age under the earnings test to age 70 in 1982 was delayed until 1983.

7. The workers' compensation offset against disability benefits was extended to several other types of governmental disability benefits.

8. Interfund borrowing among the OASI, DI, and HI Trust Funds was permitted, but only until December 31, 1982, and then no more than sufficient to allow payments of OASI benefits through June 1983.

Further action beyond the 1981 amendments was essential to restore both the short-range and long-range solvency of the OASDI program. President Reagan established the National Commission on Social Security Reform—a bipartisan group whose members were appointed both by him and the Congressional leadership—to make recommendations for its solution. Such recommendations were adopted almost in their entirety in the 1983 act.

This legislation made the following significant changes in the OASDI program (as well as some in the HI program):

1. OASDI and HI Coverage Provisions
   a. OASDI-HI coverage of new federal employees and current political appointees, elected officials, and judges. (HI coverage of all federal civilian employees was effective in 1983 under previous law.)
   b. Coverage of all employees of nonprofit charitable, educational, and religious organizations.
   c. State and local employees once covered are prohibited from withdrawing.
   d. Employee contributions to cash-or-deferred arrangements (Sec. 401[k]) and employer contributions under nonqualified deferred-compensation plans when no substantial risk of forfeiture is present are covered.

2. OASDI Benefit Provisions
   a. Cost-of-living adjustments are deferred for six months (i.e., will always be in checks for December payable in early January).
   b. The indexing of benefits in payment status is changed from being based only on the CPI to the lower of CPI or wage increases when the trust funds are relatively low.
   c. Gradual increases will be made in the normal retirement age from the present 65, beginning with those attaining age 62 in 2000—so it will be 66 for those attaining such age in 2009 to 2020, then rising to 67 for those attaining such age in 2027 and after. Age 62 is retained as the early retirement age, but with appropriate, larger actuarial reductions.
   d. Gradual increases will be made in the credit for postponing claiming (or not receiving) benefits beyond the normal retirement age from 3 percent per year for persons attaining age 65 in 1982 to 1989 to 8 percent for persons attaining normal retirement age in 2009 and after.
   e. The retirement earnings test for persons at the normal retirement age up to age 70 is liberalized, beginning in 1990, by changing the "$1 for $2" reduction in benefits for earnings above the annual exempt amount to a "$1 for $3" basis.
   f. Several minor changes are made to liberalize benefits that primarily affect women (e.g., indexing deferred widow[er]'s benefits by whichever is more favorable, prices or wages, and increasing the benefit rate for disabled widow[er]s aged 50

to 59 from 50 percent to 71.5 percent, depending on age at entitlement, to a uniform 71.5 percent).

g. The situation about windfall benefits for retired and disabled workers, with pensions from noncovered employment and OASDI benefits based on a short period of covered employment is alleviated.

h. The offset of government employee pensions based on employment not covered by OASDI against OASDI spouse and widow[er] benefits is reduced from a full offset to a two-thirds offset.

i. Restrictions are placed on the payment of benefits to prisoners receiving retirement and survivor benefits (previous law related essentially to disability beneficiaries).

j. Restrictions are placed on the payment of benefits to aliens residing abroad who have, in general, not had at least five years of residence in the United States.

3. Revenue Provisions, OASDI and HI

a. OASDI tax rate scheduled for 1985 was moved to 1984 for employers, but not employees. Trust funds receive, from general revenues, additional amount of taxes as if employee rate had been increased.

b. Self-employed pay the combined OASDI-HI employer–employee rate, minus (for 1984 to 1989) a credit (in lieu of a business expense deduction for such taxes). The trust funds receive, from general revenues, the additional amount of taxes as if the full employer-employee rate had been paid.

c. About 72 percent of the OASDI tax rate increase scheduled for 1990 was moved forward to 1988.

d. Part of OASDI benefits (but not more than 50 percent) will be subject to income tax for persons with high incomes, with the proceeds going into the OASDI Trust Funds.

e. A lump-sum transfer of general revenues will be made to meet the cost of certain gratuitous military service wage credits (which, under previous law, would have been paid for in future years).

f. Interfund borrowing (which, under previous law, was permitted only in 1982) was allowed in 1983 to 1987, with specific repayment provisions (before 1990 at the latest) and with prohibitions against borrowing from a fund that is relatively low.

g. Operations of OASDI and HI trust funds will be removed from Unified Budget after FY 1992 (subsequent legislation moved this up to 1986 for OASDI).

h. Two public members will be added to the boards of trustees.

4. HI Reimbursement Provisions

a. A new method of reimbursement of hospitals will be gradually phased in. This will be done on the basis of uniform amounts (but varying among nine geographical areas and between rural and urban facilities) for each of 467 Diagnosis-Related Groups.

    b. No change is made in the minimum eligibility age for HI benefits for the aged (i.e., it remains at 65).

5. SMI Provisions

    a. The enrollee premium rate is changed to a calendar-year basis (to correspond with the OASDI cost-of-living adjustments [COLAs]). The rate for July 1982 through June 1983 was to continue through December 1983.

    b. No change is made in the minimum eligibility age for SMI benefits for the aged (i.e., it remains at 65).

These changes in OASDI were about equally divided, over the long run, between increases in income and reductions in outgo. They were supposed to solve both the short-range problem (in the 1980s), which they did, and the long-range problem (of the following 75 years), which, as it turned out, they did not completely do.

Index

Page numbers followed by n indicate material found in notes.